MODERNIZATION
AND THE STRUCTURE
OF SOCIETIES

MODERNIZATION AND THE STRUCTURE OF SOCIETIES

A SETTING FOR INTERNATIONAL AFFAIRS

BY MARION J. LEVY, JR.

PRINCETON, NEW JERSEY

PRINCETON UNIVERSITY PRESS

FOR

CLARENCE E. AYRES

TALCOTT PARSONS

AND THE LATE

FRANK W. TAUSSIG

FROM WHOM ONE COULD ALWAYS LEARN

WITHOUT HAVING TO AGREE

ACKNOWLEDGMENTS

I owe a large debt to the National Science Foundation which made possible two years of part-time release from teaching plus secretarial aid, which in turn made it possible for me to do more work along several lines, including this one, than I have ever been able to do before or since in comparable time. I cannot overstate the admiration I have for the pleasant conditions which the Foundation made possible.

I owe a badly unpaid debt to a previous grant from the Ford Foundation which made possible my repeated references to Japanese materials though this in no way completes that bulky study of Japan which stares me down daily—which is my old man of the sea.

I owe a general debt to my university community which still makes individual research possible. My indebtedness to the Woodrow Wilson School of Public and International Affairs is especially great. Three of her mid-career students, Mr. David Munson, Dr. Kenneth E. Ogren, and Mr. Donald A. Wehmeyer, furnished valuable criticism when this manuscript was in its infancy. In general my graduate students were helpfully rebellious.

Professor M. Stanley Kelley, Jr. of the Politics Department here and Dr. Roger S. Pinkham of the Bell Laboratories helped in ways that defy identification. Indeed, they bear a certain responsibility for what appears here since our discussions were so incessant that much of what I present may properly be theirs.

I am beholden to the Princeton University Research Committee for making available the services of Mrs. Elsa Granade to edit this essay in hypotheses and for Mrs. Lorna R. Harvey's help with the index, and to Princeton's Bureau of Student Aid, which furnished the invaluable assistance of Messrs. G. Sumida and T. Mira in the preparation of the index.

I shall be most indebted of all to those who read and criticize this work. Essays in hypotheses are risky and questionable at best. Their one possible payoff is in fruitfulness for further developments, and critical scrutiny from many different points of view is the minimal prerequisite for estimating that.

[*Note for the Paperback Edition:* I owe a special debt to Dr. Johan Goudsblom of the Universiteit Van Amsterdam. His colleaguesmanship is responsible for the corrections of many of my shameful typographical errors, and he has raised substantive questions which could only be satisfied by a revised edition.]

Marion J. Levy, Jr.
Woodrow Wilson School of Public and International Affairs
Princeton University, Princeton, New Jersey

CONTENTS

MODERNIZATION
AND THE STRUCTURE
OF SOCIETIES

I

THE POINT OF VIEW

This book had its beginnings in a course designed for graduate students resolved on professional careers in public and international affairs. So broad a subject is a distillation of concerns ranging from puristic scholarship and science to casual comments—cutting across all of the disciplines of social analysis. Since this large book attempts much, it may be useful to say first what it does not attempt. It makes no attempt to deal with the history of international affairs in general or with diplomatic history in particular. Although comparative, it makes no attempt to go into any of the details of operation of conventional distinctions among governments or economies. It is not, for example, concerned with the contrasts between the British Parliamentary System and the United States Congressional System or with the differences between the economic aspects of French and German social structure. It makes no attempt to deal with either the nature or the mechanisms of the conventional organizations oriented to international affairs. It is not at all concerned with either the structure or the operations associated with the United Nations Organization, the World Court, the International Bank, the International Monetary Fund, etc. It does not concern itself with the subject of international trade directly. It pays little or no attention to problems of geography or of international communications as those are ordinarily treated. Finally, it does not attempt to go into any of the details of leadership and relations in international affairs in any particular or general case. Questions of the "British hegemony," Bismarck's leadership, the balance-of-power system, bipolarity, neutral nations, and third men are not discussed at all directly.

These are all matters of the greatest importance. What is offered here is no substitute for the voluminous writing on these matters, or for the classics of history, which form the general background of the competent and literate in this field. Whoever is not deeply acquainted with them would do well to steep himself in them before reading this. In the field of international affairs they are indispensable.

This book does attempt something highly relevant to the problems of international affairs. First, it attempts to sensitize one to the social background—to a setting—for international affairs. It discusses, on very general levels, the relevance of the varied social backgrounds of the members of different societies for the kind of relationships they are likely to have in the international field. Second, it attempts to show the interdependencies of societies as wholes in matters that are relevant for international affairs. A great deal is said about societies from the economic point of view, from the political point of view, or from the point of view of one of the many organizations that characterize societies. Nevertheless, I never intentionally concentrate on one of these points of view for its own sake; all such treatments are undertaken to show how the different elements of social structure fit together. Any attempt at such a holistic approach is in part elusory. A complete picture of how elements of even a single society fit together as a whole would entail final knowledge, not only about it and all its members, but also about everything else with which it and they were interrelated. Still, I wish to emphasize how members act in terms of their society rather than in terms of their governments, their business firms, their class positions, etc., considered as things apart from one another.[1]

Third, this book attempts to distinguish different types of societies. After brief discussion of various classifications of this sort, I use a distinction between relatively nonmodernized societies and relatively modernized societies. I judge this distinction to be not only highly relevant to general questions of social analysis but also particularly relevant to the analysis of problems of international affairs today.

Fourth, the book attempts to show something of the common elements in all societies. Fifth, it attempts to show something of

[1] One of the special bits of jargon used throughout distinguishes between units such as societies, social systems, organizations, etc., and the individual(s) involved in them. For technical reasons, I define all such units "as various sets of structures [i.e., patterns] of social action involving a plurality of interacting individuals" rather than as various sets of individuals or groups. Given such usage it is improper to speak of such units "doing" anything. Individuals or members of various sorts do things in terms of the structures of action that constitute those units. Thus the members or office holders of a government *do* things but the government does not *do* anything. To speak of a society or government in this sense as doing anything is to commit the pathetic fallacy in social analysis. I justify the more cumbersome phrasing of this usage by asserting that it avoids: (1) begging questions by substituting a phrase like "the government decided" for an analysis of the decision making process, (2) confusing individuals with organizations and hence obscuring the extent to which unofficial elements may be relevant to official actions, (3) the anthropomorphism or organismic analogy of referring to organizations as though they were men or other biological entities, and (4) the possibility of obscuring common elements among different organizations by constant reference to them as separate and more or less isolated entities. *States* are never *actors* here. Society *does* nothing to people; people do things to one another in terms of some society (ies).

the main variations among societies. For hundreds of years two saws have bestridden the field of social analysis in general and that of international affairs in particular as a paradox. One holds human nature to be the same everywhere. The other holds no two human beings to be alike. The pair is not paradoxical. Both views are correct, and, stated correctly, they are not contradictory. In extremely general respects, people and societies everywhere *are* alike. The more detailed our interest in people and societies, the greater is the amount of variation we must be prepared to handle. Finally, this book attempts to show something of the way in which the main lines of similarity *underlie* the main lines of variation treated.

Pursuit of these six objectives is in terms of three principal comparative analyses. The first is a comparative analysis of relatively nonmodernized and relatively modernized societies. Although there are difficulties about these concepts, I believe the distinction to be the most generally relevant breakdown of societies, not only for present purposes but also for the purposes of analysis of societies in general. I can illustrate this by an extreme assertion. In terms of social structure highly relevant for problems of international affairs in particular, and social analysis in general, any two cases well on either side of this classification have more in common with one another than any one of them has with a case well on the other. Despite the fact that modern English society clearly developed out of thirteenth-century English society, thirteenth-century English society has more in common with the society of the Trobriand Islanders in more respects relevant both to international affairs and general social analysis than thirteenth-century English society has in common with modern English society. One may disagree with this assertion, this example, and the point of view exemplified, but this work attempts to show where they lead.

The second comparative analysis is a comparison of those things that all societies have in common with the major lines of variation among societies. The third comparative analysis focuses on two matters that I think contain the heart of the general problem of international affairs in the present world. The first of these is the problem of modernization of the relatively nonmodernized societies; the second is the problem of stability of the relatively modernized [and especially of the most highly modernized] societies. I do not think there is any escaping the former problem, and I am not sure that there is any satisfactory solution to the latter. There are few problems of international affairs today—including the problems of the implications of nuclear weapons—that do not hinge heavily on either the modernization of the relatively nonmodernized societies or on stability among the members of highly modernized societies, such as the United States and the Soviet Union.

Before turning to the organization of this work and the basic distinctions used, two further points of view should be stressed explicitly. The first has to do with jargon and the second with the kind of statements and evidence on which this effort rests.

A great deal of jargon is used throughout this work. Some takes the form of special usage already referred to in the first footnote of this work, and much takes the form of specialized terminology of various sorts. Jargon, in the sense of a technical language used for subject matter treated in a specialized way by adepts, develops about any subject—whether it be sociology, theology, music, baseball, or physics—that becomes a focus of great attention. There is no getting away from it—especially as a field begins to get somewhere. It is, however, possible to distinguish between *justifiable* and *unjustifiable* jargon. *Justifiable* jargon is any that improves the brief expression of precise ideas that are used frequently. Most of us are thoroughly addicted to jargon, and if it is justifiable enough, we are frequently unaware of it as jargon. The sports section of any good United States newspaper is full of justifiable jargon [e.g., "filly takes dash with stretch run," "with *Columbia's* skipper pinned firmly under his lee and astern," etc.].

I have tried to use only justifiable jargon, but I have not hesitated to use quite cumbersome jargon if I could not make a passage unambiguous without it. Authors vary widely in their abilities to combine easy-to-read with clarity. In a work like this I feel the choice must go to the latter if the writer's limitations force a sacrifice of one or the other. In the presence of sin, I have tried to sin bravely—and carefully.

The ideas and materials presented throughout this work are presented primarily to stimulate, sensitize, and inform. The focus of this work is so broad and important that any approach to definitive treatment, either theoretically or empirically, is well beyond present knowledge. I have tried to present as many relevant general propositions on this subject as I can and to illustrate them by empirical examples. The examples used are taken largely from the historical materials with which I am most familiar, i.e., those on traditional China, Japan, and the United States. They are not given as demonstrations, only as illustrations.

I have not knowingly presented propositions or allegations about the facts that are false or misleading—but many of the propositions are questionable, and few, if any of them, can be considered definitively demonstrated. *Therefore,* the propositions asserted throughout this work—no matter how smugly or dogmatically I assert them—should be regarded as hypotheses, that is, as unconfirmed propositions. The references to empirical data or evidence should always be regarded as *hypotheses about the facts* and not as any definitive presentation of the facts themselves.[2] In scientific work it is more important to be fruitful for further work than to be right. I am much more concerned with being fruitful by increasing the horizons in terms of which the problems treated here are handled than in solving problems. I seek, however, neither to encourage a cavalier attitude toward evidence nor to have my enthusiasm for—even faith in—some of the propositions presented here confused with a demonstration of their tenability.

I I
ORGANIZATION

This work has four parts preceded by this introduction and followed by a summary. The introduction states the general point of view and content of the work in the first section and introduces the basic distinctions employed throughout the work in a third section. In the course of making these distinctions, some of the aspects and organizations common to societies, some of the elements of variation among societies, the general problem of modernization, and the general problem of stability are touched on briefly.

Part I is entitled *The Structure of Relatively Modernized and Relatively Nonmodernized Societies.* Its two chapters constitute the main comparative analysis of relatively modernized and relatively nonmodernized societies. Relatively modernized societies are discussed first because most of us are more familiar with them. In the next chapter the structure of relatively nonmodern-

---

[2] The presentation here of material as hypotheses about the facts is not a function of a preference for hypotheses rather than the collection of data. Throughout this work the discussion proceeds on very general levels. Even relatively noncontroversial hypotheses referring to all societies or all relatively modernized societies or all relatively nonmodernized societies cannot be said to be well confirmed by any reliable collections of data extant. I hope that all the hypotheses about the facts made here meet the first scientific requirement of such statements, namely that they be "conceivably falsifiable"—that they are neither nonempirical mystical propositions nor tautological propositions. I hope that all are fruitful in that either proof or disproof of them will teach us much more than we already know.

I see no harm in, and no alternative to, this perseverance in the absence of highly reliable confirmation as long as I have made the speculative nature of what is advanced sufficiently explicit.

ized societies is described increasingly by contrast with that of the former. In the course of the description the comparative analysis of the two emerges.

Part II is entitled *Aspects of Social Structure*. These seven chapters deal with aspects common to all societies and some of the main variations among them. The first deals with a special tool of analysis, applicable to any social relationship involving two or more individuals, and is the most technically sociologistic chapter in this work. In the following six chapters the whole question of aspects of societies is introduced at some length, and five aspects common to all societies and underlying all variations among societies are discussed.

Part III is entitled *The Organizational Contexts of Societies*. It deals with the types of organizations that constitute the most strategic subsystems of any society. As in the treatment of the aspects of societies in Part II, the common elements and main lines of variation dominate these chapters. There are five of these chapters: (1) Kinship and Family Organizations, (2) Governments and Associated Organizations, (3) Predominantly Economically Oriented Organizations, (4) Armed Force Organizations, and (5) Other Organizational Contexts: Churches, Schools, Predominantly Recreationally Oriented Organizations, etc.

In Part IV, *The Common Elements, Variations and Problem Foci,* Chapter 1 summarizes the common elements and the major lines of variation among societies from the points of view of any relationship, any aspect of society, and the organizations characteristic of any society. This chapter is especially concerned that, however dramatic the variations, one cannot be unaware of the common elements that underlie them.

Chapter 2 of Part IV concerns itself with the problem foci of this work, i.e., the problems of modernization and stability in international affairs. The analysis presented casts serious reflections on the relevance of the terms in which much of international debate is carried out. Ethically and sentimentally I could not agree more with those who speak of "respect for national sovereignty" and deny any intention to "interfere with governments or the people of other nations," but intellectually I believe this to be dangerously self-deceptive nonsense. The process of modernization being what it is and the world being what it is today, the choice between interference and noninterference in the affairs of others is not what it easily appeared to be in the eighteenth century—or even in the nineteenth or early twentieth century. The relatively high levels of self-sufficiency conceivable for the members of societies in those days gave these clichés meanings impossible for them today. As the interdependence of the people of the world increases inexorably, the question is not whether the citizens of one nation *will* interfere with those of another but whether they will interfere with one another in accord with certain ethical principles more or less generally acceptable—whether decency, honesty, dignity, creativity, humor, and health can be maintained at the inevitable levels of mutual interference. Interfere they will, and increasingly every day, unless the process of modernization is not only stopped but reversed.

The problem of stability is discussed primarily in terms of its implications for the possible outbreak of war between any two of the relatively modernized or very highly modernized societies. The stability or instability of these societies has many other implications, but for the sphere of international affairs this is the central one. Many of the often iterated major sources of international difficulties such as "the invincible rise of x-nationalism," the military threat of the "have-not" nations, the threatening development of societies involving huge populations in the midst of the modernizing process, etc.—all these problems would be relatively simple were it not for their implications for touching off a war among the members of two or more of the most highly modernized nations. The members of the nations most highly modernized in regard to their weaponry are plagued by instabilities which find ready outlets in the exercise of age-old prides and prejudices as well as new ones. The most final of such outlets conceivable for the present would be a wearisomely old-fashioned war with catastrophically new-fashioned weapons.

The concluding summary returns to some general considerations.

III
THE BASIC DISTINCTIONS

A. RELATIVELY MODERNIZED AND RELATIVELY NONMODERNIZED SOCIETIES

The distinction between relatively modernized and relatively non-modernized societies is the most important of the general distinctions used throughout this work.[3] This classification of societies is

[3] It is used instead of the distinction between relatively industrialized and relatively nonindustrialized societies. For many the term *industrial* literally means factory-ized. For this analysis the concept of the factory is not literally the heart and soul of the concept industrial; agriculture may be as highly industrialized as the production of automobiles [e.g., much of modern farming in the United States, for example, is as highly mechanized or industrialized as almost any factory production]; recreation no less than communications may be industrialized; even universities and the process of learning in general may be highly industrialized, and so forth. The term *modernized* is more readily taken as a broader term.

relevant to virtually all questions of distinctions among societies, and it is especially relevant to all distinctions used in analyses of international affairs. I use a definition of *modernization* that focuses on the sources of power and the nature of the tools used by the members of a given society. Although these are elements usually referred to as technological or economic, the approach is neither a special form of technological determinism nor of economic determinism. Simple technological or economic determinism, like all other monisms, falls in the category of theories that are either true but meaningless or meaningful but false. The definitions used here, if used carefully and properly in the sense appropriate to scientific work, do not even lead one into technological or economic biases. I define modernization in these terms because it is convenient to do so, because the continuum of classifications so set up is relatively easy to understand, because measurement in terms of the concept so defined is not difficult to imagine, and above all because its use so defined is fruitful for the formulation of hypotheses.

I seek a *definition* of the concept modernization, not a full or realistic *description* of the thing to which the concept refers. This definition, like any definition proper to a scientific field, is intended as a parsimonious tool for the identification of the class of phenomena referred to. In scientific contexts definitions are not intended to approximate detailed descriptions.[4] The elements used in a definition are not necessarily conceived to be the most important elements of the phenomena they are used to identify. They may be so conceived, but above all they are the elements that most easily and precisely enable one to make the sorts of distinctions useful for the scientific analysis intended. What are the most important elements will vary with whatever criteria one wishes to employ for the term important. In most of the discussions to follow, other elements will be far more "important" than those used in the definition.[5]

The causal significance of the defining elements is closely connected with the question of importance. I do not view the

[4] I have tried to use a parsimonious definition, confining interest to two elements, sources of power and tools, of which the latter might even be dropped. I have above all tried to avoid a definition that approaches a realistic and complete description of the thing defined. I do so for the simplest of reasons: (1) there is no end to the attempt to be descriptive, and (2) the more descriptive the definition, the more of the analysis true by definition, i.e. tautological.

[5] From certain points of view the most important thing about snakes is that an enormous number of human beings are afraid of them. There is hardly any usage of the term *snake* that would be served by defining it as something most people are afraid of.

defining elements as causing the other elements or aspects of the phenomena concerned. For example, all highly modernized societies are open class systems in some sense, but the development of such systems is by no means necessarily caused by the sources of power or kinds of tools used to define modernization. In specific cases it can often be argued that some of the defining elements were, in fact, caused to develop by some of the other elements characteristic of the systems so identified. Indeed, if monistic arguments are avoided, this is always a theoretical possibility.

In scientific analysis, elements different from those used in the definition but also characteristic of the phenomena so identified, should not follow tautologically from the definition. This is not to say the defining elements are irrelevant. It may be possible, given the setting in which such phenomena are found, to draw highly relevant deductions from the presence of a given unit as defined. It might, for example, be possible to maintain that the defining elements could not be present unless certain others were also, and hence to predict on the basis of the *known* presence of the defining elements that those other features would also be present.[6]

Finally, the definition of modernization used here is arbitrary in two senses. First, there are an infinite number of other possibilities for defining this concept in such a way as to have exactly the same referent. Second, for different purposes, one might wish to define the concept as having a totally different referent. Anyone who feels strongly that the term modernization *must mean* something other than its explicit definition here should feel free to substitute any other term or symbol provided he does so consistently.

My definition of modernization hinges on the uses of inanimate sources of power and the use of tools to multiply the effect of effort. I conceive each of these two elements as the basis of a continuum. A society will be considered more or less modernized to the extent that its members use inanimate sources of power and/or use tools to multiply the effects of their efforts. Neither of these elements is either totally absent from or exclusively present in any society.

I define *inanimate sources of power* residually as any sources of power that are not produced from human or other animal

---

[6] If such predictions do not follow tautologically from the definition, they may prove to be untenable. Even if they are, something will be learned. In the example given, a prediction could only be incorrect if: (1) the hypothesis about the mutual relevance of the predicted elements and the defining elements is in general incorrect, (2) observable data have been overlooked, (3) the unit and/or its setting are not the sort they were thought to be, or (4) some combination of the above three.

energy. I define a tool as any physical device that is ordinarily separable from the body of an individual who applies it and that is used to accomplish what he could not accomplish *at all* or could not accomplish so well without it.

It is important to much of this work that the most general differences among societies with regard to inanimate sources of power are those of degree, not kind. There is no society whose members use no inanimate sources of power, nor is there one whose members use only inanimate sources of power. If gravity is an element in gathering fruit, if sails are used to focus winds to propel a boat, if rivers are used to float logs, if fire is used to crack stones or to clear land—if anything of this sort is used to carry out any endeavor—to some extent inanimate sources of power are being utilized. The use of animate sources of energy may seem insignificant in social contexts at the other end of the scale. I do not know what fraction of the total power consumed in the United States is, in fact, produced by animals other than man or by humans directly, but it must be a small fraction in terms of units of measurement such as horsepower and watts. From other points of view, however small that fraction may be, it is of exceedingly great importance. Automation notwithstanding, most of the decision-making [and that in some way literally involves a consumption of power] is still done by human beings. There are many other contexts in which outputs of energy from animate sources are of the greatest significance. Academics like to think of teaching and research as examples.

I shall not attempt to give any precise directions for measuring different points along this continuum. I conceive the continuum to be established in terms of the ratio of inanimate to animate sources of power. As far as sources of power are concerned, the larger this fraction [or the positive number which represents this ratio], the greater the amount of modernization, and the smaller the fraction the less the modernization. Exactly how to measure this ratio and exactly how to determine where on this continuum a given society would fall are not matters about which I have any good ideas. It is sufficient for present purposes to assert that in principle it ought not be inordinately difficult to get relatively precise measures of this sort.

Throughout this work I rely upon no greater level of precision about this continuum than that relatively easily agreed upon in common sense terms. For example, despite some large dramatic uses of inanimate sources of power by the members of traditional Chinese society in the form of irrigation works, sails of various sorts, canals, etc., few would dispute the statement that the ratio of inanimate to animate sources of power was considerably lower for traditional Chinese than for modern inhabitants of the United States. Not all of the comparisons made will be as gross as this one, but in principle they do not present any greater problems than this one does.

Correspondingly, in the case of tools, there are no societies whose members employ no tools. It is also inconceivable to me that there ever be a society whose members never exert effort save through tools, whose tools operate without any exercise of effort by the members, or whose tools in some sense multiply effort as much as is physically possible. The use of a digging stick, however primitive, is the use of a tool. The digging stick is no less a tool than the most powerful and efficient modern power shovel. Both extend or multiply the effort expended upon them, though the two are used to extend and multiply effort in different degrees and ways. Here again, we have a continuum the opposite ends of which are not opposites, do not in fact exist, or perhaps are not even conceivable. Again, I have not set up any precise method of measuring the particular society. Here, I must be even more imprecise than in the case of power. I suspect that this particular continuum should in some way be based on the number and variety of tools relative to the size of the population involved and on some measure of the extent to which the use of these tools multiplies effort.

For reasons which will become obvious in discussions later, I feel that in some way this measure should reflect one special distinction among tools. It matters enormously whether given tools are such that relatively slight differences in skill in their use are significant for output. Here again, I rely on no greater precision about tools than afforded by common sense. Throughout this work, however, I shall deal only with gross comparisons. For all the lack of nicety of measurement, again, no one will disagree that in terms of such a continuum modern United States society must be judged much more highly modernized than traditional Chinese society and that traditional Chinese society must be judged much more modernized than that of the Australian Bushmen.

However cavalier I may be about the details of measurement of the continua of sources of power and use of tools, the question of one cutting-off point as far as the continua are concerned is absolutely vital. The distinction between relatively nonmodernized and relatively modernized societies is the central focus of this work. For several reasons I have deliberately set up these continua so that no one can say that there is any society completely devoid of any and all elements of modernization. First, to fail to do so is to beg an important question. That question is whether the distinction intended between relatively modernized and relatively nonmodernized societies is a binary or all-or-nothing distinction, a simple difference of degree, or a difference of kind based on different combinations of common elements as well as on differences of degree and unique elements. Although it is fruitful to consider relatively modernized societies different in kind from relatively nonmodernized ones from several points of view, it is radically misleading to imply—even inadvertently— that all, or most, of the elements crucial to the former are completely lacking in the latter. Therefore, the definition should be set up in such a way as to facilitate the recognition of common elements as well as variations.

Second, although I do not think the use of different sources of power and kinds of tools cause all or even most of the other characteristics of relatively modernized societies, given the setting of such societies and the characteristics of societies in general, such elements are interdependent enough with the others to be used as the defining elements for more reasons than the possibility of relatively simple and precise measurement.

Third, I wish these definitions to be fruitful in consideration of the process of modernization without, of course, making the analysis of that process follow tautologically from the definitions themselves. I believe that there is something peculiar, something "new under the sun," about the structures of relatively modernized societies. This new factor hinges on the fact that the structures of modernization, once they have reached certain levels of development, constitute a sort of universal social solvent. Given contact between members of relatively modernized societies and relatively nonmodernized societies, it is always possible—even easy—for some of the latter to find interest in *and* to understand some of the structures or devices of the former. By no means all of this, but part of this, is a function of the fact that no mentally competent member of any society is completely unable to understand the use of tools and inanimate sources of power. The significance of a modern milling machine may be difficult for members of a relatively nonmodernized society to grasp, but the significance of a sharper, more easily maintained cutting edge is not. The same also holds for some applications of inanimate sources of power. If it did not, the peculiarly solvent effect of the introduction of the structures of relatively modernized societies—even the introduction itself—might be quite otherwise. For one thing, the possibility of communications as between members of the two types of society, especially given difficult language barriers, would be radically different. This whole question is a critical one throughout this work.

It is important that the elements of both power and tools be considered as constituting some sorts of continua, unless there are untenable implications of doing so, but if they are to be continua, the cutting-off point used to distinguish between the relatively nonmodernized and the relatively modernized societies is essential to the analysis. If it is easier to imagine the elimination of the remaining or a considerable amount of the remaining animate sources of power, save for purposes of decision and control, than to imagine a replacement of the existing inanimate sources of power by animate ones without basic change in the structure of the society, the society is a relatively modernized one in terms of the power continuum. If not, not. If the levels of performance required for the stability of the society are out of the question without the tools used or if a return to more primitive ones and increased labor would involve catastrophic changes in the social structure, the society is a relatively modernized one in terms of the tools continuum. If not, not.[7]

The cutting-off point in terms of the combination of these two continua, is a more delicate question than the question of the continua themselves. The hypotheses developed here rest on such gross distinctions that the problem of the cutting-off point is not serious. It is not difficult to get agreement that the United States, the Soviet Union, England, France, present day Japan, and perhaps a number of other societies are well past the cutting-off point toward the relatively modernized end of the scale, whereas the societies of Burma, India, Ceylon, some of Latin America, and many others are well past the cutting-off point on this scale in the other direction. The location of this cutting-off point is, however, of first-order importance in questions such as: "When did Japan become a relatively modernized society?" or "At what rate is Communist China becoming a relatively modernized society?" Because of my difficulties in locating this cutting-off point more precisely, I shall try to stick to illustrations that are reasonably distant from the cutting-off point.

---

[7] I have not faced up to the theoretical possibility of the cutting-off point of the tools continuum being radically different from that of the power continuum. I have not set up these definitions to rule out the possibility of a society relatively modernized in terms of the tools continuum and relatively nonmodernized in terms of the power continuum or vice versa. The two continua are sufficiently interdependent that such divergencies are unlikely if not impossible.

B. INDIGENOUS DEVELOPERS OF MODERNIZATION AND LATE-COMERS TO THE PROCESS

By indigenous developers I mean the members of those societies who, acting in terms of their existing society, developed these structures mainly on their own and relatively gradually over a long period of time. Even during the eighteenth century there were international contacts and relationships, and in this sense the members of none of the societies referred to really did anything on a completely indigenous basis. Nevertheless, there is a sense in which societies such as those of England, the United States, and France can be considered the societies of the indigenous developers of modernization. Other societies are the societies of late-comers. German society was, of course, a relatively early late-comer society; the Russians were somewhat later late-comers; the Japanese still later; the members of the societies of the Middle East still later, and so forth. The late-comers who are of greatest importance from many points of view are those who did not get substantially into the process until it was already relatively highly developed elsewhere in the world.

Since the problem of modernization is one of the major problem foci of international affairs, treatment of the process of modernization as though it were pretty much the same process for all people regardless of the stage of development of the process elsewhere is one of the fundamental naïvetés of much present-day thinking. Variations among the societies of late-comers are also important. The problems associated with the process of modernization are not simply a function of the distinction between the "have's" and "have not's" of modernization. Many problems hinge on whether the "have's" have or have had, what they have, or had, as a result of indigenous development as opposed to relatively rapid importation of structures, goods and capital from relatively modernized contexts.

C. CENTRALIZATION AND DECENTRALIZATION

This distinction focuses on questions of coordination and control. As used here, it is closely related to the distinction between relatively modernized and relatively nonmodernized societies. By centralization and decentralization I mean nothing more precise than the layman has in mind when he uses these terms. I define centralization in terms of the organization of the action of the members of a social system about one or more foci. Complete centralization of a society consists of having a single member make and carry out all decisions and determine all coordination;

any departure from this constitutes some element of decentralization. Rule by members of a committee is not so centralized as rule by a single individual, etc. As will become clear, complete centralization and complete authoritarianism would be identical. Apart from this extremity or approaches to it, centralization and authoritarianism do not necessarily vary identically. In some cases they may even vary inversely. No society ever reaches the point at which the action of its members is completely centralized or completely decentralized. A completely decentralized organization would lack all structures of organization or coordination.

Despite the identities at the extremes, it is essential that the distinction between centralization and decentralization not be confused with that between authoritarian and nonauthoritarian. So concerned have men been down through history with questions of tyranny, and so relevant has centralization been to tyranny, that there has been a tendency to see nothing but centralization where other critical elements existed and to exaggerate the extent of centralization in tyrannous situations. Before the development of relatively modernized societies, no overwhelmingly centralized society could exist stably for any considerable period. Prior to these developments all stable societies save those of relatively small scale, no matter how despotic, were quite specific combinations of centralization and far-reaching decentralization. I do not mean to maintain that there were no cases prior to relatively modernized societies of overwhelmingly centralized large-scale societies or aggregations of societies. I do mean that these were short-lived, and that the "short-livedness" was related to the attempt to achieve levels of centralization beyond the technical means available. Think of the attempts at world conquest. Only with the radical increases of modernization in the last century did the possibility of combining stability and overwhelming emphasis on centralization appear. Not only did it appear, but, as will be explained, the further the process of modernization goes, the greater is the degree of centralization that must be achieved if stability is to exist. Correspondingly, with the increase of modernization characteristic of the world today, decentralized elements must play an increasingly smaller role in social organization if the societies concerned are to be stable.

The impossibility of stable overwhelming centralization prior to modernization is most simply a function of the state of development of communications in general and logistics in particular. The increasing importance of centralization as the level of modernization increases hinges mainly on the increasing levels of interdependency of the various parts of any relatively modernized society, of the members of any such society, and of the members of all of the societies of the world.

D. AUTHORITARIAN AND NONAUTHORITARIAN

Different from but closely related to the distinction between centralization and decentralization is that between relatively authoritarian and nonauthoritarian societies, organizations, etc. I shall make less of the distinction than is usually made in comparative treatments of political systems. My use of the distinction hinges on the extent to which an individual is, may be, and/or can be ordered about or forced about by representatives of the government or the state or of whatever system is involved. It also considers the relative lack of any recourse enabling him to challenge such control. As a human being, my main concern with this distinction is an ethical one; in the present work my major concern with this distinction has nothing whatever to do with ethics per se. Many of the technical problems of social engineering, the problems of correcting mistakes, and many other problems are functions of differences in these respects. These considerations, rather than anything having to do with the dignity of individuals or the like, are of concern here.

E. LARGE-SCALE AND SMALL-SCALE SOCIETIES

Scale here is reckoned in terms of the numbers of people involved and the extent of the areas inhabited by them. Large-scale societies are those that involve large numbers of people, say at least a million or more for purposes of example, and large geographical areas, say at least a few thousand square miles, also for purposes of example. The treatment of social phenomena in this work hinges almost entirely on hypotheses about societies that are large-scale in this sense. Occasionally reference will be made to small-scale societies for purposes of perspective, but whatever the significance of small-scale societies may be for us ethically, they do not in the practical world of international affairs loom large in the minds of most men.

F. RENOVATING AND REVOLUTIONIZING
SOCIAL CHANGE

Change is a central focus of this work. One of the most fundamental distinctions with regard to social change is that between renovating social change and revolutionizing social change. For some societies social change generally takes the form of radical alterations in the general social structure of the society. This sort of change has been characteristic of most societies in world history. There have been rare cases of societies that over a long period have been characterized by structures of renovating change; the changes have taken the form of restoration of a previously existing state of affairs rather than a starkly new departure in social structure. Perhaps the most dramatic case of this kind of a society is traditional Chinese society, which was characterized by structures of renovating social change for a period of nearly two thousand years. It is difficult to find a comparable case elsewhere, but there are many cases where, over much shorter periods, changes were renovating rather than revolutionizing.

Here incidentally, I should like to warn against a dangerous cliché; by the term *revolution* I refer to the radical nature of a change not necessarily to the violence of the means by which it is achieved. Many have implicitly assumed that unless there is active fighting in the street no revolutionary changes occur.[8] This unnecessary impoverishment of the language carries with it a literally awful impoverishment of perception.

One of the special features of relatively modernized societies is a peculiar set of structures of revolutionary change. The members of a relatively modernized society, unlike the members of any other societies, have the problem of socializing children for an unknown future. In relatively modernized contexts revolutionary social changes may be confidently, even if fearfully, predicted at the rate of at least one set every three decades or less. Characteristically the childhood of each man's children will be more different from his childhood than his was from his father's. This means at least a general social revolution per generation for the relatively modernized. Moreover, such rapid change may obtain without what is ordinarily referred to as a political [i.e., governmental] revolution of any far-reaching sort. If this is so, we live in a spectacularly peculiar period of history.

G. SOCIAL ASPECTS AND SOCIAL ORGANIZATIONS

This distinction is not ordinarily made when members of relatively modernized societies discuss social phenomena, but it is

---

[8] I know of no area in which revolutionary change, in the sense intended here, has been taking place at a more rapid rate than in Japan since World War II. Nevertheless, in 1960 I heard a famous and exceedingly sensitive Japanese novelist take the position that, what with the general possession of arms in the hands of a large number of soldiers immediately following the surrender, he and many others expected a revolution to take place, but that nothing had happened and nothing had happened since. The implication was clear in his words that no really important changes had taken place since.

precisely the same distinction which laymen and scientists alike take for granted and apply with skill when they distinguish between properties of an object [e.g., shape, color, weight, etc.] and objects [or parts of objects] themselves [e.g., chairs, organisms, stones, etc.]. This distinction has already cropped up above in remarks about different aspects of societies, social systems, or organizations on the one hand and the societies, social systems, or organizations themselves on the other.[9]

Organizations are much easier to define than the aspects referred to here. By organizations I refer simply to the membership units characteristic of societies. A society as a whole is itself a membership unit. Governments and families are such units. Churches, political parties, and schools are other examples. The nature and content of the social structures that constitute these units are subject to the widest variation, especially in the kind of societies with which most of us are familiar. The chapters of Part III treat the organizations that, if not universal, are at least sufficiently widespread to merit our special attention.[10]

[9] I have treated this as a distinction between analytic structures and concrete structures in *The Structure of Society*, Princeton University Press, Princeton, 1952. The general system of analysis on which this work is based is derived from that work. Any technical terms not defined herein, and technical elaboration on many that are, can be found there.

[10] Certain elements of my usage need clarification. In the first place, all organizations discussed, unless specially indicated, will be social organizations [i.e., systems of action involving a plurality of actors whose behavior is not adequately explicable in terms of the heredity of the species concerned and the nonspecies environment—in this case, of human heredity and the nonhuman environment]. Hence, for brevity, the prefix social will be dropped. The term *organization* will be used synonymously with the term *social system* and used in preference to the term *social system* when referring to units ordinarily called organizations rather than social systems by laymen. A *society*, as that term is used here, is a strategically peculiar case of the general category of social systems or organizations. A *society*, as the term is used here, is a special sort of a social system in that all social systems other than a society are either subsystems of one society [e.g., Princeton University is a subsystem of United States society] or else the result of interrelationships among the members of two or more societies [e.g., the United Nations Organization]. Although a society is a specific kind of social system or organization, it is such a special one that the term *society* will always be used here to denote it explicitly. The terms *social system* and *organization* never include societies unless modified by the adjective *any* [e.g., *any* social system] or suffixed by the phrase, including societies [e.g., social systems, including societies].

The definition of the term *society* used here is a slight variant of that presented and discussed in Chapter 3 of *The Structure of Society*. A *society* is defined as a system of social action: (1) that involves a plurality of interacting individuals whose actions are in terms of the system concerned and who are recruited at least in part by the sexual reproduction of other members, (2) that constitutes a set of social structures such that action in terms of them is at least in theory capable of self-sufficiency for

The aspect of societies are no less familiar in one sense than the organizations discussed, but the careful treatment of them in the fashion insisted on here is a source of great difficulty. The aspects most relevant here have to do with special foci of attention, such as the economic, the political, the religious, etc. In ordinary language these different aspects are frequently referred to as though they were different things. For example, one refers to *the* economic factors and *the* political factors. Usually *the economic* is defined as having to do with allocations of goods and services, or by some rough equivalent; and *the political* is defined as having to do with the allocation of power and responsibility, or by some rough equivalent. Given such definitions, there are no such *things* as *purely economic* actions or factors or *purely political ones*. In ordinary discussions of social phenomena as well as in most technical discussions we fall unselfconsciously into such expressions as, "I shall now discuss the economic, political, and social factors involved." As a minimum such statements imply that *the economic* is nonpolitical and nonsocial; *the political* is noneconomic and nonsocial; and *the social* is noneconomic and nonpolitical. But such implications are nonsensical and seriously misleading. There is no such thing as an act that involves an allocation of goods and services but no allocation of power and responsibility. There is no allocation of power and responsibility that does not involve some allocation of goods and services. Neither economic nor political aspects are nonsocial. Both are special cases of the social unless one intends to imply that the economic and political aspects are explicable in terms of human heredity and the nonhuman environment or to set up a differently restricted definition of the term social.

The terms *economic* and *social* as used here, and as used generally, do not refer to different things. They refer to different ways of looking at the same thing. As social scientists, what we observe is action and its results; that is, we observe individuals or sets of individuals doing certain things and/or what we believe to be the results of such action. There is no social action that does not involve some allocation of goods and services; there is no social action that does not involve some allocation of power and responsibility; and I might add, there are no actions that do not

the maintenance of the plurality of individuals involved, and (3) that is capable of existing long enough for the production of stable adult members of the system of action from the infants of the members. One will not be misled seriously if he considers societies to refer roughly to the systems of action ordinarily called nations, countries, or societies, though for some technical questions and some of the "new" nations such identification could be misleading.

involve educational aspects, religious aspects, etc., depending on how those are defined. From this point of view the term social is a more general term than terms like economic, political, etc. The latter refer to different ways of looking at what we describe as social behavior or social action. Social behavior in its turn is only analytically separated from nonsocial behavior. While an individual thanks a friend, buys an automobile, orders a subordinate, etc., he is "held down" by gravity, his body operates homeostatically, etc. One may view a human being from the point of view of physics, from the point of view of biology, or from the point of view of the social sciences. In so doing one does not refer to different things but so different ways of looking at the same thing.

This distinction is an especially difficult one if applied in the social field. But every individual who reads this work is in a sophisticated sense quite used to making exactly this sort of distinction in a wide variety of fields. We discuss ordinary physical objects such as a chair in terms of what I would call here, by analogy, its parts or subsystems or organizations. We refer to its legs, its seat, its back, its arms, etc. If one pulls these apart, he does a certain violence to the chair, of course. In some chairs, especially modern ones, the dividing line among these parts is not easy to discover. Nevertheless, even when the back of a chair and its seat are formed of one continuous sheet of plastic, one is still able to refer to that portion of the sheet of plastic which is serving as its back as distinguished from that portion of the sheet of plastic which serves as its seat. The dividing line may be more or less arbitrary, but it does no great violence to our thinking to conceive of them as separable—of say, putting the seat in one room and the back in another. The screws or dowels that hold the chair together are also subsystems or parts of the chair. From many points of view it is exceedingly important to be able to consider a chair in terms of concretely distinct subsystems or units. We can, and frequently do, also consider a chair in terms of a different set of concepts. We speak of its form, of its shape, of its color, of its weight, of the density of its materials, of its temperature, etc. These concepts do not refer to different parts of the chair. They refer to different aspects or properties of the chair, that is, to different ways of looking at the chair. It is nonsense to speak of physically separating the shape of a chair from its mass.[11] They are separable only analytically, not con-

---

[11] We have little or no difficulty in maintaining the distinction between the paint of a chair, which is part of the chair in the sense intended here, and the color of the chair, which is a property of the paint, which is part of

cretely; one cannot conceive of putting the mass of a chair in one room and its shape in another.

In analyzing social phenomena—in analyzing any phenomena for that matter—for some purposes it is useful to refer to concrete distinctions [i.e., distinctions of units or subsystems or parts of things], for other purposes to these aspects or properties, and for most purposes to some combination of the two. It is quite necessary, however, to avoid confusing aspects with parts or subsystems. Confusion usually takes the form of referring to one of these aspects as though it were a unit or a thing or as though that aspect exhausted all the relevant aspects of the unit. Such confusion is a fallacy which has acquired a special sort of fame. It has two particularly apt names. Professor Alfred North Whitehead dubbed it the fallacy of misplaced concreteness. Professor Morris R. Cohen called it the fallacy of reification. The most classic case of this fallacy in social-science history is, of course, the vulgar concept of economic man. The sophisticated among the early economists realized that their conception of economic man was a special sort of abstraction, but many of their followers did not. Quite apart from the aesthetics of science, such fallacies generally lead to oversights, especially of interdependencies critical for understanding the phenomena under examination.

The fallacy of reification is hardly less characteristic of the work of professional social scientists than of lay conversation, and the prevalence of this confusion is not difficult to understand. A particular kind of widespread, highly developed specialization of organizations is one of the unusual features of relatively modernized societies.[12] This is specialization of interests in one of the types of aspects discussed here. Most of the members of a modern business firm are supposedly overwhelmingly preoccupied with the economic aspects of the action in terms of the organization. The members of a government are supposedly primarily oriented to the political aspects of their organization and of the action in terms of it. Universities are presumably organizations whose members are preoccupied with educational aspects. We are familiar with endless examples of this sort of specialization, and the simple need for economy of words could account for referring to these organizations as economic organizations, political organiza-

---

the chair, if one likes. One way of changing the color of the chair may be to remove its paint. But color [or its lack] is an aspect that the chair always has if it can be seen. Color is a property that usually can be easily identified but cannot be conceived as separable physically from the other aspects of the chair. Color must be a property of something that has properties or aspects other than color.

[12] See below, pp. 38–46.

tions, educational organizations, etc. For most purposes it would be pedantic beyond belief to refer to such organizations as predominantly economically oriented organizations, predominantly politically oriented organizations, predominantly educationally oriented organizations, etc., but that is just what I do throughout. The economy of expression relinquished here is costly even in analyzing the most highly modernized of societies, but however preoccupied the members of a business firm may be with economic aspects, the political aspects of the operations in terms of such an organization are by no means negligible. Questions of control, chains of command, etc., are vital.[13] The United States government is almost always referred to as a political organization, but it happens to be *the organization* in terms of which the largest allocations of goods and services in the entire world take place [roughly 100 billion dollars a year], unless the Soviet government holds that position. No business leader, or as far as I know, no organized set of businessmen begins to have nearly the economic impact of operations carried out by members of the United States government routinely.

We do not think of the family as an economic organization, and in such vital matters as national income accounting in relatively modernized societies, we do not ordinarily take into account, save possibly by inference from the amounts of power consumed domestically, etc., the kinds of vital services which take place in a family context: such services as child care, laundry, cleaning, and the preparation of food. Though highly relevant in other respects, these probably constitute only a small fraction of the total national income characteristic of a highly modernized society. Nevertheless, our tendency to regard economically productive activity as overwhelmingly and properly carried out in terms of specialized organizations such as business firms and factories may cause us to overlook vital elements of economic allocation in terms of such nonspecialized organizations as families.[14]

As soon as we step outside the circle of relatively modernized societies however, and most of the societies in the world are still relatively nonmodernized, the problem is magnified. In these

[13] Indeed, most modern novels about life in an environment of such organizations stress political aspects and other aspects far more heavily than the economic aspects themselves. Novelists of this genre are usually exceedingly naïve about the economic aspects, and perhaps about the others as well.

[14] Exceptions are beginning to crop up. Professor Fritz Machlup attempts to measure some contributions in the form of child care. See F. Machlup, *The Production and Distribution of Knowledge in the United States,* Princeton University Press, Princeton, 1962, pp. 52–56 and 103–106.

contexts [15] organizations specialized in terms of economic, political, or other aspects, are much rarer. Analyzing these societies in terms we have come to take for granted as laymen in relatively modernized contexts leads to one of two [or some combination of the two] sorts of difficulties: (1) we tend to assume that organizations which seem analogous to highly specialized ones in relatively modernized societies have comparable levels of specialization, or (2) important implications of action in terms of relatively nonspecialized organizations tend to be overlooked because, as members of relatively modernized societies, we habitually overlook them. In the latter respect, it is one thing to ignore in national income accounting the goods and services produced on a family basis by members of United States society; it is quite another thing to overlook them in the case of traditional China. The overwhelming proportion of all economic allocation, education, etc., that takes place in terms of relatively nonmodernized societies takes place in terms of family units—at all periods of history, everywhere.

For these reasons I shall pursue the distinction with great rigor. Even for the sake of economy in communication I am not prepared to shorten phrases like predominantly economically oriented to economic. I shall persist in that level of jargonizing because the very clumsiness and awkwardness of the phrases will call continuous attention to the distinction insisted upon here. I am stubborn about this because virtually all social science literature slurs the distinction of aspects and things.

Parts II and III of this work are concerned with these aspects and organizations. Five aspects are distinguished: (1) role differentiation, (2) solidarity, (3) economic allocation, (4) political allocation, and (5) integration and expression. Briefly, role differentiation refers to the aspect of "who does what when." Solidarity refers to the aspect of "who sticks with whom" under varying circumstances, in what way, and how strongly. Economic allocation refers to the allocation of goods and services. Political allocation refers to the allocation of power and responsibility. The categories integration and expression are catch-all categories. I find them unsatisfactory, but I have not been able to improve upon them; they cover such aspects as those having to do with education, religion, recreation, artistic expression, emotional reactions, etc.

The major types of organizations discussed are the following: (1) kinship and family organizations [especially the family],

---

[15] See below, pp. 93–95.

(2) governments and associated organizations, (3) predominantly economically oriented organizations, (4) the armed forces, (5) churches, schools, predominantly recreationally oriented organizations, and miscellaneous organizations. These five aspects are relevant to any and all societies; [16] and these five types of organizations are each highly relevant to problems of modernization and as setting factors for international affairs.

H. IDEAL AND ACTUAL STRUCTURES

The distinction between ideal and actual structures is used on virtually every subsequent page of this work. Unless specific notice to the contrary is given, the term *ideal* is used with only one meaning. It is defined as what some set of individuals regards as right, good, proper, preferable, etc. When a structure is called an ideal structure, it is to be presumed that on challenge the caller is prepared to identify the individuals from whose points of view it is an ideal structure. Thus if I say, "Bullying is a violation of American ideal structures," I am alleging that, in general, if one questions members of American society, they will tell him [or he may find out in some other fashion] and that they sincerely believe bullying is bad. This allegation [or hypothesis about the facts] may or may not be tenable, but it is at least conceivably testable.

The term *actual* is defined as that which an objective omniscient scientific observer would observe, whether the people observed were aware of it or not. An actual structure refers to any structure in terms of which behavior in fact takes place. Thus, ideally speaking, Americans are against bullying. Actually speaking, there is, of course, a considerable amount of bullying indulged in by Americans.

The distinction between ideal and actual structures is one of the most vital and useful tools of analysis of any society, any time, anywhere. In one form or another men have been aware of it since time began for them. In this sense modern social scientists cannot be said to have discovered it. It is, however, so obvious and such a humble distinction that many social scientists either neglect it or overlook its importance. A large set of theoretical propositions based on this distinction can be stated. These propositions constitute some of the most general, the least questioned and the most useful—as far as developing other propositions and understanding phenomena are concerned—of any

[16] Discussion of their derivation may be found in *The Structure of Society*.

propositions in social science. Some of the most important of these follow briefly because I use them again and again in one way or another throughout this work:

1. There is not [and in all probability there never has been] a society whose members never distinguish between ideal and actual structures.

2. For no society [and for no subsystem within a society or resulting from the interrelationships of the members of two or more societies] do the ideal and actual structures of the members coincide exactly. In individual cases they may coincide. For example, there are individuals who hold that bullying is a bad thing and who, in fact, never bully anyone. Actually, however, there is no organization whose members live up to all of the ideal structures that as members of the organization they actually hold, let alone those they merely profess.

3. To some extent the members of every society not only distinguish between ideal and actual structures, but they are also aware that these do not always coincide. They may use different terms for the distinction. They may be more or less concerned with the lack of coincidence of ideal and actual structures. They are, however, never completely indifferent to the distinction or the lack of coincidence.

4. Some of the sources of stress and strain characteristic of any social system inhere in the fact that the ideal and actual structures of the members of the system do not coincide exactly. Not only are the members of societies aware that their ideal and actual structures do not always coincide but they are also upset by some of these inconsistencies.

5. To some extent, and not paradoxically relative to the preceding proposition, the possibilities of integration characteristic of any society inhere in the fact that the ideal and actual structures of the members do not coincide perfectly. Not only do people get upset because their ideal and actual structures are at variance, but also some of their possibilities of adjusting as well as they do result from the fact that their ideal and actual structures differ. For example, in traditional Chinese society the ideal structures for family size were quite different from the actual structures. Another one of the ideal structures was that of equal inheritance of family property among all the sons. The latter could not have been lived up to as well as it was—indeed, it would have necessarily been abandoned very early in Chinese history—had it not been that

relatively rarely did more than one son survive to maturity. Even with the small actual average size of the membership of traditional Chinese families, subdivision of the land was carried well past the point of diminishing returns even for the members of traditional Chinese society. People could not adjust to interaction with other members of their society as well as they do if they actually lived up to the letter of all of their ideal structures if only because some of the ideal structures are always inconsistent with others.

6. That the ideal and actual structures of a society do not coincide cannot be accounted for solely in terms of hypocrisy of the members of the society. Cynics may hold that people who do not in fact do what they say should be done are simply insincere, but that is the sort of naïveté which gives cynicism a bad name. Hypocrisy is rarely scarce. It may be defined as a discrepancy between *actual* ideal structures and *professed* ideal structures. But, by no means all, or even the vast majority, of discrepancies between ideal and actual structures fall into this category. Some hypocrisy is highly vulnerable to social techniques such as exposure and ridicule. The general failure of coincidence between ideal and actual structures could never be remedied by application of such techniques. It is one of the irreducible facts of human social existence. No dissemination of knowledge about it threatens the truth of this generalization.

7. The ideal and actual structures of a given society cannot coincide for at least two sorts of reasons. The first has to do with the cognitive capacities of human beings. Assuming that consciousness is a characteristic of human behavior, the amount of knowledge that each individual member of a society would have to "carry about with him" all the time, were the ideal and actual structures of a society to coincide exactly, would overload any known cognitive storage capacity of the human brain. Each individual would have to know exactly everything that was expected of him, ideally speaking, in every conceivable circumstance at every conceivable point in time, and he would have to act in accordance with that knowledge. The second line of reasoning is somewhat different. Any system for which the ideal and actual structures coincided exactly would be exceedingly brittle. So interdependent are so many social structures that, given such a perfect system, any change in the setting or environment that resulted in any sort of failure of the ideal and actual structures to coincide would require

complete revision of the entire set of ideal and actual structures. It is not wild to theorize that no such system could exist stably for any considerable length of time.[17]

These distinctions and the theories based on them are applied throughout this work. From time to time subsidiary theories in these terms will also be suggested. For example, differences in ideal structures as between the leaders of a given society and the general membership of the society have radically different implications in some types of societies than in others. One of the main utilities of this distinction is that if one keeps it constantly in mind, many things that otherwise seem paradoxical are no longer so. Many critical observations which should be made, but frequently are not, will be made if the distinction is kept in mind. Since some 200 years before the Christian era, the traditional Chinese family unit has been described as having a large number of members. The membership of the average unit has usually been described as consisting of individuals of many generations, many sons and their wives, etc., all living together. Never, however, did more than a small minority of the total Chinese population realize such a state. It is the actual family style approximated by the traditional Chinese gentry. Peasants rarely achieved it. Somewhere between 80 and 90 per cent of all Chinese in traditional Chinese history were peasants who rarely lived, family-wise, as traditional Chinese were supposed to live. Nevertheless, one of the most significant structural features of traditional China is the fact that the ideal structures which the gentry both held and to some extent approximated in actuality were also the ideal structures for the vast majority of all Chinese regardless of whether they were actually able to live up to them or not. Or take another example, many societies have been described as polygamous by social scientists, travelers, etc. Until recently most of these were usually described by asserting or at least implying that the average male [or even the great majority of them] had several wives. Actually that has probably never been the case. It is true there are many structures permitting polygamy of one sort or another [i.e., polygyny or polyandry]. Some members of such societies do have multiple wives or multiple husbands. Rarely if ever, however, has the segment of the population that actually had multiple spouses amounted to more than a relatively small proportion, usually a special elite group in the case of polygyny, of

[17] Elaboration of sets of theoretical propositions in terms of these two concepts is only just begun by these seven propositions.

the total membership of the society. For it to be otherwise, it would have to be an unusual society indeed, since in all known cases the ratio of male children to female children at birth is slightly in excess of one to one. Even if somewhat more males than females die off in childhood, at marriageable age the ratio of females to males is nothing like two to one unless there is systematic killing of male children. For all males of marriageable age to have two or more wives at the marriageable ages of males and females, there would have to be a ratio of roughly two females for every male or more. Alternatively, there might be structures in terms of which the older men all had several wives and the younger men none, that the younger men *always* marry widows of the older men as their first wives, etc. Structures of this sort are unusual. What have usually been described as polygamous societies are not, in fact, polygamous for the average individual. They are rather societies in terms of which, ideally speaking, polygamy is permissible or even desirable. One of the most important facts to realize about polygamous societies is that the average individual of marriageable age is not able to achieve polygamy even if it is an ideal structure for him [or her]. Achieved polygamy is usually characteristic of elite status.[18]

This sort of discrepancy is bound to come to light if one asks habitually whether an apparently descriptive statement about a social situation refers to the ideal or actual structures. Moreover, when one asks an individual to describe some part or aspect of his own society, the answer is more likely to be in terms of the ideal structures than in terms of the actual structures—especially if there are considerable discrepancies between the ideal and actual structures.[19] Ordinarily descriptive written materials are also more likely to stress ideal than actual structures. Especially in situations with which one is unfamiliar, it is well for any person to keep this distinction in mind.

[18] It has been recently shown [see P. Kunstadter, R. Buhler, F. F. Stephan, and C. F. Westoff, "Demographic Variability and Preferential Marriage Patterns," *American Journal of Physical Anthropology*, vol. 21, no. 4, pp. 511–519] that the probability is exceedingly small that the membership of any society can survive while adhering strictly to a cross-cousin marriage structure. Careful attention to the ideal—actual distinction will probably entail alterations in the whole field of kinship analysis. See Part III, Ch. 1 [especially pp. 426–430, below].

[19] As recently as the 1940's Chinese who knew perfectly well that they and most other Chinese did not live in terms of a large Chinese gentry type family, when asked what the Chinese family was like described the large gentry type. They did not do it to mislead, though it usually had that effect. In general material on China used in this work is taken from my book, *The Family Revolution in Modern China*, Harvard University Press, 1949 [Reprinted by Octagon Books Inc., N.Y., 1963].

I
THE PROBLEMS OF MODERNIZATION
AND THE PROBLEMS OF STABILITY

Finally in this introduction, return to the distinction involved in the two central problem foci: the problem of modernization of the relatively nonmodernized and the problem of stability of the relatively modernized. The main concern of this work is the analysis of modernization and the structure of societies as setting factors for international affairs. I do not wish to become embroiled in the evaluation of different goals of public policy. I am not concerned with what any of us might like or dislike in international affairs or in our future history. I am interested in extremely general statements which may be useful because (1) they are tenable, and (2) they are highly relevant to international affairs. I think the most general forms of all of the problems in international affairs may be classified under the two main headings used here. All of the present relatively nonmodernized societies will change in the direction of greater modernization. They will change in that direction regardless of whether their members wish it or whether the members of some other society or societies wish to force such change upon them.[20] In fact, some combination of the two is likely to be the case.

Most of these movements in the direction of greater modernization will be accompanied by far-reaching instabilities of the widest variety. The most important thing as far as policy implications are concerned, however, will not be the stability of the process but the nature of the process in general. If we understand this process, we will know more about what the members of such societies wish, what sorts of things upset them, and what they are likely to do. We may not like greater modernization, we may love it, we may be neutral about it, but it is nevertheless going to be terribly important to each of us. The fact that greater modernization is going on all over the world will be a much more important variable in explaining the actions of people than terms such as nationalism, freedom, human dignity, greed, lust for power, or pride. In the world in which we live, increasingly no member of any society, whether relatively modernized or not, will have for long the privilege of standing aloof from the problems of modernization. Modernization is a general process; it touches us all.

The problem of the members of relatively modernized societies, especially of the most highly modernized ones, is the prob-

[20] See below, pp. 125–129.

lem of living with the form of society they have already achieved. Relatively modernized societies are exceedingly recent phenomena. The most superficial examination of recent history reveals a constantly ascending spiral of bloodier and bloodier wars in which the leadership is taken by members of the most highly modernized societies. They did not invent wars, but they have certainly maintained a rate of technological advance in weaponry that has never been achieved before. The technical means literally to wipe out world-wide civilization was not within the reach of the members of any society prior to our time. Now our best scientists tell us it is well within the reach of the members of at least two societies.

As far as the relatively nonmodernized societies are concerned, the question of whether they are stable is not nearly as relevant to problems of international affairs as the problem of how their members will proceed in the process of modernization itself. Their societies are going to be unstable in the most profound sense in any case. For international affairs, the most extreme form of the problem is whether behavior in terms of highly modernized societies impels the members of one of them to modern wars with those of another. Do these societies contain within themselves sources of instability such that modern global wars are likely to result? Regardless of whether other societies have, or had, such sources,[21] do these? I hope our societies do not, but they probably do. If we intend to try to do anything about this, given the past record, we ought to look carefully into these matters to seek a way out. Even though we cannot eliminate problems of instability in general of these societies, if we can lower radically the probabilities of instabilities likely to result in modern global wars involving the members of two or more of the most highly modernized societies, the prognosis of a long future in which we can turn our attention to other problems of international affairs, even to other problems of living, is considerably enhanced.

[21] After all, the members of no other societies have had such weapons. Of one thing we are cynically certain! No weapons are "so terrible they will outlaw war"—however much we wish it.

PART I

THE STRUCTURE OF RELATIVELY MODERNIZED
AND RELATIVELY NONMODERNIZED SOCIETIES

THE STRUCTURE OF RELATIVELY

MODERNIZED SOCIETIES

I
DEFINITION OF MODERNIZATION

The degree of modernization has been defined above as having to do with inanimate sources of power and tools [see pp. 9–15]. The greater the ratio of inanimate to animate sources of power and the greater the multiplication of effort as the effect of applications of tools, the greater is the degree of modernization. Among the members of relatively modernized societies uses of inanimate sources of power not only predominate, but they predominate in such a way that it is almost impossible to envisage any considerable departure in the direction of the uses of animate sources of power without the most far-reaching changes of the entire system. The multiplication of effort by applications of tools is high, and the rate is probably increasing exponentially. The application of tools is constantly being pushed into new spheres.

Relatively modernized societies constitute phenomena quite new in social history. The origins of some of their aspects are ancient, perhaps, but then by definition the origins of anything can be traced indefinitely far back into history. However long their pedigrees, the specific combination of elements characteristic of relatively modernized societies do not begin to emerge with any clarity prior to the early part of the nineteenth century. High degrees of modernization are no more than roughly fifty years old at present. Indeed, some of the most striking aspects of some of the most highly modernized societies are probably not a great deal more than a quarter of a century old. The fact that a given trait exemplified by a relatively modernized society and crucial to it existed in, say, Renaissance society or early Greek society does not make it useful to consider either of the latter as modernized or relatively modernized as the terms are used here.

Although this type of society is quite new in social history, no people in history have completely lacked the elements used here to define the degree of modernization. It is partly because of the presence of some such elements as these that no society has members completely unable to comprehend or sense advantages in some applications of power from inanimate sources and tools.

As modernization is studied in greater detail, the question of the exact location of a dividing line between relatively modernized and relatively nonmodernized societies will become more important. The present state of the field and the objective of this work are sufficiently rough so that we may beg or loosely answer this question. No one is likely to contest use of the society of the Australian aborgines as an example toward one extreme of the continuum and modern United States society as an example toward the opposite end. Americans have not gone as far as it is possible to go in these directions. Indeed, they are going further every day. United States society, however is the most extreme example of modernization insofar as these defining elements are used. Among Australian Bushmen the use of inanimate sources of power is negligible quantitatively. Most of the power they use is human power. The tools they use are important to them and multiply their effort, but not a great deal. In the United States power from animate sources has become negligible quantitatively. It is certainly a small fraction of the amount of power from inanimate sources.[1] It is considerably easier to contemplate increasing applications of power from inanimate sources in the remaining fields in which power from animate sources is used than to contemplate the reverse. Any considerable attempt to return to animate sources of power in United States society could be carried through only after a massive reduction in the population and a radical change in all social systems in terms of which the members of that society operate. The same sort of catastrophic consequences would accompany comparatively small regressions in the work ratio furnished by tools in the United States. This would not be equally the case among Australian Bushmen, though in some cases one might argue that any decrease in the efficiency of their tools might plunge them below the subsistence level altogether. Despite this difficulty the contrast is on the whole sufficiently clear to be usable.

I intend none of the arguments put forward to rest on the exact location of the dividing line between relatively nonmodernized and relatively modernized societies. In principle it is unfortunate in technical works to define by example, but for present purposes I shall attempt no further refinement of this dividing line than

[1] Again, however negligible quantitatively this power from animate sources may be, it is not necessarily negligible from the point of view of direction and control. The increase of automation is making some changes even in this field, but this revolution has only just begun.

some examples of societies which fall well on one side or the other of it. Most of the western European nations are relatively modernized today. There are of course conspicuous differences in the level of their modernization. England, France, and at least West Germany represent high levels of modernization. The same is probably true of Italy, Belgium and Switzerland. Spain and Portugal are still relatively nonmodernized, though perhaps at the upper end of that scale. The same might be said of the Eastern European countries, excepting such a case as Czechoslovakia, of course. The Scandinavian countries represent interesting combinations of some highly modernized fields and some relatively nonmodernized ones, but as wholes I would place them well up in the scale of relatively modernized societies. Canada, Australia, and New Zealand would fall on the relatively modernized side of the dividing line. The Soviet Union would fall well on the relatively modernized side. Nothing in Asia would fall on the relatively modernized side of the line save for Japan which would fall far on the relatively modernized side of the line. Communist China would certainly not fall on the relatively modernized side of this line unless we are to take the pronouncements of her present leaders as the gospel of accomplishment. India's position is on the relatively nonmodernized side of the line, further toward the other side in some respects than Communist China at present, though one would doubt whether that can long continue to be the case. No Middle Eastern societies save those of Israel and Turkey would be on the relatively modernized side of the dividing line. Israel for peculiar reasons is probably well over that dividing line, and Turkey may be. No African country save South Africa and isolated portions of Algeria could qualify as being on the relatively modernized side of the line. The Latin American societies raise some of the most difficult cases of judgment. The urban segments of several of these societies are certainly relatively modernized, but the societies as a whole probably fall on the relatively nonmodernized side of the line. Some of these estimates are questionable, but I shall not knowingly make use of any save safe examples.[2]

Finally, the elements discussed here are presented solely as defining elements. One should expect no more from them; I do not. They are not viewed as a complete description of the phenomena which they define. They are not to be given any special causal significance in understanding this set of phenomena. The

[2] This is a good opportunity to emphasize once again that all of the apparently definite statements of fact used here are hypotheses about the facts.

two main elements used for purposes of definition here are regarded as good elements to use for definitions for four reasons. First, there is no alleged case of these phenomena not characterized by these two conditions. Second, no society that I do not wish to consider as a relatively modernized case has these two characteristics as far as I know. Third, of various alternative elements of definition I know of few that do not pose even greater problems of measurement than these. Measurement of these elements, moreover, depends not on the concepts of social science but rather on the concepts of the natural sciences and their engineering applications. Since these are much more highly developed disciplines than any of the social sciences, I would prefer to use their relatively better developed, relatively more precise, forms of measurement rather than those available from my own field. Fourth, although these defining elements should not be confused with causal elements, they are highly relevant to the phenomena I wish to discuss.

I I
STRUCTURAL FEATURES OF
ANY RELATIVELY MODERNIZED SOCIETY

A. ASPECTS

1. SPECIALIZATION OF UNITS

In the Introduction [pp. 19–26] organizations were distinguished from their aspects. These are the units which will be spoken of here as more or less specialized. There are at least two forms which such specialization may take. The action of the members of these units may be specialized with regard to some concrete activity, and they may also be specialized with regard to one or more of the aspects of action discussed above. Historically there are many examples of specialization in the former sense accompanied by little or no specialization in the latter sense. In these cases the specialization is in some important senses incidental to the organization whose members are specialists in the activities concerned. Throughout history craftsmen and even whole village populations have been specialized with regard to the output of certain particular types of products, for example, dolls or some special form of cloth, etc. However, the organizations in terms of which those activities are carried out—usually a family unit in the case of the craftsmen and, by definition, a village unit in the case of the village example—are not usually specialized with regard to a specific aspect of the behavior of its members such as the economic aspect or the political aspect. The units are viewed by the members who belong to them as general living units. Neither the family nor the village is more predominantly economically oriented than other families or villages. The villages, if anything, are predominantly politically oriented organizations, but even that may be questionable.

The contrast may be somewhat easier to grasp in terms of economic aspects. The economic aspects of a family-type organization are *never* irrelevant to its general character, and often they are strategic for an understanding of many other characteristics of the family. Nevertheless, the family members as family members are also much concerned with child bearing and child rearing, recreation, solidarity, etc. Orientation of family members to economic aspects of their behavior in family terms cannot be said to predominate in the sense that activities in terms of a modern business firm can be said to be predominantly economically oriented. Even the latter, of course, cannot be held to be exclusively economically oriented, which is one of the major reasons for avoiding reference even to such specialized organizations as economic organizations.

The kind of specialization of organizations that is strategic here is specialization in terms of one or more of the aspects of the action. Examples of specialization of this sort are to be found in relatively nonmodernized societies. *Governments* are a frequent example of this sort. Sometimes there are specialized predominantly economically oriented organizations in relatively nonmodernized societies. Some of the merchant firms in such societies as those of the Hanseatic League, the Venetian city-states, etc., are examples. In general, however, in relatively nonmodernized societies organizations specialized in this sense are comparatively rare and, above all, are relatively restricted in number and variety when they do appear. In relatively modernized societies without exception one encounters the large-scale possibility of organizations whose members are predominantly concerned with a single aspect of behavior or even a special form of that single aspect. In modern United States society, our most extreme case, we have an unending variety of units of this sort. We have units overwhelmingly specialized with regard to economic aspects, political aspects, education, religion, etc. If we look at the predominantly educationally oriented units, for example, we see the most bewildering variety of special cases of that type of unit.[3]

[3] Schools [see pp. 342–344 and 624–634] are just such units. In the category of schools there are elementary schools which have to do with the broadest, most elementary forms of literacy, secondary schools, col-

It is difficult to make out a case to the effect that any of these specialized units is universal in social history. The only type of membership unit that is apparently universal in social history is some sort of family unit. Yet, in no known society has the family unit ever been specialized in this sense. In some instances the extent of activities covered under the heading of family concerns is a great deal broader than in others, but even in a society like our own in which the focus of family orientation by contrast with the sphere dominated by it in other societies is restricted, the family is not such a specialized unit. The most general highly specialized unit in social history is undoubtedly a government. As defined here a government is always to some extent predominantly politically oriented. Every known society of any considerable scale in world history has a government as one of its subsystems. Even if governments are not characteristic of all possible societies, they are characteristic of all societies of major interest in this work.

Even specialized units are by no means devoid of other aspects than the one emphasized [see pp. 23–25]. There are certainly critical economic aspects of any government. Indeed, from many points of view the aspects not emphasized by the members of these units may be more important than the one which is, if only because they tend to be overlooked. The mistake of referring to these units as though they had no other aspects is a function of the fact that members of relatively modernized societies have come to take them so very much for granted. Our society is such, never mind how it got that way, that if certain political aspects of ideally predominantly economically oriented units or certain economic aspects of ideally predominantly politically oriented units come to the fore, we are virtually bereft of any explanation except one of social evil.

In the context of United States society, for example, reference to the government as though its members were primarily concerned with economic aspects or reference to the members of a business firm as though they were primarily concerned with polit-

---

leges, etc. Colleges are much more specialized in terms of subject matter. We have colleges of dentistry, medicine, law, etc. Indeed, we have developed schools specialized along almost any substantive line one may think of. We take this sort of elaboration so much for granted that we tend to overlook the fact that the vast majority of all education in world history has taken place not in terms of such doubly specialized units but rather in terms of units that were not educationally specialized at all. The vast majority of all education in world history has, in fact, been carried out in terms of family units. Only in quite recent times in terms of relatively modernized societies has this ceased to be the case for any save a relatively small minority of the population.

ical aspects is almost always done in a context of derogatory social criticism. This holds true even though the United States government has a larger budget, and a more strategic one for the budget of other organizations, than any single so-called *big business* or organized set of business firms. For the members of various business firms, allocation of power and responsibility in terms of their firms is often considered the most important one affecting them. In the context of United States society derogatory criticism focused on the economic aspects of the activity carried out in terms of the government tends to take one of two forms. Either the activity is dubbed illegitimate because it involves graft and corruption, that is, it involves an improper allocation of goods and services by members of the government to people who have no right to them, or on the other hand, it involves a drift toward socialism, that is, the activity is seen as entailing a deliberate attempt on the part of some members of the government to change the structures of the government in order to produce a greater involvement in economic allocation than the critics deem proper.

Correspondingly, if a member of our society criticizes a business firm for the involvement of its members in supposedly specialized politically oriented activities, that criticism too tends to take one of two forms. Again, it is either graft and corruption, that is, representatives of the business firm are trying "to buy political influence" for their own ends and thereby "corrupt the government," or they are trying to take over the government. Ideally speaking, in our society the right of businessmen, as representatives of their businesses, to be involved in politics at all is questionable. If they try to influence the government in this role, they are presumed to be trying to do it for the profit of the business firm to which they belong. They are trying to get a special bill favoring their business or some special advantage of another sort. This is simply graft and corruption seen from the opposite point of view. It is not a matter of chance that the question of the ethical defensibility of lobbying has always been a touchy one for us. Instead of socialism, the criticism takes the form of fascism or paternalism, if one feels that members of a business firm are trying to take over the government or the functions of government not just for personal profit but for the sake of control itself.

These attitudes toward government and business are a function of the fact that United States society is what is generally referred to as a capitalistic society or at least one in which it is regarded as quite legitimate for predominantly economically oriented units that are not directly owned or controlled on a governmental basis to exist. In a relatively modernized socialist context there would presumably be no basis for criticizing members of the government on this score. If such a state had been carried to the extent frequently referred to as an ideal by socialist thinkers, any private involvement in predominantly economically oriented activities would, by definition, be illegitimate.

Modern man in the context of relatively modernized societies moves increasingly in terms of just such specialized units. Apart from friendship units and family or other kinship units, he moves in terms of little else. He purchases and sells, he votes, he worships, he creates, he learns, he is transported, he recreates, and he thinks, all in terms of such units. Prior to his evolution, the overwhelming majority of all men in social history spent their average days and nights without reference to any such units whatsoever.

Perhaps the most obvious implication of such specialization in general is that the more highly specialized the units are in a given society, the lower is the need to generalize all skills in that society and the greater is the need to generalize some basic skills. Specialization here is discussed primarily in terms of specialization of interest with regard to a particular aspect of behavior, but specialization in the more ordinary sense always accompanies this sort of specialization. Thus, in regard to education, we not only have predominantly educationally oriented units, but we also have exceedingly detailed distinctions among those. In discussing the skills that are important for the members of a society, it is useful to distinguish between *basic skills* and *intermediate skills*. *Basic skills* are those that virtually any adult member of the society must acquire at one time or another in his life cycle, if he is to operate effectively in terms of the society of which he is a member. For a society like ours literacy is such a basic skill. Virtually every member of any society must be able to count. He must know how to use the language characteristic of his society and so forth and so on. *Intermediate skills* are those skills in which only a segment of the membership of the society need be proficient in order to operate. For example, only a small proportion of the members of our society need know how to run milling machines, how to use a computer, how to use a cyclotron in research, etc. These intermediate skills may be of the greatest significance, but they need not be possessed by more than a limited portion of the membership of the society. As the proliferation of highly specialized units mounts, there are great economies in the kind of skills that can be generated because it is possible to train only a small specific segment of the membership of the society in these special skills without worrying about whether the remainder of the members even understand them.[4]

Proliferation of these highly specialized units cuts down on the need for most skills to be basic skills [i.e., for the skills of most members to be interchangeable]. Granted, there is no society for which all of the skills of all of the members are basic skills, but it is characteristic of most of the relatively nonmodernized societies that the ratio of basic skills to intermediate skills is high. It is certainly high by contrast with that ratio among the members of any relatively modernized society.

Although the need to generalize the vast proportion of all skills diminishes, the importance of generalizing some of the skills certainly does not. One of the special features of the relatively modernized societies is the fact that perhaps a larger absolute number of basic skills must be generalized. For example, in relation to language, the average member of any society has to be able to speak and understand the language of other members. In addition to this command over the spoken language, virtually all of the members of relatively modernized societies must become literate during childhood. Even the enormous proliferation of technological devices which play to aural capacities or simple visual rather than literate ones does not make it possible to operate in terms of a relatively modernized society with high levels of illiteracy.

Closely related to the lower need to generalize most of the skills of the members of the society concerned is the question of "economies of scale" and the like. In relatively modernized contexts it is possible to do highly specialized and limited things on a very large scale. There is not space or need to discuss the technical aspects of economies of scale that are so highly developed in the works of professional economists. The implications for the interrelationships among the members of different units

[4] It is not necessary to do exhaustive reading in sociology to be aware of this. The layman may not be accustomed to being asked to marshall his knowledge of this but he certainly has it. Every layman is thoroughly aware of the fact that the ordinary housewife must know the difference between right and left and up and down and how to recognize a policeman. It is absolutely unnecessary that a housewife under ordinary circumstances be able at a glance to distinguish between a major and a lieutenant colonel of the United States Army. Most housewives cannot do this and couldn't care less. It is, however, absolutely necessary that virtually every member of the Armed Forces be able to do this at a glance because too many things depend on the conception of the line of command in his life, including, perhaps, his life itself. There is of course a special category of housewives who need this information at their ready disposal. They are army wives.

in the society, and among the units in terms of which the members of the society have different parts are the important ones for this work. As the level of specialization of these units increases, as the emphasis on intermediate skills and economies of scale mount higher, the individual member of the society plays parts in terms of an increasing number of different units. These parts are referred to technically as roles. The term *role* is defined as any socially differentiated position in terms of which an individual may and/or does act. The increased differentiation of the individual's roles in terms of different organizations increases the problem of coordination in two forms. First, there is the coordination of the various roles of the individual by the individual. Second, there is the more general problem of coordination. How are all the various roles of the various individuals coordinated? It is also important to look at the problem of coordination the other way around. This problem in any social context is simultaneously a problem of the separation of various roles. The question of separation arises a great deal more often and is a great deal more important in relatively modernized contexts, if only because so many more roles are distinguished and ideally speaking are kept separate by the members of such societies. The separation of roles is, however, a problem common to all societies.[5]

In terms of a relatively modernized society, how does a person keep his role as a citizen separate from his role as a member of a university? These are roles supposedly kept separate in many respects. As a citizen I am legitimately interested in who wins an election for the presidency. As a member of a university faculty I might use means at my disposal for imposing my beliefs on, say, the graduate students of my department. It is quite illegitimate, ideally speaking, to take advantage of these facilities.

I emphasize this "separation implication" of the general term coordination because its general connotations stress bringing things together. Coordination of roles is just as much a question of keeping certain roles insulated from one another. This insulation is never perfect, but it is always increasingly important in relatively modernized societies. There is an especially important illustration of this point in the context of family problems and the general process of modernization. One of the reasons why the process of modernization is so highly disruptive of the general structure of relatively nonmodernized societies is that the vast

---

[5] Here again is one of those similarities among societies that makes it possible for men from diverse social settings to understand one another's problems.

majority of members of the relatively nonmodernized societies orient more of their behavior to family considerations than to all other considerations taken together, and that ceases to be the case as modernization is achieved.[6]

The increase in specialization of the organizations in a society impinges on the action that is ordinarily carried out in family terms in different ways. In terms of our own society and in terms of highly modernized or relatively modernized societies in general, the question of these interrelationships is ticklish and tough. We go to great extremes in our assumptions and views about these matters. Ideally speaking, we maintain that what goes on in terms of a man's family should not interfere with what he does in terms of his occupational roles. We assume that if a man has a responsible executive position, he does not permit his executive

[6] I shall return to this whole general question at great length. The present illustration, however, requires some amplification lest it be misinterpreted. I mean that the actions of the vast majority of members are overwhelmingly family oriented in that, day in and day out, they make their decisions in terms of the implications of their behavior for the persistence of their family organizations. This does not mean, however, that family structures always occupy the same position in general social structure in all of the relatively nonmodernized societies. This is not the case. For example, in premodern Japan the average individual in fact oriented most of his behavior to family considerations, but in many contexts, if there was a question of family interests versus that of his overlord, he put the interest of his overlord first. In traditional China to behave in such a fashion would have been considered bestial. In terms of no relatively modernized society is anything like so great a proportion of even the average person's action oriented directly to family considerations.

This distinction between relatively modernized and relatively nonmodernized societies says a great deal about the place that family structure has in the general social structure of these two different types of societies. It is not, however, equivalent to the implication that "the family is more important" in relatively nonmodernized societies than in relatively modernized societies. At least this is not the case unless one defines more important as meaning that more of the individual's activities are oriented to family considerations. If one defines more important in this way, then the statement is correct, but it adds nothing to what has already been said about the proportion of an individual's actions that, ideally and/or actually, is family oriented.

There is another sense in which it is definitely not correct to say that the family is more important in relatively nonmodernized societies than in relatively modernized ones. The kind of family structure characteristic of relatively modernized societies is remarkably uniform. The place of family structures in the general social structure in such societies is also remarkably uniform. It is crucial for relatively modernized societies that the family structures of those societies take the particular form that it does, just as it is for societies like that of traditional China and premodern Japan that the family took the specific forms it did. To say that the family is relatively less important in relatively modernized societies and imply that elimination or change of the family units would have fewer implications for a relatively modernized society than for a relatively nonmodernized society is clearly mistaken.

decisions to be influenced by family considerations. We also know perfectly well that in actuality his executive decisions are affected by family considerations. It is still neither irrelevant nor hypocritical to maintain that ideally speaking these two realms of behavior are separated from one another.

One of the reasons this coordination and, if one will, separation of roles has special implications for family organizations lies in the fact that every member of every society under ordinary circumstances always has family roles in addition to whatever other roles he may have in other organizations. An individual may have a role in the government of his society and not have a role in any of its universities. He may have a role in a given business firm and not in the entertainment industry. Regardless of what other organizations he belongs to, however, ordinarily he has a role in some family organization of his society at all stages of his life. This is true of all societies, whether they are relatively modernized or not. Therefore, as problems of coordination of these interrelationships of a nonfamily sort increase, they always impinge on family structures to some degree. They also impinge in a more direct sense. A considerable amount of this increase in specialization of units is the result of conducting in other organizational contexts activities that formerly were conducted in terms of the family itself. It is not a matter of chance that (1) the impact of modernization is always felt in the realm of kinship and the family, that (2) it is commonly felt at the beginning of the process, and that (3) these changes are uniform in direction.

2. SELF-SUFFICIENCY OF THE UNITS

Another characteristic of the organizations of relatively modernized societies has to do with their degree of self-sufficiency. No specialized units in any society approach self-sufficiency. In relatively nonmodernized societies there are many units that approach self-sufficiency quite closely. These are not only family units; they may be village units or provincial units too. They are usually family units, but the important thing is that such units exist at all, regardless of what their other characteristics may be. A unit is defined as approaching self-sufficiency insofar as the activities of its members in terms of it are capable of perpetuation of the unit, more or less indefinitely into the future, with little contact with persons outside the membership of the unit. Here, is another of those touchy differences of degree, but again I shall deal only with sufficiently gross differences of degree so that the exact location of the dividing line will not raise serious problems for the analysis.

In traditional Chinese society the family unit was characterized by high levels of self-sufficiency. Due to strict rules of family exogamy, the recruitment of wives was one respect in which family units were not self-sufficient. Family members, however, generally produced most of what they consumed and would have liked to consume most of what they produced. For most Chinese the interaction of family members with others did not extend often beyond the geographical boundaries that in part defined their particular village organization. If they did, they rarely extended beyond the limits of a small number of neighboring villages. Traditional Chinese society was complicated and varied, but as societies in general social history go, the level of self-sufficiency of family and village organizations was quite high. The level of self-sufficiency characteristic of the average traditional Chinese peasant family unit is never approximated in highly modernized contexts.

To illustrate the problem of self-sufficiency and relate the illustration once again to the family question I should like to start with the problem of recruitment. Every highly specialized organization depends on other organizations for the recruitment of its members. Although the members of such units may be and commonly are trained in the context of the units, there are also many critical respects in which the members are never trained in terms of such units themselves. In the last analysis, the members of all units in all known societies are ordinarily generated in terms of family units. In all social contexts there is always a question of how personnel gets from family contexts into nonfamily contexts. The formation of these nonfamily relationships is never a matter of indifference to the members of any society, but it is particularly important for the members of relatively nonmodernized societies.

Apart from nations considered as wholes, the units which ordinarily are the foci of attention in problems of international affairs [e.g., governments, armies, international organizations, etc.] are ordinarily units whose members do not generate their own new members by sexual reproduction of existing members as do the members of a family unit. They are also units which are not ordinarily joined by new members until those new members have reached adulthood. Usually most of the general training and education which the new members need in their roles in any specialized units has been gained by these new members in contexts other than the specialized unit.[7]

[7] The general relevance of some educationally oriented system to all of these highly specialized organizations poses one of the most spectacular

Regardless of the sort of specialization of the unit concerned, there are always problems of allocations of goods and services. How does one get the means for the activities to the persons who must utilize them; how does one motivate the actors to participate in the units concerned; etc.? If the unit concerned happens to be a government, despite the fact that it is presumably predominantly politically oriented, there is still the important question of paying the personnel so they do not have to do other things in order to make a living. Whether the society is capitalistic or socialistic, this basic problem is not altered. The activities that the personnel must engage in if the governing is effective will not leave this personnel with either the means or the energy to create their own food, shelter, clothing, etc., in terms of relatively self-sufficient family units. If they are to perform specialized governmental tasks, there must be some systematic way of conveying these goods and services to them.

As the level of modernization increases, the self-sufficiency of the various units diminishes. The self-sufficiency of the family units is always directly diminished, since any increase in specialized units must in the last analysis recruit personnel from some family context, no matter by what means. The relative immunity of family members from contact with members of other units, therefore, always declines. Family members depend more and more on the members of other units for an increasing variety of things. It may be income; it may be power; it may be education. Whatever it is, these interdependencies constantly increase.

With an increase of specialized units, self-sufficiency declines

---

problems for modernizing societies. In all of the modernizing societies public educational systems on a large scale must be introduced early in the process. The late-comers to modernization cannot develop their systems by bits and dabs or on a privately financed basis. The ultimate consumers of the education produced cannot be precisely enough located, especially in advance, to finance educational systems on this basis. Observers of modern United States society, which is probably characterized by the largest systems of privately financed higher education, have seen some rather interesting developments in this connection in recent years. As the possibility of continuing this financing largely out of personal contributions from the individual fortunes of members of the society has declined, members of private corporations have come increasingly to realize that, while they cannot in any precise sense assess the value of the services of individual private colleges and universities in providing trained personnel or as centers of research, it is nevertheless to the "interest" of such corporations to make unrestricted gifts to private universities so that those benefits will not be discontinued. Various schemes are being tried. Nevertheless, in no relatively modernized social context, whether dominated by people with the ideology of socialism or of capitalism, can the general education be privately financed or treated as a commodity such as automobiles, houses, etc.

in two senses. First, there is an increase in specialized units which do not even approach self-sufficiency ideally speaking. Second, the approach to self-sufficiency of the remaining relatively nonspecialized units also declines, as illustrated in the case of the family above. In all relatively modernized societies some relatively nonspecialized units always remain. These are never confined to family units alone, though family units are probably the most important category of units of this sort in any and all societies. It is important to realize that the self-sufficiency of the relatively nonspecialized units of such societies declines despite the fact that these units are not necessarily becoming more specialized. The ordinary family unit in relatively modernized societies is no more overwhelmingly oriented to one of these aspects as opposed to another than was the traditional Chinese family. The degree of specialization and the degree of self-sufficiency are not the same things, nor are they inevitably linked to one another in any simple fashion. The following generalizations, however, will hold: (1) Taking the society as a whole, as the level of specialization increases the level of self-sufficiency declines. (2) The more specialized a given organization is, the less self-sufficient it is. (3) As the level of specialization increases in the society, even those units which are not increasingly specialized become less self-sufficient. (4) In the long run, once the process of modernization is started, the levels of modernization and specialization always increase. (5) A further increase in the specialization of a relatively specialized organization or in that of other organizations in the society does not necessarily complicate the problems of its members. Insofar as it does not, it is because the very level of specialization of the organization concerned may enable its members to minimize the implications of their other roles for their actions in terms of the organization in question. (6) On the other hand, the increase of specialization in general always increases the problem of adjustment of the members of the relatively nonspecialized units insofar as the level of self-sufficiency of these units continually declines without the level of specialization of such units necessarily increasing.

Before leaving the closely interrelated questions of specialization and self-sufficiency of the units concerned, I should like to mention three other examples: predominantly recreationally oriented units, predominantly religiously oriented units, and again the family. In most of the relatively nonmodernized societies the distinction between work and play is not so starkly drawn as it is in terms of relatively modernized societies. In some of the more advanced of the latter it has become fashionable to speak of that portion of one's life spent in work as though it were something different from living. In some respects living is what one does when one is not working. Nevertheless, there probably has never been a society whose members failed to make any distinction at all between serious activities and play or recreation. In relatively modernized societies the existence of units highly specialized with regard to recreational aspects is one of the interesting developments. In most societies the units in terms of which recreation is carried out are not so highly specialized. A good part of the recreation is carried out in terms of family units, neighborhood units, etc. Insofar as predominantly recreationally oriented units develop, the self-sufficiency of the family units even with regard to the relaxation of their members declines.

With regard to churches, some of the developments have been even more interesting. A *church* may be defined for present purposes as a predominantly religiously oriented organization. There was a time, however, in the history of European societies in which the church was more nearly a relatively nonspecialized unit. It had its specialized orientations to religion, but it was also conceived to be a general organization in community life. In some cases, for example, the church and the local government were the same. There has been a tendency with the development of modernization in European society for the churches to become more and more specialized with regard to religious orientations as such, and participation of church members as church members in other areas of social action tends increasingly to be minimized. A layman's way of putting this was that church membership became primarily a Sunday affair. Curiously enough with the development of high modernization there is a reverse tendency cropping up in the predominantly religiously oriented organizations in the United States. The Community-House activities associated with the church or with the synagogue become as important a part of the behavior of the members of a given church as the more strictly religiously oriented activities themselves. In some cases these other activities may become even more important. There are even cases of churches or other predominantly religiously oriented units whose members build their Community Houses before they build an actual church or synagogue building. In these cases religious services and the like are carried out in the Community House. Until the members of the congregation can collect enough funds to build a separate church building, the main hall of the Community House is as much a dance floor as it is a center for worship. If one wishes to be paradoxical, it may be regarded as a reversal in the trend toward specialization of a specialized organization. The incorporation of recreational aspects of activities in the church setting in this sense makes some inroads on the self-sufficiency of other relatively nonspecialized units, but it increases that of the churches concerned.

Finally, with regard to the family again, in virtually every relatively nonmodernized society the overwhelming amount of training of all sorts of an average individual, as an infant, as a young child, as an older child, as a young adult, as a mature adult, and finally in old age, is inculcated on the average member of the society by members of his own family or kinship unit. As modernization increases, elements of these training functions are almost immediately taken over by members of nonfamily units. This is especially true of the training for performances in adult roles. Training of the young by older members of their family or kinship units for adult roles is probably one of the major methods of reinforcing the structure of control of family heads over family members in general, of parents over children, of the older over the young, etc. As soon as a substantial proportion of the members of the society perform specialized adult roles requiring special training outside the family context, this source of reinforcement of family control is radically undermined. One of the major elements of self-sufficiency which is therefore diminished is the degree of self-sufficiency in the control of members of the family unit. One of the major problems in the process of modernization in all social settings is the general problem of control. In virtually every one of the relatively nonmodernized societies the family unit is a major focus of social control. Undermining the stability of the family units is most likely to increase the general problem of social control. It is characteristic of all societies with governments that action in terms of the government can and does make some inroads on control in terms of family units. Ordinarily in relatively nonmodernized contexts, one of the most important forms of decentralization lies in the fact that these inroads are made as little as possible. In the process of modernization, leaders operating in terms of the government do not have the same degrees of freedom as far as noninterference with the structures of family control is concerned. In all cases of modernization operation in terms of the government not only interferes increasingly with the structures of family control, but alternatives to family control methods must be found if chaos is to be avoided. When such an alternative is not skillfully and thoroughly developed in terms of the government organization, disintegration of family control is not avoided, but general social chaos and hardship increase.

3. AN INCREASINGLY UNIVERSALISTIC ETHIC

In Part II, Chapter 1 below I shall deal quite extensively with the concepts of universalism and particularism. For present purposes [see section E of this chapter] I shall not define these terms beyond the following. A relationship or ethic will be considered relatively universalistic to the extent that it stresses "what a person does or can do that is relevant to the action or purpose under consideration." A relationship or ethic will be considered more or less particularistic to the extent that it emphasizes "who a person is" rather than what he can do or does that is relevant. These two concepts are not binary concepts. They refer to a scale of indefinite differences of degree. An ethic or relationship may be more or less nearly universalistic or more or less particularistic.

To return to the example of bullying used before, the condemnation of the use of superior force over a weaker opponent to coerce him into a particular line of activity, regardless of who does it or under what circumstances it is done, is an example of a highly universalistic ethic. If such behavior is regarded as bullying and condemned if it involves two individuals of the same class position but not if the coercer is a nobleman and the coerced is a peasant, then to that extent the ethic concerned is a highly particularistic one. Ideally speaking, the members of the societies considered to be modern democracies pride themselves on their emphasis on highly universalistic ethics. Members of these societies frequently invoke such mottoes as "All men are equal before the law." Voting criteria are supposed to be predominantly universalistically determined. Discrimination against people in voting on the basis of race, creed, or color is regarded as an intrusion of particularistic elements, though such terms are rarely used. At one time it was a practical impossibility to elect a member of the Catholic faith to the Presidency of the United States. It is a practical impossibility today to elect a true believer in Judaism or Islam to that position. The fact that a true believer of the Catholic faith *has* been elected to that position implies an increase in the level of universalism in certain respects.[8]

There are societies whose members, ideally speaking, place

---

[8] This is, of course, not without certain tinges of arguments about particularism, however, since many allege that a large number of people voted for the candidate in question *because* he was a member of that faith rather than on the basis of his sheer merit for the position. Insofar as individuals voted either for him or against him on such a basis there was an intrusion of particularistic elements.

little or no emphasis on either a predominantly universalistic ethic or predominantly universalistically defined relationships. There is no society for whose members questions of universalism are actually irrelevant. To some extent germane abilities always get to be a criterion in some fashion or other. In ethical matters the emphasis in relatively nonmodernized is heavily on predominantly particularistic ethics. This is not always the case, of course. Roman law contained many highly universalistic elements. The Ten Commandments are on the whole a highly universalistic ethic as is the ethical injunction, "Do unto others as you would have others do unto you." In relatively modernized contexts the emphasis on predominantly universalistic ethics is always heavy and increasing. Neither ideally nor actually does the emphasis on a universalistic ethic ever eliminate all particularistic emphases. For example, specific ethics of kinship remain, and kinship is always predominantly particularistic.

Increases in emphases on highly universalistic ethics abound whenever societies become increasingly modernized, regardless of whether their governments are authoritarian or nonauthoritarian. Many of the highly universalistic ethics to which we are most accustomed happen to be closely associated with nonauthoritarianism and concepts of democracy, but it is possible to set up highly universalistic criteria that are quite undemocratic.

Why is this emphasis important in a relatively modernized society? Quite apart from judgments of good or bad about these criteria, increasing problems of scale and coordination alone require an increasing emphasis on predominantly universalistic criteria if the society is to be stable. In handling questions on a predominantly particularistic basis it is always important to know in some detail exactly *who* a person is. Only in relatively small-scale sedentary environments can one count on being able to identify accurately in personal terms most, if not all, of the individuals with whom one must interact in the course of a day. As specialization increases and as self-sufficiency declines, the increased interdependence and interaction of members of different subsystems make it increasingly impossible to keep in mind who each individual is in all the contexts in which he must interact with others. In the heyday of small neighborhood stores, a merchant could know each and every one of his customers as an individual and to some extent treat each and every one of them differently. No modern department store in either a capitalistic or socialistic society could possibly exist on such a basis. The development of mass production and of mass consumption —the increase of interaction in general—make the cognitive problem posed by a highly particularistic ethic impossible, even if that problem is considered alone.

Although the emphasis on universalistic criteria can never be complete, it increases in the transition to and the maintenance of relatively modernized societies. It will be argued later that the scale and complexity of interaction in terms of relatively modernized societies must continue to increase if the societies are to be stable. Although the stability of such societies is problematical, interaction of the members has continued to increase in scale and complexity with consequent problems for particularism.

The problem of the preparation of youth for adult roles, the socialization of the new members of these societies, adds further impetus. Their preparation has to be carried out on highly generalized objective impersonal bases at least in part because of the lack of certain knowledge in advance as to what roles these individuals will have in the society and what their future lives will be like. In relatively nonmodernized contexts the future of the individual is more predictable.

As relatively modernized societies become more modernized predominantly particularistic ethics, though never eliminated, are increasingly restricted. Actually predominantly particularistic ethics remain much stronger than they do ideally. Supporters of particularistic identifications in terms of class, regions, race, creed, color, etc., are put in increasingly defensive positions. The largest basis of particularism which remains in such societies is nationalism. National pride, national identification, the ethic of patriotism, however admirable and however broadly defined, all involve a particularistic identification. At its most nearly universalistic, the ethic of patriotism remains particularistic even in the formulation, "My country, may she always be right, but right or wrong, my country." Nationalism is so broad a form of particularism that under many circumstances it does not complicate the problems of action in terms of a relatively modernized context. Most choices of personnel have to be made without crossing national boundaries. This is much less true today than it was fifty years ago. With continuing technological improvements, it will be much less true ten years from now than it is today.

As modernization has increased in the world, not only has the self-sufficiency of the various subsystems of the societies concerned declined, but the self-sufficiency of any given society or nation has also declined. That decline poses radical problems for the doctrine of national sovereignty. We inherit that doctrine from a period in which self-sufficiency was higher than it now can be. Nationalistic ethics are becoming an increasing problem, regardless of our likes or dislikes. Some decrease in particularism on a nationalistic basis is evident in the development of organizations such as the United Nations and the European Common Market. Welcome or not, the doctrines of national sovereignty are breaking down, whether on a relatively authoritarian basis [e.g., foreign conquest, occupation, and control] or on a voluntary basis.

Men in this world will not soon cease to think in nationalistic terms. That may never come, but a great deal of thinking in highly nationalistic terms is already suspect. Nationalism might conceivably be replaced in the future by continentalism, and continentalism in its turn, especially if we feel ourselves threatened by beings from another world, might be replaced by worldism. Nevertheless, one may generalize about relatively modernized societies as follows: (1) elements of particularistic ethics will always survive in them both ideally and actually, (2) there will be many more actual than ideal survivors, and (3) the survivals tend to be either more narrowly confined [e.g., family oriented or nepotistic ethics] or diluted by being defined in terms of broader and broader identifications [e.g., the progression from localism to nationalism to continentalism, etc.].

4. COMBINATION OF CENTRALIZATION AND DECENTRALIZATION

All societies are combinations of centralized and decentralized structures of action. The most extreme form of centralization would be one in which a single individual made all decisions as to what each and every other member of the society would do at any and all times in any and all contexts. He would presumably be able both to make these decisions and to see that they were carried out. Complete decentralization would require every individual to decide what to do and when to do it without reference to anyone else. There would be no accepted methods whereby one individual could coerce or influence another. Neither such extreme could exist. No society could survive if decentralized to the extent of permitting infants to make all their own decisions. Such infants would not survive. On the other hand, the problem of cognition alone would make a completely centralized society impossible. A single mistake by the ruler would probably shatter everything. The system would have to be completely rationally planned and therefore incredibly brittle.

The degree of centralization always increases with modernization, if it has not already been high previously, and continues to increase with further modernization. Although the question of authoritarian versus nonauthoritarian practices is highly relevant, the increased level of centralization may be considered quite apart from the question of authoritarian versus nonauthoritarian structures. One of the special features of relatively modernized societies is that, for the first time in world history, it is possible to combine overwhelming centralization with the possibility of stability. None of the highly centralized systems in world history prior to the development of relatively modernized societies have been very stable, and most of the stable despotisms have not been nearly as centralized as they are sometimes described. Technological advances in communications and logistics make possible stable moves in the direction of ever increasing centralization that is not possible without them.

There is a range of variation of combinations of centralization and decentralization among relatively modernized societies despite the fact that it is possible to hold that all of them are characterized by increasing centralization. Most of us are concerned as to whether this increasing centralization is combined with increasing authoritarianism. The extremes of centralization and authoritarianism are inseparable. Apart from the extremes which cannot exist, as the level of centralization increases, the level of authoritarianism probably increases, and that probability, in turn, increases with the degree of centralization already achieved. There is an element of acceleration involved in this process.

Emphasis on authoritarian elements can, however, be carried far beyond the level required by the degree of centralization essential for a given state of modernization. United States society at present is far more highly modernized than is the society of the Soviet Union. It is also considerably less authoritarian as a society. Whether the United States society is more highly centralized than that of the Soviet Union or less so is an interesting question. Except for the element of governmental authority, United States society is considerably more centralized than the Soviet Union. At this point the comparison between the two societies may be argued along several different lines, but the net result of the argument will be to show that the degrees of centralization and authoritarianism can vary independently of one another *within restricted ranges* and, perhaps, even independently of the level of modernization actually achieved.[9]

[9] The possibilities here may be outlined as follows without actually making a choice among them. If the level of modernization of United States society is higher than that of the Soviet Union but the level of authoritarianism is lower, then to some extent the level of authoritarianism can

In the long run the level of modernization, the level of centralization, and the level of authoritarianism vary directly with one another if modernization is increasing. Over a broad range of such possible increases, however, it is certainly possible (1) for the rate of centralization to increase more rapidly than that of authoritarianism, (2) for the rate of authoritarianism in restricted areas to increase more rapidly than that of centralization in general, (3) for the rate of modernization to increase faster than centralization or authoritarianism, (4) for the rate of authoritarianism to increase faster than the rate of modernization or centralization, etc. Not all of these possibilities have the same implications for stability. If a society is to be stable once a relatively modernized stage has been achieved, unless the society was already highly authoritarian, modernization, centralization, and authoritarianism will probably increase. Furthermore, modernization by late-comers cannot be achieved without increasingly high levels of centralization and authoritarianism unless those were already at high levels when the transition began.

The problems of coordination and control steadily increase with the increasing specialization and interdependency characteristic of relatively modernized systems. Nonauthoritarianism comes to consist increasingly of protection of the rights of minorities or of dissenters in general to express themselves. The degree of freedom for the expression of either individualism by ideal or individualism by default [10] becomes increasingly small. Certainly there are variations among relatively modernized societies in the extent of such nonauthoritarianism [e.g., the relative freedom of expression of dissent in Great Britain or Japan today by contrast with Czechoslovakia or China].

The history of modernization exhibits another range of varia-

---

vary independently of the level of modernization. If the level of centralization of United States society is higher than that of the Soviet Union and the level of authoritarianism is lower, then to some extent the level of authoritarianism and the level of centralization at least do not always vary directly. If the level of centralization of United States society is lower than that of the Soviet Union but the level of modernization is higher, then, despite the fact that modernization and centralization may in general vary in the same direction, they do not necessarily vary directly over all ranges. From most points of view relevant here the level of modernization of the United States is higher than that of the Soviet Union; the level of centralization of the United States is higher than that of the Soviet Union; and the level of authoritarianism is lower than that of the Soviet Union. United States communications are more highly centralized than those of the Soviet Union if only because of the higher development and application of the technology of communications. Governmental control on the other hand is less centralized.

[10] For definitions of these concepts, see below, p. 228.

tion among relatively modernized societies. This is the political scientist's distinction between national and federal systems. It is significant only in the relatively early stages of modernization. The high element of actual decentralization connoted by the concept of federal systems decreases as the level of modernization increases, even though the ideal structures continue to receive allegiance. Increasingly members of the central government interfere with states rights, and only puristic "states righters" are prepared to make the sacrifices in other benefits that would have to be made to have it otherwise.

Stress on the possible variations of combinations of centralization and decentralization should not imply a general independence of centralization and modernization. As modernization increases, the trend is overwhelmingly and irreversibly towards more centralized structures in every case. The degree of centralization may be relaxed for a time, especially if the prior degree of centralization was higher than required by the level of modernization already achieved. One of the fundamental hypotheses of this work, however, is that in the long run modernization and centralization cannot vary inversely. Unless the process of modernization is stopped by a holocaust, the degree of centralization all over the world will continue to increase. A holocaust is quite feasible.

The minimal reasons for maintaining this hypothesis have to do with problems of coordination and control. There is a radical increase in the degree of interdependency at advanced levels of modernization. What the members do in terms of one unit of a society has increasing implications for what they and other members do in terms of other units. The implications of any slips continually increase. Thorstein Veblen in quixotically memorable phrases described this long ago. He referred sardonically to the increasingly delicate "interstitial adjustments" of the "closely concatenated processes" of societies. With increasing modernization the implications of what goes on in terms of one part of a society are increasingly manifested in terms of others. The implications of any breakdown in communications, whatever the source of the difficulty, increase radically. The increasing importance of "the traffic problem" in every increasingly modernized context is no more an accident than the ubiquity of modern forms of juvenile delinquency, regardless of the assertedly important ideological differences among societies.

The increase of centralization that accompanies increases of modernization need not be concentrated solely in terms of the government. The increasing centralization must always be concentrated in the government to some extent, however, and it must be concentrated in terms of the government to an increasing extent as both centralization in general and modernization increase. A given society may be so organized that all of its increases in centralization are increases in the centralization of its governmental system. Socialistic, communistic, fascistic, and similar societies—in the usual ideological definitions of those terms—are probably good examples of societies of this sort. This need not hold for all societies, however. In the United States context a considerable part of the increases of centralization are to be found in the increased centralization of a wide variety of nongovernmental organizations. Business firms, labor unions, universities, etc., all afford examples of increasing centralization. Relatively small organizations newly and strategically placed may radically increase the centralization of the system.

Many trends that appear to move toward decentralization from centralization turn out to increase centralization. Measurement may be difficult, but consider the movement of people into suburbs and even exurbs. Had they continued to live in our large cities, the density of population of those cities would be higher than it is now, but the decentralization of the surrounding rural areas would also be greater. The increase in centralization of activities in the suburban and exurban areas has far outrun the decrease or slowed rate of increase of centralization characteristic of the urban areas.

Increases in centralization outside the governmental context may exceed those in governmental terms. The two cannot vary at random, however. Increases of centralization in terms of organizations other than the governmental system increases the relevance of action in terms of those organizations for the actions of others who belong to the same or different societies. The more centralizing the effects of operations in terms of a given organization become for other members of, or organizations in, the society, the more acute are the problems of its relationship to the government. When representatives of the state do not, ideally speaking, control everything, it is not a matter of chance that action in terms of large-scale organizations is generally considered both easier and more important to control than action in terms of small-scale organizations. The increasing implications of any slips require an increasing interest of governmental representatives in all other systems whose centralization or centralizing effects increase. This in turn increases the level of centralization of the government.

Whether or not one likes increasing centralization, there is no denying it. The cases that appear to contradict this are those in which the levels of centralization exceed the level of centralization requisite for a given stage of modernization. Then cutbacks in the excess are quite conceivable. More decentralization than that is not likely to be long tolerated by the members of the society. It can only be carried out at the expense of what one might call *demodernization,* which cannot be stably maintained in the present day world, or in any probable future world.

Comparison of the relatively modernized and relatively non-modernized periods of any generally selected set of societies will show an increase in the levels of centralization. So will any comparison of different degrees of modernization of any society after becoming relatively modernized. No general social inventions give any hint of changing the direction of this tendency. There is no reason to believe that this tendency is a function of belief in any particular political ideology. There are ideologies that would make a virtue out of as much centralization as possible as well as ones that claim it a major vice. Advocates of neither set are responsible, and none of them show any ability to alter these phenomena.

Some decentralization will persist [e.g., on a family basis]. No society has yet existed without families, and this is not simply the result of a lack of social inventiveness. Although the family itself may remain a focus of decentralization, the growing centralization of the setting in which its members operate may actually increase the centralization of the family regardless of whether the ideal structures for the family concerned are highly authoritarian, highly centralized ones, or highly permissive, highly decentralized, ones. As more and more of the actions of family members are centralized in terms of other organizations, activities on a family basis will decrease. This decrease will increase the actual centralization of family units, whatever the wishes of their members. For example, the problems of transportation for general and special schooling result in a centralization of activities around the "family chauffeur" that is considerably greater than that around more authoritarian family heads in rural environments of fifty years ago.

5. RELATIONSHIP ASPECTS

The relationship aspects are taken up in some considerable detail below [pp. 133–174]. For the present I wish to comment briefly on four pairs of these terms, one of which has already been discussed above: (1) rationality and traditionalism, (2) universalism and particularism [pp. 52–55] (3) functional specificity and functional diffuseness, and (4) avoidance and intimacy. The first pair refers to the kind of knowledge [cognition] or thinking relevant to a given relationship. The second refers to the criteria for belonging to a given relationship. The third refers to the explicitness with which a relationship is defined and delimited. The fourth refers to the kind of emotional or affective involvement of the individuals concerned. Relevant differences of degree may be distinguished with regard to all four pairs. Thus one may speak of a greater or lesser emphasis on rationality or traditionalism, on universalism or particularism, on functional specificity or functional diffuseness, or on avoidance or intimacy.

As the level of modernization of a given society increases, the emphasis on rationality increases. That is to say, there is an increase in the emphasis on explaining one's reasons for doing a given thing in scientifically defensible terms as opposed to explaining on the basis of "we've always done it that way." The explanation that "we've always done it that way" or "that's the right way to do it for traditional reasons" is never eliminated, though in general the contexts in which such explanations are invoked diminish. In many contexts in which they are not eliminated such explanations tend to be offered with increasing defensiveness. An emphasis on traditionalism is not, of course, the equivalent of irrationality, i.e., of ignorance or error. In most sedentary agrarian contexts the methods used for tilling the soil are frequently explained or justified on what would here be called traditional grounds. Given the means available to the individuals involved, the traditional techniques probably are in fact rational ones. The great difference between emphases on rationality and traditionalism has not to do with whether a given activity is in fact rational or not. It has to do with an attitude, with whether people feel it should be rational or not. If traditionalism is emphasized, even though the actual practices are in fact rational, the implications of this emphasis are important. Problems of efficiency are not immediately posed, but if the means change and what was formerly done is no longer rational, traditionalists are likely to continue the old methods although they are now irrational. When available means are likely to be changing, this distinction means more.

One further reservation: no amount of devotion to the ideal of rationality guarantees rationality. As moderns we like to think of ourselves as exceedingly rational, but how rational we are is open to question.

A relationship is considered relatively more universalistic insofar as it emphasizes what a person can do that is relevant to the relationship, rather than who he is. An emphasis on the latter is an emphasis on particularism. A relationship is considered more or less functionally specific to the extent that everything the relationship is to cover is explicitly defined and explicitly delimited. Any departures from this are in the direction of functional diffuseness. Thus the ideal structures of a contractual relationship in United States society epitomize a predominantly functionally specific relationship [i.e., all rights and responsibilities of all parties are explicit]. The husband-wife relationship in practically any society is an excellent example of a predominantly functionally diffuse relationship. Some of the elements of predominantly functionally diffuse relationships may be [and usually are] precisely defined and even precisely delimited. Nevertheless insofar as unforeseen obligations may legitimately become relevant, the relationship contains important elements of functional diffuseness. Thus many obligations characteristic of the husband-wife relationship even in our society are relatively clearly defined and delimited, but there are also many obligations commonly covered by this relationship which are not.

Relationships characterized by avoidance rather than intimacy, are those whose members stress either emotional neutrality or emotional displays that minimize contacts and involvements, such as respect, by contrast with emotional displays that, whether positive or negative, get one deeply involved with others on a highly personal basis. Predominantly intimate relations may take the form of love, hate, etc.

Characteristically the structures of all [11] relatively modernized societies reflect an increasing emphasis on rationality, universalism, functional specificity, and emotional neutrality or avoidance. It is also characteristic of them that these emphases are much higher and more general throughout social structure than is the case for *any* relatively nonmodernized society.[12] Emphases

[11] Although this is characteristic of the structures of all relatively modernized societies, it is by no means characteristic of all of the structures of all relatively modernized societies. It is essential to stress differences of degree in the discussion of these paired concepts. As indicated below in this chapter and elsewhere in this work [e.g., pp. 64–65, 137–138, 141, 677–683] to speak of relatively modernized societies unqualifiedly as universalistic and of relatively nonmodernized ones as particularistic sinks a mite of insight in a sea of misunderstanding.

[12] The level of emphasis on emotional neutrality or avoidance may be high in relatively nonmodernized contexts. To the extent that this is the case, movement in the direction of greater modernization may for a time at least actually decrease the emphasis on avoidance. There are many respects in which modernization is likely to increase informality and hence to some extent the emphasis on intimacy. In the long run, however, there is always a sense in which the emphasis on emotional neutrality or avoidance increases as a society becomes a relatively modernized one—no

on traditionalism, particularism, functional diffuseness, and intimacy, however, are never entirely eliminated. For some organizations they may not be eliminated at all. Nevertheless, the direction of emphasis is *always* changed for the society as a whole unless the emphasis was previously in the direction of rationality, universalism, functional specificity, and avoidance. In relatively nonmodernized contexts overwhelming emphasis on rationality, universalism, and functional specificity are confined to restricted spheres. Indeed, ideally speaking, explicit emphases on rationality, universalism, and functional specificity are relatively rare and mild when present.

There are many reasons for this change in emphasis. One of the simplest ways to throw light on this is to develop some of the implications of the increasing use of increasingly efficient tools and of inanimate sources of power involved in the definition of modernization used here.[13] When one reaches relatively highly developed stages of the use of inanimate sources of power and complicated and efficient tools, rational calculation becomes much more strategic for many lines of action.[14] It becomes important in both the use and repair of the power and tools involved. Without an increased emphasis on rationality and on scientific thinking in general, it is unlikely that the increases in use of inanimate sources of power or of increasingly efficient tools can ever take place at all. The continual increases in variation and efficiency make even a relatively stable coincidence between

matter how high the emphasis before the transition. As the process continues, the number of individuals with whom the vast majority of individuals interact increases enormously, and an increasing number of these interactions are of such short duration as to preclude any considerable intimacy. In this sense in the context of relatively modernized societies, the vast majority of individuals participate in far more numerous and varied predominantly emotionally neutral or predominantly avoidant relationships than in any relatively nonmodernized social context.

[13] These are by no means the only arguments which could be used. They are not presented as causal arguments. Causal arguments involving them can be formulated, but all such arguments will also involve other strategic variables. Nevertheless, after a given stage of development of tools and inanimate sources of power is reached, they have interesting implications.

[14] One sees constant evidence of such conflicts in even the most highly modernized social contexts. The whole issue of featherbedding in labor relations contains important elements of this. What may have been quite rational from at least the point of view of specific interested parties may become quite irrational under changed conditions of technology. The same may be said of many practices staunchly defended on overwhelmingly traditional grounds by businessmen, civil servants, politicians, academics, doctors, lawyers, etc. Most of the individuals most deeply concerned in these matters are extremely sensitive about any implications that their behavior in these contexts is nonrational—let alone irrational.

traditional ways of doing things and rational methods unlikely.

Once these tools and sources of power are developed, the different implications of selecting people on the basis of what they can do as opposed to who they are become stark. As long as tools remain simple and easily mastered and combinations of tools and inanimate sources of power multiply effort only slightly, small differences in skill among the people who use them are insignificant. Some of the differences in skill of individuals available to dig with spades may be considerable, but at the end of a long day's work, they will not make much absolute difference in the amount of earth moved. Relatively small differences in skill, however, of operators of modern power shovels may make enormous differences in the absolute amount of work done at the end of a day. Not only that, small differences in skill may make a great deal of difference in terms of the repair costs, of other damage done, etc. Selection of personnel on the basis of who they are rather than what they can do means that one cannot take advantage of such differences either to maximize accomplishment or minimize damage.

If relationships are vaguely defined and delimited, it is difficult to emphasize and expect rational behavior. If one does not know what is likely to be involved in a relationship, it is exceedingly difficult to select people on the basis of what they can do that is relevant rather than on the basis of who they are. Furthermore, when levels of mass production and mass coordination are reached, if one cannot treat people on the basis of quite limited involvements, such large-scale relationships become impossible. If one has to deal with all consumers personally, regardless of whether one is a socialist or a capitalist, there cannot be mass production of food, clothing, automobiles, or anything else. Neither businessmen nor government officials can distribute the output of a highly modernized production of goods and services on the basis of functionally diffuse relationships with particularistically selected consumers.

Finally, with regard to avoidance or emotional neutrality, insofar as one becomes directly involved emotionally—especially if one becomes intimately involved—it is difficult to keep such relationships highly functionally specific. It is difficult to think of people with whom one is emotionally involved on the basis of what they can do that is relevant rather than on the basis of who they are; it is also difficult to deal with them rationally. Not only is love blind, but most of the intimate emotions certainly increase the problems of objectivity, and limited involvement.

No increase in modernization ever eliminates traditionalism, particularism, functional diffuseness, or intimate emotional involvement, and no relatively nonmodernized society is devoid of structures of rationality, universalism, functional specificity, and emotional neutrality or avoidance. Nevertheless, for most of the time most of the relationships of most of the members of relatively nonmodernized societies are carried out primarily on the basis of traditionalism, particularism, and functional diffuseness.[15] In terms of relatively modernized societies those emphases, ideally speaking at least, are increasingly restricted to the context of relatively nonspecialized organizations such as family units, friendships, etc. Even for relatively specialized organizations the trend toward emphasis on rationality, universalism, functional specificity, and avoidance is never complete. All save the most naïve are well aware of the discrepancies between ideal and actual structures. Given previous history, however, the surprising thing is not how far actual practice departs from ideal structures in these respects, but how little.

Perhaps one of the best illustrations of the meaning of this sort of shift of emphasis is the change in the attitude toward nepotism.[16] One of the hardest things for the members of relatively modernized societies to understand is the attitude of members of the relatively nonmodernized societies toward nepotism. There is no relatively modernized society for whose members an emphasis on nepotism is not a source of embarrassment in many social contexts.[17] Few members of few nonmodernized societies consider neoptism anything to be embarrassed about. They are more likely to consider a lack of nepotism as occasion for embarrassment. A great deal of nepotism continues to be characteristic of United States society, but those who practice it are likely to be on the defensive.[18]

[15] These relationships may be characterized by high levels of either avoidance or intimacy. A great deal of intimacy in the relations among some adults and children and infants and among children is, however, unavoidable.

[16] Nepotism, in this sense is particularism on a kinship or simulated kinship basis.

[17] Many parents are even embarrassed if their estimates of their children's intelligence can be shown to be highly biased by such considerations.

[18] They find it necessary to justify the special position in a business firm for the son of the owner on some such basis as: "The business is a family business." The continuation of family members in positions of responsibility is something our customers and suppliers expect and rely upon. In other words, they tend to give as nearly universalistic a justification as possible of the nepotism itself, despite the fact that nepotism is inherently particularistic. They insist that it is at least germane particularism, which it may very well be. For the concept of germane particularism, see below, pp. 142–143.

We Americans expect defensive reactions toward charges of nepotism. We think that, if we point out that members of a relatively nonmodernized society, are engaging in nepotistic practices, they will be moved to do something to correct the situation. Again and again in the past history of our relations with the Chinese we have been surprised and even hurt to find that accusations of nepotism did not automatically result in reform. The Chinese found us equally hard to understand. From their point of view not to give preference to relatives was bestial, although in general they thought us kindly. Our differing evaluations of universalistic criteria had important effects on our relations.

6. GENERALIZED MEDIA OF EXCHANGE AND MARKETS

A *medium of exchange* is defined here as any good or service that can be exchanged for two or more other goods and/or services. The more different items that a given article or service can be exchanged for, the more highly generalized it is as a medium of exchange. A *market* is defined as any organization in terms of which action is primarily oriented to facilitating the exchange of goods and/or services among its members with some choice left to them [i.e., with some degree(s) of freedom]. As defined, both are susceptible to exceedingly wide ranges of variations. A given society or nation may be characterized by many different media of exchange. Characteristically this is the case. The different media of exchange may vary widely with regard to their levels of generalization. For example, although they in fact use multiple media of exchange, the members of many societies and of *all* relatively modernized societies designate a single medium of exchange as the legal or official medium of exchange. The term *money* is generally used to describe this special medium of exchange. In all cases the structures of control, issuance, etc., of monies are to some extent governmental structures. Money is usually a highly generalized medium of exchange. It is ordinarily much more generalized than any other medium of exchange available.

The degree of generalization of a medium of exchange may vary within the following extremes: (1) The minimal level of generalization of a medium of exchange is the minimum for a given medium to be identified as a medium of exchange at all [i.e., two other goods and/or services]. (2) The opposite end of the scale is a completely generalized medium of exchange [i.e., a medium in terms of which any and all goods and/or services can be exchanged].[19] There are many variations between these extremes. The members of most feudal societies cannot ordinarily use money to buy and sell land with any great degree of freedom. Even in highly modernized contexts some land is not subject to purchase and sale, such as entailed estates in the case of Great Britain and many national monuments in the case of the United States. Although there has never been a society completely lacking some [or even several] media of exchange, there have certainly been many societies characterized by media of exchange of low levels of generalization and highly subject to *ad hoc* arrangements by the individuals using them.

The range of variation of markets is also great. It is entirely possible that there be a society with no market as such, that is to say there need be no organization set up primarily in order to facilitate exchanges of goods and/or services among the members. It is quite conceivable that the members of a society conduct all such exchanges in terms of organizations not primarily oriented to the facilitation of such exchanges. Markets, too, have varying levels of generalization. The greater the number and the variety of goods and/or services that may be exchanged in terms of it, the greater is the level of generalization of the market. The more restricted the variety and amounts are, the more specialized the market. Markets may vary in other important respects. They may, for example, be more or less highly centralized. They may be organizations with only private members, or they may be subsystems of a government. Their members may emphasize traditional bases for exchange, or they may emphasize rational bases for exchange. Their members may carry out their exchanges on predominantly universalistic or predominantly particularistic grounds, etc.

Both highly generalized media of exchange and highly developed markets can exist as elements of relatively nonmodernized societies. Both are absolutely essential, however if relatively modernized societies are to exist. For the former they are possibilities; for the latter they are requisites. All relatively modernized societies must be characterized by a highly generalized, official or legal monetary unit. This unit inevitably becomes a standard of measurement for questions considerably broader than the exchange of goods and/or services. Not the least of these other matters is

[19] For important reasons discussed below [see pp. 259–260] there can be no stable society characterized by a completely generalized medium of exchange. That is to say—views of cynics and humorists to the contrary, notwithstanding—no society can persist whose members can literally buy anything with money.

social prestige. This is not merely because of the preoccupation with material concerns of the members of such societies. It is also due to the extent to which material indicators are regarded as functions of other values rather than vice versa. Thus to a large extent, cynics not withstanding, the members in general of relatively modernized societies regard the receipt of high incomes to be a function of high merit rather than high merit to be a function of high income. It makes little difference whether one chooses to illustrate this principle from socialist or capitalist societies.[20] Members of all societies of any considerable scale have to some extent developed relatively highly generalized media of exchange and, in most cases, the use of money as well. Relatively modernized societies must be characterized by increasingly highly generalized media of exchange and monetary units of a well defined sort, if they are to persist. The problems of some sort of cost-accounting system alone, let alone problems of inventory and actual exchange, make the development of such media requisite.

All societies of any considerable scale also have markets. Here again relatively modernized societies must have highly generalized markets as well as markets that are highly specialized in terms of the goods and/or services exchanged. In both relatively modernized and relatively nonmodernized societies, there may be actual markets that do not exist ideally speaking,[21] but in the relatively modernized cases many markets must exist both ideally and actually. If one could conceive of a completely centralized, highly modernized society, the leader of which reacted in no way

[20] With relatively few general exceptions, throughout social history, high income and wealth have been generally considered—both ideally and actually—to be a function of merit. This has held true even when some roles of highest prestige were not necessarily correlated with the highest incomes or greatest wealth as in the case of the Brahmin caste in Indian history. Communists and Socialists readily grant their leaders greater incomes and command over wealth than the common man among them, and in general carefully grade material rewards for services to the people or state.

This question of money as a measure and an influence outside the narrowly confined consideration of goods and/or services is discussed below in various connections [e.g., pp. 257–262, 762–765]. The subject is one about which modern man in general and modern thinkers in particular are unbelieveably skittish. It is frequently tied to quite remarkable preoccupations with distinctions such as that between materialistic and spiritual [n.b., not usually called spiritualistic] outlooks. For the present one might ask the following question: Given a society whose members used a highly generalized monetary unit, what structures would such a society have to have were there to be no positive correlation [or no significant correlation of any sort] ideally speaking, between high merit and high income?

[21] E.g., white slave markets, black markets, etc.

to changes in taste of the other members of the society—if that leader had perfect and complete knowledge—it would be possible to conceive of a highly modernized society with no markets. All allocation would be decided upon by a single source and would be subject to no alterations. Short of such centralization and such perfect knowledge, markets will exist. These markets may vary radically with regard to the extent to which they are free markets. As modernization increases, however, the levels of generalization and specialization of markets increase and the freedom [i.e., absence of regulation in terms of another organization or other organizations—usually in terms of a government] of markets declines. In general, the higher the level of modernization, the higher is the degree of centralization of markets. Apart from this qualification, variations in political ideology do not affect this hypothesis.[22]

Generalized media of exchange and markets are presumably familiar to all readers of this work. Monetary units have varied from huge stone pieces, which certainly minimized problems of theft and maximized a sort of ease of display, to the paper monies which we take for granted. Markets vary from periodic or even *ad hoc* local organizations in terms of which one may exchange agrarian and domestic industry products to highly developed security markets, department stores, etc. As the level of generalization of the media of exchange and of markets increase, there is always an increase in the possibility of emphasizing rationality within the sphere of the allocation of goods and/or services. It is not a matter of chance that economics was the first among the social sciences in modern times to acquire many of the trappings of a genuine science.[23] From its early development to the present day, some assumptions about the rationality of behavior of individuals engaged in the allocations of goods and/or services have occupied a central position among the assumptions vital to the field. Modern developments in this field of social analysis occurred subsequent to the beginnings of a long-run secular trend toward increasing generalization of the media of exchange and of markets.[24] Within broad limits the increase of generalization of

[22] This hypothesis must be qualified by the implications of the possibility mentioned above [pp. 58 ff.] of the degree of centralization existing at the outset of the change exceeding the requisite degree for the given level of modernization achieved.

[23] I refer here, of course, to such things as the emphasis placed by economists on systems of highly general theory, models, data, explicit assumptions, measurements, etc.

[24] Prior to these developments one would hardly regard economics as more highly developed than political science given such names as Aristotle, Machiavelli, and Hobbes.

the media of exchange greatly simplifies calculations about one's interest in one kind of goods or service relative to another. Whatever the meanings of these prices [e.g., $14,000 for a house or $20 a day for wages] to different individuals for different purposes, they make certain common calculations possible for all individuals for any purpose.[25]

Interestingly enough the increase of both these elements to some extent minimizes the need for knowledge. With the increased generalization of the media of exchange, one need not know all of the characteristics of all the goods and/or services that one has to take into consideration for whatever purposes. For many purposes it suffices only to know the price of such goods and/or services, that is, the rate at which the items concerned will presumably be exchanged for a monetary unit. The existence of markets, given even minimal degrees of freedom, makes it possible for both producers and consumers to gain information from the interaction of one another rather than to rely on complete predictions with regard to everything. This again holds true regardless of whether the producers and consumers, as differentiated for these purposes, act in terms of structures of private ownership or not.

Finally, there is always a problem of the interrelationship between allocations of power and responsibility and allocations of goods and/or services. Thus the development of media of exchange and markets is always relevant to governments and vice versa. It is not a matter of chance that the most highly developed monies are virtually without exception carefully controlled by members or representatives of governments. This begins in early stages of the transition to relatively modernized societies, if not before. It certainly increases as the level of modernization increases. With increasing modernization both markets and media of exchange inevitably become more centralized, and their centralization proceeds increasingly in terms of a government, if the society is to be stable.

The close mutual relevance of monies, markets, and governments may be briefly illustrated by a special interrelationship,

---

[25] Further, had it not been for the leg up given by the analysis of economic allocation in terms of a model importantly based on assumptions of rational orientations—whatever its gross or fine faults—it would have been much more difficult for those interested in other aspects of social phenomena to make scientific headway. Vilfredo Pareto seems to have understood this more clearly than any other social thinker in history. See his volumes, *The Mind and Society*, Harcourt, Brace and Company, Inc., New York, 1935, especially vol. I.

that between merchants and government officials.[26] Whenever, ideally speaking, such relationships are illegitimate they will nevertheless continue to take place in fact, and there will be graft and corruption by virtue of the very attempt to eliminate such relationships. Classification of these relationships as illegitimate never eliminates them. Actual allocations of goods and/or services are always highly relevant for actual allocation of power and responsibility and vice versa. This has nothing to do with economic or materialistic determinism as such. Allocations of goods and/or services are not one whit more material than allocations of power and responsibility. Members of many societies have decreed such separations, but they have never been made to stick. Ironically, in this regard capitalistic societies have been a great deal more sophisticated than many others such as those of Imperial China and some modern socialist societies. Increasing centralization of all relatively modernized societies, quite apart from questions of ethics, makes recognition of the impossibility of such separations more important.

B. ORGANIZATIONAL CONTEXTS

1. BUREAUCRACY

In the heraldry of social forms the coat of arms of bureaucracy consists largely of a field strewn with epithets. There is no language in which the term *bureaucracy* exists unencrusted with derogatory connotations. In some cases it may have no connotations of any other sort. The term *bureaucracy* refers to an "organization's organization." Although there are many ways of organizing organizations, in modern times, bureaucracy has come to epitomize large-scale organizations. The term is usually defined descriptively following Max Weber. Parsons has summarized that description as follows: "Bureaucracy, as Weber uses the word, is a rather complicated phenomenon. It involves an organization devoted to what is from the point of view of the participants an impersonal end. It is based on a type of division of labor which involves specialization in terms of clearly differentiated functions, divided according to technical criteria, with a corresponding division of authority hierarchically organized, heading up to a central organ, and specialized technical qualifications on the part of the participants. The role of each participant is conceived as an office where he acts by virtue of the authority vested in the office and not of his personal influence. This involves a

[26] This matter is treated in more detail below [see pp. 333–336, 494–495, 543–548].

clear-cut distinction in many different respects between his acts and relationships in his official and his personal capacity. It in general involves separation of office and home, of business funds and property from personal property, above all of authority in official matters from personal influence outside the official sphere." [27]

Bureaucratic organizations are absolutely essential if relatively modernized societies are to exist. As the level of modernization increases, all epithets to the contrary notwithstanding, the level of bureaucratization increases. The two phenomena vary directly, though the function which interrelates them may be a complicated and largely unspecified one. Like centralization, to which it is closely related, the increase in bureaucratization has little to do with the varying ideological sentiments of members of relatively modernized societies. Both the Republicans and the Democrats of our society curse it, but the leaders of neither stem this tide. Nor will they; nor could they, save at a catastrophic cost. The Russians also use the term as an epithet, but they if anything have carried bureaucratization beyond the requirements of their level of modernization. Like centralization, bureaucratization is not confined to governmental organizations. Our business firms, our research laboratories, both profit and non-profit alike, our universities and our colleges, our grammar schools and most of the intervening schools, our churches and associated organizations—all of them [28] are bureaucratized; a substantial portion of our forms of recreation are bureaucratically organized. Apart from our families and our friendship units, most organizations to which we belong are either bureaucratically organized or are in the process of being organized bureaucratically. Since the productivity per bureaucrat cannot increase faster than the scope of activities bureaucratized under relatively modernized conditions, there can be no prospect of an absolute decrease in bureaucratization—and not a steady state either—nor, probably, of personnel involved either.

[27] See Talcott Parsons, *The Structure of Social Action*, McGraw-Hill Book Company, Inc., New York, 1937, p. 506. Descriptive definitions in addition to being unwieldy, make much of the ensuing discussion "true by definition." If the focus is on the phenomenon defined itself, that is a drawback. That was not Weber's focus, nor is it the present one.

[28] Sometimes the bureaucratization of churches and associated organizations has peculiar obstacles to hurdle. From the point of view of devout members of certain sects, any form of religious authority as such over the individual other than his own conscience is beyond the pale. For a fascinating study of what can happen when this is the case see Paul Harrison, *Authority and Power in the Free Church Tradition*, Princeton University Press, Princeton, 1959.

For those who believe in democracy and the "sacredness and dignity of the human individual" the solution for the problem of bureaucracy is not to do away with all bureaucracies. That is a visionary, childish, or meretricious view. It is rather to organize bureaucracies such that impersonality, which is one of their special utilities in relatively modernized contexts, does not result in injustices or such that, if it does, those injustices can be corrected. Varying the proportions of private and public control over various organizations and many other proposed solutions to these problems have little or no relevance to the question. Private organizations in relatively modernized societies, apart from family and friendship units, are every bit as highly bureaucratized as governmental units which correspond to them in scale and specialization. The most efficient private organizations may well be more highly bureaucratized than comparable governmental subsystems. Except for the charge that individuals are being treated in a dehumanized fashion [i.e., impersonally], every accusation about the shortcomings of a bureaucracy—even from the point of view of the accuser—is not so much a charge that bureaucracy is bad but that the bureaucracy accused is a bad bureaucracy.

The minimal reasons for the increasing importance of bureaucratic organizations are closely related to the remarks made above about the importance of problems of coordination and control in the face of increasing specialization and lack of self-sufficiency. I can illustrate comparatively, how the bureaucrats of traditional China coped with large-scale administrative decisions and planning in terms of capital formation, of individuals to be handled, and of other organizations involved. The irrigation works of traditional China, constituted, and clearly still do, one of the engineering marvels of history. It took an extraordinary amount of technical talent to conceive and build them. Management of them required continuous operation, expansion, and improvement from time to time. In spite of these demands, traditional Chinese society with its bureaucratically organized government was highly stable for 2,000 years—a record probably never equalled unless ancient Egyptian society qualifies—despite outside conquests and all sorts of internal indigenous revolts which transferred power from one set of individuals to another. The Imperial Chinese Bureaucracy was certainly not irrelevant to that strange stability.

The bureaucrats of relatively modernized societies however, are faced by an additional order of problems which were not ordinarily acute for Chinese bureaucrats. The creation of large-scale irrigation works required high levels of ingenuity, but they were characterized by slow rates of obsolescence and decay. The irrigation layouts of some Chinese provinces are not obsolete even now. In relatively modernized situations the rates of both obsolescence and decay are extraordinarily high. The equivalent of canals gradually silting up cannot be permitted. Or rather, if it is permitted, the resulting chaos, discomfort, etc., reaches far and wide—fast. Thus the scale of organization characteristic of relatively modernized societies continues to increase; the importance of technical knowledge continues to increase; the emphasis on clear-cut responsibility, quickly determinable, continues to increase; clear-cut lines of action continue to increase in importance; etc.

Ever increasing automation and increased leisure time—both prominent features of the new social revolution taking place in terms of relatively highly modernized societies—will not change this trend. The increased leisure time and increased standard of living of American families has resulted in increasing bureaucratization of leisure facilities. At one time we walked or drove on bureaucratically produced highways until we got away from it all in nature. Now the preservation of nature herself is increasingly bureaucratized as must be the preparation of facilities for increasingly large numbers to enjoy her. Increasingly we drive off bureaucratically constructed highways into bureaucratically organized parking lots, camp sites, and the like.[29]

2. FAMILY SYSTEMS

The ideal type of family unit varies widely through history. As will be discussed below, [see pp. 426–430] actual family units have not varied nearly so widely as variations in ideal structures have lead most of us to believe. Nevertheless, both within and among societies the variations have been considerable. One of the special characteristics of relatively modernized societies is their quite unusual type of family unit. Whatever the previous ideal family structure was, during the transition toward relative modernization, the ideals always change toward what anthropologists and sociologists call a *multilineal conjugal family* unless they already took that form.

The term is justifiable jargon. Ideally speaking the members of such a family unit are a father, a mother, and nonadult children,

---

[29] It is one of the ironies of modern intellectual history that, although a sense of humor is generally lacking in the treatment of these matters, one of the most important generalizations in modern social science, *Parkinson's Law,* has on the whole been highly regarded only because it poked fun at everyone's favorite target—bureaucracy. We have, alas, had more fun with it than we have learned from it.

or in the absence of children, a husband and wife. The members reckon solidarity more or less equally in terms of both the paternal and maternal lines of descent. More accurately, they deemphasize both equally. Insofar as relationships continue among the members of the family unit and their grandparents, ideally speaking, one is not expected to prefer one's maternal grandparents to one's paternal ones or vice versa. Many people would regard such lack of distinction as barbarous. The one remaining clear-cut sign of greater accent on one line of descent is the continued use of the father or husband's surname as the family name.

When the children belonging to such a family mature and marry, they organize a new family unit. Ideally speaking they do not live with the parents of either the husband or the wife. The use of the term conjugal to describe the unit accents the primary importance, ideally speaking, of the relationship between husband and wife. The children upon maturation choose their own future mates, with little let from parents or others. This form of family system, though known outside the context of relatively modernized societies, is rare. Carried to the lengths with which we are familiar, and given its relation to other subsystems, it is unique in social history.

It is frequently noted that activities in terms of the family have been radically reduced in relatively modernized contexts. This does *not* mean that the family units are less important than formerly, unless family importance is defined by the restriction of such activities. It is not at all true, however, that under these conditions the activities still performed in terms of the family are not crucial for the existence of the society. It is not correct to infer that, once the reduction of activities has reached a certain point, family units become negligible or that one can continue to restrict the functions performed on a family basis indefinitely. It is also misleading to imply that this type of family is less critical for this type of society than other types of family are for other societies.[30]

The reduction of education in terms of the family is one of the most spectacular examples. In relatively modernized societies the family as an educational unit has had its wings cut back radically. Less and less training takes place in terms of such units. Virtually none of the technical education for adult roles takes place in family terms in relatively modernized societies. The decrease in family-based education reaches into younger and younger age categories with further increases of modernization.

[30] See above, footnote #6, p. 45.

Universal schooling is one of the obvious sources of this restriction. One of the signs of relatively high modernization is the increasing generalization of the prekindergarten or nursery school. The decrease of family educational functions is never complete. More of the crucial education of the vast majority of individuals takes place on a family basis than on the basis of any other organization for the members of this as of all other societies. The family remains the organization in terms of which, everyone ordinarily first learns to eat, to walk, to talk, to perform various other bodily functions, etc. With increasing modernization, more education takes place in nonfamily contexts, but so far there has been no society in terms of which education on a nonfamily basis has been generally extended to these fundamental initial bits of learning.

In most societies in world history the family units have ordinarily been important units in terms of which production and consumption are carried out. These units have been important not only in the relevance of the kinds of production and consumption carried out in terms of them but also in the sense of the proportion of that production and consumption to the total production and consumption carried out in terms of the society. In relatively modernized societies it is increasingly only the former sense in which the production and consumption carried out in family terms is of importance. Here there is some imbalance. Family units become a much greater focus of consumption from the point of view of the members of the units than of production. Little of the total gross national product [as currently measured] of the members of a relatively modernized society is in fact produced in terms of family units, although a large proportion of personal consumption is carried out in family terms. Even with regard to consumption, because of the large amounts consumed in other organizational contexts, the relative amount carried out in family terms goes down, although the absolute amount increases enormously if one contrasts the per family consumption characteristic of relatively modernized societies with that of relatively nonmodernized ones. Certain forms of production continue in family terms. Although these are critical, they are frequently ignored. A considerable amount of food preparation, laundry, child care, etc. continue in family terms, as do their consumption counterparts. But the conception general among the members of relatively nonmodernized societies of family units as the ordinary units in terms of which most production and consumption is carried out is gone forever.

Perhaps, it it not gone forever. With certain levels of productivity and forms of income distribution which characterize high modernization as opposed to relative modernization, there may actually be developing a new form of recreational family which may modify this state of affairs. It is a new possibility on the social horizon. As the work week shortens, the possibility of the third great social revolution developed and exported in American history grows.[31] This is the *leisure revolution*. It is one of the most peculiar social revolutions in all world history.

This third revolution might also be called the altruistic revolution as well as the leisure revolution. Its leaders will turn out to be the most altruistic revolutionary leaders in world history. This social revolution is carried out by people who have the highest per capita standard of living in world history in terms of real income with an extremely even distribution of that income. For the first time in world history the *problem* facing the members of a society has become, not how one keeps people well adjusted while they work, regardless of whether they distinguish work from leisure, but rather, how one keeps people well adjusted while they are not at work. Once the work week has become forty hours, even if one discounts eight hours a day for sleep and three hours a day for meals, here remain more hours for leisure than for work. Most of the members of most societies in world history either do not distinguish sharply between work and leisure activities, or if they do, consider the overwhelming proportion of their time as spent working. The United States work week is already reduced to forty hours, and there are strong pressures about for a further reduction of it—with no loss in real income to the persons concerned, of course.

The leaders of the other revolutions produced and exported by members of United States society have had a major personal stake in the products of the revolution. In this sense they were at least as much self-interested as altruistic. They regarded themselves as benefitting from the fruits of those revolutions. Jefferson and Franklin were avidly interested in what they regarded as political liberty. This was the fruit of their revolution. Henry Ford and others were interested in the fruits of the mass production revolution. The leaders of the leisure revolution are a different breed. They consist largely of professional and administrative elite. They are lawyers, doctors, scientists, executives, etc. They operate in terms of bureaucracies. They exercise great privileges. They undertake great responsibilities. They may or may not reap

---

[31] The first revolution developed and exported in American history was the "political" revolution of the eighteenth century. The second was the mass production revolution of the early twentieth century.

great material rewards. One thing is absolutely certain, however, they do not enjoy increased leisure. A leading figure among them who works less than sixty to eighty hours a week is rare. They will not enjoy the fruits of their revolution. In this sense they are the most altruistic revolutionary leaders in world history.

Given a leisure revolution, a recreational family may become more widespread. Individuals once again will participate on a family basis in all sorts of activities that have been dying out. Craft activities such as pottery making are a possibility as a leisure activity for the members of such a society. There is already a marked example of this sort of thing in the case of "do it yourself" work at home. I have heard many of my colleagues explain that they do it themselves because they cannot afford plumbers, carpenters, etc., but I do not believe them. With rare exception, given our skills, despite the high costs of plumbers, carpenters, etc., it would be cheaper to call a professional plumber than do it ourselves. Even if the individual is unusually skillful, at home he must be terribly "overcapitalized" in tools to work efficiently. Even granting that labor costs in "do it yourself" work are zero, the cost of inefficient uses of materials, overcapitalization in tools, personal injuries, etc., make the price of "do it yourself" work exorbitant. Such poor and expensive work would be one of the great luxuries of our day were it considered apart from its recreational value.[32]

Wives do well to be tolerant of husbands when they are at the height of this mood. House repairs may do more than professional baseball teams for close parent-child associations. We may actually get a return to all sorts of family activities previously thought abandoned. Craft production as a matter of recreation rather than as a matter of livelihood is a possibility. For the talented such production may even become an important source of family income, but this is likely to be self-defeating. If it becomes really lucrative, the family members will have to give it up on a family recreational basis and go into a family business.

There are many possibilities open for the future development of the family in relatively modernized societies. None of those

---

[32] Plumbing is an excellent example of all this. Even if the "do it yourselfer" is skillful at plumbing, he must be terribly overcapitalized with regard to tools. He uses his tools no more than once every two months, if he has bad plumbing. If he has good plumbing, he uses the tools once every six months, or maybe once every two years or so, whereas the professional plumber uses them day in and day out. They each need roughly the same tools, however, if they are to work efficiently. He makes many more mistakes than the ordinary plumber, hard as that may be to imagine. He usually injures himself in the course of his work. Modest to substantial medical costs are not a small factor in "do it yourself" work, etc.

lines of development point to an abandonment of the multilineal conjugal family unit as the ideal type of unit in society. Since this type of family, with the restricted activities in terms of it in relatively modernized societies, is quite rare in social history, and since in other societies the general structure of controls is intimately hooked up to the general family structures, the disruptive impact on other societies of this feature alone is far reaching.

I I I
TWO MAJOR PROBLEMS FOR THE MEMBERS
OF ANY RELATIVELY MODERNIZED SOCIETY

Two major problems confront the members of all relatively modernized societies, whether recognized or not. One of these is new, and the other is an ancient problem posed anew in acute form. The new one is the problem of *socialization for an unknown future*. The acute form of an ancient problem is the problem of coordination and control.

A. SOCIALIZATION FOR AN UNKNOWN FUTURE

This problem is one with which laymen are more familiar than social scientists. With rare exceptions the members of relatively modernized societies are all faced with it. Adults must train and educate the young, teach them how to behave, prepare them in a myriad ways for a future neither adult nor young envisages. Such a problem has been rare in world history prior to modernization, even for elite or bizarre individuals. It has never pertained to the general population of a society. Think of what it means as a problem of knowledge alone. How does one train people so that they can act in terms of a system which the trainers expect to be radically different, in unknown ways, from the system they currently know? It is in this sense that the layman has been more sophisticated about this than the social scientists as a group. As laymen, most of us expect our children to live in a radically different world from the one in which we grew up and have lived in so far. We constantly tell them so. We are correct in doing so, for the probability is great that they will have to live in a very different world, indeed. As social scientists, we may or may not build this into our work.

The ordinary expectation for the members of all relatively nonmodernized societies has been that their children would live in roughly the same kind of world as the parents. The discrepancy began to be dramatic in our time. I grew up in Galveston, Texas, a member of a family long of that place. My father and others often told me what Galveston was like when he was a boy. Galveston traffic was then horse-drawn. When he spoke to me of this, I used to think that it would be impossible that my children would find my way of life as a child as different from theirs as my father's was from mine. I thought there would never be such a gap again. My children are still small, and the gap is patently greater. As a small child I lived in a world with practically no airplanes, except a few military planes of questionable reliability. There was no television; radio was much a plaything and a wonder, but on the whole inconvenient; atomic energy had never been heard of. The levels of centralization and bureaucratization of United States society were quite different. My childhood was even more different from my children's childhood than my father's was from mine. The normal expectation now is that their children's childhood will be more different from theirs than theirs is from mine. One must also keep in mind the fact that the time span from childhood to childhood in these cases is a thirty year gap at most. This is what has become of what we still express as a goal, "I want my child to have a better future than mine." All this has come about so quickly that it is no surprise that we have not yet learned to understand it, that we have not yet analyzed it thoroughly, and that we have not learned to cope with it.

In this context it is easy to understand the importance of a predominantly universalistic ethic. If people are taught to act on the basis of what they can do that is relevant in many contexts rather than on the basis of who they are, the possibility of individuals adjusting to a new situation is increased. It is inconceivable that there exists a situation in which achievement and objective criteria are totally irrelevant, though almost any special set of relatively personal identifications may become irrelevant overnight. There will always remain many particularistic criteria and many particularistic ethics. There will always be some clustering around the family, but as this problem increases the relevance of any such identification to other contexts becomes increasingly precarious.

Here again, then, a predominantly universalistic ethic and the emphasis upon it, without anyone planning it, is highly relevant to the general situation of relatively modernized societies. What other strategy could be devised to meet this situation? Consider the problem of knowledge posed. If one asks how one should train individuals to operate in terms of a certain corporation the immediate reply is "What kind of a corporation?" If one says, "I have no idea what kind of corporation," they will say, "How can I help you devise a training system for those people apart from devising one that will presumably fit any corporation at any time?" If one says,

"You are doing that every day of your life. You train your kids for an unknown system. You brag about it. You say that your kids aren't going to be brought up the way you were, that your kids aren't going to have the same kind of future you did, that they are going to be living in a different world." If one brings out the problem that way, people realize what it means, though it may upset them.

It is a peculiar problem. Within the memory of many living members of even our most modernized societies there existed a view of a society in which virtually every member of the society as far back as could be remembered could count on his children and his children's children growing up and living under conditions roughly similar to his own. Now virtually no one can. The one thing certain is that the future is going to be different and at a constantly accelerated pace. Whereas members of relatively nonmodernized societies teach their children roughly what their children need to know for their adult lives, we teach our children what we needed to know for our lives rather than what they will need to know for theirs.[33]

This is a problem of radical social change with a time span of twenty to thirty years. That is revolutionary enough in social history, but the pace will probably not continue to be so leisurely. There is also acceleration involved. In the discussion of stability below [pp. 770–790], the hypothesis that these relatively modernized societies must change constantly and probably at an increasing rate is suggested. It is enough to contemplate the possible meaning of one radical social revolution per generation. How is one to contemplate changes of such magnitude once or perhaps as much as twice per generation? What if the periodicity of such changes becomes ten years rather than twenty or thirty? Can it become five? I do not know the answer, but I am certain of two aspects of the problem: (1) the rate of change will continue to increase, but (2) there is some limit beyond which large sets of human beings cannot react effectively to heightened rates of

---

[33] The cognitive question alone is one of the major challenges to man. I do not begin to understand the causes of modern juvenile delinquency, although I am sure that its universal association with the modernization of societies is not a matter of chance. It is one of the most frequently analyzed, and to many one of the most vexatious, phenomena of our day. So far none of those analyses has been very satisfying intellectually or therapeutically. We have tended to overlook the cognitive element in juvenile delinquency. In addition to the relevance of rejection and questionable parental treatment, etc., one of the most relevant problems is posed in the question one frequently hears from young people whenever they do something of which others disapprove: "How was I to know?" When one is reared for an unknown future, there is no more important question.

change. Either these societies will approach such limits only asymptotically, or the prognosis is bleak.

B. COORDINATION AND CONTROL

The other problem is a much more ordinary and familiar one. It is the old problem of coordination and control. The members of every one of these relatively modernized societies are faced with this problem in an acute form. Again it has nothing to do with whether they are democratic, socialist, communist, or fascist societies. Severe problems of coordination and control exist and proliferate for any people who act in terms of the structures of increasing modernization. How do the myriad of highly specialized and differentiated activities get coordinated and regulated? How are activities kept from "getting out of hand"? For these societies the lower limit of practicable coordination and control lies in the implications of any breakdown. For example, the members of relatively modernized societies will not tolerate a modern depression. One cannot say that a depression will not take place, but one can with some confidence predict what will follow if a genuine depression does take place. There will be rapid and perhaps violent change in the personnel in control. There will be a revolutionary change in the power situation at least. It may not be by guns, but it will be radical, and it will be fast. No one knows exactly where the lower limit of necessary coordination and control is located, but it certainly has to do with the implications for the system as a whole of any breakdown. The more highly modernized the society becomes, the less such breakdowns are tolerable. The possibility that the members of any relatively modernized society will tolerate any breakdown that results in the continuation of the system but at much lower levels of productivity and the like is increasingly small. The action they take may make matters even worse from their point of view, but they will not be indifferent.

The upper limit of coordination and control is equally important. It is becoming more important all the time. Less coordination and control than the minimum is neither feasible for, nor popular among, the members of any of the relatively modernized societies. The most radical conservatives are continually being frustrated by this state of affairs. On the other hand, how far are we in some cases from approaching greater coordination and control than we can handle? Here again one runs into the twin problems of knowledge and brittleness. Quite apart from what people may or may not like in terms of coordination and control, there is the question of how much coordination and control there can be without overloading the cognitive capacities of the individuals who must plan and direct operations, or without the structures becoming so brittle that any small changes within the society, regardless of the source, will fracture the whole system. This is not to say that the attitudes people have toward coordination and control are irrelevant. The degree to which the members of a given society are habituated to centralization and/or authoritarian treatment is of great importance in scientific guesses about their reactions to increases of coordination and control. Nevertheless, even were such differences of degree of no importance whatsoever, there would still be an upper limit on the extent to which coordination and control can be carried. The lowest conceivable limit of coordination and control would be like the lowest conceivable limit of centralization—complete anarchy. The upper limit would be complete centralization. Neither limit can in fact be reached or maintained by the members of any relatively modernized society, or of any other kind of society for that matter. Well within those limits the members of every relatively modernized society face critical problems.

As indicated above again and again, those problems have little to do with the specific form that ideological differences frequently take in today's political arguments. From the point of view of the problems of coordination and control the terms *conservative* and *radical* take on new meanings. If we are to retain these terms and have them mean something in terms of the realities of the situation, it is necessary to distinguish two forms of radicalism: (1) the *fundamentalist* or *conservative* form of radicalism and the *reformist* or *radical* form of radicalism; *fundamentalist* or *conservative radicals* are radical to the extent that, usually by being naïvely antibureaucratic, their attempts to minimize the elements of coordination and control threaten to cut the effectiveness of coordination and control below the point necessary to prevent catastrophic breakdowns, and (2) the *reformist* or *radical radicals* threaten to carry the development of coordination control beyond the limits of available knowledge for adequate planning and execution and beyond tolerable limits of brittleness.[34]

Ideological wishful thinking is not helpful in these matters. I happen to like the implications of the clichés of democracy. They are my ideals, and the implications of these assertions for those

[34] Herein may lie the most tragic aspect of our poorly developed social sciences. They do not tell us nearly what we need to know for the levels of planning we already require.

ideals are dire. Nevertheless, these aspects of human society are as much a matter of human creation as are the ideals and structures of democracy. The range of variation possible for either democratic or authoritarian structures in relatively modernized societies lies within limits set by these considerations.

I · C H A P T E R · 2

THE STRUCTURE OF RELATIVELY

NONMODERNIZED SOCIETIES

I
DEFINITION
A. RESIDUAL DEFINITION AND EXAMPLES

Relatively nonmodernized societies, although defined residually to relatively modernized societies, may be identified by the following characteristics: (1) their members depend overwhelmingly on animate sources of power, (2) the inanimate sources of power utilized [e.g., rivers for transport, wind, etc.] tend to be fixed in amount or to increase slowly, (3) the tools used multiply effort modestly, and (4) the tools used are sedentary. All societies in world history prior to the nineteenth century were relatively nonmodernized. Highly modernized societies did not exist until the twentieth century. Only a small minority of nineteenth-century societies became relatively modernized. In the twentieth century the vast majority of societies remain relatively nonmodernized, but the process of modernization has begun in all of those whose members are in contact with the members of relatively modernized societies.

B. OTHER CLASSIFICATIONS

The classifications of relatively nonmodernized societies sometimes seem nearly as numerous as the scholars who have treated of them. Most beg questions rather than answer them. Most overlook the fact that, despite the enormous variety of detailed social structures, all of the relatively nonmodernized societies have more in common with one another in more general respects than any one of them has with any relatively modernized society. Nevertheless, most of these distinctions have in fact gotten at some important differences among these societies. A few may be illustrated here.

1. LARGE-SCALE—SMALL-SCALE

The distinction between large-scale and small-scale societies has already been defined [see p. 18] in terms of the number of people and the amount of space covered. The distinction is not talked of a great deal, but it is significant. Up to a point, it enables us to distinguish between the types of society on which the professional anthropologists have made so much valuable material available and the sorts that most scholars and public officials in the sphere of international relations refer to as nations. It is a distinction, if one likes, between "small" societies whose members, let us say, are confined to one island or fairly small regions and societies of much greater complexity in terms of the areas covered and number of people interrelated. It has not yet proved fruitful to seek a general theory of social structure in terms of the scale of societies, but many structural problems do hinge on differences of scale. The utility of the distinction for present purposes is that the treatment here will hinge on relatively large-scale societies rather than small-scale ones.

2. LITERATE-NONLITERATE

One of the most frequently invoked distinctions is that between literate and nonliterate societies. This refers to the question of whether or not a written language is a feature of the society. Few large-scale societies relevant to international affairs are nonliterate. Most of the large-scale societies on which we have evidence, archaeological or otherwise, have some written forms of communication. The level of literacy characteristic of these societies varies enormously, but the proportion of literate to illiterate members prior to the development of relatively modernized societies has varied less than is generally assumed. Before the nineteenth century the upper limit of literacy of the population of a large-scale society probably never exceeded 30 per cent nor dipped below 5 per cent.

For discussions of relatively large-scale societies, the important distinction is among differing rates of literacy rather than between literacy and nonliteracy. The differences in literacy rates as between, say, the Hanseatic League societies and the Venetian city-states on the one hand and the medieval German principalities on the other are significant for many purposes. This is not, however, a distinction between literate and nonliterate societies but between societies which probably had radically different literacy rates. The implications of such comparisons for the kind and type of elite that can be maintained, etc., are sufficiently obvious examples of the utility of the distinction.

The implications of the invention of printing are not entirely clear. The assumption that with the invention of printing the literacy rate automatically increases until the general membership of the society is literate is not borne out by the Chinese or Western Europeans. With or without printing, the literacy rate in neither Europe nor China ever exceeded 30 per cent until parts of Western Europe and the United States [1] became relatively modernized.

3. PRIMITIVE-NONPRIMITIVE

Another popular distinction is that between primitive and nonprimitive societies. This classification raises terrible problems because the term *primitive* has come to have such pejorative connotations. I have never encountered a really precise and rigorous definition of this distinction. The distinctions between large-scale and small-scale societies, especially if combined with that of literate and nonliterate, will probably handle all distinctions of this sort that are not intended to be invidious.

The distinction does not mean much more than the distinction between simple and complex societies without rigorous specification of the bases for judging simplicity or complexity. It is probably true that societies described as primitive have simpler structures of allocation of goods and services than do societies described as nonprimitive. On the other hand the so-called primitive societies usually have kinship structures of a complexity far beyond those of the most highly modernized societies.

4. NOMADIC-SEDENTARY

Another classification of relatively nonmodernized societies is that of nomadic and sedentary societies. Nomadic societies are societies whose members herd and/or hunt or fish. The sedentary ones are the agrarian societies. This distinction enables one to make a useful generalization: *all stable large-scale societies are sedentary as opposed to nomadic.* There are many cases of relatively small-scale nomadic societies persisting stably for long periods of time. All of the major instances in history of large-scale nomadic societies, however, have been quite unstable, es-

[1] This matter continues to be a source of fascination to many as the basis of policy proposals. For example, there are those who maintain that the literacy rate was kept low in China as part of a more or less deliberate plot on the part of the wicked Chinese bureaucrats who maintained their elite status largely by preservation of an exceedingly complicated and difficult method of writing. Chinese writing is certainly complicated and difficult. This line of argument reckons, however, without the fact that in the West relatively simple phonetic alphabetic writing has existed for something like four thousand years. Despite our debt to the Phoenicians for this, it is doubtful that our rate of literacy surpassed that of Imperial China until the nineteenth century. Arguments, therefore, that the difficulty of the writing is the primary or central villain of the piece are conclusively naïve. In qualification of these remarks, I must add that recently I have been told that the inhabitants of Iceland have been nearly universally literate for several centuries. If this is true, the case of Iceland is significant as the only known case of nearly universal literacy among the members of a relatively nonmodernized society.

pecially if their members took control over the members of large-scale sedentary societies. One of the best known examples of such societies is that of Genghis Khan. It is interesting to note that only those parts of his empire that were never converted to Mongol patterns of nomadism or from them remained stable.[2]

There is a close relationship between the management of large-scale societies and agriculture, especially if the large-scale societies are relatively nonmodernized. The proportion of the population engaged in sedentary agrarian pursuits never becomes a minority until very advanced stages of modernization. It is difficult to maintain the levels of productivity in food production required for a large-scale society solely on a nomadic basis.[3] The problems of food productivity per acre increase exponentially with population increase. There are also problems of the minimum level of communications necessary to hold members of a nomadic society together. The problems of communication seem paradoxical. They are maximized for those very societies whose members use the fastest means of communication available given their level of technology; frequently the members of nomadic societies have very fast horses or camels. One of the more obvious problems, which also increases exponentially with population increases, is that of keeping the members of one tribe or subsystem from drifting willy-nilly into the current grazing or hunting area of another. The problems of communications of sedentary agrarians are minimized by the high level of self-sufficiency which can be maintained and the very minimization of the problems of movement.

---

[2] The most dramatic case of this is the fate of the Mongols who dominated the traditional Chinese. For a bit, the fate of Chinese society was touch and go. A considerable school in the Mongol camp felt that the Mongols should wipe out, not decimate, the Chinese living in the areas of China they chose to take. They felt that the land should be turned over to grazing, that the Mongols should live there only as Mongols always had lived elsewhere. But a Chin Tartar, Yeh-lü Ch'u-ts'ai talked Ögödei out of this policy. Yeh-lü Ch'u-ts'ai was a fast tongue. He convinced Ögödei that there was more to be gotten from the Chinese as taxpayers than from the area as grazing land. Ögödei went along with this, and although the Mongols themselves resisted Sinification better than had others, they had to use buffer bureaucrats and abandon many of their own structures while they ruled China. Neither the customs nor the laws of the Mongols were adapted to the large-scale governance of a highly sedentary society. The most the Mongols could do was alter the domination of the Chinese bureaucrats in limited spheres of influence, wipe them out, become Chinese, or rule so inefficiently as to foredoom their dominance. Insofar as Mongol distinctness was maintained in China, it was at the price of the last of these possibilities.

[3] Most nomadic societies of any scale involve structures of raiding sedentary agrarians.

5. WESTERN-NONWESTERN

This classification and its associated clichés have entered most discussions of these matters and have obscured virtually every discussion they have entered. It is a distinction that is important from certain points of view. Some of the religions of the soi-disant Western societies are quite distinctive. Some of the forms of government are distinctive, and many other features of Western societies are distinctive quite apart from the fact that they are of course the features best known and understood by Westerners. It is also extremely interesting that scholars spoke little of this distinction until modernization came to be a major focus of interest. At just this point, the distinction between Western and nonwestern societies tended to beg rather than answer the important questions addressed.

It is childish to poke fun at this distinction by pointing out that what constitutes Western is to some extent a function of where one stands on the globe. The distinction means more than can be handled by that line of attack. The interest is in aspects or elements held to be inherent in Western societies as such by contrast with, let us say, Near Eastern or Far Eastern societies. This school of thought has its own prophets, best exemplified by the philosopher, F. S. C. Northrup. He is, however, only an especially articulate spokesman for a very popular point of view. The distinction aimed at is that between relatively modernized and relatively nonmodernized societies. The terms *Western* and *Nonwestern* have been plausible because of one indisputable fact. That is the fact that all of the earliest, indigenously developed, relatively modernized societies were clearly special cases of Western or European, or European-derived societies. What the usage ignores is that societies, whether Western or not, have more in common with one another structurally speaking if they are relatively nonmodernized than any one of them has with any relatively modernized society, whether Western or not. The social structure of Tokugawa Japan has more in common with that of eighteenth-century United States society than with that of modern Japan. Modern American social structure has more in common with that of modern Japan than either has with either that of eighteenth-century United States or Tokugawa Japan.

The distinction between Western and Nonwestern societies also contains elements of sheerest nonsense. Part of this nonsense has to do with the mysterious Orient. The mystery of the Orient is nothing but an elaborate unconscious euphemism for an unusually difficult language barrier. Scholars who speak and read these languages well do not on the whole find the societies concerned mysterious in this romantic sense, nor do they find many of the differences asserted to inhere in the Western-Nonwestern distinction. What is no less important, they do not find the equally mysterious assumed similarities alleged to characterize the so-called Nonwestern societies. Apart from partisans of the particular school attacked here, I know of no scholars who do not find the range of variation as among Indian, Chinese, and Japanese societies prior to modernization at least as great as the variation between any one of them and any Western society prior to modernization. Western society in this dichotomy does not refer to *any* and all Western societies. After all both Merovingian and Carolingian France as well as Spain and Portugal would have to be included along with the United States, West Germany, and England of today. The emphasis on science, the levels of specialization, the lack of self-sufficiency, the materialistic orientations, the concern with predominantly universalistic ethics, objective recruitment, bureaucracy, etc.,—these taken together are not characteristic of Western societies in general, but only of those Western societies which became relatively modernized. Furthermore the alleged impact of Western structures on Nonwestern societies vanishes strangely save for cases of the impact of relatively modernized Western social structures on relatively non-modernized societies at whatever point of the compass.[4]

Distinctions like the Western-Nonwestern one are unsatisfactory for two other reasons. First, many of the allegations are simply incorrect. For example, the contention that Nonwestern

[4] History affords a perfect comparative case. From the time of Marco Polo on members of traditional Chinese society and of Western societies had contacts that fluctuated in intensity but were continuous. The leaders of Tokugawa Japan, for reasons which need not detain us here, cut off, save for the merest trickle, all contacts with Westerners in 1638. This contact was not renewed until modernization had made considerable headway in the West. Then, as all know, Japanese society was reinvaded by Western influence following Perry's expedition in 1853. This peculiar Japanese experience enables us to distinguish between *Western influence in general* and *relatively modernized Western influence in particular* on the members of a relatively nonmodernized society. For China, where the contact was continuous, it is not possible to separate these influences with any such precision. In neither Chinese nor Japanese society do the so-called disintegrative effects of contact with the members of Western society manifest themselves until those structures referred to as relatively modernized ones have developed. It is not *any* Western structures that disintegrate others. It is the introduction of relatively modernized structures that does so. Those structures happen to have developed first in a restricted set of Western societies. No other interpretation of the Western-Nonwestern distinction will enable one to handle the contrasting cases of Chinese and Japanese societies.

societies are uniformly oriented to compromise as a way of settling disputes whereas the members of Western societies are uniformly oriented to litigation and resort to the courts, is simply fallacious. The Hindus have been among the most litigious of people, and the Chinese have never been adverse to use of the courts provided they felt that the courts were either fair or favorable to them. Conversely, there is no more favored maxim among Western lawyers of the most highly modernized societies than that the mark, par excellence, of the really good lawyer is that he keeps his clients out of court. Correspondingly, the idea that Nonwestern peoples are more spiritually oriented than Western peoples is either unclear because what is meant is not defined with any precision or is flatly incorrect. The idea that the Western mind somehow places greater emphasis on rationality than the Nonwestern one is patently contradictable in many spheres. Prior to the development of relatively high levels of modernization, the members of large-scale societies never exceeded the traditional Chinese in their emphasis on and interest in rationality, despite their great interest in and emphasis on tradition. It is all too easy for Western philosophers to forget that for many centuries in the West the light of science was barely kept alive by the efforts of a much contemned minority. The idea that Nonwesterners look at phenomena as they really are whereas Westerners see those same phenomena only through the biased or arbitrary glasses of the special concepts of science is childishly naive from the point of view of any epistemologist.

Second, the fallaciousness of the propositions asserted in terms of this distinction is by no means the worst problem connected with it. That honor is reserved for the fact that use of the distinction seems to explain a great deal but in fact usually begs the question. References to the Oriental mind form one of the best illustrations of this in the whole field of social writing. There certainly are important differences in the attitudes of the members of different societies. Some attitudes toward time, for example, vary considerably among the members of different societies. We may be told that the Chinese attitude toward time is different from that of members of United States society, and that this is a typical result of the Oriental mind. In the absence of a clear-cut and precise definition or description of the Oriental mind that is to some degree independent of this observation about the attitude toward time—and I have never known an adept of such usage to have such a definition or description—nothing has been contributed to our understanding. We have in effect been told that "their attitude toward time is different because it is different." An explanation of the difference in attitudes toward time as a function of particular physical, psychic, or even of social characteristics of Orientals as distinct from Americans would constitute a major theoretical break-through in biology, psychology, or the social sciences. No scientific improvement in any field has so far been shown to flow from any such observations. It is unenlightened to feel enlightened by them.

Proponents of the Western-Nonwestern distinction have one strong point in their favor. Relatively modernized societies did first develop in the West. They have not developed independently anywhere else.[5] The spread of structures of relatively modernized societies has so far proceeded overwhelmingly from those areas in which they first developed. Now, of course, there is an increasing spread of them from late-comers to the process, e.g., the Japanese. It is surely not a matter of chance that those structures first developed in the West, but beyond that social science is not now in a position to go definitively. Max Weber maintained that the strategic necessary but not sufficient variable in this development was the Protestant Ethic. Some would contest that, and some would agree with it. If one agrees, there arise the further questions of why the Protestant Ethic or its equivalent developed in the West and only in the West, why, if it developed elsewhere, it did not have the corresponding effect, etc. Use of the distinction is never confined to this context, nor has it illuminated this question. It has been an appealing distinction, but its use has done more harm than good.[6]

6. MISCELLANEOUS

A myriad of other classifications has been applied to relatively nonmodernized societies. Those interested in kinship have sometimes distinguished between matrilineal and patrilineal societies. A favorite in some circles has been the distinction between folk and urban societies. There have been taxonomies based on the

[5] It is by no means certain, of course, that relative modernization could not have developed anywhere else. Arguments can be presented that, had the Japanese continued unmolested, they might have developed relative modernization independently. It is difficult, however, to see how this possibility could be conclusively proved.

[6] There have been side effects—of this and other unjustifiable jargon—which one may not wish to disturb. They fall largely within the sphere of adjustment immortalized in another context by a ditty once popular among junior naval officers:

> "The officers ride in a whaleboat,
> The captain he rides in a gig
> It don't go a —— bit faster,
> But it makes the old —— feel big."

distinctions between status and contract, mechanical and organic societies, gemeinschaft and gesellschaft, etc. All of these distinctions are too specialized if used rigorously, too badly defined to be used, or too erroneous in their implications if used, to be of service here. As insisted here, although the variation of relatively nonmodernized societies is enormous and fascinating, all have more in common with one another in more generally relevant respects than any one of them has with any relatively modernized society. I shall not take up all the features that relatively nonmodernized societies have in common. Paralleling the discussion of relatively modernized societies, only a set of common structural features especially relevant for the problems of modernization as a setting for international affairs is presented here.

I I
STRUCTURAL FEATURES OF
ANY RELATIVELY NONMODERNIZED SOCIETY

A. ASPECTS

1. SPECIALIZATION OF UNITS

Relatively few of the membership units of relatively nonmodernized societies are specialized in terms of one aspect of action such as the economic, the political, etc. Despite this dearth of specialization some form of government, however loosely organized, always exists for any large-scale society. Relatively nonmodernized societies are by no means bereft of specialization in other respects. Highly specialized craft work, for example, is a frequent product of the members of such societies. Most of the organizations in these societies, however, are not specialized as a modern business firm is. Even highly specialized craft work is usually carried out on a family or other nonspecialized basis. The craft work characteristic of these societies—though it may appear bizarre and incredibly refined—is relatively unspecialized by contrast with the level of "product differentiation specialization" characteristic of any relatively modernized society.[7]

All large-scale relatively nonmodernized societies are characterized by at least one specialized unit, a government, but there is greater variation in the form of government displayed among relatively nonmodernized societies than among relatively mod-

[7] Never underestimate the specialization in this sense of a lapidary or of a craftsman who carves sixteen lacework ivory balls, one within the other, from a solid piece without splitting any of the outer balls! Never underestimate, either, the spectacular specialization reflected in any dictionary of occupational distinctions for any relatively modernized society —or even the job classifications for any large-scale factory operation.

ernized ones. It would be difficult, on general theoretical grounds, to maintain that there *must be* specialized units other than governments even in large-scale relatively nonmodernized societies. Nevertheless, ideally, and/or actually, there always are some forms of predominantly economically oriented organizations. Merchant firms are, perhaps, the best example of this. Although merchant firms are often a family enterprise, just as craft shops are usually family enterprises, when a merchant enterprise reaches any considerable scale of operations, the separation between the merchant firm and the family is greater than is common for crafts. The relevance of specialized abilities on a scale barring recruitment solely on family terms is a feature of these cases.[8]

Other specializations of units in relatively nonmodernized societies vary enormously. Organizations specialized on the basis of religion, education, entertainment, etc., are common. The degree of specialization of these units varies widely. Sometimes [e.g., traditional China or Tokugawa Japan] the specialization and differentiation of such units are highly developed, but the degree of specialization never approaches that taken for granted by the members of any relatively modernized society. The vast majority of members of a relatively nonmodernized society rarely, if ever, actually interact with others in terms of such specialized units, let alone actually belong to such units. No active member of any relatively modernized society can avoid continuous multiple involvements of this sort.

Not only are the degree of specialization lower and the extent of members involved more restricted in every way, but also relatively nonmodernized societies are not characterized by the continuous and striking increase in the specialization of organizations taken for granted in relatively modernized contexts. Increases of specialization of subsystems of relatively nonmodernized societies are usually slow, sporadic, and modest. Furthermore, a general reversal of the trend to greater specialization is never characteristic of a relatively modernized society. Such a reversal is by no

[8] Closely allied and highly relevant to these phenomena is the fate of particular craftsmen whose works catch on in major population centers. Long prior to modernization of any considerable extent it is difficult to keep the operations of the most popular doll maker of a center like Kyoto on the basis of a relatively nonspecialized unit. Such operations tend to get out of hand from the point of view of the members of the units in terms of which they originate. "Getting out of hand" frequently consists of increases in specialization of the unit in terms of which these activities are carried out. In the example used here the master craftsman is also increasingly forced into the actual roles of a merchant executive specializing in his craft product.

means out of the question in a relatively nonmodernized context. There is some reason to believe that something of a reversal of this sort took place in Europe following the fall of the Roman Empire.

The sedentary nature of the level of specialization and the reversibility of a trend toward greater specialization are important characteristics of relatively nonmodernized societies. Even more important for present purposes, however, is the restricted involvement of vast portions of the population of such societies in specialized organizations or in interrelations with the members of specialized organizations. Even hermits do not approach self-sufficiency in relatively modernized contexts. When they must interact with others, they inevitably interact with some who act in terms of highly specialized units. One of the major implications of this difference is that the members of relatively nonmodernized societies must make a major readjustment not only to an increased number of roles as modernization increases but also to an increased compartmentalization of roles. The facile making and breaking of contacts that we take for granted may seem to most of them bewildering, callous, and insincere.

It is important, however, to realize that some specialized units do exist in relatively nonmodernized societies. Just as with inanimate sources of power and tools, the presence of some such units makes possible a level of communication between the members of relatively nonmodernized and relatively modernized societies which would be much harder to understand in the complete absence of such common features. With relatively few exceptions, such as the problem of socialization for an unknown future, the major distinctions between relatively nonmodernized and relatively modernized societies rests on different incidences, emphases, and combinations of factors and aspects rather than on their presence in one case and their absence in the other.

2. SELF-SUFFICIENCY OF THE UNITS

High levels of self-sufficiency are approached by the organizations in terms of which most, often the vast majority, of the members of a relatively nonmodernized society act most of the time. This approach to self-sufficiency is particularly true of kinship and/or neighborhood units. The majority of the members expect that they, in concert with other family members, the members of larger kinship units, or the members of some sort of neighborhood unit, will produce most of what they consume, consume most of what they produce, and have little or no contact with anyone outside those units. In general they both expect and prefer this. They never attain such an ideal exactly, but they often approximate it. If cut off by a calamity of nature or some other factor from the contacts they ordinarily do have with members of other units, they are usually able to operate in terms of their preferred units with considerable stability.

There are some fairly notable exceptions, or at least qualifications, in social history. These are best exemplified by the Venetian city-states and the Hanseatic League societies. These are examples of the few great trading societies of history. A real question may be raised as to whether the social systems usually referred to as those societies in fact constituted a set of separate societies. They probably did not, but that is a technical question which need not detain the discussion here. In any case they are examples of fairly large-scale social systems with subsystems characterized by much lower levels of self-sufficiency than is common for most of the members most of the time in relatively nonmodernized contexts.

There are many implications of the high levels of ideal and actual self-sufficiency of the organizations in relatively nonmodernized societies. Relatively high levels of self-sufficiency make it exceedingly difficult to centralize such a society. The greater the level of self-sufficiency, the greater the requirement for virtually man by man supervision if one wishes to centralize in ways which are not congenial to the members. Increases in centralization involve lowering the degree of self-sufficiency. The economy in supervisory manpower, alone, that lowered self-sufficiency permits recommends it. Rulers must, however, pay a price for this stratagem. Alterations in the level of self-sufficiency have far-reaching implications for the social system as a whole. The rulers of the most stable of the relatively nonmodernized societies have not in general tried to centralize the government or other organizations of their societies to a point inconsistent with high levels of self-sufficiency.

The vulnerability of organizations and the self-sufficiency of the organizations vary inversely, but there is also a sense in which the vulnerability varies directly with the degree of self-sufficiency. This vulnerability usually shows itself in what the members of such units or observers of such phenomena are likely to consider as unconnected changes. The best example of this is training or [education] conducted outside a family context. Ordinarily the training an individual gets during his entire life as a member of a relatively nonmodernized society is carried out in family terms or simulated family terms. In the craft shop, for example, when apprentices are not actual members of the family they often acquire a sort of assimilated family rank. To train someone outside of a family context for a job which he may hold outside of a family context may seem on the surface to have few implications for the general stability of the family. Training, however, is intimately connected to the general structures of respect and control of the family. It may never have occurred to other members of the family that training could take place outside the family context. Realization that it can opens up new possibilities of action to all of the family members. To some extent it diminishes the prestige of family members of the older generation. Now the young see that some of the roles that older more respected members of the family have fulfilled can be fulfilled by others on a nonfamily basis. If families were stable despite considerable amounts of internal stress and strain among the members, the most casual opening up of such alternatives may have explosive effects. Introduction of structures of modernization has in fact had explosive effects on the social structure of relatively nonmodernized societies. The family context is commonly one in which these effects are felt earliest. One of the commonest outside influences first introduced is some training by outsiders of individuals for adult roles. Not only does the individual learn that he can prepare himself for adult roles and hence continued existence, even if he defies his family elders and runs away, but he may also be more impressed by and respectful of the new training afforded by the outsider than of the old. As his respect for his family elders declines, so does their ability to control his behavior, or even their ability to keep him a member of the family. Thus general controls are undermined, and the ability of families to persist in the face of stresses and strains generated quite apart from modernization may disintegrate explosively.

3. PREDOMINANTLY PARTICULARISTIC ETHICS

Members of relatively nonmodernized societies emphasize predominantly particularistic ethics overwhelmingly. They never approach, ideally or actually, the emphasis on predominantly universalistic criteria characteristic of relatively modernized societies. When they emphasize predominantly universalistic criteria, they do so for restricted contexts, and the emphasis is more likely to be actual than ideal. The importance of predominantly particularistic ethics in these contexts is closely connected to the enormous focus of attention on kinship in general and the family in particular. The vast majority of the members of all relatively nonmodernized societies make family considerations the major

determinant of all their decisions.[9] Even though other considerations are important and may occasionally even take precedence
over these, for the ordinary man in all history prior to the nineteenth century the most important question was, "How will this
affect my family?" Kinship is inherently particularistic; it is
specifically a sphere in which the individual is identified, above
all, on the basis of who he is. Kinship identification is determined
at least in part on the basis of an actual or fictitious biological
relatedness, on the basis of some particular sexual relationship
with a person, usually of the opposite sex,[10] or on some combination of the two. Initial kinship identification is always as
someone's child and not a function of anything the individual has
done which is germane nor of any of his special objective
qualifications or achievements. Kinship identification is never
entirely biological. There is the general, if not universal, practice
of adoption, and there is also the fact that, although it is usually
easy to determine who the mother of a child in fact is, the
question of paternity is by no means so simple.[11]

Traditional Chinese society is probably the most extreme case
of a large-scale society whose members oriented most of their
action, ideally and actually, to kinship considerations. Ideally
speaking members of that society always expected, and were
expected by others to take family considerations into account.
Moreover, those considerations ideally took precedence over all
others.[12] One of the major responsibilities of the Chinese Emperor

[9] See also pp. 120–122 and 377–435.

[10] It is necessary to be ponderously careful in these matters. Societies
vary enormously with regard to the attitude of their members toward
homosexual relationships. There are societies in terms of which it is quite
legitimate for homosexual partners to be "married." This structure is not a
great rarity in social history. Even when this procedure is perfectly acceptable, such relationships never constitute more than a small minority of the
sexual relationships which are considered legitimate.

[11] Malinowski alleged that the physiological process of conception is not
understood even in a crude sense in all societies. He gives an example of
one society whose members saw no connection between sexual intercourse
and the birth of children [see B. Malinowski: *The Sexual Life of Savages*,
Halcyon House, New York, 1929, pp. 179–186]. Some are uncertain
whether the people concerned were teasing Malinowski or Malinowski was
teasing his readers. Nevertheless, even in that setting an infant was always
connected in a kinship sense to some particular marital pair.

[12] It was even conceivable that one be forgiven for an attempt to assassinate the Emperor or one of his representatives if it were shown that one
did so in order to avenge a genuine wrong done to one's father or some
other ancestor. Practically no other excuse could justify such behavior.
Obversely, if a person did attempt to assassinate the Emperor or one of the
Emperor's officials, he was likely to pay for it with his life, and his relatives
might be wiped out too, specifically in order to prevent the possibility of
vendettas.

was to prevent the development of a situation in which family oriented actions could conflict with one another or with governmentally oriented action. Such conflicts constituted prima-facie evidence that the Emperor did not have "Will of Heaven," which was the sole legitimation of his position.

Tokugawa Japanese society presents an important variation. The ordinary member of that society was expected in most instances to be as family or kinship oriented as his Chinese counterpart. If, however, a conflict between loyalty to his overlord and loyalty to his family arose, loyalty to the overlord came first, no matter the cost. Ordinarily such questions would not arise unless one was of the samurai class or better.[13]

Kinship-oriented particularism is almost certainly the most universal form of particularism. There are, however, many other frequent forms in relatively nonmodernized societies. Particularism based on neighborhood or class identification are examples.[14] The list of possible bases for predominantly particularistic ethics is indefinite. The important thing to remember is that it is quite possible for the members of relatively nonmodernized societies to place no discernible ideal emphasis on universalism at all.

There will be some actual emphasis on predominantly universalistic criteria even if there is none ideally, because there is no society [and there can be no society] whose members pay no attention whatsoever to what a person does or can do that is relevant. The often cited emphases on universalism in relatively nonmodernized social contexts have probably been exaggerated. One of the most notable cases of this is the democratic practices of the Greek city-states. Even Athens at her height was a democ-

---

[13] In this connection I should like to digress for a moment and point to a device which may be useful for quick insight. It is always interesting to ask, "To what extent are the words appropriate to action in terms of one type of unit 'exported' to cover relationships carried out in terms of other units?" For example, traditional Chinese applied kinship terms to practically any relationship construed important to the individual but not in fact a kinship relationship. One referred to a close friend as a brother, usually by the term for elder brother, and to a teacher as an older brother of one's father; etc. Export of kinship terms to nonkinship spheres indicated the importance of the latter. Nothing could indicate a greater importance for them without violating the ethical structures of that society than this simulation of kinship.

Contrast this with our practice. It is frequently said of a given father and son that their relationship is more than that of a father and son; they are real friends; they are real companions, or they are real pals. We rarely export terms from the kinship sphere save in a derogatory sense such as in the sardonic phrase, "oh brother."

[14] To some extent class identification is always closely related to kinship because one's initial class placement is via one's kinship position.

racy only for her citizens who by no means coincided with her total population. Citizenship was predominantly particularistically defined. The degree of universalistic emphasis of Roman law may also require qualification.

There are certain obvious implications of heavy emphases on particularistic criteria. Either there must be easily and ubiquitously observable signs indicating who a person is to all other persons with whom he comes in contact, or the ordinary individual must be so restricted by himself or others that he rarely comes in contact with anyone ignorant of who he is. For most of the people most of the time the latter has probably held true. Even when signs were easily observable, the individuals concerned were not ordinarily highly mobile either socially or spatially.[15] This has obvious implications for these societies once the mobility of these people increases radically spatially and/or socially, in the process of modernization.

4. COMBINATION OF CENTRALIZATION AND DECENTRALIZATION

However despotic their rulers, relatively nonmodernized societies are never stable without major provisions for decentralization. The major structure of decentralization in the last analysis is always the actual if not ideal autonomy of the nearly self-sufficient units within the sphere of their self-sufficiency. Within this sphere the members are almost always left entirely to their own devices. Interference with individual members may be spectacular, but general behavior is centralized only slightly in terms of the government or any other large-scale unit. Traditional Chinese society had many highly centralized features, but only rarely did the Chinese Imperial bureaucrats reach down directly from the Emperor, as it were, to specific family members. Almost always the day-to-day elements of centralization were achieved by virtue of the essentially autonomous cooperation of the members of the relatively self-sufficient units. Thus, in traditional China troops were not ordinarily sent to collect the grain for taxes. The peasants made initial deliveries. Imperial troops were not ordinarily sent to punish villagers. Culprits were surrendered to the District Magistrate or kept in line at home. The most spectacular

---

[15] In Tosa Han [fief] in Tokugawa Japan members of the Eta, an outcast class organization, were required to wear a particular kind of hairdress so that others could avoid contamination. After dusk they were not supposed to stir abroad lest that hairdress be unnoticed. Even so, the Eta of Tosa probably did not move around a great deal even within Tosa Han.

cases of centralization had to do with the collection of taxes and the levying of *corvées* for purposes of public construction. The former affected most of the population but in specifically limited respects, and the latter affected a limited portion of the population in limited respects.[16]

In many of the cases, and certainly in the case of traditional China, the members of the government in a pinch were quite capable of moving troops into any village or town and thereby of controlling its members directly. It is also true that that society never could have been run on the basis of anything approaching such actual direct control. There were never that many men under arms. They were never that well organized. Transportation was never highly enough developed to shift available manpower about at the rate necessary for such centralization. The logistic difficulties made it quite out of the question. At the highest point of its development there were never enough members of the Chinese bureaucracy—certainly one of the administrative marvels of all history—to administer any such large-scale activity.[17]

Tokugawa Japan was probably the most highly centralized feudal system in world history. It was certainly the most stable feudal system in world history, persisting in its main outlines for a period of two and a half centuries. Despite genuine power available to the Shogun, most operations involved a great deal of autonomy of the members of a han [i.e. a fief]. Within the han there was important decentralization to the village level and within the village to the family level. The Shogun was in an excellent position to bring pressure to bear if he chose to do so, and from time to time he certainly did. Ordinarily, he did not do so, and for two hundred of those two hundred and fifty years few members of the hans got out of line in any manner seriously threatening to the position of the Shogun.

[16] I mention the case of traditional China in particular because this case is the main basis for the important work of Professor K. A. Wittfogel. Professor Wittfogel has increased our understanding of the centralized elements of traditional Chinese society in particular and of centralization in relatively nonmodernized societies in general. He has done this at the expense of some neglect of the importance of the elements of decentralization throughout Chinese history. He probably would not or could not have made the contribution for which we are indebted to him had he not overstated and oversimplified the case. Now that we are in receipt of his findings, considerably more limited scholarship can qualify those findings importantly [see K. A. Wittfogel: *Oriental Despotism*, Yale University Press, New Haven, 1957].

[17] The total membership of that bureaucracy including many who were not scholars probably never exceeded half a million men by the most generous estimate. Most scholars would select a much lower figure.

There certainly were cases of high centralization prior to the development of relatively modernized societies, but none of these were stable for any extended period of time. The best examples were the famous cases of large-scale conquest, but the rapidity with which these organizations broke up and decentralized is well known. Vestiges of these empires often persisted for centuries, but the centralized features which strike us so forcibly rarely survived for long the death of the leader who initiated them. The vestigial systems that persisted for centuries were always highly decentralized.

The sedentary nature of the relatively nonmodernized societies lessens the importance of centralization and also makes it in a sense inefficient. Most of these societies, if large-scale, have been sedentary in the fullest sense of the word. They not only have low rates of change, but their members are largely agrarian, i.e., they are sedentary in a locational sense.[18] The members of any highly centralized organization must gather and keep records of the activities involved. There is little point in gathering and keeping records of who is planting what and what the land distribution is, and so forth on a large scale if those matters are going to remain stable year in and year out. For most of these societies inheritance structures are highly stable. The nature of techniques and crops does not vary markedly from one year to the next. Local records suffice to avoid or settle disputes. The relative lack of change makes questions of centralization considerably less relevant than would be the case with less sedentary equally large-scale societies. It also makes such centralization uneconomic. Everyone knows that the peasants in a given area are planting rice in a given year and intend to plant it next year, and the year after that. Everyone knows that they are going to harvest with the same tools, at roughly the same time of year, with roughly the same amount of labor, and so forth and so on. Under such circumstances centralization is inefficient in a special sense. At the same time that high levels of centralization are unnecessary for most purposes, the amount of attention required for centralization is comparatively great because of the close approach to self-sufficiency of many of the organizations. Centralization may be quite important for a leader's dream of power, but as long as the general situation is

[18] Even the nomadic societies are sedentary as far as change is concerned, but they are rarely societies of any considerable scale, and it is the relatively nonmodernized societies of some considerable scale which are of greatest importance here. Nevertheless, the remarks here should apply equally well to nomadic societies if they are relatively nonmodernized.

highly sedentary, increases in centralization will not alter markedly the kinds of organization which can exist stably. Such increases are more likely to be disruptive than otherwise.

The state of technology of communications is vital for the question of centralization. In relatively nonmodernized contexts, it is too poor to support large-scale overwhelming centralization. There have been structures of efficient and rapid communication for limited purposes. Even the most spectacular examples, however, were not sufficiently developed to permit either the efficiency or the scale of communication necessary if decentralization were to be virtually eliminated or radically reduced. Neither the necessary flow of information nor that of people and goods could be handled. Bad logistics have laid low more power megalomaniacs than have ever been brought to book by heroic resistance.[19]

Among relatively nonmodernized societies the range of variation of combinations of elements of decentralization and centralization is considerably greater than the corresponding range of variation in relatively modernized societies. Here again there is an hypothesis which runs through virtually everything I have asserted so far. For all of their important differences, all relatively modernized societies are in fact becoming more and more alike all the time and the range of possible variation among them decreases all the time. The limits of stable centralization for relatively nonmodernized cases are important, but their members can carry centralization much further and remain stable than the members of relatively modernized societies can carry decentralization and remain stable. Accounts of high levels of centralization in relatively nonmodernized societies are usually overdone. Accounts of decentralization in the relatively modernized cases may not be overdone to the same degree but the allegations of the amount of decentralization possible and practicable are usually sentimental, nostalgic, and romantic. One of the wists of highly

[19] In traditional China, centuries before the Romance of our Great West, there was a pony express capable of transporting such items as True Relics of the Buddha and important Buddhist Sutras in a matter of days from India to the capital of China, across thousands of miles, many of them over exceedingly difficult terrain. Apart from the set of Roman roads probably no means of communication in world history prior to the development of relatively high levels of modernization exceeded in sophistication and complexity those developed in traditional China. Nevertheless, neither those of China nor Rome were capable of the level of transportation of either information or people which would have been necessary for the kind of day-to-day centralization which members of the United States take for granted—or anything remotely approximating it.

modernized people is that somehow increases in modernization will make possible substantial increases in decentralization.[20]

In relatively nonmodernized societies the range of combinations of centralized and decentralized elements goes all the way from the loosest sort of tribal or interkinship organization to societies in which, for all of their elements of decentralization large-scale bureaucracies exist and for which large-scale communications and public works are erected and maintained. Textbooks in anthropology, history, political science, and sociology treat these variations in a degree of detail which makes it unnecessary here. There is, however, one form of the combination of centralization and decentralization, *feudalism,* which deserves some special comment because the term is used for both analysis and propaganda. Propaganda-wise the tendency is to refer to practically any society that is relatively nonmodern as feudal. This is plausible primarily because the well-studied feudal societies were relatively nonmodernized and shared many characteristics with all other relatively nonmodernized societies. For example, the large-scale relatively nonmodernized societies are all characterized by a particular bimodal [or radically asymmetrical (see below, pp. 65–279) distribution of income. That is to say a small number of their members are wealthy people, and the vast majority of the members live on the bare margin of subsistence. All such societies are characterized by great differences in authority among their members. All have highly particularistic ethics and so forth. Feudal societies have all of these characteristics in common with other relatively nonmodernized societies, but they also have a set of special characteristics with far-reaching implications for the problems of modernization of late-comers. These implications are different, indeed, from the implications of the structures of nonfeudal societies, even though those nonfeudal societies also have the common characteristics mentioned above. I object to the use of the term

---

[20] In the late 1930's there was in this country a really delightful group who called themselves "Decentralists," I believe. They had read and misunderstood Veblen. They felt that life was dominated by huge bureaucratic organizations, and that the situation was getting worse. They developed ways and devices for getting us out of this terrible spiral. One of these was to get people back to grinding their own flour and making their own bread. These processes had gotten into the hands of the corporate colossi, and we were now not only more centralized but we got poorer bread as a result of it. They suggested that we buy wheat, grind it ourselves, make our own bread and at one and the same time interfere with the heinous trend and improve our diet. In order to facilitate this they had persuaded representatives of one of the corporate colossi to manufacture for them and their converts a little dandy gem wheat grinder for the home. If people would just buy these grinders, plug them in and . . .

feudal as an epithet for purposes of propaganda not merely because it injects a pejorative note into analyses about which it is difficult to be objective at best. I object much more because it is a debasement of the languages. Such usage [21] makes it more difficult to understand certain important social differences.

If one means by the term *feudal* the kind of society which existed in medieval Europe in many areas, a quite specific combination of centralization and decentralization is involved. Feudal societies are societies in terms of which to a high degree positions of power and responsibility are ideally allocated along with control over land. Control over land in these cases means, of course, control over certain forms of income. The members of these societies emphasize loyalty to an overlord. A given individual judges his relations to other people in important part on the basis of how his overlord is related to them. Ordinarily his loyalty to his overlord takes precedence over his loyalty to his overlord's overlord. Succession to positions in the hierarchy is ordinarily determined by inheritance on the basis of kinship. Class distinctions are usually extremely rigid. Some feudal societies are, ideally speaking, characterized by completely closed classes. In those cases there is little possibility of actual mobility between different classes though some mobility within a given class is always countenanced.[22]

The main form of decentralization characteristic of feudal societies is the considerable autonomy permitted to a given overlord within the area under his control. Usually a King or an Emperor or a Shogun is considered to be the supreme overlord. Usually his control over his subordinates is quite limited. Tokugawa Japan, probably the most centralized feudal society in world history, and certainly the most stable, was exceptional in the strength of the control of the Shogun. This is not the place for an extended discussion of feudal social structure as such, but feudalism is a specific social form, radically different from most other arrangements in which there are great discrepancies of wealth, large amounts of authoritarianism, and so forth. Furthermore the differences between feudal societies and other societies with

---

[21] This special form of unjustifiable jargon may be called *culpable* jargon.

[22] The level of actual mobility in such cases is always higher than the level of ideal mobility. The actual mobility may be highly disruptive of the *status quo;* it may also have integrative effects. Both effects are usually via the "illegitimate" mobility of talent. This contrasts sharply with societies with high mobility structures ideally. In the latter the structures of actual mobility are likely to be less than the ideal structures call for—again with both disruptive and integrative implications for the *status quo.*

which they are often confused are strategic for the problems of late-comers to the process of modernization. After all, the most successful of all of the later late-comers to modernization have been the Japanese who made the transition to high modernization specifically from a feudal basis.

Traditional Chinese society is one of the best examples of a society frequently described as feudal in the misleading sense. In the strict sense, Chinese society has not been feudal for upward of 2000 years. The social structure of traditional China, in many respects [e.g., open classes both ideally and actually, a bureaucracy whose members were recruited on the basis of a civil service in the ordinary sense, etc.] was superficially much more like the social structure of relatively modernized societies than was that of Tokugawa Japan. Furthermore there is absolutely no comparison between the extent of available natural resources of the sort generally deemed relevant to modernization in the two cases. There is also no question but that the Japanese made the transition to modernization with much greater ease than did the Chinese and that they have carried the process to levels which the Chinese do not approach, even remotely. In this comparison at least, strong feudal structures constitute a better basis for rapid and efficient modernization of late-comers than do nonfeudal social structures. This holds true despite the fact that the nonfeudal social structures may have much more in common with the so-called democratic aspects of some relatively modernized societies.[23]

[23] Many assume that, since all relatively modernized societies have open-class structures, both ideally and actually, societies with open-class structures are a better bet for rapid and efficient modernization. This is not necessarily the case. A substantial portion of the errors in thinking about problems of modernization can be classified as failures to take into account one of the following propositions: (1) The requisites [i.e., the conditions necessary for maintaining a given system] for relatively modernized societies are not necessarily the same as the prerequisites [i.e., the conditions necessary for achieving a given system]. Thus it is by no means true that by finding out what characteristics are present in a relatively modernized society can one simply say "put these into effect" in society X and relative modernization will be achieved quickly and efficiently. It may not be possible to put the requisites into effect directly. (2) The prerequisites for late-comers to modernization are not necessarily the same as the prerequisites were for the indigenous developers of relatively high degrees of modernization. It does not necessarily follow that the history of England, the United States, France, etc., give us the best clues as to what late-comers have to do if they wish to modernize. (3) The prerequisites for one set of late-comers are not necessarily the same as for another. What worked in Japan, for example, will not necessarily work in Turkey. For an understanding of these differences the most important element is careful research into the basis from which change toward modernization takes

In analysis of centralization and decentralization I urge great care about the use of the term feudal. Ordinary usage, intentionally or unintentionally injects a note of evaluation which obscures analysis of the problems involved. Many are interested in analysis of these problems primarily because of an interest in evaluations. Knowledge of the role of feudal structures in modernization is important for policy decisions with regard to relatively nonmodernized societies. To use the term as an epithet for any structures regarded as unenlightened or wicked is to gloss over critical distinctions.

5. RELATIONSHIP ASPECTS

The particular set of relationship aspects emphasized by the members of all relatively nonmodernized societies is critical. All of them emphasize traditional rather than rational action. I must reemphasize something already mentioned in the discussion of the emphasis on rationality in relatively modernized social contexts. Traditional ways of doing things are not necessarily irrational or even nonrational. Many, if not most, of the traditional ways of doing things—particularly those which become the focus of great technical advance during modernization—coincide with the rational way of doing things, given the means available. For example, in the areas of both craftsmanship and agriculture, the traditional techniques, given the available means are often rational techniques. Traditional techniques of this sort are almost never silly or superficial. Even if traditional techniques coincide with rational ones, however, the fact that emphasis is placed on doing things *because* it is traditional to do them in the given way

---

place, that is research into the previous history of the society concerned. The structures of modernization which have developed elsewhere and will be introduced from outside the societies of the late-comers are relatively easy to describe and relatively constant in most strategic respects. The bases from which the changes take place, however, vary widely. It is knowledge of these variations as well as knowledge of relatively modernized structures themselves which furnish the largest number of clues about the differences in prerequisites for one set of late-comers as opposed to another. (4) One of the special implications of the second proposition above is that social structures most like those of relatively modernized societies are not necessarily the best basis for transition to modernization.

Errors from these sources would not be so formidable were it not for the following propositions: (1) Some of the requisites for relatively modernized societies are the same as some of the prerequisites. (2) Some of the prerequisites for late-comers are the same as those for the indigenous developers, and (3) Some of the prerequisites for all late-comers are the same.

This whole matter is elaborated below, see pp. 737–740.

has different implications from an emphasis on doing things in a given fashion *because* there is a presumably rational explanation of doing them that way. If a farmer cultivates crops in a particular way because his forebears always have done it that way—even though that is rational given the means available—and the available means change, the traditionalist is likely to continue to employ the old means, even though they are no longer rational. Not only is his likelihood of changing quickly less, but if he does change, the implications for his conduct in other respects are greater, specifically because the switch involves an abandonment or defiance of the previously accepted traditional emphases. Perhaps the most outstanding feature of traditionalism is the emphasis on continuing to do something in a specific way because the perpetuation of doing it in that way is regarded as good, respectful, and right. To change a given traditional way of doing something, particularly under the kind of pressure usually involved in a more or less dramatic demonstration that another technique is vastly more efficient, is likely to call the emphasis on tradition in general into question. This is not to imply that traditions do not change. They change, and in many cases rapidly. Especially in relatively nonmodernized social contexts changes in tradition are usually not carried out self-consciously by the members. Even when the change is relatively rapid, the individuals involved are usually convinced that the new structures have been the traditions all along.[24] The continuous confrontation which the rapidly changing rational technology characteristic of relatively modernized societies affords any given set of accepted means makes unselfconscious alterations of tradition impossible, or at least, a great deal less likely. It is one of the ironies of history that the terms *conservative* and *old-fashioned* have on the whole been laudatory ones until relatively modernized societies developed. In terms of relatively modernized societies, apart from the area in which it is fashionable to be

[24] Professor Joseph R. Strayer whose special concern is medieval history is fond of pointing out that the general idea of the importance of tradition in medieval society is correct but that quite incorrect implications are often drawn from it. What is considered a tradition may be of very recent coinage. Particularly in the absence of high rates of literacy and carefully kept records, a request for a special exception to feudal dues granted only a year before may by the following year be regarded as a long-standing custom. He illustrates the process involved by a feature of universities which are strongholds of traditionalism even in relatively modernized societies. As an experienced departmental chairman he knows that a special request granted to a senior in any given year may be regarded as a "right" of hoary sacrosanct tradition by any freshman entering the university in any subsequent year.

quaint, usually a restricted area for a restricted elite, anything dubbed conservative or old-fashioned is on the defensive. One of the reasons that so many things seem to come apart at the seams at once during the process of modernization is that any self-conscious challenge to traditionalism in any area *may* bring into question traditions in *any other* area, and that it inevitably brings into question traditions in *some* other area.

In the discussion of relatively modernized societies, I indicated that it was not possible to have societies whose members place no emphasis whatsoever on traditional ways. It is possible to have societies so overwhelmingly traditionalistic that members place little or no emphasis, ideally speaking, on rationality. This would not be possible, of course, if the traditional ways of doing things did not coincide to some considerable degree with rational procedures.[25]

Once it was fashionable to distinguish between rational and prerational peoples. Taken literally such a distinction would imply that prerational people are quite incapable of understanding that injuries or at least pain could follow from a fall. They would be unable to understand the distinction between a sharp and a dull arrowhead or knife. No such people have ever existed as far as is known. Malinowski pointed out that no known primitive people confused bad workmanship with improperly performed magic. There are no people who do not think rationally in some context and who do not appreciate some rational thinking. He understood and appreciated, however, that the emphasis could still be overwhelmingly on tradition as long as what was traditional coincided relatively well with what was rational. In this sense, a complete emphasis on tradition is theoretically possible. It is exceedingly doubtful that the actual emphasis on tradition has ever been carried to such an extreme, and it certainly has not for any large-scale society.

For any large-scale society there are always spheres of action, usually the most clearly instrumental spheres of action, in which rationality is emphasized and recognized to some extent. The extent of that emphasis, however, need not be great, and it may be associated with spheres of behavior of relatively low ideal status. One of the best examples of this has to do with the activities of merchants [see also pp. 113–114 and 543–548].

[25] Ideally speaking, it is possible for the members of a society to approach an extreme pole of emphasis on traditionalism which cannot be approached by the members of any society with regard to rationality. No society, for example, has ever been characterized by completely rationally based kinship structures. Furthermore, such kinship structures are improbable and perhaps not even possible.

Merchants always understand rational operations to a marked degree and place heavy emphasis upon them. Ideally speaking, merchant members of relatively nonmodernized societies frequently have low prestige, which may continue to be low ideally, even though they may become powerful and important actually. Although relatively nonmodernized societies vary to some degree in the emphasis placed by members on rationality both ideally and actually, ideally speaking the emphasis on rationality never reaches the point at which arguments based on traditionalism are generally defensive arguments.[26]

The criteria for forming relationships tend in relatively nonmodernized societies to be overwhelmingly particularistic. Before a relationship can be formed the parties must know who everybody is. There is the widest variation in different bases for determining who an individual is. Despite this variation, however, kinship is the major basis of particularistic identification for the overwhelming majority of the members of these societies.

As already pointed out, kinship is an ineradicable basis for particularistic distinctions in all societies, and most members of most societies have oriented most of their action to kinship considerations. Under these circumstances, it is not surprising that so much of particularism is defined in kinship terms. The form of particularism emphasized is often the special form of particularism distinguished below [see pp. 140–143] as germane particularism. The criteria for belonging to a relationship depend primarily on who an individual is, but that identification is highly relevant to the nature of the relationship itself. When most of the interrelationships are on the basis of some sort of kinship unit, it may be highly germane to select work crews largely on that basis.

As indicated above [see pp. 63–65], one of the great problems of placing emphasis on particularistic criteria lies in the possibility that predominantly particularistic selection of individuals will interfere with the extent to which an emphasis on rationality can be maintained. The person selected on the basis of who he is may not be the person best fitted to carry out the job. On the other hand, what is here called germane particularism is to a considerable degree easily combinable with rationality, particularly when

[26] The reverse tends overwhelmingly to be the case in relatively modernized social contexts and becomes the more so the more highly modernized they become. Traditional emphases are not eliminated either ideally or actually, but the burden of proof comes increasingly to rest on the defenders of tradition rather than on the proponents of rationality. This is no small element in the frenetic insistence of so many moderns on a completely rational, scientific, objective ethic.

the elements of rationality are present, not so much because of the direct emphasis on rationality as because the traditional ways happen to coincide with what is rational. Again given the position of family units in such societies, it is probably rational to make up various groups of individuals for particular purposes on a family basis.

It is important to keep in mind that the vast majority of all relatively nonmodernized societies have been societies in terms of which the average individual lived out his life in contact with a quite restricted number of individuals. The number of different organizations in which a given individual has roles is also highly restricted. Furthermore, the possibility of the average individual coming into contact with individuals from another organizational context of which he knows nothing is also relatively slight. Under these circumstances it is not difficult to envisage virtually all the relationships in which he enters being predominantly particularistically defined.

There are certainly examples of great emphasis on comparatively universalistic criteria in such social contexts, especially in matters having to do with generalized media of exchange, markets, and bureaucracies [see below, pp. 113–120]. They may in fact exist quite apart from the two categories just mentioned. Although in theory it is possible that there be a society whose members placed no ideal emphasis on universalistic criteria whatsoever, such a society obviously could not continue to exist if individuals selected on a predominantly particularistic basis were totally incapable of performing tasks vital to their survival. Societies may actually have gone out of existence because predominantly particularistic selection interfered with the minimal requirements of operations in terms of them. The most spectacular cases of this are likely to be the result of particularistically selected leaders of governments.

Another emphasis characteristic of the relationships in relatively nonmodernized societies is that on functional diffuseness. Relationships in these societies are rarely precisely defined and precisely delimited, i.e., predominantly functionally specific. Frequently in such societies there are important elements of careful definition. For example, in Chinese society the minimum obligations of a wife to her husband were quite clearly stated. The relationship was, however, by no means precisely delimited. As indicated above, the modern contract relationship is an extreme case of functional specificity. In this respect the use of the term *contract* for the feudal contract is misleading. The feudal contract was typically a predominantly functionally diffuse relationship. Although there was a considerable amount of detailed definition as to some of the obligations involved, the relationship was by no means precisely delimited.

The importance of kinship considerations is highly relevant to the emphasis on functional diffuseness. Kinship relationships are always overwhelmingly functionally diffuse. Any society in terms of which a very considerable proportion of all relationships are carried out on a kinship basis is a society characterized by an overwhelming emphasis on functionally diffuse relationships. Here again, unlike the case of relatively modernized societies, the emphasis on the opposite pole may be quite slight or even nonexistent. It is quite conceivable that there could be relatively nonmodernized societies with no ideal structures of emphasis on functional specificity whatsoever. It is not possible to have a relatively modernized society with no emphasis whatsoever on functionally diffuse relationships. One of the problems of functionally diffuse emphasis in relatively modernized contexts is that, if the relationship is predominantly functionally diffuse, it is difficult to confine it to predominantly universalistic selection or to predominantly rational cognition. In societies in terms of which neither rationality nor universalism is highly emphasized this particular order of problem is not likely to arise. These emphases in relatively nonmodernized contexts are not likely to cause trouble because they clash with the implications of other emphases on their opposite extremes. The clashes and conflict in relatively nonmodernized societies among relationship structures are likely to be conflicts between one set of predominantly traditionalistic emphases and another, between one set of predominantly particularistic emphases and another, or between one set of predominantly functionally diffuse emphases and another.

These interrelationships, whether in conflict with one another or not, may have some special effects. In relatively nonmodernized social contexts effects comparable to emphases on rationality, universalism, and functional specificity are sometimes obtained by a balance of traditional, particularistic, and functionally diffuse emphases. For example, in traditional Chinese contexts a given family member of a given Chinese village would, if given the opportunity, exploit other villagers to the benefit of his own family members. Often the members of one of the families were so much more powerful than the others that exactly this sort of exploitation resulted. On the other hand ordinarily there was a more nearly even balance of power among members of different family units. In village management of various sorts not only was one family-based particularism often played off against another, but neighborhood particularism was often played off against family particularism, and frequently the result was the same sort of selection which would have been obtained had selection been on a predominantly universalistic basis. This matter of obtaining predominantly rational, universalistic, and functionally specific results as a function of varying balances of emphases on tradition, particularism, and functional diffuseness is important for an understanding of problems of modernization. Some apparently inexplicable upsets at local levels have probably been a function of the fact that initial moves in the direction of emphases on rationality, universalism, and functional specificity have actually lowered the extent to which those qualities have been achieved. This has been the result of the fact that the efforts to achieve the new structures have wiped out delicate balances of the old, which gave such results, without replacing them efficiently with the new.

6. GENERALIZED MEDIA OF EXCHANGE AND MARKETS

Highly generalized media of exchange and markets do not necessarily exist in all relatively nonmodernized societies. It is unlikely that any of these societies be totally devoid of generalized media of exchange. Nevertheless, the level of generalization of any media of exchange which do exist can be exceedingly low, and certainly there can be societies of this sort without markets. Both highly generalized media of exchange and markets, however, do exist in all known cases of societies of any considerable scale. Both the degree of generalization of the medium or media of exchange and the development of markets may be highly restricted by contrast with the extent of either of these in relatively modernized societies. To the extent that generalized media of exchange and markets exist, an element of rationality is exceedingly likely to be injected into the society even though tradition is emphasized. As indicated again and again, there is always some rationality, regardless of whether it is ideally called for or not. There is in the first place the kind of rationality that happens to coincide with the traditional forms preferred for traditional reasons. In the second place, there is the sort of rationality which comes from sources other than ideal sources. The likelihood of some rational orientation wherever there are highly developed media of exchange and highly developed markets, contributes to the peculiar role of merchants in these relatively nonmodernized societies. The role of merchants is likely to be a marginal or outcast role ideally speaking in relatively nonmodernized societies specifically because of ambivalent attitudes toward rationally oriented experts in exchange. Actually speaking merchants frequently become powerful and even prestigious, and there are even cases such as the Hanseatic League societies and the Venetian city states in which both ideally and actually the merchant is a man of great prestige, but these tend to be exceptions in world history.

There is a more detailed discussion of the basis of these assertions below [see pp. 543–548]. For the present, suffice it to illustrate the situation by the general point that anything which injects an element of rationality into a situation which ordinarily emphasizes traditionality tends to create special problems of integrating the activities concerned with the general ideal structures. One of the most flagrant examples of this is one on which sociologists dote. It is the problem of the relationship between prostitution and ideal family structures. One of the great differences between them is the setting within which sexual relationships take place. Specifically sexual relations in a family context are sexual relationships taken out of a market, taken out of a generalized medium of exchange setting. Prostitution is a sexual relationship taken in specifically that kind of setting.[27] Sex in the family context and in the context of prostitution as referred to here both involve women. In even the most highly mechanized societies no satisfactory substitute has been found, as a popular musical maintains, "There is nothing like a dame." Since exactly the same sort of personnel can be involved in either or both relationships, there are likely to be conflicts between sex carried out on a family basis and on the basis of generalized media of exchange in markets. Most of the attacks on prostitution as a social evil dwell on real or hypothetical examples in which the practice of prostitution somehow undermines a given family situation. One of the more dramatic examples always invoked to exemplify the evils of this practice is the tale of an otherwise upright family man who in resorting to prostitution finds he is expected to carry out the relationship with a member of his own family—usually in the most telling case with his daughter. This

[27] In the revolt against the restricted position of women in the nineteenth century one of the focal war cries was based on the allegation that in fact family practice was a great deal more like prostitution than the upholders of morality cared to admit. Lady Cicely Hamilton in a famous book, *Marriage as a Trade* [Moffat, Yard & Co., New York, 1909], pointed out that insofar as women accepted limitations on their freedom in return for support by their husbands, etc., or insofar as their husbands justified such subservience on that basis, the implication clearly was that marriage was only a special form of prostitution. Many of the early feminists delighted in the shock value of this point of view.

not only emphasizes the subversiveness of the practice for family stability, but also contains a high-minded emphasis on "just deserts."

It is not necessary to depend upon the prostitution—family case for illustration of this point. There is exactly the same sort of conflict implicit in the hiring of labor on a generalized-media-of-exchange-market basis. When labor is carried out in a family or neighborhood context, work as well as sexual services are ordinarily carried out without a cash nexus involved. Most of the members of most of the societies of the world carry out most of what we would consider labor and the like on just such a predominantly particularistic basis. To inject considerations of a cash nexus into those relationships can be every bit as upsetting and have every bit as far-reaching implications as to inject such considerations into areas ordinarily concerned with sexual relationships. In relatively modernized contexts so many of these other activities have long since been drawn into the generalized-media-of-exchange-market context that the example of prostitution is one of the few vivid examples left. As far as relatively nonmodernized societies are concerned, any highly developed markets or highly generalized media of exchange are always accompanied by a conflict of ideal and actual structures, by special forms of insulation of this sphere of activity from others carried out on other bases, or by highly developed cases of both. The fact that the role of merchants, ideally speaking, is frequently denigrated is one of the most frequent ways of insulating their activities from the general practices in other contexts.

B. ORGANIZATIONAL CONTEXTS

1. BUREAUCRACY

The presence of bureaucratic systems is not universal among relatively nonmodernized societies. This is one of the characteristic differences between relatively modernized and relatively nonmodernized societies. Bureaucratic systems are requisites for the former. Although they are not requisites for the latter, there are certainly some outstanding examples of them. Following the work of Max Weber, scholars tend to point to relatively few bureaucracies in relatively nonmodernized contexts, the outstanding examples being the Catholic church, those of the early Egyptian dynasties, traditional Chinese society, Roman society, etc. Instances of bureaucracies are far more frequent than this, although they are not as frequent ideally as they are actually.

This may be why so many have been overlooked.[28] Some elements of bureaucratic organization probably appear in all cases of large-scale relatively nonmodernized societies, and there is always the problem of combating the effects of particularism in a predominantly particularistic setting. When quite high levels of skill are necessary for large-scale purposes of administration, how is personnel to be recruited when, ideally speaking, ostensibly, recruitment is only on a particularistic basis? There are many fascinating variations of methods in terms of which members of these societies accomplish this purpose. Some of them are undoubtedly used self-consciously; others probably are not. The most striking method is the one seen so clearly by Max Weber. The members of these societies sometimes hit upon the device of a bureaucratic system as described by Weber, both ideally and actually. All such systems have a major problem built in. This is the problem of insulating the predominantly universalistically defined bureaucratic system from the enveloping sea of predominantly particularistic relationships.

The second method does not involve what Weber would have considered a bureaucratic system, ideally speaking. It achieves comparable results by special handling of a predominantly particularistically recruited system. The bureaucracies of Tokugawa Japan were excellent examples of this. A third device is that of selecting for bureaucratic personnel individuals who are outsiders from the point of view of the general membership of the

[28] One of the most important reasons for raising the question of the distinction between ideal and actual structures is the fact that the former are frequently taken for the latter. The reverse confusion is less likely. The reason is in one sense simple—in another complex. When a member of a given society describes his own society, whether as an informant or not, he is very likely to state its ideal structures. Ordinarily he does not do this with any intent to deceive [see above, pp. 28–30].

The fact that most individuals tend to describe ideal rather than actual structures in their own society, although they may disagree as to what the actual ideal structures are, is simple enough to observe. Why this is so general and why social analysts have been so systematically insensitive to this unintentional distortion is a much more difficult matter. Some of the reasons may be stated as follows: (1) The members of all societies learn to take most of their ideal structures very much for granted and are familiar with them. (2) The ideal structures characteristic of a given society are important empirical features of any society. In this sense it is not a distortion to describe the society in terms of them. It is only a distortion to infer that the description in these terms exhausts the relevant material on the level of generalization under discussion. (3) The ideal structures on any given level of consideration are always far simpler, better known, and better understood by the members of a society than are its actual structures. Conscious or unconscious chauvinism has probably never accounted for more than a tiny fraction of the presentation or acceptance of ideal structures as actual ones.

society and setting up methods for keeping them outsiders. The Janizariat of Turkey and the general use of eunuchs are good examples of this device. Finally, on a relatively small scale some of the effects of a bureaucratic system may be achieved by the balancing of various particularistic interests of the sort already mentioned above [pp. 112–113]. The first three of these devices are the most important in relatively nonmodernized societies, if bureaucratic systems of any large scale are involved and, I shall describe them briefly.

The traditional Chinese bureaucracy was a bureaucracy in Weber's sense both ideally and actually. Recruitment for the bureaucracy was conducted via a set of civil service examinations. When the members acted properly, those examinations were very carefully guarded. This led not only to highly universalistic selection, but also to some of the most elaborate methods of cheating on examinations seen in world history. The examinations were rather like the old British Civil Service examinations. The candidates were examined on a general classical background. Technical know-how directly applicable to the job was learned on the job. Occasionally certain categories of individuals were excluded from participating in the examinations, but on the whole the examinations were open to anyone who could achieve a sufficient level of education to enter. Once one succeeded in the examinations, he could become a member of the bureaucracy. Some levels of success in the examinations carried with them automatic appointments at high levels. No attempt was made to teach members of the bureaucracy that they should not put their family interests ahead of their bureaucratic duties. Considerable attempts were made to so insulate the bureaucrats that nepotistic inclinations could not interfere with operations in terms of the system. For example, an official was not permitted to serve in the province which was his family seat. Needless to say, in the course of a dynasty these attempts at insulation always broke down. The various forms of breakdown were as subtle, sophisticated, and fascinating as the forms of cheating developed.

The bureaucracies of Tokugawa Japan were organized along fief lines. The Tokugawa Shoguns had their bureaucracy and each of the daimyo [i.e., major feudal lords] had his own bureaucracy. Ideally speaking most of the positions were inherited ones. To this extent these systems were not bureaucracies as envisaged by Weber, but Weber, too, was so preoccupied with ideal structures that he tended to ignore actual ones. Ideally speaking the supreme obligation of a bureaucrat was not to his family but to his overlord [i.e., to his bureaucratic duty]. So fully were these ideal structures actualized that, if a son was not well fitted for a particular inherited bureaucratic position, his father might well disinherit that particular son and adopt a boy or man of suitable promise or accomplishment. Apparently the level of adoption among the samurai [i.e., the feudal bureaucrats] was considerably greater than one would have expected on the basis of normal replacement of sons for simple purposes of succession. This was explicitly not a civil service by examination, but rather a "civil service by adoption." As such it avoided a problem which the traditional Chinese were never able to lick. Given the ethics of the samurai, the greatest possible devotion to one's family name was a devotion that required even the destruction of one's family if that would serve one's overlord. Therefore, a civil service by adoption tied up the selection on the basis of relevant skills, loyalty to the bureaucracy, and loyalty to one's family in a package that minimized many of the conflicts which always resulted in graft and corruption in the Chinese case. There is some reason to be skeptical about the alleged graft and corruption of the samurai during the Tokugawa regime. One marked characteristic of the end of that regime was the high level of poverty of many of the samurai. If they were corrupt, they were the most inefficiently corrupt group of public servants in world history. The members of the Chinese bureaucracy were far more efficiently corrupt.

There was another interesting civil service device in operation in Tokugawa Japan which might be called "civil service by usury." It is probably a frequent form of civil service recruitment. Merchants in Tokugawa Japan were specifically ineligible to hold office in the bureaucracies of the various fiefs. For reasons too complicated to go into here, they were in some special respects protected by the Tokugawa Shoguns and expected to sap the financial power of the various overlords of the rest of Japan. Before the regime was greatly advanced, a considerable proportion of the daimyo were deeply in debt to the merchants. They constantly sought extensions of their loans and new loans. On such occasions, merchants sometimes pointed out that, on the basis of existing operations, they could neither extend the present loans nor make new ones, but that, if certain changes were made in the way in which fief affairs were handled, perhaps something else could be done, etc. Insofar as their suggestions were heeded, there existed a "civil service by usury." Administrators of fief affairs thus utilized the plans of some of the ablest talents available in Japan during that period. No matter how great their administrative contributions,[29] these merchants were not ordinarily, if

[29] This leaves to one side all questions of exploitation of peasants, etc.

ever, given actual samurai rank and made members of the ideal bureaucracies of the various fiefs.

The device of the Janizariat is quite well known. These men were usually slaves or captives or both. They were frequently, if not always, of a different religion than the members of the host system in terms of which they operated. They were charged with administrative offices, and to the important among them high privileges were accorded. They could not, however, have legitimate descendents. Therefore, the question of succession of their heirs to office was ostensibly ruled out. The turning over of administrative affairs to eunuchs is, of course, an obvious method of cutting down on the possible interference of some nepotistic considerations in succession to administrative posts. Both of these cases, I might add, imply quite clearly that the major source of particularistic interference with objective standards of administration of the bureaucracies concerned is likely to be kinship-oriented particularism.

The fourth instance referred to above may not be properly referred to as an actual bureaucratic system. It is at least an approximation of the results often sought by uses of bureaucracies, however. Particularly at local levels in all relatively nonmodernized societies the balancing of predominantly particularistic factors is probably the major device whereby effects equivalent to bureaucratic ones were achieved. These balances are not ordinarily devices in the sense of having been carefully thought out. Probably in most cases they are not explicitly thought out at all. Nevertheless, they do exist. Thomas C. Smith quotes Professor Ariga Kizaemon as indicating that the role of headman in Japanese villages, ideally speaking, rotated among a number of qualified family heads, but that if one of the several lineages in a village was much stronger than the rest the role of headman might come to rotate in some such sequence as 1,2,1,3,1,4,1,2, . . . rather than rotating in the order 1,2,3,4,1,2,3, . . .[30] Such balances of particularistic interests are not without analogies in relatively modernized societies. Many of the soi-disant virtues of pluralism and "countervailing forces" inhere in just such balances.

Virtually all of the bureaucracies of relatively nonmodernized societies have structures which stress on-the-job learning by the bureaucrats. Like the Chinese systems, most had to have members with considerable talent for devising and carrying out major programs, but by contrast with relatively modernized societies,

[30] See Thomas M. Smith, *The Agrarian Origins of Modern Japan,* Stanford University Press, Stanford, 1959, p. 58.

the factors overseen by the bureaucrats were not characterized by high rates of obsolescence or rapid rates of deterioration in the absence of constant detailed supervision. The day-to-day pressure on these bureaucrats never approached the pressures characteristic of relatively modernized societies with their high levels of specialization and interdependency.

2. FAMILY SYSTEMS

Relatively nonmodernized societies have the widest possible variation in family types. Their variations include the multilineal conjugal family which is characteristic of relatively modernized societies. All of the variations commonly described in standard anthropological and sociological texts are to be found among them. Indeed it is only these societies which exemplify those variations.

Two of the best known are the *patrilineal extended family* which was the ideal family in traditional China and the *famille souche* or *stem family* which was the ideal family in Tokugawa Japan. Ideally speaking, the members of the former consist of the following relatives: father, mother, sons and their wives, the sons of sons and their wives, and all of the nonadult children of the youngest married couples who belong to the unit. Daughters "marry out" of the family; wives "marry in." Such family structures call for the maximum proliferation in terms of numbers of generations represented, numbers of marital units present, number of siblings of a given sex present at any one point in time, etc. *Famille souche* units are similar save for the fact that not only do all daughters marry out, if they are patrilineal families, but also all sons save one, usually the eldest son, marry out. The sons who marry out set up branch families. Ideally speaking, families of these two types contain a large number of members. Actually, despite variations of these ideals, the average number of members of the average family has been exceedingly uniform throughout history. In brief [31] this is to be accounted for by the high death rates and the limitations of adoption characteristic of the vast majority of societies with family structures stressing the desirability of numerous family members. Regardless of what the ideals may be in a given relatively nonmodernized society, few grandparents, for example, long survive the birth of their grandchildren.

In all relatively nonmodernized societies the family unit is overwhelmingly the main unit in terms of which the socialization of individuals takes place. For most individuals in all history [and

[31] For amplification see below, pp. 428–430.

prehistory, if one may conjecture there] prior to the development of relatively modernized societies training and education has been in terms of some family organization. This continues to be true of all early socialization even in relatively modernized contexts today, but for the relatively nonmodernized man this is also true of virtually all other forms of socialization as well. When training and education of the latter take place in specialized contexts such as schools, only a very small minority of the population participates in them. As already indicated above, one of the major contrasts between relatively nonmodernized and relatively modernized societies is the extent to which the portion of socialization outside a family context continually rises in the latter context.

Not only is virtually all of the socialization in all of the relatively nonmodernized societies carried out in family terms, but also most of the behavior of most of the members of all such societies is oriented to family considerations. This does not mean that in case of conflict between family and other orientations that the family orientations always take precedence. They may, and Chinese society has already been cited as a dramatic example of this. Even when this is not the case, family orientations are more important than any others for ordinary daily operations. When, ideally speaking, family orientations do not take precedence over nonfamily orientations, conflicts between family and other orientations do not ordinarily arise. In the Tokugawa period of Japan such conflicts did arise from time to time for the samurai. When they did, the samurai was expected to sacrifice his family interests with vim and vigor. Such sacrifice was the expression par excellence of the true samurai spirit. It would be hard, however, throughout the two hundred sixty-five years of the Tokugawa regime to estimate the extent of the frustration of samurai anxious to show their mettle but denied the opportunity of such a dramatic conflict. The number of cases in which such conflict actually occurred must have been relatively small. One may even suspect that this is one of the reasons why the famous tale of the Forty-Seven Ronin became so popular in Japan. The Forty-Seven Ronin did have just such an opportunity to show what virtuosi of feudal loyalty they were. Each one of them destroyed his family, but interestingly enough, because of his tremendous loyalty to his overlord he ensured the perpetual fame and prestige of his family. The lack of opportunity for such conflicts, when they are possible, is the basis of an important distinction between relatively nonmodernized societies and relatively modernized ones. As modernization increases, the possibility and probability of conflicts between family and other orientations increase enormously. A considerable part of the discussion of various age periods such as adolescence in relatively modernized contexts moves almost exclusively in terms of conflicts between family and other orientations.

Family relationships are always predominantly particularistic relationships. Since the vast majority of orientations for the average member of relatively nonmodernized societies are family orientations, if problems of particularism arise, they are usually questions of family-based particularism. Even in relatively modernized contexts family considerations are a major source, if not the most important source, of particularistic considerations [and ignorance with its implications for capricious particularism (see pp. 141–143) is undoubtedly next], but in relatively nonmodernized societies, without exception, they constitute the overwhelmingly important source of particularism. The only close competitor is likely to be neighborhood loyalty or in some cases a particularistically defined loyalty to one's overlord or to some hierarchy of that sort.

Correspondingly, the family is the main focus of solidarity. Therefore, anything that threatens family solidarity threatens general stability. The family is the main focus of organization, and at least for day-to-day matters it is the main organization in terms of which control is exercised. If there is a structure of control that takes precedence over the family as in Tokugawa Japan, family control may be disintegrated without disintegrating the general control structures of the society. Usually, as in the case of China, this is not possible. To undermine the stability of family control is to undermine, at least initially, the prevailing structures of control of the entire society.

III
MAJOR PROBLEMS FOR THE MEMBERS OF
ALL RELATIVELY NONMODERNIZED SOCIETIES
IN THE MODERN WORLD SETTING

A. PROBLEMS OF STABILITY WITHOUT REFERENCE TO MODERNIZATION

First, one must not forget that the members of all of these societies have some problems of stability that are not functions of their involvement in the process of modernization. There have never been any societies totally devoid of problems of stability. There have been spectacular cases of stability in social history such as that of traditional China, but that stability over two thousand years held only for some of the more general structures of that society. There were many detailed changes, of course, which took place during that long period. It is useful to note that all societies, however stable, have problems of stability even in the absence of outside influences.[32]

[32] Because of the general state of sociology and related fields I must digress here somewhat technically. It has become fashionable to *define* social systems as being in equilibrium. This creates a whole range of special problems. In the first place, it implies that systems of social action that are not in equilibrium are in some respects not social. Secondly, equilibrium is sometimes defined as including both itself and its residual category. In that case the equilibrium clause in the definition does no harm except by implication. If the term equilibrium means itself and everything else, then to define a social system as being in equilibrium is to say that a social system is a system which is either in equilibrium or not. This may sound as if it gets the analysis somewhere, but of course it does not. Every system of any sort is either in equilibrium or not. In the third place, if one defines the term so that it says something, one gets into the nasty predicament of having to maintain in essence that systems which were social systems must be explicable in nonsocial terms—usually the factors of the heredity of the species involved and the nonspecies environment—if the systems get out of equilibrium. No one wishes to go to such extremes, but that is in fact where many of us have gone.

One may, of course, define terms any way one wishes in science, if one is prepared to stick by the implications of the terms so defined. If those implications are absurd or lead to nonscientific elements, or are fruitless for the formulation of theories, one must try again, if one wishes to continue the game. If one defines social systems or societies as stable or equilibrium systems or as homeostatic systems, there are a whole host of problems which cannot be treated with these concepts. Those who use this device are led by it either to beg questions which they presumably address or are led to treat those questions in terms of concepts which in fact are quite different from the ones they have defined. It is not actually a difficult problem to solve. There is no need to define these systems as being *in fact* stable or in fact in equilibrium. One may distinguish those which are relatively stable or highly stable and those which are not, those which are in equilibrium for a given period of time, those which are in partial equilibrium states, etc. Even when one uses a stable case in order to derive certain properties of the general class, it is not necessary to assume that all instances of the special class will in fact be characterized by stability. Almost every automobile maker issues a statement as to how many pounds of air *should* inflate the tires on his make of automobile for proper functioning. A random sample of the automobiles in fact on the road would indicate considerable variance from this figure. This does not mean that it was foolish of him to present the figure in the first place, nor does it mean that the figure has no implications whatsoever for automobiles on which the tires are markedly over- or under-inflated. This may seem to be a petty quarrel among the acolytes of a fortunately restricted and bizarre sect. It is more than that, particularly when the problem of modernization of relatively nonmodernized societies is under study. In this case there is no question that there is going to be instability on both general and specific levels of concern. To define the units one intends to use in such analysis as stable units is to guarantee that one either begs the questions or in fact uses definitions other than the ones presented. It is a difficulty exceedingly easy to avoid. Any careful reading of the history of science or even a casual inspection of the roles of models in the natural sciences would be sufficient to prevent any social scientist from falling into this trap.

If one does not define societies as actually stable, whether or not any particular instance of a society is in fact stable at a given point of time is an empirical question. On the completely descriptive level any society, or any other phenomenon for that matter, is constantly changing in some respect, if only that of age. The actual degree of stability allegeable about a given society is to some extent a function of the level of generalization on which one wishes to consider the society. Thus in the period of traditional Chinese society's long stability the structure of equal inheritance for all sons remained highly stable as did the structure of requiring marriage outside the paternal lines of descent. On the other hand, some of the details of the treatment of different sons and the details of marital arrangements varied. On any given level of generalization with which one is concerned, if the unit is neither stable nor unstable by definition, its stability or lack of stability is something to be accounted for. Throughout history it appears that the maintenance of stability is not easy even in the absence of outside influences. Even if the members have yearned for stability, most societies have not been stable long. Scientific propositions about social stability are not highly developed, alas.

The nature of the problems of stability that exist quite apart from the process of modernization varies at least as widely as the ideal and actual social structures of these societies vary on whatever level of generalization one wishes to consider them. I have indicated above certain of these problems in connection with both traditional China and Tokugawa Japan. In traditional Chinese society virtually the whole structure of social control was a function of family solidarity. If the family got out of kilter, the whole society got out of kilter. In Tokugawa Japan on the other hand the relationship between family interests and the interest of one's overlord existed in a strong and flexible balance.[33] Quite apart from China and Japan, there always exists the problem of socialization of what one social scientist has referred to as the periodic barbarian invasion of every society—i.e., children. Any disturbance that interferes with these socialization processes threatens the general stability of the society.

The stability of any given relatively nonmodernized society may also be threatened by the activities of members of other societies. Most relatively nonmodernized societies have not ex-

[33] One of the strengths of the Tokugawa Shoguns lay precisely in the fact that they did not do what many people have accused them of trying to do. They did not try to get overwhelming centralization of everything. It would have cost them their rule had they tried to do so.

isted in total isolation. War is an extreme case of such interaction, but some of its implications for the stability of the societies whose members participate are both too numerous and too frequently commented on to require further mention here. Even in the absence of an extreme form of social action like war, acquaintance with structures of a strange and foreign nature, interaction with members of another society, etc., may pose problems of stability in terms of relatively nonmodernized societies. I do not intend to treat of these problems in any detail here. That is a special study in and of itself. I mention them because it is naïve to think that relatively nonmodernized people were not plagued with problems of stability before structures from relatively modernized societies were introduced. In trying to understand problems of modernization it is misleading to fail to separate out those problems that were functions of action in terms of the social structures as they were before contact and those problems that are functions of the contact of the existing structures with outside, relatively modernized influences.

B. PROBLEMS OF STABILITY AFTER CONTACT WITH THE STRUCTURES OF RELATIVELY MODERNIZED SOCIETIES

There is always a motive among the members of relatively non-modernized societies for taking up some structures of modernization, with or without duress from outsiders. The problems of modernization of late-comers have almost uniformly been discussed in the context of imperialism. It so happens that all of the initial cases were in fact carried out under the spur of this particular sort of interference, but emphasis on this form of interference has grossly obscured the problems involved. Like most people today, I happen to detest imperialism as it has existed and have no desire to deny its evils. I do wish, however, to point out that the morals of imperialists are essentially irrelevant to the problems faced by members of relatively nonmodernized societies in contact with modernization. If there is contact, some set of members of that society will always attempt to take up some of those structures even if those structures are not forced upon them. They will do it for the following reasons: (1) There is no society whose members are in general unaware of material factors. (2) There is no society whose members fail to distinguish between being relatively better off and relatively worse off materially. (3) There is no society whose members in general do not prefer to be better off rather than worse off materially. (4) Peoples do vary widely, both within a given social context and from one context to another, with regard to the prices they are prepared to pay in order to be relatively better off materially and— even more importantly—in their *horizons* of such possibilities. Failure to envisage possibilities of improvement probably explain more of many alleged spiritual qualities than spiritual criteria which make people explicitly unwilling to pay prices for material improvement. One reason why increased use of money, as well as travel, is broadening is that the increased comparisons which result always extend the horizons of the possible. (5) Aesthetics, morals, and everything else to the contrary notwithstanding, the one respect in which the relatively modernized societies are always superior to the relatively nonmodernized societies, and by a considerable margin to boot, is the inordinate material productivity of their members following their ways. Once contact is made, therefore, there is always motivation for some of the members of a relatively nonmodernized society to try to take over some of the elements of the relatively modernized societies regardless of whether the initial contacts and the ensuing relations are imposed or voluntary. Unless the members of the relatively nonmodernized society are prevented from doing so by force, such attempts will always be made. Attempts to prevent them by force, short of extermination, have never been successful. (6) Furthermore, the elements common to all societies and the appreciation of some form of tools and inanimate sources of power by the members of any society guarantee that members of relatively nonmodernized societies will never be completely unable to comprehend at least some of the elements of greater material productivity with which they come in contact. In the desire to try these new methods the sources of instability inherent in the society concerned may be highly relevant. It may well be those members of a society who are most frustrated by the ordinary prevailing state of affairs who are most motivated to try the new, but someone would try something in any case.

Once the contacts are established, there will be some transfer of the relatively modernized structures to the relatively nonmodernized society.[34] When such transfers are made, they are inevitably subversive of the *status quo* of the relatively nonmodernized society, and usually explosively so. After these contacts, in addition to gradual erosion of some existing structures, many struc-

[34] Transfer of structures in the opposite direction need not concern the discussion now. Apart from occasional influences, the transfers are largely one-way.

tures with long pedigrees of stability begin to change with great rapidity.[35]

One of the most frequently cited problems bearing on social change is the so-called population explosion. I refer to the increase in the rate of population growth occasioned by the sudden drop in death rates that accompanies the introduction of modern medical technology, given much less resilient rates of fertility. Dramatic drops in the death rate can be effected quickly and cheaply. It is one of those material things which all relatively nonmodernized peoples seem to prefer and understand, at least in part. The birth rate never drops as rapidly as applications of modern medical technology can lower the death rate. Birth rates tend to be high and stable [e.g., averaging well over forty births per one thousand members of the population]. With sudden drops in the death rate—a large part of it in the lowered rates of infant mortality—the rate of natural increase for the members of such a society may easily jump from say five per thousand to twenty per thousand or more. The consequent rapid increase in population alone, especially since a good part of the increased population, initially at least, is in the least productive age brackets, poses all sorts of problems of order.[36]

Some of the problems posed by the population explosion are so obvious that for some they dominate the whole question of modernization. I would not want to detract one whit from the importance of this source of explosive implications, but it is by no means the only one. Even if we found a way to control the birth rate tomorrow by methods inoffensive to the people concerned, those methods would not preserve the general structures of relatively nonmodernized societies in their previous forms. There is still

[35] There is a tendency in considering questions of social change to imply that certain social factors are inherently slow changing as opposed to fast changing. This is not the case for at least two reasons: (1) The development of charismatic leadership can convert any social factor into a fast-changing one, though perhaps at catastrophic costs, and (2) social changes which knock out a key block in the retention of previously existing stresses and strains can be followed by spectacularly rapid alterations in general structures. Both of these sources of rapid change are quite familiar to students of the process of modernization. The second of these is, perhaps, far more likely than the first. In addition there may be all sorts of variations or approaches to both of these conditions which approach them in their implications for rapidity of change.

[36] Given a natural rate of increase of 2 per cent [i.e., 20/1000] a population will double in size in thirty-five years unless other factors intervene. Given a natural rate of increase of 3 per cent—a rate by no means out of the question—a population would double in only twenty-three years. It is not necessary to be a social scientist, a misanthrope, or a pessimist to see problems in such rates of growth.

ample reason to believe that the structures of every one of those societies would be revolutionized on extremely general levels and always in the direction of the structures of the highly modernized societies. In the modern world the problem par excellence for the members of every relatively nonmodernized society is modernization itself.

The various sources of explosive subversion of the structures of relatively nonmodernized societies will be explored throughout this work in summary below [see pp. 741–776]. I have tried to give here sufficient reasons why members of relatively nonmodernized societies cannot expect to avoid these problems. Once the contacts are made, attempts will be made to use some structures of the relatively modernized societies. Once those attempts are made, the existing structures will begin to disintegrate, some explosively. The structures of the relatively modernized societies do constitute for the first time in social history a sort of general social solvent for all other social types. The difficult aspect of the problem lies in the fact that although changes in the direction of modernization will always begin and although the subversion of the *status quo* will always reach a point of no return, successful achievement of the structures of modernization is by no means guaranteed. Indeed, conspicuously successful cases of latecomers have been few and far between.

The general subversive nature of the importation of the structures of modernization is discussed in some detail below [see pp. 741–776]. The argument there rests on four generalizations and distinguishes several basic sources of erosion. Here I shall only list the four generalizations and mention the major sources of erosion common to all of the relatively nonmodernized societies. The generalizations are as follows: (1) The structures of relatively modernized societies always will invade relatively nonmodernized societies if there is contact between the members of the two types of societies—regardless of whether force is employed to introduce them or they are taken up voluntarily. (2) The structures of relatively modernized societies can never be imported entirely piecemeal. Whether introduced by force or voluntary means, more is introduced than is bargained for or understood. (3) The structures of the relatively nonmodernized societies never coincide with those of the relatively modernized societies and are always incompatible with them to some extent. (4) Finally, with rare exceptions, the major sources of control in the relatively nonmodernized society are always eroded. Again this is independent of the intent of the members of either type of society.

Some of the most obvious sources of erosion are already implicit in what has been said in this and the preceding chapter. They are as follows: (1) The degree of specialization of organizations, (2) the decrease in self-sufficiency of the indigenous organizations, (3) changes in the emphases in relationships, (4) changes in family structures, (5) changes in literacy and the critical approach, (6) changes in the demographic situation,[37] and (7) increase in the generalization of the media of exchange and increase in the presence and specialization of markets. The history of no relatively nonmodernized society furnishes evidence which either disproves these generalizations or indicates that these sources of erosion are insignificant. The Japanese case furnishes us with the only instance of thoroughgoing late-comers who have coped with these problems with any high degree of success in terms of achieving a relatively modernized state, and that high degree of success was certainly related to their involvement in World War II. For the members of relatively nonmodernized societies in the modern world—whether they or we realize it, like it, or not—the major problem is how they will cope with modernization. All previous questions of instability, stability, social evil, etc., come to be important principally for their relevance in this context, whatever their consequences may have been before.

[37] Not only is the population explosion an increase in surviving infants, it also poses the problem of what to do with the aged. The number of surviving aged to be taken care of is also certain to increase radically.

PART II

ASPECTS OF SOCIAL STRUCTURE

ASPECTS OF ANY RELATIONSHIP

I
INTRODUCTION: DEFINITION AND EXPLANATION

This chapter gives explicit attention to a bit of analytic apparatus. I have developed it in greater detail elsewhere,[1] and I shall not try to reproduce it in full here. This will be the only chapter in this work devoted primarily to an analytic tool.

I define a *relationship* as any set of social structures that define the action, ideally and/or actually in terms of which two or more individual actors interact. I define a *social structure* as any pattern [i.e., as any observable uniformity] in terms of which social action takes place. I define *social* as the adjective descriptive of any phenomenon that is not adequately explicable [for the purpose in hand] in terms of the heredity of the species of actors involved and the nonspecies' environment. Since we are only interested in human societies here, *social action* refers to any action of human beings that is not adequately explicable in terms of human heredity and the nonhuman environment. Thus any structures of behavior that adequately describe, for whatever purposes, the interaction between two or more human beings also describes their social relationship, provided of course the structures are not adequately explicable in terms of human heredity and the nonhuman environment. The structures of interaction of two friends constitute a relationship; the interaction of individual faculty members of a university is in terms of various relationship structures; the operations of the members *qua* members of any large-scale enterprise, be it a business or governmental enterprise or whatever, involve a complicated set of relationships; etc. All relationships are social systems or membership units or concrete structures or organizations. The number of members may be as small as two or indefinitely large. The most restricted possible relationship is the most restricted possible social system,[2] and all social systems consist of one or more relationships, involving two or more members.

Since all social systems can be conceived of as sets of relationship structures, the analysis of them may be used as a tool for the

---

[1] *The Structure of Society,* Chap. 6.
[2] The most restricted possible social system would consist of structures interrelating only two members for a single act.

location of the more important social systems or organizations in terms of which social analysts must treat societies. The analysis of relationship structures is one of the tools with which we can combat the biases of ethnocentrism. There are certain social systems which we expect to find even if we study an unfamiliar society. We do not particularly expect to find these because there is anything "natural" about them, though this is frequently asserted. We expect to find them because we are familiar with them in our own experience and because most of the other societies with which we are familiar have also contained such organizations. Organizations such as families, governments, neighborhood units of various sorts, churches, business firms, friendship units, etc.—these are all organizations with which we are familiar. We are rather more surprised when we fail to find them elsewhere than when we do. Indeed, our initial approach to other societies is frequently to look for units of this sort. But there are also many types of units in many societies with which we are not at all familiar. It is quite impossible to approach any society without any conception of what you might find there. The idea that one deals with this sort of problem by approaching other peoples with a blank mind is a particularly virulent type of nonsense because it confuses inexplicitness with objectivity. To approach the analysis of any society [or of any other subject for that matter] with a completely blank mind would be like attempting to get to one's feet on a frictionless surface. In the latter case one would stay prone; in the former case one's mind would stay blank. Perhaps, if the members of that society were kindly, the person with a blank mind might be reared from scratch as though he were an infant and become thereby a member of their society but not an analyst of it.

In the absence of concepts of the specific types of units that are in fact present, one could always locate such units in a given society by observing the way in which individuals interrelate with one another and discovering which of these cluster in such fashion that one might refer to the people engaged as members of some common unit. This would be time consuming, but it would, in the long run, locate the organizations. Since we do not have blank minds and since there are some organizations common to all societies, we are never faced with the really costly problem of trying to locate all organizations by starting from scratch solely in terms of relationship structures. The analysis of any relationships is, however, useful as a tool when our preconceptions do not turn out to have a close fit with what we observe.

Another application of relationship structures is more important for present purposes. It leads to generalizations that cut across other distinctions and show common elements among them. For example, in the United States today, however different business firms and government may be, members of both organizations emphasize rationality, universalism, functional specificity, and avoidance. One can not only use these aspects of relationships to locate common features in different organizations of the sort just described; one can also use them to locate common features prominent in the conduct of different aspects of behavior. Again in the United States, outside of the family context the economic and political aspects of our behavior are, ideally speaking, carried out in terms of relationships which emphasize rationality, universalism, functional specificity, and avoidance. One may also use the same concepts to isolate variations across such lines. In the examples just given, although in business and governmental contexts we emphasize the same four aspects, and, I might add, relationships in both are hierarchically arranged, we usually expect business relationships to be predominantly individualistic whereas we expect government relationships to be predominantly responsible.[3] Thus in terms of all of the most general aspects of relationships developed here our business firms and government [and its subsystems] are identical, ideally speaking, except with regard to what will be called the "goal orientation" aspects [see below, pp. 147–149]. By no means all of the distinctions between business firms and government are explicable in terms of this one difference, but many are, and other differences are understandable in terms of differences in more specific forms of the aspects in which they are identical on more general levels. Though rationality is stressed by both businessmen and members of the government, the rationality concerns quite different matters, and so forth.

I I
ASPECTS OF ANY RELATIONSHIP

A. INTRODUCTION

The treatment here of aspects of any relationship is a development and adaptation of concepts that I have taken from the early work of Talcott Parsons. He, in turn, developed them partially on the basis of the work done by F. Toennies. The development here is not the form conceived by Toennies or favored by Parsons cur-

[3] The terms *individualistic* and *responsible* as used in this connection will be explained below.

rently. Nevertheless, Toennies indirectly and Parsons directly are the sources from which these developments came.[4]

In selecting subcategories of relationship structures two considerations are paramount. First, the distinctions should be ones that are relevant for *any* relationship. Second, the subsidiary categories or aspects should be ones in terms of which some variability is possible. If a given subcategory has only a unique value, it is only useful as a constant in hypotheses about all relationships and can only be a variable in distinctions between relationship and nonrelationship structures.

For present purposes we need aspects of relationships with subcategories capable of binary distinctions at least. Rather than binary distinctions, I have chosen polar distinctions which permit considerable variation in degree of approximation to one extreme form or another of a given aspect. These distinctions could be converted into binary ones, but only at the expense of leaving out the vast majority of cases I wish to treat since they are not at one extreme or the other.

It is also essential that the distinctions are not such that virtually all of the cases fall in one subcategory as opposed to the other or close to one pole of the distinction as opposed to the other. For example, one of the aspects chosen here is the *cognitive aspect*. One could distinguish among cognitive aspects of different relationships on the basis of whether or not explicit biological knowledge were involved. If one did, only a small number of all the relationships one would wish to analyze would be ones involving such knowledge. To think of relationships as

---

[4] In my book cited above I have discussed the distinctions between the scheme as presented there and that of Parsons. The differences are considerably greater today than they were then. In Parsons' work these aspects of relationships have developed into the famous "patterned variables." I have continued to use a form based on his earlier versions. The earlier versions [e.g., T. Parsons, "The Professions and Social Structure," *Social Forces*, vol. XVII, no. 4, May, 1939, reprinted, pp. 185–199, in T. Parsons: *Essays in Sociological Theory: Pure and Applied*, The Free Press, Glencoe, 1949], as qualified and amplified here are considerably less subject to confusion than the "patterned variables." There is another more technical reason for not using the present Parsonian version. Parsons insists that the distinctions drawn are binary distinctions. Thus a relationship is either *particularistic* or *universalistic*. Empirically this is simply not the case. The concepts so defined must always be used in a manner other than their definitions would lead one to expect. In fact the uses of the distinctions by Parsons in his own works and in that of his followers are almost always differences of degree rather than of kind. To insist that differences of degree are in fact differences of kind and to try to handle consequent overstatements by *ad hoc* qualifications to the effect that of course other elements are involved to some degree is to beg the very question one intends to answer.

biologically cognitive or nonbiologically cognitive would be useful only for extremely limited questions. We need some set of distinctions of greater general utility if the tool is to be generally applicable for the comparative analysis of any set of relationship structures.

Six aspects of any relationship have been distinguished here. They are (1) the cognitive aspect, (2) the membership criteria aspect, (3) the substantive definition aspect, (4) the affective aspect, (5) the goal orientation aspect, and (6) the stratification aspect. For each of these aspects a polar distinction is offered. Those are respectively (1) rational-traditional, (2) universalistic-particularistic, (3) functionally specific-functionally diffuse, (4) avoidant-intimate, (5) individualistic-responsible, and (6) hierarchical-nonhierarchical. These categories are defined and discussed below [pp. 138–152].

B. PROBLEMS ABOUT THESE CONCEPTS

There are considerable theoretical shortcomings about these concepts. First, I have no satisfactory theoretical explanation of why six and only six aspects are distinguished. Second, I have no satisfactory explanation of why this set of six rather than another set of six is presented. The only answer I have to such questions is that it can be shown that these six and their subcategories are in fact useful in formulating hypotheses. One may use them and get at a great number of distinctions, and those distinctions turn out to be generally relevant for social analysis and particularly relevant for the analysis of the problems of relatively modernized and relatively nonmodernized societies which are of interest in this work.

Third, I have insisted that these distinctions not be used as binary distinctions. Technically, however, in all six of the cases about which I have been able to be fairly precise, I have defined one extreme of the scale residually relative to the other. Thus perfect rationality is different in kind from any element of traditionality; perfect universalism is different in kind from any particularism; etc. Perfect instances of these extremes may not exist at all, and most of the cases of interest to us are not pure cases of the extremes. Actual classification of relationships in terms of any of these aspects is always to some degree a function of the observer's judgment, and that, to some extent, is always arbitrary. Moreover, for theoretical reasons discussed shortly, no relationship can ever be completely and purely universalistic, and it is unlikely that any relationship be completely and perfectly rational. Therefore, the differences dealt with here are differences of degree.

Moreover, it is quite useful in social analysis to distinguish whether ideal and/or actual emphases approach one extreme more closely than the other. Thus it is often useful to observe that employment structures characteristic of relatively modernized societies reflect overwhelming emphasis on universalism by contrast with those of other societies that reflect overwhelming emphasis on particularism. This is a relevant distinction despite the fact that there are *some* emphases on particularism, whether ideal or not, characteristic of even those relationships which reflect the most complete ideal structures of universalism in the most highly modernized society, and so forth. In general, to emphasize the nearly universal combinations of these elements a given relationship will be described as predominantly universalistic, rational, traditional, etc., if there is any possibility of confusion about whether the distinction intended is one of degree or kind.

C. USES OF THESE CONCEPTS

For the present two general uses of these concepts are asserted. First, as already mentioned, they can be used for the comparative analysis of any relationships. Implicit in this assertion, of course, is the assertion that they can be used to analyze any single relationship. Second, applications of the relationship aspects afford good reason to believe that different clusterings of certain of these relationship aspects are prominent features of societies. For example, if a relationship reflects heavy emphasis on rationality, it is likely also to be characterized by emphasis on universalism, functional specificity, and avoidance. This does not follow tautologically from the definition of the concepts involved. In the discussion of relatively modernized and relatively nonmodernized societies above, references have already been made to these relationship aspects. After detailed definition and illustration of these various aspects, their use for both comparative analysis and the formation of hypotheses about these clustering effects is discussed at some length.

D. RELATIONSHIP ASPECTS

1. COGNITIVE ASPECTS

Every relationship between two or more people involves some sort of knowledge, some sort of thinking, some sort of mental process, and that is defined here as its cognitive aspect. Subcategories of the cognitive aspects of any relationship are distinguished as follows: *rational* cognition is the kind of knowledge that, were it subjected to a theoretically omniscient scientific observer, would be found to violate none of the canons of science, that is to say, it would be in complete accord with the best scientific reasoning. Conclusions reached in terms of *traditional* cognition may coincide with conclusions reached on a purely rational basis. Even though this may often be the case, *traditional* cognition is defined as knowledge that is justified from the point of view of the individual who accepts it by argument to the effect that a given way of doing things is the prevailing and accepted way, and the way that should be continued because one's predecessors always did it that way. This is the essence of tradition in the social sense. Even when the conclusions of tradition coincide with those of rationality, the implications for action are importantly different. Having claimed this, let me go a bit behind this distinction and indicate some of the factors on which it rests.

This is one of those distinctions which, whatever its relevance to other species, is especially relevant to the human species. At the present stage of our development in the social sciences, it is fruitful to distinguish between the point of view of an observer and the point of view of an actor. The term *actor* is self-explanatory in this context. The term *observer* as used here is defined as a theoretically omniscient and objective scientific observer, literally a know-it-all. In considering any given act one may distinguish between the *end* of the act and the means [i.e., the methods, including use of materials] employed for that end. Either ends or means may be either empirical [i.e., can be analyzed in terms of sensory perception] or nonempirical. One may also distinguish as to whether from the point of view of the actor or the observer the ends and the means used are empirical or not. Thus if the action consists of going into a particular store to buy a pair of pliers, the end may be described as the purchase of a pair of pliers, and the means may be described as the selection of the particular store. Both ends and means are quite empirical. If the means selected by the actor are in fact adequate to the end he seeks, such action may be described as rational action. Even if he happens to have selected the wrong sort of store, such action is at least rationally oriented, although it is in fact *irrational*. On the other hand a given actor may simply pray that a pair of pliers be deposited on his desk. The end is still empirical, but the means contain an important nonempirical element. The physical act of prayer is quite empirical, but at least from the point of view of the actor the act of prayer is viewed as having some particular effect on some deity (ies) of some sort. This is quite nonempirical. The observer cannot tell one that he will not get a pair of pliers by use of such methods. The most that he can say is that many people who have behaved in that fashion have not ended up with pliers. There is no need here to elaborate on the various categories of nonrational and arational action which can be distinguished.[5] Value judgments such as the value of tradition itself in the last analysis always involve questions to which no observer can give a purely scientific answer.

In any social context the ultimate justifications of action from the point of view of the actors are standards of value to which no purely scientific solutions are possible. In this sense, if the range of action studied is enlarged, sooner or later one always encounters nonrational elements. Nevertheless, over a broad range of action, the selection of means may, ideally and/or actually, proceed much more importantly in purely scientific terms than not. When it does, I shall consider the emphasis, at least ideally speaking, to be on rational rather than on traditional action. The view that action should be as scientifically justifiable as possible is as much an evaluation as the view that action should be based on tradition as much as possible. Though both are evaluations which can be neither proved nor disproved by science, they are evaluations that have different implications for the actions of those who hold them. Those different implications can be studied scientifically and justify the distinction used here.

2. MEMBERSHIP CRITERIA ASPECTS

Every relationship is a system of action involving two or more actors who may be described as its membership. One may, therefore, always inquire why [or how] actors come to be members of such units. The reasons constitute the membership criteria. Following Parsons' early work, I have differentiated those into the two main categories of universalistic and particularistic. This distinction involves two lines of variation. The first has to do with the question of germaneness. Are the criteria concerned directly relevant to the purposes or main activities to be carried out in terms of the relationship? The second has to do with social barring. Is anyone prevented from participating in this particular relationship because of any social classifications which need not have anything to do with his abilities and/or accomplishments? The concept of social barring as used here is closely allied to the term *ascription* as it is ordinarily used by anthropologists and sociologists. Since to some extent one's life chances are always affected by one's kinship position, if one broadens the sphere of action enough, sooner or later, some criteria involving social barring come into play in every situation.

[5] For further elaboration see, *The Structure of Society*, pp. 240–248.

A relationship is defined as universalistic if the membership criteria contain no element of social barring and if they are germane. A relationship is defined as particularistic insofar as the membership criteria contain either nongermane elements, social barring, or some combination of the two. There are, therefore, three types of particularism: (1) *germane particularism,* i.e., involving social barring but germane criteria, (2) *capricious particularism,* i.e., involving no social barring but nongermane criteria, and (3) *ultimate particularism,* i.e., involving both social barring and nongermaneness.[6] I shall return to the three subcategories of particularism shortly. For the moment some more central considerations with regard to the basic distinction between universalism and particularism must be discussed. Membership criteria that tend to minimize but do not entirely eliminate particularistic elements will be called *predominantly universalistic.* Those that tend to minimize or eliminate universalistic elements will be called *predominantly particularistic.* Relationships may of course be ideally and/or actually *predominantly* universalistic or particularistic. The reason for insisting on these qualifications is simple. It is not difficult to find examples of relationships that are purely particularistic, ideally at least. The relationship between mother and son in many societies is such a relationship. Social barring is certainly involved. Unless a specifically different structure such as a structure of adoption is interposed, one and only one woman at any given point of time is eligible to stand in the relation to mother to a given son, if we define the term *mother* as it is defined in our own society. The criterion that only lords may join the hunt in a given forest is equally particularistic. A purely universalistic relationship is much more difficult to discover. As already mentioned, to some extent one's kinship position always affects one's life chances later on. Thus, if one considers the influences broadly enough, sooner or later one runs into some particularistic element since kinship considerations are inherently particularistic. On the other hand, *within a given setting,* the criteria concerned may be highly universalistic or even completely so, ideally speaking. For example, there are no doubt some particularistic elements in the determination of who is or is not admitted to Harvard College, but within the category of those admitted to Harvard College, admission to the Phi Beta Kappa honor society depends overwhelmingly, if not entirely, on

[6] The treatment of the cognitive aspects of relationships is an abridgement of the treatment presented in *The Structure of Society.* The treatment of the membership criteria aspects is an enlargement on the treatment there.

qualifications that are germane to the selection for this relationship and that are criteria from which no Harvard undergraduate is socially barred.

In distinguishing between predominantly universalistic and particularistic classifications one must keep in mind the distinction between ideal and actual structures. In our own society, for example, relationships are frequently more nearly universalistic, ideally speaking, than they are in fact. Whenever one classifies a relationship as more or less particularistic or more or less nearly universalistic, he must be prepared to elaborate on the following questions if an explanation is called for: (1) From whose point of view is the relationship so classified? (2) Is the relationship so classified ideally and/or actually speaking, and again from whose point of view? (3) Within what setting is the relationship so classified?

Germane particularism may be defined as particularism in which social barring is present, but the social barring itself is highly relevant to the purposes of the relationship. Such a situation obtains in selection for succession to the throne of England. There the relationship may be considered one of sovereign to subject. At any given point in time, ideally and actually speaking, one and only one person is eligible to succeed. Eligibility for that succession is determined on the basis of kinship. The members of Parliament can, if they wish, set the whole structure aside, but if the system continues as at present, ideally speaking every individual save one at any given point in time is socially barred from succeeding to the throne. Since one of the main functions of that sovereign, however, is to symbolize a line of tradition and a family responsibility for the welfare of England, etc., the criteria involved are germane to the purpose of the selection. To the extent that such a situation obtains, a relationship will be considered more or less germanely particularistic. It is important to distinguish this kind of particularism because it combines more readily with a heavy emphasis on rationality than do the other types of particularism. Ordinarily, for example, there is an important element of kinship-oriented particularism in succession to positions of importance in a large number of family firms. The general emphasis on universalistic criteria may be great. Sons or sons-in-law of the directors of these enterprises may in fact be set aside if they do not have sufficient levels of ability, but there can be little doubt that in most cases the fact that they are sons or sons-in-law does give them a distinct differential advantage over other possible competitors. If the level of ability which they in fact achieve is sufficiently high and if to some extent the confidence of people who deal with them is importantly oriented to continuation of the family line, these predominantly particularistic criteria for succession may be easily combined with a heavy emphasis on rationality and on predominantly universalistic criteria elsewhere in the firm.

Capricious particularism is a quixotic possibility. Criteria that involve no social barring but that are irrelevant to the purpose for which selection is made may be insisted upon. In consideration of all these types one must pay close attention to the relationship involved since what would be nongermane criteria for one relationship might very well be germane ones for another. For example, the insistence that redheads and only redheads be hired to operate the pumps in a gasoline station would probably fall under the category of capricious particularism. No member of a society like our own is socially barred from being a redhead. There are no preferential mating structures that make redheadedness especially unlikely, there is no discrimination against redheaded infants at birth, etc. But redheadedness is not germane to one's ability to run a filling station. On the other hand for certain types of color film processes redheadedness might conceivably be highly germane. Thus, what would be an emphasis on capricious particularism in the one case might be a heavy emphasis on universalistic criteria in another.

If the criteria involve both social barring and nongermaneness, the relationship may be considered *ultimately particularistic*. Many forms of social discrimination fall into this category. Typical is the kind of discrimination based on so-called racial or religious distinctions. These certainly involve social barring, and in many settings they are not germane to the purposes of the relationship unless that relationship be extended to include the preservation of racial or religious distinctions as a basis of social barring. This sort of particularism, of course, raises the greatest difficulties when other emphases are on rationality, functional specificity, etc.

For most of the general purposes in this work the broad distinction between predominantly universalistic and purely or predominantly particularistic relationships will suffice, but for more detailed applications, the additional subcategories will prove useful.

3. SUBSTANTIVE DEFINITION ASPECTS

The substantive definition aspects of a relationship have to do with the precision or lack of precision of the definition and delimitation of the relationship. This is one way of describing what is involved in the relationship. The categories distinguished here are functionally specific and functionally diffuse. A *functionally specific* relationship is one in terms of which the activities, considerations, rights, obligations, or performances that are covered by the relationship are precisely defined and delimited. The modern business contract relationship is a typical example of a predominantly functionally specific relationship. In a modern contract relationship, ideally speaking, an attempt is made to state explicitly everything covered by the particular relationship. All questions among the members of such a relationship [*in verbis legitimis:* parties to the relationship] are supposed to be settled by specific reference to the contractual document itself. The burden of proof is on whoever wishes to claim some additional obligation under the contract. To show that the special request is not covered by the contract is sufficient defense. It is obvious, of course, that all contracts are not perfectly clear-cut documents, but ideally speaking at least that is one of the criteria of a good contract.

A *functionally diffuse* relationship is one that is more or less vaguely defined and delimited. The relationship between husband and wife is always predominantly functionally diffuse. Frequently many elements in a husband-wife relationship are carefully defined, but the relationship is always to some extent vaguely delimited. If a new situation raises a question of how husband and wife should behave toward one another, it is not customary to settle such matters by seeing whether or not the situation is covered in the fine print of the marriage contract, even if there is one. When the emphasis is on functional specificity, the burden of proof is on anyone who wishes to justify an additional obligation. When the emphasis is on functional diffuseness, the burden of proof is on anyone who wishes to evade an additional obligation under the relationship. Justification of such evasion is not ordinarily based on what was clearly understood at the outset of the relationship, but rather on citation of some more important obligation to which prior allegiance is recognized.[7]

It is important to distinguish degrees of functional specificity and of functional diffuseness. One can characterize relationships as placing greater or lesser emphasis on one or the other of the

[7] In this connection, one must be careful about the use of the term *contract*. The modern business contract used as the example par excellence of a predominantly functionally specific relationship is quite a different matter from a marriage contract or a feudal contract. These contracts contain many elements of precise definition, but characteristically the extent of the relationships is vaguely delimited, even deliberately so.

extremes. Detailed and precise measurement of variations along the scale may be exceedingly difficult, but for many rough purposes a common sense reference to differences in the degree of emphasis will serve well enough. In this distinction as the others, the distinction between ideal and actual structures is also of the greatest importance.

Some of the worst misunderstandings about relationships occur when a relationship is predominantly functionally specific from the point of view of one member and predominantly functionally diffuse from the point of view of another. Thus, again, one must be prepared to give some indication of the point of view from which he is describing a relationship.

Some of the implications involved in this distinction and the other two previously made should be fairly obvious by now. To the extent that a relationship is or becomes functionally diffuse, it is difficult to emphasize rationality and universalistic criteria. After all, if one does not know in advance what is likely to be involved in a relationship, how can one emphasize rationality in its conduct or make selections on a predominantly universalistic basis?

4. AFFECTIVE ASPECTS

I do not feel at home with the concept of affect. The concept of affective aspects is an attempt to get at the kind of emotion, the degree of formality and informality, the feeling, etc., involved in a given relationship. Relationships among the members of any given society or as among the members of different societies vary considerably in the kind of emotional or affective displays made, the intensity of such displays which is expected and permitted, etc. There is no question but that the members of certain relationships are expected to emphasize elements easily recognizable as emotional displays and in considerable intensity. For example, a mother and son of our society are expected to love each other and to show it. The ticklish question for present purposes is whether or not there are nonaffective relationships, that is to say, relationships in terms of which no affectivity of any significance whatsoever is involved. This is a particularly important question if one wishes to handle relationships in a highly modernized society. In such societies there are an enormous number of relationships that are of the most fleeting and casual sort. To determine, either ideally or actually, whether precisely *no* emotional involvement is intended is even in principle a difficult proposition. Furthermore such a concept implies perfect indifference to a relationship of which one is at least in some sense aware. Such indifference is almost certainly a feat of affective virtuosity, and rare. For these reasons that concept is not used. The distinction used here is that between *avoidance* and *intimacy*. Here again the distinction is intended to be a polar distinction. Perhaps no relationship is at either pole, but the gamut that can be run is wide. It varies from relationships that are quite important for the parties concerned, but in terms of which the members must avoid any direct contact with one another, including seeing or being seen by one another, to relationships in terms of which direct, informal, almost constant contact with overt displays of emotion are both expected and demanded by the participants and/or by other members of the society. The relationship between mother and infant in all societies is likely to be intimate in this latter sense. Relations between ruler and subject or sacred figure and true believers often approximate the former.

The relationship between husband and wife is a predominantly intimate one in the modern United States. It is also predominantly intimate in some contexts in traditional China, but in the latter case it is far less so than in the former. There are also many social contexts in traditional China in which the relationship is not supposed to be an intimate one at all. According to strict Confucian etiquette the husband and wife are expected to display genuine avoidance in many contexts. The term *avoidance* may be used to cover relationships that, ideally and/or actually, are supposed to be devoid of emotional involvement as well as those in terms of which the emotional involvement is supposed to be considerable though minimizing overt contacts, etc. The most highly avoidant affect is probably that generally referred to as respect. The opposite of respect is probably contempt, and it is not a matter of chance that there is a wise old saw in many languages which holds that "familiarity breeds contempt." With regard to this aspect of relationships, as with the others, the prefix predominantly will be used. A relationship will be termed predominantly avoidant if it is one in terms of which the members or others emphasize restraint and/or formality in the overt display of affect and/or subordinate the overt display of affect to other aspects of the relationship. A relationship will be termed predominantly intimate if it is one in terms of which the members or others emphasize lack of restraint and informality in the overt display of affect and/or subordinate other aspects of the relationship to the overt display of affect. These affects may be of many different sorts. As indicated above, respect is one of the easiest affects to reconcile with avoidance; love, as that term is frequently understood, is one of the easiest to reconcile with intimacy.

For all the problems involved in their use, the concepts of

avoidance and intimacy provide a highly generalized distinction among relationships in terms of their affective aspects. The distinction has been chosen because of its general relevance to the analysis of social structure. The line of theoretical speculation that justifies this particular choice may be briefly stated as follows. In all social contexts situations arise in which the unrestrained display of emotional responses would or could be highly disruptive. There are also situations in which overt emotional expression is to a high degree adaptive in its implications. Current work in the field of personality development would seem to indicate that rather lavish informal displays of affection for infants and children are critical for the development of stable adult personalities. The distinction used here is based largely on the distinction between types of regulation of affective expression and hence is germane to this sort of consideration. More specifically, in all societies the structures of allocation of power and responsibility are of central importance. Furthermore, there are always some situations in which a premium is placed upon the efficient and even rapid exercise of power. Even slightly uninhibited displays of emotion can be extremely disruptive in such situations. Hence it may be argued that in all such situations the institutionalization of predominantly avoidant rather than predominantly intimate relationships is of adaptive significance for the members of the organizations involved. One of the most obvious cases of such a relationship is that between superiors and subordinates in military organizations. That is by no means the only case. Similar factors are involved in the relationship between a traditional Chinese father and his son. Because of the manner in which the family structures of traditional China fits into the total social structure of Chinese society, the strength of the father-son relationship is far more important than in modern American society. In general, whenever the intimate type of affective expression is not a central element of the substantive definition of the relationship, or at least whenever it is subordinated to other aspects of such a definition of the relationship, a premium is placed upon avoidant affects. It is not enough to repress intimacy in such situations; formal modes of affective expression are also needed. Because of the ubiquitous relevance of such considerations as these, the particular polar dichotomy suggested here has been selected.

5. GOAL ORIENTATION ASPECTS

The goal orientation aspect of a relationship focuses attention on some of what might be called motivational aspects of the relationship. Insofar as the ends sought in terms of a relationship are manifest to one or all of the members of the relationship, what can be said about them which is generally useful in analysis? The concepts used here are *individualistic* and *responsible*. A given relationship is more or less *individualistic* to the degree that each of the members of the relationship may be expected to calculate how best to secure his own maximum advantage from action in terms of the relationship without regard to the goals sought by the other members of the relationship. A given relationship is more or less *responsible* to the degree that each of the members of the relationship is expected to safeguard, even at the expense of some of his own goals, the relevant goals of the other members of the relationship. Again these are polar terms. Pure cases of either extreme, if they exist, constitute only a small proportion of the relationships in any society. The use of the prefix predominantly is of service here as in the other categories. A relationship will be called *predominantly individualistic* if the emphasis is placed on each member of the relationship looking out for himself. A relationship will be called *predominantly responsible* if the emphasis is placed on one [or more] of the members of the relationship safeguarding the relevant goals of the others if he is [or they are] to achieve his [or their] own goals at all. This distinction has nothing whatsoever to do with egoism or altruism, nor with selfishness or the lack of it. A relationship may be so structured that even the most selfish person must make sure that the other members of the relationship realize their goals if he is to realize his. Correspondingly, one of the most altruistic of men in terms of another type of relationship may have to take the attitude that each other member must look out for himself. Ideally speaking, for example, the most selfish of doctors *has* to behave responsibly in this sense towards his patients. On the other hand, a businessman who intends to give all of his profits away to charity must nevertheless continue to be a driver of hard bargains if he is to compete successfully for profits.

Illustrations used here will be compared in greater detail below. A business relationship in the United States today is, ideally speaking, a predominantly individualistic one. Each member is expected to seek to maximize his own interests. The relationship is not devoid of responsible elements. Presumably negotiations are carried out in terms of a general framework of honesty. Straight misrepresentation is fraud, as is payment with a bad check. On the other hand, if the buyer is willing to pay twice as much as would be necessary if he knew the situation better, the seller is not necessarily expected to enlighten him or to price the property at the going-rate despite his customer's ignorance. Students of social change could no doubt trace an interesting development of the businessman-customer relationship in the United States. At no time was the maxim of *caveat emptor* completely without limit. Members of the judiciary stood ready to act on certain practices classified as illegitimate. Nevertheless, the change has certainly been marked, and deals that were commonplace in the heyday of "captains of industry" would be considered unethical today. Despite these changes, the good businessman is expected to be able to take care of himself and is not expected to look out for the interests of others. If his concern for the interest of others exceeds the expected levels of probity, and if that concern is to the detriment of his own interests, whatever may be the evaluation of him in other respects, he has shown himself to be a poor businessman, perhaps even something of a fool.

On the other hand, the doctor-patient relationship may be described as a predominantly responsible one. Ideally speaking, the doctor is expected to protect his patient's interests. The doctor is not only expected to avoid direct misrepresentation. The doctor is also expected to protect the patient from the patient's own ignorance. If the patient wishes an unnecessary operation, the doctor, whether to his own financial hurt or no, is expected to refuse to perform it. If the accepted scale of fees for patients of a given income group is five dollars a visit, it is not ethical for a doctor to charge such a patient ten dollars simply because the patient is ignorant of the situation. Again it must be insisted that this tells one nothing of the personal character of the doctor. A doctor who scrupulously observes such standards may be selfish in the extreme, and the businessman who follows the others may be the soul of generosity. The practice of medicine is, however, differently structured than the conduct of business. The achievement of success in terms of the one is in part dependent upon the observance of this type of responsibility, and in terms of the other it is in part dependent upon the observance of this type of individualism. Two men almost identical in their personal ambitions for money, power, and prestige will behave quite differently in these respects if one is a doctor and the other a businessman. There is in all this every indication that socially acceptable behavior may be independent of individual personality factors to a high degree.

6. STRATIFICATION ASPECTS

This aspect is considerably simpler than those discussed above. *Stratification* may be defined as the particular type of role differentiation that distinguishes between higher and lower standing in terms of one or more criteria. In some relationships one member of the relationship is expected to have a higher ranking than another. The relationship between a traditional Chinese father and his son is of this type. There are also relationships such that, regardless of the rank of the members in their other roles, as members of this particular relationship their ranking is either considered equal or any question of differences in rank is considered irrelevant.

A relationship of the former type will be called a *hierarchical* one. A hierarchical relationship is defined as one for which the relative rankings of the members are different and in terms of which action is distinguished with regard to this ranking. The latter type of relationship mentioned above will be called a nonhierarchical one. A nonhierarchical relationship is one in terms of which no differential rankings of the members in any respect are considered relevant to the relationship. When the relationship is one such that its members are specifically expected to treat one another without reference to differential rankings, it will be termed *egalitarian*. The term egalitarian is used to distinguish this type of relationship from those in which differences in rank are irrelevant but are so simply by lack of definition of the relationship in this respect, e.g., in which the members are neither equals nor unequals ideally speaking.

Varying degrees of hierarchical relationships are familiar enough to require little or no comment. The example of a traditional Chinese father and his son has been given, but other examples are even more obvious. The relationship between officers and enlisted men, professors and associate-professors, employer and employee, union leader and union member, etc., are definitely of this sort. Nonhierarchical and egalitarian relationships are somewhat harder to find. Probably only relationships of short duration and ones such that any specific case of the relationship is socially defined as unimportant are nonhierarchical relationships of a nonegalitarian sort. So pervasive are rank-order structures and so strategic, if not crucial, are they structurally speaking that strong, explicit structures are usually required to keep hierarchical considerations out of the picture. Furthermore, only in rather fleeting relationships, specific cases of which matter little, would it be possible to have no definite structuring of hierarchical elements because of the great relevance of such elements to any action in terms of the relationship. Relationships of the casual-meeting or crowd-contact sort would fall into this category. This is not to argue that such relationships in the aggregate are unimportant for the society in which they occur. No relatively modernized society could exist unless a tremendous amount of action in terms of it could be carried out on the basis of the casual-meeting type of relationship. On the other hand, in many relatively nonmodernized social contexts relationships of this sort are relatively infrequent, and any great expansion of such relationships would probably be a source of disorganization.

Egalitarian relationships, though considerably less frequent than the hierarchical ones, are quite familiar to most people. Friendship is generally a relationship of this order in relatively modernized societies. Friends are expected to treat one another as equals and to consider one another as such regardless of other factors.[8] Strong egalitarian elements often enter relationships that are in other respects hierarchical. In some respects the members of a university faculty are equals despite the fact that the hierarchy of professors, associate professors, assistant professors, and instructors is of great significance to us. The faculty situation tenses instantly if we feel that the hierarchical aspects are being pushed beyond their proper sphere. The emphasis on egalitarianism in the face of hierarchical distinctions is perhaps symbolized by the official university use of the term of address Professor for all three ranks of the professor category, and by the fact that faculty members among themselves frequently avoid such terms altogether and use the more neutral term Mister.

Particularly among those who believe or profess belief in democracy there are some misconceptions about hierarchical relationships. The overwhelming proportion of all relationships in all societies contain hierarchical elements both ideally and actually. In fact, it is difficult for most individuals to give examples, apart from friendship, of relationships that are ideally and/or actually egalitarian. Family relationships certainly aren't; bureaucratic relationships aren't; relationships within the government rarely are; universities aren't; business firms aren't, etc. For men to be "equal before the law" does not imply a lack of hierarchy "before the law." A judge may *order* the defendent or the plaintiff, etc. It is common for those interested in either social analysis or social welfare to confuse predominantly universalistic criteria for treat-

[8] During World War II the egalitarian character of friendship as opposed to the hierarchical character of the officer–enlisted-man relationship was a frequent theme of conflict in comic strips, in the movies, on the radio, etc. Bosom friends who met but could not eat together because of the military distinction appeared in all sorts of stories. Whether or not old friends in uniform, meeting in a nonmilitary context, could treat one another as equals became, as it were, a test of the strength of the friendship, etc.

ment with egalitarian relationships. Societies could not persist on an egalitarian basis, nor could any other social system of any considerable membership or importance from the point of view of its members and other members in the society. Relatively modernized societies could not exist at all if social structures combining predominantly universalistic emphases and hierarchical ones did not exist in great and varied panoply.[9]

For comparative purposes the distinctions concerned with the stratification aspects of relationships are often quite revealing. Military systems seem on the whole to have been strictly hierarchical if their members were successful. But other relationships show greater variations from one context to another. Take, for example, the husband-wife relationship. Although modern, urban, middle-class Americans do not regard the relationship, ideally speaking, as egalitarian, they at least favor as close an approach to egalitarianism in this relationship as men have ever achieved. In traditional China it was definitely a hierarchical relationship with the husband much more highly ranked than the wife. There are cases in which the relationship is hierarchical but with the wife ranked well above her husband in most respects. With factual knowledge of only these three differences with regard to one aspect of one type of relationship, one can make a considerable number of predictions about other differences that must exist in these social contexts.[10]

E. APPLICATIONS

1. INTRODUCTION

First, the concepts discussed above are such that some statements can be made about any relationship, in any society, at any time in terms of them. This means questions asked about these concepts are always capable of yielding some answers relevant for comparative purposes. Second, they have been devised to illuminate the part played by specific relationships in more general social systems. Finally, like most sets of scientific concepts, these are designed to make possible the greatest accumulation of defensible knowledge about a given type of phenomena with the least amount of effort and to have that knowledge of maximum general relevance to the development of further generalized

---

[9] See below, pp. 296–300 and 670–671.

[10] Predictions based on these three facts taken alone might be extremely risky, but they would tell something, and the more such facts one has, the less risky prediction becomes.

knowledge about the field concerned. More specifically, however, this set of concepts is useful because it provides a framework in terms of which one may analyze and describe any single relationship and compare the following: (1) different types of relationships in a single society, (2) similar types of relationships in different societies, and (3) different types of relationships in different societies. For the purposes of rapid sketching of examples the following table has been set up:

TABLE 1

	X	Y
1. Cognitive aspects	Rational	Traditional
2. Membership criteria aspects	Universalistic	Particularistic
3. Substantive definition aspects	Functionally specific	Functionally diffuse
4. Affective aspects	Avoidant	Intimate
5. Goal orientation aspects	Individualistic	Responsible
6. Stratification aspects	Hierarchical	Nonhierarchical

The symbol X_1 will be used for rational [i.e., predominantly rational], the symbol Y_1 for traditional [i.e., predominantly traditional], X_2 will be used for predominantly universalistic, etc. I devised the notation to make certain typical clustering effects which will be discussed below more readily obvious, but apart from this, it is arbitrary. One could mix the various polar types between the X and Y columns at random or change the order of the rows. To do so would make the discussion a bit more cumbersome, but it would not change the implications or the meaning of the discussion in any way. Using the notation as set up, a relationship that is described as $X_1, X_2, X_3, X_4, X_5, X_6$ is a relationship that is predominantly rational in its cognitive aspects, predominantly universalistic in its membership criteria aspects, predominantly functionally specific in its substantive definition aspects, predominantly avoidant in its affective aspects, predominantly individualistic in its goal orientation aspects, and predominantly hierarchical in its stratification aspects.

In order to illustrate the use of these concepts and this notation I shall compare: (1) the doctor-patient relationship and the businessman-customer relationship in modern United States society, (2) the businessman-customer relationship in modern United States society and in traditional China, and (3) the businessman-customer relationship in modern United States society and the gentry father-son relationship in traditional China.[11]

2. EXAMPLES

a. THE DOCTOR-PATIENT AND THE BUSINESSMAN-CUS-TOMER RELATIONSHIPS IN MODERN UNITED STATES SOCIETY The doctor-patient relationship may be described in the terms used here as X_1, X_2, X_3, X_4, Y_5, Y_6. Ideally speaking, the doctor is expected to employ rational techniques in his treatment of the patient. It is well understood that, given the limitations of knowledge and the fallibility of man, the doctor sometimes acts irrationally, but the range of irrational actions is limited, and attempts are made to limit them further. Many medical errors are considered inescapable and nonculpable, but others, for example, repeated failures to diagnose correctly common ailments appearing in common uncomplicated forms, are likely to result in pressures of some sort being brought to bear on the doctor. Some irrational actions are considered sufficiently egregious to be grounds for civil suits against the doctor, and some are even grounds for his loss of license to practice. The latter form of discipline is relatively rare, probably because of the reluctance of qualified personnel to testify. This reluctance is by no means wholly understandable in terms of a "guild" or "There but for the grace of God go I" feeling. It is, at least in part, understandable in terms of the reluctance to shake by such exposure the element of public confidence in medical men. This element of confidence is certainly vital to the current forms of medical practice. Whether it would be broken down or bolstered by more frequent exposures of this sort is as yet an undetermined point. The fact that overt sanctions are not so evident as might seem justified on the basis of expressed licensing standards, medical

---

[11] These relationships have been chosen to illustrate the three major comparative applications of this scheme of analysis. I do not wish at this point to get sidetracked into any discussion of the validity of the assertions made about any of the relationships. I have not knowingly misrepresented any of the structures, but my hypotheses about the facts may be false.

The material used on the doctor-patient relationship was first brought to my attention in lectures delivered at Harvard by Professor Talcott Parsons more years ago than either of us cares to remember. Much of the material also appears in his article already cited above [p. 136] as one of the original sources for the development of this particular taxonomy of relationship structures. Professor Parsons is, of course, not to be held responsible for the present form of this material or any of the uses made of it despite the indebtedness of this treatment to his work.

I have not bothered to illustrate the analysis of a single relationship separately because that analysis can be illustrated by the description of the first two relationships discussed below.

society membership criteria, etc., does not mean that sanctions of this sort are totally lacking.

Doctors may in fact act nonrationally, or traditionally as the term is used here, in their treatment of patients. The use of traditional techniques which are not necessarily rationally justified is either definitely condemned or is not considered proper to the relationship. The complete substitution by a doctor of nonempirical means for empirical ones in the treatment of a patient is never sanctioned. Nonempirical means of some sort, for example prayers in terms of one of the established religious systems of society, are acceptable as a means supplementary to the application of scientific knowledge, but such activities are definitely not a central part of the relationship. They may be tolerated, sometimes even approved, but they are not required. Nonempirical means of other sorts are strongly condemned and are considered applications of superstitions or magic, both of which are felt to have no place in this field and to be bad. Doctors frequently carry out practices because that is the way they have been done in the past, but the usual traditional arguments are not considered justifications in this field. The argument, "We have always done it that way, and it's a good way to do it because we've always done it that way," is not in general acceptable. The argument, "We have not yet got a better scientific way of doing this than the one we have been using for quite some time," is as far as medical ethics permit the doctor to go.[12]

The patient on his side is also expected to act rationally in the following respects. He is expected to choose his physician on the basis of predominantly universalistic criteria. This involves an element of rationality since there is rationality involved in the process of understanding what criteria are germane to the end sought and in the process of judgment as to whether the doctor chosen in fact measures up to such criteria. Another rational element enters from the patient's point of view in that he is expected to know within limits when it is and is not necessary to consult his doctor [i.e., initiate the relationship], and he is expected to follow his doctor's orders rationally. The emphasis on

[12] As is well known, this is an area in which there is great pressure on the professional man to act. In similar circumstances in many societies, magical practices are frequent. They are specifically denigrated in the medical sphere. It is not a matter of accident that medical faddism is so prominent a phenomenon. Many wise doctors have pointed out that the most difficult thing for a doctor to do when his knowledge is inadequate is literally to do nothing. Fortunately, perhaps, the constantly changing nature of medical faddism—in this respect it is almost exactly the opposite of magical practices—probably minimizes any harm done by uncritical pursuit of any particular medical fad.

his rationality, however, is much less well institutionalized [13] than for the doctor.

The doctor-patient relationship is, ideally speaking, a predominantly universalistic one. The patient is expected to choose his doctor on grounds of competence and availability. The doctor is expected, within quite broad limits, to accept patients on the basis of need for treatment. These ideal structures often fail to coincide with actual ones. Patients often choose or reject doctors on bases that are medically irrelevant. Such considerations may range from liking a doctor's looks to not liking his political or religious affiliations. Doctors, on the other hand, sometimes choose or reject their patients on the basis of the patient's ability to pay, social position, etc. Again, the structure seems to be better institutionalized for the doctors than for the patient in both conformity and sanction aspects. Although the ideal structures are often violated from both points of view, the remarkable feature of the situation is that they are not violated more often, given, among other relevant factors, on the one hand the medical ignorance of the patient and on the other hand the tremendous relevance of monetary income as a symbol of success in such societies.

Ideally speaking, the relationship is functionally specific. It is the doctor's obligation to do what he can medically for the patient, and all of his orders and access to the patient must be justifiable on the grounds of their relevance to the patient's health. The patient on his part is expected to follow the doctor's orders [and to pay his fees unless he is being treated on a charity basis]. The doctor with respect to fixing fees is expected to take into consideration the patient's ability to pay. Often functionally diffuse elements creep into the relationship, particularly in the case of the general practitioner or family doctor, who may be a close friend and advisor of the patient in matters otherwise as well as medical. The appearance of functionally diffuse elements in the relation-

[13] The term *institution* is defined as a normative pattern, conformity with which is generally to be expected, and failure to conform with which is generally met with the moral indignation of those individuals who belong to the same general social system and are aware of the failure—or by some other sanctions from that source. The term normative pattern refers simply to any pattern involving a standard of conduct. Thus, "men should have only one wife at a given point in time," "no one should bully anyone else," "patients should select their doctors on the basis of their medical qualifications," etc., are normative patterns. A normative pattern may be more or less well institutionalized with regard to the level of conformity expected in terms of it or the degree and kind of moral indignation and sanctions which greet a failure to live up to this ideal structure. There is an extended discussion of this concept in the *Structure of Society*, pp. 101–109. The details of that discussion need not detain us here. All institutions in this sense are social structures.

ship almost inevitably go hand in hand with predominantly intimate rather than predominantly avoidant structures. Again, the
lead in breakdowns in these respects is more likely to be taken by
the patient than by the doctor.

The relationship is ideally a predominantly avoidant one; the
more so the more it is strictly confined to medical matters. Departures on the doctor's part are only in theory justified if they
contribute to the patient's health. Departures on the patient's
part may range from the often unobjectionable combining of a
friendship relationship with that of doctor and patient, to excur-
sions into intimacy of a sort most strongly condemned. Both
doctor and patient may be strongly condemned for some of these
departures in the direction of intimacy, and the profession as a
whole, as well as the public, is well aware of this. Doctors are so
thoroughly aware of it that elaborate precautions and procedures
have been set up to eliminate such breakdowns.

The relationship is ideally predominantly responsible rather
than individualistic. The doctor rather than the patient is primarily concerned here since he has the more active role in the
relationship. The whole structure of prestige in the medical profession is so set up as to require even the most selfish of doctors to
place the interests of his patients, both actual and potential,
before any goals of his own that do not involve their medical
welfare. The selfish doctor dares not acquire a widespread reputation for demanding assurance of payment before treating an
emergency case or for ordering profitable but medically unnecessary operations and the like. Again, the experts in the field are
reluctant to testify openly in such cases, but the sanctions
brought to bear are none the less strong. The patient on his part is
expected to heed the doctor's advice and pay his fees, but the
question of individualism or responsibility is not quite so relevant
from the patient's point of view, since he has little possibility of
sacrificing the doctor's interest for his own. Both he and the
doctor in theory share the end of restoring the patient's health.
Other goals such as minimizing the doctor's fee, etc., are not
supposed to enter since the doctor's responsibility covers making
such fees reasonable.

Finally, the relationship is of a relatively nonhierarchical sort.
Of course, the roles are sharply differentiated, but as far as
general social standing the doctor may be of either higher or
lower rank than the patient. In theory at least, none of the action
takes place because one member of the relationship is a superior
of the other in any power sense. A doctor's orders are not orders in
the ordinary sense that implies an enforcement agency outside

the person ordered and the possibility of orders not to the subordinate's best interest. Ideally, the doctor's orders are given the patient only so that the patient may achieve his own goal, i.e., restoration or maintenance of health. The only hierarchical aspect involved, ideally speaking, is that of medical knowledge, but even this is by no means a hard and fast requirement since doctors are usually patients of doctors other than themselves, sometimes of less able ones. However the members of the society as a whole may rank doctors relative to patients, and in this there is certainly a hierarchical element, the treatment by the doctor of the patient, ideally speaking, is determined by medical criteria and not by criteria of any other relative social standing.[14]

The relationship between a businessman and his customer in the modern United States may be described as an X_1, X_2, X_3, X_4, X_5, and Y_6. Both the businessman and his customer are expected to deal rationally with one another. Not to do so is bad business, and in terms of this relationship both parties are expected to behave in a businesslike fashion. Irrational action on the part of either member is the mark of a fool. Traditional action or other departures from rationality in general, simply are not considered good business, and in some cases come in for harsh criticism. The emphasis on rationality in the businessman-customer relationship is by no means complete. Some important traditional elements are still maintained, but the trend is overwhelmingly in the opposite direction. The mark par excellence of maintenance of traditional emphases is likely to be the presence of a family firm, but these in the old fashioned sense are becoming increasingly rare in all highly modernized societies.

The criteria for membership in the relation are predominantly universalistic. Both parties are expected to pick fellow members on the basis best calculated to serve the empirical ends sought.

[14] There is not space here to go into the question of how these peculiar structures developed or what their implications may be. It is important, however, to keep in mind the fact that the doctor-patient relationship, as we take it for granted, is a peculiar and unusual relationship in world history. To an unusual degree one member has a great deal of knowledge relative to the other member's concern, and the other member usually has little knowledge. In that sense the doctor could potentially do the patient great harm, if he took advantage of his knowledge. It is also interesting to keep in mind that we permit the doctor a kind of access to our bodies that is literally permitted to no one else in the society. Such access is deemed vital to modern medical treatment, but such access made available to any one on a nonmedical basis would immediately raise questions of proper conduct in general and of proper sexual behavior in particular. It is not a matter of chance that members of modern societies feel so strongly about doctors or that so much attention is given to the way in which the doctor-patient relationship is exemplified.

The businessman seeks to make a profit; the customer seeks to get the best possible value for his money. To refuse to sell at a profit to second generation Scandinavian citizens because one does not like them is bad business, as is refusal to buy from them on this ground. There are many departures from these standards by both types of members, but such departures become increasingly less common as business becomes large scale. Representatives of large-scale firms such as some of the automobile manufacturers would find insuperable obstacles in trying to enforce such predominantly particularistic criteria. Individual customers find their effect in such matters negligible and such activities likely to fall into the category of "cutting off your nose to spite your face." The accepted criteria for businessmen in selecting customers is their ability to pay, and that of customers in selecting businessmen is the ability to deliver the best goods at the lowest price.

The relationship is generally kept as functionally specific as possible. Ideally speaking, it is perfectly so from both points of view. The contract relationship is the archetype of this quality. If a contract is vague, it is a bad contract, at least from the point of view of the person who may find added unanticipated obligations as a result of such vagueness. In only a fraction of such relationships are actual contracts drawn, but the usual structures of a one-price market makes such things quite clear. A customer buys a soft drink. His obligation is confined to the payment of the price; the dealer's obligation is to deliver the product as defined by quite specific standards. If there is an insect in the drink, the dealer is liable; if the payment is less than the stated price, the customer is liable. To leave the obligations of such a relationship vague is always potentially bad business from someone's point of view.

Ideally speaking, the relationship is a predominantly avoidant one. Often there are departures in the direction of intimacy, but these departures are more likely to characterize small firms with a restricted, relatively unchanging set of customers. On the whole, the attitude in this respect is that business is business and that emotional involvement with one's customers, insofar as it is permissible, becomes inadmissible if it interferes with the profit goals of enterprise. Roughly the same situation exists from the customer's point of view.

The relationship is a predominantly individualistic one. It is not, however, completely individualistic with a completely unhindered *caveat emptor* outlook. There are restrictions on both parties. Certain standards of honesty, for example, are not only expected but are enforceable at law. Yet, neither member is held responsible for protecting the other against his own ignorance as is the case with the doctor-patient relationship. Within a certain framework of mutual regard for each other's interests, the businessman and his customer operate on an "every man for himself" basis. Ideally, this is never true of the doctor's relation with his patient.

Finally, this relationship is, ideally, nonhierarchical and in some respects even egalitarian. The customer has neither higher nor lower rank than the businessman in general, and of course, one individual may at any time be playing both roles in different operations. Ideally the members of such relationships deal with one another as equals. Proof of deliberate tinkering with this equality may be the basis for setting aside such transactions legally. Much of the antimonopoly legislation rests on the legal philosophy that the parties to a valid contract should be equals from many points of view for the purposes of that transaction. Of course there are many departures from the ideal structures in this respect.

I shall now compare these two relationships briefly on three levels. First, I shall compare them on the most general level discussed here. In that comparison the basic difference between the doctor-patient and the businessman-customer relationship lies in the fact that the former is predominantly responsible and the latter is predominantly individualistic. On this level the two relationships are identical in all other five aspects. Now, there is considerable feeling that the doctor-patient relationship, ideally as well as actually, is different from that of the businessman and his customer. For purposes of comparative analysis of the two, it is best first to see how much of the differences between the two can be explained in terms of the difference between X_5 and Y_5. Some of the differences, which we feel so strongly should and do exist, hinge on this difference at this level.

If differences on the most general level are not sufficient to explain the differences we wish to understand, we must proceed to the second level of analysis. Both relationships institutionalize structures of predominantly rational action and predominantly universalistic criteria. The specific contents of the rationality and of the universalistic criteria are, however, quite different. In the one case rational action is oriented to the restoration and maintenance of health, and in the other it is oriented to the allocation of goods and/or services. In other words, both are predominantly rational but their members are interested in rationality about different matters. In theory at least, those differences between the two relationships which are not explicable in terms of differences between X's and Y's [i.e., differences on the most general level] may be explicable in terms of the differing contents of the similar X's or Y's [e.g., both of the relationships described here are predominantly rational, but about quite different matters]. If the second level differences are insufficient to explain the differences noted between two relationships being compared, then one of four possibilities remains: (1) differences on the first level of generalization have been overlooked, (2) differences on the second level of generalization have been overlooked, (3) the list of aspects of relationships needs reformulation and/or additions at least on lower levels of generalization, or (4) some combination of the three foregoing difficulties is present.

In the third of the foregoing possibilities lies the third level of comparison mentioned above. If two relationships are in fact different in their structures but also in fact identical on the two levels of procedure cited above, the difference must be in aspects of one or the other or both of the relationships not given in the original list of six aspects. Even if the relationships are not identical on the two levels previously cited, additional differences on this third level may still be present. Any failure to explain differences between relationships on the previous two levels should lead to exploration of this third level. Its exploration may also lead to further development by discovering an aspect(s) which is (are) empirically observable in *any* relationship and hence should be added to the original list of six aspects.[15]

It is possible to discuss the doctor-patient relationship at great length, and its contrast with that of the businessman-customer in modern United States society is revealing about both spheres and about the society in general, but most of the relevant differences between these two relationships are, in fact, to be subsumed under either the most general differences in the goal orientations aspects and lower level differences in the other aspects.

[15] Two colleagues, Miss Kazuko Tsurumi and Mr. Andrew Effrat, have suggested further developments of this scheme. Miss Tsurumi has suggested a *communications aspect* with a polar distinction between *secret* and *open* relationships. Mr. Effrat in an unpublished paper has suggested a *volitional aspect* with a distinction between voluntaristic and non-voluntaristic relationships plus some six mixed forms. Both suggestions are promising, but I have not explored them enough to use them here. One of the rough rules of thumb of theory, however, is that once one exceeds six or seven distinctions on any one level [and these two aspects would give us eight] some more general less complicated level should be sought.

b. THE BUSINESSMAN-CUSTOMER RELATIONSHIP IN MOD-
ERN UNITED STATES SOCIETY AND IN TRADITIONAL CHINA
The material on the businessman-customer relationship in modern United States society need not be repeated. In traditional
China the relationship took one of two forms. If the relationship
was the expected predominantly particularistic one, it took the
form $Y_1, Y_2, Y_3, X_4, Y_5, X_6$. Ideally speaking, it was expected to be
based on particularistic criteria such as friendship, family connections, and neighborhood considerations which were already
present or established by a go-between. If predominantly particularistic connections of this sort did not exist the relationship
was likely to take the form $X_1, X_2, X_3, X_4, X_5, X_6$.

This difference between the businessman-customer relationship in China when based on predominantly particularistic rather
than on predominantly universalistic criteria of choice, explains
many differences in accounts as to the reliability or honesty of the
Chinese businessman. If he were dealing with a friend or relative
or family members who had dealt with his family members for
years, or a person from his own village or a person introduced by
a go-between who possessed one or some combination of these
connections with both businessman and customer, the businessman emphasized the preservation of the relationship. He operated in a predominantly traditional fashion. The relationship was
by definition highly particularistic, but it was also predominantly
functionally diffuse. Extra requests by the customer might well
be granted. Although something like friendship might dominate
the relationship and displays of affect in terms of it were by no
means out of the question, it must be borne in mind that the
members of that society generally placed a heavy emphasis on
highly formalized predominantly avoidant relationships. Given
the fact that, ideally speaking, the position of merchant was
frequently a lowly one, the relationship might be prominently
avoidant. Most importantly, it was a highly responsible relationship. The merchant was expected to protect his customer at all
costs even to the extent of his own financial ruin in some extreme
cases. The relationship might be hierarchical in different ways. If
the merchant were dealing with a gentry customer, the relationship was certainly hierarchical with the customer of higher rank
than the merchant, of course. In other cases it might be hierarchical in the opposite direction. The differences between ideal and
actual structures were especially important. In the strictest ideal
sense the merchants ranked below gentry, peasants, and artisans.
Actually, of course, if they were at all well off, they certainly
outranked the latter two as well as many of the gentry.

On the other hand, if the expected predominantly particularistic connections did not exist, the picture was almost exactly opposite. A ruthlessly *caveat emptor* situation existed and was carried as an ordinary matter to an extreme that United States businessmen have not tolerated for some decades. Indeed, if the businessman could get by with it, his attitude was not simply "every man for himself," but rather " 'It's every man for himself and God for us all,' said the elephant as he danced among the chickens." Under these circumstances both businessman and customer acted as rationally as possible in an attempt to maximize their material gains from the relationship. The relationship was as functionally specific as either party could make it to his own advantage, and it was an avoidant one. It was ruthlessly individualistic, and that within a framework in which force and fraud were only limited by what the parties concerned thought they could get by with. It would be hierarchical with each party attempting to utilize hierarchical factors to secure an advantage. Thus, insofar as possible, it becomes a relationship of the X_1, X_2, X_3, X_4, X_5, and X_6 type. It must be emphasized that it was not institutionally expected that the businessman-customer relationship would be of this second type, and the Chinese tried to avoid this type of relationship if they could possibly do so. Cases of it, however, were frequently observable. If one entered such a relationship without establishing proper predominantly particularistic grounds either directly or via a go-between and was badly treated in terms of it, one was considered a fool for having gotten oneself involved in such a situation in the first place.

In comparing the businessman-customer relationship in modern United States society and in traditional China, one should first consider the differences in the relationship in China. Here the distinctions are almost, if not completely, understandable in terms of differences on the most general level of relationship aspects. In comparing either of the Chinese structures with those of the United States, differences on both the most general level and the second level of generalization mentioned above are significant. These relationships have been set up in Table 2, below, along with several others for ease of comparison.

In this tabular form, it is immediately obvious that the differences between Type A and Type B in traditional China apparently lie on the most general level since the structures tend to opposite poles except with regard to the possibilities of variation in the affective and the stratification aspects. The differences between Type A and the United States type again lie apparently almost wholly on the first level of procedure, but the differences between

TABLE 2

RELATIONSHIP	RELATIONSHIP ASPECTS					
	1	2	3	4	5	6
(1) Doctor-patient	X	X	X	X	Y	Y(?)
(2) U.S. businessman-customer	X	X	X	X	X	Y
(3) Traditional Chinese businessman-customer Type A	Y	Y	Y	X	Y	X
(4) Type B	X	X	X	X	X	X
(5) U.S. husband-wife	Y	Y	Y	Y	Y	X
(6) Traditional Chinese husband-wife	Y	Y	Y	X(Y)	Y	X
(7) U.S. employer-employee	X	X	X	X	X	X
(8) Traditional Chinese employer-employee	Y	Y	Y	X	Y	X
(9) U.S. lawyer-client	X	X	X	X	Y	Y(?)
(10) U.S. architect-client	X	X	X	X	Y	Y(?)
(11) U.S. father-son	Y	Y	Y	Y	Y	X
(12) Traditional Chinese father-son	Y	Y	Y	X	Y	X
(13) Japanese Emperor-Crown Prince Old	Y	Y	Y	X	Y	X
(14) New	Y	Y	Y	Y	Y	X
(15) Engineer-client	X	X	X	X	Y	Y(?)
(16) Certified public accountant-client	X	X	X	X	Y	Y(?)

Type B and the United States type obviously must be sought in considerable part on the second level of generalization or on the third [i.e., in some additions to the list of relevant aspects]. Actually, in comparison of the United States type and Type B the differences lies largely in differences in the cognitive aspects and the goal orientation aspects, both of which on the first level emphasize rationality and individualism. Most of the differences may be subsumed under the goal orientation aspects. The much greater individualism possible in Type B behavior in China makes it possible for the cognitive aspects to be far more ruthlessly rational than would be countenanced in the modern United States case. Approved rationality in the latter case does not permit taking into consideration the possible rational implications of applications of force and fraud as in the Chinese Type B. The differences between Type A Chinese relationships and the United States type are the ones conventionally associated with discussions of the contrast between traditional Chinese ways of doing business and modern, "objective," etc., forms of businessman-customer relationships.

c. THE BUSINESSMAN-CUSTOMER RELATIONSHIP IN MODERN UNITED STATES SOCIETY AND THE FATHER-SON RELATIONSHIP IN TRADITIONAL CHINA The United States businessman-customer relationship has already been described above. It takes the form X_1, X_2, X_3, X_4, X_5, and Y_6. The father-son relationship in traditional China takes the form Y_1, Y_2, Y_3, X_4, Y_5, and X_6. On the most general level these different types of relationships in different societies have only one element, predominantly avoidant affective aspects [X_4], in common. On the most general level the relationships are almost wholly different from one another, but there are critical differences on lower levels as well. For example, the matters about which the members of the one emphasize rationality and those of the other emphasize tradition are quite different. Even in the one similarity on the most general level, there are differences on lower levels, since the types and degrees of avoidance are quite different. Whether this particular comparison is interesting may be doubtful. Some comparisons of radically different types of relationships in different types of societies are, however, of considerable importance.

d. OTHER EXAMPLES In Table 2 additional examples have been given For example, the employer-employee relationship in the United States is ideally expected to take the form X_1, X_2, X_3, X_4, X_5, and X_6. Insofar as one can speak about the employer-employee relationship in most of the relatively nonmodernized areas, those relationships, ideally speaking, take the form Y_1, Y_2, Y_3, X_4, Y_5, and X_6 as illustrated by the employer-employee relationship in traditional China. The husband-wife relationship in the United States ideally takes the form Y_1, Y_2, Y_3, Y_4, Y_5, and X_6.[16]

---

[16] That is to say, even in the United States there is still a vestigial expectation that the relationship be a hierarchical one with some male precedence. Some might argue that Y_6 should be substituted here, taking the position that this relationship should be an egalitarian one. Whatever *should be* the case, even in America, the relationship retains hierarchical elements [with male precedence] even ideally speaking. It may also be argued that the pressure is not toward egalitarianism but toward female precedence.

Since this set of concepts can be used to analyze *any* two or more different relationships, it follows that it can also be used to analyze the same type of relationship at different points in time. Thus it can be used to analyze questions of changes in a given relationship over any given span of time. For example, a dramatic change has recently been reported in the structures of the Royal Family in Japan. This appears in Table 2 as the example of the relationship between the Japanese Emperor [or the Crown Prince] and the Emperor's [or Crown Prince's son, i.e., the present or future Crown Prince] according to previous custom and present practice. In the old days that relationship took the form Y_1, Y_2, Y_3, X_4, Y_5, and X_6. According to the present reported decision of the Crown Prince to rear his own son within a more ordinary modern family setting in Japan, the relationship would now take the form Y_1, Y_2, Y_3, Y_4, Y_5, and X_6. There is every reason to believe that the relationship between the present Crown Prince and his son will be a predominantly intimate one at least by contrast with the overwhelmingly avoidant one previously characteristic of this relationship.[17]

For purposes of comparison, Table 2 also includes the husband-wife relationship in the United States and in traditional China, the lawyer-client relationship in the United States, the architect-client relationship in the United States, the engineer-client relationship in the United States, the certified public accountant-client relationship in the United States, the father-son relationship in the United States, and the father-son relationship in traditional China. Given the detailed illustrations above, these should be sufficiently clear to support subsequent allusions to them.

I I I
USE OF THE RELATIONSHIP ASPECTS
FOR THEORY FORMATION

A. GENERAL EXAMPLES

The examples given above illustrate comparative analysis of different types of relationships in terms of the concepts suggested here. Four sources of differences have been suggested. Differences arise from: (1) differences on the most general level [i.e., differences in X or Y classification], (2) differences on lower levels of generalization [i.e., the relationships whether similar or different on the most general level may be different in the kind

---

[17] Under previous custom the Imperial children were literally reared almost entirely by persons who were not their parents.

and/or degree of "X-ness" or "Y-ness"], (3) differences in aspects on the most general level of relationships or on lower levels for which no concepts have been provided [i.e., aspects of any relationship or of specific ones not included in the present list of six general aspects], or (4) some combination of the three foregoing differences. The diverse choice of relationships used for illustrations constitutes an attempt to indicate that *any* relationships, however different or similar, in the same or different societies can be compared usefully in these terms. Insofar as analysis of this sort is successful, one in effect forms theories [or gets useful insights, if one prefers], by locating differences in relationships that are relevant to the analysis, whatever the purpose of the analysis may be.

Inferences drawn from the comparison of the doctor-patient and businessman-customer relationships illustrate this. As modernization increases, if a considerable amount of decision about the allocation of goods and services is left in the hands of members of private enterprises, there is nevertheless observable a continual increase in the level of bureaucratization of those private enterprises. This increase has caused growing talk about the professionalization of the business role. The patterns of X's and Y's characteristic of the doctor-patient relationship are also characteristic of a substantial number of so-called professional man-client relationships. For example, the lawyer-client relationship is, ideally speaking of the same form, and so are those of architect and client, certified public accountant and client, and engineer and client. There are important differences among all of them on the second level of generalization, e.g., they are not expected to be rational about the same matters, but the one difference between all of them and the ordinary businessman-customer [including other businessmen] relationship is that they are predominantly responsible. Given the line of analysis suggested here and the history of the well-established professions, the inference is that, as the professionalization of the business role increases, the most general alteration in the relationship of businessmen with their customers [including other businessmen] will be an increase in emphasis on the responsibility of the more expert members of those relationships for the interest of all others involved in them.[18] Modern business history shows an increase in emphasis on responsibility by contrast with individualism. Probably noth-

[18] One can generalize as follows: All relationships characterized by high emphases on rationality will involve members who have a high probability of being cognitive equals or will be characterized by high emphases on responsibility or will be instable.

ing else is more characteristic of the discipline of the modern business school, and few themes appear more frequently in the pronouncements of leading business figures. Even so marked lapses such as those implicit in recent alleged violations of standard and generally accepted antimonopoly rules continue to crop up,[19] the ticklish question in modern business development is not *whether* such increases in emphasis on responsibility will take place, but only *how* they will take place.

In many spheres this development has gone quite far. Veblen made much of the concept of sabotage as deliberate interference with efficiency for the sake of profit. It was Veblen's irony that a word developed from a desperate labor practice of throwing a wooden shoe into machinery to confound businessmen should be applied to business practices. Today some of Veblen's irony has come full circle. For many business leaders, particularly those associated with communications, the use of "strategic withdrawals of efficiency" to gain profit are virtually out of the question. The range of choice open to labor leaders is often larger than the range of choice open to business leaders. Certainly there are emphases on individualism in the relationships between union leaders and their "customers," whether those customers be representatives of their own government or of private business firms which are at least the equal of any emphasis on individualism characteristic of other businesslike leaders in our society.

The prediction of increased emphasis on predominantly responsible goal orientations can be broadened. Not only will there be an increase in emphasis on responsibility in businessman-customer [including other businessmen] relationships, but the same will also be increasingly true of relationships involving any leaders strategically placed in terms of bureaucratic organizations of considerable relevance to the allocation of goods and/or services. Thus there will be an increasing emphasis on responsibility in the relationships between union leaders and the customers of labor and between governmental leaders whose policy decisions can seriously affect economic allocations and members of all other organizations whether those be local, state, or federal agencies on the one hand, or private enterprises or labor unions on the other. At present, the major differences of these relationships from professionalized relationships in the ordinary sense

[19] Even in these instances, however, the reaction of the accused parties, much of the general reaction of other businessmen, and certainly that of the general public is censorious of such behavior to a degree hard to imagine some decades ago. Sworn testimony in court established clearly that many, if not all, of those convicted of these lapses were violating explicitly professed standards of their organizations.

inhere overwhelmingly in the emphasis on individualism as opposed to responsibility. In every bureaucratic sphere of any importance in which the emphasis, either ideally or actually, on individualism continues at a high level that emphasis is shifting in the direction of an emphasis on responsibility. With all increases in modernization it will continue to do so, if the systems concerned are to be stable and probably even if they are not. From this one may draw a still further inference, a riskier one: With the increase of modernization and the attendant increase of bureaucratization, all roles in bureaucracies tend to become increasingly professionalized.

I shall give one further example of such theorizing. The major difference between the traditional Chinese father-son relationship and the United States father-son relationship, is that the latter is predominantly intimate and the former is predominantly avoidant. There has already been considerable discussion of family developments in relatively modernized societies as opposed to relatively nonmodernized ones above, and there will be more below [pp. 377–435]. Suffice it to say here that in all increasingly modernized social contexts there will be an increasing emphasis on intimacy in the father-son relationship, if that emphasis did not exist before. The attempt of the Chinese Communists to carry out their commune policies in greatest detail does not alter the tenability of this proposition. It is characteristic of all other societies as they change in the direction of modernization.

B. THE CLUSTERING EFFECT

Inspection of Table 2 discloses clusters of relationship aspects. If a relationship is predominantly X in any of the first three aspects it is predominantly X in the other two and correspondingly with the Y aspects. Furthermore, if there is any X in any one of the first three aspects there is an X in the fourth aspect as well.[20] What does such clustering mean? If an emphasis on rationality, universalism, functional specificity, and avoidance must go together *by definition*, and if an emphasis on tradition, particularism, and functional diffuseness must go together *by definition*, such clustering effects would add nothing to what we already know. But, they do not cluster by definition. Emphases on rationality, functional specificity, universalism, and avoidance are likely to cluster, and if they fail to, one can make further predictions from

[20] It does not follow that if there is an X in the fourth aspect that there are X's in the first three. Although one can generalize to the effect that if there is X_1 or X_2 or X_3, there is also X_4, one can not generalize to the effect that if there is Y_1 or Y_2 or Y_3, there is usually Y_4.

that variation. When rationality is involved, both ends and means must be empirical and to a high degree explicit. Functionally diffuse elements are likely to interfere with rational emphases and force inclusion of traditional or nonrational elements if only by adding vagueness to an otherwise explicit situation. Again rational factors are likely to be interfered with by particularistic selections, especially if the particularism is not germane particularism, since such selection will not maximize or safeguard the ability of the members of the relationship to carry out rational action in terms of the relationship. Intimacy, as opposed to avoidance, is more likely to involve departures in the direction of traditionality [or nonrationality], functional diffuseness, and particularism. It is difficult to confine activity to rational considerations or to specifically defined and delimited factors or to objective selections when a person is intimately involved with others. These four elements by no means always go together. For example, rather close approaches to universalism are sometimes maintained by picking wives for one's sons, whereas this relationship may be and commonly is, predominantly traditional, functionally diffuse, and intimate. Also there may be radical differences between the ideal structures and the actual structures of the relationships. The ideal structures of relationships that are predominantly X in the first four categories are extremely difficult to live up to. One of the major developments in social science in the twentieth century came from the developments of the Harvard Business School studies of just such questions. The famous studies by Roethlisberger and Dickson [21] stressed the importance of the entry of particularistic considerations even into settings that were ideally speaking predominantly universalistic.

In Part I, above, one of the major distinctions between relatively modernized and relatively nonmodernized societies was the different emphases in different spheres that the members of those societies placed on the X and Y forms of the relationship aspects. Throughout this work, there is a great deal of hypothesizing that the role of changing emphases on different clusters of the relationship aspects is of the first importance in the transition from relatively nonmodernized to relatively modernized societies. Many problems of the transitions can be understood in these terms. The exploration of just how these relationship aspects tend to cluster and under what conditions these and other clusterings take place, has only recently begun in social science. The two major clustering effects illustrated in Table 2 may be rather

[21] F. J. Roethlisberger and William J. Dickson, *Management and the Worker*, Harvard University Press, Cambridge, 1941.

confidently relied upon. For any relationship in which there is a switch in emphasis from a Y to an X category in any of the first three aspects, one should expect a shift from an emphasis on a Y category to an X category in the other two as well. There would also be a switch toward X_4 if the emphasis was previously on Y_4. If such a switch does not take place, or if one finds an emphasis on an X in any one of the first three aspects and not in the other of the first four, he can draw one of two possible inferences: (1) the relationship concerned will prove to be highly unstable, or (2) it will be fitted into and buttressed by other relationships in a peculiar fashion.[22]

There is another general avenue for theory formation in these terms. Certain emphases on relationship aspects are characteristic not only of different societies but more importantly of their various subsystems. This has many implications for general theories of social change. One of the major reasons that the structures of relatively modernized societies are in fact a sort of universal social solvent of the social structures of other societies is that for certain structures likely to be imitated intentionally or unintentionally, the members of relatively modernized societies emphasize X qualities in the first four aspects whereas members of most of the relatively nonmodernized societies emphasize Y qualities in at least the first three aspects. Moreover, the disintegrative impact of the importation of such structures is never confined to the minimal departures from emphasis on the Y categories necessary to establish firmly an emphasis on the X categories for altogether new relationships. The disintegration may go quite far even though the emphases on the X category are not at all firmly established. For example, contrary to many sentimental views, the stability of the traditional Chinese family did not inhere in the fact that it was a type of family devoid of stressful implications for its members. The stresses and strains on family members were of considerable intensity at different periods of their lives, but there were many reasons why relatively few people attempted to run away. One of those reasons certainly had to do with the fact that they had little or no place to go. Ordinary employment was in a family context on, of course, predominantly particularistic grounds. If one sought employment elsewhere, there was also a heavy emphasis on particularistic

[22] In changes in relationship aspects generally it makes a great deal of difference not only whether there is a switch from an X emphasis to a Y emphasis [or vice versa] or from one type of X emphasis to another [e.g. from an emphasis on rationality about health to one about wealth], but also the sequence of changes is important especially when clustering effects are relevant.

criteria. One of the main criteria was a person's filial character. A runaway defied family structures and was for that reason alone not to be trusted. The possibility of viable alternative employment on relatively objective grounds, if one defied one's family head and fled, hardly existed. Family rebels were likely to be forced into the byways of the society in terms of which life, though rarely solitary, was likely to be nasty, brutish, and short. With the coming of the structures of relatively modernized societies, for the first time in two thousand years, the possibility of viable alternative employment on relatively objective grounds began to crop up. The threat of the disaffected to run away unless treated better became an effective possibility.[23] The modification of the authority of the family head was far-reaching. This was one of the reasons why family structures, relatively stable for two thousand years, had already begun to change radically long before the Communist regime, despite the fact that the actual development of modernization in terms of large numbers of modern factories and the like was modest.

I V
FINAL CAUTION

Let me recapitulate and warn about the use of this tool. First, it is a set of categories in terms of which any relationship in any society can be analyzed. Second, it is a tool in terms of which any two or more relationships or any particular relationship at different points in time can be compared with one another. Third, it is a tool that provides a systematic procedure for seeking out some of the major differences and similarities relevant to any particular problem. Fourth, even elementary applications of the tool for purposes of illustration reveal that certain of these relationship aspects tend to cluster with one another. Fifth, certain types of clusters are characteristic of some social systems and not of others. Sixth, the fact that certain of these clusters are characteristic of some subsystems and not of others has considerable relevance for theories of social change in general and for those of change from relatively nonmodernized societies to relatively modernized societies in particular. Given the state of the social sciences, none of these claims is modest, but I would claim more and maintain that it is quite unlikely that either the problems of modernization of relatively nonmodernized peoples or the prob-

[23] In addition, the Chinese family was the only general structure of social insurance for the aged. If the son ran away and was able to establish himself elsewhere, he not only won his own freedom, he also left his father and mother, if they survived into old age, without anyone to take care of them.

lems of stability of highly modernized peoples can be studied at all without some form of these concepts being explicit or implicit in the analysis.

There are, however, two major cautions which anyone should observe in using this tool of analysis. First, as I have tried to indicate nontechnically, it is by no means a perfectly developed tool of analysis. There are serious problems of a theoretical nature in its present state of development—let alone its further refinement and development. As a set of scientific concepts, it leaves a great deal to be desired. Second, insofar as it is at all well developed, critical acumen is still necessary. In the treatment above I have stressed again and again that combinations of say universalistic and particularistic elements are more likely than pure cases of either, even if pure cases are possible. It is, therefore, always legitimate for anyone to inquire "Why has this particular relationship been classified as 'predominantly,' or even 'more,' X_1 than Y_1?" In answering such a question one must specify not only what the criteria for such judgments are but also the set of actors alleged to make these emphases. For example, if I claim that the relationships between employer and employee in the United States today are predominantly universalistic, I may justify it by saying that, ideally speaking, from the point of view of virtually everyone in the society, the feeling is that no one should be barred from employment on the basis of race, creed, or color and that the only legitimate criteria are the possession of skills relevant to the job for which selection is being made. Any of those empirical allegations is subject to either confirmation or disproof.

In addition to the justification of the classification of a structure as predominantly X rather than predominantly Y there is also another kind of comparison. One may wish to maintain that the emphasis in the United States doctor-patient relationship is predominantly X_1, whereas that in the traditional Chinese doctor-patient relationship is predominantly Y_1. If challenged, one must be prepared not only to substantiate the classifications in the sense discussed immediately above, but also to say in what respect, if any, one justifies differences in the comparison as between the American and the Chinese case. If the emphasis is predominantly X_1 in one case and a predominantly Y_1 in the other, such justifications are relatively simple. If both are predominantly X_1 relationships, the statement that one of them is more predominantly X_1 than the other may be difficult to demonstrate. Nevertheless, it is at least in principle possible to make such statements. For example, with regard to the employer-employee relationship in ordinary manufacturing concerns in the United States by contrast with those in Japan there are far more elements of functional diffuseness in the Japanese than in the American case. In many areas of Japanese production the acceptance of a job and the acceptance for a job imply a lasting obligation of employee to employer and vice versa. This is a less prominent feature of the Japanese labor market than once was the case, but it is often still the case. In this sense the relationship between employer and employee is less precisely delimited in the Japanese than in the United States case.[24]

This tool of analysis shares a common tragic defect with all tools of analysis. No matter how infatuated one may become with it, it is never a substitute for either hard work or good ideas. Within any given frame of creativity and hard work, however, its use does at least facilitate the development of implications.

[24] Once again I must emphasize that the statements of fact in this illustration may not be tenable, but at least in theory they are susceptible of confirmation or disproof.

II · C H A P T E R · 2

ASPECTS OF ANY SOCIETY—INTRODUCTION

I

THE DISTINCTION BETWEEN ASPECTS OF SOCIAL SYSTEMS
AND SOCIAL SYSTEMS (OR ORGANIZATIONS).

A. DEFINITION OF TERMS

This distinction has been presented above [pp. 19–26] and need
not be elaborated in technical detail. Social systems are defined as
sets of structures [i.e., patterns] that define the character of
membership units in terms of which social actions take place,
that is, units such that any given individual may be classified as
included or excluded [or some combination of the two] as a
member of the unit. Terms used here such as society, nation,
business firm, government, family units, etc., all refer to such
systems or organizations. These units are referred to technically
as *concrete structures*. What are here referred to as *aspects* of
societies or of other social systems or of organizations are referred
to technically as *analytic structures*. They are defined as patterned ways of looking at action that are not even theoretically
capable of physical separation from other ways of viewing action.
If one seeks a physical analogy to this distinction, *concrete* structures or systems refer to units such as tables, chairs, etc.; the
analytic structures or aspects refer to such concepts as the mass,
the shape, the color, etc., of the tables, chairs, etc.

B. EXPLANATION OF THE DISTINCTION

The use of this distinction is above all justified by virtue of the
fact that it avoids certain confusions. No social analysis can
proceed far without some reference to membership units of some
sort, be they as simple as some two-person relationships or as
apparently complicated as large-scale societies. Sooner or later in
social analysis one always must make reference to membership
units in terms of which actions take place. More often than not it
is sooner rather than later since only a peculiarly sophisticated
discussant of social affairs can begin his discussion in so abstract
a fashion as to refer to no social systems whatsoever. One may be
as preoccupied with process or change as he likes, but he cannot
discuss it without referring to process or change in terms of

something. That something in the social field will be some sort of social system. It holds equally that, although one may break down any given social system into subsystems which make it up, sooner or later, either in making distinctions among subsystems or in talking about the subsystems so distinguished, one must refer to some of their different aspects. The two aspects most generally discussed in the realm of international affairs are the economic aspects and the political ones. If one defines the economic aspects as having to do with the allocation of goods and services and the political aspects as having to do with the allocation of power and responsibility, and most explicit definitions of these two terms come quite close to these definitions, these terms do not refer to acts *in toto* but rather to particular ways of looking at such acts. The exchange of a watch for fifty dollars is an empirical act. One may be interested in it primarily as an exchange of goods, but that way of looking at that particular act by no means exhausts its implications. For example, if one of the parties to the exchange is holding a gun and the other party hands over his watch in exchange for fifty dollars, the implications of the exchange are quite different, even though fifty dollars has been given for the watch in this case too. If the gun is used threateningly, one might infer that the watch is worth a great deal more to the original owner than fifty dollars and that he would not have made this exchange save under duress. There is no exchange of goods or services that takes place in the complete absence of some allocation of power and responsibility and vice versa. This example is given to demonstrate that what are generally referred to as economic and political factors are never different things and are always relevant to one another. These two aspects of behavior are by no means the only two with such high mutual relevance. For present purposes I shall discuss five of these aspects. The five discussed here form a special list of aspects of *any* society, selected for their relevance to all societies.[1]

Insofar as one must, for purposes of analysis, deal with two or more such aspects as these, one commits a serious scientific fallacy if he asserts or implies that he exhaust the implications of any actual behavior by analyzing it solely or primarily in terms of one of these aspects. Indeed one does so even if he is interested in only implications for one of these aspects. It is exactly this fallacy that has been referred to as the fallacy of reification or the fallacy

---

[1] The argument for that relevance, mentioned in the introduction of this work, is pursued in *The Structure of Society* at great length. It need not be discussed here where the concepts are used as tools and not as a central focus of interest.

of misplaced concreteness. It is involved in the confusion of economic man with man [i.e., actual man]. The statement that man is by no means identical with the assumptions of economic man is not to imply that the restrictive assumptions of the latter are of no relevance for scientific development. It no more implies that than the statement that "terrestrial objects do not generally fall in a perfect vacuum" implies that a vacuum assumption is of no relevance to terrestrial physics. Since it is impossible to analyze any social phenomena [or other phenomena for that matter] scientifically without reference to both sorts of distinction made here, it is especially important to make sure that the fallacy of reification is avoided.

I have already indicated [pp. 23–25] that one of the major reasons for confusion on the score is that most of the people who indulge in scientific social analysis are used to societies in terms of which the specialization of many organizations in terms of a single one of these aspects has been carried so far that relatively less violence is done to the analysis by referring to them as though they were purely economic or purely political systems. I refer to such organizations as predominantly economically oriented, predominantly politically oriented, etc., to avoid such confusions. Such specialized organizations are by no means totally absent in relatively nonmodernized societies, but they are relatively rare especially by contrast with the frequency with which they appear as subsystems of relatively modernized societies. If one falls into the habit of using such terms as economic, political, etc., solely with regard to such highly specialized organizations, he must face up to the fact that he will have to forego almost totally their application save in restricted spheres in relatively nonmodernized societies and abandon them even in some critically important spheres of relatively modernized societies. In the context of most of the relatively nonmodernized societies, for example, most of what in a loose way is characterized as economic behavior in relatively modernized societies would disappear into action in terms of family units. Only the most extreme economic determinists undertake to describe family systems as predominantly economically oriented throughout history. Though verbally clumsy, the distinction as presented here, enables one to handle any of the distinctions that one ordinarily wishes to refer to in relatively modernized societies, many distinctions which ordinarily are glossed over even in relatively modernized societies, and either specialized cases or general cases in relatively nonmodernized societies. It also enables one to avoid the fallacy of reification from this source.

The remainder of this chapter consists of a list of the five aspects used here with a definition of the concepts involved and a brief illustration of each category. Following that there is a brief addendum. The remaining five chapters of this part consist of a detailed discussion of each aspect with many of its subcategories. Since these categories refer to aspects that are necessary [or requisites] for any society, obviously much of the discussion in Part IV about common elements in all societies consists primarily of a restatement of some of the observations in the following five chapters.

I I
LIST OF ASPECTS

A. ROLE DIFFERENTIATION

Technically the term *role differentiation* refers to any socially distinguished position. For present purposes, suffice it to say that role differentiation is concerned with who does what when. There is no society, there never has been any society, and there never will be any society all of whose members always do the same thing all of the time. That is to say, there is no such thing as a society devoid of structures of role differentiation. The number of different positions distinguished by the members of different societies varies widely. For example, the members of some of the highly modernized societies distinguish several hundred thousand occupational roles alone, whereas the members of most of the relatively nonmodernized societies have never distinguished more than a fraction as many roles in the occupational sphere. In all societies which persist, there will be definite structures of role differentiation because: (1) there are differentiated activities which must be performed if the society is to persist; (2) these activities must be assigned to capable persons trained and motivated to carry them out; (3) not all individuals are capable at all times of performing all requisite activities, and some are even incapable of performing activities on which their own survival depends; and (4) even were all individuals equally capable at all times, it would not be possible for each and every individual to carry on simultaneously all the activities that must be done if the society is to persist.

The set of roles which characterize the society, however, does not define a membership unit in the sense that that term is used here. It merely defines an aspect of social action that is observable in all such action. It defines an aspect of any social unit, but it does not define all of the aspects of any unit. There are no units the members of which do exactly the same thing all the time.

Moreover, the question of who does what when never exhausts the various relevant aspects of an organization for any given level of social analysis. In addition to the fact that different members of a unit do different things, social systems for many purposes must also be viewed in terms of structures of the allocation of goods and services, power and responsibility, etc.

B. SOLIDARITY

The structures of *solidarity* in a society may be defined as those in terms of which relationships among the members of the society are allocated according to the *content, strength*, and *intensity* of the relationships. In a somewhat less precise but perhaps more communicable sense, solidarity is concerned with who sticks with whom under what circumstances. Solidarity, as the term is used here, will cover an aspect of behavior of infinite gradation between two poles. The negative pole will be taken to mean complete antagonism—war at sight as it were. The positive pole will be taken to mean complete agreement and complete and mutual affective accord. The only element of discontinuity of the variation between these poles is at the point of perfect neutrality. This point may be ruled out for most purposes since even in the most casual of relationships some affective element is likely to be involved. Precise neutrality is rare. The term *content* refers to the type of relationship that is supposed to exist and the members between or among whom it is to exist. The content of the solidarity aspect of the relationship involving mother and child consists of the fact that it is a mother and child who constitute the members of the relationship and of certain standards of behavior of the one toward the other. By the *strength* of the solidarity I mean the relative precedence or lack of precedence taken by this relationship over other relationships of this general sort and over other obligations and commitments in the larger social sphere in which the relationship may occur. Thus for example, in the mother-child illustration, if the mother gives the child an order and the father gives the child a different order, if, ideally speaking, the child is expected to obey the father rather than the mother, the strength of the child's solidarity with the father is greater, ideally speaking, than the strength of the child's solidarity with the mother, and so forth. The strength of a given relationship is not necessarily the same from the point of view of the various members of the relationship. For example, the relationship between a mother and child may be stronger from the child's point of view than from the mother's. A mother's order to a child may take precedence over anyone else's order to the child, whereas a request or order from the child to the mother may very well not take precedence over the orders of others to the mother.

The term *intensity* refers to the state of feeling, affect, or emotion involved in the relationship. Here again I would describe the range of variation in terms of the distinction set up in the previous chapter between avoidance and intimacy. The intensity of a relationship or the intensity aspects of a large-scale social system may vary not only with regard to the kind of emotion involved but also with regard to the degree of emotion involved. In connection with the general treatment of solidarity two things must be noted with regard to intensity. In the first place, the intensity of a solidarity, like the strength of a solidarity, is not necessarily identical from the points of view of all of the individuals involved in any given social system. Thus the intensity of the solidarity of a mother-child relationship, like its strength, may vary depending on whether it is described from the mother's or the child's point of view. There is a second kind of variation, as important if not more important. It is possible for the strength and intensity of solidarities to vary in opposite directions in some sense. It is possible to have relationships of relatively low strength but high intensity. For example a child's emotional involvement with his mother may be the most intense emotional involvement the child has. It is not necessarily his strongest solidarity. There are, presumably, limits on this type of variation. Insofar as the type and degree of emotion are relevant to the strength of the solidarity, neither the actual nor the ideal kind or degree of emotion can vary at random relative to the strength of the solidarity if the system is to remain stable.

In considering large-scale social systems one cannot confine the analysis of solidarity aspects to those among the members of given units, such as family units. One must also be concerned with those structures of solidarity which relate the members of one type of unit to members of another type of unit. For example, it is necessary to ferret out the solidarity structures in terms of which relations among the members of family units and governments or of family units and business firms, etc., are carried out. One may say of social systems in general and of societies in particular two things: (1) there must always be some regular structures of solidarities, and (2) in any society there are certain minimal relationships among which the solidarity aspects must be specifically defined and in some manner generally communicated to the members of the system(s) concerned.

C. ECONOMIC ALLOCATION

The structures of *economic allocation* have to do with the allocation of goods and/or services as iterated above. The members of any society must have food and usually shelter and clothing as well if there is to be any survival of members to continue the society. Since the minimum requirements in terms of goods and services are never found in nature as completely free goods, problems of the distribution of goods and/or services among alternative possibilities always arise in the social context, if only because of the possible effect of jealousies which can arise no matter how intrinsically homogeneous the articles or services concerned. It is theoretically possible that the members of one or more types of relatively rare social systems consume virtually negligible amounts of goods and services without producing them or others save in negligible quantities. It is not, however, conceivable that this be true for the members of all the subsystems of any given society or even of a substantial portion of them. Some members of any sort of large-scale organization might survive solely by virtue of economic exploitation of others, but this can never be true of any save a relatively small proportion of the members of any society unless the society concerned is on the road to extinction. It is, of course, not conceivable that the members of any social system produce without consuming, though it is by no means necessary that the members of any particular unit consume exactly the same goods and services they produce. The relevance of goods and/or services as means for other purposes is an obvious basis for the relevance of economic allocation for other structures in any given society or social system. They are not, however, in any deterministic sense more relevant to the other structures than the other structures are to them. In the discussion below, following a convention which has come to be relatively well accepted in such discussions, the structures of economic allocation will be subdivided into two categories: the structures of production, and the structures of consumption.

D. POLITICAL ALLOCATION

This aspect, along with the preceding one, constitute the two aspects most likely to be confused with concrete distinctions. *Political allocation*, for the purposes of this work, is defined as the distribution of power over and responsibility for the actions of the various members of the social systems concerned, involving on the one hand various forms of sanctions, of which sheer coercive force is the extreme in one direction, and on the other accountability to the members and in terms of the systems concerned, or to the members of other interdependent systems. The term *power* is defined as the ability to exercise authority and control over the actions of others. *Responsibility* is defined as the accountability of an individual(s) to another individual(s) for his own acts and/or the acts of others. The existence of well understood and not at all well understood structures of allocation of authority and responsibility are well known. What is sometimes not quite so well recognized is that such structures are quite well known to most unsophisticated and inexperienced individuals as well as to sophisticates. Virtually all small children, even before they know the words used here or the equivalents in their own language, are already used to react in terms of structures of authority and responsibility. The political aspect of behavior in terms of organizations is not at all confined to the governmental sphere but is identifiable in every social context. Furthermore, it is by no means confined to individuals who are classified as adults. One of the most interesting features of modern political science is the fact that quite recently a large number of its practitioners have become acutely aware of the fact that the manner in which children are taught to react to structures of power and responsibility is vital in understanding many of the features of their behavior in what are more commonly considered by the layman and other political scientists to be more strictly political contexts. If this healthy recognition is not killed off by fatuously faddistic applications, it will prove to be a basis of lasting improvement of the field of political analysis.[2]

Four other observations need be made about the structures of political allocation in any society, or any other social system for that matter: (1) whatever the intentions of the members of the system may be, the allocations of power and responsibility are never completely rational; (2) the allocations of power and responsibility are never completely random; (3) not only are they not random, but also if the system in which the structures are found is at all stable, the elements of capriciousness in the struc-

[2] It should perhaps be added parenthetically that while the reappearance of this in recent years in what is specifically referred to as the "behavioral approach to political science" is to be applauded, insight to this effect is by no means new. It would be difficult, for example, to make out a case to the effect that St. Thomas Aquinas was unaware of the relevance of these phenomena. Here again our modern tendency to think uncritically in terms of highly specialized predominantly politically oriented organizations has obscured these matters. The Greats of political theory in the classic sense were nowise unaware of the significance of "political culture" though the term was not minted by them.

tures of power and responsibility are quite limited, and (4) the structures of allocation of power and responsibility can never be analyzed solely in terms of applications of force or threatened applications of force, i.e., even in the most authoritarian systems there are elements of influence that are neither ideally nor actually functions of applications of physical coercion or threats of such.

It should go without saying that the structures of political allocation both within nations and as between nations is one of the major orthodox foci of attention for students of international affairs. Indeed, its only close rival is the focus of attention on the structures of economic allocation. Given the interests of students of international affairs and of persons responsible for making decisions in these matters, such preoccupations have certainly not been amiss. They have, however, sometimes been carried to such extremes of exclusion of consideration of other aspects and such narrow concern with orthodox distinctions within consideration of these aspects as to be self-defeating.

E. INTEGRATION AND EXPRESSION

The structures of *integration* and *expression* remain, in this work essentially a catchall category—i.e., a residual category, despite an attempt here and below to be more explicit about these concepts. The concept of *integration* used here denotes a positive adaptation of a given individual to action in terms of a particular social system. That is to say, these are the structures which help explain the adjustment of the individual member's behavior in such a way that the maintenance of the system [never mind whether the system is judged to be good or bad for present purposes] is enhanced and so that the satisfactions of the individual as a member of the system are enhanced. The matter is not a simple one. No structures are perfectly integrative, though certainly some may be malintegrative enough so that if they continue the system concerned will break up. Thus specific structures spoken of as integrative often [or always] have some malintegrative aspects. Therefore, one is well advised to use terms such as predominantly integrative. This, of course, involves difficulties of measurement, but at least in theory it is possible to conceive of making such measurements. For example, the disciplinary procedures used in terms of family units by adult members relative to the children have critical integrative aspects for those social systems. In these days of widespread amateur psychoanalysis, the general public of most relatively modernized societies is more than minimally aware of the fact that these disciplinary procedures are by no means solely integrative in their effects. The fact remains, however, that as far as we know no little child born into this world alive is inherently endowed with reflexes that will enable him either to gain satisfaction or to interrelate at all smoothly with others without the intervention of some sort of tutelage, however unselfconscious it may be.

The concept of *expression* used here denotes the type and limits of reaction, symbolic or otherwise, on the part of individuals or sets of individuals to the various phenomena with which they come into contact. The structures of expression in a society or other social system consists of those which define the type and limits of reaction, symbolic or otherwise, on the part of individuals or sets of individuals to the various phenomena with which they come into contact. One of the most notable types of these structures have to do with affective reactions, i.e., emotional displays, displays of feeling, etc. In all social contexts some types of emotional expression are considered appropriate and others inappropriate. The circumstances may vary, but the situation is never totally undefined from the point of view of the members of the system, although it may be sufficiently ill-defined to pose major problems for them. For example, under conditions in which Frenchmen would consider weeping by men quite appropriate, members of United States society would consider such behavior effeminate. The Japanese repress overt expressions of emotion in situations in which such repression would be considered most unnatural for members of United States society, and display relatively uninhibited emotions under conditions which would be considered just as inappropriate by those Americans. As already indicated above precisely neutral emotions or the complete absence of emotions is probably on the whole rare, but even if such cases do occur, they like the others discussed here are structured ideally and/or actually. Those structures, moreover, do not constitute a set of actions concretely separable from other actions. They constitute rather a special way of looking at any concrete actions.

III
ADDENDUM

The five categories of aspects discussed above constitute a set of aspects that can be considered requisites of any society. That is to say, structured aspects of these sorts must be present, if a society is to persist. That is not to say that, if they are present, the society cannot be destroyed in other ways. It is also not to say that these structures *must* be present because they are requisites. Such an argument would be teleological. Nothing, as far as we know scientifically, predetermines that the units of which they are requisites must persist. The foundation of the discussion of those respects in which all societies are alike is this set of requisite aspects of any society. No society lacks not only structured forms of these aspects but actually institutionalized forms of them, using the term institutionalized as defined above [p. 156]. In addition, the major lines of variation of societies discussed will be variations in terms of specific or specialized elaborations of these aspects rather than of totally different ones. Even the discussion of organizations, i.e., of units such as families, governments, business firms, the armed forces, churches, schools, etc., will not be on so general a level as discussion of these aspects will be. The organizations mentioned are all ones which in fact appear in one form or another in all of the societies that are likely to be of greatest interest to students of international affairs, but only in the case of family structure [and one other (see pp. 222 and 290–291)] can we mount an argument to the effect that it not only does, but must, appear in any and all societies. Initially the discussion of all of the aspects treated below will be in terms of an elaboration of elements of these aspects insofar as they can be expected in any and all societies whether relatively non-modernized or modernized.

I would push this line of attack still further, however. Although these aspects of any society are not necessarily aspects of every subsystem of a society, they are probably requisites for any subsystem of interest here. In this work I use as an assumption the hypothesis that all social systems other than societies are either subsystems of some particular society or else the result of interrelationships of the members of two or more societies. Therefore, if one analyzes any social system, regardless of whether he knows in fact whether it is a society or not, in terms of these aspects common to any and all societies, he will find out as a minimum in what respects that system is like or unlike a society. More importantly, he will discover in what respects the members of such systems must have minimal interrelations with the members of other systems if the system concerned is to continue.[3]

Even in the elementary and incomplete sense in which they are applied here, it is easy to illustrate the utility of such considerations. For example, one of the bases of role differentiation in any society is age, and within that there is always some category of old age. In any given society, if care of the aged takes place in

[3] This is of course one of the main reasons that this system of analysis was originally developed in the volume cited above [p. 20].

terms of the family unit and if changes tend to minimize the possibility of handling the care of the aged on this basis [e.g., if the family unit changes to one in which the grandparents do not ordinarily continue to live with their children], some set of the following consequences must be expected: (1) the members of some other existing subsystem in the society will have to take over such care, (2) some new subsystem in terms of which such care can be secured will have to be developed; (3) the aged must be systematically eliminated before they can become helpless; or (4) the members of that particular society are in for a considerable amount of unrest, and the society is in for further change. This happens to be a major problem for the members of every relatively nonmodernized society changing in the direction of modernization. It is particularly noteworthy because at the very time that the family unit is less likely to continue as the major form of old-age insurance, the survival of the aged increases. Or take another example, any organization whose members are adults and only adults is an organization which must have as one of its elements both structures of recruitment of personnel and structures of disposal of members when they cease to be adults and become aged. If such arrangements cannot be made with the members of other systems, either that organization must go out of existence, or it must change radically enough so that children are produced by the interrelationships of its own members acting in terms of its own structures, and corresponding adjustments for the aged would have to be made. These would constitute radical changes indeed.

ROLE DIFFERENTIATION

I
BASIC ROLE DIFFERENTIATION

Basic roles for any social system are defined as those positions in terms of which all members act at some time during their membership in the system. The set of basic role differentiations in a society consists of all of the roles which every individual acquires sometime or other during his life cycle, and examples are familiar to everyone. All the members of every society are differentiated on the basis of age, sex, generation, etc., and also in certain respects with regard to economic and political aspects, etc. There is a common core of these for all societies, no matter how much societies may vary from one another. Later in this chapter [pp. 200–219] some of the most striking cases of this common core of basic role differentiations are taken up briefly. Since this work focuses on large-scale social organizations of the type generally referred to as societies or nations, the illustrations of basic role differentiation taken up will be those common to any society. This common core is one of the major respects in which all societies everywhere at all times are alike. Correspondingly variations in the details of these differentiations, when considered on more descriptive levels, constitute one of the major sources of variations among different societies. Although the illustrations of basic role differentiations used here exist in any society, any other specific type of social system will also have a set of basic role differentiations which may be unlike those of any other social organization. No matter how great the variation of the sets of basic role differentiations may be, one generalization about them can always be made: to some extent the basic role differentiations of any social organization will contain some of those basic for any society. This is one of the reasons why, no matter how specific one's policy orientations may be, it is useful to have a study of the general social structure of the society or nation with which one must deal. Without the more general knowledge, neither the special organization nor the implications of dealing with the members of the special organization in a particular way can be understood.

I I

INTERMEDIATE ROLE DIFFERENTIATION

Intermediate roles are defined here as any positions in terms of which some, but not all, of the members of a given system act at some point in time during their membership in the organization. In other words, it is a residual category of basic role differentiation. It is all role differentiation specialized by categories of members. Illustrations are just as easy in this case as in the other. A substantial portion of all roles we generally think of are intermediate role differentiations. The role of typist, for example, is just such a specialized role differentiation as are the roles of doctors, legislators, or professors in our society. In some societies the role of student is an intermediate role differentiation. This is not true of all societies if one uses the term *student* in the ordinary layman's sense to refer not simply to anyone who studies anything but to one who is in fact studying as a pupil "in a school" as such. In this sense for a society like the United States, in which there is a structure of universal compulsory education at the elementary and secondary school level, every individual is expected to have student roles during the early years of his life cycle. Therefore this role differentiation is a basic role differentiation in the United States. The role of student in this sense was not a basic role differentiation in traditional Chinese society despite the fact that in that society the role of student was an important intermediate role.

There are some intermediate role differentiations in every society, but societies differ widely in the number and kinds of intermediate role differentiations distinguished. It is also true that all societies have some intermediate as well as some basic role differentiations in common. Perhaps the most obvious of these has to do with sex. Some sex role differentiation is basic in the sense that all members of every society are so differentiated at some point in their life cycles. Male roles as contrasted with female roles are, perhaps, the most universal and general of all intermediate roles in social history. There are, however, much less obvious and general cases of intermediate role differentiations that a large number of societies certainly do have in common. Some sort of governmental officials are examples of intermediate role differentiations present in a substantial proportion of all societies, if not in all societies. Unlike the basic role differentiations, the intermediate role differentiations of social organizations other than societies do not necessarily contain the intermediate role differentiations of the society in general except, of course, in the trivially tautological sense that if the role is found in that particular organization it is also found in the society. The intermediate role differentiation of a given subsystem of a society might be unique in that society. This distinction is worth illustrating. Many social systems other than societies are characterized by role differentiation on the basis of age just as are societies in general. Sex is another frequent such distinction. In the field of intermediate role differentiations members of a given organization may use many distinctions which are quite common elsewhere in the society or even common in a large number of societies. The role of employee, for example, is such a role. There may, however, be specialized role differentiations which characterize a particular organization and only that particular one. Now this is, of course, true in a trivial sense if one is referring to a completely descriptive level of analysis. On this level every organization is characterized by some unique intermediate role differentiation. Even on quite general levels of great practical significance, however, one of the important differentiating characteristics of highly specialized organizations is the number and kinds of intermediate role differentiations unique to such organizations.

Relatively modernized societies are always characterized by many more intermediate role differentiations for any given level of consideration of social phenomena than are relatively nonmodernized societies. Here again it is important to give explicit meaning to the phrase many more. I cannot give it a precise meaning here, but like other distinctions of degree used in this work the relevant differences are usually so gross that the distinction is, relatively speaking, clear enough. For example, the members of almost all societies of any considerable scale, whether they be relatively modernized or not, distinguish some specialized occupational roles. These are examples of intermediate role differentiation. The difference between even a sophisticated relatively nonmodernized society such as that of traditional China and a highly modernized society such as the United States in this respect, without going into any greater descriptive detail in the one case than the other, is probably the difference between several hundred [or some few thousand] specialized occupational roles and several hundred thousand specialized occupational roles. The less highly modernized the society compared with traditional Chinese society, the less extreme is the comparison, of course.

It is also important to consider the great variation among relatively nonmodernized societies in these respects. Some relatively nonmodernized societies have a considerable number of intermediate role differentiations. The myriad special distinctions of roles in the Hindu caste taxonomy are an excellent example of how elaborate such detail can get in a relatively nonmodernized society. Depending on the taxonomy used, without going into too much descriptive detail, one may make at least several hundred distinctions on this basis alone in Hindu society. The extent to which the traditional Chinese carried role differentiation on the basis of farming was probably on the whole not great, but the extent to which they carried it on the basis of craftsmanship was almost certainly as great as the level of variation approached by the members of any relatively nonmodernized society. Moreover, in traditional Chinese society the differentiation of highly special-ized roles in the general field of learning was also elaborate. There were not only the publicly differentiated roles of scholarship; there was an even vaster proliferation of differentiated private scholars.

In considering the problems of modernization, the extent of intermediate role differentiations in a given society is of consider-able significance. If the proliferation of such role differentiations is relatively slight, it is trivial logically, but not practically, to observe that any element of the general social structure which depends for its stability on the restriction of such role differentia-tion will be threatened by the changes which will follow increases in modernization. If the proliferation is carried quite far, it does not necessarily follow, however, that there will be less disturb-ance. The extent of disturbance will depend on the appropri-ateness of the range of intermediate role differentiation for con-version to relatively modernized forms of role differentiation just as much as it depends on the fact of the existing proliferation itself.

I I I
ACHIEVED AND ASCRIBED ROLES

The distinction between achieved and ascribed roles is now one of ancient tradition as the field of social analysis goes. This distinc-tion is close to, if not identical with, the distinction already used in another context under the heading of universalism and partic-ularism. I use it in this form here simply because the reader will meet it in this form in many other contexts, and it costs little additional effort to mention these terms here.[1] *Achieved roles* refer to those positions that an individual has acquired on the

[1] Purists about consistency should simply substitute predominantly universalistic for achieved and predominantly particularistic for ascribed.

basis of his qualifications or accomplishments relevant to the actions carried out in terms of the position. *Ascribed roles* refer to those positions that an individual receives on the basis of qualifications that are not necessarily directly germane to the action in terms of the roles and that are attributed to him by virtue of his social classification in other roles. The role of Nobel Prize winner probably is as close to an approximation of a purely achieved role as one can come; the role of successor to the throne of England is an ascribed role. Kinship roles are always in some sense ascribed roles, though the basis of ascription is often germane to performance in terms of kinship roles. Roles attained through competitions and the like always contain some elements of achievement. There has never been a society without some examples of both achieved and ascribed roles, both ideally and actually, but the difference in emphasis placed on achieved as opposed to ascribed roles varies widely not only from one subsystem of a given society to another but from one type of society to another. The members of some societies, as one would expect from the discussion of the distinction between universalistic and particularistic membership criteria, emphasize achieved roles little, though probably never as little as some social-science accounts might lead one to infer. Highly sedentary societies with relatively little differentiation of skills and social structures overwhelmingly oriented to family considerations are probably ones whose members most minimize the emphasis on achieved roles. In even the simplest societies, however, some roles focusing on craftsmanship or presumed virtuosity in magic, hunting, fighting, or the like are frequently achieved roles.

Those societies whose members emphasize achieved roles are always ones whose members place a major emphasis on ascribed roles as well. As a minimum there is always an important emphasis on kinship considerations in some contexts, and roles in kinship structures are on the whole ascribed roles. Relatively modernized societies are characterized by members who place much greater emphasis on achieved roles than do the members of relatively nonmodernized societies for any given level of detail on which the societies can be compared.

Since no society totally lacks ascribed roles ideally and/or actually, and since the members always consider some ascribed roles important, there is no society whose members do not to some degree understand an emphasis by themselves or others on ascription no matter how much the members of that society may emphasize achieved roles. To use kinship as our major example again, there is no society whose members do not understand or are completely unaware of the practice of nepotism, regardless of whether it is approved or not. Indeed, one of the problems posed by considering nepotism an evil in certain contexts inheres in the fact that there are always contexts in that society in which nepotism is not only respected but preferred by the members. There are always contexts in the most highly modernized societies in which one is expected to put some of his relatives first. Thus, insofar as there are any contexts in which one is not expected to place any of his relatives first, those contexts require careful differentiation from the others.[2]

[2] Even in societies in terms of which other ascribed allegiances take precedence over family allegiance, the problem of the separation of action in terms of those roles from action in which family considerations are supposed to take precedence is always a special problem. Although there are no societies totally lacking in critically important ascribed roles, there are societies in terms of which an emphasis on achievement is relatively little understood or appreciated by the members. It is necessary to be careful how one states and understands this. There is no society whose members are unable to distinguish differences in achievement. There is no society whose members fail completely to distinguish between good and bad workmanship, for example. It may well be, however, that there are societies whose members place comparatively slight emphasis on different levels of achievement. As modernization increases in a given context, the preexisting emphasis on the ascription of roles or on particularism in selection, as indicated above, is always a source of problems because, in the process, it always becomes necessary to increase the emphasis on achievement or on predominantly universalistic selection of persons for roles. Furthermore, even after high levels of modernization are achieved there always remains the possibility of conflicts of interest of every member of such societies because of potential conflicts in the interdependencies of various social contexts in some of which he has ascribed roles and in others of which he has achieved roles.

With the continued increase of modernization in the context of societies already highly modernized, a rather interesting and new extreme question is raised for the social future. Are human beings able to adapt easily to great emphases on achievement? It is not a simple question. With relatively rare examples such as the nationalistic spirit of the Japanese, we in general regard the spirit of nationalism as a concomitant of relatively modernized societies. A nationalistic ethic is a predominantly particularistic one. Membership in a particular nation is usually a function of ascribed rather than achieved roles, though one may achieve citizenship in a nation to which one did not previously belong. Of all of the popular bases for ascription of roles, national identity is the largest and the least likely to interfere in the ordinary arena of emphasis on achieved roles. Thus in areas in which predominantly universalistic selection is emphasized, ordinarily one is not faced with a choice from among individuals belonging to two or more nations. Until quite recently at least in most of the nations in the world an employer who wished to employ only members of his own nation usually had only such members to select from in the first place. With modern communications what they are, the sense of identification which seems to inhere in heavy emphasis on ascribed, nationalistic roles may raise increasing problems for efficient and well-organized operation of an increasing number of activities.

I V
FOCI OF ROLE DIFFERENTIATION:
CONCENTRATED OR DIVERSIFIED

All societies have a common set of foci of roles plus variations around those foci. This again is but another exemplification of the fact that there are respects in which all societies are alike as well as of the fact that there are lines of variation along which societies differ at more specific levels. For most of history and before, however, all role differentiation has taken place in terms of a relatively small number of social systems. Again, kinship units in general and families in particular are the best examples of this. For most of the members of the vast majority of all societies to date, the family has been the overwhelming focus of role differentiation most of the time. Most societies have been relatively nonmodernized ones, and for all of them the family unit has been the overwhelming focus of role differentiation for most of the members most of the time. Although roles outside the family context may have taken precedence over family roles, most of the roles have actually been family roles. As already indicated above, even in the most highly modernized contexts the family continues to be a focus of a considerable amount of role differentiation.

In addition to the role differentiation on the basis of families, all societies are characterized by some differentiation on a non-family basis. Nonfamily role differentiation may be concentrated in a small number of alternative organizations. When the number of social systems in terms of which the ordinary individual acts is relatively small, the foci of role differentiation may be thought of as *concentrated foci*. For most of the members of most of the societies in world history the foci have been concentrated in this sense. When, however, a relatively large amount of the role differentiation in terms of which the ordinary individual acts falls not only outside the family context but also is in terms of a relatively varied and numerous set of alternative social systems, the foci may be termed *diversified foci*. The case par excellence of this is, of course, the relatively modernized society. The more highly modernized the society, the more diversified the foci of role differentiation by contrast with all other societies.

Corollarially, for the members of these societies there are always special problems of the separation of roles from one to another context. Whenever an individual has roles in two or more organizations the possibility of role conflicts arises. Those societies characterized by concentrated foci of role differentiation are also characterized by a well-understood hierarchy of precedences among the different roles. These characteristics make it relatively easy for the members of such societies to minimize the problems of role conflicts, though these problems are by no means eliminated. There is no society for which the conflict of the actions called for in terms of different roles is not a serious theme of such drama as its members create. The Japanese, for example, in days gone by not only held that death was lighter than a feather whilst obligation was heavier than a mountain, but the dramatic theme of themes for the Japanese was that of conflict between two or more loyalties.

When the proliferation of social systems in terms of which the average individual has roles increases radically, the problems of these adjustments also increase radically. One of the marked characteristics of relatively modernized societies is that so many of the relationships into which one enters emphasize either avoidant emotions or, insofar as possible, an approach to neutral ones. The rapid adjustment of different expressions of intimacy is difficult for anyone. When the foci of role differentiation become highly diversified, one of the major forms of diversification is in terms of the kind of specialization previously discussed [see pp. 38–46 and 93–115]—specifically in terms of predominantly economically oriented as opposed to predominantly politically oriented roles. This particular distinction of roles always poses additional special problems of adjustment because of the considerable relevance of allocations of goods and services for allocations of power and responsibility and vice versa.

V
THE MUTUAL REINFORCEMENT OF ROLES

The various bases on which roles are as a minimum differentiated in every society will be sketched in brief detail below. There are not only a large number of different bases on which roles are in fact differentiated by the members of every society, but in addition to those differentiations that are, as it were, requisites of any and all societies, the number of different bases on which roles may be differentiated in any specific society or subsystem of any given society is, of course, enormously greater, if not in principle infinite. This variation raises the problem of the possibility of the implications of one role differentiation, or one set of them, contradicting the implications of another. If a given social unit is to be stable, as a minimum the role differentiations must be such that in no radical sense do they contradict one another in their implications. In all societies, if there is stability, the various sets

of role differentiation in fact reinforce one another, although
there may be many cases of contradiction among the implications
of role differentiations. For example, if one looks at a family role
such as that of the family head and one looks at various bases of
role differentiation in terms of which precedence within the family context is usually reckoned [e.g., such bases as age, sex,
generation, etc.], without going into any questions of origin, ordinarily in stable families the family head is in fact the oldest
member of the family, a representative of the oldest generation,
male, etc.—assuming that this is a society for which there is
precedence on the basis of relative age, of representing the oldest
generation, and of being male. In such situations the expected
reinforcement may get out of kilter in individual cases. For example, the family head may be younger than another family
member whilst representing an older generation, or a woman of
older generation may take over command. It is the possibility of
such conflicts which sometimes enables us to distinguish which
of these various bases of precedence matter most to the members
of the society concerned.[3]

The mutual reinforcement of the various different forms of
role differentiation is considerably easier to illustrate in terms of
societies in which kinship is *the* major focus of orientation. The
reason for this is not obscure. Since kinship is always *a* major
focus of orientation for the members of every society, there is
always a potential problem, if there are any role differentiations
which lie outside the kinship structure, of the implications of
those role differentiations for the ones carried out in terms of
kinship. If the kinship focus is expected to take precedence, or in

[3] In traditional China, for example, precedence within the family context rested on generation, age, and sex in that order. Ordinarily the family
head was the eldest male of the oldest generation represented. If the
family head died and had a brother younger than the family head's son,
that brother took over as family head, ideally speaking. Generational considerations were so important that they even enabled women to take over
effective headship, though ideally speaking this was considered improper.
Nevertheless, the Chinese matriarch, almost always the widowed wife of
the family head, was a famous figure in traditional Chinese life and literature. Despite the fact that she was supposed to bow to her sons in her
widowed state, their maleness rarely triumphed over the filial piety
owed a person of the older generation if she chose to be strong-willed. Had
life expectancy been what it is, given modern medical technology, this
possible conflict of precedence in terms of role differentiation in the
family might have changed the structure of Chinese society radically. As
it was, relatively few women survived long enough to threaten male
claims to the family headship [see Marion J. Levy, Jr., *The Family
Revolution in Modern China*, Harvard University Press, Cambridge, 1949
(Reprinted by Octagon Books Inc., N.Y., 1963), pp. 129–132 and
140–41].

specific cases to yield way to loyalties to members of other units, it is relatively easy to visualize sets of role differentiation which reinforce one another. If, on the other hand, kinship considerations are not expected to take precedence, or do not have a specific relationship to the activities in terms of other units, two sets of problems inhere. First, there are the problems occasioned by the implications of the role differentiation in terms of other units for the stability of the kinship units. The second set consist of the reverse of the first. What are the implications of role differentiation in terms of the kinship units for the role differentiations carried out in terms of the other units? In the former case, for example, if a son can get a job away from the supervision of family members and without needing any family influence to get the job, the father's control over the boy is likely to be radically diminished. In the latter case, if the son pays close attention to his father, and if his father wishes him to exploit his nonfamily connected job for the benefit of family members, he is likely to do so at the expense of the stability of the organization in terms of which he holds his job.

The greater the degree of diversification of foci of role differentiation, the greater must be the attention paid to insulating one set of roles from another. This is one of the respects in which the relatively modernized societies are peculiar and exotic in terms of general social history. For some years social scientists have been extremely aware of the extent to which predominantly particularistic considerations actually become quite important in what are, ideally speaking, the most predominantly universalistically oriented settings.[4] Given the general nature of social history before the development of relatively modernized societies, the surprising thing is not how much this is the case, but how little it is the case. The vast majority of all societies have had relatively concentrated foci of role differentiation. Before relatively modernized societies developed, the systems in which diversified foci of role differentiation existed were, to a great extent, restricted to such systems as cities and towns. The persons involved in such systems on a day-to-day basis ordinarily constituted only a small fraction of the total membership of the societies concerned. In the relatively modernized societies almost exactly the reverse obtains. The members of such societies whose role differentiations are highly concentrated—except for infants and small children—constitute a small minority of the total membership. They also constitute a minority that diminishes every day.

[4] The work of Roethlisberger and Dickson in this connection has already been mentioned above [see p. 170].

We are accustomed to thinking of actors in the theatrical sense as individuals with specially developed skills in switching with the greatest of ease from behavior appropriate to one set of roles to that appropriate to a radically different set of roles. In this sense the great emphasis of modern social scientists on the term actor in their analyses is especially apposite since, in fact, most of the social scientists concerned deal largely with the phenomena of relatively modernized societies. In this special sense these are actors' societies. During the course of an ordinary day the average actor in such societies not only plays several different roles in terms of a given organization. That is not unusual in social history, perhaps, though in relatively modernized contexts this too is carried to great extremes. He also plays an enormous number of different roles in terms of an enormous number of different organizations, and hardly gives thought to his passage from one to another. The daily behavior of such actors constitutes quite a performance. Probably no one fully understands how and why men can act in terms of such systems with as little friction from such sources as they in fact do. The ability to operate effectively in such a complex situation is certainly related to the emphasis in such spheres on rationality, universalism, functional specificity, and avoidance. Relationships in terms of which facile switches from role to role are made with the unconscious ease of monkeys swinging through the trees require such emphases.

In this whole problem of role reinforcement, family life is of special importance. The family is a peculiar social organization in all societies in world history. First, it is unique in that we are relatively sure some form always exists and always has existed in every society. There is another peculiarity about it. Later in this chapter role differentiation on the basis of age will be discussed and divided into two parts: (1) role differentiation on the basis of absolute age and (2) role differentiation on the basis of relative age. Absolute age role differentiation is concerned with distinctions like infancy, childhood, adulthood, old age, etc. All societies are characterized by such distinctions, and the average individual throughout all of his absolute age distinctions always has a role as a family member. The traditional Chinese had a way of putting this with regard to women. They said that as a daughter she was subordinate to her father, as the wife to her husband, and as a widow to her son. This covered her life cycle as far as subordination was concerned. Males and females of all societies ordinarily belong to some kinship unit all their lives. This means that for every individual member of every society there is a major problem of role reinforcement within the family context and between the family and any other organizational context. In addition, all nonfamily organizations may be put in one of two categories. First, there are those whose members are supposed to consider family matters in determining their behavior in terms of the organization. Action in terms of family role differentiation is expected to determine many of the things which go on in terms of the role differentiations of such organizations. If the role differentiations of the family units do not reinforce one another, the resulting instability has implications for the other organizations as well as for the families. Second, there are organizations for whose members, ideally speaking, family considerations are not supposed to matter in determining their behavior in terms of the organizations. Such organizations are not unknown in relatively nonmodernized societies, and they are extremely common in relatively modernized societies. Although, ideally speaking, the structures of role differentiation in the family are supposed to be irrelevant to action in terms of these organizations, actually such is not the case. Each of us who has lived in a relatively modernized social context knows perfectly well that although ideally speaking family matters are not supposed to affect our behavior at work, they do in fact affect it and importantly, whether we or anyone else likes it or not. Thus ideally and/or actually the problems of role reinforcement within the family are reflected in all other organizations in any society.

Highly diversified foci of role differentiation pose significant problems of role reinforcement quite apart from the family considerations mentioned above. For example, it is not only necessary that role differentiation problems in the family context impair operations in terms of these systems as little as possible; it is also important that the structures of role differentiation within these organizations reinforce one another. In such organizations something like a chain of command is always important. The limits within which the authority of the director of such an enterprise can be undermined are restricted. In an extreme form military organizations, in terms of which the problems of authority are always a critical focus of concern, illustrate this. Among military personnel, especially in the context of a society whose members are as antimilitaristic as members of United States society, there is no more often repeated refrain than the observation that one is "saluting the uniform, not the man." There could hardly be a pithier way of putting the point that it is the office which any subordinate of that office must respect regardless of the personal qualifications of the incumbent of it. Whole dramas and operas such as the *Caine Mutiny,* and *Billy Budd* have been written about the theme of the inviolable importance of the office even in the face of the most obviously justifiable challenges on the basis of excesses committed by the incumbent thereof. A considerable portion of the talk about morale problems in various organizational contexts is to be understood in terms of maintaining reliable reinforcement of the role differentiation characteristic of such systems. Few such organizations reach any considerable scale without some differentiation of what might be called line and staff personnel. The line personnel are especially endowed with responsibility, and the staff personnel are in some sense expected to be especially competent intellectually, perhaps more so than the line personnel themselves. Still the line personnel are supposed to command the staff personnel. All sorts of problems arise if staff personnel take over line functions. In general, however, these problems do arise in any social context in which mental ability is supposed to be one of the prime qualifications for positions of authority. The fact that in relatively modernized social contexts a special aura of benign [sometimes malignant] impracticality is associated with all personnel in the society whose talents and interests are highly specialized along intellectual lines is not independent of the problems of mutual reinforcement role differentiations.

The extent of mutual role reinforcement is always relevant to the problems of control in terms of any society or any social system. One of the best examples of this is one of the phenomena most closely associated with the explosively disintegrative effects of the structures of modernization when they are introduced into a relatively nonmodernized social context. As indicated above in other connections, the members of most of the relatively nonmodernized societies ordinarily learn most of their roles from an adult in some authority over them within their own family context. The older members of the family are not only the individuals from whom affection, food, shelter, clothing, etc., flow; they are also the usual source of all relevant learning and training. In the context of relatively modernized societies the grousing of parents about the lack of respect of the young for the old and especially of the younger members of the family for the elder members of the family is always a rising crescendo. With the age of schooling in the specialized sense beginning as early as the age of two or three, there is hardly a period of conscious memory in the life of a relatively modernized child that is not increasingly associated with outside experts as well as those who belong to his own family. For those schools to work, it is absolutely important that the child respect his teachers, but in some respects what parents or other older family members tell the child is bound in fact to conflict or is bound to be conceived by the child to conflict with what teachers tell him. In any case in one sphere after another having to do with knowledge and skills the child becomes at least as dependent on people outside the family membership as on family members. One of the grimmest reflections of this sort of thing is the standard joke associated with the United States college graduate.[5]

When elements of modernization are introduced into a relatively nonmodernized setting, one of the first changes is that a large number of the individuals are trained by persons outside of their family setting. Frequently they are not only nonfamily members but probably quite young individuals to boot. At one and the same time, the feeling of dependency on and respect for family members is to some extent challenged; so is respect for those older than one, and so forth. Furthermore under these circumstances one can challenge family control and still find an alternative place to work, at the same time that one also sees that it is not necessarily more respected members of the family from whom all blessings flow. The introduction of structures of modernization provide alternative foci for respect as well as alternative bases for employment. Members of relatively modernized societies take it so much for granted that this sort of training will take place on a nonfamily basis that it almost never occurs to them that this particular introduction into a relatively nonmodernized social context is from many points of view far more dramatic in its implications than the gigantic dam with which such training may be associated or the new factory whose strange machines are such an obvious symbol of the transition. As has already been indicated above and will be taken up again below, when one adds to this that, in general, the structures of control of such societies rest importantly on family structures of control, the general implications of the problems of role reinforcement for general problems of control in such societies come to sharp focus.

V I
TYPES OF ROLE DIFFERENTIATION

A. ROLE DIFFERENTIATION ON THE BASIS OF AGE

In every society there are always structures of role differentiation on the basis of age. These structures are always oriented to at

---

[5] This is the story of the young man who on his graduation from college, after seeing relatively little of his father during the four-year period, remarks to someone that it is astonishing how much his father has learned during that four-year period.

least two different considerations with regard to age. First, there are always structures of role differentiation on the basis of what may be referred to as *absolute age*. Second, there are always role differentiations on the basis of what may be referred to as *relative age*. Absolute age classifications refer to distinctions such that an individual is classified in one and only one particular category at any given point in time. Absolute age distinctions of this sort are known as the categories of infancy, childhood, adulthood, etc. They are not absolute age classifications in the sense that everyone always begins his participation in one of these categories at the same point of elapsed time in his life cycle. The point may differ from individual to individual, but they are absolutely classified in the sense of being classified in one and only one of these categories at a given point in time. For purposes of praise or derogation one may refer to him as participating in two or more at a given point in time. For example, one may say that he is a child who acts like an adult or that he is an adult who acts like a child, but clearly in either case one is not in fact classifying him as being in more than one category at a given point but rather as being a person who has characteristics appropriate to another absolute age distinction than the one to which he properly belongs.

As a minimum, absolute age distinctions in every society cover at least four differentiations: (1) infancy, (2) childhood, (3) adulthood, and (4) old age. In every case with which I am familiar more than these four are in fact distinguished, but these four periods of development are always covered in some fashion by such distinctions. In the modern United States as a minimum we distinguish the following: (1) infancy, (2) young childhood, (3) older childhood, (4) adolescence, (5) young adulthood, (6) middle-aged adulthood, and (7) old age. Another social analyst might wish to distinguish the categories differently, but all would distinguish some set of categories which would cover the four minimal ones for any society. The specific distinction of adolescence, while not unheard of in other societies, is always present in the context of relatively modernized societies. In societies like that of traditional China such a distinction was made with regard to the gentry but not with regard to others. Members of all societies have relatively specific expectations and reactions to the performances of individuals in terms of these different categories. Although there may be many variations in these classifications on the basis of membership in different subsystems of the society, absolute age categories covering the life history of the ordinary individual are parts of the basic role differentiation of every known society.

Relative age role differentiation is role differentiation on the basis of age oriented to some consideration of lapse of time from a given starting point. As a minimum in all societies to some extent this is reckoned in terms of elapsed time since birth or some point of origin taken as birth by the members of that particular society, not necessarily the exact moment of physiological birth. Some differentiation of roles on the basis of relative age is characteristic of all types of families so far reported in the world. In some cases role differentiation on the basis of relative age is carried quite far. In traditional China, for example, precedence among sons was reckoned on the basis of age, and many societies in world history have structures of primogeniture about property as well as titles. In such social contexts relative age is a matter of the greatest importance in determining one's future.[6]

Relative age reckoned from birth is by no means the only form of role differentiation on the basis of relative age. Role differentiation on the basis of elapsed time spent in terms of a given organization is another important form, and this is, of course, exactly what is ordinarily referred to by the term *seniority* in both relatively nonmodernized and relatively modernized social contexts. The members of some societies consider it to be like any other predominantly particularistic criterion, they consider seniority good in and of itself. In terms of relatively modernized societies seniority is usually justified on the basis of a predominantly universalistic or a pseudouniversalistic argument. Thus one bases arguments in favor of seniority on "greater experience," "greater contribution to the joint effort," etc., in such contexts. In fact, of course, seniority in relatively modernized contexts frequently becomes a highly particularistic consideration and may interfere quite seriously with standards of performance, etc. This is especially true in spheres of rapidly changing technology.

In some societies role differentiations on the basis of age cut through practically all other social distinctions. This is especially likely to be true to the extent that the members of the society are

[6] I shall return to his matter [pp. 400–403] of patterns of primogeniture. Such societies must always be characterized by a *cadet class*. These cadets consist, of course, of the younger sons. In the context of such societies, the younger sons as well as the eldest son of a given family must be prepared to succeed to the family headship or whatever else is determined on the basis of primogeniture should the eldest son fail to survive long enough to succeed. Not all of the individuals so educated can in fact succeed to positions for which they have been prepared. Thus, there is a built-in set of members prepared for a set of roles which in fact many of them cannot live up to. In addition these are likely to be a highly articulate and important set of individuals, and they are always a source of unrest in the social contexts concerned.

overwhelmingly family oriented. Such societies are relatively nonmodernized. Even in terms of relatively modernized societies or other societies whose members do not expect age considerations to cut uniformly across other social distinctions, they remain important. For example, one does not ordinarily think of role differentiation on the basis of age in modern armed-force systems, but there are at least three major considerations based on age characteristic of such systems. First, armies are supposed to involve only adults. An individual is not permitted to become a member of the armed forces before he reaches maturity in some sense, and when old age is reached the individuals concerned are expected to retire. Second, for the army system, seniority is certainly an important factor. Length of membership is relevant to pay and other considerations. Third, even in reckoning such factors as promotion and the like, certain qualities presumably must be demonstrated before a given age is reached. Thus there is a sort of absolute age distinction with regard to eligibility for promotion. After a certain amount of time as a captain, if one has reached a certain age, he must be promoted or retire from the service.

Societies vary widely in the emphasis placed by members on relative age. Sometimes it is roughly uniform in all spheres of social action throughout the entire life span of the individual. In deciding on his behavior toward others with whom he comes in contact one of the major considerations is whether they are relatively older than he both in lapsed time since their birth and in membership in the particular organization in terms of which they are interacting. There are, however, other societies for whose members relative age role differentiations are important at one period of an individual's life, and much less important at other periods. For example, in terms of modern United States society, relative age is a matter of great importance in early years, but particularly as a person comes into full possession of his faculties, as those are generally reckoned, considerations of relative age receive, ideally speaking [and to a high degree actually speaking as well], minimal emphasis. In the latter part of life the emphasis on relative age increases. The period of minimal emphasis coincides, of course, with that period of the individual's life during which there is a maximum emphasis on predominantly universalistic criteria in an enormous number of the contexts in which individuals interact with one another. Even when seniority considerations are present in those spheres of action, the emphasis on relative age is less than the emphasis on relative age in the family context. Furthermore, seniority is rarely defended forthrightly as good in and of itself. Those who favor it tend to defend it as a practice on predominantly universalistic grounds, however transparently irrelevant those grounds may in fact be. The family context remains even in this society the one sphere in which predominantly particularistic criteria do not excite defensive reactions generally.[7]

The major variations of emphasis on absolute and relative age cut heavily along lines of the distinction between relatively modernized and relatively nonmodernized societies, as do so many others in this work. In this particular case they are in addition closely connected to the relevance of family structure for the total social structure. Both of these considerations are even more prominent in the next basis of role differentiation found in all societies.

B. ROLE DIFFERENTIATION ON THE BASIS OF GENERATION

The term *generation* is generally used in the sense in which I have used the term *absolute age* above. Thus in ordinary language, one frequently speaks of teachers and students as belonging to different generations. What one means is that the teacher and the student ordinarily belong to different absolute age classifications and that the teacher is likely to be of the same absolute age classification as the student's parents or grandparents. The term *generation* came to be used in this sense because of the implications of its use in terms of kinship structure. It is to its original and precise meaning that I intend to return the use of the term here. Accurate reckoning of similarities or differences in generation will be a function of kinship reckoning throughout this work. Generational similarities or differences will be determined solely in terms of the relationship of the two or more individuals concerned to some one or more common

---

[7] Even this statement requires some qualification. Family structures in United States society probably go further than any in world history in the extent to which elements of universalistic emphasis intrude. The relevance of this as a special sort of family training in a society whose members emphasize predominantly universalistic criteria so highly outside the family context is obvious enough. Relative age distinctions in particular tend to be justified on increasingly universalistic grounds even within the family context. Fathers, for example, are less defensive if accused of preferring sons to daughters [or vice versa] than of preferring the eldest [or the youngest] to the other children. Insofar as privileges within the family context are correlated to relative age distinctions, those in turn tend to be justified on predominantly universalistic grounds ["Your older brother can cross the street by himself *because he is better able to look out for the cars!*"], etc. Although members of United States families may seem increasingly to emphasize differentiated aspects rather than the "whole man" [or child], even for us the home remains the "castle of the me" as in all known societies.

ancestor(s). Thus father and son belong to different generations; brothers belong to the same generation, etc.[8]

Role differentiation on this very specific basis is characteristic of all societies. In a quite obvious sense, role differentiation on the basis of generation is confined to family and kinship circles. In terms of no society do the children do exactly what their parents do. The representatives of different generations do not do the same things and are not expected to do the same things at the same time in terms of kinship and family structures.[9] Depending on the position of family structure in the general social structure, the importance of role differentiation on the basis of generation will vary enormously from one society to another. The more important the position of the family in the general social structure, of course, the greater is the relevance of role differentiation on the basis of generation to the general social structure of the society concerned. More specifically, the greater the relevance of family considerations, ideally and/or actually, for action in terms of any other social system in the society, the greater are the implications of role differentiation on the basis of generation for action in terms of that other subsystem.

Matters of care and attention to children are always importantly differentiated on the basis of generation. Even in those societies in terms of which older siblings participate prominently in the care of their younger siblings, the role of older siblings in child care is quite different in kind from the role of family mem-

[8] Depending on the permissiveness of the structures of kinship endogamy or exogamy, generational comparisons of this sort can become quite complex. For example, in terms of United States society it is not inconceivable that the great-grandparent of one individual be a grandparent of another whilst another relative be a grandparent of each. Under these circumstances—especially given the more or less equal emphasis on all lines of descent characteristic of the members of American society, the individuals concerned are in some respects representative of the same and in others of different generations. Granted second marriages and adoptions, it is even possible for an individual to become his "own grandpa" as one popular record once had it, though this is not biologically feasible [hear: "I Am My Own Grandpa," Dwight Latham-Moe Jaffe, Lonzo and Oscar with the Winston County Pea Pickers, R.C.A. Victor 20–2563A].

[9] Representatives of one generation are, however, always expected in general to repeat in some future family context the roles of corresponding representatives of older generations in terms of the units in which they were reared. Thus sons are expected to become fathers, nephews to become uncles, etc. This is not inevitably the case in all individual instances, of course, but it is nevertheless true in general of all societies that an intergenerational relationship is predictive of a future one with the representative of the younger now representative of the older generation in a manner that does not necessarily hold true of relationships involving individuals of different absolute age categories.

bers or other relatives of older generations. The generational distinction is always an important focus of the allocation of power and responsibility in kinship structures in general and families in particular. Insofar as those are highly relevant to the general structures of control of the society, role differentiation on the basis of generation is an important general focus of political allocation. Even in relatively modernized ones in which governmental structures are ideally and relatively easily separated and carefully insulated from family considerations, role differentiation on the basis of generation remains an exceedingly important factor in understanding the general structures of political allocation because it is largely by means of behavior in terms of intergenerational relationships that the average individual in the society learns his initial responses to patterns of authority and responsibility. Those may be offset by later experience, but they are never irrelevant to later developments.

There is one other consideration with regard to role differentiation on the basis of generation which is so strategic for this work that it requires special mention here. In all of the relatively nonmodernized social contexts the vast majority of all teaching and training is carried out on the basis of generational role differentiation within a family or pseudofamily context. This is so overwhelmingly the case in most relatively nonmodernized societies most of the time for most of the members that any introduction of any set of structures in terms of which the role differentiation of teacher and student does not coincide with role differentiations on the basis of generation—is specifically not supposed to involve kinship or family considerations—is bound to have far-reaching general implications for change.

C. ROLE DIFFERENTIATION ON THE BASIS OF SEX

Unlike the term *generation,* the layman's use of the term sex is quite precise enough for present purposes. Role differentiation on the basis of sex is a prominent feature of all societies. There is an enormous amount of variation in the type of role differentiation on the basis of sex, but as a popular musical of the twentieth century maintains, it is a distinction which seems to "come naturally." There are, of course, in all societies the minimally expected correlations of role differentiation on various bases with role differentiation on the basis of sex. Biological kinship and social kinship never coincide exactly, of course.[10] The biological aspects

[10] The fundamental distinction in here is best put by a popular record referred to above [p. 205]. That song sings of the sad state of affairs of a young man who has married an attractive widow. That widow has an at-

of kinship certainly never exhaust the social aspects, nor do they determine them uniquely, but they are never completely irrelevant either. Thus for known societies women, not men, are mothers even though men may actually go through simulated birth pains as we know from the famous couvade. Not only do women bear the children, but of course they nurse them if they are nursed [and until high levels of modernization are reached, the vast majority are nursed]. There are always role differentiations on the basis of sex in courtship, though they need not necessarily coincide with ours. Sex role differentiations closely dependent on physiological sex differences never exhaust the role differentiations on the basis of sex characteristic of any society. However much the members of a society may consider sex role differentiation to be biologically explicable, much of it certainly is not at present or envisaged states of development of the science of biology.

There are two universally present types of role differentiation on the basis of sex that are especially relevant for the present work. First, sex is always to some extent a focus for political role differentiation. There are spheres in which the males are expected to take precedence and vice versa. The exact allocation of power and responsibility on the basis of sex varies enormously, but there is no society, and there never has been a society, in terms of which the sex of a member is completely irrelevant to that member's positions in matters of authority and responsibility. Many societies are radically patriarchal in their ideal structures at least. The traditional Chinese structure has already been cited above. Family units are always major foci of this sort of distinction because such units are universal in all known societies and also because the degree of orientation of the average members of most societies to family or kinship structures is, and has been, overwhelming. Political role differentiation on the basis of sex always extends beyond kinship and family spheres of behavior. Even among the members of the most highly modernized

---

tractive daughter of precociously mature development. That daughter then marries the hero's father. The song complicates the tale further by the discussion of infants born to each of these marital pairs, but those are elaborations which need not detain us. If a man is married to a woman whose daughter is married to that man's father, that man has become "the saddest thing you ever saw," i.e., his own grandpa. However facetious this song may be, in kinship terms it is thus conceivable that a man become his own grandfather because in the social sense of kinship it is true that the husband of one's grandmother is one's grandfather. It is only barely necessary to point out that no present advances in medical technology and none conceived in the future make it possible biologically for a man to be his own grandpa.

societies, ideally and/or actually, the biases against women being in positions of supreme or crucial authority remain impressive. In terms of relatively nonmodernized societies no matter how much descent in the female line is emphasized, crucial roles of authority in both the kinship context and elsewhere are inevitably roles held by males, ideally speaking. In this respect the situation is little different as between the most highly modernized and least modernized of societies. In the history of the most highly modernized societies no woman has yet attained the major executive role in a governmental system if a single such role is distinguished. The number of women who occupy roles of any considerable authority in either the government or other organizations is certainly quite restricted given the general distribution of members of that sex throughout the general population and the inevitable accent among the members of such societies on "the equality of the sexes." Most, if not all, of the women in the greatest positions of power in world history seem to have held such power in terms of societies whose members did not for a minute consider themselves oriented to either the "equality of the sexes" or "female superiority"—rather the reverse.

Second, to some extent role differentiation on the basis of sex is always a specific basis for occupational role differentiation. Here again the differences always go far beyond those more or less obviously associated with the bearing and nursing of children. In all societies work may be divided into three categories: "men's work," "women's work," and work which may be done by either men or women. How work is differentiated on these bases varies enormously, but so differentiated it always is. Moreover, there is always in operation a sort of Gresham's Law about occupational role differentiation on the basis of sex. If a given occupation is identified with individuals of one sex and individuals of the opposite sex begin to enter that occupation, there are three possibilities: (1) the new entrants are immediately driven out, (2) the occupation ceases to be identified as exclusively male or female work, or (3) the individuals of the sex which previously was identified with these positions are driven out of those positions. The analogy to Gresham's Law inheres in the fact that to some extent when such invasions are made the individuals of the sex originally identified with the position are always replaced. One of the more spectacular examples of this in United States history was the replacement of male teachers at the elementary and secondary school level by female teachers.[11] The implications of

[11] An interesting development in educational circles today is the increasing reappearance of males in teaching roles at the elementary

the recruitment of women as regular members of the armed forces of the United States following World War II, as far as I know, have never been examined systematically from this point of view.

Members of relatively modernized societies go to lengths to minimize the focus of attention on sex as a basis for the differentiation of many roles. This, like so many other factors mentioned throughout this work, is one of the peculiar features of relatively modernized societies. The reduction of emphasis on this distinction characteristic of such societies, and the preoccupation with this reduction as an ideal to be sought should not obscure for a moment the fact that the members of none of these societies have come even close to eliminating this distinction either ideally or actually. Sex role differentiation continues to be exceedingly prominent and important in the kinship sphere, in the structures of political allocation, in the structures of economic allocation, and in most other contexts. In some respects it has certainly become even more important than it was previously. For example, the radical separation of the "production of family income" from the "consumption of family income," the overwhelming identification of the former as the male's responsibility and the latter with female supervision has almost certainly left women in the most highly modernized of such societies with far greater powers of decision and administrative responsibility with regard to income expenditure than women have ever known before in world history. At the same time this has left the home even more completely identified as the woman's sphere of influence. The last implication of these developments has frequently been underestimated.

Since sex role differentiation cannot be eliminated from the family sphere and in fact is never completely eliminated from other spheres either, this role differentiation remains in all societies highly relevant to both allocations of power and responsibility and the problems of allocation of goods and services, as well as to other aspects of social life. Since (1) the probability is exceedingly high that there will be far greater emphasis on the subordination of women to men in general by the members of relatively nonmodernized than by those of relatively modernized societies, (2) that subordination is likely to be an important feature of the general structures of control, and (3) that subordination is likely to be an important focus of stress and strain in such societies, we

---

and secondary school levels. They come in, however, on a different basis from what they had when they at one time dominated teaching in this as in most other fields.

have here another set of reasons why the transition to increased modernization has explosive effects on the social structure of relatively nonmodernized societies even though the absolute amount of influence introduced is relatively slight.

D. ROLE DIFFERENTIATION ON THE BASIS OF ECONOMIC ALLOCATION

To some extent roles are always differentiated in all societies on the basis of who does what when with regard to the allocation of goods and/or services. Perhaps the simplest and most universal distinction of such roles is that drawn between the roles of *consumption* and *production*. Here it is necessary to observe a note of caution. No activity is inherently either consumption or production. Its classification depends on the point of view from which the activity is observed. What the members of General Motors "do" is from the point of view of the members of the United States Steel Corporation *consumption;* they are consuming steel plates among other things. From the point of view of automobile buyers what is going on is the *production* of automobiles. Nevertheless, the members of all societies draw some distinctions between consumption and production.

The most important consideration with regard to role differentiation on the basis of economic allocation has to do with the sort of social systems or organizations in terms of which role differentiation on the basis of economic allocation is carried out. The vast majority of all social experience has been with relatively concentrated foci of such role differentiation. The example par excellence has been the family unit. This has never been the only unit in any society, but it has been the major unit for most of the members of most of the relatively nonmodernized societies in world history, and it remains an important unit in all of the relatively modernized societies as well. In relatively modernized contexts an important distinction emerges systematically. What are *considered* to be production roles tend overwhelmingly to be concentrated in highly specialized organizations whose members are, for their productive activities, radically separated from and insulated against the organizational contexts in terms of which they regard themselves as carrying out their consumption roles. This is carried so far that production roles tend to be regarded as roles in terms of which action is conducted outside the family context, and family roles are considered to be *the* major roles of consumption. In many senses this is a naïve point of view even with regard to the most highly modernized societies. An enormous number of roles crucial in their productive aspects continue to be conducted in family terms. Most obvious among these are the roles having to do with food preparation, at least the early care and rearing of infants and children, the provision and regulation of sleep and relaxation, much of the production of cleanliness, etc. There are also, of course, major foci of attention to consumption which fall outside the family sphere.

One of the major results of this degree of specialization, and of this level of naïveté about it, has been a tendency to regard the spheres of production and consumption as spheres isolated from one another in a radical sense never before approximated in history despite the fact that people have never failed to distinguish between the two to some extent. Actually this has resulted in the implicit development from the point of view of the individuals concerned of at least two radically different kinds of production and consumption: family production and consumption and nonfamily production and consumption. Since that distinction is ideally and actually implicit in the point of view of the vast majority of members of all such societies, there has been a systematic underplaying of the aspects of production in the family context and of the aspects of consumption in the nonfamily context even by professional social scientists. Since these distinctions ordinarily are not carried to such lengths by the members of relatively nonmodernized societies, once again the contrast implicit in the introduction of structures of modernization is likely to be great.

E. ROLE DIFFERENTIATION ON THE BASIS OF POLITICAL ALLOCATION

Political allocation is defined here as the distribution of power over and responsibility for the actions of the members of the social systems concerned, involving on the one hand various forms of sanctions, of which sheer coercive force is the extreme in one direction, and on the other accountability to the members and in terms of the systems concerned, or to the members of other interdependent systems. *Power* is defined as the ability to exercise authority and control over the actions of others. *Responsibility* is defined as the accountability of an individual(s) to other individual(s) for his own acts and/or the acts of others. As in the case of production and consumption, the concepts of power and responsibility are in a sense the obverse of one another. If an individual, A, has power over another, B, then to that extent at least B is responsible to A. This does not mean, however, that the power in a given system is balanced by the responsibility in that system. For example, although A's power over B, is B's responsibility to A, A is not necessarily responsible to anyone for the power that he wields over B. In Chapter 6, below, in the fuller discussion of the structure of political allocation, the instability inherent in any cases of imbalance of this sort is discussed. For the time being it is only necessary to point out that the distinction between power and responsibility, though different ways of looking at the same thing, is nevertheless an important basis for distinguishing roles from the point of view of the members of any society.

This distinction in and of itself implies some distinction in the allocation of roles in terms of any society. An individual may be involved in roles so defined that he and others with whom he interacts have identical roles with regard to power and responsibility. Friendship as we understand it in our society is just such a relationship. Ideally speaking, if a friendship is what we consider a true one, the powers and responsibilities of the participants in the relationship are equal.[12] Even so, the power roles of a given individual are not the same as his responsibility roles. He acts in terms of his power over his friends and his responsibilities to them, but these aspects of his activities may and must be distinguished.

Apart from the minimum necessity of distinctions among roles with regard to the allocation of power and responsibility in the above sense, the convenient and familiar case of the implications of infancy may be cited again as a basis for further universally necessary distinctions. Infants cannot in their own persons either wield power or bear responsibility in any effective sense. At the same time they must be subjected to controls to prevent harm to themselves as well as to prevent activities which might become a menace to others. In a modified form the same remark may be made about young children in general, though at quite early ages children do begin to operate in terms of structures of power and responsibility.

In all social organizations of any sort role differentiation on the basis of political allocation always goes beyond either the minimal distinction between power and responsibility or the implications of infancy and early childhood cited here. There are always important differentiations of roles politically on the basis of age, generation, sex, economic allocation, etc. Perhaps the most familiar case of interrelationship among these aspects is that between

[12] Despite all the talk of egalitarianism in many social contexts, egalitarian types of relationships constitute a restricted set of social relationships. The vast majority of all social relationships are in some respects hierarchical ideally speaking. Relationships are sometimes nonhierarchical if casual and fleeting, but rarely egalitarian [see above, pp. 150–152].

economic and political allocation. So highly specialized are many roles in relatively modernized societies that we tend to think of them as primarily concerned with one or the other of the two, but no observer is so naïve as to be completely unaware of the implications of allocations of goods and/or services for the allocation of power and responsibility, if only because of the minimal relevance of goods and/or services as means in the wielding of power and responsibility. It is also true that no one is so naïve as to be completely unaware of the implications of the wielding of power and responsibility for the allocations of goods and/or services if only because of the relevance of either confiscation or chaotic conditions for relationships predominantly concerned with exchange. But these two are no more involved with one another than each of them is with all of the other aspects so far referred to. This, again, is why these are distinguished as *aspects* rather than as different things. Economic allocation is quite important in understanding political roles. It is relevant regardless of whether one feels that possession of considerable power should be closely coordinated with possession of great wealth or not.[13]

Great wealth, however, is certainly no more often a high correlative of power than is a particular differentiation on the basis of sex or age. For example, throughout social history within virtually every society and certainly across the history of all societies the correlation between being male and having high power is far more consistent than is the correlation between having great power and having great wealth. The correlation between certain roles of power and responsibility and age roles is also marked. Since absolute age categories always differ more broadly than the general dichotomous role differentiation on the basis of sex, the situation with regard to age is much more complicated. Neverthe-

[13] Quite sophisticated references to this sort of thing appear in the current humor of any given society. In recent United States history the success in attaining important leadership roles in the political arena of a number of individuals coming from family backgrounds of great wealth has been widely commented upon as indicating a basic change in the American attitude toward elected officials. In the United States today, it is obviously quite possible to succeed in a political career despite the fact that one has been born with a silver or even a golden spoon in his mouth. There have been periods in American history in which such origins would have been more of a liability for one seeking high elective office. American ideals in these matters call for predominantly universalistic standards. It is certainly an intrusion of particularistic factors if an individual has an advantage in an elective race because of great personal wealth. It is equally an intrusion of particularistic standards if he suffers specific disabilities as a result of being born into a family context of great wealth. In actuality wealth and power cannot be distributed randomly relative to one another, but whatever their distribution in actuality may be, attitudes about their proper relationship certainly do change.

less, it is almost banal to point out that, ideally speaking, important roles of political leadership are never identified with nonadults.[14] In general, political leadership is likely to be heavily concentrated in the age category that we call middle-aged adults. There are numerous reports of so-called gerontocracies in which the aged members of the society wield power. More often than not, however, both the powers and responsibilities of the aged members of such societies are delegated to subordinates, or there are relatively early retirement structures for the aged, even though, ideally speaking, they hold power and bear responsibility.

There is one particular reason for paying considerable attention to role differentiation on the basis of political allocation. As indicated above again and again, one of the very few specialized organizations found in practically every known society of any scale, whether relatively modernized or not, is a government. Thus, for all such societies—if that does not, indeed, mean all societies—there are always some individuals who hold political roles with far-reaching implications for other individual members of the society regardless of whether the other individuals belong to the government or not. Political roles are by no means confined to governmental and closely associated organizations such as political parties. Political roles are distinguished in some way in terms of any and all organizations. Ordinarily the political roles which are most significant to an individual at any given point in time are those of the organization(s) in terms of which he is acting at any given moment. Governmental roles are always a potential exception to this. The stronger [i.e., the more effectively centralized] the government, the greater the exception. This holds true regardless of whether the individual is more oriented to governmental considerations than to, say, family ones and regardless of whether or not he gives priority or precedence to governmental considerations by contrast with those having to do

[14] Some of the social structures in terms of which this is realized are interesting. Structures of regency are usually invoked when infants and small children legitimately inherit roles of political leadership. On the other hand individuals who might otherwise be classified as nonadults may be considered to be adults as soon as they take over certain roles of leadership. The second type of structure is more likely to be a source of instability, if it recurs frequently, than the first.

In general role differentiations on the basis of age, generation, and/or sex are more likely to underlie other bases of role differentiation than the reverse. Political role differentiation, for example, is more likely to be a dependent variable of sex role differentiation than vice versa. It is far more common in human history, both ideally and actually, to regard individuals as weak because they are women than to regard them as women because they are weak. See also pp. 659–660 below.

with any other organization. Since problems of control are strategic for the members of any organization, and since a government is always an organization specialized with regard to problems of control, action in terms of a government, however weak, always has potential implications ideally and/or actually for action in terms of all of the other organizations in a given society.

This last consideration leads to the final emphasis in this connection. Nothing could be more mistaken than to consider role differentiation on the basis of political allocation to be confined largely to role differentiation in terms of a governmental structure. Because of our preoccupation with highly specialized organizations, we have come to think roughly in these terms, but it is misleading to do so. Role differentiations on the basis of political allocation are characteristic of every organization in terms of which an individual operates. Furthermore, those role differentiations are always of the greatest importance in understanding action carried out in terms of any given organization. The structures of political allocation in such organizations may be loose, permissive, even egalitarian in rare cases, or rigid, authoritarian, and hierarchical, but they are never irrelevant.

In this connection again the problem of reconciliation or reinforcement of roles is raised. The greater the proliferation of organizations in terms of which the ordinary individual operates, the greater is the number of political roles that he must coordinate in some fashion.[15] In relatively nonmodernized social contexts the fact that the ordinary individual operates in terms of few organizations means that this particular problem is minimized. Fewer possibilities arise. In relatively modernized social contexts these problems are mitigated by the presence of specific structures more or less carefully inculcated on the members. For example, ideally speaking, operations in terms of one of these organizations are insulated from operations in terms of another by virtue of the fact that operation in terms of one is supposed to

[15] It has become popular for intellectual winds to blow over whether a given approach overemphasizes integration and underemphasizes conflict. These arguments frequently seem to blow themselves out with the conflict people devoting most of their attention to the relevance of conflict to integration and vice versa. Since such controversies usually tell us more of the values of the participants than of social phenomena, they are avoided here. If there is to be any social organization, there must be some mutual reinforcement of differentiated roles, and the more highly differentiated and specialized the roles of individuals are, the more complex is the problem of interdependence among such roles. Both of these statements hold true quite apart from this sort of revival in new guises of old dichotomous logomachies like heredity versus environment, the dialectic [usually presented with a tone of authority as an undefined argument quencher], statics versus dynamics, etc.

be irrelevant to operation in terms of the other. Actually speaking, this insulation is never complete. Only under the most brittle circumstances, with extraordinarily high levels of self-conscious rational knowledge and emotional self-control could it conceivably be complete for any single individual let alone the membership in general of the society.

F. ROLE DIFFERENTIATION ON THE BASIS OF RELIGION

The term *religion*, as used here, refers to aspects of action directly oriented to ultimate ends or goals, that is to ends or goals that are not conceived as means to other ends but that are conceived as desirable in and of themselves, as their own basis of justification, etc. This definition of religion does not coincide with many of the conventional ones. It would cover major aspects of most of the phenomena which in common parlance we consider religious. It would also cover major aspects of many phenomena not ordinarily classified in that category. For example, regardless of whether one likes them or not, by this definition Communism and Nazism as followed in many respects by their true believers are as much forms of religion as are Judaism, Catholicism, Taoism, Shintoism, etc. Organizations or social systems will be considered *predominantly religiously oriented* if the religious aspects of the structures of action take precedence over all other aspects.[16] Such organizations are not uncommon as subsystems of either relatively nonmodernized or relatively modernized societies. Role differentiation within such specialized organizations always has an important religious element, of course, but there is nevertheless a great deal of role differentiation on the basis of religion that is not confined to such specialized organizational contexts. Frequently the family head has special religious roles. In traditional China he was, as it were, the high priest of the family's ancestor cult. In all societies there must be some role differentiation on the basis of religion, though there need be no such differentiation in many specific organizations. Religious role differentiation is no less strategic for societies in general than the other forms mentioned above, but all of those are exceedingly likely, if not inevitably, to be found in any organization within a society as well. This is not the case of role differentiation on the basis of religion. It is quite possible to conceive of organizations in terms of which no action directly oriented to ultimate ends is expected of the actors involved. There is an important distinction between relatively modernized and relatively nonmodernized so-

[16] A given organization might be predominantly religiously oriented ideally and/or actually.

cieties in this respect. In terms of relatively modernized societies role differentiation on the basis of religion tends to take place overwhelmingly in terms of specialized predominantly religiously oriented organizations while role differentiation on the basis of religion in terms of other organizations becomes increasingly less emphasized. In terms of relatively nonmodernized societies role differentiation on the basis of religion, while often present in terms of some specialized religious organizations, is also very widely distributed among other organizations that are not necessarily specialized in any religious sense.

G. ROLE DIFFERENTIATION ON THE BASIS OF COGNITION

Cognition may be defined as knowledge or understanding of the situation or of phenomena in general. Unless one falls back solely upon an instinct theory of human behavior or into metaphysics, some concepts of learning and knowledge are necessary in the analysis of human action. The presence of some differentiation of roles on the basis of knowledge is not only obvious but also necessary in every society. Infants must be taught the various forms of knowledge necessary if they are to operate in terms of the society. This, of course, implies the minimal distinction between teacher and student. Hardly less obvious are the implications for role differentiation of different types of knowledge. The distinction between *basic* and *intermediate* which was used with regard to roles in general can be applied to cognition. *Basic cognition* is that which, under ordinary circumstances, every member of a given society or organization ideally and/or actually acquires and uses. *Intermediate cognition* refers to those forms and bits of knowledge which ideally and/or actually are acquired and used only by specialized personnel, not by every member of the society or organization concerned. The more specialized the distinctions among forms of intermediate cognition, the greater is the role differentiation on the basis of cognition. As far as basic cognition is concerned, roles are not necessarily differentiated apart from the teacher-student distinction, some distinctions among different levels of skill, and the distinction between "have's" and "have not's" [e.g., literacy is an element of basic cognition in our society, but preschool children are usually have not's in this respect. See further pp. 663–664.]. In addition, the more highly developed the distinctions with regard to intermediate cognition, the more important it becomes that roles in fact be differentiated along these lines.

There is another basis for cognitive role differentiation. One may distinguish at least two types of cognition which are of great importance in understanding human behavior generally. First there are the *technologies*, i.e., the knowledge that serves as the basis for rational action of whatever sort. Second, there are forms of cognition about value standards, the normative patterns of the society, including both the values involved in ultimate and intermediate ends. These are different bases for cognitive role differentiation. The different subcategories possible within each serve as still further bases for cognitive role differentiation. In relatively modernized social contexts the elaboration of the technologies is carried out to a degree of differentiation and on a scale unparalleled in previous history. In the nontechnological sphere of cognition it by no means necessarily holds true that the differentiation in relatively modernized social contexts will be carried further than in relatively nonmodernized ones. Except for forms of cognition which are specific outgrowths of the kind of knowledge associated with modern science and technology, there is probably no cognition having to do with normative standards or other matters in relatively modernized societies that does not find some sort of reflection, echo, or source in relatively nonmodernized social contexts.

Finally, differences in cognitive ability, whether physiologically innate, socially determined, or some combination of the two, always open the possibility for the distinction of the expert in cognition. Because of the importance of knowledge for action in terms of any society, the expert in cognition is always important in some respects. As societies become increasingly complex in their technologies or in their general social structure, the role of the expert, and consequently the distinction between the expert and the nonexpert becomes of greater importance for the stability [and simultaneously for the lack of stability, of course] of the system and for future operations in terms of it.

H. ROLE DIFFERENTIATION ON THE BASIS OF THE NONHUMAN ENVIRONMENT

In all societies, even in the most homogeneous contexts, roles are differentiated on the basis of climate, geography etc. Members of the society do not do the same things in the spring of the year as they do in the winter. There are certainly societies whose members live in areas unmarked by dramatic seasonal variations, but in even the most equable climes, there are some seasonal variations, and some roles are differentiated with regard to these. There is also no society whose members have lived in a territory so uniform that no roles are differentiated on a geographical basis. In relatively nonmodernized social contexts differentiation of roles on the basis of these factors in the nonhuman environment are likely to be of great importance. It is commonplace in anthropological field work that one is likely to overlook something important unless observations cover a full year's time. The importance of such distinctions is so obvious that it would be hardly worth emphasizing were it not for two factors. First, social scientists fought so long and so hard against naïve biological determinism that some came to analyze social phenomena as though the factors of the nonhuman environment have nothing whatever to do with the case, or can be taken as constants without examination. Second, social scientists are usually members of relatively modernized societies. In such societies there are marked differentiations of roles on the basis of factors in the nonhuman environment, but technological developments certainly enable the members of those societies to offset the implications of elements in the nonhuman environment for social action to the maximum known degree. To a certain extent this makes it possible for many to ignore variations in the nonhuman environment. From a slightly different point of view, however, these very developments may radically increase the implications for role differentiation oriented at least in part to the nonhuman environment. In those societies whose members live in areas with marked seasonal changes, for example, the more highly modernized they become, the greater is the development of specialized goods and/or services specifically oriented to coping with elements of seasonal variation. Thus increasingly there develop roles oriented at least in part to the seasonal variations. We have, for example, not only experts in the manufacture of tires, but also people who are expert in the manufacture of snow tires. With the increase of leisure time and the increasingly even distribution of high incomes, a seasonal set of resort specialists is growing. It is perfectly true that modern technology to some extent does make it possible for many individuals to ignore variations in the nonhuman environment, but it is essential to keep in mind that to overcome or, from an individual actor's point of view, to make it possible to ignore those factors is by no means the same thing as ignoring them *in toto*. From this point of view increases in modernization may actually lead to a substantial increase in the differentiation of roles oriented to factors in the nonhuman environment.

SOLIDARITY

I
DEFINITION AND INTRODUCTION

The structures of solidarity have been defined [p. 179], formally, as those in terms of which relationships among the members of a society or any other social system are allocated according to the *content, strength,* and *intensity* of the relationships. In a more laymanlike sense it has been defined as directing attention to the question of who sticks with whom, under what circumstances. The fact that the strength of the relationship need not be identical from the point of view of all the members of a relationship was pointed out. The same fact was pointed out about the intensity of the relationship. Finally the possibility of solidarities whose degrees and kinds of strength and intensity do not reinforce one another in any neat sense, or even vary in opposite directions was mentioned [pp. 179–180].

For any society to exist, there are some requisite structures of solidarity. The factors that make role differentiation a requisite of any society also require relationships of some sort in terms of which different roles can be coordinated, as it were, i.e., relationships in terms of which different individuals interact in terms of different roles. As a minimum, for example, the care and rearing of children require that some structures of solidarity exist if they are to survive. If infants are to be cared for, there must be solidarities of some sort as between infants and adults. Considerations of solidarity always involve considerably more difficult problems than these which make it easy to see that some structures of solidarity are necessary. There are not only those structures characteristic of the relations among the members of a given organization; there are also the solidarity aspects of the relationships among the members of that organization and the members of any other organizations in terms of which the members of the first organization also act. In studying United States society, for example, not only the solidarity structures among the members of an individual family organization but also those relating the family members to members of the government, business firms, etc., must be considered. This draws attention to the general relevance of structures of solidarity for the relative positions of different subsystems in a society.

II

SOLIDARITY STRUCTURES AS A BASIS
FOR DISCOVERING ORGANIZATIONS
OR SOCIAL SYSTEMS

There is a fairly obvious relationship between the structures of solidarity as discussed here and the general analysis of relationship structures discussed above [pp. 133–174]. The content aspect of solidarity involves some of the matters considered as the aspects of membership criteria and substantive definition of any relationship. The strength consideration is closely related to the stratification aspects, and the consideration of intensity is closely related to the affective aspects of any relationship. There is, however, a difference in the point of view involved. In considering the aspects of any relationship interest was focused on tools of analysis which could be applied to any conceivable relationship in any society. In considering the structures of solidarity, interest is focused upon the fact that relationships are universal in any society, however difficult it may be to prove that specific relationships as they are specifically institutionalized are a requirement for any society. Chapter 1 of this Part concerned itself with aspects of any relationship; the present chapter is concerned with the structures which inhere in any society or any other organization by virtue of the fact that there will be relationships that constitute subsystems of that society or that organization. The requisite basis of the structures of solidarity rests in the most general sense on the fact that the various requirements for the members of any society cannot be produced unless the members of that society enter into relationships with one another. Over the minimal basis for alleging that structures of solidarity are requisites of any society, there are many other equally compelling and not a great deal less obvious reasons. This gives the social analyst an extremely helpful hand with a rather difficult problem. Although it is difficult to maintain that a particular kind of social system is a requirement of any society, despite the ubiquity of families and governments, it is not difficult to show that certain structures of role differentiation and solidarity must be present.[1]

---

[1] It cannot be emphasized too strongly that none of these discussions in terms of what is required if a society is to survive is intended to imply that any given society or that societies in general must survive. That would be teleology, pure and simple. From a scientific point of view, at least, the continued existence of no society, let alone the welfare of its members, is foreordained. Whether such arguments can be supported on theological or metaphysical grounds need not interrupt the argument here. There has been a great tendency in recent social science literature to

The reason it is exceedingly difficult to allege that even a ubiquitous social system such as a family is a requisite of any society lies in the extreme flexibility and adaptability of membership units of many sorts. What can be done in terms of such a unit is subject to enormous variation. How is one to prove that an alternative to such an organization could not be invented such that operation in terms of that alternative organization would have all of the results which are necessary for the existence of a society? [2] The extraordinary flexibility of social systems and

assume that all social systems are in some special sense homeostatic. Some authors have even used an equilibrium assumption as part of their definitions of social systems. This is a quite fruitless strategem of analysis in most instances. It tends by either assumption or definition to establish something which is frequently at variance with the facts; it is a needless restriction on the range of variation of social phenomena which can be handled, if one uses these assumptions or definitions as one has set them up. There certainly are some social systems such that the actions of members in terms of them will have equilibrium or homeostatic properties, and there are certainly some that lack such implications unless one wishes to decide this issue by definition or assumption. The fact that one uses a stability assumption of some sort to ask a question such as, "What would a given society have to have *if* it were to survive?", in no ways implies that any society to which the results of such analysis are applied will in fact be one that survives. If, for example, I am able to maintain that certain types of attention by adults to infants are necessary for a society to survive and if I observe a society in which such structures do not exist, I can immediately conclude one of three or some combination of those three things: (1) my argument that such a relationship had to exist for society to exist is an untenable argument, (2) the system I am examining is not the kind of system which has to have that sort of a structure to survive or it is a society which is in the process of going out of existence, or (3) I have misobserved, and if I go back and reexamine the data more carefully, I will in fact find data on such a relationship. It is always teleological to say that a given structure must exist because it is a requirement of such and such a unit, although it may be quite correct to say that if that structure is a requisite of the unit and if the unit exists, that structure will also be found to exist.

There are various reasons having to do with the elegancies of scientific method which dictate that one should be exceedingly careful about such problems. Those reasons need not concern us here. What is of concern is that carelessness in these matters can lead to serious misjudgment of social situations. The idea that the traditional Chinese family had to continue to exist in its old form because it was essential to traditional Chinese society is misleading unless one also points out that traditional Chinese society did not have to continue to exist or that some form of Chinese society might continue to exist in a changed form such that the traditional Chinese family be no longer a requirement of that society. Arguments in terms of the requirements of a given system or situation are exceedingly dangerous if they get translated somehow into arguments either that a given structure must continue to exist because it existed before or that the system of which that structure is a part cannot change in so radical a fashion as to eliminate the necessity of that structure for the new system.

[2] Actually I am convinced that such an argument can be maintained, but it is too technical and too tentative to be presented here. Even so,

the ingenuity which individuals of the human species have shown about them make this a difficult question to answer in the relatively neat sense in which structures of role differentiation, solidarity, economic allocation, political allocation, and integration and expression can be shown to be requisites.

This is more galling to students of social phenomena whose major interest is in public affairs specifically because they must make decisions and act in terms of organizations rather than in terms of aspects of those organizations—however useful those aspects may be for analysis. The analysis of requisite structures of solidarity gives leads on what the organizations present in any situation are likely to be both in general and specific cases. Since certain solidarity structures must exist if any society is to exist, and therefore certain types of relationships must exist, organizations which incorporate those relationships must exist. This does not tell us the exact form those organizations must take, but it does indicate certain types of individuals who must be in some way or another organized in close relationships with one another.

There is no need to treat this in great detail here. Illustrations should suffice. If one considers role differentiation on the basis of absolute age alone, there are certain minimal implications for solidarity structures in any society. There must be such structures as between infants and adults, adults and children, adults and the aged, and adults and other adults. It is, perhaps, conceivable that there not be structures interrelating infants and other infants, infants and children, infants and the aged, children and other children, children and the aged, and the aged and other aged. If the solidarities dubbed necessary are in fact necessary, it is unlikely that those can be organized apart from some units in which these relationships appear as a set. It is also exceedingly unlikely that some if not all of the solidarities mentioned as not obviously necessary be either absent or neatly separated from those dubbed necessary.

There must also be some organizations in terms of which individuals of different relative ages interact and there must be some involving role differentiations on the basis of generation, sex, economic allocation, political allocation, and so forth. The most obvious example of an organization in which all of these solidarities inhere is, of course, a family organization. Claims of the Chinese Communist leaders and of students of the kibbutzim

---

the family and some organization in terms of which members of two or more families are interrelated are the only organizations about which I can mount such arguments that would apply to any society.

in Israel notwithstanding, no society has ever been reported by any observer and reliably found to be devoid of families.

To some extent therefore, whether it is done self-consciously or not, we in fact always do locate organizations in terms of some considerations of solidarity structures. One of the bases for discriminating membership as among different organizations can be answered in terms of the question of who sticks with whom under what circumstances. In addition to that, any given organization can be described in terms of the varying solidarities of different members which, taken as a set, characterize that particular organization. By studying the content, strength, and intensity of solidarity aspects of relationships one can always isolate the various organizations in terms of which people act in any given social setting even if one lacks other means of identifying them.

I I I
RANGE OF VARIATION AND ITS RELEVANCE

In consideration of the structures of solidarity in a given social system one of the easiest questions to raise has to do with the number of solidarities self-consciously differentiated by the members of the society or the organization being studied. Is the number differentiated, for example, small or large? Here again we have our old numerical difficulty, but we are not concerned with dividing lines such as whether two hundred is a large number and fifty a small number but rather with whether one is dealing in terms of let us say several hundreds of solidarities by contrast with several thousands or tens of thousands or more. In general, the number of solidarities knowingly and importantly differentiated by the members of relatively nonmodernized as opposed to relatively modernized societies is small. There may be considerable differences among relatively nonmodernized societies. By contrast with the traditional Chinese, the Australian Bushmen differentiate relatively few solidarities, but the members of both societies differentiate relatively few solidarities, especially from the point of view of the average member of those societies, by contrast with those differentiated by virtually any member of any relatively modernized society.

The family is always a focus of solidarity differentiations in any society. So far there has been in world history no known society in which the solidarities distinguished in family terms have not been exceedingly important in explaining the development of the individual as well as in explaining the general set of interrelationships which characterize the society. In some societies the family unit may be in a sense *the* major focus of solidarity structures. Certainly one of the most extreme cases is that of traditional China. Proper behavior in terms of that society literally required that the individual put family considerations before all others. In solidarity terms that meant, for example, that ideally speaking the solidarity of a Chinese with his family head was the strongest solidarity he knew in terms of the entire society. Actually many individual Chinese no doubt transgressed against this moral standard, but there is little reason to doubt that, ideally and actually, for the overwhelming majority of all traditional Chinese the strength of the solidarity of any family member with his family head was stronger than his solidarity with any other family member or anyone who was not a family member. Perhaps few societies are as extreme as this, but a fairly close approach to it is by no means uncommon. In the Tokugawa period the solidarity of a Japanese with his overlord was stronger than his solidarity with anyone else, and second to that in strength was his solidarity with his family head. Thus, unlike the case of traditional China, the family was by no means the major focus of solidarity ideally speaking for everyone. Actually, however, for the average Japanese most of the time his family solidarities were the strongest solidarities in terms of which he acted. The vast majority of the members of that society never faced a situation in which the strength of their solidarities with family members was challenged by the strength of their solidarities with members of the society outside the family circle.[3]

One may generalize about societies throughout world history as follows:

(1) The family unit is always an important focus of solidarity structures.

(2) In some of them, ideally speaking, it is clearly *the* major focus of all solidarities.

(3) In all of the relatively nonmodernized societies, even if the family is not *the* major focus ideally speaking, it is always *actually the* major focus for the vast majority of the members for the vast proportion of their time.

[3] The samurai of Japan were supposed to be the great virtuosi of sacrifice of self-interest and family interest to the interests of their lords. For two hundred and fifty years relatively few of them had the opportunity to make such sacrifices and so attain the highest pinnacle of virtue distinguished by the members of that society. For the Tokugawa Japanese the focus of literature that took the place of romantic love or success in some other societies was this romantic sacrifice. For members of the society below the rank of samurai it was romantic even to consider one's self eligible for such sacrifices. Indeed, it was almost the commission of the sin of *lèse majesté* to act as though such a one were eligible to make such sacrifices. See above, pp. 121–122.

(4) In relatively modernized societies the family continues to be an important focus of solidarity structures, but neither ideally nor actually is it ever *the* single major focus of solidarity for the majority of the members of the society for the largest proportion of their time.

(5) The members of relatively modernized societies always have a large number of solidarities the strength of which in specific areas is always stronger than the strength of the individual's family solidarities.

(6) In all societies and in all subsystems of societies save those very few which are explicitly egalitarian, there always exists a hierarchical arrangement of solidarities. Even friendships which are usually institutionalized as explicitly egalitarian are in actuality often characterized by a hierarchical arrangement of solidarities. Indeed, this is more likely to be the case than not, despite the explicit ideal to the contrary.

(7) Explicitly egalitarian systems can never be developed to any great length in terms of either numbers of individuals involved as members of a single system or in terms of geographical areas or areas of social action covered. As the scale of social organizations increase, hierarchical arrangements of solidarities become increasingly important. It is also true, however, that in most of the small-scale social organizations the arrangement of solidarities is hierarchical rather than egalitarian.

(8) The dimension in terms of which solidarities are hierarchically arranged is most likely to be the dimension of strength of the solidarities. This is not inevitable. It is certainly possible to have a hierarchy of solidarities based on intensity, for example.

(9) Hierarchical arrangements of solidarities vary enormously in many ways even though the dimension of strength is likely to be the most strategic basis for such hierarchies. One of the most important lines of variation has to do with the degree of clarity with which the hierarchy is defined, whether it is based primarily on the strength of the solidarities or not.

The last of these generalizations is one of the most fruitful. In the illustrations given above of traditional Chinese society, one of the striking features is the clarity with which, at least ideally speaking, the hierarchical arrangement of solidarities is defined. An individual's solidarity with his family head is expected to take precedence over his solidarity with literally any other member of the society. In cases in which conflicts arise, the major criterion for settling the order of precedence of different solidarities is in the last analysis how one's family head would order one to settle such a controversy. One can generalize about societies or subsystems of societies further in the following fashion: the smaller the number of social units in terms of which an individual distinguishes different solidarities [i.e., the more concentrated the foci of solidarity], the easier and more likely it is that there be a clearcut hierarchical arrangement of such solidarities. This generalization follows almost trivially from the problem of cognition involved in appreciating the hierarchical arrangement of solidarities.

One of the special problems associated with relatively modernized societies is that the problem of clarity about the hierarchical arrangement of solidarities is vastly complicated in all these social contexts. The complications are minimized to the extent that many of the solidarities have to do with predominantly universalistically and functionally specifically defined relationships. To the extent that this is the case, the problems of solidarity arrangements are kept as much within a single organizational context as possible. The real case of conflict is conflict between a solidarity within one such context and some other solidarity which also characterizes an individual. This usually involves the question as to whether the individual should leave one of the organizations or the other. The greatest likelihood of conflict in these cases is not so much conflict involving members of two or more of these predominantly universalistically defined organizations, but rather conflict involving the solidarities an individual may have in terms of such an organization and in terms of a predominantly particularistically defined organization such as a family unit. However much emphases on predominantly universalistic criteria and functional specificity may simplify the matter ideally speaking, such emphases do not guarantee actual clarity. Some of the problems inherent in this situation are reflected in the frequent iterations of feelings that the members of such societies lead highly fractionated rather than whole lives. Individuals complain in their novels and in their letters to the editor that they are torn among too many "competing claims."

The flexibility of the human individual is generally conceded to be enormous. The inhabitants of relatively modernized societies accept as a matter of course, for all their difficulties of adjustment, a complexity of solidarities that would bewilder virtually any member of a relatively nonmodernized society. Here again inheres another of the special problems of adjustment in the transition from a relatively nonmodernized society to a relatively modernized one. Consideration of an emphasis on *individualism* is especially pertinent. In every society and indeed in every sub-system of a society there is some basis on which the individual member makes and/or is expected to make decisions affecting his future and the future of others with whom he interacts. Insofar as the individual himself is supposed to be or is the major basis for those decisions, *individualism* exists. Insofar as the individual is *actually* the major basis for the decision, *actual individualism* exists. Insofar as others with whom he interacts and he himself feels that he is *supposed* to make decisions on this basis, *ideal individualism* exists. In some cases individualism exists both ideally and actually. Elsewhere, considering this question, I have differentiated between *individualism by ideal* and *individualism by default*.[4] *Individualism by ideal* is present when individualism exists both ideally and actually. Individualism by ideal and ideal individualism are by no means the same. The latter may exist without the former but not vice versa. *Individualism by default* refers to a form of actual individualism in situations in which ideal individualism is explicitly not present. It does not, however, refer to the case of an individual who is supposed to and could make decisions on a nonindividualistic basis, but in fact makes them on the basis of his own considerations in defiance of custom. I shall call that form of actual individualism *deviant individualism*. Individualism by default refers rather to actual individualism which exists because the individual concerned cannot make decisions on any basis other than an individualistic one, whether he wishes to or not.

Individualism by ideal is a relatively rare social invention. Most people most of the time in most social settings have not been expected to make decisions on the basis of their own considerations. The general attitude toward individualism by ideal by members of societies other than the rare ones in terms of which individualism by ideal is institutionalized in some spheres has been parodied in a motion picture [5] by the statement of a traditional Chinese father who says to his son growing up in the United States, "When you are old enough to think for yourself, I will let you know." Neither individualism by default nor deviant individualism is so rare. There are always some individuals in any society who by force of one set of circumstances or another are not in a position to make nonindividualistic decisions, whether

[4] See: "Some Aspects of 'Individualism' and the Problem of Moderniza-tion in China and Japan," *Economic Development in Cultural Change*, vol. X, no. 3, April, 1962, pp. 225–240. I have benefitted from discussions of individualism with my colleague in history, John William Ward.

[5] See *The Flower Drum Song*.

they wish to or not. Furthermore, there are always some individuals who do not follow the nonindividualistic ideal structures even when they can.

Whenever individualism is present, there are special problems for stability in terms of the structures of solidarity in the systems concerned. After all, ideally and/or actually, whenever a conflict as between solidarities arises, the issue of how to settle it is thrown open. In situations that ideally speaking are nonindividualistic, when such a conflict arises, the issue of *how* to settle it does not necessarily arise. In many such cases the only issues which arise are: what is the nature of the conflict and what are the rules which one is supposed to apply to settle the order of precedence of solidarities. There is no question but that ideally and/or actually an emphasis on individualism always calls into question the going structure of loyalties or makes it easier to do so. This in turn has far-reaching implications for the general structures of control of the social systems involved. The rare cases of societies in terms of which individualism by ideal has been highly developed are also the rare cases of societies whose members heavily emphasize social change as an ideal.

In this connection a special problem in terms of solidarities and individualism inheres in the continual increase in the degree of centralization and of bureaucratization characteristic of relatively modernized societies as they become more and more highly modernized. It becomes increasingly difficult for individual members of such societies not only to move with sufficient flexibility from one place to another, but also to alter their actions from one role to another with sufficient flexibility, unless they behave on something approaching an individualistic basis. If some technique is not found of making the individual the major referent of his behavior, the detailed attention to detailed orders from a central source must be multiplied unbelievably. On the other hand, to the extent that the individual is made the focus of decision in these matters, the possibility that he may not make the correct decision is, of course, increased. Individualism in general and individualistically decided solidarities in particular may turn out to be one of the peculiar structures without which a highly modernized society cannot survive and with which it may not be able to survive either. For the most highly modernized societies such problems are well on the way to requiring us to revise our most seriously held predictions about social life as it will be lived in the penultimate decade of our century.

In summation, about the structures of solidarity in any society the following remarks may be made. As a minimum there will always be structures of solidarity oriented to the minimal interrelationships which must exist if the minimal differentiation of roles in a society are to be successfully coordinated with one another—if that society is to exist. That is to say, there must be solidarities oriented to role differentiations on the basis of absolute and relative age, generation, sex, economic allocation, political allocation, religion, cognition, the nonhuman environment, and finally solidarity itself. As a minimum in every society which survives there must be actual organizations in terms of which these solidarities are conducted. The number and detailed description of these organizations are subject to enormous variation, but insofar as the set of them for a given society must cover all of these solidarities, the substantive structures of those organizations are by no means completely arbitrary. Although it is difficult to prove this in a detailed sense, one of the clear-cut implications of this argument is that one of those organizations is exceedingly likely to be [or inevitably is] a family organization of some sort. In the study of any society, if one has not covered all of these minimal solidarities, something is seriously lacking in the analysis. If one does not cover this possibility, he may be suddenly faced with a difficulty which is a function of the fact that action in terms of a solidarity that he did not anticipate has taken precedence over action in terms of a solidarity that he previously believed invulnerable or unthreatened. Although they have not been worked out here, corresponding hypotheses can be developed with regard to the minimum presence of solidarity structures in any particular organization with which it is necessary to deal. Whenever roles are differentiated and the activities in terms of those differentiated roles have to be coordinated and those roles involve different individuals, some more or less explicitly recognized structures of solidarity must be present, if action is to proceed effectively.

ECONOMIC ALLOCATION

I
DEFINITIONS

A. STRUCTURES OF ECONOMIC ALLOCATION

Structures of economic allocation are defined as those structures having to do with the distribution of goods and/or services making up the income of the members of the social systems concerned and of the goods and/or efforts making up their output among the various members of those systems, and among the members of those systems and other systems with whom they are in contact. Structures of economic allocation may be subdivided into structures of production and structures of consumption.

B. STRUCTURES OF PRODUCTION AND CONSUMPTION

1. INTRODUCTION

Structures of production include all of the structures in terms of which the members of a given social system create or modify the goods and/or services which accrue in the name of the system [i.e., accrue in some fashion however transitory to its members]. These goods and/or services may be taken from the members or some set of them in a variety of ways as quickly as they accrue. *Structures of consumption* include all of the structures in terms of which goods and/or services are allocated to and utilized by the various members of the social systems concerned for the purposes recognized by the members of those systems. As already indicated above [pp. 210–211] production and consumption exemplify a special sort of distinction. What is production from one point of view is consumption from another. Nevertheless, it makes a considerable amount of difference whether a particular activity is looked at from the point of view of production or from the point of view of consumption. There are always some organizations in every society in terms of which distinctions between production and consumption are considered unimportant if made at all. These are, of course, never predominantly economically oriented organizations. They are either differently specialized or relatively nonspecialized organizations. The best example of this is again a family unit. In every society families are actually units in terms of which important forms of production and consumption take place. The activities of the members in terms of a given family are frequently not [or hardly ever] differentiated on the basis of production and consumption as such either by the members of that family or others of the society. It may nevertheless be of the greatest utility for an individual in attempting to analyze family units to make this differentiation. In relatively nonmodernized societies the families are units which combine most of the production and consumption of most of the members. The vast majority of the members of any relatively modernized society consider the family overwhelmingly as a unit in terms of which consumption rather than production takes place. But even from the point of view of those most accustomed to differentiate in these specialized terms, the actual activities carried out in family terms are rarely differentiated into those of production and consumption as such. What goes on in the family context is spoken of as consumption from the point of view of nonfamily activities of the members and the society as a whole. Within the family context it would be unusual to differentiate activities into those of production, e.g., preparation of food, cleaning of the household, rearing of children, etc., and those of consumption, e.g., eating of food, watching the television set, enjoying a good night's sleep, etc. In relatively nonmodernized societies the family context encompasses activities which would be sharply differentiated by the members of a more modernized society as predominantly production-oriented activities or as predominantly consumption-oriented activities [if considered from an economic point of view (on the asymmetry of the concepts of production and consumption see below, pp. 247–248, 504–513, and 522–523], but those actually involved consider their activities as family activities and not as specialized predominantly economically oriented activities in any sense.

The fact that such specialized differentiations are not commonly made in any sharp form by the members of a given society makes a great deal of difference to anyone who seeks to analyze and understand these phenomena. For example, in terms especially relevant to the problems of modernization, the tendency of any observer more used to the practices of members of a relatively modernized society to view family activities as legitimately primarily a special focus of consumption, if considered from the economic point of view, is likely to be viewed by members of a relatively nonmodernized society as either unfeeling, unknowing, or even as an interference with appropriately family-oriented activities. To pursue an occupational role outside the family context is to have a whole new world open up for most of the members of such societies. To do so is also likely to undermine a whole set of characteristic reinforcements for the stability of family structures and hence usually of more general structures as well.

2. STRUCTURES OF PRODUCTION

In analysis of the structures of production, one of the terms most frequently encountered is the division of labor. The term *division of labor* is defined here as role differentiation on the basis of production. It is important to realize that the members of a given society or of a given organization within a society may not make these differentiations in any sharp fashion. I have already indicated above that such differentiations are much more likely in relatively modernized societies and are most likely in terms of the highly specialized social systems that characterize such societies. Even in those settings, these differentiations are not made neatly within relatively nonspecialized organizations such as family units. Some distinctions among forms of production are minimally required in any society and are necessary in analyzing the division of labor in any society. These may be divided into three categories: (1) the production of raw materials [i.e., materials or objects which exist in a nonhuman environment and are either directly dissipated upon their acquisition or are dissipated in the creation of other goods or services], (2) manufactured goods [i.e., all goods which are modified by human activities for human purposes from a raw material state], and (3) the actual allocation of goods and/or services itself [i.e., the production of management, delivery services, salesmanship activities, gift bestowals, regardless of whether these activities are germane primarily to production for further production or to delivery for consumption].

Even in the simplest of societies, to some extent, structures of all three types of production exist, though they are by no means neatly differentiated one from another in a highly specialized form. The members of relatively modernized societies, of course, differentiate these in considerable detail in neatly specialized forms.

a. RAW MATERIALS The production of raw materials may take many forms. Certain minimal raw materials are necessary for survival itself, e.g., for food, clothing, and shelter. Raw materials may be subdivided into animate and inanimate products. Animate products may in turn be divided into those of a botanical character and those of a zoological character. Raw materials for products over and above the minimum necessary for survival may be similarly subdivided.

Structures of production of botanical raw materials are confined to structures of simple collection and structures of collection based to some degree on processes of cultivation. Collection in the absence of cultivation may vary all the way from structures such as gathering nuts and berries to structures involving the use of complex machinery in a planned deforestation for the purposes of timber production or a highly modernized fishing fleet. No society of any considerable scale can exist if the members resort solely to collection activities in order to secure a supply of organic materials. Insofar as the members of any society do depend on such collection activities, the range of variation of such a society will be to that degree more narrowly explicable in terms of human heredity and the nonhuman environment than would otherwise be the case. The addition of mechanical aids for collection increases flexibility to some extent, but it is safe to say that no considerable development of such mechanical aids can itself develop unless some structures other than simple structures of collection exist in the society or in other societies with which the members of the society concerned are in contact. When such mechanical aids exist, the requirements of their production and their maintenance introduce inflexibilities of another sort, usually those involving an increase in the interdependency of the subsystems within the societies concerned.

Although structures of simple collection cannot be completely ignored because of their role in the economic aspects of a society, the most cavalier reading of social history impresses one with the importance of structures of cultivation in all relatively stable societies of any considerable scale, and of clearly developed organizations in terms of which cultivation of whatever sort is carried out. Indeed, relatively few societies of any sort seem to survive in the absence of such a development. There are examples, however. Certain Eskimo peoples exist [or have existed] for whom concentration is perhaps overwhelmingly on animal rather than botanical sources of raw materials. On the whole, some structures of cultivation of plants are, if not ubiquitous, at least present in the overwhelming proportion of all known societies. The term *agrarian* will be used here to apply to those structured aspects and subsystems of any society which are concerned with the cultivation of plant materials.

Agrarian elements in a society always limit nomadism. Some of the members of such a society must be tied to specific areas during planting and harvesting seasons. The implications go well beyond this, however, since constant care and attention between planting and harvesting activities are necessary in most cases if there is to be any considerable harvest at all. The limits on nomadism are not the only implications of the presence of agrarian elements in a society. Some concepts of rights and obligations in locational factors [i.e., property rights in the land] and some conceptions of their distribution among the members of such societies are an inevitable concomitant. Conflicts over these, as well as other matters, must be held within certain limits; certain minimal responsibilities for cultivation must be allocated; and there must be specific structures of distribution for the products of such production, as there must be for any forms of production.

A large number of aspects of agrarian production have far-reaching implications for general social structures. The different plants themselves, the different characteristics of different soils, climates, and seasons, the different types of work units—all have widespread implications which cannot be ignored. The differences between relatively modernized and relatively nonmodernized structures of agrarian production are especially significant for present purposes. As pointed out before, the term *modernized* permits of indefinite degrees of variation despite the fact that the distinction between the terms *relatively modernized* and *relatively nonmodernized* identify social states characterized by other distinctions that differ far beyond the elements of tools and power in their definitions. It is useful to differentiate societies with respect to the degree and kind of modernization or lack of it. The range of variation possible for relatively nonmodernized societies is widely different from that possible for relatively modernized ones. In many respects the range of variation possible and actual in relatively nonmodernized agrarian systems is much greater than in relatively modernized ones. Furthermore, the higher the level of modernization, the greater is the isomorphism of the systems concerned. Members of relatively nonmodernized societies, for example, may organize such production in terms of an almost indefinite number of different types of differently [though usually predominantly particularistically] recruited units. Members of relatively modernized societies must increasingly emphasize more predominantly universalistically recruited units. The degree of self-sufficiency of the organizations is much higher in the relatively nonmodernized cases. Variations in the scale and variety of products, degree of specialization, etc., are much higher in the relatively modernized cases. The relative ease of comparability, especially as the level of modernization increases, increases the importance of the recognition of these factors for purposes of comparative analysis.

I have focused overwhelmingly on botanical raw materials above rather than on animal raw materials. With regard to animal raw materials, again the distinction between simple collection and cultivation [i.e., animal husbandry in this case] is drawn. Here the possibilities of combining both simple collection and animal husbandry with nomadism are considerable. In both cases the details of the nonhuman environment, the size of the membership of the society, and the type of animals involved place definite limits on the degree to which nomadism can be avoided and the degree to which it can be practiced if the society is to persist.

The greater mobility of animal as opposed to plant stocks means, of course, that animal husbandry does not have the same implications for sedentary structures as agrarian production. Structures relative to the use of space are also considerably different. The clear demarcation of hunting and fishing preserves as well as grazing possibilities is both more difficult and less practicable than is the clear demarcation of plots of land for cultivation of plant stocks. Extremely small, highly parcellated land holdings of the type characteristic of many agrarian-based societies are quite out of the question in animal-husbandry-based societies. The implications of greater spatial mobility of the membership of such societies for the organization of different social systems are considerable as are the requirements of locomotion and the like.

Sedentary animal husbandry also has different implications for social structures than does sedentary agrarian production. Given land capable of both agrarian cultivation and animal husbandry, other factors being equal and quite apart from the differences in mobility of plants and animals, the amount of land necessary to support human life via animal husbandry is much greater. For all of the inefficiencies of agriculture it is more productive per acre in terms of food and other raw materials than is animal husbandry, assuming land adaptable to either purpose. Given land adaptable in physiological terms for either purpose, animal husbandry can be more profitable than agriculture in terms of food production only under certain conditions. There must be a comparative advantage for animal husbandry between the area concerned and other areas with which its users are in contact, i.e., it must be possible for exchange to take place among the inhabitants of these areas such that persons involved in animal husbandry can more than equal their possibilities of agrarian food production through the exchange of the products of animal husbandry for agrarian products. Even apart from differences in productivity, animal husbandry would still require different social structures. The types of knowledge required vary widely, and different organizations are both feasible and necessary. The differences involved are well illustrated in history when members of societies characterized by agrarian production and animal husbandry and/or different types of animal husbandry have come into contact with one another. Conflict among the members has been a frequent feature. Conflicts between cattlemen and sheepmen, cattlemen and farmers, etc., in the history of the United States were not only notorious for the violence and bitterness involved, but also clearly reflected different ways of life. In England the enclosure movement and in China the contacts between the Chinese and the Mongols contained important elements of this sort. Throughout history cases of change from cultivation to animal husbandry or from one type of cultivation or animal husbandry to another have had far-reaching social implications. It is not necessary to be an economic determinist to learn the lesson that they really did have to teach us, namely that the structures of production are never without some implications for other types of structures in any society.

As in the case of agrarian production, animal husbandry too can be carried out on a relatively modernized or relatively non-modernized basis. In animal husbandry, too, the implications of the difference are far-reaching. Modernization in animal husbandry increases the practicable scale of production units and in fact places minimal requirements on the scale. The productivity of labor is tremendously increased, though the absolute productivity of all of the other factors involved need not necessarily be increased, at least not to the same degree that the productivity of labor is increased.

Modernization in this field requires the integration of raw material production with some manufacturing. The further modernization is carried, the greater becomes the interdependence in these respects and the lower the degrees of self-sufficiency possible for the organizations in terms of which animal husbandry is conducted. In a highly modernized society, for example, an obscure grievance precipitating a strike of power workers could create a major crisis within a matter of hours in the dairy production of the area concerned. Prior to the invention and spread of automatic milking machines, such interdependency was unknown. Increases in modernization both increase and decrease flexibility. As far as self-sufficiency is concerned the decrease is the more noticeable. Flexibility with regard to product differentiation, elaboration, etc., is increased. The possibilities of disposing of a product are increased, but the necessity of such disposal outside the membership of the organization in terms of which production takes place is also increased. It is always the essence of modernization that the use of machinery and power so multiplies the effort of the people engaged in production that the members of the unit in terms of which production takes place can never hope to consume directly all or even most of the products they produce. It is quite out of the question to set up a modern dairy production organization solely to supply the dairy needs of the individuals involved in the unit itself.

Apart from growing crystals and the like, the possibilities of self-propagation under control are out of the question with regard to inanimate products. One is confined to collection techniques, though these may vary widely. There is a difference between the ways in which the production of animate and inanimate raw materials may or must fit into a society. It is conceivable, perhaps, that puristic vegetarians use little or no animal or inanimate raw materials. A society whose members are similarly focused on animal products is also at least conceivable. Similar concentration upon inanimate raw materials is, however, quite out of the question because of the relative unavailability of inanimate raw materials as foodstuffs. Therefore, inanimate raw material production must, to some extent, be integrated with some structures of production of animate raw materials. In all the societies of concern here some inanimate raw materials are always involved, but the difference in degree of preoccupation possible on a raw material level as between animate and inanimate materials is nevertheless significant. Hunting, fishing, agrarian, or animal husbandry structures can conceivably well nigh, if not completely, exhaust the raw material production of the members of a society. This cannot even conceivably be the case with regard to inanimate raw material production such as mining and the like. In the production of inanimate raw materials distinctions among the degrees and types of modernization must also be explored.

b. MANUFACTURED GOODS As the term *manufactured goods* is used here, some element of manufacture enters the raw material picture whenever the production of raw materials passes the most rudimentary collection procedures. In both cultivation and animal husbandry, for example, almost at once some modification in selection of stocks takes place. Such elements enter the picture to a marked degree with increases in the level of modernization. Elements of manufacture in the production of raw materials must, therefore, be carefully distinguished. Structures of production of manufactured goods obviously cannot stand alone in any society or in any subsystem of any society. No matter how specialized organizations become, in relation to any manufactured goods, two other types of questions relevant to economic aspects inevitably arise. First, there is the question of the materials which are modified. What are they? How are they produced? How do they get to the manufacturers, etc.? Second, there is the question of the process of modification itself. What further goods and/or services are required for this process? Where do they come from? How do they get to the manufacturers, etc.? It may be conceivable for there to be a society in which virtually all of the structures of production are confined to raw materials and the services of allocation without any manufacturing, but if there is any manufacturing at all, there must be both structures of production of raw materials and structures of allocation as well.

Manufacturing, as conceived here, covers quite rudimentary modifications—rudimentary enough to make structures of manufacture an inevitable component in any society of any scale. Cooked food, sharpened tools, as well as modern blast furnaces are all examples of manufactured goods as that term is used here. Virtually all raw materials used by the members of any society of any scale undergo some modification by human activity prior to consumption. It is important to distinguish between raw materials and manufactured goods, nevertheless, since to some extent raw materials may be directly consumed without a modification beyond the gathering thereof. Such structures can never exhaust the structures of production in a society because of the helplessness of some of the members of the society, but they may be present for many. As soon as the question of modification arises, however, questions of the source and character of the things modified and the things used to modify them arise. The problem of sources of goods for modification plus modification itself always makes any altered or manufactured good different in kind as far as its social significance is concerned from any raw material.

As in the case of raw materials for present purposes the most important distinction with regard to manufactured goods is whether or not they are manufactured on a relatively modernized or a relatively nonmodernized basis. Here again relatively nonmodernized manufacture is subject to a wider range of variation in many respects than is relatively modernized manufacture. This is particularly true with regard to the types of organizations in terms of which such production may be carried out. The emphases, associated with high levels of modernization, on rationality, universalism, and functional specificity, for example, limit the possibilities of relationships in terms of which manufacturing can be carried out quite sharply. The organizations in terms of which manufacturing is conducted by the members of relatively nonmodernized societies are likely to be predominantly particularistic—indeed, they are usually family units. They are by no means inevitably so, however. In relatively nonmodernized societies the units in terms of which manufacturing takes place are also ordinarily the units in terms of which most of the consumption of the goods manufactured also takes place. In relatively modernized contexts, however, only restricted manufacturing can be carried out in terms of the same units in terms of which consumption of these items takes place.

c. ALLOCATION The production of *allocation* is more likely to be ignored than the production of either raw materials or manufactured goods. Two categories of allocation are distinguished here: (1) allocation in the *managerial sense,* i.e., the planning and supervision of the productive processes themselves, and (2) the *distributive sense,* i.e., the distribution of the goods and/ or services produced to the persons or sets of people who will consume them. Both forms of allocation must take place if any society is to survive. Goods and services can neither be produced nor dissipated at random if a society is to survive. Allocation in both senses is always carefully structured in every known society.

What is production from one point of view is, simultaneously, consumption from another point of view, but the consumption of a given article is by no means necessarily simultaneous with its production. There is one sense, however, in which the production of allocation differs from the production of either raw materials or manufactured goods. The processes of allocation are at one and the same time produced and consumed. Both types of allocative processes share this characteristic. A given act involving allocation may be only one step in a further chain of allocation, but as it is effected it is consumed. The organization of a hunting party is done when it is done. Its members may stand idle for months, though organized, but they are in essence consuming their organizational characteristics all the time. Goods delivered to a wholesaler's warehouse may sit there forever, but the production and consumption of their delivery are simultaneous. An additional peculiarity of the managerial form of allocation is the possibility of its being consumed indefinitely. However indestructible the goods may be, they have some span of life as a particular type of goods. Some types of services are indefinite in these respects. The planning of a given activity is one of these. One of the interesting distinctions as far as allocation is concerned between relatively modernized and relatively nonmodernized societies is precisely the fact that in the context of relatively modernized societies the managerial sense of allocation is usually quite short lived. In the context of relatively nonmodernized societies the managerial sense of allocation may have a very long life indeed.

There is one important distinction between managerial and distributive allocation. The former is not separable from the production to which it is relevant whereas the latter is. Managerial allocation of some sort inheres in every process of production and is consumed simultaneously with the process of production. The distribution of the fruits of such production may be handled in terms of separate organizations altogether. No activity can exist without some direction whether centralized or decentralized. From the point of view of the general members of a society there must also be actual distributive mechanisms, but these need not be operated directly in terms of the units in terms of which the goods and/or services to be distributed are in fact produced. The members of one organization may build automobiles, and the members of another quite distinct one, either private or state, may drive them away.

Finally, the general relevance of the allocation of goods and services for the structures of political allocation must be noted briefly. Managerial allocation is inseparable from the allocation of power and responsibility in the productive processes. The actual distribution of goods and/or services is no less inextricably involved with questions of power and responsibility, but it is involved in a different way. Without some command over the allocation of goods and services, neither power nor responsibility holders would be alive to carry out their roles, but the matter goes far beyond this. The relevance of the allocation of goods and services as an instrument of coercion, persuasion, and influence in general, cannot be overlooked. One need not go to the unjustifiable extreme of holding that "man lives by bread alone" for such factors to be relevant. It is only necessary to realize that "no man lives by nonmaterial factors alone." As indicated [pp. 125–126] there is a limit to the degree of other worldliness possible for the members of any society which persists, even though some minimum of this may also be inescapable. No study which ignores the implications of the allocation of goods and services for the allocation of power and responsibility, and vice versa, can handle the problems which inhere in the general field of public and international affairs.

3. STRUCTURES OF CONSUMPTION

Much of what has been said immediately above would apply also to the consumption aspects if only because of the fact that what is production from one point of view is consumption from another. Nevertheless, implications of viewing economic allocation in terms of both of these concepts are quite different. It is primarily from the point of view of consumption that we learn how one set of activities implements another in terms of a given society. It matters, for example, whether the factors consumed are raw materials, manufactured goods, or allocation services. It matters whether or not they are produced under relatively modernized or relatively nonmodernized conditions. Just as revealing, however, are the implications of how command over consumption implements the allocation of power and responsibility, how much and what sorts of consumption are allocated to what sorts of educational activities, etc. Distinctions among the things produced have direct implications for how they may be produced because of the empirical nature of the processes involved. What is consumed also has relevance for how it may be consumed. Since goods produced by either relatively modernized or relatively nonmodernized processes can sometimes serve the same consumption purposes, the *purposes* of consumption become in a sense the more directly relevant part of the analysis. Three questions must be considered in the analysis of any organizations in terms of which consumption is to be studied: (1) what is the source and type of income of the members of the organization qua members, (2) how and by whom is the distribution of the income controlled, and (3) to whom and for what purposes is income allocated? These questions enter any consideration of the structures of consumption. Many of the factors touched on above have implications for the possible range of variation in these respects. The helplessness of infants, for example, at one and the same time precludes their services as managers and requires that the roles of others be so differentiated as to make consumption possible for infants.

In general, if one looks at economic allocation from the point of view of production, one stresses the manner in which given things get done. If one looks at economic allocation from the point of view of consumption, he tends to stress the implications of what gets done for subsequent events. The analysis of action from the point of view of production stresses the implications of action in terms of various organizations and general structured aspects of social systems for economic allocation; the analysis of action from the point of view of consumption stresses the implications of economic allocation for action in terms of various organizations and general structured aspects of social systems.

I I
SELF-SUFFICIENCY VERSUS
INTERDEPENDENCE OF SOCIAL SYSTEMS

One of the most important distinctions among different sorts of social systems has to do with the extent to which action in terms of a given system combines most of the production and consumption of the members of the system, that is the extent to which its structures cover most of the economic aspects of the member's behavior. Obviously no social systems can be highly self-sufficient unless they are organizations of this sort. Because of general preoccupation with economic aspects of behavior as well as because of the relative ease of perception and measurement of goods and services, observation of the relative self-sufficiency of a given system with regard to the production of and consumption of goods and services by its members is, in fact, probably the quickest key to the question of whether or not it is highly self-sufficient in more general respects as well. Such a key should not be used uncritically. While economic self-sufficiency is a *sine qua non* of more general self-sufficiency, it is certainly not the only matter to be considered in making such a judgment. Despite the enormous mutual relevance of economic and political allocation, an organization may be highly self-sufficient economically without being highly self-sufficient politically.

A given social system will be considered economically self-sufficient to the degree and in the respects that its membership can and does both produce and consume all the goods and/or services necessary to and resulting from the operations of the members in terms of the unit. In this sense, no unit of any society is completely self-sufficient economically, though the society may be. To the extent that complete self-sufficiency is impossible, there are minimal requirements for relations among the members of any given unit and the members of some other unit(s). This is obviously true from the point of view of production aspects of economic allocation. The members of an organization in terms of which shoes but no food are produced must have contact, directly or indirectly, with some members of organizations in terms of which food is produced. This is no less true from the point of view of consumption aspects of economic allocation. The members of a unit who cannot and do not consume all that they produce must have interrelationships with members of other organizations who can fill this function of consumption or they must accumulate unconsumed products endlessly. The only alternative is to cut back production with the structural changes that would thereby be involved. The implications of the self-sufficiency of the units are, in general, all implications for the involvement of the members of the units concerned with the members of other units in the society, and specifically in this case, the implications are the implications of the economic aspects of the units concerned for other aspects of these and other units. Self-sufficiency may vary widely if not infinitely in degree and type. This is true of both consumption and production. Some specific formulation of the degree and type of self-sufficiency of the units concerned from both the point of view of production and consumption is necessary in the analysis of any society. From the point of view of production, self-sufficiency of a unit varies in two main respects: (1) to what extent do operations in terms of the unit produce all the necessary factors for the production carried out in terms of it, and (2) to what extent do the operations in terms of the unit produce the factors necessary for the consumption of the members of the unit apart from that involved in the production itself? The first question is always involved in considering any organization. The second is only involved directly in those organizations in terms of which both the production and the consumption of the members are combined ideally speaking. Examples may illuminate this distinction. The typical factory unit of relatively modernized societies is oriented consumptionwise to those materials necessary for the production carried out in terms of it. Raw materials, labor, machines, power, etc., are involved. Insofar as it has any self-sufficiency, its self-sufficiency is to be reckoned in those terms. The consumption activities of its members, apart from the factors mentioned above, are expected to be carried out in terms of quite different units. Some of these different units are always family units, but there may be many other types of units as well. The lack of self-sufficiency in production of these other units is not directly germane to the factory unit's self-sufficiency unless this lack of self-sufficiency interferes with the ability of the members of the factory to operate in terms of the structures of the factory. Thus housing for workers is not ordinarily a concern of the members of the factory units as such. On the other hand, if a decision is made to locate a plant in a place such that housing is inaccessible for workers, some provision of housing itself or of transportation for workers from available housing is directly germane to the self-sufficiency of the factory organization from the point of view of production.

On the other hand, in a society like that of traditional China, quite a different picture obtains. In that society the basic unit in terms of which production was generally carried out was the peasant family unit. Unlike the factory illustration above, that unit was also, ideally speaking, the unit in terms of which most of the consumption as well as most of the production of most of the members was carried out. In the case of the traditional Chinese family both types of consideration relative to self-sufficiency were germane all of the time. The traditional Chinese family unit lacked economic self-sufficiency not only if its members could not produce the tools, seeds, etc., necessary for agrarian production, but also if they did not produce the food, clothing, shelter, and services necessary for all of their consumption. Ideally speaking most of the members of that society were expected to carry out both types of production in terms of the same unit. They also expected to consume those goods and services in terms of the same unit. These peasant families were never completely self-sufficient. To some degree the peasants were involved in some interdependencies because of the import of goods from nonfamily sources—goods such as iron for tools, salt, etc. Had this been the sum total of the involvement of the members, interdependencies with the members of other units could have been kept at an absolute minimum by exchanging goods and/or services produced in the family context for the ones just mentioned. Actually interdependency was forced further because of exports in the form of taxes, rents, and interest on loans. Taxes were virtually unavoidable, and in many parts of China at many different periods of history the rates of tenancy rose quite high.[1]

The degree of economic interdependence of units of the second

[1] There was another interesting interference with the self-sufficiency of the peasant Chinese family, as China was, ideally speaking, an open-class society. Its class structure got badly clogged, and perhaps relatively few people did rise in proportion to the total population, but to rise was always a goal to be striven for. In a genuine sense, for members of a family to rise in the social scale in China, they had to get involved in increased interdependency with the members of other units. As a minimum they had to find some way to export and exchange goods and/or services produced in terms of their family for other goods and/or services or for money which could be used to buy additional land or still other goods and/or services for exchange.

type is less than in the case of units of the factory type, if operations in terms of the units take place according to expectations. This distinction is not only significant, however, when the operations take place according to expectations. They are equally relevant when this doesn't happen. Cases like that of the factory unit, for example, require carefully structured forms of economic interdependence of far-reaching proportions. Cases like that of the traditional Chinese peasant family do not, and commonly such societies lack a comparable development of carefully structured forms of economic interdependence. A given economic failure in the context of highly developed factories is likely to result in spreading the problems of the failure along the lines of this expected interdependence. Failure to dispose of factory products brings unemployment of factory workers; their unemployment lowers their ability to purchase foodstuffs, etc.; this in turn affects operations in terms of other units of production; and depending on the degree of interdependence, the effects of such an economic dislocation spread widely and rapidly among the members of the society concerned and among those of other societies economically interdependent with them. In the case of the Chinese peasant family such spreads are far more restricted. Only conditions such as drought, floods, and insect scourges which wipe out simultaneously the production of the members of large numbers of families bring widespread economic depression. When such depressions occur and spread, they are not generally understandable in terms of the units and the interstitial adjustments of their members. Furthermore, the problems of relief in such situations are further complicated by the fact that ordinarily in those systems the very units dislocated are the standard relief units. Organization of relief in the case of highly self-sufficient units generally requires the erection of structures of economic interdependency of a type not previously in existence.

Finally, a special observation is necessary with regard to the close interrelationship of the structures of economic and political allocation. The higher the level of self-sufficiency of an organization from the economic point of view, the greater is the problem of exercising centralized control over the members of the organization. To the extent that such units are highly self-sufficient in goods and services, control of the flow of goods and/or services is unavailable as a means of enforcing conformity on or requiring other performances from the members concerned. Given the general relevance of the allocation of goods and/or services for other aspects of behavior, one of the first things which must be done if one wishes to increase centralized control in societies with subsystems that are highly self-sufficient economically is to break down the degree of economic self-sufficiency of those systems. On the other hand, the less economically self-sufficient the subsystems of a society are, the greater are the implications for the existing structures of control of any breakdown in the allocations of goods and services in terms of the society. Highly self-sufficient peasant units are more difficult for members of a central government to control, but highly interdependent factory units pose much greater problems for the continued stability of a government if governmental control is inefficient or irrational from the economic point of view.

I I I
SPECIALIZATION OF THE SUBSYSTEMS

Specialization of the subsystems of a society from the economic point of view is subject to very wide variation, but limits are possible. For every society major elements of consumption always take place in a family context. There are no known exceptions to this. They are, of course, many societies whose members do not make the distinction between consumption and production as glibly as members of our society have been trained to do. Nevertheless, in both relatively modernized and relatively nonmodernized societies the family units are always a focus of consumption from the point of view of the members of the society in general and the members of the various families in particular. As indicated above, the members of relatively modernized societies frequently speak as though family units were the only units in terms of which consumption takes place save for individual exceptions of more or less unapproved hedonism. There is always some element of production in a family context too in all known societies, but the production element is more likely to be overlooked in critical respects. This is characteristic of relatively modernized societies. No one can look at the family organizations of relatively nonmodernized societies without being struck by the fact that a vast proportion of the production aspects of behavior are conducted in family terms. There may be examples of relatively nonmodernized societies in terms of which only a small proportion of the general production-oriented activities are carried out in family terms, but if such cases exist, they are rare. In relatively modernized societies, however, the development of specialized predominantly economically oriented organizations has gone quite far. The vast majority of these are not only specialized with regard to their economic aspects, but within the range of their economic aspects they are specialized from the point of view of their production aspects. In these societies there are not only predominantly economically oriented organizations, but almost certainly all of those are predominantly production-oriented as well. In considering such societies one hardly thinks of the family as a unit in terms of which production takes place, despite the fact that a considerable proportion of child care, the preparation of food, and other forms of production are still, even in the most modernized societies, carried out in family contexts. In both relatively modernized and relatively nonmodernized societies there are examples of specialized predominantly economically oriented organizations that are specially oriented to production. In no known social context, however, have organizations been specialized as predominantly consumption-oriented, predominantly economically oriented organizations. Such organizations may have existed as special forms of hedonistic expression, but they have probably never been generally approved or sanctioned by the members of the societies in which they have existed. From the point of view of the people who work in terms of them the most specialized recreationally oriented organizations such as night clubs, for example, are predominantly production-oriented rather than consumption-oriented if considered from the economic point of view. Even in societies in terms of which the members feel that most of the consumption is carried out in family terms, the family is never generally considered to be overwhelmingly oriented to consumption rather than to noneconomic aspects of behavior. Even in the most modernized societies family units are not considered to be more oriented to consumption than to solidarity, education, child rearing, etc. I mention this because there is an element of asymmetry here with regard to the concepts of production and consumption as they are actually embodied in social practice.[2]

The specialization of social systems is, of course, closely interrelated with the question of the self-sufficiency. Family units can never be specialized units in this sense, and organizations that are specialized in this sense can never approach the level of self-sufficiency that can be approached by family units. Members of organizations other than family units, whether specialized in these respects or not, must always have interrelationships with members of family units and other nonfamily units. The members of family units, if those units are self-sufficient enough, need

[2] This asymmetry is disturbing and/or interesting theoretically given the fact that what is production from one point of view is always consumption from another. Its possible significance is discussed in greater detail below, pp. 504–513.

not have relationships with members of other family units save for the minimal exchange of personnel necessary to comply with whatever form of incest taboo applies in the particular society concerned. As iterated before, the greater the specialization of a given organization, the lower is its self-sufficiency. The reverse is not necessarily the case, however. Relatively unspecialized units may be highly interdependent ones.

I V
FORMS OF PRODUCTION

From the point of view of observations strategic for the analysis of societies in general and for the analysis of relatively modernized as opposed to relatively nonmodernized societies in particular, volumes could easily be written on the forms of production alone. Some of what has to be said as a minimum has already been said above in the initial elaboration of the distinction between production and consumption itself. Here I shall only reiterate a few special considerations that are likely to be overlooked. A great many of the most essential observations about forms of production are fortunately treated at great length in the general literature of economics, and in the special literatures of industrial sociology, business school publications, and the field usually referred to as human organization and human relations.

First, no matter how varied societies may be, there are always some forms of production common to all societies. One of the best examples of this is infant and child care. The common details of this form of production are by no means as abstract as the observation that some form of production of food is common to all societies. It is possible to go into considerable detail as to what the minima of child care are for the members of any society. They not only involve food, shelter, clothing, and the services necessary for some level of cleanliness, but also, very importantly indeed, education and training, including virtually all of the training in those skills that form the foundation on which all other skills and learning rest in later life. This matter will be gone into in greater detail below [pp. 377–435]. For the moment, suffice it to say that these skills involve speaking, eating, sleeping, locomotion, perception in general, modes of thought, and initial adjustments to role differentiation, solidarity, economic allocation, political allocation, and integration and expression. Not only are these forms of production common to all societies, but a considerable portion of such production always takes place for the overwhelming majority of all of the members in terms of family units. Leaving to one side the so far inadequately examined claims of such devices as the Chinese communes and the kibbutzim of Israel, the members of the family organizations characteristic of the modern United States probably go further than any other family members in world history in the export of child and infant care to social contexts other than family ones. Even in the modern United States, however, the observations above hold.

The common core of forms of production always extends beyond infant and child care, but family units are an exceedingly good place to seek out most of the minimal common forms of production for all societies. The reasons for this should already be obvious from much of what has been said above. Prior to the development of relatively modernized societies, the family unit was more likely to be the unit in terms of which economic allocation took place for most of the members of any given society, most of the time, than any other organization. Neighborhood units of some sort and/or government units of some sort would be second to family units in these respects. It is one of the ironies associated with the most highly modernized societies that at the very time the level of specialization and the increase of material productivity characteristic of the most highly modernized of societies makes possible the most radical export of various forms of production from the family context, the increased time available for time spent in a family context as opposed to a specialized occupational context—the time made available by the leisure revolution referred to above—may actually increase the amount of time spent in a family context in activities of interest from the point of view of their implications for various forms of production. Insofar as this is the case, the members of the families concerned are more likely to view such forms of production as predominantly recreationally rather than as predominantly economically oriented.

Apart from generalizations about the importance of food getting and the like, two other forms of production are especially significant for understanding societies both from general points of view and more specifically from the point of view of the problems of modernization and stability. First, no matter how decentralized the organization of a given society may be, there must be some production of communication among the members. Insofar as one can measure these matters, the proportion of the output of the members of a society spent, as it were, on communications is a figure of great significance. When that proportion is low, the degree of self-sufficiency of the units *must* be high if the society is a stable one. In both general and specific cases many implications for problems of control and the like follow from these hypotheses.[3] Second, the members of any given society must, if the society is to be stable, engage in actions which may be viewed as producing governmental services. As a minimum every society must have some subsystem whose member(s) have especially general responsibilities for the maintenance of order, decision-making, etc. In societies of extremely small scale such services may be quite restricted, but no matter how decentralized any society of any considerable scale may be, these services can never be negligible from the point of view of the general structures of production in the society. To some extent both the minimal forms of productivity necessary for communications and government must be carried out in terms of an organization(s) other than ordinary family units.

If the members of a society are to survive, either the members themselves or other members with whom they are in contact must be capable of producing food. It is characteristic of all relatively nonmodernized societies of any scale that the overwhelming proportion of the members for the overwhelming proportion of their time are involved in the production of food. Some of the various forms this may take have been discussed briefly above, but actually in relatively nonmodernized societies of any scale the form of such food production in the vast majority of cases has been sedentary agriculture. Those societies whose members have depended for food primarily on nomadic husbandry, whether plants or animals, have in general been relatively small-scale ones. For societies of any considerable scale even animal husbandry is usually sedentary rather than nomadic and associated with sedentary plant husbandry. One of the great problems of the all-conquering Mongols lay in the fact that they really had only two choices in handling the territories they conquered. They could literally wipe out the existing population and turn over the lands to grazing land, or they could govern the existing population on a basis different than that on which they were accustomed to govern themselves. They could not govern sedentary agrarian populations on the basis of social structures adapted to one of the

---

[3] This subject is a major one in and of itself. One further implication would be that the proportion of income spent on communications always increases with modernization regardless of declines in cost per unit of communication, however those may be currently measured. The problems of centralization of governments and of modernization in general as special problems in the more general field of information theory have hardly been touched on. They will become increasingly critical questions for all persons concerned with public policy.

more radical forms of nomadism. Indeed, once the areas controlled were large enough and their own people increased sufficiently, they would not have been able to govern even those by the old laws. For all the destruction they visited on others, the further they pushed their conquests and tried to hold them, the more certainly they destroyed their own society.

One of the inevitable corollaries of modernization has been the declining proportion of the population engaged in food production. Even when food production remains or increases as an important proportion of the total national income, the personnel involved in its production declines radically with modernization. The earlier applications of inanimate sources of power and radically productive tools to manufacture in the narrow sense has led to a lag of thinking in which, somehow, food production, even under the most modernized circumstances, is regarded as less industrialized than activities carried out in factory buildings. Nothing could be more naïve. To consider our cities as the symbol par excellence of the state of our modernization is to overlook obvious gambits in the gamesmanship of world affairs. Latecomers to modernization find it far easier to reproduce our urban centers with their manufacturing productivity than to reproduce the manufacturing productivity of our agrarian production.

In this sphere it is not so much the productivity of labor which is the special mark of modernization, but rather the productivity per acre. Prior to modernization, no societies in world history have ever had structures of production such that one could expect long-run increases in productivity per acre more or less indefinitely projected into the future; virtually all such increases were sporadic and relatively long separated in time. With high levels of modernization such increases can be systematic and relatively rapid. For reasons which are by no means clear, developments in the modernization of food production is the basis of one distinction which has split relatively neatly along the increasingly outmoded distinction between capitalistic and socialistic societies. So far even the most highly developed of the so-called socialistic societies have been spectacularly less remarkable in these developments than the United States which is perhaps the epitome in these ideological terms of a so-called capitalistic society. The same contrast can be seen in a comparison of the development of agrarian productivity in China and Japan. Lack of motivation on the part of leaders in these cases cannot be argued since increase in productivity per acre of foodstuffs is usually sought by the officials controlling these developments.

For late-comers, especially, modernized production in an urban setting may be much easier to develop specifically because there is a sense in which this form of production does not replace anything but develops in an area in which there may have been little or nothing before. Relatively modernized agrarian production, however, almost inevitably replaces something in an area in which there was something before, something about which the members involved felt deeply, and something which, in its structures of organization, literally touched on, if it did not completely encompass, the entire lives of all who were concerned in it.

Nonagrarian production in all social contexts may be divided into three general types: (1) domestic or local production in terms of nonspecialized organizations, (2) production in terms of specialized small-scale units [e.g., some craft organizations], and (3) production in terms of specialized large-scale units [e.g., factories]. In all of the relatively nonmodernized social contexts a considerable part of nonagrarian production takes place in nonspecialized domestic or local units. The most obvious example of this is craft production on a nonspecialized basis in terms of a family unit. Much production of this sort is also carried out in neighborhood terms. Often, if not usually, such production is for the direct consumption of the members producing it. It is frequently a spare-time occupation. For various reasons, the emphasis on production carried out on such bases sometimes increases radically, and the products so produced are exported by the members from the social contexts in which they are produced. The so-called domestic or "putting-out" industries are obvious examples of this. Nevertheless, the organizations in terms of which these activities are carried out do not ordinarily become specialized predominantly economically oriented units. The most common of these nonspecialized units is, of course, the family. Such developments always to some extent make the members of the family concerned vulnerable to influences from without the family context, but the unit remains different from any specialized predominantly economically oriented organization. The maintenance of this difference is one of the special features of stress and strain in such social contexts. The fact that the family unit, which ideally in these cases is usually highly self-sufficient, becomes increasingly vulnerable because of its members' involvement in production for export is usually a focus for a special feeling of outrage and injury on their part. They usually have to operate in contact with specialists in exchange—i.e., *merchants.* As has been mentioned above and will be gone into in some detail below, this is one of the reasons why, ideally speaking at least, merchants have more often than not been considered marginal men regardless of how powerful they have become in actuality.

I know of no societies of any scale in which specialized units of production on a small scale do not exist. Even in the context of quite small-scale societies specialists in craftsmanship seem to develop more or less inevitably. The organizations in terms of which these individuals produce are considerably more specialized than the domestic or local units mentioned above. Even when the former are likely to be domestic or family units, as they often are, they differ from the others in that the specialized output of their members is a far greater proportion of their total production. Furthermore, the export of their finished products is overwhelmingly expected to be the source of the main proportion of the income of the members of the unit concerned. When the members of domestic or local organizations produce for export, that production is usually supplementary to some form of food production, usually sedentary agriculture, which the members of the family units concerned regard as their main occupation. The relatively specialized units of craftsmen regard their main occupation as the production of a particular good or service, e.g., doll production, blacksmithing, shoemaking, etc. Insofar as these activities are carried out in a family context the organization cannot be considered predominantly economically oriented. Even when the organization is not a family unit, one may question whether it is specialized in such a way as to be considered predominantly economically oriented. There is no doubt, however, that as far as self-conscious attitudes toward production are concerned, the attitudes of the members of those units are overwhelmingly focused on particular goods or services, that those goods or services are ordinarily disposed of to individuals who are not members of the organization in terms of which it is produced, that from the exchange involved in such disposal both new materials for further production and much of the means of living of the members of the organization are derived. For the members of such organizations the focus is on the production of the goods or services concerned.

Inseparable from this, but secondary to it from the point of view of the artisans, is the disposal of the product and the acquisition of a new supply of materials for further production. One or more members of such a unit must specialize his activities to some extent in the direction of exchange, and the members become importantly dependent upon the activities of specialists in exchange [i.e., merchants] for these reasons. The specialists in exchange have many important implications for the life of the artisans, but they are at best generally thought of as outsiders and a necessary nuisance. Once again the specialist in exchange is likely to be resented if anything goes wrong.[4]

A *factory* as that term is used here, is usually a large-scale unit. That is to say, the forms of production in which its members specialize usually involve a considerable number of individuals. I would not place the main burden of definition of a factory on the number of individuals involved, however. Either domestic, local, and craftsmen organizations may involve considerable numbers of people without becoming factories in the sense in which I would use the term. A factory is distinguished by virtue of the fact that it is a specialized unit predominantly oriented to production. In terms of its structures labor, materials, power, and tools are coordinated. In this sense factories may exist and have existed in relatively nonmodernized societies. Nevertheless, the great proliferation of factories—proliferation to such an extent that they are familiar organizations from the point of view of the general membership of the society—occurs only after change toward relative modernization has begun to gather way in a given social context. Factory units imply special sets of relationships between the members of the factory and their family members as a minimum. They also imply additional relationships of the factory members with specialists in exchange. Materials for production are imported and finished products are exported by factory members.

A factory, as the term is used here, does not have to be an organization in terms of which all activities take place under a single roof. The term refers to a particular form of social organization, not to a building. In this sense it is perfectly correct to say that in many cases there exist today factories in the field. Whatever the history of a society before the development of relatively modernized structures, factories always come into being. Even if they were present before, their proliferation and development are radically accelerated. In relatively nonmodernized societies, because of the specialized orientation of factories, they pose special problems of organization and coordination with the rest of the social structure. In such societies relatively few other social organizations are so highly specialized with regard to one of the aspects of action as are factories. The initial establishment of a

[4] There is a further element of strain inherent in the fact that the more successful any set of artisans become, the more the individual(s) among them who specializes his activities in exchange is forced into the roles appropriate to a merchant. This happens despite the fact that the role of master craftsman is usually far more prestigious.

factory in such a setting, therefore, always has far-reaching implications.

Finally, I must return to an emphasis on distribution as a special form of production. This has already been mentioned [pp. 233, 240–241]. The lower the degree of self-sufficiency and the higher the level of specialization, the greater is the importance of *distribution* as a form of production. Correspondingly, the higher the level of self-sufficiency and the lower the level of specialization, the more specialists in distribution are likely to be regarded as marginal individuals from the point of view of both producers and consumers. These specialists are always outsiders from the point of view of both producers and consumers in other contexts in relatively nonmodernized societies. This attitude is not a function of the popularity of Marxist doctrine. This element of Marxist doctrine is rather more explicable as a particularly effective distillation of an age-old attitude of distrust and distaste for specialists in exchange—an attitude that has been characteristic of the members of all save a small minority of societies.

To some extent distribution develops as a specialized form of production in every society. The development of some minimal means of communication implies this and so does the development of some governmental system. With the development of modernization, the importance of specialists in exchange increases radically if only because of increases in communication and specialization. The growing importance of such specialists is not affected materially by whether or not the society is organized on a socialistic or capitalistic basis. The distinction between capitalism and socialism may tell us a great deal about the manner in which specialists in exchange are employed, but the level of modernization achieved is more indicative of the role which will be played by such specialists than is the question of state versus private ownership.

In the history of modernization we have not only seen radical shifts in the proportion of the population employed first in raw materials production, later in manufacturing, and at present "in services." The proportion of services which can be classified under the heading of distribution have increased both radically and rapidly. In the United States context this is not only reflected in the development of all sorts of specialists in communication, it is also reflected in the strategic power of the leaders of labor organizations whose members are involved primarily in services having to do with distribution such as transportation.

There is one other special feature of distribution as a form of production. In relatively nonmodernized contexts most forms of production are organized in terms of relatively nonspecialized units. This is much less likely to be the case of distribution as a form of production. Merchant firms can be, and often are, family organizations, but most of the activities of merchants and other specialists in distribution fall outside the family context. Even hawkers frequently do not hawk with other family members. There is a sense in which specialists in distribution must live on what they can charge for distribution per unit of whatever is distributed. There is thus for them a minimum viable scale of operations and constant or at least continuing pressure toward an increased scale of operations. There is also constant emphasis on thinking in terms of the possibilities of increasing scale. Specifically to the extent that the specialists in distribution are successful, their activities become less possible to organize on a relatively nonspecialized basis. Even when merchant firms are largely family firms, merchant activities tend to be separate from other family activities to an extent which is almost never the case for the activities of craftsmen or farmers in a relatively nonmodernized social context.

V

MEDIA OF EXCHANGE

In all societies there exist media of exchange, i.e., there are goods and/or services that may be exchanged for two or more different goods and/or services. *Money* is a special case of a medium of exchange. Money may be defined as something that is specifically perceived as a medium of exchange. There may be different media of exchange in a given society, but at elementary levels of development of complexity some monetary units are likely to emerge. As monetary units develop in a given social context, it is exceedingly likely that a single unit that is regarded as a *legal monetary unit*, i.e., the monetary unit controlled by the representatives of the government of the society concerned, will develop. For all of the societies of concern here, some sort of monetary unit is present. Usually there is a legal monetary unit as well, whatever other monetary units may exist. Whether there are monetary units or not, there will be other media of exchange, but the significance of other media of exchange decreases as the acceptance of a legal monetary unit becomes general, as levels of specialization and interdependency increase, and, in general, as modernization increases. There is not space here to discuss money or the social systems specialized with regard to it in any detail. These matters are considered in careful detail and sophisticated theoretical terms by highly professionalized social scientists and men of affairs—the economists. In relatively modernized social contexts money is a question about which many academics, laymen, and government officials are highly sophisticated. In many relatively nonmodernized social contexts there have also been some laymen and some governmental officials highly sophisticated in these respects.

There is not even space here to discuss in any detail the obvious, close relationship between money and government. Monetary units and social systems importantly oriented to monetary matters are rarely developed to any sophisticated degree without a vital concern with monetary matters on the part of the members of the government developing as well. Tokugawa Japan, for example, was a genuinely feudal society, but the members of the Shogun's government were much concerned with regulation and control of the monetary units used.

This is a good opportunity to draw attention to a set of considerations closely associated with the relevance of money for governments and money in other respects as well. This is a respect that we take for granted as members of relatively modernized societies. Perhaps for that reason it is not often treated explicitly. Media of exchange in general and money as a special case of such media can vary radically in the level of generalization to which they are developed. A medium of exchange has been defined here as anything which can be exchanged for two or more different things. A given medium of exchange, for example money, is relatively *more generalized* the larger the number and the greater the variety of goods and services for which it can be exchanged. The *least generalized* medium of exchange would be one which could be exchanged for only a specific pair of other things. The highest level of generalization for a medium of exchange would require something which could be exchanged for literally anything—any good or any service. For relatively modernized societies the level of generalization of the monetary units tends to be high by contrast with levels of generalization of media of exchange in past social history. An extraordinary number of things can be exchanged in such social contexts on a monetary basis.[5] Even among relatively modernized societies there are con-

---

[5] One may even, as a matter of speculation, consider the possibility that the reason that economics developed earlier and in a more highly generalized form than the other social sciences, qua science, lay in the fact that increases in the generalization of the media of exchange in parts of Western Europe made possible, with increasing relevance, the application of a rational model to problems of economic allocation. The fact that to some extent one could measure the most diverse forms of goods relative to one another in terms of their respective prices, regardless of whether

siderable differences in the levels of generalization of the media of exchange to which the members are accustomed. For example, in Great Britain entailed estates are not subject to purchase or sale. There are many national monuments in the United States which are not subject to purchase or sale. We need not get involved in the monetary sophistication of special blocked currencies and the like to realize that there are important variations in terms of what can be bought and sold among members of even the most highly modernized societies. Every one of those variations implies some differences in the level of generalization of the media of exchange involved.

There is a special problem connected with the level of generalization of media of exchange. We have all frequently heard or read cynics who maintain that *anything* [or anybody] has its price, that anything can be bought and sold if one has enough money. This is tantamount to alleging that the society referred to is one for which there exists a *perfectly generalized* medium of exchange, i.e., a medium such that literally anything can be exchanged for it. Cynics to the contrary notwithstanding, this has never been the case for any society in world history. If one is interested in the niceties of theoretical sociology, one can develop an argument to the effect that it cannot in fact ever be the case for any stable society. In doing so it is not necessary to rest the argument on the character inherent in the defiance of a distressed maiden who wails melodramatically, "You cannot buy my caress." There are always some things other than national monuments or a lady's virtue which cannot be bought or sold. As cynical as one might wish to be about the folkways of awarding honorary degrees in the United States, it is nevertheless true that in terms of the first-class universities of this country and probably in terms of most of the others as well it would not be possible, openly and with no avoidance of publicity, literally to purchase an A.B. degree. A novelist has recently based his work on the conception of a person who in fact wishes to buy a child despite the fact that we ostensibly have long since left the practice of slavery behind. In no open and obvious sense can an individual as such be bought and sold in the context of modern United States society. If there existed a perfectly generalized medium of exchange in a society, there could be no ethics, no

---

these prices reflected their true values or not, made possible such calculations. One may even speculate further that the other social sciences, as sciences, might not have developed at all had not the infant science of economics begun to bring some order into the general consideration of the patterns of allocation of goods and services on the basis of such rational models.

standards of any sort, that could not be reversed in a twinkling by the offer of sufficient accumulations of capital. Given the very extent to which men are capable of attempting to behave rationally, such a possibility would preclude the possibility of a stable social structure.

It is equally true that there has never been a society in terms of which absolutely nothing could be bought. That is to say there has never been a society in the context of which nothing could be exchanged. It is true, however, that there are [and have been] many, many societies in terms of which the generalization of media of exchange that we take for granted is simply out of the question. The works of anthropologists are full of examples of so-called primitive people who could not be easily traded with in terms of the European's beads and mirrors. Cases have even been cited in which the entering wedge of such exchange was an appeal to what the Europeans would have regarded in their own social contexts as a set of neurotics rather than the well-integrated substantial members of the society concerned.

One can generalize as follows about where within the two extremes of levels of generalization the level of generalization of a particular monetary unit in fact lies: (1) The more highly modernized the society, the more highly generalized do the media of exchange become. (2) On any given level of modernization, save some theoretical level of complete modernization, whatever that might mean, there are possibilities of variation in the level of generalization of the media of exchange. (3) For any given level of modernization, there is a level below which the generalization of the media of exchange cannot fall if the society is to remain stable. (4) There is also a level of generalization up to which it cannot rise if the society is to be stable, and that is always far short of the level of complete generalization.[6]

Increases in the level of generalization of the media of exchange have implications for the general ethical [or normative or ideal] structures of the society. The more the level of generali-

[6] These generalizations pose a problem for the general stability of relatively modernized societies. If as maintained elsewhere in this work relatively modernized societies will continue to become more highly modernized [or be instable] and if the level of centralization in long [and most short] runs always varies directly with increased modernization, then at some point the degrees of freedom inherent in the necessary increases in generalization of the media of exchange become inconsistent with the necessary level of centralization. Presumably from such a point on, either increases in direct allocation [with consequent decreases in the level of generalization of the media of exchange] and/or instability ensue.

I am indebted to P. D. Bell, A. G. Bischoff, H. P. Gassner, and J. R. Himes who, as graduate students of the Woodrow Wilson School of Public and International Affairs, forced this implication to my attention.

zation of a medium of exchange increases, the more vulnerable to exchange becomes any commodity, activity, or standard for which any goods or services are relevant. In a stable social context there are always some forms of honor that cannot be bought, but the more highly generalized a medium of exchange becomes the more vulnerable becomes honor to exchange in monetary terms. To this extent there is something in what the cynics have said. There is a corollary to this: although there can be no society whose members can be completely materialistic in this sense [i.e., bought], the more generalized the medium of exchange, the greater becomes the relevance of monetary measurement for *all other standards*. In relatively modernized social contexts it is not surprising how much monetary measurement is used as a yardstick of accomplishment or general worth. The surprising thing actually is that it is not used to an even greater degree than it is. As modernization increases, it becomes increasingly difficult to have, for example, a high-prestige occupational role whose effective incumbents receive a lower income than is received by individuals of less prestigious occupations. This is not less true of socialist than of capitalist societies. Indeed, there is a genuine sense in which socialist societies probably run far ahead of nonsocialist societies in these respects if only because of the explicitness of the planning of their leaders. Income is probably more highly correlated with social prestige in the Soviet Union than in the United States. In the United States there is a genuine sense in which the absolute pinnacles of general social prestige *cannot* go to those with the highest incomes. The very identification of an individual with such high incomes has a connotation inconsistent with the aura of self-sacrifice associated with the highest levels of prestige. The fact that the salary of the President of the United States is even a piddling one by contrast with the salary of a quite substantial number of business executives, let alone movie stars, and with no reference to gamblers and others of even lower general prestige, is a matter about which we are ambivalent. We are made uneasy by the fact that what many regard as the most important and difficult job in the world is by no means the best paid or by many standards even adequately paid. At the same time, there is a feeling of reassurance about presidential character in the feeling that no one able to get the job would ever seek it solely for the pay involved. We expect our President to be dedicated and to be more dedicated to almost anything than to his monetary income.

Regardless of the tenability of this particular speculation about the comparison of the correlation of income and social prestige in the United States and the Soviet Union, it is still interesting to keep in mind the assertion that, short of the upper limit already mentioned: the more highly modernized the society becomes, the more generalized the medium of exchange becomes; the more generalized the medium of exchange becomes, the more accurate is likely to be the inference, ideally and/or actually, of standings in terms of other criteria from ratings in monetary terms. At any given level of modernization so far achieved, considerable variations in the degree of generalization of the media of exchange and hence to some extent variations of relevance of the monetary unit(s) to the measurement of other criteria are possible. Nevertheless, the more highly modernized societies become, regardless of the bases from which their development took place, the smaller is the range of variation possible among them in these respects. Proponents and contemplators of modernization whoever they may be, may want to reflect on the prediction that the more highly modernized a society becomes, the greater becomes the likelihood that distributions of income will reflect distributions of social prestige accurately, that the members of such societies will take this for granted either consciously or unconsciously, and that the members of these societies will increasingly come to believe that this should be the case—if they don't already.

V I
MARKETS VERSUS TRADITIONAL EXCHANGES

A *market* has been defined above [p. 66] as any organization in terms of which action is primarily oriented to facilitating the exchange of goods and/or services among its members. There are societies which are not characterized by markets in this sense, in which the organizations in terms of which exchange takes place are by no means primarily oriented to such an exchange. From the point of view of exchange, I would refer to these methods of exchange as *traditional exchanges*. Such exchanges may be exceedingly important in the structures of economic allocation of a society. Frequently ceremonials of various sorts and especially important *rites de passage* are attended by traditional exchanges of this sort. Exchanges of gifts among the family members of a bride and groom are frequent examples. Although there are certainly societies without markets, I know of no society of any considerable scale totally lacking in markets. The presence of even highly developed markets does not by any manner of means imply the absence of traditional exchanges. Elements of such exchanges remain characteristic of even the most highly modernized societies, though these elements tend with modernization to become relatively insignificant in any attempt to reckon the national income. However tedious the repetition, it is characteristic of all societies that some exchange takes place in terms of family units. Such exchange is never unimportant for an understanding of general social structure, but in the sense intended here such exchanges are never market exchanges.

Markets vary widely from society to society, and they vary in many different respects. Markets may be more or less generalized, that is to say, the number and variety of items which may be exchanged in terms of the market organization may be greater or less. No completely generalized market, i.e., a market in terms of which everything or any combination of things may be exchanged for some other thing or combination of things, exists, though highly specialized markets, i.e., markets whose members specialize in dealing in even a single commodity plus some medium of exchange may and do exist. Markets also vary very widely in terms of the degree of centralization or control with which the market is organized. As indicated above [p. 68], there may be actual markets [e.g., prostitution and drugs] which ideally speaking do not exist.

From the point of view of societies in general four possibilities of allocation exist, assuming that the various subsystems that constitute a society are not completely self-sufficient—which they never are. First, there may be market structures. Second, there may be structures of traditional exchange. Third, the various exchanges of the members of the society may be planned and determined explicitly by a member(s) of a centralized authority. Fourth, there may be some combination of the first three. For societies of any considerable scale, some combination of the first three is standard. The first is never carried out to the exclusion of the second and third; the second may be for societies of small scale and great stability. The third possibility has so far in history never been successfully carried out to the exclusion of the other two. That is to say, there has never yet been a stable society in terms of which all exchange has been completely planned and determined explicitly by a member(s) of a centralized authority. To carry out such an extreme form of exchange would imply complete and perfect knowledge about the society. History has seen plenty of examples of far-reaching controls on exchange though these have by no means always been highly stable.

Amusingly, a market mechanism, which certainly does emphasize rationality in exchange, minimizes the problem of knowledge. Traditional exchanges do not accent rationality in exchange as such; they are rather ones in terms of which rational considerations are subordinate to other considerations surrounding the exchange. However the participants in terms of a given market be conceived, whether they be individuals, firms, etc., to the degree that they [or their representatives] act for themselves, to the degree that they can adjust subsequent action in terms of previous actions, reevaluate their moves etc., and to the degree that no one of them in his transactions constitutes the entire membership of the market—to that extent—the problems of knowledge are always subdivided and allocated in a special sense. The implications of irrationality for either success or failure in the market are cut down, and the risks of the implications of inescapable inadequacies of knowledge are spread. In the absence of perfect and complete knowledge on the part of the members of a central authority, operations in terms of a market mechanism, especially if regulated against excesses on the parts of individuals who participate in them, are more likely to minimize fluctuations than operations in terms of any completely centralized system. This is true, regardless of whether or not the society be considered a capitalistic or socialistic society. In both there are markets, and they will continue to exist.

In the context of relatively nonmodernized societies the proportion of exchanges that can be carried out on traditional rather than market bases is considerably higher than is conceivable in the context of relatively modernized societies. The more highly modernized societies become, the smaller the proportion of exchange carried out on a traditional basis becomes. Over the total scale of variation in modernization, particularly in some of the relatively nonmodernized segments of the scale, more complicated functions may be possible for this relationship. In general, however, they may be said to vary inversely—the more modernized the society, the smaller the proportion of exchange carried out on a traditional basis and vice versa. Insofar as traditional exchange exists in terms of a society, many problems of rationality are minimized. Not the least of the problems minimized is the problem posed by the fact that one individual or set of individuals in acting rationally may profit from far-reaching disruption and interference with the interests of others. There is also the possibility that in attempting to be rational even without deliberate disruptive intent, a given individual may make mistakes that have far-reaching implications. Exchanges carried out on a traditional basis may not maximize the possibilities of material productivity, but they are not likely to be subject to such fluctuations as emphases on rationality in exchange are likely to accompany.

There is another feature of the distinction between market exchange and traditional exchange which is of special relevance here. Structures of traditional exchange never furnish vital stimuli for systematic increases in productivity. The main focus of attention is not on the exchange of goods and/or services as such but rather on the occasion to which they are ancillary. In market exchanges, since the focus of attention is on exchange as such, there always exists the possibility that one or more individuals who are parties to the market can or will benefit from increases in productivity. There is no denying that markets can be set up in such a way as to discourage or damp down technological improvements, but on the whole it is difficult to rig a market so over long periods of time. The members of market systems are always sensitive to some degree to the implications of increases in material productivity. Markets vary in the extent to which operation in terms of the market actually stimulates technological advance, but even so market structures rather than structures of traditional exchange are far more likely to maximize the rapidity of adoption of technological improvements which arise from sources other than operation in terms of the market structure itself. Whenever there is contact with the structures of a relatively modernized society by members of a relatively nonmodernized one, the outsider makes inroads into the relatively nonmodernized social context via market mechanisms, and in this sense breaks down the structures of traditional exchanges. In addition, however, the basis of exchanges among the members of the relatively nonmodernized society themselves must always break down into an increasingly clear-cut market system [or set of market systems]. Although markets in highly organized and highly specialized forms as well as in more casual forms are taken for granted by the members of relatively modernized societies, they are not unknown or rare in relatively nonmodernized societies. Some markets exist in any relatively nonmodernized society of large scale, and some highly developed markets have existed in all cases about which we have historical records in any appreciable depth. There are, no doubt, many special and peculiar features of the sophistication of the Osaka merchants of Tokugawa Japan, but merchants who are highly sophisticated in some general respects are by no means rare in social history.

VII

STRUCTURES OF INCOME DISTRIBUTION

The structure of income distribution characteristic of a given society and its implications are explored by economists at great length. Given the niceties of its technical development this subject is no longer a fit one for an amateur like myself. Even an amateur, however, may with some safety observe that most of the work on income distribution has been done primarily on a restricted range of societies—or for *any* society only insofar as any society approximates the criteria of the specific models used. This is a scientifically legitimate procedure, and nowadays economists in general are sophisticated about such procedures. Outside the technical literature of economics on income distribution, there is an enormous amount of discussion of distributions on the basis of status and contract, slavery and wages, class distributions, feudal systems, etc. Most of that discussion is focused on special types of societies. There are, however, some generalizations about income distribution which may be made about any societies and which have special implications in terms of the distinctions between societies of relatively small scale and relatively larger scale and between relatively nonmodernized and relatively modernized societies.

Specialized development of the economic aspects of society, while by no means unknown in relatively nonmodernized contexts, has on the whole been much rarer and much less emphasized than in the case of relatively modernized societies. This contrast has had marked corollaries. One of these has been the fact that neither individual income nor the income of the members of the society as a whole has been such a major focus of attention for the general members of any relatively nonmodernized society as it is for the general members of all relatively modernized societies. Particularly in terms of relatively nonmodernized societies of small scale, specialized orientation to income as such exists rarely if at all, despite the fact that, in such societies of any considerable scale, reckoning in terms of wealth and hence to some extent in terms of income is always commonly understood. Regardless of how much attention is placed on income as such from the point of view of the individual members of a society, an observer or social scientist may always speak of the *actual distribution of income* characteristic of any society. This may be more or less difficult to measure in different cases, but the remarks to be made here do not hang on fineness of distinction in measurement of this income. If one considers the distribution of income on either a hypothetical per capita or a hypothetical set of family members in any social context, one may distinguish among three measures of such distribution. These are quite conventional, well-understood measures. I refer to the three m's of statistical techniques: the mean, the median, and the mode. In the following discussion it will be necessary to refer to the three curves illustrated below as curves I, II, and III. These curves illustrate income distribution. The number of individuals with a given income is measured on the Y axis. The amount of income per individual is measured on the X axis.

The simplest remark about curve I is that the income distribution is such that a very large number of people have very low incomes; a very small number of people have high incomes; and very few people have incomes spread thinly in the middle income region. Such a curve is sometimes referred to as bimodal [or as

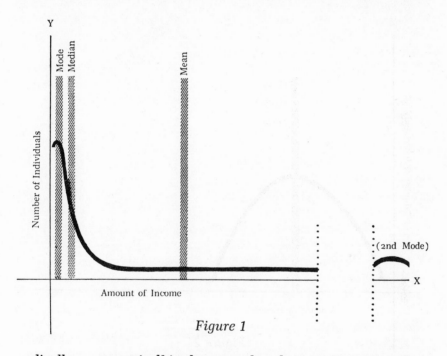

Figure 1

radically asymmetrical] in the sense that there are two important clusters of income distribution. The first is the *true mode* which is at a low income figure, and the other a slight clustering at high figures [far out to the right of the curve]. It is not difficult to envisage curves of this sort with more than two clusters. Thus trimodal or even quintimodal curves are conceivable. In curves of this sort the mean, median, and modes may fall at widely separated points on the curve. It is usually misleading to refer to curves of this sort in terms of one of these measures without any references to the other two. Many different implications may inhere in these separations of the mean, median, and mode.

Curve II pictures an income distribution such that relatively few people have very low incomes and relatively few people have very high incomes. The vast majority of incomes are bunched in the middle income range. In a sense this inverted U-shaped curve is an opposite extreme of the not so U-shaped curve I. As a curve of this shape is approached the median, the mode, and the mean of income distribution come closer and closer together. It is conceivable that an income distribution exists such that these three measures coincide exactly as in curve II. Such a curve would be a perfectly symmetrical inverted U-shaped curve. Even among curves with perfect symmetry there could still be

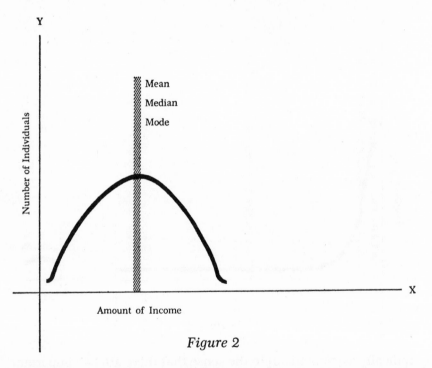

Figure 2

significant differences in terms of the spread of the curve, its height, etc. These would not necessarily be variations reflected in variations in the location in the mean, median, and modal measures.

For present purposes I would consider all cases of multimodal distribution or the like as special cases of curve I which carries with it a bimodal quality of income distribution frequently referred to in discussions of problems of economic development. It pictures an income distribution in which the vast majority of the population are relatively badly off as far as income is concerned and a small proportion of the population have very high incomes, indeed. Curve II will be referred to as a unimodal curve of income distribution. It will be considered the more nearly perfectly unimodal insofar as the three measures used here coincide. It is possible, of course, to have a unimodal distribution of income in the strictly technical sense with considerable distinction in the location of these three measures of income [see curve III for purposes of illustration].

With so much by way of nomenclature let us speculate. All income distributions in all societies may be classified as falling somewhere between the extremes of a perfectly unimodal curve

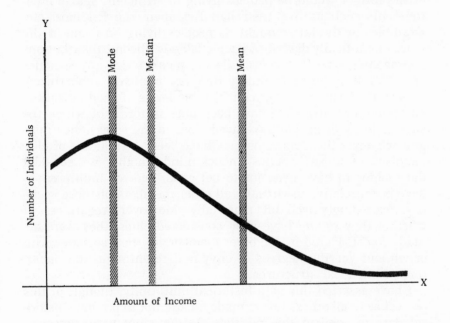

Figure 3

in the sense used here or some extreme form of curve I. Prior to the development of relatively modernized societies, virtually all societies were characterized by curves of income distribution roughly conforming to curve I. Furthermore, the main modal point of income distribution for the members of all those societies was as close to the Y axis as was consistent with survival of the populations concerned, assuming that the society did persist. That is to say, before the development of relative modernized societies the vast majority of all members of all societies lived close to the margin of subsistence. There is, perhaps, one general type of exception to this, though I doubt that this exception was ever frequent. In comparatively isolated societies of quite small scale, there may well have been income distributions of type II. Even in these small-scale societies, if they were of type II, either the societies were such that it was touch and go whether anyone would survive, given the extreme difficulties of producing a subsistence income for the members of the society, or the societies were ones characterized by a physical environment so benign from the point of view of the members that relatively little effort was involved in the collection of what the members of the society considered a quite adequate income. Examples of the former would be peoples living in stringent, sparse environments such as the Australian Bushmen, the Eskimos, etc. Examples of the latter might be peoples living on some of the more romantically described Pacific Islands. Income distributions approaching type II, however, do not characterize any societies of relatively large scale unless they are relatively modernized. Before the development of considerable levels of modernization, all societies of any scale have been ones in terms of which the vast majority of people have lived close to the subsistence margins whatever those margins may have been. A small set of elite members of those societies—never mind whether we consider those elites to have been [or to be] good, bad, or indifferent—have been, relative to virtually all other members of those societies, exceedingly well off materially. Moreover, regardless of whether they *should* have been considered elites, they were actually so considered by the other members of their societies with or without varying degrees of envy and resentment and departures from ideal structures.

I have asserted this as a historical uniformity, though in this respect as in all others I have made no attempt to produce historical data to confirm this position. As generally here, however, there are theoretical reasons for holding that this is the case. All societies of any considerable scale require some forms of specialized knowledge as has already been indicated above. In addition, some special forms of reasonably large-scale capital formation and the like are also necessary. No matter how far decentralization is carried, some centralized control exists, and so does some centralized planning. To some extent the levels of material productivity on which income production rests are a function of the existence of these specialized forms of knowledge and capital formation. In the absence of the somewhat specialized training associated with the specialized command of knowledge, neither the knowledge nor the capital formation necessary to maintain levels of productivity as they are could be maintained. Individual members in that society cannot be kept at the bare margin of subsistence and given the specialized training necessary for such forms of knowledge. Therefore, in any such social context—regardless of how wicked one may judge the relatively high income elite to be, and regardless of how much harm they may in fact do—whatever criteria of harm may be invoked—were there intervention that immediately transformed the curve of income distribution into a unimodal one approaching type II, not only would the more equal distribution of income per capita fail to improve substantially the standard of living of the general population [the more extreme the discrepancies in wealth, the less likely an equal distribution would be to improve radically the average income of the average individual], but also in subsequent income earning periods the average standard of living would probably fall further. As a result, after the initial distribution of income from the wealthy to the poor, the poor would be even worse off than they had been before. However romantic we may be about the principles of equality, and however wickedly conducted may have been the extremes of income distribution, the hard fact remains that the level of productivity actually achieved by the members of any relatively nonmodernized society of any considerable scale is importantly a function of the fact that income was [and is] actually distributed unequally among the members of the society.

In societies in terms of which the vast majority of people live at the bare margin of subsistence, whether members of private organizations or representatives of public organizations such as the government select special individuals on the basis of nepotism or predominantly universalistic, competitive examinations to receive the special education necessary to keep up the level of productivity in such societies [never mind increasing it], they will have to create of the students so selected a special elite whose income, at least in terms of the amount of resources devoted to their cultivation, will be much greater than that of the vast majority of the members of the population. The extremes of differences in income distribution for individuals need not be so radical as they frequently are, but regardless of how much income the elite may fritter away, some of the services and inevitably some of the other capital formation which account importantly for the maintenance of levels of productivity at the levels attained are functions of the special preparation which these individuals receive. No relatively nonmodernized society of any scale can continue as the system of action for members who function even at the margin of subsistence unless some proportion of the membership of that society has sufficient leisure and special command over resources to function above the generally accepted margin of subsistence. Furthermore, no matter how many other inequities may be removed, the basic form of this curve cannot be changed until the levels of material productivity characteristic of relatively modernized societies have been to some extent achieved. There may be some question as to whether income distribution will become more equitable when such levels of productivity have been achieved. Nevertheless, whether we like to face up to this picture or not, apart from circumstances made possible by subsidies from outside, the income distribution characteristic of societies in the process of modernization will remain strongly bimodal, [i.e., strongly of type I] for a considerable part of their development, whether under capitalistic or socialistic auspices.

Indeed, in the initial stages of the process, the more successful and the more rapid the modernization is, the greater is the likelihood that strategic differentials of income distribution will be maintained. Whatever our views of ethics of other standards, the distinction between capitalism and socialism has little to do with this matter. The development of modernization requires substantial capital formation and substantial specialized training for special individuals. The situation is not quite like getting "blood out of a turnip." In this case the turnip is in part the resources of the elite high-income groups. In all cases these people do have some income that from the point of view of facilitating modernization can probably be spent in more effective forms of capital formation and training than has hitherto been the case. Whatever blood does exist in this turnip, however, it is never enough without further contributions from the productive efforts of the vast majority of the members of the society to finance either the level of training or the amount of capital formation necessary for effective modernization. Not only have all developments of modernization under capitalistic direction developed by exactions from the peasant population and the laboring force in the cities, but to no lesser degree so have all developments of this sort conducted under the aegis of socialists, communists, or fascist imperialists. Indeed, one may add another generalization. The later a comer to the process of modernization, the greater is the likelihood that, apart from subsidies from outsiders, exactions from the peasants, i.e., the agrarian-based population, will have to furnish a greater proportion of such resources. This follows from the hypotheses that: (1) the vast majority of the members of all such societies will be agrarian based, (2) the later the members of a given society come into the process, the greater are the demands for performances on considerable scales both in the field of capital formation and in training, and (3) the longer the members of a society of this sort lag behind modernization which has taken place in the rest of the world, the less likely is it that the actual accumulation of wealth in the hands of the wealthy elite will amount to a sufficient accumulation to carry out these requirements without additional exactions from the vast majority at the opposite end of the income scale.

With the development of relatively modernized societies, it is possible for the first time in world history to have societies of considerable scale with curves approaching type II. Furthermore, the higher the level of modernization achieved, the greater is the possibility of approaching a perfectly unimodal distribution with adequate capital formation for maintenance and growth of the rates of productivity. The inordinate productivity of methods of organization, given the tools and sources of power characteristic of relatively modernized societies by contrast with the productivity of methods of organization characteristic of any other kind of society, has already been mentioned. Such methods of organization would not have had such implications for productivity and might not even have been feasible in the absence of such tools and sources of power. Whatever the origins, the further this process went the more it became possible for the first time in world history to produce a sufficiently high per capita income such that the mean, median, and modal incomes could approach one another without wiping out the minimal differentiation in terms of income required for the specialized knowledge and capital formation which were in turn necessary to maintain operations in terms of the society. Furthermore, these are the only societies in world history whose members have not only attained such levels of productivity and approached such distributions of income, but have also attained systematically increasing levels of productivity.[6]

Apart from relatively nonmodernized societies of relatively small scale, various elements of the productivity picture of relatively modernized societies for the first time in world history not

[6] Without pausing even to argue this assertion here, I would add that such societies cannot continue to exist stably unless the levels of productivity associated with them continue to increase. It may even be that none of them can exist stably unless these levels not only increase but continue to increase more rapidly than before. The members of such societies must not only attain some minimal velocity of productivity; they must attain some minimal rate of acceleration of productivity as well. And even so, it may not be possible for them to be stable [see pp. 783–788].

only make curves of income distribution approaching type II possible, but, historically speaking, they also make them highly probable. There are in existence, as all know, classical theories about capitalism which have broad appeal and which maintain that the longer capitalistic domination continues the greater become the discrepancies in income distribution as between the general population and the capitalist elite. This implies that the longer capitalism continues, the more the curve of income distribution takes on an extreme form of curve I. This has, of course, been neatly and precisely contradicted by the developments of history.[7] Again the distinction between capitalism and socialism has nothing whatsoever to do with the case save within narrow limits. The more highly modernized a given society, once relative modernization has been achieved, the more unimodal the income distribution in terms of it has become in every known historical case, regardless of whether it was under socialist or capitalist hegemony. Since the turn of this century the income distribution picture in the United States, which is generally considered by its own members and others to be one of the more purely capitalistic countries in the world, has been characterized more by the extent to which the mean, median, and mode of income have approached identity than by the increase in the mean of income, though that has been dramatic enough.[8] Japan is another country generally considered staunchly capitalistic. It is a country whose intellectuals and labor leaders continually talk about the bimodal distribution of income in the old sense at a period in which the trend is overwhelmingly and rapidly in the opposite direction as one may judge from the effective mass demand for heavy consumers goods which has already appeared in substantial development there. Whether the Japanese are more capitalistic than other late-comers to modernization I do not know, but of all of the non-European late-comers to relative modernization, there is absolutely no question that the Japanese are much the most highly modernized. They also ap-

[7] One of the great services of this particular formulation so often attributed to Marx lies in the sterling refutation it affords of the position held by some that nothing can be either *proved* or *disproved* in social science. This formulation is one of the few useful to social scientists because it is, to use Wilbert E. Moore's phrase, "precisely false."

[8] There are some who would make their assertion that this could not happen under capitalism true by definition by asserting that, to the extent that this has taken place, the United States is a socialistic rather than a capitalistic society. The argument need not be detained by the tautologies of the political religions of either the right or the left.

proach a unimodal distribution of income more than any of the others.

Among the nations under socialist control, which certainly has a meaning in the ideological sense regardless of whether it means what believers in either the ideology of capitalism or the ideology of socialism think it means, distinctions in the levels of modernization enable us to predict more about income distribution in terms of these curves than does anything else. Income distribution in Communist China is much more of type I than is the case of the Soviet Union which is, of course, much further along the road of modernization. China as a whole cannot yet be described as a relatively modernized society in the sense in which the term is used here.

The comparison between the United States and the Soviet Union in this respect may be speculated upon with some interest. There may be special difficulties in measuring the income of the Soviet elite, but even discounting these difficulties it is highly probable that the absolute discrepancy between the highest incomes and the lowest incomes in the Soviet Union is not so great as in the United States. It is also highly probable that there is a closer approach to identity of mean, median, and modal incomes in the United States than in the Soviet Union. Structures of automobile ownership alone suggest this unless automobile ownership is not at all closely correlated with other items in the standard of living. The vast majority of the population of the United States consider themselves radically disadvantaged if after the age of maturity they are unable to become automobile owners or to have access to automobiles as a minimum. In the Soviet Union automobile ownership or control over or access to automobiles is much more a mark of the privileged. Never mind how universalistically or justly those privileges may be gained in the one case as opposed to the other. With regard to housing, clothing, food, and many other categories the same sort of comparisons can be made despite the fact that the discrepancy between the poorest and the best housing or the cheapest and the most expensive housing in the Soviet Union may be considerably less than the corresponding discrepancy in the United States.

To close this line of speculation one additional theoretical element is necessary. I mention it only briefly here [see also below, pp. 777–790]. As far as societies of any considerable scale are concerned, not only are curves approaching type II possible only for relatively modernized societies, but the more highly modernized a society becomes, the more such curves of income distribution are required structures, if the society is to be stable. The technological possibilities opened up by action in terms of relatively modernized societies are sufficient to explain the possibility of such structures of income distribution. The levels of productivity obtained are sufficiently high that income can be allocated in such a way that there is sufficient provision for capital formation and both the freedom from other services and the means necessary for a portion of the membership to acquire the specialized intermediate forms of knowledge necessary to maintain the system without the sorts of discrepancies in income distribution illustrated in curve I. But would it not be possible, at least theoretically, for such societies to continue indefinitely with income distributions of type I pushed further and to the right? Or even not pushed further to the right? Could there not be a relatively modernized society, the vast majority of whose members stayed very poor by contrast with the elite or even stayed close to the margin of subsistence with enormous resources left over for the amusement and development of the elite and further capital formation? There could not. Not only must the mean, median, and modal incomes be pushed further to the right, that is increase in all such cases, but they must increasingly approach one another. They must do so for several reasons. First, one cannot handle people by coercion alone in terms of any society. Second, for relatively modernized societies, especially, the delicacy and fineness of adjustment of interdependencies are such that increasingly coercion, despite the radically increased efficiency of the means of coercion, cannot account for the organization of the members of such a society. Third, the adjustments of human beings to the structures characteristic of relatively modernized societies require, whatever other ways may be available, constantly increasing standards of living to keep them coordinating their activities within the limits of coercion which can be applied efficiently if necessary. Fourth, the more radically communications increase in efficiency, the less likely it is that radical discrepancies in income distributions can be kept from being generally recognized. Fifth, given the increase in generalization of the media of exchange and the increasing correlation between criteria of performance other than monetary income and monetary income distributed for those performances, if there is not an increasingly unimodal distribution of such factors, people will become just as dissatisfied as they will if their minimal incomes are not continually rising. If they become so dissatisfied, the amounts of coercion necessary to keep them functioning in terms of the system without breakdowns will rise beyond the levels of coercion consistent with such operations. Finally, as modernization increases, an increasing proportion of the members of a society must be moved away from a subsistence minimum—regardless of views of social justice, physical welfare, and human dignity—if only because of the radically increased demand for greater basic knowledge [and hence schooling] for the population in general and far more numerous highly specialized forms of intermediate knowledge for an ever increasing proportion of the total population. No doubt other reasons could also be adduced, but these will serve as a *minimal* set.

The hypothesis, the more highly modernized a society the more unimodal the allocation of income, in no way implies the limiting possibility of identical income distributed to every member of the population. On the contrary, such a distribution is quite out of the question. In connection with increasing levels of generalization of media of exchange, I pointed out that the surprising thing is not how highly merit was deemed to be correlated with income but that it is not deemed to be more highly correlated than it in fact is; that the more highly modernized a society, the more highly correlated judgments by the members of merit and income would be and would be expected to be. This does not imply that a member of such a society becomes increasingly likely to be deemed meritorious *because* he has a high income, but rather that he is more likely to have his high income attributed to his meritoriousness. Correspondingly, with regard to income distribution, insofar as members of the society continue to regard merits of whatever sort as unevenly distributed and not only to perceive differences in merit but also different degrees of merit, and given the other generalizations about increases in the generalization of the media of exchange—to that extent—discrepancies in income distribution at least sufficient to correspond to some of the discrepancies actually maintained in such judgment will be vital to operations in terms of the system. If in fact most of the members of the society without being coerced can regard all performances by their fellow men as roughly equivalent in value, the hypothesis just asserted need not hold true.

There is another point with regard to income distribution that is relevant here. Towns and villages, as those terms are generally understood, are distinguished as subsystems of all societies of considerable scale, whether relatively nonmodernized or modernized. Both towns and villages refer to types of residential systems. The members of a village are generally individuals engaged in agrarian pursuits [or fishing or the like] and some small number of additional personnel deemed necessary to provide certain services relevant to the individuals who constitute the main population of the village. Family units always exist as subsystems of villages, and most of the members of villages are organized primarily on a family basis. Towns are not only considerably larger in scale, but they also involve much greater foci of manufactured goods in the most general sense of that term used here. Most of the members of a town are not engaged in any form of raw-material production. As a minimum townspeople include ordinary workers, craftsmen, merchants or specialists in exchange of some sort, administrators or government personnel, etc. Villages, as the term is intended here, probably never involve memberships of more than a few hundred people at the very most, whereas the members of towns may vary from several hundreds to several millions.

Before the development of relatively modernized societies, a special relationship as regards the flow of goods and/or services existed between all towns and villages or between the towns and the general sedentary agrarian base of the society concerned. A substantial proportion of the income of the townsmen consisted of a flow of goods and services "exported" by the villagers. This holds true of course in an obvious sense with regard to materials such as food. From the point of view of the villagers this was considered a one-way flow of income. It has classically been received from villagers in the form of rents, taxes, interest, and profits on goods sold to the villagers. With the exception of the last item the villagers have regarded this as a one-way flow, but it has been one that, up to a point, the villagers have taken for granted as an inescapable aspect of the facts of life.

With the exception of some of the goods on which a profit is usually made, little in a tangible sense is seen by villagers as being exported by the townspeople to them. Specifically in relatively nonmodernized social contexts nothing is exported by the townspeople that systematically raises the productivity per acre of agrarian production [or corresponding productivities in activities such as fishing]. There are activities of the townspeople and even goods exported by them that certainly are relevant for the maintenance of given levels of productivity and even for occasional rises in productivity. The export to the villagers of iron tools is such an instance. In traditional China the planning and management for canals and the like and usually the direction of the actual production of such irrigation devices served from time to time to increase productivity in the agrarian areas, and the maintenance of such work certainly served to maintain productivity. Nevertheless, continuous rises in productivity, and certainly accelerated continuous rises, have never in any relatively nonmodernized social context flowed from any source at all to any other let alone from the townsfolk to the villagers. The towns, of course, were usually the focal points for the maintenance of order in the society and were the context within which governmental services were generally provided, but it was also true that the villagers of most of these societies were highly self-sufficient. In general, the more the representatives of the government left the villagers alone, the better the villagers liked it.

With the development of relatively high levels of modernization the situation changes radically. For the first time in world history there are both goods and services that (1) are produced in town environments, (2) can be exported to rural areas, and (3) can be used to raise systematically the productivity of those areas. In the context of all relatively nonmodernized societies villagers take a certain level of export to town environments as par for the course. They are accustomed to it; they do not feel themselves exploited thereby. In all such social contexts, however, if the export to the town environments is increased beyond those levels, sooner or later the members of the society do get involved in peasant revolts and the like. Only with the development of relatively modernized societies is it possible to alter the one-way flow-of-income aspect of the relationships between the townsfolk and the villagers. Usually in the early stages of modernization this is not done. The flow of goods and services from the villagers continues to be one of the main sources of capital formation for modernization. Sooner or later this situation must be changed if the relationships between townspeople and villagers are to be stable. The problem is particulary pressing if there is, as there is in most cases of relatively nonmodernized societies, the prospect of a population explosion resulting from importations of modern medical technology which drop death rates while birth rates remain high. Again, whether or not such one-way flows of income are maintainable is not a question of ethics or ideology. Quite apart from views about exploitation of peasants and the like—whether it is good, bad, or indifferent to behave so if one can get by with it—the really interesting thing is that such a procedure cannot be gotten by with indefinitely. As modernization increases, the old relationship as between villagers and townspeople must be altered in the direction of a reciprocal relationship in which the productivity in the village areas is not only maintained but systematically increased and probably systematically increased at an accelerated rate as a function of goods and services produced at least partially in a town context.

VIII
PROPERTY

I find the most sophisticated sociological treatment of the concept of *property* in the work and thought of Wilbert E. Moore. As early as 1943 he defined the concept as follows: "property consists in institutionally defined and regulated rights of persons (or other social units) in scarce values." [9] The literature concerned with property is voluminous in at least several specialized fields. The obvious fields are law, political science, economics, and sociology. Even to survey that literature would be a full-scale task in itself. Here again I shall not attempt to go into those matters treated at such length elsewhere. Despite the fact that I feel strongly that there is a profound insight implicit in the observation that a great many situations in social life can be better understood if the observer is aware of "whose ox is gored," I have not found the concept of property to be as illuminating as certain other concepts. In some of the major uses of this concept, the analysis has become so intertwined with ideology and special pleading, regardless of the point on the political compass from which the ideology or special pleading comes, that I find the reward of using the concept hardly worth the effort required to keep the analysis on the level of analysis. This no doubt, constitutes the shortcom-

[9] See, "The Emergence of New Property Conceptions in America," *Journal of Legal and Political Sociology*, vol. 1, nos. 3–4, April, 1943, pp. 34–58. This definition has many excellent aspects as a scientific concept. For one thing, it fits in well with the layman's conception of property without falling into some of the problems frequently associated with the concept from the layman's point of view. Given this definition, it is exceedingly easy to distinguish between tangible and intangible property in the layman's sense, but the concept of property as defined is easily distinguished from the physical factors in which property from the layman's point of view frequently inheres. One of the most strategic rights from the layman's point of view and from the point of view of many specialists such as economists and lawyers of the property concept is one of the rights of transference, for example, the right of sale of the property concerned. This characteristic form of transferability is in no way inconsistent with Moore's definition. In addition, however, Moore's definition is consistent with certain references to properties which are in no ordinary sense salable. The old question of entailed estates is one possible case. The reputation of a professional man is an example of a property right which Moore likes to cite as one which can be stripped from the owner but which he himself may not transfer. Good will is sometimes regarded as a property right which the owner can transfer or at least try to transfer, etc. Another implication of this definition is that the concept of property always implies a relationship. As a minimum that relationship involves the owner or possessor of the property right, the referent, whether tangible or intangible, of the property concerned, and at least one or more individuals or members of other organizations who might claim, buy, participate in or in some other way relate to the particular rights concerned.

ing of permitting certain aesthetic standards of theory construction to bias actual theory construction, but in many of these areas it is possible to go quite far in analyzing problems in terms of the interrelationships as among the members of different organizations and in terms of different aspects of their behavior without too frequent invocation of the concept of property. There are, however, a few generalizations, some of them of a rather specialized character, about property phenomena especially relevant to the arguments here.

First, there has never been a society whose members did not have some concept of property in the sense that property has been defined here, regardless of whether they attach the ownership, domination, or control of properties to specific individuals or to representatives of specific organizations. Actually, it is doubtful that there has ever been any society whose members did not attribute specific instances of property to both individuals and organizations to whom and to which they are conceived as belonging. Short of a social setting in which all goods and services are in fact free goods and services in the strict economic sense of the term one would hardly expect otherwise—and there never has been such a social setting. Indeed, even if all goods and services were in the strict definition of the term free goods by the criteria most frequently involved in that definition, if individual actors, however irrationally or arationally, acted as though any particular goods or services were in fact not a free good or service, the implications for property concepts would still inhere.

I shall distinguish three different property structures: (1) feudal structures, (2) private ownership structures, and (3) community or socialized structures. *Feudal structures* may be defined as those in terms of which the allocation of property to either individuals or members of organizations qua members of those organizations is both ideally and actually closely correlated with the allocation of power and responsibility. Feudal property is generally invested in an individual at any given point in time, but a transaction in terms of feudal property is both ideally and actually a transaction that specifically alters the political allocation. Usually societies with feudal property structures also have structures that radically restrict the purchase and sale of those properties which are most clearly defined as feudal properties. The best example of this is, of course, land. In social contexts characterized by nonfeudal property structures, at least ideally speaking and frequently actually speaking as well, there may be transfers of property without any alteration in the structure of political allocation, but this is never the case as far as feudal property is concerned. In feudal contexts political roles and ownership are closely correlated. Wherever feudal property is concerned, the allocation of loyalty, ideally speaking, is carefully correlated with the ownership of feudal property.[10]

Private ownership structures may be defined as structures in terms of which property is allocated to individuals and/or to the members of a specific organization qua members of that organization in such a way that the individuals, or the legitimate executive of the organization concerned, within considerable limits have discretion over use and transference of the instance of property concerned. Given structures of private ownership, allocations of power and responsibility may in fact be correlated with allocations of property, but ideally speaking the two are not necessarily closely correlated, and in many cases as a minimum, actually speaking, they are not. There is no such thing as a society in terms of which the allocations of private property are totally irrelevant to allocations of power and responsibility, but transference of property does not necessarily imply a transference of positions of power and responsibility in general political allocation nor is it expected to do so by many of the individuals acting within a private property context. Ideally speaking at least, the members of societies characterized by private ownership structures expect quite wide alterations in the allocations of goods and services to take place without corresponding alterations in allocations of power and responsibility. Ideally speaking the members of such societies take it for granted that all sorts of transferences of property among individuals and groups and in the name of organizations can take place without alterations in the general form or detailed substance of the government. Specifically speaking in such social contexts to use transferences of property to alter the form or effect of the actions of members of the governmental systems is to utilize property illegitimately. It is graft and corruption.

[10] I define a society as *feudal* insofar as it has the following characteristics: (1) closed social classes, (2) a well-defined hierarchy of power holders, (3) identification, at least ideally speaking, of each individual as responsible to some particular individual higher than himself in the hierarchy and related to others outside that direct line by virtue of his overlord's relation to them, (4) a distribution of goods and services, most especially land ownership and control, primarily on the basis of the ranks distinguished in the hierarchy of power and responsibility, and (5) succession to both such ranks and property, ordinarily determined on the basis of inheritance via kinship. There are, no doubt, problems about such a definition of feudal society, but it is at least more exact and considerably less misleading than the prevalent habit of referring to practically any relatively nonmodernized system, especially one which the referrer finds shocking and reprehensible, as a feudal society.

Community or *socialized structures* of property are ones such that property is not owned by individuals. It is only owned by organizations. That is to say, it is only owned in the name of organizations or by a set of individuals whose relation to the property concerned is a function of their membership in general and their specific roles in detail in the organizations concerned. In highly socialized examples of community property structures, in theory at least, the only legitimate ownership may inhere in the government as such. Any property structures will fall into one of these three categories. Community or socialized property structures always have more in common with feudal property structures than either set of structures has with the structures of private ownership. This is a result of the fact that the community or socialized organizations which are the owners of property in the third case are also usually systems that are important foci of political allocation for the members of the society in which they exist. The administrative heads of such organizations, whether they be family heads or government chiefs, in effect have major discretion with regard to the property conceived of as owned by the system. In this sense the correlation of allocations of power and responsibility and of goods and services are much more closely identified than is either actually or ideally the case given private ownership structures. Unlike the feudal structures, community and socialized structures do not necessarily involve closed classes, inheritance of office via kinship, and they need not focus discretion over property in the hands of a single individual. Discretion may volve into the hands of the members of a council of some sort, though ideally as well as actually some individual is likely to be singled out. The close coordination of the power hierarchy and discretion over property, however, is characteristic of both the feudal and the community structures.

Never has action in terms of any set of social structures succeeded in removing the political implication of allocations of goods and services, but in a peculiar sense action in terms of private ownership structures has, in fact, probably gone further in reducing those implications than any other structures of property ever realized. The amount of power associated with vast accumulations of property in the context of societies in which private ownership is institutionalized is in no way surprising. The surprising thing is that there have ever existed societies in terms of which private ownership has been carried to any considerable length and in terms of which there has been any considerable separation of allocations of goods and services and of power and responsibility. In the history of the United States, for example, it is not at all remarkable that the possessors of great wealth have sometimes succeeded in uniting their efforts in such a way as to control the government and determine the outcomes of elections at the presidential level and at lower levels. Given the inescapable relevance of allocations of goods and services for allocations of power and responsibility and vice versa, the really surprising thing about the history of the United States is that there ever should have been elections in which the possessors of great wealth were quite unable to handle matters in this fashion. There have certainly been presidential elections at least in United States history in which, despire considerable unity of opinion among the wealthy, such control has eluded them.

I X
APPROACH TO ECONOMIC SELF-SUFFICIENCY
OF A SOCIETY OR A NATION

In days gone by there were, no doubt, numerous cases of societies of some considerable scale which from the point of view of economic self-sufficiently were closed systems. The members of some of these societies had little or no contact with the members of any other societies, and insofar as they did, those contacts did not affect them substantially. In some cases these were closed systems simply because the members of the societies concerned were physically isolated from the members of all other societies. There have, no doubt, even been cases in which the closest neighbors of the members of such societies did not know of their existence. Even among those societies whose members were in constant contact with the members of other societies, there have been many cases in world history in which the individual societies concerned were to a high degree self-sufficient. As far as quite general levels of operation were concerned it would have mattered little if at all to the members of these societies had their contacts with members of other societies been totally cut off. In a setting of this sort ideas of national sovereignty and complete independence could and did develop and are quite easy to understand. Before the development of relatively modernized societies in Western Europe and the United States, a substantial number of societies were in this sense to a high degree self-sufficient. Even in cases in which members of one society were taken capitive via invasion by members of other societies and ruled by people whom they considered outsiders from the economic point of view, they may well have remained to a high degree self-sufficient, i.e., they may still have produced most of what they consumed and consumed most of what they produced. Even the early stages of imperialism did not usher in the high levels of interdependency which we take for granted nearly everywhere today. The societies of the Viking raiders about whom Veblen wrote so insightfully and with such a sense of humor were among the most extreme departures from such economic self-sufficiency.[11]

The radical decline in the possibility of such closed systems from the economic point of view is a matter of exceedingly recent history as a general phenomenon, though prior to this, all through history, there were certainly individual instances of it. The level of interdependency from the economic point of view which people take for granted today is a function of quite modern developments in the efficiency of communications. The members of Japanese society made perhaps the last and most dramatic hold-out of any considerable scale in history. After all except for a relatively small trickle of annual trade via the Dutch at Deshima in Nagasaki Harbor the Japanese from 1638 to 1853 were to all intents and purposes completely self-sufficient economically. In the economic sense as well as in others, the Japanese became importantly interdependent with the members of other societies following 1853. From the latter part of the nineteenth century on, hardly a day passed without a decline in the level of economic self-sufficiency of most of the societies of the world. Today in the economic sense, as well as in other senses, the level of self-sufficiency of individual societies, with rare exceptions, is so clearly a thing of the past that many of the arguments which developed a meaning and an appeal in an era of relatively high self-sufficiency of both societies and nations have completely lost their actual meaning except for the one imparted to them by the intense feeling associated with these conceptions as ideals of human conduct. Economic self-sufficiency is not the only element or the primary causal element involved in this change. It may not even be the most important element involved, but the increase in economic interdependency of societies, alone, is quite enough to make a special form of mockery out of the continually increasing emotional investment in the conceptions of sovereignty and complete independence which were the flowers of social philosophy of the eighteenth century. The doctrines of independence and sovereignty of that period have a high positive emotional value for me, but as they are discussed today, I know that my identification with them is primarily a matter of sentimentality—nostalgic sentimentality—by a member of a society whose earlier members

[11] See Veblen, T.: "An Early Experiment in Trusts," *The Journal of Political Economy*, vol. XII, March, 1904, pp. 270–279.

experienced such structures. It is an utterly naïve wishful sentimentality for anyone who hopes to achieve such a state of affairs
for his own nation in the future.

From the economic point of view as well as from other points
of view, there is probably not a society of any considerable scale
left anywhere in the world which approaches the degree of self-
sufficiency fairly widely achieved by the members of many different societies in the late eighteenth century. As relatively closed
social systems became increasingly less feasible with the passage
of each day and each improvement in the technology of communications, the problem facing the members of various nations in
the world has long since ceased to be a problem of protecting their
rights and their freedoms, such as they are, by the achievement of
independence and of sovereignty. The problem of maintaining
those freedoms and rights realistically becomes increasingly a
problem of whether they are compatible with the minimally necessary forms of cooperative behavior among the members of
different nations and societies. It may continue to be true as some
would maintain that it always was and always will be that "God
helps those that help themselves," but as far as rights and freedoms for the members of a given nation or society are concerned,
in the world in which we live now and are going to live in the
future, that precept will have to be modified at least to the extent
of maintaining that "God helps those who help themselves in
some sort of cooperation with others."

Insofar as the economic self-sufficiency of a given nation or
society declines, its members are involved to some extent in what
economists refer to as international trade. There is no point in
trying to handle questions of international trade in any detail
here. This is certainly a field in which immense technical sophistication exists among bankers, governmental officials of various
sorts, academic economists, general businessmen, and many
other types. There is, however, one special tool in the kit of the
economically sophisticated not generally discussed in treatments
broadly oriented to general social structure as opposed to profes-
sionally oriented to the economic analysis of international trade. I
refer to the "doctrine of comparative advantage." Any student of
international affairs or any individual charged with responsibility
in this field who is unacquainted with this doctrine had best
acquaint himself with it, and the more quickly, the better. This
imperative covers any student of public affairs, whether he thinks
he is interested in international matters or not, since increasingly
there are no problems of any importance in domestic affairs
without international implications or vice versa. The relevance of

the doctrine of comparative advantage does not depend on whether the members of a nation are aware of it or not, whether their government is fascistic, socialistic, democratic, capitalistic, or tribal. In its essence it is a simple doctrine. It maintains that as long as there are differences in the relative costs with which different goods and services are produced by the members of different countries, there is a basis for trade among the members of these countries, which can be of mutual benefit insofar as benefit can be reckoned in the maximization of goods and services per capita available from any given quantity of productive resources. The doctrine also indicates that in the absence of absolutely uniform relative distributions of resources of all sorts including skills of organization, some such differences in costs will always exist. It does not imply that the members of a given society will in fact rationally maximize the possibilities of their comparative advantages by trading internationally, but in any given case it is at least in theory possible, if one knows how to analyze situations in terms of this doctrine, to form some conclusions as to what the implications of failing to do so will be. The most rudimentary knowledge of the doctrine of comparative advantage makes absolute nonsense out of the frequently reiterated statements of highly placed statesmen that they are quite unable to compete or engage successfully in international trade because another nation's members produce everything more cheaply than the members of their nation are capable of doing. To speak in this fashion is to speak from an ignorance needless in this time and day.

Whether one likes to admit it or not, any increase in international trade is a decline in economic self-sufficiency. Any such decline increases the vulnerability of the members of a given society to the members of other societies as far as some influence is concerned. Once contacts of this sort are made, not only vulnerability but also desires relative to other societies and the products produced in terms of them are likely. Both vulnerability and desires increase as the proportion of the gross national product involved in international trade increases. The proportion of gross national product involved in international trade need not be great for the international trade to be exceedingly important in understanding the economic aspects of the society. Here again the professional economist, whether he be academic, governmental, or private, has a great deal to say. Even if only 5 per cent of the gross national product is involved in international trade, the effects of its abandonment will have far-reaching implications. As such trade continues, it is doubtful whether either the vulnerability or other desires of the people concerned can be kept from continually increasing even though the ratio of international trade to the gross national product may not increase radically.

Many years ago Fei Hsiao-T'ung in a remarkable book [12] illustrated this without full awareness of all of its implications in an exceedingly stark fashion. In a village in Eastern China somehow someone of entrepreneurial talent recruited the young girls of the village into a rudimentary factory-type organization for the reeling of silk. The venture prospered, the villagers exported the silk so produced, and not only was the standard of living of the villagers raised, but previously quite stable and strategic social structures began to alter visibly. Notably the position of women in that community began to change. Whereas formerly one married daughters off as soon after puberty as practicable, thenadays girls at that age acquired a new value as continuing members of their parental families. Marital age increased, and some marriages were put off indefinitely. The girls became independent. There were many other attendant changes. Where the silk went when it left the village, the villagers neither knew nor cared. They knew little of the outside world, and they were completely unsophisticated in the field of international trade. They were sufficiently concerned with their prosperity and the changes afoot among them without trying to understand the international scene of which they had unwittingly become a part. In 1929 the Great Depression hit. One of the first markets to suffer was, of course, the market for luxury goods in the United States. It is hard for many people to remember that such a thing ever existed, but in those days most of the best of ladies' stockings and underclothes were silk. With the radical cut-back in demand in the United States for such items, silk reeling in the small village in Eastern China suddenly became uneconomic. A depression in the United States which Chinese members of that small village neither knew nor cared about had spread to their village. The villagers not only found themselves with their incomes reduced, but more importantly in all probability they found themselves with numerous unmarried daughters, overage and out of hand. A set of remote villagers in Eastern China was tied into an interdependent set of world societies. Not a single ill-intentioned or Machiavellian hand had been raised against them, and yet their freedom and their sovereignty, such as it had been in the heyday of their higher self-sufficiency, had certainly been radically interferred with.

The degree of economic self-sufficiency of a given society always has implications for other aspects of the social organization.

[12] Fei Hsiao-T'ung, *Peasant Life in China,* E. P. Dutton and Co., Inc., New York, 1939.

This does not follow from any sort of economic determinism. The degree of economic self-sufficiency of a given society is never the sole relevant variable in understanding that society, but it is never totally irrelevant either. For that residue we are all indebted to Marx.

POLITICAL ALLOCATION

I
DEFINITION

Political allocation has been defined [p. 181] as the distribution of power over and responsibility for the actions of the various members of the social systems concerned, involving on the one hand, various forms of sanctions, of which sheer coercive force is the extreme form in one direction, and, on the other, accountability to the members and in terms of the systems concerned, or to the members of other interdependent systems. The term *power* was defined as the ability to exercise authority and control over the actions of others. The term *responsibility* was defined as the accountability of an individual (s) to another individual (s) or group (s) for his own acts and/or the acts of others. What is power from one point of view is simultaneously responsibility from another—that here again, as in the case of production and consumption, power and responsibility constitute in a sense obverse forms of one another.

I I
SPECIALIZED PREDOMINANTLY POLITICALLY ORIENTED SYSTEMS: GOVERNMENTS

In all known societies of any considerable scale there exists as a subsystem at least one specialized predominantly politically oriented organization that will be referred to here as a government.[1] All social action involves some allocations of power and responsibility, just as all social action involves some allocation of goods and services. At least three questions always arise about the allocation of power and responsibility. Those are the questions of *locus, definition,* and *procedure.* That is to say, it is important in analyzing any social organization to know: (1) where power and responsibility lie, (2) how they are defined [including in the question of definition whether they are defined explicitly or implicitly, etc.], and (3) what behaviors in the implementation of

---

[1] I would actually hold that one is able to distinguish some sort of rudimentary governmental organization in any society regardless of its scale. There is certainly no society of the scale which is a matter of general preoccupation for those concerned with public and international affairs that is not characterized by the presence of such an organization.

power and responsibility are expected and supported by the members of the various social systems concerned. No society could consist of a single subsystem or a single type of subsystem such as a family unit. Certainly in all known societies the subsystems and types of subsystems are always numerous. Given the possibility of conflict, let alone the inevitability of conflict, it is unlikely that any society could continue to exist in the absence of some organization that differed from others in that its members somehow regulate the relations among the members of other organizations when some questions are disputed among them. Thus, although *any* social organization always has some political aspects, these aspects of one type of organization can never be the sole type of political aspects for the society as a whole. In addition to the ordinary structures of political allocation that may be present in other organizations, there must be at least one additional organization characterized by structures of political allocation having to do with the regulation of behavior among the members of other organizations. Such an organization *must* be present, if the society is to be stable, but the presence of one is not a guarantee that the society will be stable. One type of organization is of special relevance from this point of view, a predominantly politically oriented organization, i.e., a *government*. It is possible that there be a society characterized by an organization somewhat different from others but not predominantly politically oriented. It is also conceivable that in fact regulation of the relationships among members of other structures when questions of dispute arise take place in terms of that organization. All societies of any scale, however, show considerably more sophisticated development in this realm than would be implied by this possibility.

When governmental units do appear, certain implications of their existence in the society are necessarily clear. They must be oriented to the regulation or supervision of relationships among the members of other units. The only conceivable exception to this would be an organization for whose members the internal allocation of power and responsibility was an end in itself, but this would not be a true exception because such an organization would not be predominantly politically oriented as that concept has been set up here. It would rather be an organization predominantly oriented to expression of a particular sort. It would actually be a specialized religiously oriented unit in which the religion concerned focused on what might be considered a political fetish. All of the known governmental units in history have to some extent been oriented to the regulation of interrelationships among the members of other membership units. Usually it is in terms of governmental structures that in the last analysis responsibility is enforced on the members of other social systems, if action in terms of the special structures of neither of those systems nor cooperative interrelationships among the members of different ones have enforced responsibility on their members. In social history, the ability of the representatives of different governments to enforce responsibility on the members of other social systems has varied widely. There have been cases of multiple governmental organizations within a given society. There have been cases in which representatives of the legitimate governmental structure have not been nearly so powerful as members acting in terms of other organizations in the society. There have also, of course, been governments in whose representatives, not only ideally but actually as well, the legitimate monopoly of power has been overwhelmingly concentrated.

Insofar as interrelationships among the members of other social organizations are regulated by members of a government and insofar as they frequently enforce responsibility on the members of other organizations, other implications follow. Governmental organizations by their mere presence always to some extent limit and define the political allocation that takes place in terms of other organizations. To some extent the activities of members of the government are always oriented to the control of behavior that is regarded as disruptive by the members of the society in general.

The importance of a balance of power and responsibility in understanding social organizations will be discussed immediately below. Here it may be pointed out that in all societies governmental organizations furnish one of the primary sources of balance for the allocation of power and responsibility in a total society, if they are actually balanced. In many cases the members of a society expect the government to be *the* primary source in this respect. This is so much the case for relatively modernized societies, and in general has been so much the case since the development in European history of relatively strong centralized states that most modern social science analysis in the field of government, either implicitly or explicitly, takes it for granted that all governments are *in fact* the primary source of such balance or that they ought to be. This is reflected in the persistent tendency to define a government or state as "having a monopoly of the legitimate use of force in the society" or in some roughly equivalent manner. Using such a definition, there are certainly many societies of considerable scale that lack governments altogether.

Most feudal societies, for example, lack governments in this special limited sense. The mistaken implications that all governments are *the* primary source of such balance, or that the members of societies characterized by such governments feel that the government should be the primary source of balance, or that the members of the government themselves feel that they should be such a source of balance—to accept those points of view, however, is to make absolutely certain that one will misunderstand a considerable part of social history as far as government is concerned.

Various forms of governments will be discussed to some extent below [pp. 436–502]. It will not, however, there or here be necessary to go into the details of governmental organization at any great length. Many of the critical questions are thoroughly and carefully investigated by professional treatises of varying sorts. The pedigree of the discipline of political science itself is an ancient and honorable one. The field of public administration is highly developed, and the literature widely produced by, of, and for governmental leaders, administrators, and employees in general is increasingly abundant. The treatment of the structures of political allocation here will refer importantly to governments but it will also be concerned with the patterns of political allocation in the society generally.

I I I
BALANCES OF POWER AND RESPONSIBILITY

A. GENERAL HYPOTHESIS

It has been indicated above that power and responsibility refer to the same phenomena looked at from different points of view. In this sense there is always as much or as little power as responsibility in any relationship. It does not follow that the power that is or can be exercised in terms of a given system is balanced by the responsibility that is or can be assessed on the members either in terms of the system itself or in terms of another system. It also does not follow that the members within a given system necessarily have power either gained in terms of that system itself or in terms of some other system to execute the performances for which they are held responsible. Thus any given individual may be a locus of power that is not balanced by responsibility, or he may have responsibilities without being endowed with corresponding powers. Cases of power without balancing responsibility are a characteristic of TV Westerns. The villain par excellence of such Westerns is often a man of considerable power who, until the hero appears, cannot be brought to book by anyone. The true or unvarnished TV Western, as distinguished from the psychologically sophisticated or TV Western *manqué*, is one in which the villain is not responsible to anyone nor is he responsible to any code which he imposes on himself. Most cases described as "arbitrary exercises of power" are cases of power not balanced by responsibility. Cases of responsibility not correspondingly balanced by power are equally familiar to any readers of modern fiction from soap opera to the *New Yorker* short story. This is the classic case of the individual who has laid upon him, never mind how, an obligation that he cannot hope to fulfill. All such fictions have endings somewhere on a triangular scale with apices of neurosis, psychosis, and mayhem.

The balance of power and responsibility in a sense referred to above is relevant for the analysis of organizations because of the following hypothesis: Any organization for which the locus of power is not balanced by the locus of responsibility is inherently instable. The balance, if one exists, may be a function of the interrelationship of the members of one organization with those of another, but the larger the scale of an organization the more likely and the more important it becomes that a considerable proportion of the balances of power and responsibility be *internal* [2] to the organization. It is essential that no one jump to the conclusion that, because imbalances of power and responsibility are inherently instable, balances of power and responsibility are inherently stable. The latter hypothesis in no way follows from the former.

The sources of instability from an imbalance of power and responsibility are of two sorts. First, individuals who possess power without responsibility for the exercise of that power always raise the possibility of exercises of power that are capricious as

[2] A relationship or other phenomenon will be spoken of as *internal* to a given system if it involves members of a given system only in their roles as members of that system. Correspondingly a relationship or other phenomenon will be spoken of as *external* to a given system in the respects that it involves a member (s) of a system (s) other than the one. Even if only members of the given system are involved but one or more of them are involved in their roles as members of some other system as well, the relationship or phenomenon will be regarded as external to the given system to that extent. Thus, a father assessing responsibility on a son for some power the son has exercised in terms of a family system represents a balance of power and responsibility internal to the family system. Arrest by the county sheriff of the father for assessing responsibility on a son in such a way as to cause his death is a case of external balancing of power and responsibility regardless of whether the sheriff is also a son of the father arrested [see pp. 307–310 below].

far as maintaining the stability of the organization concerned and that cannot be stopped whatever their consequences may be. Sooner or later, however, there are always bound to be some capricious exercises of power if only because of lack of knowledge as to what would constitute completely rational exercises of power. With even the best worked-out balances of power and responsibility the exercise of power may well be capriciously disruptive, but if so, it is not so difficult to curb. The problem of balancing power with responsibility is always posed in an especially difficult and obvious form by highly autocratic and authoritarian systems. Enforcement of responsibility on persons with power in terms of such systems always limits the scope of their power to some extent. Failure to limit them to some extent opens the possibility that their actions may destroy the stability of the social structures in general and the very basis of their own power as well. Nero and Caligula, as ordinarily portrayed for the benefit of children, are classic examples of power figures of this sort. Modern history has already supplied an interesting number of examples of this breed, and there is as yet no indication that such figures are in short supply.

Second, responsibility that is not balanced by corresponding power is no less a potential source of instability. The implications for stability of responsibility for which an individual has not corresponding powers inhere in the extent to which the action for which he is responsible is germane to the maintenance of the system to which he belongs in the given instance. If one holds someone responsible for something that he lacks the power to execute, one can even go so far as to execute him, but that will not get the task done. Furthermore, insofar as the accomplishment of that task is relevant to the stability of the system, this stability is thereby threatened.

These generalizations about the balance of power and responsibility and stability are certainly not new. In one form or another realization of them underlies all sage advice and wise description of administrative systems. Although knowledge of the implications of capricious exercises of power in the absence of responsibility and of the bootlessness of responsibility in the absence of corresponding power is as hoary as any knowledge one may wish to speak of, it is rather surprising that systematic use of this knowledge in the analysis of governments and the like has not become an outstanding element in the general quiver of political science theory. Analysis of order and change is always germane to social phenomena and particularly to those with which students of public affairs are concerned, and the balance of power and responsibility is always germane to problems of order and change.

B. FOUR TYPES OF BALANCES

The question of balances of power and responsibility can be explored at great length. I shall explore them only briefly in terms of four ranges of variation that, if not common to all societies, are certainly common to all societies of any considerable scale and hence to any questions of general interest to men of public affairs. I shall discuss these under the following four headings: (1) hierarchical versus nonhierarchical balances, (2) empirical versus nonempirical balances, (3) specific versus diffuse balances, (4) internal versus external balances.

1. HIERARCHICAL — NONHIERARCHICAL BALANCES

A system with a *nonhierarchical balance* of power and responsibility is one in which the balances of power and responsibility are mutual and equal for all members of the system. This is the type of system in terms of which every member has the same powers and responsibilities as every other member. This type of system has been discussed briefly above [pp. 149–152] in connection with the discussion of relationships that are specifically egalitarian as far as their stratification aspects are concerned. There, however, attention was focussed on the question of hierarchy as such; here the attention is focussed on the allocation of power and responsibility. Friendship as that relationship is generally described in a country like the United States is one of the very best and one of the few examples of a balance of power and responsibility that is nonhierarchical [i.e., egalitarian] by ideal. In terms of such a system, friends are expected to have equal powers over one another and equal responsibilities to one another to the degree that the similarity of their circumstances and the degree of friendship permits. Powers and responsibilities are mutually held and mutually owed. What they do in terms of their relationships with one another certainly has implications for other spheres in which they behave, but from the point of view of the friendship relationship the primary question is the mutual relevance of what they do for one another.

Nonhierarchical political balances can never be the sole type of political structures in any society. Most, if not all, of the crucial organizations as well as the more or less strategic ones in any society *must* have institutionalized hierarchical political structures if they are to be stable. If the balances of power and responsibility in a relationship are nonhierarchical, either ideally or actually, the relationship is one that can be dissolved by any party to it. Only simultaneous desire by all the parties concerned to such a relationship can both preserve the status quo and continue action in terms of the organization. Whenever or for whatever reason that mutual desire breaks down from one side or from all sides, as a minimum the political structures change radically, and in many cases the organization characterized by those structures will be dissolved or radically changed. Organizations with such structures of political allocation are obviously not well adapted to the curbing of disruptive behavior. In the field of international relations the instability characteristic of organizations whose member nations [or other organizations] ideally speaking are equals—even when the ideal is not that the balances within the organizational context be completely nonhierarchical—has been all too obvious. The periodic collapse of such organizations and the restoration of stability in terms of the establishment of a new hierarchically organized system either by virtue of a passage of arms or a recombination of "member organizations" [3] has been seen again and again in modern diplomatic history. The instability of a subsystem with a structure of egalitarian balance is no less

[3] I have placed this phrase in quotation marks because organizations as such are not members but are rather subsystems of other organizations. Action is in fact always executed by individuals or sets of individuals. Even when one can speak of sets of individuals operating in concert or unison of some sort, one of the most important questions about them is what are the structures of action [and how do they come into being, what are the implications of one set of them as opposed to another, etc.] in terms of which the individuals in the set so behave as to be identified as a set. International organizations have a general characteristic not shared by all social systems by any means. All of the members [or a very important portion of them] of such an organization are members by virtue of representing the members of some other organization. Specifically, of course, they represent nations which are a still more specific form of organization with a whole set of special properties that need not detain us here.

The important contrast here is between organizations such as these and families, universities, business firms, boys's clubs, etc. Ordinarily none or only a quite restricted portion of the members of such organizations as the latter are members of the latter specifically because of their roles as representatives of the members of some other social system. As far as I know, this is never true of family members. It is also possible to have mixed forms. For example, some members of a government may well be members by virtue of their roles as representatives of others and some may not. Thus, senators in the United States government are members of the government by virtue of being representatives in this sense: the secretaries of those same senators are not members of this sort.

Perhaps the crudest and most obvious example of the difference such distinctions can make is the question raised as to whether a given set of remarks addressed by one representative member of an international organization to another is an exchange of personal insults or an exchange that insults the members of the systems represented as a set.

obvious, even though it exists wholly within the context of a single society rather than as the result of interrelationships among the members of two or more societies. Unlike some attempts made in the international field, however, as far as is known, there has never been a conscious attempt nor an unplanned development of a society in which, ideally speaking, the structures of political allocation rested on a nonhierarchical structure of mutual balance. The problems of rearing children and keeping them from harm would, alone, necessitate some hierarchical elements.

Not only have there been no societies organized completely on a nonhierarchical basis, but there have been few social organizations of any sort that have not to some extent been organized on a hierarchical basis. Hierarchical political structures always pose the problem of maintaining a balance of the loci power and responsibility. It is the essence of such systems that responsibility is owed from the bottom up, from the less to the more powerful members, and that power is wielded from the top down. In a hierarchical political structure responsibility is never owed directly to the individual(s) over whom power is wielded in the specific respects in which that power is wielded. This is true by definition. If the contrary were true, a mutual balance would exist, and the possibility of the interference with the exercise of power would exist at every point at which power could be wielded. Despite the obvious nature of this point, emotionally charged discussions of democracy and egalitarianism which have ignored it, especially in connection with new nations, are not pauce.

An ordinary military system is one of the most clear-cut examples of the hierarchical allocation of power and responsibility. Ideally speaking the greatest power is concentrated in the role of the highest ranking official; members of the organization at every level owe responsibility to those in the ranks above them, and have power over those in the ranks below them. It is essential that the chain of command be clearly defined. To facilitate this, uniforms and insignia of rank have their utility. For quite far-reaching purposes such insignia alone are sufficient to indicate these relationships with sufficient clarity for members of the system to operate efficiently in terms of it even if no one has been properly introduced to anyone who, ideally speaking, has power over him or to anyone over whom he has power.

All authoritarian systems are by definition hierarchically structured from the point of view of the political allocation involved in addition to whatever other hierarchical structures inhere in such systems as a minimum. Because of the intense emotion that generally surrounds all discussions of authoritarian versus democratic structures of organization, there is a broad tendency to regard any hierarchical arrangement as inherently undemocratic. The ontological status of concepts like "democratic" and "authoritarian" as used in the field of political philosophy is of no concern here. If one wishes to define any democratic organization as inherently nonhierarchical and any hierarchically organized system as inherently authoritarian and nondemocratic, then all that is necessary to say here is that we must forego discussion of democratic systems so defined. They may be pleasant to contemplate as an ethical ideal, but in that sense they are a utopian ideal only, a type of system that for societies as a whole has never existed and never will exist. Most of the democratic systems in this sense that the world has seen have been essentially friendship systems, and those on the whole have not been highly stable forms of social organization.[4] I yield to no one in my personal sentimentality for the motto of the French Revolution but if the term *equality* is taken literally, the slogan is an impossible ideal for social organization in general, let alone the other two terms. If the term *democracy* is to be meaningful as a descriptive term

[4] However hostile and aggressive it may seem to observe it, no stable society has ever been based overwhelmingly on friendship. Neither has any stable social system of considerable scale in any known society. No social system common to societies in general or to any considerable set of them apart from friendships themselves in the most literal sense have been based on friendship either. Stable governments, for example, are never so based although it is quite possible to have governments based on kinship. Friendship is a genuinely peculiar form of relationship even when considered on very general levels. It is puzzling that so few social scientists have concerned themselves with it as a form of relationship that is at one and the same time universal or well-nigh universal and exotic. It is universal in that it seems to exist in some form at least among children, in all known societies actually if not ideally. It is exotic in that it has little in common with other relationships in any society. It is, for example, one of the very few relationships that is ideally egalitarian, even if not so by definition. It always injects a note of individualism into even the least individualistically oriented contexts if only because of the emphasis placed on individual appeal of one candidate for the relationship to the other (s) as the major basis for the relationship. Even if one defines the relationship by such criteria, it is interesting that there seem to be instances of such relationships in all known societies.

The implications of friendship roles for an individual's other roles always pose interesting problems. Ideally every individual is expected to have some friends. Despite the irony implicit in such pleas as, "Lord protect me from my friends; I'll take care of my enemies myself," the friendless one is an object of pity or scorn or fear in the context of all known societies. It is especially interesting that a type of relationship so inherently fragile as any placing emphasis on nonhierarchical structures of power and responsibility should be so generally regarded as a strong relationship, that so apparently fragile a relationship could be considered so important integratively, etc. Friendship is a most bizarre phenomenon.

with some utility in the description of actual social organizations, apart from egalitarian friendships of a particular type, it must refer not to nonhierarchical social systems but to hierarchically organized ones in terms of which certain rights and privileges of individuals of lower ranks in the hierarchy are protected from or guaranteed by those of higher ranks in the hierarchy.

Among hierarchical structures of political allocation there are two extremely general methods of maintaining balances of power and responsibility: either ideally or actually or both. One type of balance is that in which the power holder owes responsibility directly and explicitly for the results of his exercise of power to some other actual individual or group of individuals. It is characteristic of the military forces of the United States, for example, that the balance is maintained by the requirement of responsibility of the highest officer of the armed forces to members of the civilian government and of the members of the civilian government to the population at large via elected representatives and their appointees. The commanding officer can never be called directly to account by his subordinates, but only by his superiors, to whom the subordinates may appeal under specific rules.[5] In the last analysis the commander-in-chief of the United States armed forces is a civilian official, responsible, ideally speaking, in quite specific ways to the electorate.

2. EMPIRICALLY—NONEMPIRICALLY ORIENTED BALANCES

Balances of the sort just discussed involve an unending chain of powers and responsibilities. The method of balancing power and responsibility, ideally speaking at least, is clear in any specific case at any specific stage of its development. It is a balance such that enforcement of responsibility need not interfere with the exercise of power. I shall call such a balance an *empirically oriented balance*. It is characteristic of the kind of political hierarchy with which most of us are most familiar. There is, however, another type of political hierarchy that I shall call a *nonempirically oriented balance* of power and responsibility, that is, one in which power is balanced by responsibility by virtue of the power holder's faith in and allegiance to nonempirical entities. These entities may be ideals such as justice, honor, etc., or they may be nonempirical entities in the ordinary sense such as gods, the

---

[5] Famous novels have been woven about the theme of what happens when, even under the most extreme provocation, subordinates in such a hierarchy act in defiance of those in positions above them in the hierarchy. *Billy Budd* and *The Caine Mutiny* illustrate this theme.

spirits of ancestors, etc. The balance of power and responsibility in terms of a traditional Chinese family was of this sort. Ideally speaking, a traditional Chinese father who was the head of his family had complete power over his son, for example, and owed no responsibility directly to his son in any way. He also ordinarily owed no responsibility to the district magistrate or to anyone else for his treatment of his son. If he were not the family head, he owed responsibility only to his father and/or to the family head. A properly brought up Chinese father did, however, from his own point of view as well as that of other members of the society, owe responsibility to the ancestors for the continuation of the family line. With the possible exception of incestuous relations between father and daughter-in-law, there was *no* justification for a son resisting his father in *any* way. If the father were also the family head, no other family member was qualified to interfere, ideally speaking. On the other hand, the father knew full well that, if he acted in such a way as to destroy his son or to fail to prepare him properly for adult life and continuation of the family line, he might commit the greatest of the three unfilial sins, i.e., fail to have posterity. In modern sociological and psychological jargon all such nonempirical balances of power and responsibility should probably be described as internalized balances of power and responsibility, that is they are effective by virtue of the power holder's belief or perception of obligation to something or some ideal that as far as any scientific observer can tell would not intervene actively regardless of the behavior of the power holder. In such nonempirical balances as the one described, there was at least an empirical element in the fact that the responsibility the father owed to the ancestors for the maintenance of a family was quite clearly defined in empirical terms. Even that sort of empirical element need not be present in the case of such extreme forms of nonempirical balances as that implied in the concept of the "divine right of kings." [6] Charismatic leaders, in the sense that Max Weber intended the concept, may also be in the position of leaders whose power is balanced nonempirically in both senses intended here. I do not know what a term like internalization means in any precise scientific sense, but I do know that given nonempirically oriented balances of power and responsibility, if the power holders are not somehow carefully trained to act as though their responsibilities for those

[6] This must not be confused with the concept of the "Will of Heaven" in traditional China. As in the case of the father's responsibility to the ancestors, the emperor's fulfillment of conditions that indicated that he retained the "Will of Heaven" required that a quite definitely and explicitly empirical state of affairs be maintained.

over whom they have power were in fact empirical and as though a failure to fulfill those responsibilities would in fact bring disaster, such systems can not remain stable. It is especially difficult to ensure stable operation in terms of such a system in the case of charismatic leaders. The power of such a leader is primarily a function of the blind faith that his followers have in him. The charismatic leaders of history have by no means ordinarily been individuals carefully trained in responsibility. Organizations characterized by charismatic leaders have on the whole been highly unstable in social history.

In nonempirically oriented political balances, if the power holder is not somehow motivated in such a way as to balance his exercise of power with responsibility—and here it must be kept in mind that it is not enough for him to be motivated nicely, he must also be motivated correctly [7]—the organization in terms of which he wields his power will be instable. A Chinese family head who is not properly indoctrinated with a sense of responsibility to the ancestors for the continuation of the family can in fact become a little family Caligula and literally destroy the whole basis for the continuation of the family line. Not only can he do it; there are plenty of cases in Chinese history in which he has in fact behaved so; and in the Chinese case there has rarely been any critical problem of knowledge in these respects.

There is another reason, in addition to the question already mentioned of the proper indoctrination of the power holder, to expect elements of instability in nonempirically oriented political balances. There is the question of whether or not, even if he is so indoctrinated as to try to be responsible, he knows enough to wield his power responsibly. In the case of charismatic leaders there is even a third difficulty. They are likely to develop in situations of extreme tension and dissatisfaction. Their followers in general seek a change in the status quo. One of the surest ways for a charismatic leader to undermine the basis of his power is for him to sit tight. Such political balances are certain to produce changes, though not necessarily the ones looked for by the adherents of such leaders, assuming that those adherents know what changes they look for, which, of course, they may not.

Hierarchical political balances facilitate the wielding of power by minimizing the possibility of interference by those over whom power is wielded. Their interests may be protected in many different ways, or they may not be directly protected at all. If the balance of power and responsibility is empirically oriented, it is to

[7] There is, therefore, always a critical problem of rationality involved in such balances.

that extent somewhat easier for social scientists to analyse. If their analyses are successful, such balances may, therefore, be somewhat easier to alter on the basis of some form of explicit social engineering. From the point of view of those with roles in public affairs, the distinction is important. Even assuming adequate knowledge for social engineering, if the political balances in a given social context are nonempirical, it may be necessary to convert the members to a preference for empirical balances before some specific alterations can be effected.

In the last analysis, however, some nonempirically oriented political balances must be involved in every society, if only because one of the possible ranges of variation of human behavior is the orientation of human behavior to ultimate ends. Furthermore, some such orientation seems to be present in all known cases of human society. The allocation of power and responsibility is always relevant in some respects for any action, whether, from the point of view of the actor, that action is oriented to ultimate ends or not. To the extent that this is so, political aspects inhere also in actions with nonempirical orientations. From this point of view, if a society is to be stable, that stability will vary with the degree to which the ultimate ends are identified clearly with empirical states of affairs and hence can be paralleled by an empirically oriented hierarchical political balance.

United States social structure is interesting from this point of view. The structure of checks and balances, which we learned to take for granted as children, is one of the most explicitly empirically oriented balances of power and responsibility in world history. It is not a matter of chance, however, that most Americans, nevertheless, feel that ours is a "system of checks and balances under God." Margaret Mead was quite correct when she took as a leitmotif of her description of American society, an application of the old Cromwellian edict: "Trust God and keep your powder dry." Probably most members of United States society believe fairly devoutly that we exist with God's help, but most of those also believe equally fervently that "God helps those who help themselves."

In the field of international relations the problems of the balance of power and responsibility are raised in an acute form. It is not difficult to devise a structure for the delegation of power to a world or international organization, but how can the members of such an organization be held responsible for their acts? If any member can call the other members of the organization to a halt in their exercise of power over the members of the nation he represents, the power exercised in terms of that organization cannot be effective in times of crises. It is difficult to conceive of getting an effective nonempirically oriented balance in terms of such an organization if only because of the widely different conceptions of the nonempirical held by the various potential and actual members of such an international organization. The technology of the allocation of power at specific levels of application is highly developed, indeed, in the modern world, but the technology of the allocation of responsibility at general levels in terms of large-scale organizations has not received corresponding intellectual attention, public interest, or advance. In theory, at least, there seems to be no a priori reason as to why it should be a more difficult problem.

3. SPECIFIC–DIFFUSE BALANCES

Another major range of variation in terms of which balances of power and responsibility may be discussed is variation between *specific* and *diffuse* powers and responsibilities. This range of variation is obviously closely related to the functionally specific and the functionally diffuse aspects of any relationship. The powers at the disposal of any individual may be quite explicitly defined and delimited ideally and/or actually speaking. The same may be true of the responsibilities that an individual owes. On the other hand the extent of the powers and the nature of the responsibilities may be only vaguely defined and delimited. To the extent that the balance [or lack of balance] has the former character it is called a *specific* balance here; to the extent that it has the latter, it is called a *diffuse* balance. It is this type of variation which poses one of the greatest difficulties in determining whether in fact or in fancy a balance of power and responsibility exists. Not only are many different combinations possible with many different degrees of distinction among them, but variation may be considerable from the point of view of different parties to any given relationship or different members of any given organization. To sketch only the most obvious possibilities of variation in terms of the distinction between specific and diffuse balances of power and responsibility alone, and leaving questions of degree aside, there is the following list: (1) an individual may have specific powers and specific responsibilities, (2) he may have specific powers and diffuse responsibilities, (3) he may have diffuse powers and specific responsibilities, and (4) he may have diffuse powers and diffuse responsibilities.

It is not difficult to find examples of all four of these. Ideally speaking, offices in most bureaucracies are offices whose holders have highly specific powers and responsibilities. In the actual sense, and to some extent in the ideal sense as well, a primary school teacher in most areas of the United States has specific powers and quite diffuse responsibilities. Examples of individuals with diffuse powers and quite specific responsibilities are more likely to be found as actual than as ideal cases. Frequently the confidential secretary of a person quite important in an administrative hierarchy has rather diffuse powers and quite specific responsibilities to his [or her] own employer. Finally, the case of a father-son relationship is a typical case of diffuse powers and diffuse responsibilities. Neither side of the balance is both clearly defined and clearly delimited, though many elements about it may be quite precisely defined and delimited.

At this point some of the lines of complication of this question must be mentioned. If one considers the simplest of all possible relationships, a two-person relationship, one not only has the possibilities of the four types of balances mentioned above, but, identifying the two persons as A and B, the following main lines of variation also exist: (1) from the point of view of A, his powers may be specific and his responsibilities may be specific, (2) from the point of view of B, A's balance of power and responsibility may be seen as A sees it or as any one of the other combinations that obtain with regard to A, [see p. 304 as a minimum] (3) the same is true of B, of course, from A's point of view (4) possibilities corresponding to the foregoing three [the second of which contains several summarized] exist for each of the other three combinations given above [p. 304], and (5) the ideal-actual distinction may cut across [i.e., multiply by three: *a.* ideally and actually, *b.* ideally but not actually, and *c.* actually but not ideally] each of the preceding sets of possibilities. Every one of the possible variations of the situation from A's point of view as distinguished from B's and vice versa has implications not only for operation in terms of the relationship but for any other operations that either A or B has which interrelate in any other way with other individuals or the members of other organizations in any way affected by the actions of A and B in terms of their own particular relationship. There is no space here to go into this matter, but in even the most casual analysis of power and responsibility in terms of a society or a social organization, it is important for the observer to try to ascertain whether the allocations of power and responsibility are similarly or differently defined from the point of view of different members of the relationships concerned.

Another important line of variation has to do with whether or not these political balances are specific or diffuse, not with regard to the definition of the powers and responsibilities as such, but rather with regard to the individual or individuals over whom one has power and/or to whom responsibility is actually and/or ideally owed. Thus an individual may have power over, or be responsible to, one or more specifically identified individuals. The individuals concerned may be identified either personally or by virtue of the roles they hold in various organizations. On the other hand he may have power over, or owe responsibility to, an individual or individuals who are only vaguely identified. Again the variation of relationships is complicated by the fact that the description of the political allocation of a given relationship may be perceived quite differently by the different members of the relationship.

The various permutations and combinations of specific as distinguished from diffuse balances of power and responsibility can become exceedingly complex in organizations with large numbers of members. The possibilities may even be complex in relatively restricted organizations. Probably none of the permutations and combinations are totally lacking in implications at some levels of analysis. One may give obvious examples of some of the differences such variations may make. By contrast with Mr. Johnson's position as President of the United States, we tend to assume that the position Mr. Khrushchev held in the Soviet Union was one of relatively diffuse responsibilities as well as diffuse powers. Certainly in the field of foreign affairs an individual in Mr. Khrushchev's position is capable of more rapid alterations of fundamental foreign policy than is a person in Mr. Johnson's position. It is difficult for a President of the United States to execute a complete about-face in foreign policy overnight, if that foreign policy has received any general discussion by the members of the society as a whole or even by certain segments of the membership [e.g., Congressmen]. A leader in Mr. Khrushchev's position seems less inhibited. On the other hand, if such a leader does get launched on a disaster course, it is much more difficult for others acting in terms of his society to stop him without far-reaching consequences than is the case with Mr. Johnson. Here the differences in the balances of power and responsibility have implications for the ease and freedom of maneuver in the practical arena of foreign affairs.

Variations in the specificity and diffuseness of power and responsibility are considerable from society to society and from organization to organization within a given society. Variations in the specificity and diffuseness of balances of power and responsibility probably constitute one of the major lines of variation that longest survive considerable increases in the level of modernization in societies. Although in general there is a high and increasing uniformity among relatively modernized societies, they certainly do exhibit considerable differences. Some of the most noteworthy of those structured differences have to do with allocations of power and responsibility. In the long run even those increasingly get washed out, and all such societies become more similar rather than more different, but at any given point of development so far attained, the differences in these respects may be of the greatest moment. The range of possible variation among relatively nonmodernized societies in these respects is, as one would expect, much greater.

4. INTERNAL-EXTERNAL BALANCES

The distinction between internal and external balances of power and responsibility and consequently internal as opposed to external politically oriented hierarchies are specific instances of a general form of distinction. The terms *internal* and *external* are used here as defined above [see footnote 2, p. 294]. Whether a given structure [and hence action in terms of it] is internal or external cannot be determined unless the social system(s) involved are identified. In this sense the political structures relating representatives of the United States or other members of the United States to the representatives of the United Nations or other members of the United Nations are at least in part external to United States society. Relations between a member of the Federal Bureau of Investigation and any one who has broken a law of the United States are internal to United States society, though they involve external elements from the point of view of the member of the Federal Bureau of Investigation. The terms internal and external, in this sense, cannot be used fruitfully unless one is prepared to identify the units concerned. What is internal from the point of view of members of one unit may, of course, be external from the point of view of another.

The distinction between internal and external balances of power and responsibility focuses attention on two considerations relevant to public affairs. The first has to do with the sources of stability or change in terms of a given social system insofar as its structures of political allocation are germane to stability and change. The second, but closely related matter, is that of the relationship of the members of a given organization to members of other organizations with whom they are in contact. There is a sense in which a considerable portion of the balances of power and responsibility for any society is internal to the society as such, at least ideally speaking. The more highly self-sufficient any organization is, the more likely it is to be characterized over-whelmingly by internal balances of power and responsibility. This, for example, was strikingly true of the traditional Chinese family. On the other hand the members of an enormous number of organizations depend in a genuine sense on external contacts for balances of power and responsibility. One of the aspects of nations or societies whose leaders have absolute power or some near approach to it and diffuse and rather weak responsibilities, if any, rests on these considerations. If such leaders embark on extreme courses, it may be virtually impossible for any individual or any set of individuals belonging to their own society to curb such an extreme course. In such cases the course of action may be halted by members of other societies acting on a massive scale. There is a quite genuine sense in which no members of any German organization and no individual German alone could hold Hitler accountable. It required a massive alliance and a costly war to curb the activities he set in motion.

As one would expect, given the much higher level of self-sufficiency of organizations in relatively nonmodernized socie-ties, the extent of internal balances of power and responsibility characteristic of the subsystems of such societies is much greater than is characteristic of the subsystems of relatively modernized societies. Most of the balances for most of the subsystems of those societies depend at least in part on the specialized predominantly politically oriented organizations, i.e., various governmental sys-tems, to afford the structures of action in terms of which the members of all sorts of other organizations are in the last analysis held responsible. In a context like that of United States society, if a father mistreats his children, the members of some governmen-tal body will take action. If the president of a corporation misap-propriates funds, representatives of the government will act, etc. There are, of course, many important internal balances of power and responsibility characteristic of organizations even in rela-tively modernized societies, but there can be no denying that in general the more highly modernized a society becomes, the more do the balances of power and responsibility internal to the various organizations in the society depend on external balances of which the most important are those brought into operation in terms of governmental systems.

The whole issue of internal versus external balances of power and responsibility is related in a quite obvious way to the whole question of centralization and decentralization. Before turning to that question in somewhat greater detail, one further line of gen-eralization may be presented on this score. The greater the dependency of the members of subsystems of any nation or society on internal balances of power and responsibility, the less social planning is required for general operations in terms of the society. Under such circumstances, however, when centralization is desired, it is much harder to realize, and other things being equal, it requires a much larger involvement of manpower. It is not difficult to get students of public affairs to pay close attention to the implications of the interdependency of various organizations when one considers their interdependency in terms of their economic aspects. To observe that members of a given unit can be easily and quickly brought to heel by having their food supply cut off by members of another organization is to say something that can be and is quickly and easily understood by any member of our society. The implications of interdependency viewed in terms of political allocation as such rather than the means frequently associated are no less extreme and should be no less obvious. Any organization the stability of which depends on a balance of the power of its leaders by their responsibility to members of yet another organization is no less vulnerable to those interdependencies than it is to interdependencies viewed in terms of goods and services in the more conventional sense. If the members of the organization to whom responsibility is owed do not enforce such responsibilities, they open the way to capricious behavior [or close the means of preventing misuses of power] by the leaders of the other organization as surely as if they gave them material means of other sorts such as weapons, for in such instances internal balances are specifically lacking. When internal balances are lacking, and especially when the individuals concerned are long accustomed to the lack, it is difficult under any circumstances, let alone in crises, to shift to internal balances and much more difficult, if not impossible, to shift to internal balances quickly enough to handle a crisis. The implications of these hypotheses emerge more strongly when an additional hypothesis is considered, i.e., that motivation for such shifts is quite unlikely to occur in the cases mentioned except in times of crisis when the external balancing elements fail to work.[8] The shaman of a primitive village may be a key figure in the maintenance of the stability of village organizations because he is considered so powerful, given his contact with the gods and the incomprehensible forces of nature, that he is actually looked upon as an important assessor of responsibilities for individual members of the society who cannot otherwise be held to account. To prove to one and all of

[8] Some of the phenomena associated with the Fall Affair [1962] in Oxford, Mississippi, can be understood in these terms.

the members of such a village that the shaman's cures [or, worse, that his spells in general] are without sound foundation may do more than rid the village of superstitious health practices. It may rid the village organizations of stability for reasons that seem difficult to understand. There are close analogies in other fields in which we are not so quick to seek more explicitly rational structures. The patient's confidence in his doctor, whether in fact justified or not, is so vital to effective medical therapy in general that there are always several reasons not involving self-interest to justify the exceeding reluctance of doctors to testify against one another in cases where the competence of a doctor is in question. Balances of power and responsibility are critical for all organizations. The interdependencies relevant to them and vice versa are no less strategic than interdependencies viewed in economic terms, although analysis of them is much less highly developed. Pursuit of even the most laudable goals of reform ignore such interdependencies at the expense of the goals specifically sought and more.

I V

CENTRALIZATION AND DECENTRALIZATION

Centralization and decentralization have already been discussed [pp. 16–18, 55–60, and 100–107]. It will suffice here to mention three combinations of special interest in matters of public affairs: (1) cases of high decentralization and low centralization, (2) cases in which centralization is greater than decentralization but for limited purposes only, and (3) cases of high general centralization and low decentralization. All of the cases of relatively nonmodernized societies that have had any considerable pedigrees of stability have been cases of the first or second type. High general centralization and low decentralization has not been a possible basis for stable large-scale societies until relatively high levels of modernization obtained in communications as well as other respects. Most of the feudal societies of world history and large numbers of small-scale societies have been societies characterized by high levels of decentralization and low levels of centralization. In the history of feudal Europe there have been many cases in which the so-called king of a country was considerably less powerful than one or more of his vassals.[9] Anthro-

[9] It is important to note in such cases, however, that this is a high level of decentralization and a low level of centralization at what we would consider today to be the national or society level. It does not follow that the social systems associated with the lands held by a given vassal were in turn organized in an equally decentralized fashion, though this was probably frequently the case.

pologists and other students of relatively small-scale societies have from time to time reported cases in which the elements of centralization on the society level were so tenuous as to call into question whether or not any such thing as a government could be said to exist at all. The case of the Jivaro Indians of South America is a notable example of this sort.[10]

All stable societies characterized by high levels of decentralization and low levels of centralization are, as one would imagine, societies characterized by subsystems capable of high degrees of self-sufficiency. The main bases of decentralization are likely to be family and village units. There are alternatives, however. Kinship units larger in scale than family units can be the major basis of decentralization,[11] and guilds and other organizations may be important bases of decentralization. Whenever one deals with members of societies characterized by high levels of decentralization, considerable alterations may sometimes be made in such centralized organizations as exist without immediate and far-reaching results, but *any* general tampering with the organizations in terms of which decentralization takes place is likely to have implications far beyond the intention or expectation of those designing the interference.

Among relatively nonmodernized societies there have been spectacular cases of highly stable large-scale societies in which important elements of centralization have far exceeded elements of decentralization, but this predominance of centralized elements has only held true for limited purposes. Two of the most spectacular of these cases are the cases of traditional China and Tokugawa Japan. The main outlines of the social structure of traditional China were stable for close to two thousand years. Tokugawa Japan was a feudal society, but it was certainly the most stable feudal society in all world history, lasting for roughly two and a half centuries. There is absolutely no question in either case but that during most of the periods concerned the central

---

[10] See, Mathew W. Sterling, *Historical & Ethnographical Material on the Jivaro Indians,* Smithsonian Institute, Bureau of American Ethnology Bulletin 117, Washington, 1938, and R. Karsten, *Blood Revenge, War & Victory Feasts among the Jivaro Indians of Eastern Ecuador,* Smithsonian Institute, Bulletin 79, Washington 1923.

[11] In all societies, however, the family unit will be *an* important basis of decentralization. No society has been characterized by structures eliminating all major elements of discretion from the family scene. Deeply respected structures of what proper conduct in a family context should be probably limit discretion in a family context more than actual transfer of decision making to another organizational context in even the most highly centralized societies. No matter how generally inculcated such respect is, it is quite another matter than centralization.

authorities could have brought overwhelming pressure to bear on any particular segment of the population in any particular area of the land had they so wished. The members of no single family, of no single locality, of no province threatened the stability of traditional China irrevocably for two thousand years, and certainly none of these ordinary foci of decentralization could stand against the power at the disposal of any emperor at the height of vigor of any dynasty. Correspondingly no daimyo could have withstood any Shogun during the Tokugawa period, or tried to.

In neither case, however, was the day-to-day conduct of affairs on a highly centralized basis. Most of the operations in terms of most of the organizations in both societies depended on internally regulated activities of the members of the various subsystems of the societies. Both Tokugawa Japan and traditional China were spectacularly effective cases of relatively high levels of centralization restricted to quite limited purposes. Nevertheless, even though they constitute spectacular cases, this type of structure is on the whole more frequent than the structure of very high decentralization and very low centralization of the sort discussed above in connection with feudalism in general and small-scale societies like that of the Jivaro Indians in particular. In the context of societies characterized by high levels of centralization for limited purposes, especially if the centralization is sufficiently great for almost any given isolated display of power, manipulation of the organizations in terms of which centralized power is exercised is a considerably more complex matter than in the case of feudal societies or ones similar to Jivaro society. In the latter, any general tampering with the organizations in terms of which decentralization takes place is likely to have far-reaching unforeseen side effects. In the former the same may be said of any tampering with the organization(s) in terms of which centralization ordinarily proceeds. In both traditional China and Tokugawa Japan, despite the fact that an enormous amount of discretion was left to individuals at the local level, changes in the focus of centralized power had far-reaching implications for the local levels. Tokugawa Japan is a case in point. Before the development of the level of centralization achieved or at least maintained by the Tokugawa Shoguns internecine warfare all over the land was rife. The elements of centralization were vital to the maintenance of peace; it in turn was vital to the fact that the warriors of Japan were one of the most peculiar military castes in world history—a set of militarists who were explicitly forbidden to engage in military exploits. Finally the forms of centralization that did exist in Tokugawa Japan account for the development of structures of *absentee administration* in terms of which no ruler administered and no administrator ruled. In general, arguments about the levels of despotism that have in a fact been maintained on a stable basis in relatively nonmodernized social contexts are exaggerated, but they have not been exaggerated in one very important sense. The implications of what went on in terms of the governments of such societies for even those organizations in terms of which members ordinarily acted on an overwhelmingly decentralized basis were far-reaching and important. Whenever and wherever high levels of centralization, even for limited purposes, can be and are attained, it is important to be skeptical about local appearances of self-sufficiency.

Here it is necessary to reiterate that stable large-scale societies characterized by very high general centralization and very low decentralization are impossible until a relatively high level of modernization of communications is reached. Most treatments of centralization hinge, either implicitly or explicitly on centralization of the political aspects of social systems and especially on centralization of the governmental systems. It is always necessary to keep in mind that the allocation of power and responsibility is by no means the only respect in which a social organization can be highly centralized. Here again the habit, characteristic of all people accustomed to thinking in terms of relatively modernized societies, of considering social systems in terms of some specialized orientation to either political, economic, or some other special aspect of social life poses difficulties for the analyst of relatively nonmodernized societies. It must also be reiterated that such societies constitute the vast majority of all the societies distinguished in world history and even of all of the societies with whose members one has to deal in international affairs. There certainly have been cases of highly centralized governments in relatively nonmodernized societies, but none of these have been stable for very long periods of time as social history goes. These cases have, however, been sufficiently rare, though spectacular, that they are not likely to pie the analysis of students of international affairs. There are, on the other hand, a large number of cases of relatively nonmodernized societies for which this point of view of analysts reared in relatively modernized social contexts is exceedingly likely to pie the analysis. These are the cases like those of traditional China and Tokugawa Japan just described above. They are examples of societies which may be quite large in scale and quite stable, although the same difficulties can arise in the case of unstable examples of such societies. These are societies characterized by important elements of centralization in the governmental subsystems of the society. They may be societies in terms of which for limited purposes in general, and almost any limited purpose in particular, members of a governmental organization can dominate any other set of members of the society regardless of the degree of decentralization in terms of which affairs may ordinarily be conducted.

There is some danger that the actual levels of despotism or authoritarianism or centralization characteristic of the governments of these societies may be taken to indicate what comparable structures would indicate in a relatively modernized social context. High levels of centralization in the political sphere go hand in hand with high levels of centralization in other spheres in a manner taken for granted by the members of highly modernized societies. Furthermore, centralization in one of these spheres is never irrelevant to other spheres in any social context. Nevertheless, in a social context like that of traditional China the government [and to that extent the general allocation of power and responsibility] may be relatively far more centralized than the allocation of goods and services. Even among highly modernized societies variations of this sort may be observed. The government of the Soviet Union is surely more highly centralized than that of the United States though in some respects the latter is the more highly centralized society overall. For example, communications, economic allocation, and entertainment are in many respects— regardless of the intentions of the members—more highly centralized in the United States than in the Soviet Union. They are certainly more completely interdependent. We run a risk, even in regard to the societies we know best, in identifying governmental centralization with centralization in general, and the less modernized the society we study, the greater is the risk. The *appearance* of overwhelming centralization, which is so frequently commented on by students of relatively nonmodernized societies, is usually explicable at least in part by virtue of the fact that the vast majority of members of the society do not ordinarily get into the act as far as the actual wielding of power by members of the government is concerned. In these circumstances the important trick of analysis is not to be deceived into thinking that the level of centralization of governmental control is carried further than it actually is. Informants high in governmental circles in such societies are not necessarily the best informants on these matters, and this, of course, further complicates the problem.

The elements of centralization achieved may be great enough, as in the case of traditional China, so that vast engineered works of irrigation, canals, etc., can be constructed and maintained.

The power of the kings or emperors of such societies to work their will, however horrible it may be, on any given individual or even on considerable sets of individuals, need not be doubted either, but neither of these observations implies the level of general centralization which, whether we like to admit it or not, is increasingly characteristic of all of the relatively modernized societies, despite the very great variations of authoritarianism in governments among those societies.

Certainly no example of governmental centralization in a relatively nonmodernized society which has remained stable over any considerable period of years has approached the level of centralization attained in some of the relatively modernized despotisms such as that of Germany under the Nazis, the Soviet Union, Japanese society in the late 1930's and early 1940's, etc. For what it is worth, so far none of those cases of extreme centralization among relatively modernized societies has yet proved to be highly stable, though certainly the Soviet Union has the longest record so far. Among relatively modernized societies the most spectacular cases of instability associated with the highly centralized governmental systems have generally been functions of the international relations among the members of these societies and other societies. Germany, Italy, and Japan were all societies whose members got involved in major wars and became societies whose leaders were held responsible, as it were, for their exercises of power by external coalitions of the members of other societies. Apart from the danger, from the point of view of the members of the society concerned, of inciting some coalition of members outside the society, the limiting problem of governmental centralization, as of any other centralization, is that of adequate knowledge for the planning that must go along with such centralization. If it is possible for the members of relatively modernized societies with highly centralized governmental organizations to avoid entanglements in war and consequent instabilities, we may have an opportunity within the next few decades to see whether or not the level of centralization outruns the knowledge at the disposal of the leaders who direct such organizations, or whether to some extent there are increases in decentralization. Presumably this increase in decentralization would be possible only if the actual degree of centralization was considerably greater in the governmental sphere than was minimally required by the level of modernization so far achieved.

Finally, in considering higher levels of centralization in political allocation in general and the government in particular, I would emphasize once again that, despite compartmentalized thinking, centralization is never solely a political phenomenon. We have exceedingly little knowledge of the kinds and degrees of variations possible. Nevertheless, it is possible to assert, first, that centralization can never be solely a matter of political or governmental centralization. Second, although such centralization always has implications for other aspects or other organizations in the society, there are quite important ranges of variation possible. There are, for example, certainly some limits within which centralization of the government can increase or even decrease while the centralization of the allocation of goods and services remains constant or even in peculiar cases varies inversely. Third, although we do not know the regularities of these variations with any clarity or precision, if we do not take the attitude that such variations are at least in principle lawful and that the laws which will enable us to describe and predict their behavior are discoverable, we must in general resign any hope for public policy based on scientific analysis.

V

LEGISLATIVE, EXECUTIVE, AND JUDICIAL ASPECTS

The distinction of legislative, executive, and judicial aspects of government is a familiar one. It is dealt with at length and in depth in at least two of the major divisions of modern knowledge, the field of law and the field of political science. The behavioral science sphere of political analysis of the problems of relatively nonmodernized societies is a recent development, and a major work in it replaces the three terms used here by the terms *rule-making, rule application,* and *rule adjudication.*[12] I would use the terms *legislative, executive,* and *judicial* to refer to aspects of behavior or organizations rather than to concrete acts or organizations. Other than that I would use the terms roughly as I understand the layman to use them. The term *legislative* pertains to the establishment of structures defining who shall wield power

---

[12] This application of a special form of the "3-r's" to the field of political science is accompanied by no new definitions of these concepts nor even by any citation of old definitions. The author asserts that these ". . . are the old functions of 'separation of powers,' except that an effort has been made to free them of their structural overtones—rule-making rather than 'legislation,' rule application rather than 'administration.' " Since I find in this contribution to concept formation no greater precision of meaning or increased fruitfulness in application, either by the author or his followers, I regard this particular set of neologisms as one of the more clear-cut cases of unjustifiable jargon in the social sciences. See G. A. Almond, "Introduction: A Functional Approach to Comparative Politics:, *The Politics of the Developing Areas* [edited by G. A. Almond and J. S. Coleman] Princeton University Press, Princeton, 1960, p. 17.

and/or bear responsibility, in what respects, and how. The term *executive* pertains to the wielding of power or bearing of responsibilities. The term *judicial* pertains to the interpretation of the structures of political allocation, the judgment of what the structures mean in specific circumstances, and the decision of when and how they apply.

It is characteristic of all of the relatively modernized societies that some form of the distinction of the legislative, executive, and judicial aspects of governments is made and to a noteworthy degree generally disseminated among the members of the society concerned. A general understanding of this set of distinctions by the members of most of these societies is furthered because some of the subsystems of the governments of such societies are usually labeled specifically as legislative, executive, or judicial organizations. In the United States context, for example, where ideally at least the doctrine of the separation of powers is strongly held by the members, we distinguish with careful exactitude among legislative, executive, and judicial bodies. In the federal government, for example, we refer to *the Executive* [or *the Administration*], *the Congress,* and *the Judiciary.* It is also true that any sophisticated observer of the United States government is perfectly well aware of the fact that there are administrative and even legislative aspects of the behavior of the members of the Judiciary, that there are executive and even judicial aspects of the behavior of the members of the Congress, and that there are judicial and legislative aspects of the behavior of the members of the Administration. Despite these obvious realities of the political aspects of life in the United States, just as one can speak of the government as being a predominantly politically oriented organization, one certainly can speak quite legitimately of the Congress as a predominantly legislatively oriented organization, of the Administration as a predominantly executively oriented organization, and of the Judiciary as a predominantly judicially oriented organization.

Such a clear-cut specialization of organizations along the lines of this distinction is relatively rare even among relatively modernized societies. One need only mention the fact that in Great Britain, for example, the executive and legislative aspects are by no means so neatly compartmentalized, even ideally speaking.[13] Such specialized organizational development is, on the whole,

---

[13] There is no point whatsoever in arguing here as to whether it is better or worse to have such a clear-cut separation of powers. For the moment the discussion is only concerned with whether such separations are empirically frequent, and what forms, if any, they take.

rare, and the extreme form exemplified in a relatively stable society like that of the United States is, perhaps, unique. Moreover, not only is such organizational specialization rare, but it is even rare for the members of the society concerned to think generally in terms of such a tripartite distinction. It is not rare in social history for an observer to distinguish these aspects of governments. They may always be distinguished by an observer, and indeed these aspects can be distinguished in the observation of any organization, though the members of many organizations devote relatively little attention to such aspects and do not distinguish among them in their own views of their organizations. It is relatively rare for members of societies, apart from relatively modernized societies, to think of these aspects as separate aspects, let alone as separate organizations, however useful it may be from the point of view of an observer to make such a distinction. Furthermore, outside some of the societies of Europe, the United States, etc., the societies generally considered as Western societies, it is especially rare for much thought to proceed in these terms.[14]

Before the development of relatively modernized societies, the members of most societies considered themselves actually governed primarily by men of good judgment rather than by law, if, indeed, they did not feel that it was right and proper that they be so governed. This in the main held true even of societies among whose members quite clear-cut conceptions of law developed. There are relatively few cases of relatively nonmodernized societies for whose members anything like so clear-cut a conception of law as that developed in terms of Roman society exists. There are, however, plenty of cases in terms of which quite generally understood and disseminated statutes exist, are generally observed, and are expected to be observed by the members. Even in many of those cases, however, few members think in terms of this tripartite division. In the highly developed bureaucratic system of traditional China the district magistrate, who was the clearest embodiment of government with whom most individuals in that society came into contact, was not conceived of as now an executive, now a legislator, and now a judge. He was considered and almost certainly considered himself as *the district magistrate* in whose activities all these aspects could but need not be distinguished. He was above all a man of good judgment fitted to govern by virtue of his knowledge of the Classics. The sedentary

[14] This may be one of the rare useful uses of the concept of Western societies.

nature of relatively nonmodernized societies and the high degree of decentralization of power and other aspects of the society, the high levels of self-sufficiency of the various organizations which make up the society—all of these factors as well as others are easily compatible with "government by men of good judgment" as opposed to "government by law." All relatively modernized societies, however, must be characterized by structures of government by law rather than by men of good judgment if they are to be stable. This in no way implies that good judgment ceases to be important in such societies.[15] The increased emphasis on law is rather an implication derived from the fact that in the context of relatively modernized societies problems of scale, the frequency of change, the high level of interdependency, and all of the other factors that have been mentioned so frequently above combine to make the conduct of the allocation of power and responsibility in terms of a governmental organization out of the question in the absence of relatively precisely defined, easily located, carefully authenticated statutes, etc. One may add another, perhaps cynical, consideration. In the context of relatively modernized societies it has so far proved exceedingly difficult if not impossible to count on a sufficient number of men of good judgment sufficiently willing to serve in governmental roles to do the job on that basis even if it were practicable or possible from other points of view.

The more highly developed government by law becomes, the greater is the likelihood of the tripartite specialization under discussion. This is true both of the distinction of these aspects by the members of the society and the actual specialization of governmental subsystems in terms of these aspects. The distinction among these aspects developed long before relatively modernized societies. Even the specialization of governmental subsystems in these terms developed long before such societies appeared on the scene, but whereas the members of relatively nonmodernized societies *can* make such distinctions, the members of relatively modernized societies *must* make them if the society is to be stable. Since thinking in such terms is by no means universally distributed among the members of relatively nonmodernized societies, the development of adeptness of thinking in these terms is likely to be a special problem of transition toward higher levels of modernization.

[15] Though in nonnegligible respects, the higher the level of modernization, the greater is the effort to reduce the area of decision based on good judgment.

V I
THE USE OF FORCE

The use of force is perhaps the most striking form taken by the allocation of power and responsibility, but the use of force is never the sole means at the disposal of the members of a government or any other organization. It is in fact only an extreme in one direction as far as procedure in terms of political allocation is concerned. The idea that any system can be maintained or understood solely in terms of the use of coercive sanctions is wildly naïve. Allegations to the effect that coercion is the sole means of maintaining order in terms of a stable organization never cope successfully with the question of who guards the guards themselves. The members of highly authoritarian systems like that of Nazi Germany certainly have carried the uses of coercion to extreme lengths, but even that society is by no means understandable solely in terms of applications of coercion. Faith in Hitler as a charismatic leader was a vital element in that society. The Nazi leaders themselves and many of their followers to some degree clearly understood the importance of elements other than sheer coercion, as have authoritarian rulers in virtually all cases in history. The Nazis relied heavily on propaganda in education in their special ideal structures for lasting support. They never hesitated to use coercion as a means of insuring the success of propaganda and education or for the maintenance of the motivation to support the regime. Opposition was frequently removed by coercion, but support was by no means completely secured in that fashion. Had coercion been the sole support of the Nazi regime, it would not only be impossible to understand that regime, but it would be impossible to understand the fact that the military defeat of Nazi Germany did not eliminate all vestiges of Nazi attitudes and ideals.

Although coercive sanctions never constitute the sole form of political procedure in terms of a society, the extreme efficiency of coercive sanctions for limited ends cannot be ignored either. The careful structuring of the use of force to secure responsibility or to eliminate disruptive individuals from whom responsibility cannot be secured is essential to some extent to the stability of any society. It is certainly essential to the extent that conformity cannot be motivated in other ways, although conformity can never be secured solely in this fashion. In the context of all societies characterized by broad ideal structures of tolerance of deviant behavior special problems arise. The civil liberties institutionalized in the United States, for example, furnish a basis of protection for individuals who may even seek to overthrow that society itself. When operation in terms of the system fails to motivate conformity or to drain off the energies of possible dissident elements in other ways, as was probably done in the past to some extent by the geographical frontier and is done to some extent today and always by frontiers of activity, deviant individuals may arise who actually threaten to use the area of tolerance as a basis to gather strength to overthrow the very structures in terms of which they operate. Even if they do not actually threaten and intend to do this, they may well be considered by other members of the society to have such intentions. If they actually intend to do so, failure to close the area of tolerance may result in a closure of it by virtue of the success of the deviant individuals and their consequent rise to power. If they are considered a threat, whether justified objectively or not, a closure of the area of tolerance may be invoked to prevent such an overthrow. In any case, societies characterized by accepted structures for such an area of tolerance are peculiarly liable to social change in the political realm from real or fancied threats. In the long run in all of these cases stability of the area of tolerance is more likely to be a function of the fact that the structures of socialization prevent the rise of genuinely dissident elements or elements conceived to be dissident by other members of the society in great strength. The areas of tolerance, whether one likes to admit it or not, in such societies are more likely to persist to the degree that they are not actually put to serious test.

The problem of maintaining structures of power and responsibility by means other than coercive ones is difficult. The whole problem of motivation and of the process of inculcation and maintenance of social structures is involved. Even the general possibilities cannot be treated here, most importantly because of ignorance, and less importantly for lack of space. The relatively easy observability of applications of coercion and their extremely dramatic character when evidenced in torture, killings, concentration camps, jails, economic sanctions, and the like have tended to preoccupy students of the political aspects of phenomena with the question of the uses of force that take place both ideally and actually in terms of all societies. Nevertheless, in the context of relatively stable societies, the essence of the problem of the allocation of power and responsibility is not how they are allocated by the uses of coercion, but rather how power and responsibility are allocated in the absence of coercive sanctions. The famous French sociologist, Emile Durkheim, was partly famous for his observation that it was impossible to understand the phenomena of contracts unless one appreciated what he dubbed the "noncontractual elements of contracts." Something of an analogy may be maintained here. The noncoercive exercises of power and responsibility must be analyzed, if a society or other organization is to be understood. It is equally tenable, however, that the noncoercive exercises of power and responsibility must be analyzed if the coercive exercises are to be understood.

The tenability of these observations is not affected by whether one refers to relatively modernized as distinguished from relatively nonmodernized societies. The enormous increase in efficiency of communications and of many of the instruments especially useful in coercion certainly does increase the level of coercion that can, at least in theory, be attained and maintained. We have at our disposal today not only weapons but elements and aspects of social organization which would make sadistic despots of less technologically developed periods of history green with envy. Tyros of coercion today can, at least in theory, perform feats which virtuosi of coercion could not perform before, but neither these technological advances nor these new developments in social organizations have cut either our governmental or our general social leaders free from the irreducible bastion of concern for the views of some individuals some of the time posed by the question "who guards the guards themselves?".[16]

V I I
SPECIAL QUESTIONS

Before leaving the discussion of generalizations about the structures of political allocation I wish to touch on four questions which do not lend themselves easily to the abstractions above.

[16] Appearances to the contrary notwithstanding, there is little cause in this observation for hopefulness for those who feel that a decent consideration for the opinions of the ruled *should be* of concern to rulers. In these very societies the radically increased efficiency of communication devices makes feasible a level of mass indoctrination never before feasible for rulers. Although there are levels of coercion which cannot be exceeded, recent history has by no means been uniform in indicating any mass reluctance on the part of members of societies when they are contacted in large numbers to accept and, in some cases at least, enthusiastically endorse quite large-scale and far-reaching invocations of coercive sanctions. There have been frequent cases of this in relatively modernized social contexts such as Japan, Germany, Italy, the Soviet Union, and even in special instances in the United States [e.g., the removal of the United States citizens of Japanese ancestry from the West Coast during World War II despite the absence of a single authenticated case of sabotage or espionage on the part of any American of Japanese ancestry in the areas concerned]. Examples of the ease of quite wide-spread public acceptance of high levels of coercion in the context of relatively nonmodernized societies as they change in the direction of modernization are practically universal today.

They are the following: (A) mass appeals, (B) bureaucratic government, (C) the relevance of the structures of economic allocation to government, and (D) the interdependence of governmental systems and the underlying political allocations of any society.

A. MASS APPEALS

1. IN GENERAL

The use of mass appeals as an extremely general device by members of governmental systems—and here the concern is so overwhelmingly with governments or with individuals trying to take over a government that I shall refer only to governments rather than to the structures of political allocation in general—is quite a modern question. It is ironic that we get the major term we use for leaders who orient most of their concern to playing on the public opinions of the masses of the members of their societies from the Greek word demagogue. The Greek demagogues were not at all what we consider demagogues to be today, anymore than the so-called democracy of the Greek city-state was what is considered to be democratic organization today. In the Greek city-state only a minority of adults had any right of participation in the government. The citizens were not the general membership of that organization, but rather an elite group among the total membership. In this context the demagogues were those who played on the emotions of the elite. Before the development of relatively high levels of modernization, rarely if ever did there exist in social history the possibility of mass appeal to the membership in general of societies of any scale. With the increase of modernization and the radical increase in the efficiency of communications which is both possible and necessary for such a development, a radically different situation obtains. In the context of relatively modernized societies, it is not only possible to have mass appeals, it is impossible to avoid them. Any ruler of any relatively modernized or any increasingly modernized society who attempted to avoid all uses of mass appeals himself or by members of his government would submit himself to the risk that mass appeals would be used by others who would eventually unseat him. Today, General de Gaulle is one of the few powerful public leaders who has shown himself capable of surviving the epithet aloof, but he has mass appeal despite the extent to which he cultivates his air of aloofness. As far as relatively modernized societies are concerned, it is not a question of whether there will or will not be mass appeals that are vital to the understanding of the actions taken in the name of governmental organizations and hence are vital to an understanding of the societies concerned. There will be; it is only a question of how the mass appeals will be conducted, who will control them, etc. In the lore and literature associated with relatively nonmodernized societies one of the most persistent tales of revered leaders who sought to improve their rule and the lot of their people is the tale of the leader who simply puts on modest clothes, leaves his retinue, and moves unperceived among his people to observe what his millions do and how and why his people prosper or suffer. Without the use of an adept make-up artist and a dramatic coach to teach him to avoid his typical gestures, hardly a single modern political leader could hope to move abroad in such easy anonymity. Radio, television, picture magazines, and newspapers guarantee that the masses of the members of their societies will know him on sight and by sound.

There are two special problems associated with mass appeals of special relevance here. One is the problem of mobs, and the other is the problem of parties.

2. MOBS

I would define a *mob* as a peculiar form of social organization. A mob is a social system characterized by a minimum of explicit, planned organization, involving a sizable group of members [for arbitrary purposes let us say not fewer than several tens of individuals, and in most cases relevant here, several hundreds or several thousands of individuals] who are, in general, not acquainted with one another, who interact on relatively short notice in a manner not generally foreseen in advance in an atmosphere highly charged with emotion—most notably the emotions described by the terms hate, anger, and fear. By this definition the Nazi storm troopers were certainly not members of a mob. The storm troops were much too carefully and explicitly organized. The large aggregations of highly disciplined demonstrators frequently marshalled to display disapproval by throwing ink, carrying signs, smashing windows, etc., of a hated embassy in a given country are usually not mobs either. On the other hand, in Iran under the leadership of Mossadegh, the mass demonstrations incited and executed against the properties, policies, and personnel associated with an oil company as the hated symbol of imperialism were certainly examples of mob action in the sense intended here.

As structures of political allocation, mobs are interesting social systems. The members of a government or other individual members of a society can in a genuine and realistic sense *give* the members of a mob power. This can be done by the careful use of mass appeals to attract a large aggregation of individuals who are potential members of the mob one seeks to endow with power. One can incite the individuals so gathered, work them up to what is generally referred to as a frenzy, until in some sense the mob is formed, and its members begin to move in some concert. Finally, if one has behaved as previously indicated and if one has coercive power at his disposal and does not invoke it to stop the concerted action of the members of the mob at this point, then he has endowed the members of that mob with power.

At that point it is *his* very own mob, and at that very same point it ceases to be his since he cannot endow its members with effective responsibility. If he has sufficient determination and sufficient force at his disposal, he may find it possible to stop the activities of the members of the mob, and he may even be able to punish them in some sense. In the nature of the case, however, the effective life of a mob is one of short duration. Mobs are among the most volatile of social systems. The activities of the members of the mob are not only unpredicted in detail, but they are usually also unpredicted in quite general respects. Even if one has in the most carefully calculated sense incited the members of the mob and endowed them with power, he cannot count with certainty on what the members will do with the power which he has so painstakingly given them. They may be aroused to wreck a store and end by wrecking a government. After they are done, they can, of course, be punished, but this does not constitute effective responsibility. Such punishment in no way constitutes any sort of restoration of the effects of their exercise of power, nor is such punishment likely to be a deterrent to future mobbists. Like crimes of passion, mobbish acts are not primarily deterred by the individual mobbist's estimates in any rational fashion of what the consequences of his behavior may be.

Action on any considerable scale by members of a mob always to some extent calls into question the stable allocation of power and responsibility in terms of any government within the jurisdiction of whose representatives the members of the mob act. Mobbists do not inevitably bring about the downfall of a government, but there is a sense in which such a potential always exists for them.

Mob action may threaten governmental stabilities in many ways. It may lead to chaos in which new leaders take power, or it may paralyze or destroy important facilities for production and hence spell economic disaster. In any case, however carefully

calculated the formation of a mob and the endowment of mobbists with power may be, short of being stopped, the members of
the mob know no effective control. It follows, therefore, that the
attempt to use the development of mob action as an instrument of
policy is, in this sense at least, always folly from the point of view
of the members of the government in power, if the members of
that government have any interest in staying in power and in the
continuing stability of the government of which they are members. On the other hand, deliberate resort to the incitement of
mobbists by individuals or members of organizations who are out
of power and wish to create a situation in which the opportunities
for an increase of their power are good, regardless of what other
immediate costs may be—for any such individuals—the attempt
to create a mob and endow its members with power may be
rational even though ruthless. Incidentally, I would add that,
from the point of view of such individuals, the particular focus of
attention of the members of a mob is not of the essence of the
matter as long as the individuals desiring to use activity in terms
of the mob are not likely to become targets themselves. Especially
if they are out of power, it is not difficult for these individuals to
keep out of the way, as it were, of the members of the mob once
they begin to move, especially since to the extent that they have
participated in the creation of the situation they have some fore-
warning. Even so, there is always some risk of being hoist by one's
own mobbists.

In the world today with its increased facilities of communication, the creation of mobs as a deliberate policy is easier than it
once was. Especially in areas where stresses and strains are likely
to be at a high pitch, as in the case of areas whose inhabitants are
undergoing modernization, the emotional climate of the population is likely to be relatively favorable for the development of
mobs. In situations of stress and strain mob action has an additional appeal. Vilfredo Pareto cited as one of the six residues,
which were for him what might be described in a loose sense as
"forms taken by the well-springs of human action," the "need of
expressing sentiments by external acts [activity, self-expres-
sion]." [17] Whether one wishes to go as far with this idea as
Pareto was prepared to go need not bother us here, but insofar as
there was anything in his point of view at all, one should expect
the actions of the members of the mob to be satisfying to them
from this point of view. After all, one of the major techniques of
inciting the members of the mob is in some form or another to

[17] Vilfredo Pareto, *The Mind and Society,* Harcourt, Brace and Co., New
York, 1935, 4 vols, Vol II, p. 517.

urge the potential mobbists, "Don't just stand there, do something!," as anyone who has ever watched the villain of a TV western create a lynch mob knows perfectly well.

The utility of the action of mobbists as a technique of creating instability, and consequently the threat such action represents to the stability of a government whose members are in power, is quite well known. It is alleged by many, and as far as I know, it is probably correct, that the members of Communist Parties in societies in terms of which the members of the Communist Party do not control the government are always willing and anxious to create, or aid in the creation, or stimulate in other ways the development of mobs. It would be quite rational of them to aid and abet the formation of mobs focused on almost any subject, though if the mobs can be so developed that its members are more likely to attack the specific enemies of the members of the Communist Party or to carry the banners and slogans of that Party, so much the better. These allegations may or may not be exaggerated, but there is absolutely no doubt about the fact that no members of the Communist Party have so far knowingly encouraged or aided in the development of mobs in the societies in terms of which the members of the Communist Party were in control of the government. In all the societies dominated by Communists the use of mass appeals are carefully organized. The members of Communist governments make effective use of mass demonstrations, but the better organized those demonstrations are, the more disciplined the individuals involved, and the more predictable the actions taken, the better do the leaders like it.

For many reasons, ideological and otherwise, mass demonstrations and mass audiences have great appeal for political leaders of all sorts including members of the government in power as well as leaders who aspire to governmental positions of considerable power. Unless such mass demonstrations and mass audiences are carefully disciplined, and perhaps even if they are, there inheres in them the possibility of the development of mobs. As indicated above, this potentiality may be a virtue rather than a drawback of such audiences and demonstrations for leaders who are not members of the government in power [or who are not in power in terms of that government]. This potentiality may also be a virtue from the point of view of governmental leaders who do not care what happens to their government. For those leaders who do care what happens to their government, mass audiences and mass demonstrations are more ticklish phenomena than they may realize. Especially if these leaders specialize in emotional appeals, there exists always the possibility that mass enthusiasm once worked up may result in the development of a mob and the development of further consequent difficulties. In some cases such leaders may even feel that they can use a mob without fear of the consequences to themselves or for their governments. Such may have been the attitude of Premier Mossadegh of Iran. It seems that he deliberately attempted to make use of mobbists in his struggles and that he utilized the Anglo-Iranian Oil Company as a symbol at least. His regime did not survive that usage, and there is a serious question as to whether the price paid for what resulted was a bargain—quite apart from whether one looks at this from the point of view of Mossadegh, the Iranians in general, the British, or the owners of the Anglo-Iranian Oil Company.

3. POLITICAL PARTIES

The problem of political parties is another of the special problems of mass appeals. I would distinguish *predominantly politically oriented parties* from *predominantly politically oriented cliques* of various sorts. Probably no society has ever existed in which some of the members did not form some sort of organization, however loosely organized, in terms of which those members attempted to influence the allocation of power and responsibility in general and the activities carried out in terms of the government in particular. As long as the members of such organizations, seeking to influence the various activities carried out in terms of the government, are drawn from relatively restricted elite groups, whatever the basis of their elitism, I consider them here to be predominantly politically oriented cliques. If the membership in such organizations is potentially at least a mass membership, if ideally and/or actually the aim of the members of such organizations is to involve as large and as broad a segment of the population [or at least the adult population] as possible in their organization, and if the orientation of the members of that organization is toward governmental influence, via elections or what not, I consider such organizations to be predominantly politically oriented parties. Given this definition, there are obviously different degrees of development of such parties. I suspect that most parties grew out of predominantly politically oriented cliques, but regardless of origins in the history of societies like the United States and Great Britain, there were clearly periods in history in which the actual membership of what might here be called predominantly politically oriented parties, and perhaps even the ideal membership, were restricted to much smaller segments of the adult population than is the case today. In both countries today certainly predominantly politically oriented parties exist in the fullest sense of the term used here. In this sense one may wish to question whether the Communist Parties in countries controlled by the Communists are in fact predominantly politically oriented parties in this sense. There is certainly no doubt about the orientations of their members, but it is alleged by some, whether correctly or falsely I do not know, that the leaders of such organizations neither seek nor desire a full mass membership in their particular organizations. Insofar as they do not seek, ideally at least, to generalize the membership of their organization beyond the alleged and presently restricted limits, those parties differ importantly from what I have here defined as predominantly politically oriented parties.

Predominantly politically oriented parties in the sense that the term is used here are also quite modern phenomena. Developments in this direction have certainly existed in the context of relatively nonmodernized societies, and relatively highly politically oriented parties certainly exist in many such societies today. Before the development of relatively modernized techniques of communication, however, the kind of mass contacts necessary for predominantly politically oriented parties in this sense to be of great moment in a general social context were not generally available. Such parties *can* exist as subsystems in relatively nonmodernized societies today specifically because these techniques can be introduced even though the general level of modernization has not advanced very substantially.

Implicitly or explicitly predominantly politically oriented parties represent an attempt to generalize participation in and influence on governmental affairs beyond any presently possible limits of highly developed knowledge about these matters. Such parties, if highly developed, always involve the implication that many people will develop strong views about and attempt to influence policies as well as selections of personnel about which they cannot possibly have expert knowledge. The development of political parties, therefore, always poses problems of the participation of individuals in areas in which they are not experts. Since such parties cannot develop until some levels of modernization are relatively highly developed or until they are being developed, there is a sense in which participation of nonexperts increases at just the point that the importance of expert knowledge for members of governments increases.[18] This is no place to argue the

---

[18] I have suggested that one of the important implications of degrees of freedom in a market is that the operation in terms of a market may mitigate inadequacies of knowledge—that the market mechanism in fact serves as an alternative to knowledge. Just the opposite inheres in opera-

virtues of mass participation in governmental affairs from the point of view of how desirable democratic participation might or might not be. Whatever our views on that sort of value question may be, there is no escaping the fact that any general attempt to involve large portions of the population in active influence and participation in the operations in terms of their governmental organization or in actions highly relevant to such operations is always to some extent a matter of exciting interest and action in spheres in which adequate knowledge is in exceedingly short supply. There are many implications of this. It may be that one of the major problems involved is that of inciting participation and interest up to but not beyond a particular level. Even if we could be absolutely clear-cut about our evaluative criteria, it is still an exceedingly difficult matter to calculate the optimum location and nature of such a level of participation.

There are further special problems posed by the existence of predominantly politically oriented parties in relatively nonmodernized societies, especially if those societies exist in the world today. By importation of techniques of mass communications, it is certainly possible to develop general participation in predominantly politically oriented behavior on a mass basis to the point at which a fairly high level of development of predominantly politically oriented parties can be said to exist. In such cases there exists not only all of the problems mentioned immediately above, but also an additional special set of problems. In these cases the development of predominantly politically oriented parties is likely to disseminate influence and interest not only beyond the levels of existing expertise but also well beyond the possibilities of control and direction from other points of view. In such cases, for example, the development of predominantly politically oriented parties may radically alter the general levels of self-sufficiency and insularity to which the members of the society are exceedingly well adjusted in other respects. The development of such parties in areas in which ordinary individuals have not interacted with anyone much beyond the confines of their villages or some particular kinship unit may not only set in operation particular activities relative to which adequate knowledge and means of controls are not in existence. Such developments may also con-

---

tions in terms of predominantly politically oriented parties. Operations in terms of them magnify problems of irrationality and arationality. Part of this difference inheres in the greater probability of various nonrational elements in the one context than in the other. It is conceivable, perhaps, that predominantly politically oriented parties be so devised as to have effects more like markets in these respects but neither motivation nor creativity about how to do so seems high.

tribute to the breakdown of previously existing structures of control—again regardless of whether or not new or alternative structures have developed.

B. BUREAUCRACY

Government in terms of bureaucratic organizations is not confined to relatively modernized societies, but it is always necessary in such societies. Not only that but the level of bureaucratization always continues to increase in relatively modernized social contexts, and bureaucratic organizations are always and everywhere increasingly carried out on the basis of highly specialized personnel. In the context of relatively nonmodernized societies the members of the bureaucracy may, at least on entry, be relatively nonspecialized in their qualifications. As government largely or solely on the basis of men of good judgment becomes increasingly impossible with the development of modernization, bureaucratic organizations whose members are relatively nonspecialized personnel also become increasingly impossible. Even in the context of relatively nonmodernized societies, however, whatever the recruitment system, whether by civil-service examinations, whether by civil service by adoption, civil service by usury, etc.,—to some extent the members of the bureaucracy in the course of their services always become relatively highly specialized.

One of the special problems always posed in a bureaucratically organized government is the problem of the insulation or separation of the members of the government from influences viewed as in conflict with the interests proper to their offices. There is always the possibility that these individuals may use their offices to serve themselves or others rather than to realize the purposes that operation in terms of their bureaucratic roles is supposed to serve. As has been indicated above, either ideally or actually, kinship considerations are always likely to be important in this connection. In essence one may handle this problem in one or some combination of three different manners. First, one may simply attempt to insulate or separate members of the bureaucracy from possible conflicting influences. This was the route taken in traditional China. The Chinese forbade a member of the bureaucracy to serve in the province in which his family resided, for example. Second, one may attempt to so unify the interest associated with all other interests which may impinge upon the individual office holder that a divergence of the two sorts of interest is unlikely. To some extent this was attempted and realized in the peculiar bureaucracy of Tokugawa Japan. As mentioned above in that bureaucracy most offices were inherited and the office holder's obligation to his family members was great. His obligation to his overlord and hence to the bureaucracy in which he served, however, not only took precedence over his obligations to his family members, but one of the greatest disgraces which he could bring upon his family members was a reputation for putting their interests before those of his overlord. Third, one may attempt to erect a set of ideal structures such that the individual is not supposed to be influenced by any other interests save those consistent with his office. Actually such ideals are never completely realized, and a relatively high degree of realization of them is only to be found in social contexts in which there exists a large number of highly specialized and highly differentiated organizations in terms of which the average member of the society operates habitually. Such situations never exist save in relatively modernized social contexts. In those social settings to some extent, and particularly insofar as these relatively specialized and differentiated organizations are concerned, the average individual is expected to operate in terms of a predominantly universalistic ethic. Such radical separation of one sphere of activity from another cannot be realized to any significant extent at all unless the general membership of the society is to a high degree used to such behavior. Even in this case problems always inhere. Notable among them is how the individual handles the implications that are relevant to what happens to him in other specialized contexts or in the context of his nonspecialized organizations, notably his family organization.

In all these cases there are not only the problems of how a given individual separates [or has separated for him] various and possibly conflicting contexts in terms of which he acts. There is also the problem of how he is able to switch back and forth among these various contexts. Not only must he keep them distinct, but he must in a sense combine them in his own behavior. After all, as a minimum, the average member of a bureaucracy in such a society goes from his home to his office and from his office back to his home. He is neither, ideally speaking, away from home while he is in office in the full sense characteristic of traditional China nor is he primarily concerned with the performance of his office even while he is at home should these two interests come into conflict as was expected of him in Tokugawa Japan. In this connection one must bear in mind an additional special difficulty of all who are late-comers to modernization. They must and do develop modern bureaucratic governmental systems before the general development of highly specialized bureaucratic organizations is carried very far. For most of them, no other import is more foreign.

C. THE RELEVANCE OF STRUCTURES OF ECONOMIC ALLOCATION TO GOVERNMENTAL SYSTEMS

However much one may think of a governmental system as a predominantly politically oriented organization, the structures of economic allocation in the society in general and in the government in particular are never irrelevant to other aspects of a governmental system. Because we are so accustomed to such specialized orientations we think of the United States Government, for example, as a political organization [instead of as our more cumbersome predominantly politically oriented organization], but the United States Government is overwhelmingly the organization in terms of which the greatest known allocation of goods and services takes place. The annual budget of the United States Government alone, let alone the capital value of the assets held in its name, is out of all scale with the budget of any other organization in the world. It certainly has no competition in this sense from any other subsystem of United States society. It has no competition from any other in world history either unless one considers the Soviet Union in terms of which, given the ideals of socialist organization, literally all economic allocation associated with the members of that society can be said to take place. From the general considerations already mentioned one would expect economic and political aspects always to be highly relevant to one another, if only because they are different ways of looking at the same thing. There is no actual allocation of power and responsibility that does not involve some allocation of goods and services and vice versa, anymore than there is a concrete instance of either that involves no role differentiation, etc. In no simple sense, however, can concrete economic allocations be said in general to cause political allocations. The obverse determinism is equally meaningless or untenable. Although variations in the allocation of goods and services are always to some extent relevant to variations in political allocation and vice versa, many variations in political allocations are possible within a constant state of economic allocations and many variations in economic allocations possible within constant political allocations, at many important levels of consideration. Furthermore, some of the most important policy questions, as well as some quite important theoretical insights into human behavior, may well hinge on what sort of variations in economic allocation may take place within what sort of constant political allocations and vice versa. And, of

course, similar questions may be raised about both of these allocations and role differentiations, solidarities, and states of integration and expression as well.

From the point of view of problems of government the interrelationship between economic and political aspects poses many
problems. A large number of these such as the problem of taxes
have been handled at exhaustive length in generally available
treatises. The problem of taxes is in one form, of course, the
problem of how the members of a given government get the goods
and services vital for operation in terms of the government. There
is, however, one special problem posed by the relevance of economic and political allocation for one another that is not generally treated explicitly. This is the problem implicit in the attempt
to separate completely the general economic allocation of the
members of a society from the political allocation carried out in
terms of the government. This state of affairs exists when in some
sense highly relevant allocations of goods and services are
regarded, ideally at least, as in some sense illegitimate or nonle-
gitimate. When, for example, members of the government are not
expected in any way to "dirty their hands" with trade, and merchants, ideally speaking, are considered as so marginal a group as
to have no legitimate standing vis-à-vis members of the government, this sort of situation exists. But the operations of the
specialists in exchange is always to some extent highly relevant to
the operation of the members of the government, and the allocations of power and responsibility at the disposal of the members
of the government is always to a high degree relevant to the
operations of the merchants—even if the latter seek only to
protect themselves from what they may regard as arbitrary expropriations. Whenever such separations are attempted, there will
exist a situation of graft and corruption. The merchants will seek
to influence the government officials for protection, for profit, or
for aesthetic reasons, and some of the governmental officials will
seek in some way to benefit from the activities of the merchants.
No social engineering can make economic and political allocation
irrelevant to one another on any such scale as this. Any social
engineering that appears to make them irrelevant to one another
or that makes any interaction among people whose interests are
more or less specialized in one or the other sphere illegitimate will
not eliminate such interactions. Such structures will simply guarantee that they continue on an illegitimate basis and on a basis
fraught with important elements of instability. What the ideal
structures have ordered asunder, the actual structures will unite.
From the point of view of the governmental organization, the

important element of that instability is likely to be the undermining of the ideal structures other than, but interdependent with, those directly violated. It is not just that a district magistrate may get a rake-off for designating a given contractor. That contractor may build an inefficient irrigation works. It is not just that one man buys freedom from punishment, but that the general administration of justice may be called into question, etc.

D. INTERDEPENDENCE OF GOVERNMENTAL SYSTEMS AND THE UNDERLYING STRUCTURES OF POLITICAL ALLOCATION

Until quite recently, so preoccupied have individuals generally been with governments and associated organizations as the major vehicles of political allocation that it has been standard procedure for most discussions of the political aspects of phenomena by both laymen and social scientists to ignore a considerable portion of the structures of political allocation in the societies concerned. Especially experts reared in terms of the relatively modernized societies discussed these matters as if the allocation of power and responsibility in a society started and ended with governments and their associated organizations. Most individuals were not conceived to participate in such matters until they reached adulthood, and at that level somehow, more or less magically, they became political individuals. This is certainly one of the greatest prices that has been paid for thinking of the political as a separate set of things or an entirely separate and disparate field or sphere of action from others such as the economic. Wherever governments appear, they are, of course, major foci of allocation of power and responsibility, and the members of many of the societies in which they appear generally expect that a government will be *the* major focus of allocation of power and responsibility. This attitude is frequently conveyed by a clause which appears in a large number of definitions of governments. This clause usually defines governments [or states], at least in part, as "organizations that have a monopoly of the legitimate use of force in a society."

No society ever existed with so sharply demarcated a political sphere, of course. However overwhelmingly attention may be focused on the government as far as allocation of power and responsibility is concerned, the members of the government always operate in terms of a more general set of structures of political allocation. There are, after all, structures of allocation of power and responsibility characteristic of every known organization in every known society, and the government is never the sole organization of any known society. Societies vary enormously from one another in the extent to which organizations other than the governmental organization are major foci for the allocation of power and responsibility as well as in the kind of structures characteristic of such organizations. However much they vary, these other organizations are always relevant to governments and vice versa. Although predominantly economically oriented organizations may be of great significance in these respects, they are by no means the only significant ones, and from many points of view they are not necessarily the most significant ones by any manner of means. On the whole their importance has been so obvious and intellectually clouting as to pie the general analysis of these phenomena.

In every known society the family organizations are especially relevant to these phenomena. It is characteristic of all societies that the average member of the society learns some [even most] of his [or her] initial responses to structures of power and responsibility within the context of some particular family organization. Action in terms of structures of allocation of power and responsibility is not, after all, something the individual in the United States can be left to learn at the age of twenty-one simply because that is the age at which voting is permissible in most of the states of the union. Most of the relevant attitudes in these respects have long since been formed. One's reactions to the details of substantive issues may change radically later in life, but general reactions to structures of power and responsibility almost certainly are as deeply ingrained as structures of eating, speaking, sleeping, and emotional display. Even in so rapidly changing a social context as that of the United States, reactions to many of the details of substantive issues seem to get fixed early in life in a family context. There is neither time nor space here to go into all of the various ways in which pressure groups lobbies, and many other nongovernmental organizations are relevant to understanding operations in terms of a government. These matters have been written on at great length. The remarks made here about the relevance of family organizations to government are made as examples of the kind of relevance of activity in terms of other organizations which until quite recently have been ignored for the most part in standard treatments by political scientists and other social scientists as well.

There is a sense in which for all known societies experiences in family terms have more relevance for the general setting as viewed from the political point of view than have any others. This generalization would hold true if only because initial learning of behavior in terms of structures of power and responsibility has always been in family settings. The only exceptions to this are, of course, the small number of people, relatively speaking, who have been reared outside family contexts, and most of those have been reared in some form of pseudo family contexts. Moreover, the relevance of family experience goes much further than is implied in this point of initial learning. In one way or another throughout most of world history the exercise of rule in governmental terms has in one fashion or another depended on the stability of family organizations. For most if not all of the relatively nonmodernized societies the final unit of decentralization of power and responsibility has been the family rather than the individual. This has been the case despite widespread variations from society to society of the actual position of the family unit in the general social structure. A member of traditional Chinese society would take it for granted that a considerable amount of discipline would be exercised in terms of requiring that the head of a given family make sure that the behavior of his family members accorded with the desires of governmental officials. The same was true in the last analysis in Tokugawa Japan, despite the fact that the family in that society was not the overriding major focus of concern for individual orientation as in traditional China. This is not to say that these societies lacked means or structures of controlling individuals as such. The representatives of the government could control individuals as such and did so in many cases, but ordinarily control was exercised in terms of family units, and there was a preference for such behavior. Given the extent to which most relatively nonmodernized societies are family oriented this should not be surprising. There is an important sense in which in most of these societies for most of their history one could find more about the interrelationships of members of nongovernmental and governmental organizations by an examination of geneological tables than one could learn by examining the account books of such organizations. There is apparently no society lacking in some conceptions of family or kinship influence—whether deemed good or bad—in governmental circles if a government exists. Increasingly with the development of modernization, however, governmental representatives never can rule through families either ideally or actually. Despite all ambivalent references to possible dynastic interests of the relatives of the past President of the United States, both ideally and actually, family interest could not rule there; the President might have been able to help his brothers succeed to the Presidency if they sought to, but he could not leave it to them. Moreover, if the members of the family who

held governmental office slipped at all importantly from justification of their positions through works into maintenance of their
positions by nepotism alone, their careers would have been short-
lived and might have endangered his to boot.

The limitation of modern governments, however, is not merely
a matter of the increasing improbability of inheritance as the
structure of succession to major governmental positions. The
members of modern governments ordinarily cannot exercise
power through family units. There are many reasons for this.
Some of them have to do with the nature of the family units
which characterize such societies. More important than the
change in family units in this respect, however, is the fact that
increasingly in terms of these societies individuals have to be
treated on predominantly universalistic bases in many contexts.
Governmental officials increasingly have to deal with individuals
on the basis of what they can do or have done rather than on the
basis of who they are. Given the past history of mankind, the surprising thing about modern governmental organizations in the
most highly modernized societies is not how much family connections still count, but how little they have come to count.

In relatively modernized social contexts, just as in relatively
nonmodernized ones, initial training and habituation to structures of political allocation continues to be in family terms. Thus
in terms of all societies there has always existed and always will
exist some question of the relationship among individuals considered in the family context and individuals considered in the
governmental context. In cases where these are supposed to be
relevant to one another, accommodations are built into the system, if the system is stable. In feudal contexts, for example, one's
place in the political hierarchy is inherited for life, and this in a
sense is true for everyone from the top of the hierarchy to the
bottom. It is in relatively modernized social contexts in which
this sort of relationship as between the governmental and the
family organizations is specifically not supposed to exist [19] that
the mutual influence as between persons considered in their family context and persons considered in the governmental context
poses its greatest problems. In all such contexts there is not only
the problem posed by virtue of the fact that the family is no
longer an instrument for the exercise of governmental power,
ideally speaking, nor is it likely to be, actually speaking either,
save for juveniles in cases considered trivial. There is also the

[19] Either ideally by the members of the society or actually by many of
the social scientists analyzing it.

problem of just how one does interrelate organizations that are in fact of enormous relevance to one another but that ideally speaking are supposed to exist in entirely separate spheres. There are specific problems of this sort in all sorts of areas. For example, there is no relatively modernized society without a system [or set of systems] of public education. Public education, particularly at the elementary and secondary school levels, is education in which other family members as well as the children are most intimately involved. Virtually all children enrolled in the elementary schools are in fact living in a family context, most of their time. They leave the family environment for certain periods of the day, a certain number of days per week, to participate in schooling. They return to the family environment after school. With rare exceptions among the members of such societies, there is a general expectation that there be public schooling, and therefore that the schooling be conducted via governmental organizations. Other family members are expected to feel strongly about the operation of the schools on a governmental basis. Especially to the degree that broad expression of opinion is freely permitted, any considerable change in the structures of public schooling is likely to result in a storm of indignant parents raising questions for the members of the governments. It is characteristic of most such societies that the professional politician, at least, would much rather deal with indignant citizens in general than with indignant parents.

In all of the relatively modernized societies the increasing bureaucratization of governmental organizations increases the separation of governmental interests and the interests of specific sets of family members. There are also changes in general family structures that are highly relevant. In recent decades there has been much comment on the fact that in some of the most highly modernized contexts psychiatrists and others detect an increasing tendency for parents to award or withhold affection on increasingly universalistic grounds. Some apprehension about the possible effects of this on the children has been expressed. There is neither space nor basis for arguing here whether the effects of such treatment in terms of increased insecurity on the part of the child, etc., are good, bad, or indifferent. I would raise one question, however. Given the fact that increasingly the average child as he moves increasingly outside a family context will in fact be met with increasingly universalistic treatment, would he adjust to such treatment by others better or with greater difficulty if within his family context he encountered no treatment on such a basis whatsoever? The older he becomes the greater is the likelihood that he will move increasingly in a governmental context in which he must be so treated and so treat others. Regardless of the causal explanation of such changes, the mutual relevance of modern family structures and those of modern governments is hard to ignore.

INTEGRATION AND EXPRESSION

I
INTRODUCTORY DEFINITIONS

The structures of *integration* of any society or of any other social organization consist of those structures operation in terms of which makes for the adaptation of the members or members-to-be of the organization to the structures that constitute the organization. Unfortunately this is not a simple matter. Few, if any, structures are perfectly integrative. Therefore, those which are spoken of as more or less integrative may also have important malintegrative aspects. The use of the term *integrative* to describe a given structure will imply that its adaptive implications outweigh its maladaptive ones. The difficulties of measurement involved in this concept are too obvious to require comment here.

The concept of *expression* denotes the type and limits of reaction, symbolic or otherwise, on the part of the individuals who belong to a given organization to the various phenomena with which they come into contact. One of the most obvious forms of expression is emotional or affective expression. What sort of emotional displays are the members of a given organization expected to indulge in under given circumstances? As indicated above [pp. 25 and 183–184] the aspects of integration and expression constitute a catch-all category. I am not pleased with it, but under this heading it is possible to refer to aspects of societies which cannot and should not be ignored.

I I
INTEGRATION AND EXPRESSION
A. INTEGRATION

1. SOCIALIZATION

What are the structures in terms of which the ordinary individual in every society learns to act as a member of that society? I assume that the behavior of an individual as a member of a society is never adequately explicable without reference to the interaction of the individual concerned with other human beings. There are methods of educating new-born infants associated with all societies. To some extent associated with every sub-system within every society there are some explicit structures, as well as some implicit ones, in terms of which new members learn how to behave as they are expected to behave, ideally and/or actually, and how to inculcate such behavior on others. I would define these as the structures of *socialization*. It is characteristic of all known societies that a considerable part of the socialization of all individuals is carried out in family terms. Even in the context of the most highly modernized of societies where the amount of socialization in general and education in particular that is carried out in terms of a variety of nonfamily organizations is great, it remains true that far more of an individual's initial basic learning from practically every point of view, including especially interaction with others, takes place in family terms than in terms of any other organization.

Apart from this generalization about socialization which applies to any and all societies, the socialization that takes place in terms of units other than family organizations must be considered. These units may be divided into two general types. The first consists of relatively unspecialized units such as friendship units, neighborhood units, etc., and the other consists of specialized units such as schools, business firms, governmental organizations, etc. For all societies, including the most highly modernized, considerable amounts of socialization take place in terms of organizations which are not particularly specialized with regard to one of their aspects as opposed to another. A given individual learns something from his interaction with friends, from his interaction in terms of neighborhood organizations of various sorts, etc. These organizations, however, are not specialized either with regard to education or socialization or anything else necessarily. In this respect they share some of the characteristics of socialization or education in family terms. This is socialization which goes along with action in terms of the organization, but is not necessarily thought of as a specialized form of activity. In this sense learning by doing has a very hoary tradition indeed.

It is not true that all societies are characterized by highly specialized organizations such as business firms, schools, etc. It is probably true that a government of some sort exists in all known societies and certainly in all societies of any considerable scale, but apart from this, specialized organizations need not be highly developed at all. In all relatively modernized societies such specialized organizations become increasingly important, and in all known societies of any considerable scale, whether relatively modernized or not, to some extent specialized organizations of this sort do exist. From the point of view of socialization or education these specialized organizations may be divided into two categories: (1) organizations specialized with regard to socialization or education, and (2) organizations specialized with regard to something other than education or socialization [e.g., predominantly economically oriented organizations]. Schools are the example par excellence of the first category. Schools, as that term is ordinarily used, have many other important aspects, but they are as predominantly oriented to education as governments are to political allocation. In most of the relatively nonmodernized societies some schools have developed, if the societies were of any considerable scale, but for the vast majority of the population, little if any socialization or education took place in terms of schools. Overwhelmingly in these societies such education as takes place in terms of schools is education of the elite. In relatively modernized societies schooling in this sense must become well-nigh universal. As a minimum it is not only true that universal schooling is an ideal in such societies, but also that many of the elements of basic knowledge are taught in school contexts rather than in any other organizational context. In such societies more basic elements of education continue to be carried out in family terms than in terms of any other organization, but it is also true that for the average individual some other important forms of basic learning are carried out in terms of schools. This is not true of any relatively nonmodernized society. Never until modernization was well advanced was any basic, as distinguished from intermediate knowledge, taught to the membership of any society in terms of a specialized predominantly educational oriented organization. Prior to this, schools in such societies were devices for inculcating intermediate knowledge. One of the special phenomena possible for late-comers to modernization is that for them schools can be used to inculcate new or old forms of basic knowledge for the members of the society before modernization has proceeded far in other respects.

Whenever specialized organizations exist, to some extent regardless of their orientation, their members must receive special training if they are to learn to behave in terms of them. Thus members of a government must know how to operate in terms of the governmental organization in terms of which they serve, and the same is true of members of school systems, business firms, churches, etc. Unlike relatively nonspecialized organizations, however, the specialized nature of these makes it the more difficult to prepare the members for their roles in them in completely different contexts. Therefore, no specialized organizations ever lack education as one of the functions which must be carried out in terms of the organization. Unlike schools, however, and like the relatively nonspecialized units mentioned above, education and socialization in terms of these organizations is incidental to their other operations. As in the case of nonspecialized organizations, some of the socialization and education carried out in terms of these organizations is always implicit rather than explicit. There is an important difference, however, between specialized organizations not predominantly oriented to education or socialization and nonspecialized organizations in these respects. The very preoccupation with specialization in general which is so characteristic of the members of these organizations is likely to result in the development of a specialized subsystem of these organizations oriented to socialization or education. Although in these organizational contexts as in all others, some socialization and education of members always takes place in ways that neither they nor their fellow members understand, increasingly an effort is made by the members to put training on as explicit a basis as possible. Thus unlike the socialization or education ubiquitously associated with relatively nonspecialized organizations, the socialization or education associated with specialized organizations not specifically oriented to socialization or education tends increasingly to take place in terms of subsystems of such organizations developed specifically with these purposes in mind. In this sense, schools of some sort tend to emerge as subsystems of all specialized organizations.

For all peoples in and out of history the learning [and hence socialization] curve has no doubt been steepest in the early years. Apart from that, the shape of the curve varies with the type of society and the roles of the individual member. One of the unusual features of relatively modernized societies is the extent to which for an increasing proportion of members there are steep climbs of the curve after infancy and childhood. The structures of these societies is such that there can even be steep rises for the aged for whom the curve has probably been at its flattest for most of mankind ere now.

2. MOTIVATION

The structures of socialization or education have to do with the inculcation of knowledge and the general learning of reactions. *Motivation* is concerned with the establishment of the ends of action, whether these ends of action be empirical or nonempirical, intermediate or ultimate—whatever they may be. How are individuals brought to desire or to seek those ends that would permit the maintenance of a society or other organization, or that will result in the dissolution or change of the organizations in terms of which they act for that matter? As in the case of learning, motivation is apparently not adequately explicable in terms of human heredity and the nonhuman environment. To some extent, given the present state of our knowledge, the ends men seek in terms of all known societies are a function of the interaction of men with one another. This is not a realm in which I feel much at home, but it is necessary to point out that there are structures of motivation in all known societies and that there cannot be societies without them. This brings up the distinction between *ultimate ends* on the one hand and *intermediate ends* on the other. For present purposes I would define *ends* or *goals* as future states of affairs toward which action is oriented.[1] *Ultimate ends* may be defined as those ends or goals of action which are regarded as ends in themselves by the individuals who seek them or in other respects orient action toward them. They are not justified as means to any further end. They are regarded as good or worthwhile in and of themselves. *Intermediate ends* may be defined as any future state of affairs regarded as a means to still further future states. Whether these future states of affairs in fact exist or are only conceived to exist by the individuals who orient their behavior to them need not detain the discussion here. From the point of view of the individuals they are ends of his action in some relevant sense if he so conceives them regardless of whether an observer views the situation this way or not. Discussion of ultimate ends in relation to motivation carries the discussion into the realm of religious aspects. *Religion* may be defined as aspects of action directly oriented to ultimate ends. Such a definition is both broader and narrower than the ordinary use of this term. Therefore, if this usage is disturbing, another word should be substituted for the word religion as that is used here. It is broader than much ordinary usage because religion in the sense defined here need not involve conceptions of superhuman deities or the like. The belief that man is good in and of himself and that man should prosper on this earth for the sake of that prosperity alone—that belief is as much a religious belief in the sense intended here as many of the beliefs associated with what we generally refer to as the organized religions. Furthermore, in this sense Nazism, Communism, as well as Catholicism, Judaism, and Taoism are religions. The definition is narrower than the

---

[1] In doing so I follow the lead given in the early work of Talcott Parsons, *The Structure of Social Action*, McGraw-Hill Book Company, Inc., New York, 1937, p. 44.

ordinary referent of the term in the sense that to pray for the recovery of a loved one from illness is not predominantly religiously oriented action as the term is used here. The recovery of that loved one is not, ordinarily speaking, an end in itself but a means to further ends and as such is not encompassed by the term as defined here. In the sense of the term used here all societies are characterized by structures of religion. These religions may be divided into at least two categories. One of these may be called *ethical religions* and the other *supernatural religions*. This distinction is based on whether or not the orientations involved are characterized by a belief in supernatural elements. Thus Epicureanism and Humanism in some of their forms might be considered ethical religions. Judaism, Mohammedanism, Buddhism, Christianity, etc., are supernatural religions in this sense. Most if not all of the societies in world history have been characterized by supernatural religions. Quite a number of societies have been characterized by what are here called ethical religions in addition to supernatural religions, and the members of some of the societies currently existing in the world insist publicly that in the long run supernatural religions will disappear from their societies altogether. This argument need not detain us here. The ultimate questions of neither ethical nor supernatural religions are subject to solution in purely scientific terms.

Organizations predominantly oriented to religious action will be called *predominantly religiously oriented systems*. Such organizations are not necessarily present in any society. Predominantly religiously oriented actions may be carried out in terms of organizations not predominantly oriented to them. Nevertheless, such organizations do exist quite commonly in social history. The ordinary term for such organizations is the term *church*. That term may be used here. Though not necessarily ubiquitous, churches are extremely common organizations in social history. Churches, like schools, may have as members only a relatively small portion of the members of the general society.

Another distinction is useful for understanding of public affairs. This is the distinction between what may be called *exclusivist* and *nonexclusivist religions*. *Exclusivist religions* are those whose adherents believe that one may believe in one and only one religion at any given point in time without being considered a hypocrite. *Nonexclusivist religions* are those whose adherents have never raised the question or believe that one may believe in an indefinite number of different religions without any insincerity being implied. Most European or American reared scholars and laymen tend to think overwhelmingly in terms of exclusivist religions. Catholicism, and all the other sects of Christianity, Judaism, Mohammedanism, and the like are exclusivist religions. One cannot believe in two or more of them at the same time, ideally speaking. On the other hand, Buddhism, Taoism, Confucianism, Shintoism, etc., are nonexclusivist religions. For many societies there may actually be a single religion, but when the members of such a society come in contact with other religious structures, they may not regard it as insincere to participate in two or more religious beliefs at once. Quite apart from whether or not one has missionary interests, some implications of this distinction for understanding interrelationships among people who tend to look at these matters differently should be obvious.

The difference between exclusivist and nonexclusivist religions has implications for stability and change. From the point of view of stability, a single exclusivist religion has certain obvious advantages. It permits all or none answers to problems affecting the broadest framework of motivation since competing ultimate ends are eliminated. As such, it tends also to freeze the structures of intermediate motivation at least insofar as they are deemed relevant to the ultimate ends. On the other hand, exclusivist religions may interfere seriously with operations in terms of a society for whose members fairly high rates of change are important ends. If the exclusivist religion concerned is incompatible with such an emphasis on change, one or the other will have to give way.

Perhaps the major source of instability associated with exclusivist religions arises, however, from the cases of societies whose members believe in more than one religion of which at least one is an exclusivist religion. Here conflicts among adherents of the different sets of religious ideas are much in the realm of possibility if not probability. Social history is replete with many examples of such conflicts—including some of the bloodiest wars in all that history.[2] There is another source of conflict. Especially in the context of relatively modernized societies exclusivist religious ideas with which members are preoccupied are likely to be those associated with supernatural religions. These are likely to ignore ethical religious ideas which are important elements of the societies concerned. Nationalism in many cases is just such an ethical religion. Unless the interests and direction of attention of the adherents of the exclusivist religions correlate neatly with those of the not fully appreciated ethical religions concerned, poten-

[2] The substantive content of the religious ideas is curiously irrelevant to the probability or extent of the violence associated with such conflicts. True believers in some of the most pacifistic and spiritual of creeds have been known to fall on others and on one another with vim and vigor. See: Eric Hoffer, *The True Believer,* Harper & Brothers, New York, 1931.

tials of all sorts of conflicts both among the members of given churches and elsewhere in other contexts inhere.

The nonexclusivist religions are not so likely to be a source of instability by virtue of the possibility of conflicts carried out in religious terms. Religiously oriented conflicts *are* likely to inhere in a conversion of a given religion from a nonexclusivist one to an exclusivist one. On the other hand, the presence of nonexclusivist religions in a society makes the inculcation and maintenance of the basic value orientations characteristic of the society, and hence its general structures of motivations, somewhat more vulnerable to change than is the case with exclusivist religions. One should be cautious about such statements, however. Traditional Chinese society was characterized by relatively nonexclusivist religions, and despite this fact remained highly stable in its general social outlines for upward of two thousand years—the longest pedigree of such stability of any known society of very large scale. Societies characterized by exclusivist religions, on the other hand have been much more vulnerable to change at many points in history than has traditional China.

In the definition of motivation attempted roughly above, I made reference to nonempirical as well as empirical ends. Whether one regards individuals as in fact trying to get to Heaven or merely as believing that this is what they seek to do, from the point of view of a scientific observer, they are orienting their behavior to nonempirical ends. After all, no conceivable scientist could verify whether a given individual in fact achieved such an end or not. On the other hand, ends such as success in business, education of one's children, achievement of a given position in the social hierarchy—these are all empirical ends. They may be complicated ones. It may be difficult to measure whether they are in fact achieved or not, but at least in principle it is conceivable that we find a way of measuring the degree of achievement of such ends with accuracy. Throughout social history a large proportion of the members of the general population have at least thought of their action as being oriented to nonempirical ends part of the time. Insofar as this is the case, a peculiarity exists. If these nonempirical ends are in fact to be relevant to an understanding of behavior, they must to some degree be identified by the individuals who orient to them with certain empirical factors. Either the individuals who believe in such ends, with or without realizing it, equate some specific empirical state of affairs with those ends, or at least they conceive of some specific forms of actions as conducive to those ends. Even if the individual believes the nonempirical ends are completely inscrutable, some empirical elements are involved, since only inaction or relatively unstructured action could result from motivation to seek completely inscrutable ends. After all, the opening words of the *Tao Te Ching* attributed to the sage Lao Tze when literally translated carries such inscrutability to the ultimate possible lengths. This opening passage can be rendered "The way that can be known is not the true way." [3] Perhaps no one has ever defined inscrutability more rigorously than this, but belief in the principle embedded in even that text had implications for the behavior of Lao Tze and for many subsequent generations of devout Taoists. Many of them, at least, interpreted this as implying that for the true believer as little involvement with the affairs of the present world as possible is implied by this doctrine. Whether the true believer likes to think of it as so or not, this implies some identification with empirical affairs of even such an inscrutable end as seeking the true way so defined. In the early history of Protestantism, some of the members of certain sects took the doctrine of the complete unknowability of God's will, the doctrine of predestination, and the injunction to work out God's will on earth quite literally and followed them to conclusions considered logical. The result was an almost random experimentation with all sorts of actual behavior including demonstrations with or without clothes. These demonstrations as a minimum got the devotees of such principles branded as disturbing to the general social order. The concept of Nirvana in Hinduism and Buddhism is as thoroughly nonempirical an end as any, perhaps, and yet it, as in the case of ascetic Taoism, comes to be identified with action oriented to as little involvement with the empirical aspects of ordinary life as possible. From the point of view of observers or individuals who must deal with believers in such ultimate nonempirical ends, the result may be as close an approach as possible to pure apathy, complete avoidance, and withdrawal by means of trances, etc., from other forms of action and other forms of involvement with human beings. Such behavior has important implications for the action of the believers, for their relations with others, and for anyone who has any responsibilities with regard to planning or administration of social organizations to which such individuals belong, regardless of whether those individuals consider themselves as belonging to the organizations concerned or not.

This sort of consideration is not, however, only significant because of the fact that one may have to deal in any given society with highly ascetic individuals. The number of rigorously ascetic members of any society is relatively small in proportion to the

[3] Literally in Chinese, Tao k'o tao fei ch'ang tao.

total population. Genuine ascetic virtuosity is rare. Certainly there is no a priori reason to assume that the incidence of virtuosity in asceticism is higher than that of any other form of virtuosity. Even in periods of history in which large numbers of individuals have flocked to monasteries, it cannot be inferred that the monasteries of those periods were highly ascetic organizations for all or even most members.

The relevance of this extreme consideration for much broader spheres of action is directly connected with the role of a particular kind of leadership generally referred to, after Max Weber, as *charismatic leadership*. There are important elements of nonempirical sort in the general motivation of the members of any society. As a minimum, the ultimate ends of the members of a given society as well as a large number of the more or less intermediate ones are likely to contain important nonempirical elements by *lack of specification* if not by specific ideals. In the case of the Taoists the nonempirical element is a specific ideal. When, however, an individual orients his behavior to, say, "working out God's Will on earth," or to the "greater glorification of the German Reich," or to the achievement of an anarchist's "paradise on earth," or to the "fullest realization of the human spirit," or the achievement of a "just and equitable democracy," etc., there may remain an important element of nonempiricality or its equivalent by virtue of the fact that neither the individual himself nor anyone else can in any neatly provable form state exactly what those ends cover and what they do not cover in empirical terms. There is as always *some* relatively undefined element in any statement of such broad goals as these.

A *charismatic* leader may be defined as a leader in whom his followers have blind unquestioning faith. In the eyes of a true follower of a true charismatic leader, as that term is defined here, the fact that the leader says that a given thing is right is enough to make it right. The tremendous impact of such leaders on social structure may in part be interpreted as a result of the fact that in the eyes of their followers such leaders are specifically individuals qualified to identify infallibly certain empirical action or behavior as identical with or conducive to these broad goals to which the followers orient their behavior. Insofar as charismatic leadership develops, no matter how stable that society may have been in the past, for a time at least the charismatic leader may produce a situation in which radical social change is rapid. His reign may be short-lived, since what he does in the course of it may make any stability impossible. Nevertheless, whilst he leads, he can institutionalize change with great rapidity as far as his followers are concerned. Thus, for example, a Hitler can tell the Nazi faithful what new behaviors are to be identified with their end, "greater glorification of the German Reich," whether these be a new invasion, a pact with the previously damned Russian Communists, a new attitude toward illegitimate conceptions induced by warriors, etc. A government characterized by charismatic leadership is a government characterized by enormous flexibility in policy formation—for a time at least. A charismatic leader may shift with ease and rapidity from one course violently supported by his followers to another supported with equal vehemence, despite the fact that the two seem radically incompatible from the point of view of a nonbeliever in that leader's charisma.

From the point of view of the general student of public affairs, there are two main implications of lack of definition or inscrutability in ultimate ends or even in intermediate ends held to be of great significance to broad segments of the membership of a given society or social organization. If those ends, whether rigorously defined as nonempirical or simply left in part undefined with any precision, are radically inscrutable and a powerful focus of orientation, the result is always to some degree either apathetic behavior or a radical and rigorous withdrawal from participation in ordinary daily affairs, i.e., radical asceticism. Such behavior on the part of any considerable portion of the membership of a society or any other social organization dooms the persistence of the organization concerned. On the whole, apathy is more likely to be a general condition posing problems of this sort than rigorous radical withdrawal. An apathetic state of affairs can be produced in individual actions from sources other than this. Thurber's story, "The Secret Life of Walter Mitty," is from this point of view not only a creation of literary genius, it is also the sophisticated embodiment of a level of social insight and commentary that probably deserves to rank with any of the last century. No one has described with greater depth of insight, clarity, or economy of means the type of apathetic withdrawal under circumstances of extreme frustration that Thurber chronicled through Walter Mitty.

The flexibility involved in the lack of complete definitions of ultimate ends in easily verifiable empirical terms is of the greatest importance in understanding the freedom for adjustment of the members of a given system to unanticipated daily events. It is also relevant to the adjustment of the members of a given system to social change. Both ideally and actually social change is built into the relatively modernized societies, and whether the members of any given relatively nonmodernized society like it or not, those societies are going to change, and they are going to change in the direction of the structures characteristic of the relatively modernized societies. To the extent that the ultimate ends or basic value orientations of the members of a society or of any other organization are not, from the point of view of those members, tightly tied to known and understood empirical states of affairs, room is left open for the reinterpretation of older orientations as an important basis for the legitimization of new departures. Even in terms of societies whose members pride themselves on the attitude that change is good in itself, older statements of value of this sort are frequently cited as a source of legitimacy. In the context of United States society today the words of the writers of the Constitution and the Declaration of Independence are often cited as evidence of far-sighted prevision on the part of the Founding Fathers to meet just the situation that the person citing them has in mind. In the context of Russian society today nothing gives greater legitimacy than to be able to maintain that just such a policy was exactly what Marx and Lenin meant. No matter how sharp the breaks with the past may be, there must be some elements of continuity. The greater the extent to which easy reinterpretations of the implications of older standards of value can be made, the greater is the ease with which modern changes can be stimulated and even engineered. The clarity with which the average member of traditional Chinese society knew what the ideal structures of that society meant in actual empirical terms was probably a major factor in the poor success of the Chinese in early moves toward modernization. A major redefinition of quite general goals was probably required on quite a far-reaching basis before modernization could proceed efficiently. Whether one approves of their means or not, the Communists in China would certainly seem to have accomplished this if only by completing the destruction of alternatives. On the other hand, Tokugawa Japan had a more or less built-in equivalent of charisma. The belief that all individuals who counted in power questions were supposed to do what their overlords told them was carried over and focused on the restored position of the Emperor. The belief in the sacredness of the Emperor meant that any statement which could be authentically attributed to the Emperor or believed to be authentically attributed to the Emperor automatically became a statement that identified empirically the proper ideals for all proper Japanese. The modernization of Japan cannot be understood without an understanding of the importance of the position of the Emperor in that modernization and the part played by the carryover of the previous orientation to the hierarchy of overlords to the role that was to be played by the Emperor once he was restored to a central position in governmental affairs. Even if the term religion is used more conventionally than it is here, it would be difficult to understand this phenomenon in purely political terms without any reference to the religious aspects involved.

By no means all of the motivational structures of a society are phrased in terms of ultimate ends. The set of ultimate ends constitute a framework in terms of which social action takes place. Motivation in terms of intermediate ends is no less relevant for an understanding of social behavior. It is, in fact, in terms of intermediate ends that the vast proportion of all activity takes place. Intermediate ends are to a high degree capable of being classified as empirical. To some extent even when they contain important nonempirical elements, they also contain empirical ones. For example, prayer may be an end of some activities and the means for further ones from the point of view of the individual at least. However much prayer may be regarded as a specific way of putting oneself in contact with a given deity, and to that extent not adequately analyzable in scientific terms, prayer does, after all, also involve empirical behaviors such as kneeling, standing silently with bowed head, etc. The fact that intermediate ends are themselves means to other ends makes it quite feasible to analyze action in terms of intermediate ends as either predominantly rational or predominantly traditional. Insofar as the intermediate ends are empirical ones, it is possible to judge whether or not the means chosen to reach them and those ends, when they become means for something else, are rationally employed or not. From the strict scientific point of view, choices among ultimate ends may be considered a matter of taste. From a strict scientific point of view choices among intermediate ends, given certain choices of ultimate ends, is by no means a matter of taste in all cases. It is quite possible to indicate quite objectively that some intermediate ends are not in fact conducive toward the achievement of more distant ends to which they are conceived to be related.

From the point of view of social change as well as from the point of view of the maintenance of stability of social organizations, one of the most significant aspects of motivation in terms of intermediate ends is that much of such motivation must be maintained on a voluntary basis. The use of coercive sanctions to maintain motivation is always to some extent an indication of malintegration. As a minimum it indicates that from the point of view of the individuals exercising the sanctions, some other members of their organization are not behaving as they should. Furthermore, the actual extent to which pure coercion may be relied upon by the members of any social organization is strictly limited. Only those uses of coercion that will motivate subsequent voluntary conformity will contribute to the integration of a society or other social organization—and the limitations on the use of coercion even for these purposes are considerable. Spanking a child for bullying other children may stop that action and may convince the child that he should not do it in the future, regardless of whether subsequent spankings will ensue. This will increase the adjustment of the child in terms of a society whose members contemn bullying, provided that such spanking itself does not have unanticipated consequences which will decrease the child's adjustment. There may be psychiatrists who will take either side of this argument, but I doubt that today one can find a psychiatrist anywhere who will maintain that such methods of child rearing can be pursued safely without let.

The problem of intermediate motivation is a ticklish one from another point of view, since motivation in terms of the various organizations of the society cannot be mutually incompatible without limits—if stability is to result. Furthermore, to the extent that motivations in terms of different organizations are relevant to one another, if there is to be any considerable level of stability, the motivations in terms of the different organizations that make up a society must on the whole reinforce one another. The more highly involved and complicated the development of differentiated social organizations, the more highly involved and complicated must be the general structures of motivation. For all of the complexity of traditional Chinese society, from this point of view it was relatively simple. Two types of social organization were of overwhelming importance in that society; one was the traditional Chinese family and the other the Imperial bureaucracy. Radically subordinated in interest to one or the other of these two, if not to both of them, were organizations such as friendship units, neighborhood units, etc. Few members of the society carried out many of their operations in such a sphere that conflict between these two major types of organizations could arise. As was well understood in the doctrine of the Will of Heaven in traditional China, as far as social stability was concerned, the real problem of motivation was to ensure that no situation could exist such that family interest could contradict that of the members of the other organizations concerned. From the point of view of the members, things were well in that society when action in family terms and family interests were such that one could not do ill in other spheres. Though a somewhat extreme case, the case of traditional Chinese society in these respects is roughly the order of the case for all other relatively nonmodernized societies of any considerable degree of stability.

The contrast of the relative simplicity of this picture with the problem in any relatively modernized social context—with the enormous proliferation of highly specialized, highly interdependent social organizations—is not difficult to understand, even though many of the details of the discrepancy might be exceedingly difficult to state with precision. In such societies, many of these organizations, though specifically insulated from one another, are absolutely crucial for one another. Membership in them is highly mobile both ideally and actually. Orientation of the members to many of these organizations ideally speaking, is finely detailed and strictly limited—perhaps more finely detailed and more strictly limited than the members are capable of carrying out as an actual compartmentalization of their personalities. In such cases concentration on any standard of loyalty as simple as that of family loyalty would have catastrophic implications. Concentration on the individual mobility necessary for many of these organizations may create substantial problems for family stability. Inculcation on the children of belief in predominantly universalistic criteria for all sorts of selections, including some for affection and intimacy, is no doubt absolutely essential if they are to be prepared for the type of occupational sphere characteristic of any relatively modernized society. It is doubtful, however, that such emphases can be obtained effectively without an increase in the fragility of family units in general and of the bonds between parents and children and the bonds among siblings in particular. To the extent that participation of the average individual in highly interdependent, highly specialized organizations as well as in some relatively unspecialized organizations increases, the structures of intermediate motivation must also increase in actual complexity, regardless of what the ideal may be for the members of the society concerned.

There must be some indeterminacy in the sets of ultimate and intermediate ends. If some general principles such as family loyalty, etc., were not inculcated on the members of the society, no society could exist. Complete determinacy of all intermediate and ultimate ends would be like the problem of complete knowledge; indeed, it would involve complete knowledge. Every individual would have to know exactly what to do in every situation. No society or organization has ever existed, for whose members the element of judgment has been completely eliminated. Highly coercive situations tend to minimize it, but every time the problems of individual judgment are minimized, the problems of some sort of social planning are to that extent increased. Correspondingly, the problems of socialization and education, whether carried out in terms of specialized or unspecialized organizations are increased.

This problem of indeterminacy with regard to motivation is closely related to another matter already stressed above. The increased development of bureaucracies in every relatively modernized society has as a lower limit the level of coordination and control necessary to keep such a society in operation and as an upper limit a level of organization not in excess of the possibilities of knowledge necessary to plan the organization. Exactly the same upper and lower limits in terms of motivation may be asserted. In addition, for given types of societies it is important that sooner or later we go a great deal further in specifying what types of indeterminacy can [or will probably] exist with what types of implications. For example, a relatively modernized society may be compatible with considerable indeterminacy and variation in motivation as to how increases in material productivity are to be utilized. Such societies are not nearly so flexible with regard to whether or not increases in material productivity must be motivated. Such societies can not survive without increases in material productivity being motivated continuously. Morever, although relatively nonmodernized societies may exist in terms of which the emphasis on achievement as such for the average individual is quite a modest one, with increases in modernization the motivation of the average individual to achieve in manners that can be judged more or less objectively by other members of the society must increase continuously. The details of what constitutes such achievement may change, but more and more people must be motivated to seek achievements that can be recognized with increasing objectivity by an increasing segment of the membership of the society.

Finally with regard to motivation, areas of social behavior in which specific motivational structures are lacking are often quite as significant as those in which such structures are present. Since, whether we like it or not, students as well as men of responsibility in public affairs are increasingly concerned with questions of planning in general and planned social change in particular, areas of behavior in which motivational structures have not been developed may be the essence of many concerns. In such areas there always arises—in terms of any society, any time, anywhere—the question of whether or not other existing structures of motivation can be utilized to cover this situation or whether new structures have to be developed.

3. UNCERTAINTY AND RELATED QUESTIONS

B. Malinowski was perhaps more famous for his explanation of magic than for any other single contribution. *Magic,* defined as the use of nonempirical means for empirical ends, Malinowski held, developed in social situations characterized by high levels of uncertainty. He did this in a classic case of comparative analysis in which he pointed out that some people he was studying used magical practices in connection with deep-sea fishing but not in connection with lagoon fishing. Deep-sea fishing was dangerous, uncertain in yield and important to the people concerned. Lagoon fishing was safe, highly certain with regard to its yield, and also important to the people concerned. Malinowski also pointed out that these people distinguished with great precision between the effects they regarded as due to bad workmanship and those which they attributed to improperly performed magic. Malinowski thought that the practice of magic enabled the people concerned to adjust themselves to these important situations characterized by high levels of uncertainty.[4] Professor O. K. Moore has added to this picture by his hypothesis that those forms of magic that have the same effect as rational behavior would have under the circumstances diffuse more rapidly from one set of peoples to another than do other forms of magic.[5] There are societies totally lacking in practices of this sort. On the other hand, in relatively modernized social contexts, the emphasis on rationality is likely to become so great, ideally speaking, that magical practices are themselves a specific source of stress and uncertainty.

Another form of behavior highly relevant to uncertainty situations may be described as faddism. *Faddism* is defined here as the relatively rapid and intense alteration and application of means

[4] See B. Malinowski, *Magic Science and Religion and other Essays,* The Free Press, Glencoe, Ill., 1948, pp. 11–16.

[5] Moore points out that, for example, for a given set of island peoples a magical practice that in effect randomizes the direction in which one sets off in search for fish is the best solution the people concerned could possibly find in the absence of more detailed specific knowledge of just where to look for fish. Such practices as muttering prayers and throwing a feather in the air and going out to seek fish in the direction pointed to by the large end of the quill would in effect randomize the search for fish. See: O. K. Moore, "Divination—A New Perspective," *American Anthropologist,* vol. 59, no. 1, Feb. 1957, pp. 69–74.

for relatively fixed ends. Such action may be highly rational over limited periods of time which is not the case of magical action. The rapid alteration of fashions in clothing in many social contexts, of some of the techniques of therapy in modern medical practice, of recreational forms, etc., are all examples of faddism. Uncertainty elements are usually marked in situations in which fads are frequent. The element of novelty is the essence of fads, and integration to uncertainty via faddism is in terms of the faith of the actors that the new method may serve to secure or maintain an old end. That end may be social prestige, restoration of health, etc. In a field like medicine, fads may result in either greater or lesser use of a given technique of therapy than is in fact medically justified. This may enable doctors better to adjust to situations in which the level of uncertainty is high, in which some of the participants react with intense emotions, and in which there is great pressure on the physician to do something. In the field of medicine it is also possible to combine some types and levels of faddism with a high level of emphasis on rationality. The use of a given drug or a given technique may in fact be a fad, but the physicians using it may firmly believe at the time that its use is scientifically justified. Faddistic behavior is not confined to members of relatively modernized societies, but it is likely to increase in relatively modernized social contexts for at least two reasons. First, it by no means follows that uncertainty declines in relatively modernized social contexts, despite the radical increases in scientific knowledge. Second, as a form of integration to uncertainty situations, faddism is much less vulnerable to emphases on rationality than are magical practices.[6]

The problem of integration to uncertainty is one frequently commented upon by social scientists. There is, however, another problem of equal importance, much less frequently treated. This is the problem of integration to *certainty* situations. Thomas and Znaniecki treat it explicitly when they speak of the desire for new experience as characteristic of all people.[7] Nevertheless, boredom has been on the whole a much less glamorous subject for social scientists than uncertainty. Some types of activity, however, are probably not explicable save in terms of the problem of integration to certainty situations, i.e., the problem of boredom and the problem of avoiding the certain for other reasons. The most

[6] This view of the relevance of faddism to uncertainty in the medical context first came to my attention in Talcott Parsons' lectures more than twenty years ago. He has since referred to this in *The Social System*, Free Press, Glencoe, 1951, pp. 467–470.

[7] W. I. Thomas and F. Znaniecki, *The Polish Peasant in Europe and America*, Boston, 1918, vol. 1, p. 73.

notable of these is gambling. Perhaps the outstanding aspect of gambling as a special form of activity is the deliberate creation of uncertainty in a situation in which otherwise the outcome would be a great deal more certain. I refer here, of course, to honest gambling. The outcome of a horse race that has not been fixed is highly uncertain for even the most expert judges of horseflesh. By wagering money or anything else on the outcome of a horse race, one makes a specific allocation of goods or services uncertain to the extent that the outcome of the race is uncertain. To some extent the gambler always feels that the result of his wager may be a windfall gain, though he is certain there will be no such gain from any other source. It is not a matter of chance that both magic and fads are closely associated with gambling wherever it appears in world history.

Faddism has been described as a technique of integration to uncertainty situations, but it may also be a technique of integrating to certainty situations by destroying the certainty of those situations. Again, the essence of faddism is novelty, and the essence of certainty is the absence of novelty. The short-run contributions at least that can be made by faddism to situations of boredom are patent enough. Unlike magical practices, which do not seem highly appropriate as a form of integration to certainty situations, faddistic behavior may integrate simultaneously to both elements of certainty and uncertainty. In modern medical practice, for example, faddistic procedures may exist in spheres in which it is certain that established techniques will be of little use and the uncertainty which attends doing nothing is difficult to bear.

In any case it is well to keep in mind the fact that elements of both certainty and uncertainty pose problems of adjustment for human beings. Human beings are alike everywhere in the sense that there have never been social settings in which humans were incapable of being anxious, or bored, or both. Magic, gambling, and fads are closely associated with such problems. Social engineers and social reformers would do well to be sure of the parts played by such practices in integration before attempting to change them. In the attempt to design new social structures we must keep in mind that certainty as well as uncertainty poses problems of adjustment. As the levels of centralization and social planning increase, as they do characteristically in all of the relatively modernized social contexts, there is a sense in which, despite the vast areas of ignorance of social phenomena, problems of certainty are likely to increase more rapidly than problems of uncertainty. It is hard to conceive of any element of social planning or increased centralization which does not have in it, implicitly if not explicitly, a decrease in the degrees of uncertainty in the social situation. As modern men we are extremely fond of pointing to the high level of boredom which we feel must have inhered in an enormous number of situations in the context of highly sedentary relatively nonmodernized societies. We are also fond of pointing to the great sources of uncertainty that characteristically pose problems for the members of those societies—problems which are not problems for us with our inordinately productive sciences. It is, nevertheless, unlikely that we shall ever know enough to eliminate uncertainty situations. As the discussion above [pp. 79–81] of the problems of socialization for an unknown future indicates, accelerated change always carries elements of uncertainty with it.[8] We may, however, come to know quite enough to increase boredom, assuming that any accurate measurements are possible.

B. EXPRESSION

My lack of expertise makes the category of *expression* as much a problem as that of *integration*. Unlike many of the spheres referred to under the headings of economic and political allocation, these are not matters adequately and fully treated in the general literature of social science on the level of societies in general or even on the level of the types of social organizations most frequently encountered as subsystems of societies. Despite the fact that I am unable to treat them to my satisfaction, I feel these categories cannot be ignored because they are all too often ignored by students of the social sciences and men of responsibility in the field of public affairs. Recreation, for example, is not usually considered at any great length or seriously in these contexts apart from ethnographic treatments carried out on a largely descriptive level—possibly because, for modern man acting in terms of highly modernized societies, one of the aspects of great specialization has been that the term recreation has acquired a connotation of frivolity and superficiality. I shall try to point out below that it is quite possible for recreational aspects to have quite far-reaching implications for the allocations of power and responsibility. I have also heard quite recently a highly sophisticated representative of Mexico point to the fact that the great development of modern art in Mexico influenced by Picasso and others was of enormous practical signifance in the Mexican pro-

---

[8] It is also not a matter of chance that so much faddism is associated with the educational periods of the young members of relatively modernized societies.

gram of economic development, if only because of its attractiveness as a stimulus for tourism. If I understood him correctly, he would go so far as to counsel the representatives of most relatively nonmodernized societies or nations to pay special attention to the cultivation of their artists as a major strategy of economic development. I would not rest the justification of these considerations on their implications for the allocation of goods and services and power and responsibility. It is one of the firmest contentions of this entire treatment that, although men in any considerable organizational context are never indifferent to either bread or power, they never live by bread and power alone.

The treatment of expression here is divided into a brief treatment of recreation, artistic activities, other emotional reactions, and politics and recreation.

1. RECREATION

Recreation as the term is used here refers to a specific aspect of behavior. Insofar as given behavior is viewed as furnishing relaxation and release from the usual duties and concerns of daily life, they will be considered as at least in part *recreational*. Games, gossip, dancing, many forms of reading, drinking, feasting, vacationing, and a variety of other similar and related phenomena certainly contain aspects of recreation. One of the most obvious significances of activities with strong recreational aspects is the extent to which the actual activities involved do provide a release from the tensions and strains of everyday life and hence contribute to the general adjustment of the individual to his environment. One of the first distinctions to raise with regard to recreation has to do with the point just mentioned. Most of the social scientists and most of the men of responsibility in public affairs, who comment on these matters, are so used to thinking in terms of relatively modernized social structures that recreation is generally thought of as a separate thing just as economic activities and political activities are thought of as separate things. In relatively modernized social contexts there is a considerable development of what might be called predominantly recreationally oriented activities and organizations, just as one can distinguish with the greatest of ease predominantly economically oriented organizations and activities, etc. One of the most general distinctions is that among societies or organizations within societies in which recreational aspects are combined simultaneously with the usual duties and concerns of everyday life and those in which the two are sharply separated from one another. The contrast between relatively nonmodernized and relatively modernized societies is sharp in these respects. Both types of situations exist in both cases. In traditional Chinese society, for example, there certainly existed relatively specialized predominantly recreationally oriented activities and organizations. Attendance at opera and the telling and listening to stories were activities by no means confined to a small elite.[9] On the other hand, the most dedicated of executives and professional men in our own society are frequently described as finding in their work their main, if not their sole, recreation. This again is one of those distinctions in which, despite the fact that there are vast differences in emphases as between relatively nonmodernized and relatively modernized societies, there are enough elements common to both so that mutual understanding between their members is not necessarily difficult. Over a decade and a half ago in a song sometimes still played [10] a hypothetical nonliterate savage states that he has no desire to seek the delights of civilization since civilized people seem to him to suffer most of the year in order to practice for two weeks the delights he pursues day in and day out.[11] The song, no doubt, distorts both the life of nonliterate savages and life in a highly

---

[9] In this there is one of the intriguing hook-ups between recreational aspects and other aspects of social organization. The vast majority of peasant members of traditional Chinese society were illiterate, but to a degree probably seldom equalled by members of other large-scale societies, these illiterate peasants were, on the whole, surprisingly well informed about the past history and the traditions of China. Their knowledge was certainly not scholarly, but it was not pauce either. The role of the story teller, itinerant and otherwise, the role of opera troupes, etc., were of great significance in this respect. A considerable portion of the stories and the operas and the like were built around incidents of Chinese history and themes of the Chinese classics. Though slow and leisurely, as methods of mass indoctrination go today, these phenomena have some interesting implications for the number of people who are preoccupied with what has come to be called "mass culture" and is generally treated as something quite modern and perhaps even a little gross.

[10] Popular songs constitute an interesting phenomenon in any social context. Relative to a society like our own whose members generate an enormous number of popular songs with a rapid turnover, there is hardly a single point in social theory which, however abstruse, cannot be aptly illustrated for purposes of general communication [though perhaps in a somewhat oversimplified form] in terms of the lyrics of some popular song. I tried for many years to give students a precise grasp of the distinction between biological kinship and social kinship without any notable success despite the development of some fairly highly refined concepts. The revival and popularity of the old song entitled "I'm My Own Grandpa" [Lonzo and Oscar and the Winston County Peapickers, Dwight Lathan— Moe Jaffe #20–2563A, R.C.A. Victor records], solved the problem neatly since it is quite easy to convey to students via that song that, although this situation is conceivable in terms of social kinship, it is quite out of the question as a matter of biological kinship.

[11] Hear: *Civilization* (Bongo, bongo, bongo), words and music by Bob Hilliard and Carl Sigman, Edmond H. Morris and Co., New York, 1947.

modernized social setting, but there can hardly be any doubt that in general the daily routine of the members of modernized societies is from their point of view something to be escaped from in a sense that is probably not true of the daily routine in many relatively nonmodernized situations. Romantic pastoralism to the contrary notwithstanding, probably most of the members of the relatively nonmodernized societies have been miserable a good part of the time, but it is nevertheless doubtful that they drew the kind of sharp line of demarcation between working and living that is so frequently drawn by the members of relatively modernized societies. The phenomenon of vacation [with pay] during which the individual seeks to differentiate his behavior as much as possible from his usual behavior is certainly not the center of emphasis in any relatively nonmodernized social context that it is increasingly in relatively modernized social settings. In some of the relatively nonmodernized societies, if not most of them, such structures may be altogether absent.

Insofar as the members of a given society think in terms of specialized predominantly recreationally oriented activities, and so much so that they tend not to recognize recreational aspects in other activities, important consequences follow. The essence of recreation considered as an aspect of activities is certainly not the restfulness of those activities in the sense of lack of expenditure of energy. Many of the most highly prized forms of recreation in any social context, notably games, sports, dances, etc., are often exceedingly vigorous activities from the physical point of view. The essence of the difference lies rather in the fact that to be worn out by a day at the office is considered highly unpleasant and sometimes even productive of insomnia whereas physical exhaustion from a day's recreation is usually considered both pleasant and conducive to a good night's sleep. Insofar as an individual's attitude toward activities is that they are highly recreational, the integration of the individual to the usual duties and concerns of daily life may be presumed to be increased. If this aspect is considered by the members of the society to be built in, as it were, into those duties and concerns themselves, the motivational structure necessary to maintain them may be presumed to be bolstered to that extent. If the activities viewed as recreational are sharply differentiated from the usual duties and concerns of daily life, it may be increasingly difficult for the activities viewed as recreational to have the effect of such increased integration. If the distinction reaches the point at which a considerable proportion of the members of the society conceive of themselves as living only in the relatively restricted periods which they regard as overwhelmingly recreational, some of the motivational support for all the other forms of activity comes to hang increasingly on the extent to which behavior in nonrecreational periods makes possible the activities seen as overwhelmingly recreational. Under such circumstances recreation, as such, becomes the major goal of other behaviors.

Such a situation has apparently been reached in some relatively modernized social contexts. The requirements of highly mechanized mass production and many associated occupations such as secretarial work and the like are such as to call for unremitting attention and effort. Even conversation with fellow workers may be highly disruptive under such conditions. It is not accidental that cliques and special personal freedoms are so jealously guarded by and play so important a role in the morale of industrial workers.[12] Recent years have witnessed an enormous preoccupation of many leaders of organizations with attempts to provide facilities which have a high recreational content and which do not interfere with unremitting attention and efforts. Musical programs piped into plants and many other stratagems have been devised. Such stratagems are regarded successful to the extent that they are enjoyed, do not interfere with, and even increase productivity.

To the extent that activities and organizations become highly specialized recreationally, they pose exactly the same problems from the point of view of general social organizations posed by other forms of specialization. These are the two problems of how one can specialize these aspects out of what were formerly unspecialized contexts, and how, having specialized them, one can interrelate the activities carried out in terms of the specialized forms with other specialized forms of activity as well as with the activity of the individuals concerned in terms of their relatively nonspecialized social organizations.

Closely related to the question of whether or not the members of a given society consider recreation as a relatively undifferentiated component of many of their daily activities or whether they consider it to exist only when it exists in highly specialized forms is the distinction between *escapist* and *nonescapist* recreation. The distinguishing mark of *escapist recreation*, as the concept is used here, is what might be termed the nonreality of the activities as far as the individual conceived of as recreating is concerned. Recreation is escapist to the extent that the recreational value of

[12] The pioneering work of F. J. Roethlisberger and W. J. Dickson, *Management and the Worker,* and the subsequent work of many others is illustrative of this point.

an activity from the point of view of the individual lies in the fact that the individual is able to identify himself in part or in whole with a state of affairs that is actually not his own and by that identification lose to some extent contact with his own state of affairs. Some of the uses of drugs and alchohol are an extreme example of almost purely escapist recreational structures. The action of these substances is sometimes such as to take the user out of effectual contact with the empirical world as far as his own consciousness is concerned, and to give him at least temporarily either a feeling of ease and content or a state of oblivion. A less extreme form of escapist recreation is recreation via the role of spectator. Spectators at sport events, for example, in many cases appear to gain a considerable amount of relaxation and enjoyment from vicarious participation in the events they witness. Motion picture and television viewing are remarkably widely diffused forms of escapist recreation from this point of view, but a considerable portion of attendance at serious theatre, performances of string quartets, etc., also consists of varying forms of escapist recreation. On the other hand, actual participation in sports and games, amateur painting, participation in amateur theatricals, etc., are *nonescapist* forms of recreation from this point of view. This distinction might perhaps more aptly be described as a distinction between *vicarious* and *participant recreation*.

It is difficult to discuss a distinction of this sort and avoid evaluations. The term *escapist* itself has evaluative overtones for many people, especially in our own social context. Regardless of how good or bad the movies or television may be from the point of view of a given set of artistic standards, the recreational impact of such performances may be high, and they may have important implications for the adjustment of the individuals who enjoy vicariously the experiences portrayed specifically in part because they are not necessarily high art. For example, there are individuals, even individuals of sensitive and sophisticated taste, who find a considerable amount of enjoyment in TV westerns specifically because, in a world in which a distinction between virtue and vice is often difficult to discern, in that medium one can absolutely count on the fact that the bastards of this world will get their just deserts within the half hour or the hour.

As far as social stability is concerned, there are radically different implications of escapist as opposed to nonescapist forms of recreation. Activities with important elements of nonescapist recreation have signal possibilities for the direct reinforcement of daily routines at the same time that they afford relaxation from them. Participation in competitive sports, for example, in the United States clearly emphasizes predominantly universalistic criteria of selection and many other standards of the greatest significance in other activities.[13] Childhood participation in competitive sports in probably one of the most important educational elements in United States society. At an early age it inculcates an understanding and faith in predominantly universalistic criteria. His experience in sports tempers the highly particularistic treatment of the child as a family member and prepares him in part for the increasingly great emphasis that others with whom he will come into increasing contact as he matures are likely to place on such criteria in selecting or rejecting him for an extremely wide range of relationships. Activities with a strong nonescapist recreational component may play vital educational as well as other supportive roles in many spheres of activity.

Activities with a strong escapist recreational component make their contribution to social stability, insofar as they do contribute to social stability, in that they remove the individual at least temporarily from the whole realm in which tensions and conflicts arise. The malintegrative implications of nonescapist recreational activities inhere in the possibility that absorption with them may interfere with the level of attention necessary to other activities. The malintegrative implications of activities with a strong escapist recreational component inhere primarily in the possibility that they may fail to buttress other forms of activity in any explicit sense. Secondarily, if tensions are sufficiently high and the activities are sufficiently compelling forms of escape, those activities may become a goal of such primacy that the individual no longer operates effectively in terms of his other roles at all. Alcoholism, insofar as it can be considered as an activity with strong escapist recreational aspects, is a clear-cut though extreme case of this possibility.

Activities may, of course, combine escapist and nonescapist recreational components. The most romantic movies may picture more or less correctly the ideal structures of a society while, at the same time they distort the actual structures. Viewing them may thus at one and the same time reinforce the ideal structures and

[13] All sorts of symbols are closely associated with this. It is practically obligatory that the chief executive of the United States be an active participant in some form of sports. Franklin Delano Roosevelt, despite his infirmity, was an ardent fisherman and sailor. Harry Truman is a brisk walker. Dwight Eisenhower is an enthusiastic golfer and hunter. John F. Kennedy, until his problems with his back, was an ardent participant in touch football as well as several other sports. President Johnson is, of course, a horseman. Such brisk participant sports reassure the public that these men will not hesitate to do something.

offer the movie goer escape into that fairyland in which the discrepancies between reality and ideals is not a source of anxiety. The complexity of these possibilities is no argument against attempts at social engineering in the recreational sphere. It is simply an argument to the effect that social engineering with regard to recreation is not necessarily a simple or trivial matter. The problems of social engineering in this sphere are no less complicated than those associated with economic or political allocation—and no less serious either. Reform of recreational structures in conformity with sophisticated standards of art and ethics may be desirable, but on the other hand it may not be. Even if there is agreement on what the goals of reform should be, the rational choice of means to those goals is by no means simple or obvious in the context of any known society.

2. ARTISTIC ACTIVITIES

The term *artistic* as used here has reference to such forms of expression as sculpture, painting, literature, music, drama, etc. Artistic aspects of behavior, especially in the case of the enjoyment of the results of artistic efforts, certainly contain major recreational aspects as well. Relaxation, pleasure, and relief from the usual duties and concerns of everyday life are certainly involved. Activities usually classified as predominantly artistic, however, place a special emphasis on other factors. Most notable, perhaps, is the emphasis placed on the skill of execution within the medium chosen, the ability of the use made of the chosen medium to stimulate the observer emotionally, and the handling of the medium concerned in terms of new and distinctive ideas. It is difficult to separate the terms *artistic* and *creative* and retain any of the major elements ordinarily associated with the term *artistic*. Given the recreational aspect of art, it is possible to make the distinctions made above with regard to recreation in general. Artistic aspects may be built into daily activities, or they may be sharply separated from them in the context of different societies or even within different contexts of a single society. Escapist and nonescapist forms of artistic expression may be distinguished with some of the same types of implications already sketched above. The accent on creativity, however, makes it quite well worth while to separate artistic expression from recreation in general and consider it on the same level of generality. Since art emphasizes skill of execution, the ability to produce emotional responses, and treatment in terms of new ideas, attention is always focussed on what special or unique qualities are contributed by the artists regardless of whether they make their contri-

butions in a spectacularly individualistic fashion or as an anony-
mous group. Focusing attention on the quality of creativity, the
following questions arise: (1) is the creativity expected to exist
within a rigidly and narrowly defined framework, (2) is the
latitude of expression which does exist regarded favorably or
unfavorably, or (3) is creativity considered to be a matter of
spectacularly individualistic performance or as a product of a
group of individuals, each of whom remains more or less anony-
mous? Perhaps it should go without saying that the greater the
emphasis on latitude of expression from the artistic point of view
the greater the possible implication of the effect of artistic production in other spheres of social life either insofar as those
effects may be viewed as tending to support or alter the status
quo—but it doesn't.

3. OTHER EMOTIONAL REACTIONS
[AFFECTIVE EXPRESSION]

The difficulty of the concept of affects or emotions has already
been stressed above. I shall not attempt to go into this genuinely
formidable problem in any depth. It requires neither great depth
nor great knowledge in general to maintain that some regulation
of the expression of emotions is absolutely necessary if any society or any social organization is to persist. There has never been
a society whose members were perfectly free to express themselves emotionally in any way they might choose at any time. In
this respect one can distinguish a range of variations between the
extreme poles of complete repression and complete freedom of
expression. Neither pole can be fully realized by the members of
any society or of any subsystem of one. Different emphases,
however, are quite possible. I would distinguish between an emphasis on *repression* of emotional reactions and an emphasis on
permissive expression of emotional reactions. Given this distinction, there are two main lines of variation. The first has to do with
the location of general emphasis. Is emphasis placed toward the
one extreme or the other? It is at least in theory possible to rank
societies with regard to whether or not their members tend to
repress overt shows of emotion or permit them to be expressed
freely. No society can exist whose members are precisely neutral
on the matter of repression versus permissiveness, nor can there
be one whose members are purely repressive or purely permissive
about affective displays. The second main line of variation has to
do with the fact that societies vary from one another, and there is
considerable variation within a given society or other social organization, as to what emotions are more or less repressed or

more or less freely expressed, how they are expected to be repressed or more or less freely expressed, and why they are expected to be repressed or more or less freely expressed by the members of the society or the social organization concerned.

If overt affective expression is to be highly repressed, there must exist highly elaborate, rigidly defined structures that will cover actions in situations likely to have strong affective effects on the individuals concerned. It is not enough merely to forbid certain forms of overt affective expressions, if it is in fact to be repressed. In such situations elaborate structures of overt affective expression must be inculcated on the individual regardless of whether these particular forms of expression in any specific case are sincerely felt or not. Elaborate sets of honorific expressions such that the very habits of speech formalize overt affective expression constitute a frequent structure with such effects in social history. I have specifically refrained from referring to such structures as a device or mechanism, since there need not be any self-conscious contriving of the structures with such effects in mind. When such structures are well and generally accepted, relatively slight breakdowns in conformity are highly noticeable. Social systems so characterized may be precariously balanced. A hydraulic theory of emotions, i.e., that emotional repression must find some outlet sooner or later, may not be tenable. It is, however, at least plausible to hold that not *all* forms of affective expression can be so rigidly repressed or rigidly defined for the general membership of any society. It is probably not even possible to maintain such structures all of the time even for a single individual. In all such straitly defined social contexts, there are usually quite specific phenomena that can be interpreted as outlets. Abandonment of ordinary formalities while drinking, feasting, and dancing are frequent examples of this sort. At one period in Japanese history, the Japanese, who by our standards at least were relatively impassive as far as emotional displays were concerned in public, were reported as engaging in veritable orgies of sentimental weeping in darkened movie houses. If it is reasonable to expect that such outlets will exist in the context of straitly defined systems, and insofar as they actually do exist, social changes affecting the outlets may have quite dramatic consequences for other apparently unrelated ranges of behavior.

Another element of some significance in societies in which overt affective expression is rigidly regulated is the likelihood that the members of such societies or organizations will behave as if radically cut loose from affective regulations if they find themselves in situations in which their habitual standards of judging behavior and of having their behavior judged have little if any reference. Again, Japanese history affords an example. The behavior in Nanking of Japanese soldiers must certainly have contained elements of this sort. The type of emotional display that took place in the non-Japanese setting of Nanking would have been out of the question in Japan proper at that time. In the usual Japanese context crimes involving personal violence, especially those of a sexual sort, are far rarer than in the United States. There is no question but that a considerable number of crimes of violence were committed by a considerable number of American soldiers during World War II, but the sort of mass berserker phenomena reported at Nanking was certainly not reported about the atrocities of either American or German soldiers.[14] The structures of affective expression characteristic of United States society permit more markedly violent displays in daily life than do the structures of Japan. Nevertheless, because of the emphasis on predominantly universalistic rather than particularistic standards of affective display, for a well-indoctrinated American of this period of history, by contrast with a correspondingly well-indoctrinated Japanese, there were no social situations that could be considered as thoroughly undefined. The more particularistically defined structures of the Japanese left situations far more open to individualism by default in the absence of what, from the Japanese point of view, constituted a qualified judge of behavior.

For the members of societies or organizations characterized by highly permissive structures of affective expression the problem of maintaining outlets for affective expressions is not great, though the problem of controlling the outlets may be. The contrast between standards emphasizing predominantly particularistic as opposed to predominantly universalistic elements in affective expression is interesting here. In the context of systems that are characterized by highly repressive structures, strait positive definitions of affective expression are of the greatest importance. Regardless of the causal explanation, the structures of such systems are characterized by a trend to emphasis on predominantly particularistic elements in the standards of affective

---

[14] Quite interesting inferences about affective expression may be drawn from a consideration of the atrocities reported in World War II. United States atrocities, for example, were on the whole highly individualistic; German atrocities tended to be carefully disciplined "by-the-numbers" performances; Japanese atrocities tended to be either highly disciplined performances or berserker performances, etc. A study of the structures of atrocious behavior in military or quasi-military situations might be valuable to students of national character.

expression. Affective expressions, after all, refer to a way of looking at reactions to what has been done at some time or other. Restrictions on such reactions in terms of who the persons involved are makes possible the formalization of specific forms of affective expression independent to a high degree of what has been done. Predominantly universalistic standards, emphasizing as they do what is done, tie affective expression to detailed variations in what has been done or what the individual thinks has been done. Since the range of variation of action actually open to an individual is always greater than the range of variation of the ideal definitions of his roles, the potential flexibility of predominantly universalistic standards is always much greater than that of predominantly particularistic ones.

It would be quite difficult, if not silly, to maintain that affective expression is more important in relatively modernized than in relatively nonmodernized social contexts. The variation of situations in which the ordinary individual acts, the number and variety of others with whom he interacts, etc., however, are certainly increased radically in relatively modernized social contexts. The relevance of such increases to the increased probabilities of emotional reactions in far more varied less predictable contexts may be as important an element in understanding the increasing emphasis on predominantly universalistic criteria characteristic of such societies as the quite obvious relations of such emphases to the efficiency of performances having to do with the production of goods and services in situations in which inanimate sources of power and extremely productive tools are involved. Predominantly universalistic criteria not only increase the flexibility of adjustment of given relationships to given purposes; they also increase the flexibility of reaction in emotional terms to an increased range of experience.

Usually in societies or other large-scale organizations there exists an extremely complex structured mixture of emphases on repressed emotional expression and permissive emotional expression. Displays of anger may be repressed and expressions of love encouraged; expressions of grief may be highly formalized. In all social contexts variation in these terms has to do with four major criteria. First, there is variation in what emotions may be more or less freely expressed. Second, there is variation in who may express them. Third, there is variation in what is considered a legitimate stimulus for such expression. Fourth, there is a range of variation in the socially acceptable procedures of expressing such reactions.

There are ranges of variation here that do not necessarily

become increasingly similar as societies become more and more highly modernized. Differences along these lines that make mutual understanding of individuals habituated to different systems extremely difficult are quite possible. For example, in the United States setting it is generally considered effeminate of a grown man to cry in public or perhaps even to cry at all unless under the most extreme circumstances of pain, grief, or anxiety. In the context of French society, which as societies go is also relatively highly modernized, the restriction of crying as a form of emotional expression by mature males is not nearly so rigid. The average American seeing a Frenchman cry, if he is charitably inclined, assumes that the situation is a very extreme one. Informed that this is not the case, he tends to assume that there is some element of effeminacy in the individual concerned. The range of variation in such forms of expression of emotions as kissing, embraces of various sorts, etc., and their differing interpretations on the part of people used to different types of structures are familiar to any individual of reasonably broad experience or reading. Although it is difficult to generalize with regard to affective expression on the basis of the distinction between relatively modernized and relatively nonmodernized societies, one generalization will certainly hold. In those spheres in which the emphasis on bureaucratization increases, in general there will be an increasing emphasis on the repression of overt affective displays. Increasingly the emphasis is on taking experiences in these contexts as they come as neutrally as possible as far as affective reactions are concerned with one exception. In such contexts an able individual is expected increasingly to make highly calculated instrumental uses of affective expression. He is expected to react in such a way that the effect of his displays of emotion on his equals, his superiors, or his subordinates is such that their behavior with regard to the maximization of what are presumed to be the goals of the members of the organization as members of that organization are maximized. In this sense in such contexts one, ideally speaking, seeks to maximize contributions to what he regards as the goals of the organization. Increasingly in all highly bureaucratized contexts affective expressions that contribute to what has come to be called *group dynamics* [a term that is much more an evaluation than it appears to be] is the approved form of affective expression.

4. POLITICS AND RECREATION

From a careful theoretical point of view these considerations probably should have been taken up under the general discussion of recreation above. They are of sufficient practical importance to be worth treating separately here. Reference will be made to these matters again in Part III, Chapters 2 and 5. So hard and fast has our thinking become in terms of highly specialized organizations that we do not ordinarily associate politics and recreation. We tend to associate the two relatively slightly despite political picnics, political dinners, etc. Even though the recreational elements in political dinners are increasingly minimized, there remain remnants in everyday language which refer to political figures. These remnants bespeak a different attitude of an earlier period. We speak of political virtuosi who love politics, for whom politics is a game, etc. Nevertheless, we tend not to think of politics as recreation or of recreation as politics. There is, however, a sense in which a new and different political history of the United States could be written about the theme that one of the most important changes in United States society has been the shift from an emphasis on politics as recreation to an emphasis on recreation as politics. One has only to read or look at the pictures of the types of gatherings that took place in the early and middle nineteenth century at which political orators by custom spoke for two or three hours at a stretch. Perhaps nothing is more often commented upon than the fact that Lincoln's Gettysburgh Address was so short, whereas Mr. Edward Everett's far longer one was at the time considered a more proper political address under the circumstances. People gathered in considerable crowds to listen to political oratory, and they made of it a festive occasion. This was, after all, one of the first periods in history in which most of the able-bodied males above the age of adulthood had the franchise. In that day, there were relatively few highly specialized forms of recreation for the average member of society. The right to listen to one's prospective political leaders, assess what they said, and choose among them was for the average man a novelty—a novelty in all social history. There was a certain zest about it. These were major recreational occasions for the participants. Remnants of this attitude persist in the United States today. One may judge this from occasional shouts such as "give 'em hell, Harry," from the interest in the Nixon-Kennedy television debates, and from the great attention which focused on the first occasions on which the national conventions were televised. On the whole today, however, the average member of United States society is really quite cynical about politics and is usually quite bored by political oratory. Unless great effort is expended, it is easier to see instances of recreational experts such as movie stars and the like devoting themselves to politics or to see various forms of entertainment viewed as political expressions than to regard politics as such as entertaining.

The point of view of those who can be thought of as late-comers to modernization is more likely to be akin to that which obtained in the United States in the nineteenth century. Politics is a major form of recreation for the members of the relatively nonmodernized societies in process of modernization. I have heard a great deal of discussion in terms of political ideologies and in terms of other political clichés about the so-called political demonstrations by the members of various African nations in which the persons demonstrating chant "Freedom! Freedom!," and about such demonstrations as those of laborers and the members of the students' organization in Japan [the Zengakuren]. Insofar as I have actually viewed such phenomena or seen films of them, I would assert that one may learn more from consideration of their recreational aspects than from the ordinary terms in which they are discussed. Whether they fully understand what they are doing or not, persons of extremist [from our point of view] political persuasions, i.e., Communists, Nazis, etc., have made far more sophisticated use of the consideration of politics as recreation than have the representatives of the less extreme [from our point of view] political ideologies. Since the vast majority of the people living in the world today live in social contexts in which the importance of politics as recreation is likely to be extremely high for some decades to come at least, this is something to think about.

PART III

THE

ORGANIZATIONAL CONTEXTS

OF SOCIETIES

KINSHIP AND FAMILY ORGANIZATIONS

I
INTRODUCTION AND DEFINITIONS

The choice of kinship and family organizations as the first social systems of high relevance to any society for discussion here is deliberate. In the past most attempts to describe and analyze societies—whether they have been carried out by travellers, anthropologists, sociologists, or government officials—have begun, after establishing a few details such as the geographical location of the peoples concerned and some discussion, perhaps, of the material resources in the area, with a description of the family structures characteristic of the societies concerned. There are good reasons for beginning so, although there is usually no explicit consideration to why it comes so naturally to begin with a description of these structures of behavior rather than others. Shorn of technical elaboration, this practice is highly justified for any society for the following five reasons:

(1) The first and most obvious reason, despite the fact that it is not the most important theoretically, is that some kind(s) of family organizations exist as subsystems of every known society. Claims to the contrary have never been borne out. (2) For biological reasons, explicable in terms of the physiology of pregnancy, parturition, and post-pregnancy the probability is great that the average biological mother will seek a solidary relationship with her biological offspring if that is possible for her. This probability can, of course, be offset in individual cases, but it is never generally offset for the set of biological mothers of the members of a society as a whole. If it were, the frustrations involved, again explicable at least in part in physiological terms, would pose serious problems of adjustment. To the extent that this is the case, it is highly probable for physiological reasons alone, that some sorts of kinship units did, do, and/or will exist in any society. At least one male other than the infant is highly likely to be associated with this pair, for reasons not so easy to hypothesize about neatly, and that male is likely to be a male involved in more or less regular sexual relationships with the mother of the child concerned. (3) In the absence of the kind of close affective attention that

the biological mother is likely to give to an infant for physiological reasons, if for no other, stable adults cannot be developed in sufficient numbers to maintain any society. This is not to say that individual stable adults cannot be produced by other means or that in individual cases this kind of affective attention cannot be given by others than the biological mother. It is to say that for members of the population as a whole it is not likely to be given primarily from other sources nor can large masses of stable adults be produced in the absence of such attention. (4) In all known societies family organizations have another peculiar property. Absolute-age distinctions such as those mentioned above [pp. 200–204] in some fashion cover the life span of the individual from birth to death [and even continue after death in societies whose members emphasize ancestor worship]. At all stages of those distinctions, the average individual always has membership in some one or more family organization(s). There is no other type of subsystem of societies for which this hold true for the average individual. The human is not only a gregarious animal; he is also a family animal. (5) Since the average member of every society is always a member of some one or more family organization(s), to some extent his membership in any other organization has implications for his family membership or vice versa if only because both involve him. Other organizations than his family organizations(s) can be classified into one of two categories. Either they are organizations in terms of which family considerations are supposed to dominate or influence the behavior of the individual concerned even in the context of the other organization, or they are organizations in terms of which family considerations are explicitly not supposed to dominate or influence the behavior of the individual members. In the former case, both ideally and actually, the relevance of what happens to the individual in his family context will be important in understanding what he does in terms of the other organizations, and therefore important to some extent in understanding what happens generally in the other organizational context. In the latter case some family influences intrude actually even though they are not supposed to. Social organizations differ as to whether family influence is supposed to be relevant or not, but there are no organizations in terms of which, actually, family influences are completely irrelevant. This generalization holds true despite the fact that characteristically relatively modernized societies contain subsystems in terms of which the degree of actual, let alone ideal, relevance of family influence is confined strictly.

Insofar as these assertions hold true, analysis of the family structures first in the study of any society, in addition to producing information easily marshalled in terms of the life cycle of the individual, is more likely to produce more relevant information about different areas and aspects of social structure than the examination of any other single subsystem of any society.[1]

In other words, the probability is great that more can be learned more quickly about any new and strange form of society by a sophisticated analysis of its family structures than by the analysis of any of its other forms of organization. To this, however, one special caveat must be added. As will become obvious as the treatment progresses, the ways in which family organizations fit into the general structure of a society vary enormously. The extent to which the general orientation of the members of a society is to family considerations ideally and/or actually, the number and variety of performances which are ideally and/or actually expected to be carried out in terms of the family unit, etc.,—all of these are subject to wide fluctuations from society to society. This has led to much casual reference of the following sort: "The family is much more important in traditional Chinese society than in modern United States society." This is only true in a restricted sense—rarely stated and frequently not intended. In its usual form the statement is misleading to social scientists and laymen alike. If the term *important* means the extent to which action is oriented to family considerations and/or the number and types of performances actually carried out on a family basis, the traditional Chinese family is, indeed, far more important in understanding traditional Chinese society than is the United States family in understanding United States society. If the statement implies that somehow it was more important for traditional Chinese society that the traditional Chinese family took the specific form it did rather than some other, whereas the level of variation open to United States society in this respect is much greater—if that is the intent or implication—the statement is not merely misleading; it is also false. It may be that one of the ways in which societies or nations vary from one another is the extent to which variations in family organization can be tolerated with-

[1] For those interested in a more elaborate and careful presentation of these hypotheses as well as some strong reservations about them, see: Coale, Fallers, Levy, Jr., Schneider and Tomkins, *Aspects of the Analysis of Family Structure*, Princeton University Press, Princeton, 1965.

out producing instability, but family variations in societies have hardly been explored with this sort of question in mind. Few assertions about it exist with any firm empirical foundation, and few exist that have been carefully thought out on any general level at all. It is perfectly true that if one could by some magic have introduced a modern United-States-type family system into the society of traditional China, that society would have come apart at the seams and changed radically. It is equally true, however, that if one were to replace the general type or types of family organizations in the United States with radically different ones, say for example those of traditional Chinese society, modern United States society would also come unseamed and change radically.[2]

For reasons, which will become increasingly obvious in the remainder of this chapter, I hold that the members of no society can tolerate any considerable variation from their existing family structures without the implications of those changes spreading widely throughout the rest of social structure. Family determinism is just as dangerous and just as idiotic as any other monistic determinism. Nevertheless, family structures have as much relevance for changes in other spheres as those of any other organization and a great deal more than any other organization in most if not all societies. Just as one cannot study the position of men as members of a society without simultaneously studying the position of women, one cannot be interested in social change without being interested in social stability and vice versa.[3] All persons interested in public affairs must be interested in problems of both change and stability. In a sense those with responsibilities and interest in these realms are by definition interested in the reform of some items and the maintenance of others. It is unlikely that in the context of any society, whatever its variations in other respects, the possibilities for change and stability not be importantly conditioned by the state of family organization or vice versa.

[2] See above, pp. 45 and 75.

[3] One must not be misled by the wars in which social scientists berate each other for preferring static to dynamic analysis, for averring self-critically that we have social theories but none of social change [though, of course, we have theories of changes within systems but not of systems], or by those who begin by saying that conflict has been ignored in favor of integration and end by saying conflict must be treated because of its relevance to integration. The problem is rather that we do not have highly developed theories of any sort. If we did, it would be comparatively simple to develop their implications for either change or stability. Certainly no one has ever been able to carry general social studies to any length without referring knowingly or unknowingly to concepts of both stability and change.

I would define the term *kinship system* or kinship organization in general as any social organization, membership of which is importantly oriented to questions of real or assumed biological descent and/or sexual intercourse. I would define a *family unit* or family organization or family as any kinship system [organization], the membership of which is determined at least in part by orientation to the facts of biological relatedness *and* sexual intercourse. I would add that one can identify the family unit as the smallest kinship organization generally treated as a unit for generalized purposes by the members of the unit itself and by the members of other organizations in the society. According to the structures of modern United States society, for example, one's grandparents are certainly kin in this sense, and there are some kinship units in terms of which grandchildren and grandparents interact. Ideally speaking in terms of our society, however, grandparents are not part of one's family unit. One's family, ideally speaking, consists of one's father and mother and one's unmarried [and usually not fully adult] brothers and sisters or of one's wife [husband] and nonadult children. For some purposes in terms of our society brothers and sisters may be considered as belonging to a special social system of their own, but usually they are considered as constituting the members of such a unit only for quite limited purposes. In traditional Chinese society the ideal picture was vastly different. There, ideally speaking at least, the family members consisted of father, mother, additional wives, if any, of the father, all their nonadult children, all their married sons, the sons' wives, the sons' nonadult children, and so on for as many generations as had live representatives. Actual Chinese families of that period frequently only involved as members a single father, a single mother, and their nonadult children, but if a parent or parents of the father were alive they were as inseparably members of his family unit as were his wife and his children. Under such circumstances one could distinguish the set of father, mother, and nonadult children. The Chinese, after all, were careful about *whose* children given children were. If the parents of the father were alive, however, neither the father nor the children, neither the parents nor the grandparents, neither other family members nor any Chinese who was not a member of that unit would have referred to that set of father, mother, and nonadult children as constituting a separate family of the larger kinship organization. Under those circumstances in that social context, ideally speaking at least, and to an extraordinary degree actually as well, it would have been as easy [or as difficult] to think of the family as involving the grandparents, the father, and mother as members and not involving the nonadult children as to think of a family as involving the father, mother, and nonadult children but not the grandparents when the grandparents were alive to live with them.[4] According to the ideals characteristic of the society of Tokugawa Japan the members of a family consisted of a father, mother [and concubines, if any], their nonadult children, one married son [no matter how many sons there were], that son's wife, that son's nonadult children, and so forth. In Japan of that period, unlike traditional China, younger sons and their wives were not members of the sons' parental family unit. In both Chinese and Japanese social contexts, sets of family units of the type described here constituted larger kinship organizations such as clans, etc.[5]

The Chinese and Japanese ideal families [i.e., *extended* and *famille souche* types respectively] are relatively well known variations in family types. They hardly scratch the surface of variation which is in fact known to exist—at least ideally speaking—in the various social contexts of world history. For reasons which will be brought out below [pp. 426–430], the actual variations in family organization throughout social history have not been as great as the variations in ideal structures lead one to expect. Despite the enormous variation ideally and the considerable variation actually speaking, it is nevertheless possible to generalize broadly about the role of family organizations in kinship organizations generally and also in the general social context.

[4] For those social analysts who insist that because father, mother, and their nonadult children are recognized and distinguished they must be recognized as constituting *the* family unit, certain implications must be faced. If that is the case, the relationship between every Chinese mother-in-law and her daughter-in-law was an *interfamilial* rather than an *intrafamilial* relationship and was so regarded by the people involved. If a mother-in-law had two daughter's-in-law [even if both were wives of a single son] her relationships with them represented permutations and combinations of interrelationships among the members of three distinct families. Finally, those interrelationships could never be internal to the membership of any single family since the mother-in-law and a daughter-in-law could never be members of any common family unit. Without complicating the picture by further possible relationships, the implications of such distinctions for structures of incest taboos, terms used for kinship units, and the like are too quixotic to be taken seriously as an account of how *all* members of all societies regard kinship or even of how it might be fruitful for social analysts to regard it. For the members of many societies the nuclear family constitutes a separable family system only when other members not called-for as members by such a system are dead or are unavailable for other reasons.

[5] The picture is actually more complex, but in ways that are not germane here. Unlike traditional China, one may not speak of *the* ideal family unit of Tokugawa Japan—there were at least six different ideal forms, let alone actual variations.

I I
THE FAMILY AS A FOCAL POINT
OF KINSHIP STRUCTURES

Some kind of family organization always has a strategic position in the kinship structures characteristic of any society. By definition, the family is always one of the social systems in terms of which kinship-oriented behavior takes place. This is true regardless of whether one accents a form of definition that holds that a family unit is that portion of kinship structures in terms of which the membership is oriented at least in part to *both* biological relatedness and sexual intercourse or whether one accents consideration of the family unit as the *smallest* kinship system treated as a system for generalized purposes by other members of the given kinship system and by the members of the society in general. There is no known society which is not characterized by subsystems that are families, nor one characterized by kinship units other than family units but not by family units. Even in societies in terms of which kinship organizations other than family units are of great significance, the family units are still the overwhelmingly important kinship units for many if not most purposes. In other words, family units may be far more significant for the general analysis of a given society than any other kinship systems, but other kinship systems can never reduce family systems to comparative insignificance for purposes of general understanding. Traditional Chinese society is a case in point. Other kinship organizations such as the clan or *tsu* were of great importance at different periods of Chinese history, and in many given situations decisions of the clan head or leader would in effect determine the action of individual family members, but at least ideally speaking one owed one's loyalty first to the family members as personified by the head of the family [the *chia-ch'ang*] and one put clan interest ahead of family interest only if the family head saw them that way. In Tokugawa Japan the situation was somewhat different. For most purposes most of the time the family unit was the overwhelmingly important one in that society too, but there were many decisions made by the head of the *main family* [the *honke*] which were quite binding on the members of *branch families* [the *bunke*] both ideally and actually. Whether the societies concerned be relatively modernized or not, it is possible for the family units to be the *only* kinship units of any great consequence in the general social setting. This is the case of modern United States society which is so familiar to most of us. To all intents and purposes in the United States today there are virtually no important kinship systems other than family units. On occasions such as Thanksgiving or Christmas there are sometimes gatherings of kinfolk which extend well beyond the membership of any single family. There are even cases in which some elements of clan organization remain. For example, there are instances in which the members of several different family units gather periodically, say every Friday evening, for dinner at the home of, say, a grandparent or great-grandparent who is regarded more or less as the leader of that set of kin. The former instance is now far more general than the latter. Instances of this sort probably involve a large number of individuals in the society, but insofar as it is a kinship system, it is only an exceedingly fleeting, ephemeral sort of kinship system. The latter is certainly neither ephemeral nor fleeting for those who experience it, but today such practices obtain for no more than a small number and a minuscule percentage of the members of United States society in general.

Thus it is conceivable that there be a society in which the *only* type of kinship unit is the family. It is, however, neither conceivable nor is there any society known to exist [or to have existed] in terms of which there are kinship units but *no* family units. If one seeks minimal reasons as to why the family occupies a strategic position in the general consideration of kinship structure the above should be quite sufficient. It is possible, however, to go into much greater detail as to the strategic position of the family among kinship structures generally. In citing these considerations, it is necessary to list almost exactly the same factors that one must take into consideration in considering the position of the family as a focal point for social structures in general. These considerations are taken up in the following section of this chapter. Given the concern with precision necessary for a puristical theorist, these should be treated separately since in some cases the strategic position of family structures among general kinship structures as distinguished from their position among other social structures in general must be differentiated, but it would be less than frank not to admit that such puristic theoretical cleanliness need not delay the argument here.

III

THE FAMILY AS A FOCAL POINT FOR
SOCIAL STRUCTURES IN GENERAL

A. THE FAMILY AS A FOCUS OF ROLE DIFFERENTIATION

The family is the only social system about which the following proposition can be defended as an hypothesis: "The family is the only type of social system in terms of which the ordinary member of every known society always has some roles." In some particular societies the ordinary individual may always have roles in terms of some other particular organization throughout his life history as well, but no matter how important in this specific sense another type of organization may be in a particular society, it is never as important in this sense in all known societies as the family. If one distinguishes the various stages in man's development in terms of any given society on the basis of age as was done above [pp. 200–204], he will find some such age classifications as infancy, childhood, adulthood, and old age distinguished in terms of any society. Throughout every one of those age classifications the ordinary individual ordinarily always belongs to some family organization, and therefore, he always has some role (s) differentiated on a family basis.

One may make an even stronger statement with regard to the role differentiation of every ordinary member of every society on a family basis. The family roles of every ordinary individual are always of some considerable importance for *all* of his other roles ideally and/or actually. All of an individual's roles can be divided into: (1) those which he has as a member of a family organization and (2) those which he has in an organization other than his family organization whether that be another kinship organization or a nonkinship organization altogether. In turn all of the non-family organizations in which an individual has roles may be divided into two categories: (1) nonfamily organizations relative to which family considerations or orientations are expected both ideally and actually to influence the individual's behavior, and (2) those nonfamily organizations relative to which the individual's family experiences are, ideally speaking, specifically not expected—that is to say, are specifically not supposed—to influence his behavior in terms of his nonfamily roles. If the nonfamily organization is of the first type, family experiences will influence what he does in terms of the other organization unless he is a virtuoso of social deviance. If the organization is of the second type, the individual may maintain a considerable amount of separation of his family roles from his roles in the other organizations, but we know quite clearly enough that, no matter how firmly these two spheres of operation are *supposed* to be separated, a good many things which happen to the individual in his family setting whether he intends them to or not will *in fact* influence his behavior in terms of his nonfamily organization.

In traditional Chinese society, for example, nonfamily organizations were for the most part of the first type. Ideally speaking, the one thing one was never expected to forget was what was expected of one as a family member and what the relevance of any particular situation was to the interests of his family. In terms of modern United States society a professor at a university is not supposed to permit his family experiences to influence his dealing with students; the family experiences of a general are not supposed to influence the orders he gives his troops; the family experiences of a judge are not supposed to influence his charge to the jury; the family experiences of an executive in a major business firm are not supposed to influence his decisions with regard to economic allocation as far as his firm is concerned. Ideally, none of these are supposed to have any such influence, but actually, especially in these days of practically universal amateur psychoanalysis, we know perfectly well that the family experiences of the individual are likely to influence such behavior with or without his being aware of it. Furthermore, family experiences may effect his operations decisively—and the more so the less he is aware of then. Thus, even for nonfamily organizations in terms of which family considerations are specifically supposed to be set aside, actually some family considerations are likely to be of great importance.

Nepotism may be taken for granted in organizations of the first type since it is ideally expected, and nepotism is exceedingly likely in some instances of the second type no matter how much one tries to prevent it. Nepotism in the technical sense, moreover, is only one form of the spread of family considerations to nonfamily contexts. More general family influence is a great deal more pervasive in any society—whether relatively modernized or not—than nepotism in the most narrow technical sense.

Thus in every known society either ideally or actually or both, the family organization is the only one in terms of which the individual's experiences are always of great importance in understanding the operation of every other organization in the society. This holds true regardless of whether the society may be spoken of as overwhelmingly family oriented, as in the case of traditional Chinese society, or whether the orientations to family considerations, ideally speaking, are as sharply curtailed as we think of them as being in the context of relatively modernized societies. Family structures are always crucial for an understanding of the general political and economic aspects of a society. This is no less true if the society is one in which there are highly specialized subsystems specifically oriented to economic and/or political considerations. This is obviously the case when the individual is supposed to put his family interests first, and less obviously but none the less importantly, it is also true when this is not supposed to be the case. In the context of relatively modernized societies, it is extremely doubtful that differences such as those between socialist and nonsocialist societies is of any considerable importance from this point of view. Indeed, the careful separation of the spheres of governmental operation and private business firm operation may make it much more difficult for members to concentrate family influences effectively than would be the case if all organizations were governmental organizations, and to that extent were relatively less differentiated for the individual actor.

Without going into any of the details of role differentiation, another hypothesis about family organizations in every known society can be stated. Without exception, for the average individual, indeed for the overwhelming majority of individuals, the family unit is always the unit in terms of which first roles are learned. Not only are first roles learned in a family setting, most of the basic role differentiation as distinguished from the intermediate role differentiation is learned in a family setting by the members of every known society. In addition, there is probably no society in which quite important elements of intermediate role differentiation are not learned in family terms as well. For example, the most members of all societies first learn to distinguish the "most general" of all intermediate role differentiations, sex role differentiation, in a family context. With regard to intermediate or specialized role differentiation societies vary enormously as to the extent that these are ordinarily learned by the ordinary individual in his family setting. In general the more highly modernized the society becomes, the fewer of his intermediate role differentiations are learned in a family setting. The less modernized a society is, the greater is the probability that virtually all of his role differentiations will be learned in a family setting.

B. THE FAMILY AS A FOCUS OF SOLIDARITY

In all known societies the family unit is always a major focus of solidarity. Some of the most intense and strongest solidarities in every society are family solidarities. As a minimum these include that of husband-wife, parent-child, brother-brother, sister-sister, and brother-sister. In societies in which the family units involve individuals other than father, mother, and nonadult children, the range of these solidarities is to that extent expanded. Whatever the range of solidarities carried out in family terms, they are *never* negligible for the vast majority of the members of any known society. To the extent for any given society that an individual has solidarities outside a family context, and this is always true to some extent, either those solidarities are regarded as inferior to his family solidarities or there is likely to be some sort of a situation of stress and strain. In the context of most of the relatively modernized societies, the whole problem of maturation with its special focus on adolescence is sometimes phrased in terms of the individual learning to adjust himself to solidarities on a nonfamily basis that frequently take precedence or are ideally speaking irrelevant to his solidarities on a family basis. Specifically it is a painful adjustment for both the individual and his parents. There is a sense in which the difficulty of adjustment may inhere because this is the period during which the average individual must learn as never before to ignore his family solidarities without hurting the feelings of his other family members. This is not the sort of social problem which has an easy solution.

The family unit in every known society is the unit in terms of which the ordinary individual receives his first lessons in solidarity. Here again I refer not merely to the ordinary individual in the sense of a statistical average. This holds true of the ordinary individual in the sense of the vast majority of members of the society. Family relationships are overwhelmingly the first relationships experienced. It is in family terms that one first encounters not only the question of what a relationship means but what variations in the strength and intensity of relationships mean as well. In addition, among family relationships, that between mother and child, is overwhelmingly likely to be the first one "learned" by the infant in any intensive fashion. There is a sense, then, in which all subsequently learned solidarity aspects to some extent appear as similar to or specifically different from family solidarities. To be indifferent to family relationships is to be considered psychologically abnormal in terms of any society in world history. For human beings it is a great deal easier to understand hatred among family members than precisely balanced neutrality of emotions or indifference.

The question of solidarity brings the discussion back once again to the question of nepotism. This time the term nepotism will be used in a somewhat more precise sense, that is to refer not simply to the inclusion of any family consideration into any nonfamily sphere, but specifically to refer to the preferment of one individual as opposed to another for a nonfamily appointment, recognition, etc., not on the basis of merit but on the basis of a family relationship or some kinship relationship. Even in this restricted sense there has never been a society whose members were totally lacking in nepotistic behavior. Regardless of the ideal structures, to some extent family solidarities actually always carry over into nonfamily contexts. The most important variation among societies from this point of view is not the actual presence or absence of nepotism, but rather the question of the ideal structures with regard to nepotism. The members of some societies regard nepotism as a positive virtue. In the context of traditional Chinese society one was expected, ideally speaking, to give preference to a relative on almost any occasion that this was possible. In the context of modern United States society, on the contrary, nepotism is overwhelmingly considered to be a vice. It is a violation of the ideal structures. It nevertheless occurs, and in some specific contexts it is not considered as vice.

The difference in attitude of the members of different societies toward nepotism is of considerable pragmatic importance, especially in considering the problems of modernization. Since members of United States society are almost without exception used to considering nepotism to be a vice in most contexts, they tend more or less unconsciously to assume that all other people so regard it. Since in the context of United States society one easily puts someone else on the defensive by pointing out that he is indulging in nepotistic practices in any nonfamily sphere, Americans abroad tend to assume that this observation has a corresponding effect on other peoples operating in the context of other societies. The person being "accused" of this may regard the "accusation" as a compliment and be puzzled by the fact that the American by his attitude seems to imply that what is obviously a compliment is not a compliment at all. The members of all relatively modernized societies come to regard nepotism increasingly as a vice. This is not simply a special form of the increasing emphasis on predominantly universalistic criteria in the increasingly specialized interdependent context of life characteristic of relatively modernized societies. It is also significant as one of the by-products of the universal trend in all such social contexts for family orientations to become less and less the overwhelming focus of orientation of the average individual and more and more a confined focus of unusual importance. In the context of relatively modernized societies there might, for example, for a period at least, be increasing emphasis of some predominantly particularistic criteria such as political party membership, nationalism, religious affiliations, etc., at the same time that the emphasis on nepotism in the strict sense is declining. In the long run characteristically the members of all relatively modernized societies tend to increase their emphases on predominantly universalistic criteria and decrease those on predominantly particularistic criteria, especially in the highly specialized spheres of interaction. Even in the presence of short or fairly long-run contradictions to this trend, however, the tendency ideally speaking, in any stable development of high levels of modernization, is always for a decreasing acceptance of nepotism. For the members of all relatively modernized societies increasingly family life and, hence, family solidarities become things apart, ideally speaking, from the rest of life.[6] Actually speaking this process can never go as far as the ideals are easily pushed.[7]

C. THE FAMILY AS A FOCUS OF ECONOMIC ALLOCATION

In all societies the family has always been critical as a system in terms of which activities, important because of their aspects of production and consumption, are carried out. From the point of view of members of relatively modernized societies, the family unit is deemed especially noteworthy only as a focus of consumption, and family life might almost be described as the "seat of consumption." We speak of the women of the family, especially the wife, as the major determinant of consumption, etc. It is certainly true of relatively modernized societies, as of all the other societies, that a great deal of behavior considered to be important from the point of view of consumption—food, shelter, and

[6] In a curious way family matters increasingly take on sacred overtones in the context of highly modernized societies. This is curious in that the whole trend in such societies is so often regarded as predominantly secular and critics of changing family structures often decry secular trends in that context too. Nevertheless, as Durkheim has observed, the apartness quality is one of the special aspects of the sacred. The mere fact that the family context becomes such a special context while remaining both ideally and actually an extremely important one, whether appreciated and understood by family members or not, may actually enhance the sacred aspects of the family by contrast with those contexts in which the family is a much more taken for granted focus of most everything.

[7] The unreality of some of these ideals is specifically realized in certain contexts. Ideally speaking, no one is supposed to testify falsely under oath under any circumstances. Nevertheless, it is quite unlikely that an action for perjury be brought against a mother who lies during the trial of her son, and explicitly a husband or a wife cannot be required to testify against his or her spouse. Actually, we even carry the matter much further. A doctor does not like to treat members of his own family in any serious situation, and any individual in a position of great responsibility for objectivity such as a judge is expected to disqualify himself in any actions involving close relatives. It is generally assumed that for such an individual to attempt to maintain his objectivity in the face of such potential strains is to imply a level of virtuosity in objectivity that approaches the inhuman. This is an attitude any traditional Chinese could well appreciate despite the fact that it is found among members of the most highly modernized of societies.

clothing—is carried out in family terms. This is true of a considerable portion of expenditure on entertainment, etc. The members of relatively modernized societies, however, tend overwhelmingly to think of production, serious production that is, to take place in terms of activities carried on outside the family setting. All of those societies are characterized by highly specialized occupational roles, and those roles, almost without exception, lie outside of family contexts. It is from activity in terms of those roles that most of the income of any given set of family members is earned, and the person(s) earning that income is the producer of the family income. We tend to ignore the aspects of consumption of an individual during pursuit of his occupational role. Thus rarely, if ever, do we comment on the fact that while an individual is at work in a factory or in an office, he is carrying out an important part of his consumption, that he is, as it were, consuming the food that he ate the evening before and the morning before he came to work, that he is in a sense consuming the results of the rest he got "at home" the night before, etc. So, correspondingly, as members of relatively modernized societies, we tend to ignore the important production aspects of activities carried out in the family context. Even in the most highly modernized of our societies, however, the family is still the context in which most of the preparation of food takes place, in which most of the earliest infant care takes place, in which most laundry is done, in which most house cleaning is done, in terms of which a considerable part of child care in addition to infant care and, of course, the corollary element of training is done. The productive aspects of these activities are absolutely vital for understanding the societies concerned.

In all, or virtually all, of the relatively nonmodernized societies the family organization is the organization in terms of which the vast majority of the productive aspects as well as the consumption aspects of the behavior of the vast majority of individuals is carried out. Most of the members of most of these societies are engaged in agricultural enterprises and almost inevitably these activities are carried out largely on a family basis. The same is likely to be true with regard to the productive aspects of nomadic people, hunting people, etc. In such societies organizations larger in scale than family units are likely to be kinship units of some other type in the areas of greatest relevance to the allocation of goods and services in general and production and consumption in particular. Even when an enormous amount of the important behavior from the point of view of production is carried out outside the family context, as in relatively modernized cases, the family nevertheless remains an important focus of such behavior, though it is not often discussed in those terms in general discussions of economic allocation.

Regardless of how much activity, whether it be considered important from the point of view of other members of the society or from the point of view of a social scientist attempting to analyze the society from the economic point of view, is carried on outside the family context, in all known societies the family is always the unit in terms of which some of the structures of behavior appropriate from the point of view both production and consumption are first learned. What might be called the basic structures of production and consumption, that is those structures in terms of which all of the members of the society are ordinarily expected to act are always learned by the ordinary individual in a family context. This is not simply true of structures of eating, sleeping, and the like. It is ordinarily true of structures of cooperation, individual effort, etc. In addition, as one would expect from the above, for most of the individual members of virtually all, if not all, of the relatively nonmodernized societies not only is initial and basic learning with regard to structures of production and consumption carried out in family terms, but the vast majority of *all* learning is carried out in family terms.

In those societies in which either structures of production or structures of consumption are carried out in terms of units larger in scale than is possible for the family units in the society concerned, the larger units, if not some larger kinship units such as clans, are generally based on family organizations. For example, if the unit of such behavior is a neighborhood unit, organization of the members of the neighborhood is likely to be on a family or other kinship basis. The structures of control, especially, usually rest on family considerations.

For the vast majority of relatively nonmodernized societies, certainly for those of any considerable scale, there is a tendency for the members to maximize general family self-sufficiency from both the point of view of production and consumption. Most of these societies are predominantly agrarian as far as the vast majority of their members are concerned, but this generalization will probably hold true at least as well of nomadic societies of any considerable scale. The extent to which the self-sufficiency of the family unit is maximized in terms of economic allocation has far-reaching implications for the rest of social structure. This is especially true from the point of view of questions of control. To the extent that general family self-sufficiency is maximized, the problem of exerting control requires much greater direct interference than would be necessary if the family units were highly interdependent or highly dependent on operations in terms of other units. It is practically out of the question to control action in terms of highly self-sufficient units of any sort from afar if the members of such units are in fact serious about any wish to go their own way. Thus, if one wishes to organize family members in projects which might not meet with their liking, the problems of organization are maximized to the extent that their family units are highly self-sufficient. On the other hand, as far as operation in terms of the general society is concerned, in the absence of any desire to organize or control family members in a fashion which does not meet with their approval, the amount of central organization and control necessary for smooth operation in terms of the system is correspondingly minimized by the level of self-sufficiency of the family units. This question will come up again and again in other contexts. The structures of economic allocation in the family are by no means the only structures relevant to these questions of self-sufficiency and their implications and they are not necessarily the most important ones, but they are not ordinarily negligible ones either.

D. THE FAMILY AS A FOCUS OF POLITICAL ALLOCATION

In all known societies, the family is always a major focus of political allocation. As societies become increasingly modernized, other organizations outside the family sphere become increasingly important as foci for the structures of power and responsibility. There is in addition a general age variable in this connection. In the context of relatively modernized societies, the older an individual becomes up to the peak of his nonfamily career during full adulthood, the greater is the likelihood that the individual will have increasingly important foci of power and responsibility that lie in organizations outside his family or kinship context. Even in very highly modernized societies, however, for most of the individuals during the periods of infancy and early childhood practically none of the critical foci of power and responsibility lie outside the individual's family context. With the beginning of participation in school systems, of course, this picture changes radically and abruptly. Despite this attenuation of the family as a major focus of political allocation with increasing age and adulthood in relatively modernized societies, the family remains for all of these individuals in the ordinary case a major focus of power and responsibility as far as the individuals themselves are concerned and as far as others are concerned with them.

Again, families in all known societies are always the systems in terms of which structured political aspects of behavior are first learned. Some of the recent preoccupation with the permissive attitude of parents characteristic of some societies has obscured the fact that there are no societies in terms of which the behavior of infants and children is totally devoid of restraint by others. The sage Mencius, in trying to prove that human nature was inherently good, observed that even a complete stranger would not stand idly by and permit a small child to fall into a well. In general traditional Chinese parents were highly permissive with infants and young children, and strangers were even more permissive by virtue of the fact that they did not wish to be involved at all, but even so, Mencius and everyone else took the amount of restraint necessary for the survival of the child for granted. It is hardly to be doubted that certain amounts of restraint necessary for the survival of those who had to live with children was also taken for granted.

I have alluded above to the fact that the high level of specialization of organizations characteristic of relatively modernized societies has led most political scientists until recently to speak of structures of political allocation as if, by default of treatment at least, they develop miraculously with adulthood and legitimate participation in terms of governmental and associated organizations such as predominantly politically oriented parties, etc. This has, of course, never been the case of any society. Some basic structures of political allocation in every known society are learned in a family context. Societies vary with regard to how much of the basic as well as the intermediate structures of political allocation are first learned in a family context. Nevertheless, initial behavior and some, if not most, of the basic behavior in these terms is *always* learned in a family context save in the case of a relatively small number of unfortunate orphans or children somehow left more or less abandoned or isolated. The chances of such children developing into stable adults in terms of any society is slight. No activities of the members of any government can be fully understood in terms of the structures of the government alone. The structures of political allocation in terms of which the members of the society operate in organizational contexts other than that of the government are always to some extent relevant to operation in the governmental context itself. The number and varieties of other organizational contexts crucial for understanding behavior in the governmental context vary enormously from society to society, but behavior in general and training in particular in the family context is always crucial for a thorough understanding and analysis of governments and/or operations in terms of them. Implicit, if not explicit in any understanding of governments or operations in terms of them are assumptions about how the members of the society concerned will react to different exercises of power and responsibility. Family experiences are always relevant to those reactions.

Frequently kinship organizations in general and families in particular constitute the most important basis for political allocation in a society. This is never the case ideally speaking in relatively modernized societies. In all such societies the governmental organization is a more important focus of general control than is the family unit. Among relatively nonmodernized societies, however, there are two major types of which it may be said that kinship organization in general or the family in particular constitute the most important basis for political allocation. One type is the traditional Chinese type. In that society family control was the keystone of the whole structure of political allocation in both the family and in the society as a whole. In traditional China under ordinary circumstances the level of family self-sufficiency was relatively high. The family head was the focus of the control structures of the family organization. Ordinarily the members of other organizations exercised control in terms of their organization over individuals through the given individual's family head rather than directly. The government in particular was so organized that its members could exercise control directly over individuals if it became necessary, but the general maintenance of order did not hinge on such direct control. In such a society, if the structures of family control are weakened, the general structure of control in the society as a whole is weakened. Exactly that happened during the early highly unsuccessful moves in the direction of modernization in China.

Another major type is that in which the direct allocation of power and responsibility in the society as a whole is on kinship terms. This is the case in societies in terms of which rule is determined on the basis of kinship actually as well as ideally. This involves more than an hereditary monarch since it is possible to have an hereditary monarch in a society like that of Great Britain. On the other hand, feudal societies are definitely societies of this sort. In such societies virtually every relevant position from the point of view of structures of control, ideally speaking, is allocated on the basis of kinship. In terms of such societies positions in the hierarchy of control are obtained on a highly particularistic basis.

Since that is the case, it is exceedingly difficult in the context of such societies to count on having individuals of high levels of ability in such positions. In Tokugawa Japan this was to some extent obtained via "civil service by adoption" which has already been referred to above [e.g., p. 118]. In general, however, in the context of such societies either the level of ability necessary for stability is not on the whole great, or these societies are highly unstable. There are plenty of examples of both sorts in social history. There are many cases of relatively stable but small-scale societies in which the government is based almost entirely on clans and tribes and the like. There are also plenty of cases of societies of considerable scale which were highly unstable. Feudal societies in general were cases of this sort. As far as I know, the society of Tokugawa Japan is the only genuinely feudal society of any considerable scale that has a pedigree of high stability for a period of as long as two hundred and fifty years. In general in feudal social contexts a stable hegemony of power lasting as much as fifty years is unusual.[8] One of the major contrasts between the second type and the first type lies in the fact that members of societies of the first type must, if the society is to be stable, be overwhelmingly family oriented and in addition family orientation must take precedence over all other orientations, ideally speaking at least. In the second type, orientation to the hierarchy may take precedence for the individual over family orientations. In the second case, the family becomes the most important basis for political allocation by virtue of the fact that the hierarchy itself is allocated on a kinship basis. In general as far as societies of any considerable scale are concerned, the first type is more stable but less readily convertible to modernization and the second is on the whole less stable but relatively more convertible to modernization. In the first case the weakening of the family position in the structures of allocation of power and responsibility wipes out the general structure of control. In the second, the weakening of the family position may leave important elements in the structure of control intact. The experiences of the Chinese and Japanese with modernization are the best illustrations I know of these variations. Those cases at least establish the possibility of such variations.

Finally, although the family is always a major focus of power

[8] The case of Tokugawa Japan is so unusually stable that for that reason alone some historians would prefer not to consider Tokugawa Japan as a feudal society despite the fact that the society seems to meet the other criteria of the definitions generally used save for the one of instability which is sometimes added when the case of Japan comes up.

and responsibility, in relatively modernized societies the position of the family as a major focus of power and responsibility rests increasingly on the position of the family with regard to early and basic learning about the structures of political allocation rather than on more general control functions realized in terms of the family, i.e., it rests increasingly on the role of family members in socializing the new members of society to behavior in terms of political allocation and to the maintenance of order within the family context itself. In all other societies the position of the family unit as a major focus of power and responsibility goes far beyond these limits. As indicated above, kinship organizations in general and the family in particular constitute for some societies *the* most important basis for political allocation. Even in societies in which this is not the case, however, the family organization is almost inevitably coequal in importance or second in importance only to the governmental organization. For the average member of a relatively nonmodernized society only the governmental organization ever rivals the family organization as a focus of power and responsibility as far as he is concerned. This situation always changes as societies become increasingly modernized.

E. THE FAMILY AS A FOCUS OF INTEGRATION AND EXPRESSION

As far as religion and recreation are concerned, the family once again is always a major focus of attention in any society, and it is frequently *the* major focus of attention in these respects. It is not quite tautological to point out that the more highly self-sufficient the family unit is, the more likely the family is to be *the* major focus for religion and recreation in the society concerned. With regard to these aspects of behavior too, initial structures and basic ones in every society are ordinarily learned in a family context. In most relatively nonmodernized societies most of such structures for most individuals are learned in a family context at all stages of their lives, but this is increasingly less likely the more highly modernized the society becomes.

Within the general category of integration and expression, however, it is in consideration of the socialization of the individual that the special importance of the family unit emerges most clearly. Consideration of the process of socialization is virtually a summation of what has already been discussed above under the preceding four major headings. In every known society a considerable portion of the basic socialization [i.e., that socialization common to all the members] of a society takes place in a family context. Frequently the most important intermediate or specialized socialization also takes place in family terms. The more highly modernized the society becomes the less likely this is. In the context of every society, including the most highly modernized ones, however, some intermediate socialization always takes place in a family context. For example, it is always to some extent in family terms that the average individual learns to differentiate between the conduct appropriate to women and the conduct appropriate to men [see p. 387]. Even in the most highly modernized societies the average individual learns something about work habits in a family context, though the more highly modernized the society becomes the more likely occupational socialization is to take place completely outside a family context. Indeed, one of the most radical contrasts between relatively modernized and relatively nonmodernized societies lies precisely in the diminishing significance of the family in the intermediate socialization of the average individual.

This is, of course, one of the reasons why the structures of relatively modernized societies are so subversive of those of relatively nonmodernized societies. In such societies family control is exceedingly likely to be a vital element in the general structure of control of the society as a whole. Part of the reinforcement of the structures of control in the ordinary family system is a function of the fact that family members of an older generation who generally control family members of younger generations are also ordinarily the only individuals from whom those of the younger generation can learn their adult roles. In virtually all of the relatively nonmodernized social contexts for the vast majority of individuals the father and mother are not only one's parents, but they are also ordinarily the only teachers one ever knows. They are at least ordinarily the most important teachers one ever knows. As modernization progresses, increasingly one does not rely on his own family members as a source of instruction for performances in adult roles, and particularly in the early stages of modernization one cannot even count with certainty on the fact that his teachers will be older and thereby reinforce the precedence on the basis of age in the family context to which one is accustomed. In general in highly modernized contexts even professional teachers are unlikely to teach their own children the specialities in which they are technically expert. Furthermore, they are generally as reluctant to try to do so as doctors are to treat their own family members in the case of serious illness.

Closely related to this whole question is the matter of initial social placement. For all known societies the initial placement of virtually every single individual is to some extent in family terms.

There are a few spectacular exceptions such as the Dalai Lama. At the moment of the death of the present Dalai Lama, men go about the countryside of Tibet seeking a baby born at that exact moment. By divination or by other methods some baby is picked out, regardless of what his family background may have been. That child, if he survives, is the Dalai Lama. But that is a peculiar case and does not alter the general argument to the effect that initial social placement in all known societies for virtually all known people has been to some extent in family terms. The implications of this for general discussions of caste, class, and social mobility are fairly obvious. A given member of any society either retains roughly the position into which he is first socialized, or he does not. The overwhelming majority of individuals have tended to retain roughly the positions into which they were first socialized. In some of these societies the lack of social mobility has to do with a special set of ideals. Many of these societies were characterized by closed class or caste structures. That is to say, many of these societies are societies such that if one is born a peasant, not only is one not likely ever to be anything else, but it is not considered right and proper to strive to be anything else. The classical caste structures of India were certainly some of the most extreme examples of this sort known to social history. There have also, however, been many societies characterized by class structures that were highly sedentary, not because this was preferred by the members of the society, but rather because there were relatively few opportunities for social mobility even if social mobility was considered a good thing by the members of that society. Whatever the reasons may be for a lack of social mobility, for the members of societies in terms of which one tends to keep the general social position into which one is born, the importance of the family structures in socialization is overwhelming.

To the extent that a given individual is either upwardly or downwardly mobile, he must be socialized in terms of the different structures characteristic of his new position. The usual examples of this are generally cases that have to do with upward mobility, though the problems of adjustment of the downwardly mobile are no less acute, as will be seen below. The classic case of this is the problem of the *nouveau riche*. Take the case of the member of a society in terms of which achievement is both emphasized and rewarded, who starts out as a member of a family of humble origins and through great ability climbs to the top of the social ladder. As a matter of course, we assume that he is going to have a long difficult period of adjustment because he does not know how to behave when he reaches his pinnacle. The comic strip, *Bringing up Father* [starring Maggie and Jiggs], for several decades was based on just this problem. Jiggs is a man who made a lot of money, presumably because he was a man of great ability, and basically the man remains a simple Irish soul whose greatest ambition is to eat corned beef and cabbage with Clancey and the boys, despite his great wealth. His wife, Maggie, wants to be upperclass in every sense of the word. Jiggs is at least sincere in his tastes, whereas Maggie, though admirable after her fashion, is primarily socially ambitious—a social climber in the fullest sense of the word. No value is too shallow for her to pursue if she thinks it is identified with the right people. Neither knows how to behave among individuals who have comparable incomes and resources or who have been long used to the structures considered appropriate to persons of such income.

All relatively modernized societies are ones whose members place great emphasis on social mobility. In such social contexts those who are mobile always face the question of how to become socialized to the structures appropriate to their new stations in life. They are always faced with the question of how and from whom they are to learn these new structures. Hundreds of novels, movies, TV dramas, etc., have been based on the plot that initially at least these individuals are not even well adapted to judge who is a good model to follow in these respects and who is not. In societies characterized by little social mobility, the problem of such socialization apart from one's initial family context is a relatively rare problem. In terms of societies in which the classes are, ideally speaking, closed, it is usually a special offense [e.g., *lèse-majesté*] for a person of one class even to aspire to behavior appropriate to one born into another setting. In societies whose members do not regard this as in any sense reprehensible but in terms of which actual social mobility is relatively infrequent, once again the problem of late socialization is stressy only for a small portion of the population at any given point in time. When such changes do take place, the fact that the individual must be resocialized, as it were, poses not only the problems of reeducation for him, it is also likely to pose problems for members of many of the relationships in which he previously participated, especially for those in which the strength and intensity of his solidarities were considerable and for those which continue. The *nouveau riche* always face a special dilemma. They are uncomfortable with their new friends and acquaintances, and their old friends and acquaintances are uncomfortable with them.

There is a special case of the relation between socialization and initial social placement in a large number of relatively nonmodernized societies, and even a special form of it in relatively modernized ones. There are some societies in terms of which there is a kind of enforced mobility, especially downward mobility, even though the ideal structures of the society may call for closed classes and as little social mobility as possible. I refer to the problem of *cadets*. It arises whenever great accumulations of wealth or important roles in the government or the like are inherited on the basis of primogeniture or some other structures in terms of which a single representative of a given generation of the family is selected as the sole or major inheritor of fortune and/or position. The members of some societies have avoided this by ideal structures of equal inheritance among all sons or even among all children. In traditional China this was specifically one of the devices which ended feudalism and feudal accumulations over two hundred years before the Christian era. In the history of large-scale societies the Chinese practice is on the whole relatively rare.

All societies characterized by the *cadet problem* have been relatively nonmodernized ones. In all such social contexts, the life expectancy of any individual at birth, whether he is from a wealthy and important family setting or not, is relatively short. To the extent that succession to family position and wealth is important to members of the society, in order to guarantee succession there must be several possible candidates in any given generation. The most usual structure in this respect is primogeniture among sons. Given structures of male primogeniture, the eldest son alive at the death of the previous holder of fortune and/or position inherits. But given the woeful state of medical technology characteristic of such societies, it is necessary to have several sons, to ensure succession. Since it is impossible to know in advance that the initial eldest son will in fact survive to inherit, it is not only necessary to have, if possible, more than one son, it is also necessary to socialize and educate *all* of the possible inheritors in such a way that, no matter who among them die before succession can take place, someone will remain who is ready and able to succeed. Once succession does take place, if any of those also socialized so that they could succeed are still alive, one of two things must take place. Either they must be disposed of, or they must live out at least a portion, if not all of the remainder of their lives, in a social position somewhat inferior to the one which they were at least in part trained to inherit. This is likely to result in a set of dissatisfied frustrated people highly articulate in the social contexts concerned and in positions in which actually if not ideally influence comes easily to them because of their past associations. There have been societies in terms of which the person who inherited [e.g., a sultan] was expected to be relatively cold-blooded and to execute, as soon as possible, any younger brothers who might be disgruntled by his succession. This drastic resort, however, is not likely to serve stably for any numerous class of individual members of any given society.

Commonly in history there have rather been instances in which young men of this sort were a source of unrest unless their talents and energies were drained off into the army, the colonies, the clergy, or the like. It is not a matter of chance, for example, that in the literature associated with Great Britain and similar societies there are certain stock villains. These stock villains are likely to be younger sons who wish to get the position of their virtuous older brothers, virtuous younger brothers who are debarred from succession by virtue of the fact that they have a wicked older brother, etc. The situation is further complicated by whether a given son is illegitimate or not. These instances all involve individuals, reared so that they could or might succeed, but forever doomed under the ordinary course of inheritance not to succeed. The state of medical technology characteristic of all societies prior to the development of modern medical means was such that in many cases only one son was in fact left to succeed, but whenever this was not the case, and the increased availability of food, clothing, and other care for the children of the relatively well-to-do was more likely to result in the survival of more sons per family unit than was the case among the general population. there were still plenty of cases in which the cadet problem was bound to arise.

In all relatively modernized social contexts, regardless of how much the members of those societies pride themselves on the social mobility characteristic of their societies, there is a possibility of a somewhat analogous problem. Those societies are not ordinarily characterized by structures of primogeniture. This is especially unlikely to be the case with regard to powerful and important positions which tend to become increasingly positions which have to be gained by achievement rather than by inheritance. Under these circumstances, there is no question but that the children of people highly placed are likely to have advantages in background and schooling which, given the general possibilities of mobility, will keep them roughly on the level of their parents. To the extent that this is not the case, there arises once again the problem of individuals used to life on one level of social prestige and forced to live out the remainder of their lives on a less highly regarded level.

In the case of relatively modernized societies, however, there is an added special problem. In general in all such societies not only is there the possibility of social mobility on the basis of achievement, but a great deal is done to motivate individuals to strive for achievement and the recognition accorded to it. In such social contexts the greater the recognition achieved by one or more representatives of the parental generation the greater is likely to be the pressure for achievement placed upon the children. It is unlikely that the son of a Supreme Court Justice will in fact succeed to that Bench. It is not at all unlikely that he become a lawyer. In relatively modernized social contexts the children of persons of high achievement, especially the sons,[9] are notoriously subject to great psychological pressures to live up to the standards set by their parents. Parents and others begin to exert pressure in these respects early in the child's life, and the pressure continues to grow in intensity. In the United States today, for example, one sees especially striking instances of this as one of the major problems centering around admission to college. The son of a brilliant academic who is not able to gain admission to his father's prestigious alma mater or stay in once he is admitted is likely to encounter serious problems of personal adjustment.

In the context of relatively nonmodernized societies whose members accent primogeniture there always exists a cadet class of younger brothers. In relatively modernized social contexts the cadet problem tends not to be one of younger brothers but rather one of family members of a younger generation in general. To some extent these problems are alleviated by virtue of the fact that the general standard of living for the average member of the population increases so steadily and so markedly. At least in terms of material acquisitions a considerably less able son may still achieve as much or more than his father even in a social context in which there is a fairly high correlation between achievement and the material resources at one's disposal. To the extent that this is the case, the tendency to consider material acquisitions in general and achieved income level in particular as a general measure of social achievement and worth may be a basis for something other than high-minded denigration.

[9] But not the sons alone. This is especially true of sons only insofar as, despite all of the emphasis on achievement, in even the most modernized of the highly modernized contexts, there remains a differentiation on the basis of sex with regard to how hard one is supposed to strive to achieve and what one is supposed to strive to achieve. Sexually oriented particularism never dies.

I V
VARIATIONS IN THE FORMS OF FAMILY AND KINSHIP UNITS

A. INTRODUCTION

There exists now in the work of anthropologists, sociologists, etc., an enormously complicated and detailed literature on variations in the form of family and kinship units. There is no more point in attempting to reproduce that literature here than there is in attempting to reproduce the literature in the field of political science on the distinctions among different types of legislative bodies. Some of these extremely generally used distinctions, however, are especially pertinent to questions of social analysis generally, the distinction between relatively modernized and relatively nonmodernized societies, and the problems of modernization of relatively nonmodernized societies and the maintenance of stability in terms of relatively highly modernized societies. I shall touch briefly on the following six: (1) the family of orientation and the family of procreation, (2) distinctions based on lines of descent, (3) distinctions based on precedence and power, (4) distinctions based on residence, (5) distinctions based on the integration of family units into larger kinship units, and (6) three other major types of family units. The development of theory in this field is in such an elementary, inchoate stage that I am unable to justify this particular selection for attention on any basis other than personal judgment. The problem posed by the state of theory in this field is not that the distinctions presented here are likely to be irrelevant ones, but that there are likely to be equally relevant ones and perhaps much more relevant ones which have not been presented here and may not yet have been conceived in the literature.

B. THE FAMILY OF ORIENTATION AND THE FAMILY OF PROCREATION

In any society it is possible to distinguish between the family [or families] in terms of which a given individual is reared from infancy to some state of maturity and the family unit in terms of which he [or she] ordinarily becomes a parent and has to do with the rearing of children considered to be his [or her] own or representatives of a younger generation than the one to which he [or she] belongs. It is conventional in anthropology and sociology to refer to the former as the individual's *family of orientation* and to the latter as the individual's *family of procreation*. In the discussion here I shall speak of the matter as though there were only a single family of orientation for each individual and a single family of procreation for each individual, ideally speaking. Neither is necessarily the case. Especially with regard to families of orientation, it is quite conceivable that there be a society in terms of which the average individual belongs to two or more families of orientation. For example, an individual might be reared from infancy to say the age of six or seven as a member of a family unit of which the other members were his father, mother, and other young siblings, but at the age of six or seven he might go to live as a member of the family unit of his mother's older brother. As a member of that unit he might be reared from the age of six or seven to the time of his own marriage. Such an individual would belong to two distinct families of orientation. A comparably complicated picture as far as the family of procreation is concerned is also quite conceivable, given various possibilities of multiple spouses, divorce, etc. Thus it is an over-simplification to speak as though every society were characterized for any given individual by only one family of orientation and only one family of procreation. The over-simplification, however, does not seriously distort the situation in any of the societies of considerable scale of most interest in these volumes. Such an over-simplification is preferable to turning this into a general treatise on kinship.

For some of the members of some societies the family of procreation is a continuation of the family of orientation. For example, ideally speaking in traditional China, a man was reared as a member of his father's family. When he reached marriageable age, a bride was brought into that family membership for him. He and his wife subsequently had their children and reared them as members of that unit. Sometimes the representatives of the grandparental generation died before the individual concerned had fathered his own children and reared them, but ideally speaking his family of procreation was in this sense a continuation of his family of orientation. In some societies the family of orientation and the family of procreation are, ideally speaking, different for every member of the society. For example, members of modern United States society are expected to belong to different families of orientation and procreation. A member of United States society is reared as a member of his parents' family. When he marries, ideally speaking, he and his wife become the members of a new and separate unit which is specifically not a continuation of either his family of orientation or his wife's.

Although there are societies in terms of which the family of orientation and the family of procreation are, ideally speaking,

different for every individual, there can be no society for which
the family of procreation is expected to be a continuation of every
individual's family of orientation. For this to be the case both sons
and daughters would have to make their spouses members of
their specific families of orientation by marrying other members
of their own family of orientation. If they brought in spouses who
were members of other families, the spouses brought in would
have different families of procreation from their families of orientation. On the other hand, to marry members of their own families of orientation would sooner or later violate incest taboos
which in some form are characteristic of every known society.[10]
Usually the members of a society who are ideally expected to have
different families of procreation from their families of orientation
are defined either on the basis of sex role differentiation or relative age role differentiation. Thus the female members of many
societies, such as that of traditional China, are expected to marry
out of their families of orientation and join their husbands'. In
Tokugawa Japan not only did women marry out as was the case
typically in China, but in addition to that younger sons, when
married, were exceedingly likely to set up new family units separate from their families of orientation. These were considered
branch families of their family of orientation, but they were separate systems.

This distinction is important because it is an easy and immediate indicator of certain problems of adjustment. In social contexts like that of traditional China, women are to some extent
always marginal members of the families in terms of which they
participate. The other members of a girl's family of orientation expect that she will someday leave it. Furthermore, she is likely to
give up her membership in that family at just the point in time at
which her services might from other points of view be most
helpful to other family members. In the context of her family of
procreation she is ordinarily the newest member and the most
obvious focus for treatment as an outsider. The members of
societies like that of Tokugawa Japan regard the average woman
as a marginal member of her family of orientation just as in the
case of China, but in addition to that, younger sons are also
regarded as marginal members of their families of orientation
once the eldest brother reaches maturity and is able to succeed to
the headship of the family. Characteristically, members of a
society like that of the modern United States regard neither men
nor women as marginal members of either their families of orientation or of their families of procreation. In that social setting
both men and women must adjust to the problems of life in terms

[10] See below, pp. 419–423.

of a family of procreation without there being a line of continuity for either—thereby maximizing those problems of adjustments.

C. LINES OF DESCENT

The most frequently encountered distinctions in terms of lines of descent are the distinctions among patrilineal, matrilineal, and multilineal systems. There may be other possibilities of organization in terms of lines of descent, but these will suffice for present purposes. *Patrilineal descent* refers, of course, to descent reckoned in terms of the male line; *matrilineal descent* refers to descent reckoned in the female line; and *multilineal descent* refers to descent reckoned in terms of both lines of descent accented equally or in some more or less complicated form. Most of the societies on which we have historical materials have probably been characterized by patrilineal family and kinship structures. Modern United States family structures were at one time much more strongly patrilineal than they are now. At present ours is properly described as a multilineal kinship structure with only one major remnant of patrilineality. That major remnant is, of course, the fact that the family name is the father's surname. These structures of reckoning descent always tell one something of the kind of relationship individual family members are expected to have with other people who are considered kinfolk. Multilineal family children, for example, are not expected to prefer their paternal grandparents to their maternal grandparents. Actually, as any modern American parent whose parents are still living and interested knows, as far as the child is concerned the relationship with grandparents is a sort of popularity contest. The children in a sense are granted a great deal of freedom to make up their own minds which grandparents they prefer. Insofar as the grandparents are interested, this results in much competition among the grandparents for the attention of the grandchildren. Sometimes it leads to quite strong feelings among the grandparents. Almost inevitably it complicates the relations of the parents concerned with their own parents. This is a typical multilineal situation. Ideally speaking, this sort of problem did not arise at all in the traditional Chinese context. Paternal grandparents were of enormous significance to a child; maternal grandparents were of relatively little significance.

Distinctions based on lines of descent are, of course, of considerable significance in explaining the kinds of kinship-oriented solidarities that are expected, ideally speaking, in a given society. Relatively nonmodernized societies are rich in examples of all three sorts of lineality mentioned here. Relatively modernized and modernizing societies, however, are all characterized by multilineal conjugal family units or are changing in that direction if that type of unit did not characterize the society prior to movements in the direction of modernization. Among other things this uniformity is always accompanied by a lessening of the importance of kinship apart from the family units as a major focus of solidarity for the members of the society concerned. The switch in emphases from, say, a previously existing set of patrilineal structures to a multilineal one never means that the individual's relatives in the paternal line continue to be as important to him as they were before but that in addition his relatives in the maternal line become more important than they were. *Any* change in the direction of multilineality that accompanies a change in the direction of modernization is indicative of a decreasing emphasis on lines of descent in general. Given the fact that in general the orientation of behavior to considerations of the family and kinship organization in general always decreases radically with the increase in modernization, this is exactly what one would expect. There are special problems connected with this, however, because the ordinary experience with modernization, especially of late-comers to the process, is that the stability of the previously existing kinship and family organizations as foci of solidarity in general and of control in particular is radically undermined long before the process of modernization has proceeded far in other respects.

D. PRECEDENCE AND POWER

When one analyzes family systems in terms of precedence and power one runs into the classic distinction of patriarchal, matriarchal, and what one might call the egalitarian forms of the family. This set of distinctions is primarily oriented to the allocation of precedence and power among family members on the basis of sex. *Patriarchal families* are those in terms of which the males take precedence over the females, other things being equal, and the family head is ideally expected to be of the male sex. The *matriarchal family* is one in terms of which females are supposed to take precedence over males, and the family head is supposed to be a female. The *egalitarian family* would be one presumably in which neither males nor females took precedence over one another but shared equal powers and equal responsibilities. Actually the vast majority of all family units has certainly been patriarchal. Indeed, despite frequent usage of the term, the question is now raised by social scientists as to whether any society ever had a truly matriarchal form of organization. Even the societies whose members are known to stress matrilineal descent are always characterized by some male leadership of the family subsystems of the society. Insofar as matrilineality is stressed, that male is more likely to be a brother of the wife than her husband, but the family head is usually a male.

It is becoming increasingly popular to speak of the ideal family structures in relatively modernized societies as emphasizing egalitarianism especially as between husband and wife. There has certainly been a trend in this direction, at least sentimentally,[11] but neither the ideal nor the actual family situations characteristic of those societies are in fact close to being egalitarian. In general that sort of precise balance would be rather difficult to envisage. What is far more likely is that the family unit in relatively highly modernized societies will become increasingly matriarchal. In relatively modernized social contexts the overwhelming majority of males earn the major income for the support of family members via occupational roles which they pursue in a context completely separate from the family one. To an extent never true of members of any other society the average married male member of such societies is literally away from home when most of the day-to-day decisions which have to be made for the operation of the family members as a set or as individuals are in fact made. Ideally speaking, the male is still expected to dominate his family, especially in crisis situations, but actually this is probably increasingly less the case. The great increase in leisure time, i.e., time away from work, characteristic of the most highly developed of these societies may to some extent change this picture, but it is by no means clear yet to what extent the increased leisure time will be spent by family members in the family context.[12]

The extent to which the actual power and precedence of women in the family context is likely to increase in any situation in which the mature male members of the family are taken out of the family context for a major portion of the waking hours of the family members each week is incompletely understood by both

[11] For brief discussions of egalitarianism see above, pp. 150–152 and 296–300.

[12] In the modern United States setting this change has gone so far as to have its own special body of humor and wit. We have become somewhat bored with having personality development explained primarily in terms of momism. We still, however, circulate jokes such as the one in which the husband maintains that the secret of his ideal marital adjustment is that he makes all of the important decisions and his wife makes all of the minor decisions. Minor decisions, it develops, cover such matters as whether they buy a new home, where the children go to school, what sort of automobile they purchase, what sort of vacation they shall take, and when and where, how much they shall try to save, and so forth. Important decisions cover such matters as, "whether or not we declare war on Bulgaria."

technical experts and laymen. For example, if one reads the work of modern scholars on Japanese history or the documents which circulated during the Tokugawa period, one gets the impression that the wives of samurai, i.e., the wives of the warrior retainers, were the most completely powerless, downtrodden, victimized women in Japan. Peasant wives who worked in the fields with their husbands are frequently cited as having had far greater precedence and power in their family environments than did the samurai wife. Contemptuous references by samurai husbands to women as "borrowed wombs" and tales of the callous slaughtering of concubines after they have borne a family heir reinforce the generally accepted interpretation. There is reason to believe quite otherwise. These samurai, though ideally speaking warriors, were in fact the civil servants of their particular lords. To an extent only equalled by some of the larger merchants they left home each day to go to work. Sometimes they had to make long trips which kept them away from home for weeks or months on end. The day-to-day decisions had to be made by the wife or the mother of the samurai when he was absent. When he was home, he may well have been the boss, but most of the occasions for being bossy came up when he was not even present. Futhermore, as his young son grew up, the father was not available day in and day out to serve as a direct model and instructor for his son. When a question for family decisions came up for the peasants, the husband was usually quite near enough for the wife to consult him. When the peasant's son was a young child, he went to work with his father or with his older brothers in the field. The average samurai wife actually dominated the development of her son far more than any other wife characteristic of Tokugawa Japanese society. She in fact made more important decisions with regard to family affairs than any other type of wife in Tokugawa Japan with the possible exception of the wives of fishermen who were also likely to be away from their villages a good part of every day and often for many days at a time. Time away from home—and who spends it —is important for understanding family phenomena. Absence may or may not make the heart grow fonder, but some of its implications for allocations of power and responsibility are undeniable.

Although most discussions of power and precedence in the family context tend to emphasize sex role differentiations, there are always other important bases for these distinctions. In every family in every known society there are structures of precedence on the basis of generation and age. Older generation family members have both precedence and power over family members of the younger generation. To some extent absolute age distinctions are always a basis for distinctions of precedence and power in the family context. In addition, relatively older people always have some sorts of precedence over relatively younger ones. The extent of precedence on both the basis of age and generation tends to decline in the context of relatively modernized societies, but it is never eliminated. It is true that, in relatively modernized social contexts, once a man is married he is expected to give greater consideration to his wife and to his children than to his own parents, but in terms of all of those societies, when he reaches that stage, ideally speaking at least, he is no longer a member of the same family as his parents. His family of procreation is a new and different one from his family of orientation, ideally speaking, and generational precedence and power continue to hold in that context. It is also important to realize that however much precedence and power in other organizational contexts in the society are achieved on the basis of predominantly universalistic criteria, precedence and power in the family situation in all known societies is ideally expected to be ascribed on the basis of overwhelmingly particularistic criteria. Even in the most highly modernized societies in the family context *who* an individual is is always more important than *what* he can do, ideally speaking.[13]

E. RESIDENCE

Another conventional way of distinguishing among family organizations is on the basis of the residence of family members. Societies may be distinguished on the basis of whether or not

[13] The sense of kinship identity of the past President of the United States and his relatives was often commented upon. In gatherings of the family members of his brothers', sisters', and his parents' families, Mr. Kennedy was certainly the person of greatest achievement present. Nevertheless, the precedence and power within those settings of Mr. Kennedy's father might be assumed, although he was reported on at least one occasion to have delegated that role to his son. It is interesting to note that his son was not reported to have assumed that role on his own initiative. It is also interesting to note that many of Mr. Kennedy's political opponents specifically raised the question as to whether or not domination by his father influenced or interfered in any way with his performance of his duties as President of the United States. Even in the United States where people are generally considered to be quite lacking in respect for their family elders, most Americans would be shocked and dismayed if their President did not show a proper respect and deference for his father's wishes in the kinship context at least, regardless of what American public opinion might be about the President's father. It is further interesting in general that, in a society whose members are so widely and naïvely commented on as having reduced the position of the family to virtual insignificance, the very strong sense of family identification, loyalty, etc., of Mr. Kennedy and his kinfolk was so widely regarded by political friend and foe alike as a great source of his appeal as a public figure.

family units are *patrilocal, matrilocal* or *neolocal*. That is to say, do the family members tend to reside where the members of the father's family of orientation reside, where the members of the mother's family of orientation reside, or are the members of each new family supposed to or likely to locate in a new place altogether. The vast majority of all families have been either matrilocal or patrilocal, and this has usually coincided with whether or not the family structures were matrilineal or patrilineal. There are, however, numerous examples of relatively nonmodernized societies characterized by neolocal structures. In all relatively modernized social contexts, ideally speaking, married couples expect to have the right to neolocal families. The married couple may choose to reside where one or both of them have previously resided, but this is not necessarily expected, and it is certainly not required. The ideal structure in the society is that the married couple should be free to set up a household wherever they wish to, and the expectation is that the actual location chosen will be more a function of the occupational opportunity open to the husband than anything else. The relevance of this for participation in specialized organizations sharply separated from the family sphere of action is fairly obvious. To the extent that predominantly universalistic criteria are applied in selection for roles in these organizations, members of these organizations cannot count on living where their parents have previously resided. One of the clear-cut respects in which family units in even the most highly modernized societies are not ideally speaking egalitarian is quite visible in connection with the location of the family unit. If both husband and wife have careers in nonfamily contexts and the development of the husband's career requires that he move to another location, ideally speaking his wife is expected to go with him even if such a move means the sacrifice of her career.

F. INTEGRATION OF FAMILY UNITS INTO LARGER KINSHIP UNITS

Another organizational focus for family units is the incorporation of such units into larger kinship units such as clans, lineages, etc. The literature of anthropology is full of examples of the ingenuity, conscious or unconscious, displayed by men in the creation of organizations of this sort. In the vast majority of relatively nonmodernized societies some fairly substantial integration of this sort is present. It is not necessarily present, however, and the degree to which it is present can vary from society to society and within the historical development of a given society. For example, the integration of family units into clans was a quite common phenomenon in traditional Chinese history, but there were considerable fluctuations as to how important clan organizations were in fact. When these larger kinship units are present, they are usually quite important as forms of organizations in terms of which the interests of the members of the individual family subsystems are protected. Frequently the only close approach to what we might consider public relief is carried out in terms of these organizations; the only specialized schooling available to their members may be provided in terms of them, and the same may hold true of predominantly religiously oriented organizations for kinship purposes, etc. Often individuals have more influence in governmental matters as representatives of clans than as representatives of families.

None of these integrations of family units into larger kinship units appear to be consistent with the development of relatively high levels of modernization. As modernization develops in terms of a given society all vestiges of such organizations do not disappear immediately, but increasingly none of the vestiges which remain continue to take effective precedence over the other obligations of family members in general. In terms of such societies even family obligations do not necessarily take precedence over obligations to the government, to the church, to one's employer, etc. Obligations to support or interact with other members of a larger kinship organization are much less likely to take precedence over these other obligations than are family obligations. The vestiges may linger long. Persons of Scottish descent may continue to regard themselves as clansmen, but in actuality this is a question of sentimental, nostalgic, ceremonial kinship rather than a question of participation in an effective social organization whose members are in competition, or conflict with the members of other social organizations. In relatively nonmodernized societies on the other hand, membership in these larger kinship structures may constitute the most important nonfamily membership of the average individual throughout his life.

G. THREE MAJOR TYPES OF FAMILY UNITS

The actual variation in family types has not been nearly so great as the variations in ideal structures would lead one to believe. The ideal structures of kinship constitute one of the most variable forms of social structures. There are an indefinite number of points of view from which one could distinguish different types of families, especially if one were considering the ideal structures. In the material above, I have already discussed some of these variations from specific points of view. I would now like to discuss three different types of family with far-reaching implications for both general family analysis and other social analysis. The distinctions used here are focused on the nature and criteria of the membership of the family units concerned. The distinctions used are old and familiar ones. They are the distinctions among the *extended family, the stem family,* and *the conjugal [or nuclear] family.* These distinctions do not exhaust relevant differences, but they do hinge on certain elements always important in understanding family organizations. These are considerations such as the following. How many different generations are ideally or actually represented in the family? How many different conjugal pairs are likely to be subsystems of the family? How many individuals are likely to be members of a given family unit? What is the sex distribution of family members likely to be? What is the age distribution of family members likely to be [i.e., the age distribution in terms of both relative age and absolute age]? What is the ratio of siblings to spouses likely to be, of children to parents, etc.? These questions are always important in understanding family organization. It is rather simple to get precise measurements of the answers to these questions, and in addition the answers are not only intrinsically significant for understanding the operations of family members, but they also always have important implications for such questions as the allocation of power and responsibility, the allocation of goods and services, etc.

As far as family membership is concerned, proliferation may be along two axes. The vertical axis may be considered that of generations. The horizontal axis may be considered that of family members of a particular generation and their spouses who in the family context take on the generational status of their mates by virtue of their marriage. The *extended family* represents the maximum proliferation of family membership from this point of view. Extended family structures may be defined as accenting one line of descent, usually the patrilineal line, and including as members of the family unit individuals of as many generations as have living representatives, the spouses of those in the main line who are mature, and the nonadult children of all of the marital pairs. The ideal family of traditional Chinese society was of exactly this sort. Ideally speaking, the family head was expected to be a male. The family membership consisted of that male, his wife [or wives], all of his sons and all of their wives, his daughters until they reached marriageable age, at which time they married out of the family of orientation, all of the nonadult children of his sons and their wives, the wives of all of the male grandchildren when they reached marriageable age, and subsequently all of their nonadult children, and so forth indefinitely. Such a family type represents maximum proliferation both vertically in terms of numbers of generations ideally represented and horizontally in terms of the number of siblings of a given sex plus their spouses represented on any given generational level. As will be indicated below, the operation of the incest taboo is sufficient to determine the fact that one or the other line of descent will be singled out for continuation in the family unit, and persons of the opposite sex will marry out and leave the family unit [i.e., cease to be members of it] under ordinary circumstances. It is not difficult to imagine family units of this sort involving several tens of members. Families of this sort could become fairly large-scale organizations.

The *stem family,* as a concept, is generally attributed to the pioneering sociologist Frederic Le Play [14] who referred to this type of family as the *famille souche.* The classical formulation of the stem family is that of a family in terms of which one of the sons [or daughters] marries and continues to live with his parents as long as they live while all of the other sons and daughters marry and go out and join or set up other family systems. The daughters, however, marry into the family unit of their husbands whether their husbands be older or younger sons. The sons, other than the one who stays with his parents, set up what are considered to be branch families. The members of these family units maintain important relationships with the members of the main family, the most important one being the supply of succession in case none of the males of the main family are capable of carrying on the family line. When the stem family is the ideal form of the family, membership in the main family is always to some extent preferable to membership in one of the branch units, ideally speaking.

The third type of family unit is the *conjugal [or nuclear] family* unit. Ideally speaking, membership of such a family unit consists of husband, wife, and any nonadult children who are living. When the children of the husband and wife mature, they form families of procreation of their own. At that time the membership of the childrens' families of orientation reverts to the conjugal pair who originally formed it by marriage.

Certain implications of this threefold distinction should be immediately obvious. First, these three family types represent roughly a scale with the extended family at one extreme, the conjugal family at the other, and the stem family somewhere in

[14] See F. Le Play, *Les Ouvriers Europeens,* Tours, 1879, I, p. 457.

between in the possible proliferation of family units as far as considerations such as those mentioned above [e.g., generations present, numbers of members, sex distribution, etc.] are concerned. The extended family represents maximum proliferation; the conjugal family represents minimal possible proliferation, and so forth. There is a special set of implications of the stem family as an ideal structure. If health and other conditions were exactly right, it is conceivable that every family in a given society could approximate quite closely the extended family ideal or the conjugal family ideal. This has been actually realized in the case of the conjugal family unit as an ideal in such societies as, for example, the modern United States, although it has never been even approximately realized in the case of an extended family system for reasons which will be brought out in the section of this chapter which follows below. Such approximations to the ideal structures are not even conceivably possible in the case of the stem family type. When this family type constitutes the ideal structure of a given society, the preference is always for membership in the main family unit in terms of which, if the family is patrilineal, for the eldest son, at least, the family of procreation is always a continuation of his family of orientation. All other brothers, however, if they are to have families of procreation at all, must at least begin them as conjugal family units unless the brother who has remained a member of the main family dies before it is time for one of his other brothers to marry. Thus given societies in which the stem family is an ideal structure, there is always a substantial portion of the membership who for part of their lives at least must live in terms of a type of family unit which is not preferred. The branch family members cannot in their turn become main family members until at least one family member of the younger generation of the conjugal unit has been reared to maturity, married, and sired children of his own. Thus within the context of family organization itself, every society whose members hold to a stem family ideal has a sort of built in cadet structure, since some younger sons are bound to have to live for a considerable portion of their time in terms of families of procreation that are simple conjugal units rather than in terms of the three [or more] generational type of family which they have been reared to hold in special esteem.

A classic example of the extended family as an ideal structure is found in traditional Chinese society. A classic example of the stem family as an ideal structure is that of Tokugawa Japanese society. A classic example of the conjugal family as an ideal is found in modern United States society. There are many examples in social history of relatively nonmodernized societies in which one can find any one of these three types or many of the possible combinations or permutations of them as ideal structures. The vast majority of relatively nonmodernized societies are likely to include as ideal structures either some form of an extended family or a stem family type. The great emphasis on kinship units in general and family units in particular, already mentioned as characteristic of relatively nonmodernized societies, would indicate that the emphasis on continuity of some family units would be significant to the members of such societies. Structures of both the extended family type and the stem family type make great emphasis on family continuity possible. The conjugal family structure placed no emphasis whatsoever, or certainly no great emphasis, on the continuity of any given family unit. The family units are expected to change for everyone with each generation when the conjugal family type is the ideal structure for the membership of a society as a whole.

There are all sorts of reasons to expect an emphasis on the first two types by the members of relatively nonmodernized societies. For example, most such societies are completely lacking in any explicit set of specialized organizations for the care of the aged, who are cared for in family terms. Nevertheless, there have certainly been relatively nonmodernized societies in which conjugal family units were ideal structures. Many of the references in various literatures to the conjugal family unit as a typical family unit in relatively nonmodernized societies probably refer to the extent to which conjugal family units always exist in any society, regardless of the ideal structures, if no representatives of the older generation survive the birth of their grandchildren, no more than one son per marital couple survives to maturity, etc., and when the stem family is an ideal, the ordinary operation of members in terms of those structures leads to the existence of a large number of conjugal family units as already indicated above.

Whatever the case may be in relatively nonmodernized societies, the level of variability with regard to the ideal structures of family types is not of this order in the relatively modernized societies. Every society, regardless of the basis from which change took place, which has changed in the direction of relatively high levels of modernization has been marked by a change in the ideal structures for family types toward multilineal conjugal family units, if they were not multilineal conjugal family units before. So uniform a characteristic is probably not a function of chance. Extended family units and even stem family units are in some respects highly incompatible with other structures endemic in relatively modernized societies. There are, in the main, two types of reasons for this.

The first should be clear from much of what has been said above. The emphases on mobility of individuals, on predominantly universalistic criteria, on interdependency, on the lack of priority of family orientations, ideally speaking at least, etc., in relatively modernized social contexts are *all* incompatible with the stable existence of either extended families or stem families, as a general ideal. The second is somewhat more subtle. It will be treated somewhat more fully in the section below on the discrepancies between ideal and actual structures. Briefly this has to do with the fact that, although the extended family or some close approach to it has been quite frequently an ideal structure, it has probably never in fact been realized for more than a small minority of the members of any given society. Those who did realize such ideals on the whole constituted some elite set of member of the society rather than the general membership. With relatively high levels of modernization, for the first time, medical technology reaches a level at which it is possible for members of the general population to attain their ideal of life in extended family contexts, if they wish it. The actual problems of administering and adjusting to life in terms of such a large-scale unit probably do more to undermine it as an ideal than any other factor.

The ideal structures for large-scale family types tend to disappear in relatively modernized social contexts for two reasons: (1) adherence to such ideals makes nonfamily life difficult, and (2) achievement of those ideals makes family life difficult. Insofar as the conjugal family has not been the ideal in any given society, the change of structures in the direction of the conjugal family ideal, which accompanies modernization and frequently runs far ahead of the achieved level of modernization in a given society, is always broadly subversive of general social organizations specifically because so much of social organization in relatively nonmodernized societies is oriented to questions of significance to family members qua family members.

V

SOME SPECIAL PROBLEMS OF FAMILY STRUCTURES

There are three special, but extremely general, problems of family structures that I should like to emphasize separately here: (1) the problem of internal and external relations of the members of a given family unit, (2) the problem of adoption, and (3) the problem of some of the discrepancies between ideal and actual structures.

A. INTERNAL AND EXTERNAL RELATIONS

There is always to some extent among the members of every known society a distinction between the internal and the external relationships of family members. To some extent family members of all societies have relationships which are, from the point of view of the persons concerned, conducted entirely in family terms with other members of the family, but they also always have some relationships which are never conducted solely in family terms and/or solely with other family members no matter how family-oriented general action may be. The former relationships are those I define as *internal* to the family; the latter are those I define as *external* to the family. External relationships, as far as the family is concerned may be of two sorts: (1) relationships involving only family members but not conducted exclusively in family terms, and (2) relationships involving nonfamily members. The former of these two might be called *substantively external* and the latter might be called *ultimately external* relationships.

Some of the internal relationships characteristic of family organizations are always conditioned by external relationships. The opposite point has already been made in great detail above, i.e., to some extent the external relationships of family members are always a function of internal family considerations ideally and/or actually. In social analysis as in any other scientific analysis, it is never necessary to give all the reasons why a given hypothesis may be held. If a single reason why a given state of affairs *must* in all probability exist can be given, that is quite enough. In this connection the contention made may be justified by reference to the phenomena of marriage and the incest taboo. The ordinary layman's use of the term *marriage* will not cause trouble here. The incest taboo, on the other hand, is a concept that probably merits definition. It may be defined as follows: The term *incest taboo* refers to the set of prohibitions on sexual intercourse insofar as those prohibitions are specifically oriented to questions of membership in one or more of the various kinship units. That is to say, an incest taboo exists whenever it can be said that they are classified as kinfolk.[15]

[15] Interestingly enough the incest taboo never seems to cover homosexual relationships. There are societies, of course, whose members do not frown upon homosexual relationships at all. Insofar as homosexual relationships among family members or other kinfolk are prohibited, the prohibitions are generally in terms of the type of relationship rather than on the basis of the fact that kinfolk are involved. Thus in terms of our society homosexual relations between brothers would be frowned upon not primarily because

The incest taboo is an exceedingly interesting phenomenon, which is obviously closely related to the general question of marriage. An incest taboo of some sort exists among the ideal structures of every known society in world history. To some extent this generalization has not been explored for its full implications, partially because of what seem to be exceptions to the generalization. There certainly have been societies in terms of which specific elements in the incest taboo have been suspended for specific members of the society concerned. These especially exempted members, however, never constitute more than a tiny fraction of the general membership of the society concerned. The case of the ruling family of Egypt, the Pharaohs, is the most frequently cited. When the incest taboo is set aside as an ideal structure, it is usually set aside for some special elite group such as the members of a ruling family, but even then, only elements in it are set aside; the incest taboo as a whole is not set aside even in those cases. The incest taboo is never set aside for the general membership of a society either ideally or actually, although there may be numerous actual violations of it.

Not only does an incest taboo exist in every known society in the sense of applying to the general membership as a whole with only quite restricted exceptions if any. In all societies there is also a certain uniformity about the incest taboo as well as a range of variation in its definition. It prohibits, for members of the society in general, sexual intercourse between father and daughter, mother and son, and sister and brother.[16] Beyond these universally stipulated prohibitions which constitute the core of the incest taboo for the general membership of all known societies, the range of kinfolk covered by the incest taboo varies widely from one

they were kinfolk but because homosexual relationships in general are taboo. On the other hand sexual intercourse between brother and sister is frowned upon by members of our society specifically because a brother and sister are involved. The fact that either party to the relationship might be a minor, and hence that the relationship contribute to the delinquency of a minor, or the fact that either or both parties might be married to other individuals, and hence that the relationship be adulterous—neither of these other violations of our ideal structures with regard to heterosexual intercourse would be regarded as nearly as important in this case as the fact that the relationship involved a brother and sister and hence constituted a violation of the incest taboo.

[16] In some social contexts the biological father of a child may not be known or the concept of father may be quite different from the one to which we are ordinarily accustomed. In all cases in which the father is known, sexual intercourse between father and daughter is taboo for members of the society in general. When the father is not known, intercourse between any male who occupies a position *in loco parentis* relative to a girl of a younger generation is prohibited from having sexual relations with her as far as the membership of the society as a whole is concerned.

society to another. In traditional Chinese society, for example, from the point of view of a strict Confucian any two individuals of the same surname were regarded as being related to one another through the paternal line. Any heterosexual relations between any two such individuals were in violation of the incest taboo—even if the members of the girl's family had lived, let us say, in Peking for a thousand years and the members of the boy's family had lived in Canton for a thousand years with no contacts of any sort among the members of the various families during all that time. In modern United States society, apart from the common core of relationships tabooed as incestuous everywhere, the incest taboo does not reach out much beyond the range of first cousins and in some areas of legal jurisdiction it does not include first cousins. In terms of traditional Chinese society the incest taboo would cover any relationship between first cousins who were related to one another via the male line, but it would not cover those whom we would consider first cousins of other types. Indeed, in some Chinese circles, marriages between first cousins of these other types were preferred marriages.

In any society the incest taboo forbids certain types of sexual relationships internal to the family membership. Insofar as the prohibitions are observed and insofar as there is any interest whatsoever in perpetuating that family unit or forming others, operations in terms of the incest taboo require that family members have external relationships at least to the extent necessary to marry sons and/or daughters into other families or to form new families. Correspondingly, there must also be external relations to the extent necessary to acquire sons and/or daughters from other family contexts either to continue their own by becoming spouses of existing family members or to form new family units involving the family members of the younger generation and their spouses.

Thus as a minimum, given the observation of some form of the incest taboo, the practice of marriage always requires that there be some external relationships among existing family members and the members of some other families. Furthermore, once spouses marry into a given family unit their internal relationships in the family unit into which they have married will to some extent be conditioned by the fact that they come into the family environment from outside, as it were. To some extent for a time at least, they are marginal insofar as they are strangers. Frequently, these individuals come into their new family settings relatively quite low in the order of precedence and power, ideally and/or actually speaking. This was certainly dramatically the case in traditional Chinese society. When family members must get involved in external relationships in order to acquire a spouse, even if the new family of procreation is an entirely separate family for both spouses, the fact that the relationship is based on what were previously considered relationships external to the family background of each party will to some extent condition and determine their behavior in their new family setting. The higher the emphasis in general in the society on family orientation, the more important these considerations are likely to be.

The minimal implications of the incest taboo and the formation of marriages never exhaust the external relationships or their internal implications. In any society in which governmental organizations exist as subsystems, and these certainly exist in any society of any considerable scale, there is always the possibility, if not the probability, of some interrelationships among family members and members of a governmental subsystem. The implications of marriage and the incest taboo are never the only limits on family self-sufficiency. In societies of any considerable scale, in addition to some interfamily relationships, there are always some relationships with members of local or neighborhood organizations and governmental organizations. There are also probably always some with members of some predominantly economically oriented organizations, predominantly religiously oriented organizations, etc.

In the context of relatively modernized societies, of course, the problem of external relationships is enormously significant as far as family analysis is concerned. After the period of quite early infancy and childhood, almost all members of such societies spend a great deal of their time outside their family contexts. The time spent outside is not spent in terms of a single or a small number of nonfamily organizations. Increasingly as the individual matures, he operates daily in terms of an enormously complicated assortment of highly differentiated, highly specialized organizations. These operations, ideally and/or actually, always have implications for his internal family relations and vice versa. Even when ideally speaking the individual's relationships outside the family are expected to be kept carefully separated from his internal family relationships or his other external relationships carried out at least in part for family purposes or in family terms, these relationships always have at least the implication of having to be kept carefully separate. In relatively modernized social contexts, the high evaluation on many such separations to the contrary notwithstanding, the surprising thing is not how often family and nonfamily considerations which are expected to be kept separate in fact impinge importantly on one another; the surprising thing is that they can be kept separate at all. The relative ease with which members of relatively modernized societies keep such things separate to the degree that they do is one of the minor exotic miracles of life in terms of relatively modernized societies.

B. ADOPTION

Social kinship is never identical with biological kinship. Kinship phenomena in general would be a great deal simpler if they were identical, since the mechanics of biological kinship are identical for all members of many species, and it is certainly identical for all human beings as far as we can tell. At the present state of our knowledge, however, we cannot account for such phenomena as differing emphases on lines of descent, places of residence, the incest taboo, etc., in purely biological terms. Moreover, we know of no society with kinship structures lacking in some elements nonbiologically determined in this sense. The phenomenon of *adoption* is a special case of the structures of social kinship as distinguished from biological kinship. As far as I know, individuals of no other species have structures of adoption, though there are certainly instances of abandoned or orphaned young of some species who have been taken in by adults who are not their biological parents. *Adoption* may be defined as the acquisition of some individual to fulfill, at least in part, a specific family role ordinarily fulfilled by birth [in the case of marriage by adoption the individual involved is always absorbed in some family role ordinarily filled by birth prior to the marriage].[17] The person adopted may be a complete outsider or may be shifted from some other kinship role. Since adoption involves the endowment of an individual with some particular family role not previously held by him [or her], the expectations and procedures ordinarily present with regard to the role in question are likely to be high-lighted during the process of adoption. This is particularly the case if the adoption is not made in infancy. The problem of socializing and integrating an individual in a role different from his past one after action appropriate to that past one has already been taught him always requires some special procedures. Since the process of adoption must throw special emphasis on matters which might otherwise be taken for granted, it may in many cases serve as a

[17] This definition, with a slight change in wording, is taken from *The Family Revolution in Modern China*, pp. 34 and 35. In this discussion I have taken over that definition and some of the following remarks with only slight modification.

sort of socially underlined or spotlighted example of the particular relationship for which it substitutes. In some sense the roles of an adopted family member are always different from that of a member who acquires his roles by birth, but they need not be different in the respects relevant for many particular questions. Insofar as they are different, the strategic value of attention to adoption is not diminished thereby, since the very difference makes the phenomenon particularly revealing about the relationships for which it substitutes.

Adoption is crucial for family stability. Even given modern medical technology, it is impossible to count with complete reliability on all of the roles important for the kinship structures of a given society in general or for the family structures in particular to be fulfilled by operation in terms of the ordinary structures of kinship apart from adoption. A given married pair may, for example, have only daughters when the kinship structures of the society stipulate the reckoning of descent in the male line. Parents may die before a child can shift for himself as even a precocious adult, etc. There are many other reasons for adoption. These vary with the ideal structures of kinship in a given society. It should be quite possible to infer much about adoption structures from a knowledge of ideal kinship structures in general. Societies vary with regard to how much difference family stability makes both to general stability and the preferences of the members of society. For example, adoption is not pursued by members of modern United States society primarily in order to ensure family stability but rather with regard to the creation of a fuller life for both parents and children. Ideally speaking, in modern United States society, family units are stable as intergenerational units only for the nonadult life of the children. A marital pair without children is under no great pressure to adopt children out of loyalty to the ancestors, etc. Couples without children are not considered by many to lead a full family life, but the choice is regarded as entirely up to them. On the other hand, the stability of any individual family unit is not only regarded as of relatively little significance to the members of the society as a whole, but its implications are not necessarily significant for the members of that family themselves. In America, for example, care of the parents in their old age is not ordinarily dependent upon their having children—certainly it is not ideally dependent upon that.

For most societies the situation is and has been quite different. Usually filling of the various proper family roles is a matter of the greatest interest and concern to other family members. Whether this has to do with the needs for protection, the needs for labor, orientation to ancestor worship, or whatever, need not detain the discussion here. Some form of adoption is universal in all known societies, and prior to the development of relatively modernized societies at least, from the point of view of the actors involved in the process, adoption has always been justified by more than personal hedonism, however altruistic, or charity. To some extent in the contexts of all of these societies, adoption has to do with the maintenance of family units as family members and others in the society generally feel they should be. In those social contexts, usually, family members cannot fulfill their family roles or their nonfamily roles if they do not have the various roles of their family units properly staffed. It is, of course, true that not every member of a society in terms of which adoption is both approved and enjoined is in fact able to adopt the individuals desired, but in most societies—certainly in the relatively nonmodernized ones—adoption procedures are considered important by the general membership of the society.

The way in which adoption procedures fit into the structure of family stability varies not only with the structures of the family concerned, but also with the manner in which family units fit into the rest of the social structure of the society concerned. There is, however, a special case in which adoption is important for those who study social phenomena with a view to their implications for problems of public and international affairs. Most societies have been relatively nonmodernized ones, and even today few societies have achieved high levels of modernization. The lower the level of modernization in a given society, the greater is likely to be the general orientation of behavior to family considerations. Various positions of considerable administrative importance are correspondingly likely to be staffed on a kinship basis ideally and/or actually. Sometimes this goes so far that, ideally as well as actually, most important positions are inherited. Talent for such positions, however, is not necessarily inherited. Adoption may serve as a special sort of civil service structure in such societies. There is reason to believe that this took place and was important for Tokugawa Japan.[18] The adoption of individuals who showed special talent for a given administrative role not only improved the quality of individuals in such roles, it also wedded the family interest of those individuals and the objectives sought in terms of the offices they held in a fashion such that there were few or no contradictory possibilities for them in terms of the various systems to which they belonged.

[18] See pp. 117–118, and 396.

The Japanese case of civil service by adoption is particularly intersting, because it is an example of a predominantly particularistic device—specifically of a nepotistic one—which has effects that we associate only with predominantly universalistic means. It resulted in the utilization of a much higher level of talent with a lower level of self-interested exploitation of office than could otherwise have been achieved in terms of that society. In this respect the results compare favorably with the results achieved in terms of the Chinese bureaucratic system which to all outward appearances was considerably more modern and placed much more easily recognizable emphases on predominantly universalistic criteria. By the standards of members of highly modernized societies the intrusion of kinship considerations into selection for important offices outside the kinship sphere is generally taken for granted to be not only evil, but also subversive of the interests of the organization into which administrators are so introduced. This is not inevitably the case. In the process of modernization it is frequently of the essence of public policy to find methods of combatting nepotism. It is also of the essence of subtle public policy that one be able to distinguish among nepotistic practices so that one does not weed out those with at least temporary positive implications for development along with those which are likely to cause nothing but trouble in the process.

C. SOME DISCREPANCIES BETWEEN IDEAL AND ACTUAL STRUCTURES

Consideration of these discrepancies points to considerations about families not ordinarily made explicit. There are a great many commonplaces generally accepted about family and kinship matters which upon close examination prove to be neither commonplace nor acceptable. For example, when a society is referred to as polygamous, we generally think of one whose average adult male member has two or more wives [polygynous] or whose average adult female member has two or more husbands [polyandrous]. Probably no such societies have ever existed. There no doubt have been societies, perhaps many of them, in terms of which, ideally speaking, every man hoped to have two or more wives, or every woman two or more husbands, but actually speaking such a society would have to have a whole set of bizarre customs for this to be the case. In all known societies the ratio of males to females at birth is slightly in excess of unity. For the average man to have two or more wives would require either an unusual death rate among men, a singular structure of inherited wives, an exotically varied structure of divorce, or some combination of those improbables and others. This is especially the case since the concept of polygamy is not ordinarily considered fulfilled unless the husband or wife concerned has multiple spouses at a given point in time. Thus the high divorce rate of some individuals in highly modernized contexts, though referred to sarcastically as serial polygamy, is not considered to be true polygamy. Whatever the ideal structures may or may not be, the actual structures of every society referred to as polygamous turn out to be ones in terms of which some members literally do have plural spouses. Ordinarily such individuals constitute an elite set and they always constitute a minority of the eligible members of the society concerned. Plural wives were certainly considered a good thing by traditional Chinese, but only a small minority of adult Chinese males ever achieved this felicitous marital state.

Insofar as the existence of multiple spouses is viewed as a problem, it is more likely to increase as a problem with generally prosperous conditions in terms of any society and especially with the rapidly rising standard of living so characteristic of increasing modernization. Under these circumstances many individuals who would not have been able to have multiple spouses under previous circumstances are, by former standards, able to afford them. It should also be kept in mind that any increase in multiple spouses under all save the most unusual circumstances goes hand in hand with an increased problem for other members in the society in achieving the kind of marital state considered minimally satisfactory. Given the ordinary ratio of males to females, if one man has more than one wife, at least one other man is unable to acquire any at all. Thus in actuality any society in terms of which the members of an elite set practice polygamy is also a society in terms of which some other set of individuals is certain to be maritally deprived. The maritally deprived are extremely likely to be disaffected by this state of affairs. Lots of individuals have endured such a state of affairs throughout the entire period of their lives during which, ideally speaking, they were expected to be married. Specific organizations in specific societies have regarded celibacy as a good thing, but the practice has never been institutionalized for the general membership of any stable society as a whole and has rarely proved popular even if the society were doomed. The sect of Shakers is fascinating, among other reasons specifically because the religion of the members forbade any sexual relations among members, and on the whole the membership lived up to those precepts. Since outside recruitment failed, the religion was doomed long before the last of its true believers died.

With the development of modernization, the increase of polygamous practices is always confined, if it takes place at all, to the initial stages of modernization. In that period, former ideal structures of multiple spouses may continue while the new developments increase the number of members of the society who can in fact afford multiple spousage. The increase is not likely to continue long. For a whole set of reasons, which need not detain the argument here, no relatively modernized society has structures of polygamy as ideal structures.

The question of polygamy, however illustrative, is a relatively small matter in the tendency to read the ideal structures with regard to kinship and the family as the actual ones. The most important set of implications of this distinction has to do with what members generally belong to the *actual family unit* in a given society. There are many ways in which a family unit may vary. It is by no means easy to get at all of these important types of variation in any quantitative sense, but there are some lines of quantitative variation that are relatively simple to get at. Ideal family structures vary widely from society to society with regard to the numbers of generations represented, the number of members, the sex distribution of the members, the age distribution of the members, the number of siblings plus their wives who belong to the family unit, etc. In the discussion above of the extended family, the stem family, and the conjugal family, much of the discussion rested on what was referred to as the vertical and horizontal proliferation of family membership.[19]

In the relatively nonmodernized societies of world history, insofar as the ideal family unit has been other than the conjugal or nuclear family, for the vast majority of members of the society

[19] There is a considerable body of opinion among sociologists and anthropologists which holds that the conjugal family, or the nuclear family, is *the* ideal family unit for every known society. I take the position that this is not the case either ideally or actually in the vast majority of all societies. I would go further and say that not only is this demonstrably false empirically, it is also not a fruitful assumption theoretically. The details of this argument are technical and need not detain us here. Anyone interested in the controversy can pursue it in the following works: G. P. Murdock, *Social Structure*, The Macmillan Company, New York, 1949; T. Parsons and F. Bales, *Family Socialization and Interaction Process*, The Free Press, Glencoe, 1955; N. W. Bell and E. F. Vogel (ed.), *The Family*, The Free Press, Glencoe, 1960; A. J. Coale, L. M. Fallers, M. J. Levy, Jr., D. M. Schneider, and S. S. Tomkins, *Aspects of the Analysis of Family Structure* (Princeton University Press, Princeton, 1965); T. Parsons "The Incest Taboo in Relation to Social Structure and the Socialization of the Child," *British Journal of Sociology*, vol. 5, no. 2, June, 1954, pp. 101–117; and M. J. Levy, Jr., "Some Questions about Parsons' Treatment of the Incest Problem," *British Journal of Sociology*, vol. 6, no. 3, Sept., 1955, pp. 277–285.

attainment of that family ideal has been impossible. Those ideals generally call for the inclusion of representatives of more than two generations as members of the ideal family unit, at least two marital pairs, etc. In general these ideals have not been attainable for reasons which become obvious as soon as one considers the birth and death rates. Relatively few grandparents have survived the birth of their grandchildren for any considerable period, and relatively few siblings in excess of two per marital pair have survived to maturity as members of any given family unit. Thus unless the structures of adoption go far beyond the adoption of nonadult children who are orphaned prior to maturity for a large number of people or beyond the adoption of sons, for example, to continue the family line of family members lacking sons for one reason or another, the attainment of ideal families with numerous members has been out of the question for the vast majority of all people throughout all history. Given the kind of demographic rates characteristic of relatively nonmodernized social contexts, the average size of family units, given an extended family ideal of the type discussed above with adoption structures roughly like those of traditional China, is only seventy-five per cent greater than would have been the case had the ideal in fact been a nuclear family. With the kind of distribution of families by size one would expect under these circumstances, well over fifty per cent of the units would be ones in terms of which the distribution of generations, numbers, ages, sex, etc., would be what would have occurred had the ideal been a nuclear family one. There is reason to believe that societies are conceivable and not unknown in which special structures of adoption or other forms of fictive kinship permit large family aggregations, but in most societies of considerable scale this has probably not been the case. It certainly has not been the case of many quite large-scale societies which have frequently been described as though their members actually did achieve their large ideal extended or stem type family units.[20]

[20] Demography is too powerful a tool of analysis to be "wasted on" [i.e., left confined to] professional demographers. By no means all social phenomena can be predicted from a knowledge of birth rates, death rates, age and sex distributions, etc., but these are almost never irrelevant either. Furthermore, in attempts to gather social data across difficult language barriers, there are likely to be fewer boners when demographic questions are asked than when most others are. Finally, the level of analytic and statistical sophistication of the professional demographers about their materials and the increasing comparative scope and quality of those materials raise the value of the tool still further. It might well make sense with regard to most general hypotheses in social science to inquire initially as to their demographic implications and check them out via those *façade hypotheses* in demographic terms.

The argument that the nuclear family is not the ideal family for all societies is an important one, however, since the variation in ideal structures from one society to another, despite the much greater uniformity of actual structures than has generally been assumed, has important implications. Some of the sources of stress and strain implicit in those societies are a function of the fact that the ideal and actual structures do not coincide. Just as importantly, some of the possibilities of adjustment and stability which do exist from the family point of view are also a function of the fact that the ideal and actual structures do not coincide. In addition, insofar as family ideals call for large family memberships, once modern medical technology is introduced, actual family sizes are likely to balloon. Particularly in the early stages of modernization, the implications of the fact that not all societies are characterized by nuclear families as ideal families are likely to be striking, just as in the case of ideal structures of polygamy. For the first time in the history of many of these societies one gets actual family units approaching in size of membership those which people have always said they wished to live in terms of. This approach to the ideal structures may account as much as anything else for the fact that in all of the relatively modernized societies the ideal structures have changed to or toward conjugal or nuclear ones. No matter how earnestly such large memberships are desired, they are not necessarily easy to hold together or administer. As these ideals become actual, stresses and strains develop along with them. The previous discrepancy between ideal and actual structures may make it even more difficult to live with the old ideal structures as they are approached. This as much as the classical citation of the greater certainty of survival of descendents and the possibility of weighing additional children against additional income and advantages for the other children may account for some of the changes in ideal family structure characteristic of all societies after their members sustain contact wth the members of relatively modernized societies and after the change in the direction of relatively modernized structures begins for them.

V I
FAMILY AND NATIONAL STRUCTURES

Despite the recent vogue for national character studies with many of the attendant explanations of Japanese character in terms of toilet training, of Russian character in terms of swaddling, and United States character in terms of lack of breastfeeding, the general subject of the relation between kinship structures in general [and family structures in particular] and nations has hardly been begun. For present purposes I would not want to initiate the discussion beyond the categories of kinship-oriented nations and nonkinship-oriented nations and the subdivision of the former into explicitly kinship-oriented nations and implicitly kinship-oriented nations.

A. KINSHIP-ORIENTED NATIONS

1. EXPLICITLY KINSHIP-ORIENTED NATIONS

I define a nation as *explicitly kinship-oriented* insofar as its government is directly based on kinship structures. From this point of view it is necessary to differentiate at least three types of nations. The first is a nation characterized by an hereditary ruling house whose members genuinely rule the members of the nation. The second is a nation characterized not necessarily by a single ruling house but by a set of hereditary feudal lords. In both these cases the family structures of the ruling house and of the hereditary lords are of the essence in understanding the government of the nation itself.[21] The third case is a nation characterized by a governmental organization in terms of which action is largely oriented to interrelating members of specific clans, lineages, tribes, etc. In this case too the structures of the kinship units in general and probably of the families in particular are of the essence in any understanding of the governmental organization. Such cases are usually a special case of one of the first two since they tend to be characterized by hereditary ruling houses or sets of hereditary feudal lords. It is at least conceivable, however, that this not be the case. Such a govenment could well be a government by a council involving the heads of clans or lineages or tribes, etc., and not thereby be characterized by any hereditary ruling house or any set of hereditary feudal lords.

2. IMPLICITLY KINSHIP-ORIENTED NATIONS

I define a nation as *implicitly kinship-oriented* if kinship orientation is the major or even secondary orientation of the vast majority of the members of the nation regardless of whether or not it is specifically characterized by an hereditary ruling house or one of

[21] I would leave aside for the moment whether one wishes to use the term nation in so narrow a sense that one cannot speak of nationalism as having developed until quite recently. For those for whom the term nation has such a connotation the term *country* may be substituted without alteration of the meaning intended here. The intent here is to use a term which tends to identify closely the concept of the society and the government which is a subsystem of that society.

the other two forms mentioned immediately above.[22] In such a society in the last analysis a considerable part of the structure of control over all of the members of the society would depend on the stability of family control for the individual members. This type of society is perhaps especially difficult for the highly modernized to understand. Traditional Chinese society was an explicitly kinship-oriented nation in the sense that it was characterized by an hereditary ruling house, but it was even more importantly an implicitly kinship-oriented nation in that the general structure of control of the society in general and of the government in particular depended upon the stability of family control throughout the society. The government of such a society need not necessarily be based on particular hereditary units. It is, however, a society in which family particularism must have a high place in all ethical decisions, all criteria for selection, etc., with relatively rare and/or carefully worked out exceptions. Ideally speaking, the Chinese bureaucracy was always such an exception. Actually speaking, the structures of graft and corruption which characterized Chinese bureaucracy were importantly a function of the fact that such exceptions could not be maintained.

B. NONKINSHIP-ORIENTED NATIONS

All of the so-called relatively modernized nations are in this sense nonkinship-oriented nations. A few like Great Britain and Japan may have nominal hereditary ruling houses, but their members do not in fact rule. The effective governments of these nations are not hereditarily recruited organizations nor does the general structure of control in the society rest primarily on family control. Rarely, if ever, in the context of these societies do the individuals representing the government depend on family units to control other individuals as the members of the government would have them controlled. In the United States setting, for example, one can see this clearly in the problems immediately raised if someone proposes to hold parents responsible for the acts of juvenile delinquents. Not only are these societies in terms of which the sins of the fathers are not, ideally speaking, visited upon the children to the second generation, let alone the third or fourth. They are also explicitly societies in terms of which, ideally speaking, the sins of the younger generation individuals are not visited upon individuals of the older generation as is exceedingly likely to be the case in either explicitly or implicitly kinship-oriented nations.

There are special problems for these societies too. In the two

[22] Therefore a given nation can be both explicitly and implicitly kinship-oriented.

types of nations mentioned above one of the major problems is how it is possible to get narrow family interests set sufficiently aside so that the national organization is not undermined in order to serve particular family interests. The problem in nonkinship-oriented nations is how sufficient control and prestige can be maintained in terms of family units so that stable and mature adults can be developed, at least partially, in terms of them. There would seem to be a dilemma in general facing the members of any society. If kinship has a sufficiently high priority, it is easy enough to ensure for children the kind of family attention which makes the development of stable adults possible, but it is difficult to keep kinship considerations from interfering with other ones. If kinship considerations do not take a sufficient priority, it may in the long run prove difficult to hold family units together sufficiently long to ensure for children the kind of affective attention necessary for the development of stable and mature adults. In addition in relatively modernized social contexts, the problem is further complicated by the fact that in terms of those family units, as already pointed out above, it is necessary to socialize children for an unknown future. The children of the members of all relatively modernized societies from early stages of development learn not only that their families do not count for everything, but that in an enormous number of contexts neither their family units nor the most important members of them count for much of anything at all. It may not seem too difficult under these circumstances to maintain on the part of individuals of the older generation a sufficient interest in and attention to the individuals of the younger generation of their family units. It may, however, prove increasingly difficult to maintain sufficient levels of respect by individuals of the younger generation for individuals of the older generation so that the effects of that attention can produce adults capable of operating in nonfamily contexts for the overwhelming proportion of their time. Increasingly it is characteristic of our kind of societies that the young come to realize not only that their parents do not necessarily count for much outside the family context, but also that even within it they do not necessarily know what it is they are trying to rear their children for.

VII

CLOSING REMARKS

There are few phenomena of concern to man which have received so much attention as those of the family and kinship. These phenomena figure prominently in artistic literatures of all sorts, in theology, in philosophy, in ethical discussions, in history, and in all of the so-called social science disciplines. From the modern scientific point of view, exploration of these phenomena are in the stage of infancy. There is one special form of naïveté in these matters against which I would warn. Again and again the creative imagination of writers has led them to a description of future societies in which family phenomena have been eliminated or virtually eliminated. Political leaders have actually made claims of the same sort of achievement as in the case of the early claims asserted about the Chinese communes. Social scientists have claimed on occasion that the role of the family has been eliminated or reduced to virtual meaninglessness. None of these claims have yet held up. The kibbutzim of the state of Israel are frequently cited as examples of organizations in terms which children are no longer reared by their parents. The description of life in terms of these organizations has been used or interpreted as raising the question of whether family organizations are requisites for a society. So far the researches indicate no such thing. In the kibbutzim case, family organizations were not entirely eliminated nor was the role of parents in the rearing of their children negligible. In the second place, it has not yet been shown definitively that children reared as they in fact were in the kibbutzim turned into stable mature adults, though they may well do so. Finally, even were both these things true of the kibbutzim, it would not follow that this state of affairs could exist for society as a whole, since the members of these organizations certainly do not constitute the whole or even a large proportion of the total membership of that society, nor do they appear to constitute the membership of independent separate societies. The claims of the rulers of China today on this score were greeted with an almost mediaeval awe. They need not have been. There was no reason to believe that the communes had in fact been put into effect in the way and to the extent claimed by the leaders. Later the leaders themselves withdrew such extreme claims.

It is improbable that there will ever be a stable society not characterized by some form of family organization. In relatively modernized societies the position of family organization in the general social structure, ideally speaking at least, is a great deal more restricted than has been the case in any other form of society in world history. Even in all known cases of relatively modernized societies, however, a transition from a society in which family organizations exist and in terms of which the kinds of socialization already noted here take place to a society in which for the average individual no such organization whatsoever exists will constitute a social change more far-reaching in its implications than the invention or the dropping of any other type of social organization. The implications of such a change will go well beyond those of the industrial revolution, the "political" revolution of the eighteenth century, the communist revolution, the development of capitalism, and the development of relatively modernized societies. It may be difficult, if not impossible for the present, to prove theoretically that such a development cannot take place and have societies remain stable, but the implications of such a development would be sufficiently radical and dramatic to justify a high level of skepticism in the face of any future unsupported claims that a social revolution of such magnitude has been achieved with ease overnight.

GOVERNMENTS AND ASSOCIATED UNITS

I
DEFINITIONS AND INTRODUCTION
A. GOVERNMENT

A *government* is defined here as a predominantly politically oriented organization considered by its members and the other members of the society to be the organization in terms of which the general problems of order as a whole for the society, including in those problems questions of order insofar as they involve the members of that society and members of other societies, are handled. The concept intended here is generally handled in the literature of social science by defining the government as an organization whose representatives have a monopoly of the legitimate use of force. The latter, however, is a concept of government somewhat too narrowly defined for general purposes. The government of traditional Chinese society, for example, was certainly conceived as the organization in terms of which the most general problems of order for that society were handled, but its representatives certainly did not have a monopoly of the legitimate use of force. There were quite legitimate uses of force on the basis of family units, village units, etc. These were not conceived of as subsystems of the government in the ordinary sense, though they were highly significant for the general structures of control on which governmental representatives relied. The members of relatively modernized societies certainly conceive the government to be at least the overwhelming focus of the monopoly of the legitimate use of force. Their use of force, even within the family context for purposes of discipline, is quite restricted and above all subject to legitimate review by governmental representatives if excesses exist or are suspected of existing. In some societies, feudal societies being a good example, governments may be extremely *weak* in that relatively few questions are considered to be general problems of order for the members of the society as a whole and the ability of representatives of the government to exert control over others in these matters is quite limited. Under such circumstances governmental subsystems, say a given fief, may be turned into a separate government or even become a subsystem of another government with considerable facility. If the representatives of the government also have a monopoly of the legitimate use of force, and especially if it is effective, i.e., if they are *strong,* such facile changes in subsystems are unlikely.

Like all of the other organizations discussed here, a government is conceived as a system of action in terms of which the members of the government operate. It is not conceived as a set of individuals, though it certainly involves a set of individuals. The membership of a governmental organization is rarely, if ever, identical with the membership of the society at large. Members of the society at large who are not members of the government may influence the operations of others in terms of the governmental systems by such obviously politically oriented behavior as voting, but they may also influence them in other ways as well. For example, recently in the United States the members of a leading business firm in the steel industry influenced by their actions developments in the structures of the government of the United States in a dramatic and generally unpredicted fashion. These individuals were certainly not acting in any ordinary sense as members of the government at that time. Nevertheless, they contributed considerably to the increase of centralization in terms of the government regardless of whether they or the governmental officials involved intended this or not.

Among relatively nonmodernized societies there may be instances in which no governmental organization as such is specialized out of the general set of social subsystems. Governments in societies of considerable scale, however, vary widely, both ideally and actually, with regard to the extent to which the general problems of order are handled in governmental terms and to which their members, qua members, are regarded as having a legitimate monopoly of the use of force; they vary greatly in strength and stability; but in some form they always exist as subsystems of such societies. Parenthetically, the range of variation possible in these respects, if a society is to be stable, is considerably less for relatively modernized societies. If any relatively modernized society is to persist, its governmental organizations must be clearly specialized out of the general social structure; their members must be regarded as having a monopoly of the legitimate use of force; and they must be strong and stable.[1]

[1] This has nothing whatsoever to do with whether governments in such societies are likeable. In relatively modernized societies if the governments are not strong and stable the society cannot be stable. The term *strength* is used here to refer to the effectiveness of the force at the disposal of the members of the government if they feel called upon to use it as a means.

B. ASSOCIATED UNITS

In many societies there are predominantly politically oriented organizations closely associated with governmental organizations though quite distinct from them. As a minimum these organizations are predominantly politically oriented by virtue of the fact that, from the point of view of their members, action in terms of them is predominantly oriented to influencing action in terms of the government. There has probably never been a society characterized by a government which did not include to some extent nongovernmental predominantly politically oriented cliques of some sort, but the type of associated unit of greatest relevance here is the political party. Political parties have already been mentioned briefly [see pp. 328–330] as predominantly politically oriented parties. In general discussions of government today few concepts are more often invoked than that of political parties, but relatively little seems to be known about them in any highly abstract sense, and much of the general thinking about them by politicians, the general public, and political scientists is exceedingly naïve. In many areas of the world, especially the so-called underdeveloped areas it seems to be broadly assumed that if a certain amount of campaign literature, enough arm bands, and the like are issued that a political party has been created. Nothing could be more misleading. Mass stimulation and participation is no substitute for party organization.

Armed forces in general, i.e., armies, navies, air forces, are sometimes treated as though they were associated units in the sense intended here. They are not save in the cases in which they are nongovernmental armed forces. Most of the armed forces of concern to students of, and persons of responsibility in, public affairs are specific subsystems of the governments concerned. From my point of view they are sufficiently important, and for quite general academic reasons as well as others sufficiently neglected, to justify treatment in a separate chapter [pp. 571–605].

If there were no governmental organization as a subsystem of a given society, there would be no need for the concept of associated units. Even if a government is separated out of the general social structure, the various interrelated units need not be politically specialized associated units as that concept is defined here. Apart from relatively small-scale predominantly politically oriented cliques which are always present, actually [or both ideally and actually] whenever there are governments, there need not be any predominantly politically oriented nongovernmental units. When there is a government, in some sense all other units in the society are in some respect interrelated with the governmental unit. Even the most isolated highly self-sufficient family unit is potentially subject to such interrelationship via taxes and the like, though in fact its members may have little or no direct contact with the members of governmental organizations. It is by no means unusual for influence to be brought to bear in governmental contexts via action in terms of kinship organizations, predominantly economically oriented organizations, predominantly religiously oriented organizations, etc. None of these are predominantly politically oriented associated units, and this constitutes another of those major lines of variation which characterize societies. There is no case of a relatively modernized society lacking in either a government or predominantly politically oriented associated units. It is quite conceivable that there be relatively nonmodernized societies characterized by governments but not characterized by such associated units.

I I

SOME GENERAL PROBLEMS OF GOVERNMENT

A. THE PROBLEM OF STABILITY

It is still fashionable to consider the problems of stability of governments as having two major foci: (1) the problem of *external stability* and (2) the problem of *internal stability*. The problem of external stability has to do with what might generally be considered the ordinary field of international relations. Is a given governmental organization going to continue to exist in stable form, given the interrelationships carried out, at least partially, in terms of it with the members of other governments? Is it likely to become a subsystem of other governments? Are its members likely to get involved in warfare with the members of other governments and win, lose, or draw? Can it be maintained either in isolation or in a state of interdependency with other sets of governments, etc.? The problems of external stability seen in this light are partly functions of the size and strength of the membership of the society in which the government is found, of the type of society, and of the membership of the government itself, but these factors must also be considered in conjunction with the international settings in which the government exists. Problems of external stability of governments are generally discussed in terms of war, diplomacy, subversion, international trade, etc.

In this chapter the problem of internal stability is the major problem for consideration, and that problem is so important in understanding governments that it will be taken up separately below [see pp. 475–495]. For the moment suffice it to say that the problem of internal stability of a government is the problem of the way in which the government is interrelated with other organizations in the society. It is a problem that is subject to a large number of solutions, if not an indefinite number of solutions. Under given circumstances it may have no solution at all, in which case both the government itself and the society in which it is found will be unstable. For some types of society, however, considerable amounts of instability of the actual governmental organization may be combined with relatively high levels of stability of the general society. This is certainly not the case of relatively modernized societies. For such societies the viable range of change in governmental organizations is closely related to the viable range of social change in general. The relative lack of self-sufficiency of units in the society generally *means* that changes in any unit are to that extent the more likely to spread generally throughout the social structure. The implications of changes in a unit as strategically placed as a government in the general social structure of these societies spread far, fast, and inevitably.

Increasingly in all the world today, there are no domestic problems of any considerable importance that lack international implications, and there are no international problems of any considerable importance that lack domestic implications. If at some future date there exists, either ideally or actually, an effective world government, this may cease to be the case, but it will only cease to be the case to the extent that what we formerly viewed as the governments of separable societies have become governmental subsystems of the government of some more general society of the world. Short of that development, or some catastrophic war during which a considerable portion of mankind and the techniques and possibilities of communication of the mankind left are destroyed, the old-fashioned separability of these two problems of stability is never likely to make sense again. The increasing degrees of interdependence among the members of societies in general and of governments in particular have made concepts such as the freedom, independence, and total sovereignty of governments a method of begging questions, however appealing they may be ethically. Increasingly it has also made the problems of internal and external governmental stability one.

B. THE PROBLEM OF RECRUITMENT

A government is not a society, and though it may be family-based, it is not a family either. There are societies in terms of which individuals are born into the government. For example, the eldest son of an autocratic ruler may have a governmental role from birth—in fact it is difficult for him to escape one even though he has no awareness of it.[2] There are, however, plenty of societies in terms of which governmental roles are not acquired at birth, and even in societies in terms of which some governmental roles are acquired at birth, by no means all of them are. Thus in the context of all societies there is a problem of recruitment of members for the government. How are individuals made members of governmental organizations?

Parenthetically, there is also a question of the *derecruitment* of individual members of the government i.e., the question of discharge and retirement. Mortality takes care of this if a long enough time span is involved. The role of death as an acceptable means of flushing out members of any organization has decreased radically with the improvement of medical technology. Prior to the development of modern medical technology, the life expectancy was such that problems raised by the senility of members of the government were, on the whole, infrequent, although they could be critical.[3] Even so, in the vast majority of governments of relatively nonmodernized societies, there have been retirement structures. It should also be added that there are always reasons other than senility for getting people out of organizations in general and governments in particular, as well as into them. In relatively modernized social contexts these problems are much more acute. The life expectancy of the members of such societies takes care of relatively few such problems. In the absence of quite specific structures of discharge and retirement the incidence of senility could make the government of any relatively modernized society unstable.

The structures of recruitment frequently imply the structures of elimination. This is necessarily the case if the structures of recruitment are predominantly universalistic, but it is by no means so well defined if the structures are predominantly particularistic. The presence of the latter either ideally or actually—and even the unintended development of such criteria after initial recruitment on a predominantly universalistic basis—always carries with it a redundancy of personnel in the government.

The individual in most cases does not become a member of the

[2] Malice domestic may strike him dead before he can pronounce such words.

[3] One should be cautious; in the absence of modern medical technology with the accompanying states of diet, etc., senility may be more precocious than we like to think it.

government until he is considered to be a mature member of the society. Indeed, membership in the government or eligibility for membership in the government is frequently taken to be one of the signs par excellence of general maturity. There are fascinating phenomena associated with this consideration. In Tokugawa Japan succession to important governmental positions was generally hereditary. Life expectancy was relatively short. Legitimate successors to such positions were, as it were, members of the various governmental organizations from birth. Given the factors of life expectancy, many of them had to succeed to their positions at early ages. If they were young children, the regency device was utilized, and as in the case of all regencies, the problem of getting the regent to let go was not negligible. Only one of the subtleties of this problem in Tokugawa Japan is especially relevant here. The ceremony par excellence denoting maturity for those of the warrior or *bushi* class in general was known as the *gempuku* ceremony. This ceremony characteristically took place for a young bushi or *samurai* at the age of fifteen or sixteen. For the sons of the main feudal lords such as the *Shogun* or the *Daimyo* this ceremony took place at a much earlier age, sometimes as early as the age of five or six. This was a society whose members placed a tremendous amount of emphasis on the precedence associated with age. To go through the ceremony of maturity at a much earlier age was a special mark of prestige, and incidentally it gave the added precedence of simulated greater age. It implied that people of such exalted position matured earlier than others. It had the additional effect in these cases of increasing the burden of proof on a regent if he were to justify a prolonged regency, since from the age of five or six on, ideally speaking, the rulers whom they represented were supposed to be fully mature and ·capable.

Even when individuals become members of the government by birth, as is frequently the case in explicitly family-oriented nations, such individuals do not become effective members of the government until they are considered mature. If they succeed to positions prior to their maturity, some form of regency or the like has to be invented for them. The problems of recruitment for a governmental organization are, therefore, always different from the problems of recruitment for kinship organizations. For kinship units recruitment of members by marriage, adoption, etc., may be somewhat similar to the problems of recruitment in general for governmental organizations. For families, however, a major portion of the total recruitment is via birth, and *from birth* the infants are actually, if not ideally, fully effective members of their family units despite the fact that their roles will change and expand with increasing maturity.

The concepts of particularism and universalism developed above [pp. 140–143] applies here. Recruitment for governmental membership may be on the basis of predominantly particularistic criteria. If recruitment is predominantly particularistic, kinship is likely to be the main basis of the particularism. Ideally speaking, membership in the government may be determined on the basis of predominantly particularistic criteria alone. Actually speaking, even in the most particularistically defined governmental organizations some recognition of ability, some selection on the basis of predominantly universalistic criteria, generally takes place. On the other hand, this is not necessarily the case. The levels of talent necessary for governmental purposes may be so evenly distributed among the available members of the society that recruitment on the basis of predominantly particularistic criteria does not create any particular problems for efficiency, or if it does, the members of the government and the members of the society may simply suffer the consequences.

In some social contexts recruitment for governmental purposes is, ideally speaking, predominantly universalistic, overwhelmingly so. This is necessarily characteristic of relatively modernized societies, but many instances are known in terms of relatively nonmodernized societies, though the degree of emphasis on predominantly universalistic criteria characteristic of such societies is relatively more restricted than it is in relatively modernized contexts. Whatever the difference in emphasis between relatively modernized and relatively nonmodernized societies, in any society in terms of which predominantly universalistic criteria are emphasized there will in fact always be a considerable intrusion of predominantly particularistic criteria. There will be a far more massive intrusion of predominantly particularistic criteria in a context in which predominantly universalistic recruitment of governmental personnel is emphasized than there will be an intrusion of predominantly univeralistic criteria in a context in which predominantly particularistic recruitment is emphasized. The reasons are simple. First, there can be no such thing as absolutely purely universalistic criteria in any society since in any and all societies some kinship experiences [or lack of them] do influence the life chances of every individual to some extent. Second, it is much easier to insulate predominantly particularistically recruited organizations against the intrusion of predominantly universalistic criteria than it is to insulate predominantly universalistically recruited organizations against the intrusion of predominantly particularistic criteria. In a society whose members emphasize predominantly particularistic criteria in the governmental sphere, there are probably no great interdependent spheres in which predominantly universalistic criteria are emphasized. Whenever predominantly universalistic criteria are emphasized in the governmental recruitment, however, there are always some critically important organizational contexts in which predominantly particularistic criteria are emphasized. All of these societies always have some kinship organizations, i.e., families as a minimum, and in addition there are always other predominantly particularistically recruited organizations as well. Third, whenever predominantly universalistic criteria are emphasized, there is not only the probability that there will be departures in the direction of particularism because actually some social barring in recruitment will be considered; there are in addition those departures from predominantly universalistic criteria because nongermane considerations will also enter. Ideally speaking, the ability to pay for a given governmental position certainly does not constitute social barring in some relatively modernized contexts, but ideally speaking, it certainly does represent the intrusion of nongermane criteria into the recruitment process. Finally, to some extent, such criteria are bound to enter, if only because of the dearth of adequate knowledge. Therefore, it is always more difficult to maintain given levels of predominantly universalistic recruitment than to maintain corresponding levels of predominantly particularistic recruitment for any governmental organization—or for any organization for that matter. What are generally considered to be modern governments are much harder to maintain in any close approximation to their ideal structures than are relatively nonmodernized governments insofar as members of the latter emphasize predominantly particularistic criteria, ideally speaking, and the members of the former emphasize predominantly universalistic criteria.[4]

Since the problems of recruitment on a predominantly universalistic basis have a great deal of relevance for the problem of stability of governmental organizations in relatively modernized social contexts, this is tantamount to holding that the problems of stability of governmental organizations in the context of rela-

[4] These reasons tell why, as a minimum, it is naïve to attempt to differentiate Western from Non-Western [or modern from nonmodern, or underdeveloped from developed] governments by alleging the latter to be characterized by cliques, nepotism, etc., and presumably the former not to be. The probability is overwhelming that both are and that in both such phenomena are important. The differences inhere more importantly in differences between ideal and actual structures in the two cases, how these structures interrelate with others, etc.

tively modernized societies, in one respect at least, are greater in principle than the problems of stability need be in relatively nonmodernized societies.

Another problem of recruitment has to do with whether or not the governmental organizations tend to be bureaucratic or nonbureaucratic. Societies of any considerable scale, if stable, tend to be organized at least in part on a bureaucratic basis. In relatively nonmodernized societies that part is overwhelmingly likely to be in the governmental sphere. To some extent this tendency has been ignored for two reasons. The first of these is probably the fact that Max Weber who is both justifiably and to a stifling degree the patron saint of studies of bureaucracy listed only six major examples of bureaucratic systems in world history. It has not occurred to many to question the *maître,* and in addition they have had relatively little reason to since few have been interested in any cases of bureaucracy other than the ones described by Weber as characteristic of relatively modernized societies. The second reason that other cases have been ignored is that which probably led Max Weber himself to overlook them. Every case mentioned by Max Weber is a bureaucratic system, ideally speaking, but Weber was on the whole not deeply interested in the "ideal—actual" [5] distinction as a general matter although he was capable of making adroit and sophisticated use of it, either implicitly or explicitly, in specific contexts. Tokugawa Japan is a classic case of quite highly developed bureaucratic subsystems, actually speaking, in a setting which, ideally speaking, calls for nothing of the sort.

There are three types of problems of recruitment connected with the bureaucratic–nonbureaucratic distinction. First, there is the problem of selection, via ideal and/or actual structures, of personnel for such service. Second, there is the problem of insulating bureaucratic personnel from non-bureacratic pressures of all sorts—keeping them recruited, as it were. Third there is the problem of keeping the bureaucratic influence on bureaucratic personnel from undermining their proper functioning in nonbureaucratic contexts—that is the problem of insulating the non-bureaucratic contexts from bureaucratic influence. I shall illustrate in terms of two types of societies in which bureaucratic systems exist ideally speaking as well as actually, and one type of society in which bureaucratic systems do not exist ideally though they do exist actually.

Whether or not a society is relatively modernized is relevant to

[5] This concept *ideal* is not to be confused with Weber's *ideal type*—a concept in which he was deeply interested.

discussions of ideal and actual bureaucratic systems. The distinction does not arise with regard to the situation in which a bureaucratic system(s) exists actually but not ideally since that situation characterizes only relatively nonmodernized societies. In all relatively modernized societies, bureaucratic systems, in vast profusion always exist ideally as well as actually in the context of governmental systems and many others as well.[6]

The development of a bureaucratic system, ideally speaking, in a relatively nonmodernized society poses, in an especially acute form, the question of how one can select certain individuals out of a predominantly particularistic, traditional, functionally diffuse set of relationships and introduce them on a predominantly rational, universalistic, and functionally specific basis into a system of operation in terms of which the latter standards are expected to be maintained. In such recruitment one must either find some method of selecting a set of individuals and schooling them in a generally different set of ideals for conduct, or one must find some specific device for insulating individuals chosen for these positions from the ordinary context of social affairs. The problem is further complicated by virtue of the fact that principles subversive of smooth operation in terms of the bureaucracy are not only widely prevalent actually in the society, but they in fact constitute the ideal structures of that society for most relationships of most of the people most of the time. It is virtually out of the question to get the general membership of such societies to regard the extension of the principles which they ordinarily take for granted in nearly all other social contexts as unwarranted in the bureaucratic context. Most of the relatively nonmodernized societies whose members have developed such bureaucratic systems are societies whose members have attempted to use specific methods of insulation. In the traditional Chinese context one forbade an official to serve in the province in which his family lived, for example, although this device never really prevented nepotistic influences. There are cases in social history in which eunuchs have been used for such positions. Their special mayhem pre-

[6] It is absolutely essential that no one be misled by the extent to which the word *bureaucracy* itself has become the butt of virtually everyone's annoyance with the behavior of some governmental personnel in relatively moderized societies and the extent to which it in humor or in serious conversation tends to figure as a derogatory term. Despite all this, if one leaves such words out of the discussion and asks members of relatively modernized societies to describe the fashion in which they feel the governmental personnel ought to work, ought to be organized, the way their recruitment ought to be handled, etc., he will get from them a relatively clear-cut description of a bureaucratic system.

sumably insulated them from the nepotistic influences which would ordinarily attend to succession by inheritance. For the famous Janizariat, young children presumably from a different social setting and of a different religious faith were selected and specially trained outside of the general context of the society in which they would operate as officials. They were given great power, but forbidden legitimate marital relations.[7] Ideally speaking these devices were presumed to keep the members of the Janizariat out of the main stream of particularistic influences in the society in which they operated.

None of these devices worked very well. The surprising thing is that any of them worked at all. The price of universalistic criteria in even the most highly modernized societies is eternal vigilance. The members of relatively modernized societies, however, do not have to attempt to maintain a small island of predominantly universalistic criteria in a social sea of overwhelmingly particularistic influences. At least in relatively modernized societies there is an ocean of general relationships which ideally speaking, at least, are predominantly universalistic as well as important land masses of predominantly particularistically recruited organizations. In relatively nonmodernized societies, whenever bureaucratic structures exist, ideally speaking, those structures never show any great likelihood of spreading throughout the general population. Rather the reverse. Those structures are continually under pressure, if they are to be maintained at all. In the long run they always break down radically. One of the unique features of traditional Chinese history lay in the fact that, despite the fact that the structures continually broke down in just this fashion they were continually refurbished and restored in virtually the same form once every few centuries for approximately two thousand years.

The trick of bureaucratic recruitment in a social context in which a bureaucracy(ies) exists as a governmental system actually though not ideally lies in the method in which it can be combined with major foci of nonbureaucratic forms of organization. It is overwhelmingly probable that this combination will involve some sort of explicit hook-up between family [or other kinship] organization and the government. In other words all such cases are likely to be cases of predominantly kinship-oriented nations. This was certainly the case in Tokugawa Japan. In relatively nonmodernized societies whenever a bureaucratic

[7] See H. A. R. Gibb and H. Bowen: *Islamic Society and the West*, vol. I, part I, Oxford, 1950, and A. H. Lybyer: *The Government of the Ottoman Empire in the Time of Suleimen the Magnificent*, Harvard, 1912.

system exists, ideally the trick is to keep family considerations [8] from being relevant to operations in terms of the bureaucracy. As a practical matter this is out of the question. In the case in which the bureaucratic system exists actually though not ideally the trick is just the reverse. The problem is to get the system to the point that nothing is so relevant to family considerations as proper behavior in terms of the bureaucratic system. The only really highly developed case of this with which I am familiar is that of Tokugawa Japan. This, of course, was a system in which actual bureaucratic office was hereditary on the whole. The loyalty of the members of the bureaucracy to their bureaucratic offices not only took priority over other family considerations but was considered the number one priority from the family point of view as well. As far as recruitment was concerned, initial recruitment at least was overwhelmingly on the basis of kinship, but if the kin concerned were not well suited to the position, one's highest duty lay in making sure that properly qualified kin were available—by adoption if necessary. This structure of recruitment was considerably less vulnerable to general particularistic influences, indeed such invulnerability as it had was a function of those influences.

For the members of relatively modernized societies the problems of bureaucratic recruitment are quite different. They are greatly eased by the widespread general emphasis on the kind of criteria ideally suited to bureaucratic systems. The problems here are of two sorts. The first is the general problem of maintaining high and general emphases on predominantly rational, universalistic, functionally specific relationships in general. The second has to do with the daily interaction of members of the bureaucracy in the bureaucratic and the nonbureaucratic contexts of their lives. Here, as in any bureaucratic system, there is always the question of nepotistic influences in the classic sense, but there is another set which is subtly different. In general the emphasis on family organizations and the like does not threaten to undermine the bureaucratic structures as a set of ideal structures at all. If anything, the reverse is true. The implications of behavior in bureaucratic contexts continually raises problems for the maintenance of stability of other types of organizations—especially of family units. To the very extent that, ideally speaking, a given bureaucratic unit is completely separate from the family units of its members, individuals acting in terms of the bureaucratic sys-

[8] And one is not likely to get into any difficulty by using family considerations to symbolize if not summarize the kind of predominantly particularistic influences which are likely to be brought to bear.

tem are used, use others, and behave in general without consideration for the implications of their behavior for the other organizations in which they have roles and in terms of which they interact with other individuals. Those implications, however, are none the less inescapable. They are likely to be implications which are major foci of stress and strain. Insofar as this is the case, the effects on operations in terms of the bureaucratic structure are primarily a function of what those stresses and strains do to the motivation, efficiency, responsibility, energy, etc., of the members of the bureaucracy. There is a sense in which in relatively modernized social contexts neuroses which are importantly a function of the implications of action in terms of bureaucratic systems for one's operation in family contexts—that such neuroses—are a much greater problem for the members of bureaucratic systems in relatively modernized societies than nepotism.

Nonbureaucratic structures of recruitment are usually characteristic of governments in relatively nonmodernized societies. They become increasingly peripheral under relatively modernized conditions. When nonbureaucratic structures of recruitment are characteristic both ideally and actually of the governmental organizations of relatively nonmodernized societies, they tend to be small in scale, subject to high levels of decentralization, and/or relatively unstable. Governments characterized by nonbureaucratic structures of recruitment pose serious problems for the transition to modernization. These are serious problems in most of the so-called emerging new nations. For many of these existence as a nation is fortuitous organizationally speaking. In some cases the nation is arbitrarily constituted of the set of social systems found in a particular territory previously under colonial administration. One of the first problems, once colonial administration is removed, is the creation of some sort of coherent relatively stable social system from a set of what are except for the imposition of colonial administration entirely separate or at least highly decentralized small-scale social systems. Most of the previously existing governmental devices are replaced, and the implications simply of increasing the interdependence of these social systems is far-reaching and unsettling though the exact form taken may vary widely.

In all governmental contexts there are special problems of recruitment of the personnel of what may be regarded as the central foci or the central focus of governmental organization—governmental leadership. In the thinking of modern social scientists the question of governmental leadership tends to be identified overwhelmingly with the executive aspect of the government. This is particularly a problem for social scientists reared in the United States, since we tend to think of the executive aspects of government as not only sharply differentiated from the legislative and judicial aspects, but as especially embodied in separate organizations to boot. For the vast majority of governments, as has been pointed out above, this has not been the case. Governmental leadership covers all three aspects as indeed it does for modern United States society, in fact, regardless of what our ideal structures of separation of powers may be.

There are in general three forms of recruitment of the central foci or focus of governments: (1) recruitment on predominantly particularistic grounds, (2) charismatic recruitment,[9] and (3) predominantly universalistic recruitment.

When the recruitment of the governmental leadership is predominantly particularistic, the basis of those criteria, ideally and actually, is overwhelmingly likely to be kinship in some form or other. Hereditary monarchs, nobles, chiefs, etc., are well-known examples. Such criteria maximize the stability of governmental systems insofar as stability is related to clear-cut criteria for succession to office. These criteria can be exceedingly clear-cut, and insofar as they are overwhelmingly likely to be based on kinship, they are clear-cut criteria which are generally extremely well understood by the members of any society. When the criteria for recruitment for the central foci are ideally overwhelmingly particularistic, the societies are always relatively nonmodernized societies. It has been noted again and again above that the members of all such societies place heavy emphasis on kinship orientations in general and family orientations in particular in most matters of selection. The great problem posed by such criteria lies in the fact that abilities germane to crucial roles in government are not necessarily highly correlated with the criteria for succession to the role. The greater the relevance of specific abilities to success in these roles, the greater is the problem of stability of governments characterized by such ideal structures.

[9] Charismatic recruitment is probably always, in the last analysis, predominantly particularistic despite the fact that charismatic leadership roles usually rest on important elements of achievement. In the "making" of charismatic leaders, however, social barring is frequently involved as is nongermaneness. As the relationship of leader and followers continues, nongermane elements are likely to increase, if only because the faith placed in the leader is sure to outrun the adequacy of his knowledge. Thus in a sense the category of charismatic leadership is redundant given the other two, and/or represents a departure to a different basis of classification. However, charismatic leadership is sufficiently important to merit the separate stress given it here.

At the same time even in the most highly modernized societies particularistic elements enter into recruitment—even recruitment of the most important leadership roles. Insofar as they enter, they tend to enter actually rather than ideally speaking. Ideally speaking, the members of virtually every relatively modernized society feel that achievement relevant to the offices concerned and that alone should determine leadership. In recent years the election of President Kennedy in the United States was considered an outstanding demonstration of the fact that devout belief in the Catholic religion did not bar one socially from the Presidency.

Insofar as particularistic elements enter into leadership choices in relatively modernized societies, they tend increasingly to do so by way of nongermane criteria rather than social barring. It may be necessary for one to belong to a particular political party from which no one is socially barred in order to hold a particular office. In some cases membership in that particular political party may be germane only in the sense that it is impossible to hold one of those offices without being a member. It is quite possible to be a member of the party concerned and not have the relevant ability. Nevertheless, in those cases the members are overwhelmingly likely to feel that achievement is what is being emphasized and should be emphasized. As will be taken up in the third case below, the members of relatively modernized societies are almost inevitably placed on the defensive if they are accused of recruiting their major leadership roles in the government—or any other organization for that matter—primarily on the basis of predominantly particularistic criteria.

Charismatic leadership is a special phenomenon in social history. The general question of charisma has already been discussed [see pp. 350–353]. Charismatic leaders have followers who have blind faith in their leaders. It is a classic case of the attitude "theirs not to reason why, theirs but to do or die." Charismatic leaders may characterize either relatively nonmodernized societies or relatively modernized ones. Governments dominated by charismatic leaders are inevitably unstable no matter where they appear. Such leaders have maximum flexibility for rapid and extreme alteration of governmental policies. If their policy choices are disastrously wrong-headed, they can literally pull their houses down about their ears. There are excellent examples in history in general and in modern history in particular. Adolf Hitler was exactly such a leader.

There are two sources of instability associated with charismatic leadership. First, like any other important political leaders, charismatic ones can make calamitous policy choices. After all, like any other leaders, it is unlikely that they make the correct choice for stability every time. Theirs is, however, a special sort of complete power unbalanced by responsibility. If charismatic leaders make an incorrect choice in this sense and do not change their minds, there is not likely to be any member of their societies or any organization whose members can stop them.[10]

The second great source of instability for charismatic leaders is the problem of succession. The greater the charismatic power of such a leader, the more difficult is the problem of succession. The more blindly his followers believe in him, the greater is the gap between himself and any successor, regardless of whether he designates his successor or not. Furthermore, within the lifetime of such a leader, the more any other individual is built up as a successor, the more likely he is to be viewed as a threat by the charismatic leader. The role of charismatic leadership is usually an achieved role; indeed in some sense it is always an achieved role. Down through history, from Alexander the Great on, such leaders have not been able to direct stably the inheritance of their charisma. In the contexts of relatively modernized societies some of the problems of charismatic leadership are intensified. From many points of view, the great asset of a charismatic leader in these contexts is that the problem of coordination and control of the general membership of the society is minimized to the extent that he is blindly accepted. They will do what he tells them—at least they will try to do what he tells them. Under such circumstances however, the problem of his having exactly the right knowledge at his disposal, of making exactly the right decisions, is maximized. The effects of any incorrect decision spread with maximum rapidity and maximum implications for instability throughout the social structure in general. This, by contrast with the implications in a relatively nonmodernized context, would follow from the high levels of interdependency characteristic of relatively modernized societies.

Recruitment of the crucial leadership of a society primarily on the basis of predominantly universalistic criteria is rare in general social history. There are examples of it in terms of relatively nonmodernized societies, but in such contexts, it is likely to be actually rather than ideally the case. There probably are cases of

[10] For example, it was no one member and no set of members of German society who were able to stop Hitler even when some of his policy decisions were known to be catastrophically irrational from the point of view of Germans. He was stopped by a coalition of members of other societies.

relatively nonmodernized societies in terms of which such recruitment has existed both ideally and actually, say via tests of strength or the like, but they certainly are not characteristic of any large number of cases of societies of any considerable scale. In general the recruitment ideally and actually of the leadership roles of the government on the basis of predominantly universalistic criteria is quite modern and quite rare. None of the societies whose members emphasize such ideal structures so strongly have ever carried the actual structures of recruitment nearly so far as their ideal statements might lead one to expect. Cases like that of Great Britain are certainly no exception. The monarch of Great Britain is not the central focus of government. She [or he] is only the symbol of government.

The problem of the ability of the leadership of the governments of relatively modernized societies increases steadily. At the same time, the probability of any single individual having all of the relevant abilities decreases at least as steadily. As far as stability is concerned, one of the most important implications of selection of leadership on predominantly universalistic bases is that, if such leaders fail, they are relatively easier to get rid of on exactly similar bases insofar as actual structures approach ideal ones. As far as the problem of succession is concerned, predominantly universalistic recruitment is also highly relevant for an understanding of such societies. Neither of the other two types of recruitment necessarily accents relevant abilities. Neither of the other two types of recruitment increases the ease of rejection of leaders on the basis of failure. But above all, in relatively modernized social contexts neither of the other two sets of criteria for governmental leadership fits in so well with the general criteria for recruitment in the governmental sphere and, increasingly, in other nonkinship spheres. If one were to try to institutionalize overwhelmingly particularistic criteria for such leadership in the context of relatively modernized societies, one would be faced with the obverse of the problem of the traditional Chinese bureaucracy. One would have to insulate this position from an increasingly general emphasis on universalism in relevant spheres. Quite apart from the implications of predominantly particularistic criteria for selection on the basis of ability, in relatively modernized social contexts one would find it even more difficult to try to keep the recruitment ideally particularistic than to strive to make it completely universalistic. The emphasis of the members of such societies ideally speaking is so overwhelmingly on predominantly universalistic criteria *in such spheres* that we tend to be preoccupied with the extent to which particularistic elements continue to enter no matter how much we attempt to eliminate them. In this preoccupation we loose sight of the extent to which it is quite out of the question to go back to overwhelmingly particularistic criteria, ideally speaking, in such recruitment.

C. THE PROBLEM OF ECONOMIC ALLOCATION

In relatively stable social contexts, even in the case of small-scale societies, whenever a government is distinguished, the government is usually the largest single organization involved in the allocation of goods and services in the society. If it is not, the government tends to be unstable and perhaps the society is as well, or what is considered to be the government, ideally speaking, is not the government actually. In feudal societies, for example, if the fief of some noble is larger and more important than the king's, the king usually has an unstable position or an ineffective one as a focus of government. In Tokugawa Japan the Emperor did not head the largest or most important single unit in the allocation of goods and services in the society, but he was certainly not the major actual focus of government either. In that society the central government was the Shogun's government. It definitely was the largest such unit, and it was carefully calculated to remain so. If one takes as the governmental system of feudal societies the systems of the king plus his major vassals, then once again there is no question that the governmental unit is the largest unit in terms of which the allocation of goods and services takes place, however much the attention of the members of the government may be focussed on the allocation of power and responsibility.

The major elements relevant here are not difficult to specify. First, there is the general paraphernalia of government. There is the capital required for the members of a government to operate, the personnel who somehow must be supported, etc. The accent on centralization evidenced in the government of relatively non-modernized societies may be quite restricted, but insofar as it is present at all, it requires some effectively greater magnitude of the government than any of the major organizations in the decentralization, if the government is to be stable.

Second, there are the armed forces. Some conception of these is always present even if the use of armed forces is only visualized for the internal maintenance of order, and even if the members of the armed-force organizations are only called up in an emergency. If the armed-force personnel at the control of the members of the government do not exceed those at the control of members of other units in the society, the stability of the government is precarious. A pure monopoly of the legitimate use of force need not characterize such governments, but some predominance in the use of legitimate force is necessary if they are to be stable. Armed-force organizations are notoriously expensive.

Third, associated with the governmental unit is likely to be what may be considered the general equipment of the society, especially that equipment having to do with the general means of communications. A government whose members cannot dominate the means of communication of the members of a society cannot dominate the members. All governments, like all other units, have to be characterized by sources of revenue to cover costs of the operations in terms of them. General taxation of one sort or another is one possibility. Insofar as taxation is general, the government in terms of which it is handled is likely to be the largest single unit in terms of which the allocation of goods and services takes place for this reason alone. In many cases, ideally speaking, the major leader of the government is expected to have the biggest personal fortune of any member of the society. This is generally the case of feudal societies at least as far as the actual leader is concerned. Whatever the case may be, ideally speaking, if the government is stable, it is unlikely that the personal fortune of the head of the government is the sole source of revenue of the members of the government. Even if that personal fortune is larger than the resources at the control of any other member or even set of members of the society, it is usually supplemented from other sources.

Fourth, whenever money and markets exist, and they tend to exist in all societies of any considerable scale, sooner or later members of the government as representatives of the government must take a hand in them if the government is to be stable. The general relevance of economic allocation to the allocation of power and responsibility and vice versa make some such involvement inescapable. It is important to realize that the *laissez-faire* ideal in its classic form was specifically a movement for the elimination of special private privilege sanctioned by governmental power. It was never an argument for eliminating all concern by members of the government with the allocation of goods and services. The *laissez-faire* ideal certainly held that the "government should get out of business," but it also held that the "government should keep business out of government" and keep an individual business from turning into the effective government in the sphere of operations of its members.

III
MAJOR FORMS OF GOVERNMENT

A. INTRODUCTION

The treatment here is not directly concerned with any of the conventional distinctions among the major forms of governments such as monarchy, aristocracy, democracy, etc. The concern here with the major forms of governments turns not upon their forms in general but on specific aspects of their forms especially relevant to the interdependencies of governmental organizations with other organizations in the society. For these purposes I shall return again to the distinctions among predominantly particularistic, charismatic, and predominantly universalistic forms, but this time the concern will be with the forms in general and not solely with the central foci or leadership of governments. The distinctions among local, feudal, and national governments will be pursued briefly, and other differentiations such as democratic versus authoritarian and capitalistic versus socialistic forms of government will be discussed briefly from the point of view of the problems presented by such concepts.

B. PREDOMINANTLY PARTICULARISTIC, CHARISMATIC, AND PREDOMINANTLY UNIVERSALISTIC FORMS OF GOVERNMENT

When I speak of predominantly particularistic governments, I mean quite simply governments in terms of which personnel are, ideally speaking, chosen on the basis of who they are rather than on the basis of what they can do. In the technical discussion of particularism above [see pp. 140–143] I defined the term particularism so that it could be used to refer to criteria which either involve social barring or nongermaness or some combination of the two. As far as the ideal structures of government are concerned, the element of particularism tends to inhere in the category of social barring rather than in the category of nongermaness. From the point of view of the members of the society, the basis of social barring is generally considered highly germane to the purposes of selection. Even in societies whose members, ideally speaking, suppose the government to be a predominantly particularistically recruited unit in general, the particularism inherent in nongermaness is more likely to enter actually than ideally. Personnel is never deliberately and self-consciously chosen for governmental purposes on irrelevant bases.

Prior to the development to relatively modernized societies, the overwhelming majority of governments of considerable scale were predominantly particularistic, and kinship was the major basis of that particularism. There were exceptions, of course. Traditional Chinese society was characterized by a governmental organization which, ideally speaking at least, was predominantly universalistic save for the central focus of the government, the Emperor. Actually there, as in so many other cases, particularistic influences easily infiltrated despite the ideals to the contrary. Most of the infiltration was kinship influence, but there were other forms as well. Nevertheless, prior to the development of relatively modernized societies, there were few cases of societies of any considerable scale for which predominantly universalistic criteria for the selection of governmental personnel even appear as ideal structures.

If these, or any governments, are to be stable, and if the societies in which these governments exist are to be stable, some of the members of the government must be men of genuine achievement. Predominantly particularistic governments, however, are not ones for which the qualifications for genuine achievement can be set and individuals sought who fill them. In these governmental contexts, save for the uncertainties of life expectancy, it is generally known far in advance *who* will fill given positions. There may be some uncertainty as to whether the individual concerned will in fact have the proper qualifications and there are usually devices—actual if not ideal devices—for some shifting about if he lacks the relevant qualifications, but the overwhelming emphasis has to rest on methods of socialization such that the particularistically preordained incumbent will in fact have the minimum qualifications necessary. Thus, to some extent, there must be specialized socialization structures for the preordained governmental personnel.

Since the basis of their preordination is generally kinship ideally speaking, those specialized structures of socialization are associated with the specific kinship organizations of the persons concerned. They appear as subsystems within such organizations, as an aspect of ordinary operation in terms of the structures of such organizations, or as specialized organizations set up by the members of some particular set of kinship units. These individuals constitute an elite set, of course, and in most relatively nonmodernized contexts they get most of their special education for their future government posts from other family members, special tutors brought into the family setting, and on the job once they have assumed their positions. It is not easy to transform such a system overnight since some new basis for creating the necessary qualifications in persons selected on a different basis is a prerequisite if any departure from the existing system is to succeed.

Another consideration is relevant here. Although any government must be staffed by some able personnel if it is to be stable, particularly in relatively nonmodernized contexts characterized by high levels of decentralization, the level of abilities required may be such that the general recruitment from a predominantly particularistically defined set of individuals may make relatively little difference in the talent available by contrast with alternative methods of selection. This is by no means always the case in relatively nonmodernized societies, and it is never the case in relatively modernized ones.

I have indicated above that it is not only conceivable that a given government have a predominantly particularistically recruited central focus but a relatively universalistically recruited operating force as in the case of the Imperial Bureaucracy of traditional China. The governmental systems of relatively nonmodernized societies tend to be overwhelmingly particularistic throughout. Having the central leadership recruited in one way while the generally operating members of the government are recruited differently poses special problems in and of itself. The major problem of such governments is the problem of the necessary levels of ability. As already indicated, the levels of abilities needed are not necessarily high even in cases of considerable scale, provided that the general society is sufficiently nonmodernized and the level of decentralization sufficiently high. To the extent that ability is needed, it can be created by use of specialized socialization structures or even by use of specialized schools. There is yet another solution to this problem. This is one mentioned above in other connections—the possibility that results similar to those which would be obtained if predominantly universalistic criteria were employed can be obtained by balances of various particularistic criteria, whether those be intended or unintended. A frequent though modest instance of this is to be found in village government in a wide variety of relatively nonmodernized societies. These organizations are frequently run primarily by representatives of the different familes whose members reside in the village area. Representatives of one of those families, if sufficiently more powerful than the representatives of the others, will frequently exploit all the others for their own ends, but usually there is a balance of family interests such that solutions are not narrowly identified with the interest of any single set of family members. In the government of a fairly large-scale society the structures of civil service by adoption referred to in the case of Tokugawa Japan constitute an example of this sort.

Most of the societies characterized by predominantly particularistic governments, ideally speaking, are sedentary societies. In such situations careful study of history and respect for precedent will go a long way toward substituting for high levels of intellectual ability and imagination. If what the ancestors did was "right," it is likely to continue to be right more or less indefinitely. In addition, predominantly particularistic selection of governmental personnel—especially insofar that this is likely to be done on the basis of kinship—minimizes the problems of succession to office, not just for the most important leaders, but for the membership of the government in general. This in turn has implications for the level of ability required of the general leadership.

Such recruitment, however, commonly does carry with it one special problem. This is the problem previously referred to as the cadet problem. The number of positions in a given governmental organization cannot be expanded indefinitely. Insofar as succession is inherited and the number of positions fairly stable, some sort of selection must be made among siblings of the same sex to determine who succeeds. The usual principle is that of primogeniture, but whatever the principle, it would inevitably imply some set of individuals who are reared for a type of life they cannot expect to follow in the fullest sense. This problem has in the past been minimized in turn by virtue of the fact that life expectancy in terms of such societies has usually been such that not many more than one son, for example, per family have survived to maturity. On the other hand, *somewhat more* than one son *always* survived to maturity for some individuals, and this was more likely to be the case among the members of wealthy or more elite families than among the population at large. Many different factors would have to be explored before one could determine what the maximum percentage of cadet members of a system could be without there being special problems of handling them, but in theory there is some such percentage for any given society in terms of which cadets are systematically created. Moreover, in theory that percentage is probably a relatively modest one. There is another reason why the cadet problem is likely to be especially great when an important office is largely determined by kinship. The cadets are not only educated so that they could succeed and likely disgruntled because they have not, they are also likely to know where every major "body is buried" both in the various governmental contexts and in the family contexts that count. Cadets from the point of view of the observer of any given society are likely to combine the maximum of temptation, facility, and opportunity for mischief.

Charismatic governments differ radically from what I have refered to as predominantly particularistic or predominantly universalistic governments. The latter two terms can characterize the basis for selection for the vast majority of the personnel, ideally speaking, in a given governmental organization. There is no such thing as a charismatic government in the sense that the vast majority of the personnel in the governmental organization are recruited on a charismatic basis—only the leader is charismatic. Ordinarily the general personnel in such a government, whatever the ideal structures of selection may be, are importantly selected on predominantly particularistic grounds—and on capriciously particularistic grounds at that. There may be relatively little emphasis on social barring in the selection of these personnel. The real problem as far as their selection is concerned is generally the nongermaneness of the criteria. One of the most important features in their selection is the question of whether or not they have happened to strike the fancy of the charismatic leader [if they are high enough up in the hierarchy] or whether or not the people who selected them thought they would strike the fancy of the leader. At lower levels many of these personnel may be selected on predominantly universalistic grounds, but the selection criteria are always subject to change—capriciously. Whatever the ideal structures for the general selection of personnel for charismatic governments, for a host of important positions the selection is likely to be on the basis of capricious particularism.

Charismatic governments have had spectacular short-run histories. They have in general been highly unstable. Two types of instability are characteristic of these governments. First, charismatic governments are inherently unstable with regard to problems of succession. Second, the instability has to do with the fact that charismatic leaders and their subordinates are exceedingly likely to make mistakes that lead to internal chaos and/or create a situation such that the members of other societies feel that they must somehow unite and bring the government under such leadership "to its knees." There have been many charismatic leaders in history who were not governmental leaders, but there have been virtually no charismatic governmental leaders who have not been substantially identified with military exploits, both at home and abroad.

To an extent seldom achieved by any other form of government charismatic governments are governments of men rather than governments of principle, or of law, or of whatever. The personality of the charismatic leader is of overwhelming importance in understanding such governments, and that personality is crucial as far down into the ranks of general governmental personnel as he chooses to dip, either systematically or by whim. The general phenomenon of charismatic leadership has been spectacular in social history and far-reaching in its significance. We lack systematic materials on the major similarities and the major variations in the personalities of the outstanding charismatic figures in history. We do not know what sort of conditions are likely to produce such individuals, and beyond banalities, we do not even know with any precision what sort of circumstances are likely to predispose considerable masses of the members of a given society to create charismatic leaders by having blind faith in them. It is not enough to say that such leaders tend to develop and devotion to them increases under circumstances of considerable stress and strain, of high uncertainty, of confusion and despair, etc. They are in fact relatively rare in social history, and there is a sense in which any relatively rare phenomenon in social history which has far-reaching implications for other elements is likely to be a source of stress and strain from the point of view of some members of the society.

Although it may be difficult to predict with any certainty when and where charismatic governmental leaders will arise and put generally charismatic governments into effect in their wake, such phenomena are certainly not confined to relatively nonmodernized societies. They have arisen quite recently in social history in the context of several relatively highly modernized societies, and they will probably continue to arise. Furthermore, they have arisen, and they are extremely likely to arise again, in the context of societies in transition to a relatively modernized state. Whenever they arise, they will prove unstable, and usually within a relatively short period of time. In the societies in transition toward relative modernization, one quality of charismatic governments is likely to seem particularly attractive. This has to do with the fact that the leaders of such governments can coordinate and control large masses of the members of their societies with relative ease. In both relatively modernized societies and those in transition, however, any errors in policy decisions on the part of the charismatic leaders will have especially far-reaching implications because of the much higher degree of interdependency characteristic of such societies in general and the ticklish problems of transition in particular.

Predominantly universalistic governments are not necessarily democratic governments. It is quite possible to have a governmental organization into which people may be admitted solely on the basis of their abilities or largely on such a basis and in terms which they may rise to great heights on predominantly universalistic grounds without those governments having much in common with what are generally considered to be democratic governments. Apart from the capricious particularism oriented to party membership, most of the members of highly authoritarian governments in relatively modernized societies have actually placed great emphasis on predominantly universalistic criteria within quite broad limits, despite the fact that some of those governments have been charismatic ones. Apart from party particularism, there are probably few governments in the world today characterized by more predominantly universalistic structures, according to the lights of their own members, than the present government of Communist China.

Predominantly universalistic governments must be governments of law rather than governments of men. In the last analysis it is impossible for a charismatic government to be a government of law, and the element of capriciousness so introduced is one of the main vulnerabilities of charismatic governments in relatively modernized and also in relatively nonmodernized social contexts. In relatively modernized societies the levels of interdependency and specialization required for day-to-day operation cannot be achieved unless individuals in governmental roles can be shifted about, substituted, and replaced. This requires explicit, well codified rules.

From the point of view of governmental stability, the greatest asset of predominantly universalistic governments lies in the emphasis placed on recruitment for ability and the check on incompetence in office. The great vulnerability of such governments is the problem of how governmental personnel are to be insulated against predominantly particularistic considerations. Such insulation must exist both in the process of selection and in the operation of such personnel after selection. These problems are much greater in relatively nonmodernized societies in which the general nongovernmental setting of activity of governmental personnel is far more highly particularistic than in the case of relatively modernized societies. It is never eliminated in the latter either, though.

Closely associated with this question of vulnerability is the problem of training prospective personnel for office. Unless access to the training facilities is widespread, important elements of particularistic selection remain. If any educated man may aspire to office, but only a few relatively wealthy individuals can afford education for their fellow family members, the universalistic criteria apply only within a restricted range, no matter how purely universalistic they may be within that range. The members of traditional Chinese society placed an emphasis on universalistic criteria for membership in the government organization rarely equaled in relatively nonmodernized social contexts. Actually, however, access to the relevant educational opportunities was quite restricted. To some extent, interestingly enough, there were some overwhelmingly particularistic devices which increased the actual levels of universalism in that society. For example, sometimes the members of clan organizations would set up special schools so that poor members of the clan, who ordinarily would have been unable to afford either the tuition or associated costs, might get the kind of education necessary. Nevertheless, the level of universalistic emphasis called for by the ideal structures of that society was radically interferred with by restricted educational opportunities.

The problem of recall for incompetence without creating a chaotic situation is endemic in the context of predominantly universalistic governments. First, the necessity for such recall is inescapably a reflection of the methods of selection. Much more important than this, however, is the fact that, human beings being what they are, there tends to develop a sort of *particularism on the scene*. As individuals work together, it is exceedingly difficult to maintain predominantly universalistic relationships without the impairment of morale. The parties to such continuing and important relationships, even in the most highly modernized social contexts, apparently like to be considered as individuals. To consider them so is, of course, to consider them, at least in part, on the basis of who they are rather than on the basis of what they can do that is relevant. To the extent that anyone so considers them, he [or she] becomes involved. To this extent he is more likely to become reluctant to discharge them for incompetence with speed and ease, if that is one of his responsibilities. Indeed, he becomes increasingly unlikely to recognize what an uninvolved observer would easily identify as predominantly universalistic grounds for recall. In general the greatest amount of attention paid to the maintenance of predominantly universalistic criteria in governmental contexts as well as in organizational contexts as a whole has had to do overwhelmingly with the problem of initial selection. Subsequent to such selection, predominantly universalistic criteria are best exemplified with regard to those who are promoted, that is to say with regard to those who are reselected again and again. One of the major devices, implicitly or explicitly, in all such organizational contexts for the weeding out of incompetence is a device by default. Incompetents tend to be eliminated more because they become discouraged at the lack of promotion in terms of such organizations than because they are fired. The more highly bureaucratized and the larger the scale of an organization, the greater is the probability that those incompetents who are purged will be purged by lack of promotion. This law is not inconsistent with Parkinson's laws.

Finally, in addition to the actual problem of firing for incompetence, there are certain universal questions about replacement. Leaving spectacular cases of incompetence aside, what is the reason to believe that the newly selected individual will be a great deal more competent than his predecessor? Furthermore, even if he is more competent, will he be sufficiently more competent to off-set the minimal readjustments necessitated by the change in the personnel. No matter how carefully or how predominantly universalistically defined a given job may be, it is impossible to create a situation such that members of an organization are as readily interchangable with as slight a problem of adjustment as are parts of mass-produced machines. Quite apart from the particularism inherent in family membership, there is this other minimal particularistic aspect of human organizations in general. Save for virtuosi of coolth, people do get involved with people as people when they interact a great deal.

Actually speaking, no governments in history have been as predominantly universalistic as the ideal structures of some governments lead some to believe. Governments with highly developed ideal structures of universalism are also quite rare in general social history. Among relatively nonmodernized societies, even the most dramatic emphases on predominantly universalistic structures in governmental contexts have contained both ideally and actually quite important elements of particularism. The head of the government in the case of the Imperial Chinese bureaucracy and the balances of particularism in the case of Tokugawa Japan are important cases in point. There are many others. The so-called democratic Greek city-state was only democratic for a highly particularistically defined set of elite who were citizens. Similar reservations may be raised about the levels of universalism which held ideally or actually in the case of Roman society. Insofar as predominantly universalistic criteria have been ideal structures of governments in relatively nonmodernized societies, those governments have inevitably fallen prey to predominantly particularistic considerations which led to intolerable increases in either graft and corruption or incompetence, or both. No matter how many devices are erected to thwart this sort of disintegration, it always has its effect whether the societies be relatively nonmodernized or relatively modernized ones. The devices created to thwart the red tape may become a special source of capricious particularism within the organizational context.

Successful maintenance of predominantly universalistic governments must rest on two considerations at least. The first of these has to do with the structures of socialization of the members of the society in general and of the prospective members of the government in particular. All of these individuals must be conditioned to think in terms of predominantly universalistic governmental organizations. They must not only think that this should be the case, they must in general be so conditioned that in many instances at least it will not occur to them that any evasion of these criteria can be anything but sinful. It is important that, if the members do not live up to these ideal structures they at least feel guilty about their failures to do so. In relatively modernized social contexts the extent of achievement of this condition is quite remarkable, but it has been virtually out of the question in relatively nonmodernized societies. In the latter context, when characterized by predominantly universalistic governments, the average individual must be trained to think this way about one relatively restricted sphere of social behavior while he does not feel this way about the vast majority of all other spheres. The members of relatively modernized societies are expected to feel this way about a broad sphere of highly differentiated activities in addition to the governmental one. It is difficult even in relatively modernized social contexts for people to live up to their ideals in this respect, but to a remarkable degree these ideals are in fact inculcated generally in such contexts.

The second requisite for success is not one about which there is nearly so much reason for optimism. The more predominantly universalistic a governmental system is, the more relevant is predominantly rational knowledge in terms of it. In relatively modernized contexts the diminution of sedentary structures reduces the reliance that can be placed on history and precedent—and hence on predominantly traditional knowledge. The importance of predominantly rational knowledge and the implications of the lack of adequate rational knowledge increase with every increase in the level of modernization. On the whole the level of rational knowledge available has never been adequate to what the members of most societies have considered to be the need for knowledge, and our current needs increase daily. Nothing in the history of the social sciences or other disciplines gives us reason to expect that the increase in predominantly rational knowledge available is likely to keep up with the "need." As indicated earlier in connection with the general discussion of the problems of centralization [pp. 55–60, 79–84, and 315–316] one limit of present lines of development may well be lack of sufficient rational knowledge to plan and execute what must be done for such systems to exist within tolerable ranges of accuracy.

C. LOCAL, FEUDAL, AND NATIONAL FORMS OF GOVERNMENT

Normally some reference to territory is second only to reference to sovereignty in discussions of governments. That question has been largely ignored up to this point. I would now turn briefly to three distinctions which explore the implications of a territorial element in the definition of government for the place of the government in the general social structure. Although these three types of government are presented here because of the territorial elements involved in the conception of them, all have other aspects and other sources of interest to various scholars as well as to people with practical interests.

A *local government* may be defined as a government the jurisdiction of whose members is limited to their geographical horizons—the horizons a member of the government can see with the naked eye—or less. Such governments are usually about as loosely organized as one can imagine. In general the members have neither the interest nor the ability to coordinate their affairs and those over which they have jurisdiction in some sense with the affairs of others on a larger geographical scale. These governments are usually found in primitive societies of small scale. From the point of view of the ordinary man of public affairs, and even from the point of view of many social scientists, such societies are probably frequently described as not having any government. The members of such social systems tend to be described as simply living in the areas concerned, getting together every once in a while, etc. Given the extremely general definition of government used here, these are governments, however. They are probably the instances of government which epitomize the emphasis on decentralization in its most extreme form. Usually the individuals living within the jurisdiction of the members of such a government do not constitute the membership of a society by themselves. The total society of which they are members usually involves members of at least several such units. In some cases it may be difficult to find any traces of any more general governmental system, though some such system exists, no matter how weakly centralized it may be. The major interest of such governments for this work lies not in the elaboration of the point that probably some more general form of government exists in all such cases, but rather in the fact that such governments may form subsystems within larger social units which are of great interest for present purposes. The members of these units may or may not conceive themselves to be members of the larger units. Whether they do so may be one of the major problems for the members of the larger units as well as for the future of the members of these governments and those under their jurisdiction. In the so-called emerging nations in an area such as Africa the problem of coordinating and reorganizing members of such local governments is clearly recognized, even if the phenomena themselves have not been adequately analyzed and even if no solution seems in sight. The general form of this problem can be simply stated. It is not a question of whether the motives and intentions of the members of larger scale units are going to be good, bad, or indifferent in taking over these fascinating, untrammeled, local people. Regardless of the motivation of those members of the larger units and regardless of whether the members of the local units think of themselves as significantly members of a subsystem of the larger units, localism always "goes" with the increase of modernization. Local units never hold their own; their level of self-sufficiency always declines. Attitudes favoring localism may be an obstacle to the main line of development, but even if they stymie developments toward modernization, localism will not survive. Ideologically these governments are of great interest. They are the closest approaches in human history to most of the ideals specified in the utopian structures of anarchism. Although no advocate of anarchy has ever used a realistic description of one of these social systems as an exemplification of the ideals called for in his prospectus, most of the descriptions of anarchic governments are either exceedingly romantic versions of what such highly localized social life is like or involve such complicated sets of social interdependencies as to make the concept of anarchy ridiculous.

The general concept of feudal society has been defined above [p. 282]. For the present discussion two of the elements in that definition are most important. The first is the extent to which the allocation of land and power and responsibility go together. The second is the emphasis on loyalty in terms of relationships oriented to landholding and power. Feudal governments are of two sorts. First, there are those in terms of which, ideally speaking at least, the land allocations to a given lord are expected to be a single territorial unit all the parts of which are contiguous. Second, there are those in terms of which the allocation of territories under a given governmental leader are not necessarily contiguous, ideally speaking. Both types of feudal governments are specific combinations of centralization and decentralization. The degree of centralization achieved depends either on the head of the centralized government controlling a single bigger or specially advantageous fief or some combination of fiefs fitting such a description. In feudal contexts the vulnerability of the focus of centralization is usually maximized. The territory of the centralized ruler is rarely big enough to outweigh any possible combinations of his vassals. In many cases it may be considerably smaller than several of them. The elements of centralization may be weak indeed; the central government may be to all intents and purposes a figurehead government. The feudal government of Tokugawa Japan is one of the few examples in social history of a feudal government with a very long period of stability. It was a feudal government of the first type. Feudal governments of the second type have been even more unstable than those of the first type.

No relatively modernized society has ever been characterized by a feudal government. All transitions to or developments of such societies have followed the destruction of feudal structures if they existed. Contrary to many expectations, however, such a governmental structure may be an exceedingly good basis from which to start modernization although highly vulnerable to modernization. Such governments, and the general structures which accompany them, may in fact be a better basis for the start of such a process than governments which appear at least much more centralized, with many of the elements already associated with modernized society such as open-class structures, etc. The relevance of feudal governmental structures as an easily adaptable basis under some circumstances for purposes of modernization—especially for late-comers to the process—lies in the peculiar combination of the emphasis on loyalty and the stability of the governmental units at the local level. Contrary to local governments, the elements of decentralization in a feudal government never approach the anarchic either by ideal or by default. The level of discretion left to the members of the local governmental units characteristic of feudal societies is, ideally speaking, a function of the grace of the overlord. It may be true that the member of a feudal society will try to switch his loyalty to another overlord if his particular overlord attempts to interfere too much at the local level, but the fact remains that discretion at the local level is presumably a function of a grant from an overlord. The level of decentralization in fact maintained is closely related to the general level of self-sufficiency of the local units of the society. The combination of localism and loyalty to an overlord can be adapted to modernization in such a way that the emphasis on localism may be continued more or less intact for a bit and then systematically brought under the control of the new overlords, i.e., the new representatives of a new type of government. The instability characteristic of feudal societies in general is focused not at the local level but on the more centralized governmental organization. Shifts in hegemony take place among the feudal lords themselves, but the village organizations and the family units of the vast majority of the population remain highly sedentary despite the fluctuations of the fortunes of the elite.

In the case of what have been called local governments above, any new forms of centralized government change the system radically; for different reasons the same tends to be the case for what might be called national governments. At least in the early stages of modernization, the structures of feudal governments hold out the possibility for late-comers of maximizing the stability at the local level until reorganization at the central level is far enough along to increase the extensions of new forms of power at the local level without chaotic results. From this point of view one might define feudal governments as the most centralized form of what have been called local governments above. To some extent the struggle for power in terms of feudal governments is to a high degree separated from the local community.

I would define *national governments* as those governments seen by their members as the central government of the territory occupied by the members of the society concerned. In national governments the union of whatever governmental systems are involved is regarded as more important than the right of any participant member to secede from the organization.[11] Whatever the degree of actual decentralization may be in such governments, the emphasis, ideally speaking, has already shifted to the side of centralization as opposed to decentralization. All of the peoples in all of the territories associated with a society having a

[11] The Civil War of United States history certainly constitutes a classic struggle in terms of this conception of a government. Today even the most ardent advocate of States Rights is unlikely to urge the right of the members of the individual states to dissolve the federal union.

national government are conceived of as living under a single government rather than as making up a single government. Action in terms of national governments, by contrast with the other two types of government mentioned above, maximizes problems of coordination and control. Implicity or explicity the members claim that such governments have sole jurisdiction in the territories associated with them. Even if the members do not claim a monopoly of the legitimate exercise of force, they claim a priority for their exercises of force in terms of the government. National governments always constitute the most general form of organization for the societies of which they constitute a subsystem.

National governments in this sense appear to be the only governmental form under which transition to a relatively modernized society and/or maintenance of such a society can take place. All relatively modernized societies are characterized by national governments in this sense. All relatively nonmodernized societies which have become more modernized have moved in the direction of national governments if they did not already have them. Prior to the development of relatively modernized societies, there existed many examples of national governments. Among the relatively nonmodernized national governments, stable combinations of relatively high levels of decentralization were compatible with the general emphasis on centralization characteristic of national governments. The members of such societies might generally understand that the representatives of the national government would not seek to handle specific problems on a governmental basis, but implicit in these societies at least was the fact that if the national governmental representatives did decide to handle problems on this basis, they were the only governmental representatives who could make such a decision legitimately. In relatively modernized societies, on the other hand, a stable sedentary relation between centralization and decentralization even with a somewhat greater emphasis on centralization is not possible. In all such cases the trend is away from decentralization, and that increasingly. There may be instabilities inherent in such a trend, but there is certainly no stable case of any society which has become relatively modernized without a national government or without consistently increasing centralization.

The territorial divisions associated with national governments do not necessarily coincide neatly with any previous definitions of the social systems whose members exist in whole or in part within the territories concerned. Nevertheless, the position of governments in relatively modernized societies is so strategic that the members of the various systems who inhabit the territory under the jurisdiction of the representatives of the government concerned, whatever their previous connections outside those territorial distinctions, tend increasingly to become the members of a society whose members inhabit that particular territory and none other. Whether voluntarily or no, those subject to the jurisdiction of the representatives of the government tend to become members of the society of which that national government is *the* government. The concept of a nation does not coincide neatly with the concept of a society, but once a nation in this sense is formed, the various social systems whose members are under the jurisdiction of its representatives tend to become a society if that national government persists stably. If this does not take place, the national government is shattered, and the result is the emergence of two or more national governments where one existed before with an attendant division of territory, regardless of how little sense such territorial divisions may make on any geographic basis save one oriented to the distinction of the territories of the members of the subsystems which could not be homogenized.

D. SOME OTHER DIFFERENTIATIONS OF GOVERNMENTS

There are other distinctions I should like to mention only briefly, e.g., those between capitalistic and socialistic governments, between democratic and authoritarian governments, between business and labor governments, etc. Anent such distinctions, arguments are not primarily in terms of the analysis of the political aspects of the phenomena but rather in terms of ideology and evaluation. As an individual, I pledge my own allegiance to certain of the concepts in these discussions, but as a social scientist I feel that while many of these concepts may have had a precision of reference some decades ago, today they constitute calls to the colors rather than tools for analysis.

Take, for example, the distinction between capitalistic and socialistic governments or between business and labor governments. How would one characterize the government of the United States today? To some extent, of course, it depends on who is doing the classification. For those individuals thinking of President Eisenhower as a tool of the Communists if not a dedicated Communist conspirator and of President Kennedy as almost certainly a dedicated Communist conspirator, there is very little question. There is no more question for them than there would be for a properly certified representative of one of the major newspapers of the Soviet Union. Their answers would differ but their faiths in faith would identify them forever. People committed to less extreme positions, however, would generally agree that the government of the United States, ideally speaking, is a business, capitalistic government and that of the Soviet Union is a socialistic and labor government.

In such discussions there probably is in fact more of an element of truth in what some of the soi-disant conservatives [they are in fact some of the most genuinely radical people in the society] say. There is absolutely no question but that the government of the United States is becoming less capitalistic and the members of the society are becoming less "free" every day of our history. In the name of the government, the members of government have entered into all sorts of private and business arenas on a massive scale. This will continue to be the case even if some of the conservatives should come to dominate the government. In this sense, the radicals who maintain that the government is more capitalistic and more dominated by business every day, are somewhat at a disadvantage. Leaving to one side such organizations as the public schools and the post office system—both examples of enterprises which at one time were not governmental subsystems, let us compare the American Telephone and Telegraph Company and its various subsidiaries with the modern International Brotherhood of Teamsters. Which is a private capitalistic concern? There is certainly a sense in which action in terms of many union organizations today furnish more examples of unfettered private enterprise than do actions in terms of large-scale corporations. The relation of the activities of the members of such organizations to activities actual or potential in terms of different types of governmental organizations is also instructive. If the members of the city government of Chicago did something radically displeasing to the head of the International Brotherhood of Teamsters, it is by no means out of the question that he could and would close down a considerable part of the activity generally associated with that city. Particularly if a certain amount of supplies were permitted to flow to service hospital patients, etc., it is difficult to say how long such a strike would be effective. In recent history, activities in New York were partially closed down for a considerable number of days by the members of a much smaller and less potent union organization. On the other hand were the members of the city government of the city of Chicago to pass thoroughly discriminatory legislation effecting the operation of telephone service, would the directors of the companies concerned think of cutting off telephone service to that city? I doubt that this would even occur to them as a means today, and if it did, they would not be permitted to get by with such a decision for any length of time at all. Does this mean that the government of the United States is a labor government as distinguished from a business government? Conversely if any given set of laborers in the Soviet Union disliked a decision of the governmental representatives, would it occur to them to strike in protest against those decisions? What would happen if they did? Does this indicate that the Soviet government is nonlabor or nonsocialist?

These questions are more fruitfully considered as questions of the interdependencies of large-scale bureaucracies rather than in terms such as capitalistic enterprises, labor organizations, etc. The real elements of private entrepreneurship left in highly modernized social contexts are left primarily by virtue of the fact that the areas concerned are so exceedingly difficult to regulate. In the context of modern United States society, given the existing legal system, labor unions are exceedingly difficult to regulate because laborers are not conceived to have property rights in the job and labor is not a commodity in the ordinary sense. Any law or court ruling which requires work of an individual is hard to distinguish from slavery or penal incarceration. At one time in United States history many felt that if only a "property-right-in-the-job" were recognized the difficulties of labor would be solved. Having achieved large-scale bureaucratic organization in spite of such a lack of equity at law, it is difficult to hold union members responsible by suit in the ordinary sense. To some extent as union treasuries become wealthy and the investments held in the name of unions increase, union members are becoming vulnerable to suit, but specifically they become vulnerable to the extent that they become organized large-scale business investors. On the purely business side, it is increasingly the activities of the members of small businesses which are exceedingly difficult to regulate. Activities in terms of big businesses are really quite easy to regulate once the decision is made to regulate them. Either directly or indirectly it is easier to regulate the activities of the leaders of major steel companies than the corner grocery store proprietors in a social setting like that of the United States today.

It is even difficult to understand these matters if one raises such criteria as private decision with regard to economic allocation. In the context of neither the Soviet Union nor the United States are critical decisions in such allocations made by individuals who own the facilities about which they make decisions. The separation of ownership and control in business contexts in the United States is well beyond serious question. In the Soviet

Union, ideally speaking, there is no private ownership on the level of large-scale enterprises. Do individual businessmen in the United States context have a more decisive area in which they can make personal decisions than do individual governmental administrators in the Soviet Union? In either case, there will be results if those decisions are wrong decisions, but in both cases the criteria for a right decision are increasingly similar. In both cases they have to do with the increase in scale and efficiency of operation, capital formation, etc., in terms of the organization relative to which the decision is made.

Some of these distinctions place more emphasis on the ideals for which men strive and the evaluation they place on the things which have been striven for than they do on what governments are actually like. Take for example the distinction between democratic and authoritarian governments. Is the United States government becoming more democratic or more authoritarian? I believe that the United States government is considerably more democratic and less authoritarian than is the government of the Soviet Union. I do not believe, however, that these distinctions tell us a great deal about where we are going, nor do I believe that the current differences I perceive between the system of the United States and that of the Soviet Union have any chance of remaining as they are. Both are examples of relatively modernized societies. In the long run both will come to resemble one another more in these respects than they will come to differ from one another, regardless of how importantly different they may be now. American society has an increasing membership and is an increasingly more delicately balanced system. The implications of getting that system out of kilter spread more and more rapidly and more and more catastrophically to more of the rest of the system with every passing day. No form of governmental organization is going to remain stable in the American context with any trend but one, and that trend is going to be toward more and more regulation of the individual. The individual American is going to be left less and less room to act as he pleases except insofar as he pleases to act rightly, i.e., in an increasingly regulated, disciplined fashion.

It is not difficult to get the most devoted adherents of democracy to agree that there is no such thing as democracy if one means by that the right of an individual to get up and shout "fire" in a crowded theater if such a whim seizes him. No one will stand up for his right to do that, if any sort of stable society is desired. But the real problem is what constitutes "shouting fire in a crowded theater." To an increasing degree as a system becomes more and more heavily populated and more and more interdependent, with various upsets in terms of the system spreading more and more rapidly to all other parts of the system, more and more things come under the heading of "shouting fire in a crowded theater." Increasingly under these conditions what we consider to be an emphasis on democracy comes to consist in a determination to make every increasing regulation of individual behavior thoroughly justified before it is committed and to provide some sort of protection for the right of dissent as long as the right of that dissent can be guaranteed without disruption of the general system. But this is not the usual sense of the term democratic as distinguished from authoritarian.

There are many governments in the world today characterized by specific forms of authoritarianism which have probably been pressed much further than is required by any level of modernization so far achieved by the members of the societies concerned. These forms of authoritarianism may well be loosened up in the direction of greater personal initiative, but in the long run, the more the increase in modernization, the greater will be the centralization of the governments concerned regardless of how they started out. It is bootless to argue the question of what must be done to maintain democratic governments unless one is able to decide what he means by such governments and whether or not such governments are likely to be viable in the present and the near future. Ideology to the contrary notwithstanding—arrantly pessimistic though I judge it to be—the upper limits of increasing centralization, and such authoritarianism as always accompanies that increase in the long run, have more to do with the structural limits of modernization in general and of available knowledge in particular than with my ethical preferences.

I V

THE PROBLEM OF STABILITY

A. THE PROBLEMS OF CHANGE AND SUCCESSION

No governmental system has been immune to the problems of change and succession. Even societies whose members have regarded the preservation of the status quo as the ultimate ideal have not been immune to such considerations. Succession in the ordinary sense has been discussed above. Here I wish to discuss it only in connection with the problem of governmental change in general. There are three types: the first is change that is *automatically justified* from the point of view of the members of the society; the second is the case of *orderly change* within limits;

and the third is the case of *revolutionary change*. In the last case I shall distinguish among systems characterized by palace revolutions, governmental revolutions, and/or general social revolutions.

I would consider a govermental system characterized by *automatic justification* insofar as changes in the government were legitimized simultaneously with the action which constitutes the change itself. The most extreme form of such automatic justification is that implicit in the doctrine of the Will of Heaven which characterized traditional Chinese society. Given the ideals of that society, if anything went wrong, that was prima-facie evidence that the ruler no longer had the Will of Heaven. Successful revolt or challenge to the power of the ruler was proof par excellence that the person previously claiming to be the ruler was not in fact the legitimate ruler, but rather that the person [or persons] who successfully challenged his rule was the legitimate ruler. Such automatic justification does not inhibit forces making for a threat to the established governmental structures, but it does reduce the problem of restoring order after such a threat, since the initial success of the opposition is the source of its legitimacy. The problems of adjustment of the leaders of a new government [or of the new leaders of an old government] are complicated as little as possible by claims and counterclaims of legitimacy. Societies with such structures are ones in terms of which whatever is and is stable is right. Charismatic governments are characterized by automatic justification only as long as the charisma of the charismatic leader continues. In traditional Chinese society automatic justification was not tied to the charisma of any individual. Such governments cannot be stable in relatively highly modernized social contexts, and in relatively nonmodernized societies they are likely to be stable only if alterations in the general governmental system relatively rarely have far-reaching implications for the importantly decentralized elements of the society.

The ordinary governmental system consists of structures in terms of which orderly change within limits is possible though not generally emphasized or sought. Unlike governmental systems characterized by automatic justification, those emphasizing orderly change within limits focus more on ordinary problems of stability than on the problem of adjustment in the face of revolutionary changes. In modern history the government of Great Britain has been the clearest example of a governmental system in terms of which orderly change within broad limits could take place. After all, from the day of William of Orange, change in Great Britain, as every school boy knows, has been "evolutionary rather than revolutionary." With the single major exception of the Civil War the same has been true of the government of the United States since the achievement of independence from England. There is a sense in which any government of any stability is a government in terms of which orderly change can take place within certain limits, but the governments under consideration here are characterized by the fact that some conception of orderly change within limits is an explicit ideal of the members of the government. This characteristic as much as any defines what is generally referred to as constitutional government. There has never been a government in terms of which no change at all took place, but there have been many in terms of which change was neither intended, desired, nor forseen. The most explicit form of constitutional governmental systems are those characterized by written constitutions. In terms of those documents, quite far-reaching changes by orderly methods are envisaged as is change in the constitutional document itself. Perhaps the purest case of the ideal structure, however, is the case of governments effectively stable on such a basis with an unwritten constitution, but such cases are rare.

In general stable cases of governmental systems in terms of which orderly change within limits is explicitly emphasized are relatively rare, until the development of relatively modernized societies. Once the process of modernization gets under way, the common state of vulnerability to continuous change and development rapidly becomes obvious to most. Reactions to this realization vary with the members of the society, but few, if any, fail to get the message. Under these circumstances the members of any and all governments and the members of the societies in which these governments exist seek a governmental system in terms of which orderly change within limits can take place. In fact the broader the limits the better. The fact that relatively few governments of any considerable scale have long periods of stability does not necessarily imply that the constitutional concept itself is the source of this instability. Since these governments have been governments in societies in terms of which relatively high levels of modernization have been reached, it is quite difficult to untangle the constitutional point of view with regard to orderly change from the sources of instability which are inherent in relatively modernized societies. *The fact that we may see little alternative to taking the possibility of stability in such societies for granted is in no way support for the proposition that the possibility of stability in such societies is to be taken for granted.* It may be out of the question.

There is a category of governments which by a slight act of oversimplification may be labeled *no-change systems*. These are not in fact governments in terms of which no change takes place at all, but they are governments whose structures are so overwhelmingly traditionalized that changes take place in spite of the intention, desires, or predictions of the members of the government or the members of the society in general. It has already been pointed out above that socialization for an unknown future as a matter to be taken for granted is the sign of modernity par excellence. Orientation to change in terms of governments is less dramatic, but in a highly developed form it is no less a sign of modernity.

With the development of relatively modernized societies, an ancient idea began to slip out of existence. There was a time in which exercises of power in terms of governments, especially power of those abroad, were regarded as the major means of alteration of governmental systems. People conceived of the members of one government establishing hegemony over the members of other societies and other governments. With this went a change in political allegiances, the flow of taxes, etc. Somehow or other far-reaching social change in general and even far-reaching governmental change specifically were not expected to follow from these changes in allocations of power. With the development of modernization, international warfare reached a level of violence hitherto undreamed of in social history at the same time that people began to realize en masse that a government was not simply a bank of power as it were. The realization became general that any considerable changes in the government—including radical increases in the extent of power and influence of the members of a government—meant general changes in the rest of social structure as well. The general level of decentralization common to relatively nonmodernized societies meant that all sorts of struggles associated with the government could take place over the heads of the general population. With the increase of interdependency characteristic of modernization this quickly and dramatically ceased to be the case. The possibility of no-change systems vanished save for an evidence of psychopathology. The change in no way implied an increase in political determinism. It was not necessarily a change in which governments became more important in determining other elements in social structure, but rather one in which all organizations in societies became more tightly interdependent with one another than ever before. Hence, any change relevant to any one—whatever its cause—was far more likely to have repercussions in all the others.

No discussion of the problem of stability in the governmental context would be complete without some discussion of the concept of revolution. The term, *revolution,* has come to be overwhelmingly associated with the idea of violent change. Such change somehow has come to be identified as the most extreme and far-reaching kind of social change. This is not necessarily the case, of course, and the problem is further complicated by another step in this development of connotations. The concept of revolution has become so thoroughly identified with the concepts of violence and far-reaching change that: (1) if there is no violence of the sort connoted, many consider that no important change has taken place at all, and (2) if there is violent overthrow of the leadership of a government, far-reaching social change is often assumed to have taken place more or less simultaneously. Nevertheless, not all revolutions constitute far-reaching social change, and not all far-reaching social changes involve revolutions in the violent sense.

If we are to retain any of the general flavor of the term, *revolution,* however, it must be used to refer to questions of change. One of the most fundamental considerations about any question of change is one most frequently glossed over by social analysts. Change can only be judged, analyzed, or perceived in terms of some specific unit, system, or object which is regarded as being changed or remaining unchanged. The object or system concerned, however, is never considered on the completely descriptive level, i.e., in its complete reality as some would have it. The object or system is always considered on a particular level of abstraction, i.e., on a given level of generalization. The reason for this is quite simple. If one tries to handle any given phenomenon on a completely descriptive level, there are two difficulties. In the first place one cannot discuss change because one can never complete his description. In principle the number of descriptive statements needed to exhaust the description of anything, if not infinite is at least so large finitely as to exhaust one's time on this earth. In the second place, if one could ignore the first place, on the completely descriptive level change always takes place between any two points in time. As a minimum the thing observed is always older after the passage of time, and in some respects the phenomenon of aging alone makes a difference. Whether one realizes it or not, whenever one speaks of change, he not only specifies the unit about which he is talking, but also the level or type of abstraction in terms of which he is discussing change. One does this either implicitly or explicitly. If the discussion is intended to be rational, it is preferable that these matters be made explicit. To the extent that these matters are unclear no discussion of change makes any sense at all.

If one wishes to know whether or not the government of the United States is changing he must specify the level of generality on which to consider it and the criteria in terms of which to discuss it. Since Franklin Delano Roosevelt, once every four years or once every eight years the Presidency of the United States, ideally speaking, has changed hands via elections. At some levels of consideration this always makes a difference. Depending on one's political persuasion and his estimate of one incumbent as distinguished from another, opinions vary widely as to *how much* difference such a switch makes and even as to *what* differences it makes. Nevertheless, none of these switches have changed the general form of the government from a republic to a nonrepublic. Ideally speaking, at least, none of these changes have challenged the separation of powers as an ideal structure, etc. From certain points of view the government of the United States has changed little if at all since its beginning, but from most of the points of view in which most of us are interested, the government of the United States has changed quite radically since its inception.

I use the term, *revolution,* to refer to a fairly radical form of change. Any change which changes the unit under discussion on the most general level on which it is being discussed is a *revolutionary change.* A revolutionary change is thus a change of the system under discussion, but no change in terms of a subsystem of the system, no matter how bloody or violent, is a revolutionary change in this sense unless at least one of its implications is a change of the system within which the subsystem is found. Violent and bloody changes within subsystems often result in some changes of the system of which they are subsystems. The interest of an observer is not necessarily in the system considered on the level at which change of the system can be considered to take place. For abstract purposes, if one were interested in the question of *any society,* then the only change which could be revolutionary in this sense would be a change which made the continued existence of a society impossible. If one were interested in relatively modernized societies a given change would be revolutionary if it made any and/or all relatively modernized societies impossible, regardless of what the results of the change were likely to be. If one were interested in the particular form of a relatively modernized society exemplified, for example, by the modern United States or modern Japan, a given change would be a revolutionary change if it altered the system in those respects in terms of which modern Japan or modern United States society had been identified.

From the point of view of politics three types of revolution are often usefully distinguished. These are palace revolutions, governmental revolutions, and general social revolutions. A *palace revolution* is any revolution that results in a change of the personnel in the major positions of leadership in the government without such changes having any implications for a general change in the form of the government concerned. The focus of attention of such revolutions [i.e., the system concerned] is the set of executive roles of the government. A *governmental revolution* is any revolution that results in a change of the form of the government. A *general social revolution* is any revolution in which the implications for change in subsystems inhere in changes in the general form of the society under examination. Technically, any change at all in the systems described above as no-change systems is revolutionary from the point of view of the members of such systems. Whether the members realize it or not, however, systems characterized by automatic justification or by orderly change within limits may under many circumstances be revolutionary systems. Indeed, one of the most striking features of systems characterized by orderly change within limits—constitutional systems in particular—is the possibility that they have held out for extremely general social revolutions without violence and general political chaos. Thus, in one respect or another, all systems are capable of becoming revolutionary systems. Some systems are such that practically any change has to be revolutionary from the point of view of the members concerned at least, since they think of the system as remaining completely unchanged or almost completely unchanged. Moreover, some systems are predisposed toward revolutionary changes in that the sort of factors which tend to undermine the going system are factors which inevitably involve changes on the level of generalization most likely to be under scrutiny. One of the best examples of the latter is, of course, the process of modernization. There is probably no level of generalization on which governments or other social systems can be considered for which the process of modernization does not involve revolutionary changes—including the level of any society.

Palace revolutions by definition imply only a change of leadership by unorthodox means. Such revolutions are most often carried out by individuals of extremely conservative turns of mind.[12] Attention is usually focussed on personalities. The usual example of a palace revolution is the struggle for power as between two or more individuals. Such revolutions have often turned into governmental or even general social revolutions, but these further results were probably unanticipated consequences as far as the leaders were concerned. When leadership roles are determined on overwhelmingly particularistic grounds, especially kinship grounds, palace revolutions constitute one form of correcting the situation when the minimal relevant abilities fail to characterize the legitimate successor. They do not always have such effects. In many contexts revolutions cannot be held to the level of palace revolutions. The more highly interdependent with other systems and the more highly centralized a government or the society of which it is a subsystem, the smaller is the probability of a palace revolution which does not turn into a governmental or even a general social revolution. Essentially a palace revolution consists of a shuffling of the persons in control with only a temporary alteration in the structures of succession to office. In relatively nonmodernized social contexts those alterations in the governmental structures may be exceedingly short-lived and restricted in their implications. The younger brother of a king, for example, may kill the king, take over the throne, and continue on the ordinary grounds of hereditary succession accepted by the members of the society. To understand palace revolutions, a detailed knowledge of the personalities involved in the particular historical incident is necessary. Analysis of the general social structure is much too general a tool to permit accurate predictions in the individual case of the detailed possibilities of palace revolutions though it may be quite revealing about the probability of some palace revolutions.

With increases of modernization it becomes increasingly less likely that any revolutionary change can be confined to the level of palace revolutions. This does not mean that the question of palace revolutions loses its interest for the student of public affairs. There are at least four types of interest in palace revolutions of great importance. First, there remains a great deal to be learned from the study of previous examples of palace revolutions. Second, palace revolutions may be frequent and important in the history to be written of societies in the early stages of modernization. Third, as modernization increases, more general forms of change are more likely to start out as palace revolu-

[12] In general more revolutionaries are conservative personalities than most revolutionaries like to think.

tions, given some of the bases from which change takes place rather than others. In highly authoritarian governments with extremely concentrated leadership—especially dictatorship-type governments, whether charismatic or not—palace revolutions are likely to be a major form of initiation of more general changes. Under these circumstances a close appreciation of personalities is likely to be essential for understanding the timing, at least, of phenomena with more general social implications. Palace revolutions are quite unlikely to take place on any scale in the context of societies characterized by governments with well worked out structures of orderly change. In those societies the role of personalities in general social change is likely to be considerably less vivid.

Fourth, in governments in which the actual governmental structures are at wide variance with the ideal ones, especially in governmental systems in which there exist such phenomena as the oft-cited power behind the throne, palace revolutions are likely to take place in terms of the actual governmental structures and thereby affect the ideal ones. In any kind of society, whether relatively modernized or not, the detailed social sanctioning and acceptance of the actual governmental structures are likely to be considerably less explicit and well worked out than would be the case if there were a closer approximation between the ideal and actual structures. Therefore, these actual structures are more open to manipulation by adventurers and the like than might otherwise be the case. In the discrepancy between ideal and actual structures lies much of the opportunity for political creativity.[13] Thus there have certainly been cases in the history of American government in which at least at the state and local levels actual palace revolutions have taken place because of changes in party bosses and the like. Changes in mayors and governors are rarely palace revolutions in this sense. Here again one of the most interesting implications of these phenomena lies in the fact that it is exceedingly unlikely in relatively modernized social contexts that palace revolutions can be confined to the level of palace revolutions alone. Thus, in all modernizing societies whether involving late-comers or not, discrepancies between the ideal and actual structures of government are strategic in open-

---

[13] Most of what posterity considers creative politics in a positively evaluated sense is viewed as brazen assertion of illegitimacy by contemporaries. The transformation of actual to ideal structures as well as the creation of new structures of any sort always involves some venture into illegitimacy. This is one of those elements common to all creativity, regardless of the sphere in which it falls.

ing up the determination of future developments on the basis of current personalities.[14]

In governmental revolutions the accent is not on personality struggles, and at least a considerable portion of the individuals involved regard themselves as striving in terms of concepts as to how power and responsibility should be allocated. The effect of their behavior, if not their aim, is to change the form of government. Governmental revolutions do not necessarily involve violence. Quite far-reaching governmental revolutions have been carried out peaceably. Many of the changes in the form of government of Great Britain during the nineteenth century were of this

[14] In considering the role of personality under these circumstances one must not go to the opposite extreme of maintaining that personalities and only personalities are relevant to the understanding of these situations. For many of the purposes important to a student of public affairs the general analysis of social structures is not at its present stage of development anything like a sufficiently fine predictive tool, but it is always a relevant tool at least by virtue of the fact that such analysis sets the limits within which such personalities may or may not operate effectively. General social analysis is not likely to enable one to predict who might or might not take over by some method of eliminating Chairman Mao Tse-Tung, but such general analysis can enable one to distinguish what sorts of changes any such successor can get by with. That is to say, it is in terms of general social analysis that one can come to conclusions as to what sort of policy, no matter who introduces them, will be effective in maintaining rates of development, what sorts of policies are likely to lead to radical instability of the government, etc. In most governmental circles the tendency is to be overly preoccupied with detailed predictions of the political future in terms of knowledge of the personalities involved or likely to be involved. After all, no responsible student of public affairs can afford to avoid speculation as to who is likely to succeed such figures as Comrades Brezhnev, Kosygin, or Mao Tse-Tung, Messrs. Johnson or Wilson, Gen. DeGaulle, etc. At the same time not nearly so careful attention has been given to the sort of basic research that might enable students of public affairs to make far longer range predictions as to the major possibilities of variation in the various large-scale social systems of the world. For such analysis thorough research on the bases from which changes can or are likely to take place is at least as important as detailed knowledge of the current situation in the social contexts concerned. The process of modernization contains the potentiality of at least one far-reaching social revolution per two decades. Barring a mystical approach, however, those social revolutions, as every other social revolution in past history, are developments out of what preceded them. It is one of the fundamental assumptions of any social scientist qua scientist that any radical future [or its probability] can be predicted on the basis of the present and some past had we only the theoretical developments which would tell us what variables and what constants are likely to be most strategic. Louis Pasteur killed off for all times the now naïve biological conception of spontaneous generation of germs. We assume that spontaneous combustion is in no way inexplicable or without a causal sequence. There is absolutely no reason any longer for students of public affairs to proceed as though important political or other social changes were a sort of human spontaneous combustion explicable primarily in terms of personality and spontaneous by a lack of any detailed predictability for individual personality developments.

order. In the history of relatively nonmodernized societies palace revolutions are a great deal more frequent than genuine governmental revolutions in this sense. Sometimes the palace revolutions have involved general participation and considerable amounts of violence but their main effects have not been to change the form of government but rather the details of leadership in violation of ideal structures of succession. Whether violent or not, governmental revolutions in this sense do not necessarily imply general social revolution. The French Revolution certainly constituted both a governmental and a general social revolution. Even in relatively nonmodernized social contexts, a governmental revolution is more likely to imply a broader revolution than a palace revolution. In the context of relatively modernized societies it is virtually out of the question for a governmental revolution not to involve quite far-reaching elements of general social revolution. The relevance of the general analysis of social structures to an understanding of governmental revolutions is, therefore, greater than is likely to be the case with palace revolutions even at the present state of the field. This follows trivially from the fact that many more social structures than succession are involved. The less highly modernized the society, the greater the importance of personalities is likely to be in trying to understand a governmental revolution.

At least one major qualification of this position is necessary. In relatively modernized social contexts questions of personality associated with governmental revolutions may be of the essence in predicting chaotic results from a given revolutionary change. This would ensue when governmental revolutions are put into effect by a charismatic leader, for example. The best lead on the changes which are in fact likely to be put into effect initially by the leader is in terms of the ability to predict on the basis of his personality. Even if one is able to predict or know what he will do, however, the prediction of the implications of those actions for other elements in the system will be the more illuminated by general social analysis than by any detailed knowledge of the personalities involved. Finally, it is possible to have governmental revolutions without general social revolutions, but it is not possible to have general social revolution without governmental revolution.

Like governmental revolutions and palace revolutions, general social revolutions may be gradual and quiet or violent and noisy. Practically all degrees of variations in between are at least conceivable. Most of the revolutions generally discussed are violent governmental revolutions. Laymen and scholars used to systems of government characterized by orderly change within considerable limits are so struck by disorderly and violent governmental change that they tend to regard any change of this sort as in some sense more far-reaching social change than peaceful social change can possibly be. We admit to few nonviolent revolutions of either the governmental or general social sort. General social revolutions need not be attended by any particular fluctuation in the more obviously politically oriented levels of concern though in the long run it would be out of the question that there be no repercussions on this level.

I should like to illustrate the category of general social revolutions by reference to three major social revolutions in the history of the United States. All three have to some extent reached a flowering in the American social setting and have as social structures been exported from that social context to others. The third of these is just coming into flower, but its export is already underway. The first of these was the general social revolution of political liberalism of the eighteenth century. This had its most striking effects in a new form of government and the social changes attendant upon that. The accomplishment of that revolution may be dated from the winning of independence from Great Britain and the starting of an explicitly democratically oriented republic as the ideal form of government. It was by no means solely a governmental revolution. It was a general social revolution. It involved the institutionalization of the "rights of man," the ideal of an open class society, the overwhelming emphasis on upward mobility with no limits in sight, etc. The timing of this general social revolution was not identical with that of the governmental revolution, which was in its day its most obvious manifestation.[15]

The second general social revolution was not as explicitly and obviously associated with a governmental revolution as was the first. This was the mass production revolution of the industrial revolution in general. The American Civil War as a political struggle may well have been a part of the creaking of the wheels which preceded this development, but remember the Civil War was fought and over before mass production developed. There was no direct and obvious governmental change attendant on the invention of the assembly line, but that invention symbolized a

[15] Herein lies the irony of the current popularity of de Tocqueville and the fascination of the man himself. As late as the mid-point of the twentieth century he remained the clearest voice scholars could find to tell them what de Tocqueville learned from listening to and watching people—that what scholars thought of as a governmental revolution was a profound general social revolution far beyond its political aspects.

radical far-reaching general social revolution now spread around the world touching even those societies whose members are late-comers to modernization and by no means yet relatively modernized. Following this revolution certain changes in governmental systems became inescapable. All governments become governments involving mass participation in one way or another; all governments increasingly have to have structures of rule via means of mass communications, etc.

If one wishes to call the Revolutionary War of the eighteenth century the form of violence of the first of these three revolutions, that revolution should be classified as a violent one, but the second revolution was gradual and on the whole nonviolent save for sporadic and relatively restricted outbursts in the relations between employers and employees.[16] The third of these general social revolutions is again on the whole a nonviolent one. This is the leisure revolution which I have already mentioned [pp. 77–78]. It is developing in the United States at a faster and faster rate every day. It is going on at a time when, ideally speaking, we have never been more conservative politically as far as self-conscious realization of what is going on is concerned. The governmental revolution implicit in this general social revolution as in the case of the mass production revolution will be one of the less dramatic implications of this general social revolution.

One of the many peculiar characteristics of relatively highly modernized societies is the fact that these societies have periodic general social revolutions built into the general social structure. Furthermore, these general social revolutions are more likely to be nonviolent than violent. Perhaps it would be more accurate to say that as modernization continues, if the general social revolutions are not nonviolent, the implications are increasingly likely to be in the direction of a destruction of human beings and associated social systems on a mass scale. In other words, if the structures of relatively modernized societies in general and those of the governmental organizations in particular are not such as to make general social revolution a question of orderly change within limits, there is real question as to whether relatively modernized societies can survive at all. In the past, few societies were

[15] The violence involved in these relations amounted to much less than the violence associated with the many peasant revolts of the Tokugawa period of Japanese history. Those revolts are one of history's best examples of violence defining revolution for scholars. More conservative acts of violence have never been witnessed as far as general change is concerned. These revolts were overwhelmingly oriented to redress of specific wrongs viewed as improper given the ideal structures. Even when the peasants had sufficient power at their command to demand and get a redress of their grievances, they did not seek to go further and alter the ideal status quo.

characterized by renovating structures of social change as was traditional China. Nevertheless, general social revolution or far-reaching change in general was not expected, was not a part of the ideals of the members of those societies, and was in retrospect generally viewed as the result of improper functioning in terms of the system by the members of the social system concerned. Whether the term, general social revolution, is used or not, what has here been called general social revolution is expected, preferred, and regarded as the sign par excellence of proper functioning in terms of the system by the members of relatively modernized societies.

B. COMBINATION OF CENTRALIZATION AND DECENTRALIZATION

For present purposes it is not necessary to reiterate the whole discussion of centralization and decentralization already given above [pp. 310–316]. As far as the question of governmental stability is concerned the major boundary factors in these respects are clear-cut. In relatively nonmodernized social contexts for any given scale of the society in terms of numbers of individuals and extent of territory involved, the state of communications alone always poses an upper limit on the level of centralization that can be achieved without instability. In such social contexts the only lower limit on centralization is such decentralization that no general governmental organization for the society can be said to exist at all. Again and again in the history of relatively nonmodernized societies the level of centralization achieved by leaders of the governmental organization has gone well beyond the practical limits of the state of communications of the times. Those governments have never been stable. There may be many other reasons for the instability of those governments, but what from this point of view would be called overcentralization is certainly one of the major factors in the explanation of such instability.

In relatively modernized social contexts the implications of the relation between centralization and decentralization for the stability of governments lies in the opposite direction. The state of communications is more than adequate for any practicable level of centralization desired. The trend of all governments in all such societies in the long run is overwhelmingly in the direction of greater centralization. These governmental organizations may be spoken of as overcentralized to the extent that the explicit knowledge necessary to run such societies on the level of centralization achieved is inadequate, if the society is to be stable. Such a government may be regarded as overly decentralized if the level of centralization does not permit of sufficient coordination and control, to maintain stability of the general society. The question of centralization and decentralization nowadays always becomes involved with important ethical preferences, especially those having to do with the concepts of democracy, authoritarianism, etc. Whatever the ethical merits or demerits of decentralization, i.e., relative freedom of action from control in terms of direct decisions by members of the government, certain implications which hinge on the level of available knowledge relevant to public administration are inescapable. In the absence of adequate knowledge, the location of powers of decision in organizations other than the governmental organization does not necessarily imply that by some randomization process the likelihood of correct decisions is increased. What it does mean over a broad area of differences of degree of modernization is that a given incorrect decision is likely to involve a less strategic organization in the general social structure than the government. The larger the scale of the organization involved and the more strategic its place in the general social structure, the greater is the likelihood that any incorrect decision will be on the one hand more difficult to correct and on the other hand more far-reaching in its implications for the society as a whole. To the extent that decentralization under these circumstances makes it easier to correct mistakes, it may for any given state of knowledge improve the possibilities of stability. *However,* as the level of modernization increases and the necessity of centralization, if stability is to result at all, increases, the possibility of degrees of freedom of this sort declines. Whatever the specific legal forms or ideal structures in general, the distinction between governmental and nongovernmental organizations, if the other organizations are of any considerable scale, will decline. The more highly interdependent the various elements in a relatively modernized society become, the less any administrative ingenuity in the form of decentralization of power can substitute for detailed adequate knowledge about the areas in which decisions must be made. If governmental stability is to be maintained, limitation of the amount of actual planning will be a function of the level of adequate knowledge available rather than of preferences for or against planning.

C. BALANCES OF POWER AND RESPONSIBILITY

The general problem of the balance of power and responsibility has already been discussed [see pp. 293–310]. Increasingly, when societies become relatively modernized, the governments tend to become systems based on explicit empirical balances of power and responsibility. Ideally speaking at least, they move in the direction of some set of structures of checks and balances such as is familiar by both ideal and actuality to citizens of the United States who have not managed to escape the civics courses of primary and secondary schools. As far as stability is concerned, such explicit empirical balances have obvious advantages. To the extent that they are actually explicit and empirical, problems of differences of opinion are reduced to a minimum; knowledge of what to do in a given situation is detailed and clear. There exist in such situations relatively clear-cut criteria of what constitutes overstepping the bounds, what should be done under such circumstances, and who should do it. On the other hand, the great vulnerability of such systems lies along three lines. First, the checks and balances are never perfectly explicit and perfectly empirical. To the degree that they are ideally expected to be perfectly explicit and empirical, many individuals will avail themselves of the opportunity of meretricious intrepretation of the relatively unclear areas for private and special purposes. This, however, is the age-old governmental problem of the instability which can be a function of the hyperrational attempts at manipulation by those whom other members of the society consider clever but wicked. At least in theory it is not out of the question to handle the clever but wicked by matching them against equally clever but virtuous individuals. Insofar as the members of the government represent what other members of the society consider the virtuous position in such contests, the members of the government have on their side the fact that the deliberately "villainous" strain toward rationality, and that always increases the predictability of their behavior.

Much the greater threat to the stability of these governments is the second line of vulnerability. There are well intentioned individuals who neither understand nor appreciate the explicit empirical set of checks and balances—those who blunder with the best intentions in the world. The difficulties they pose are far more difficult to predict. Finally, the third line of vulnerability is the greatest difficulty of all, especially as modernization increases—when one considers the problem of stability of governments in continually and radically changing societies. For there to be operation in terms of an explicit empirical system of checks and balances, there must be adequate explicit knowledge of that organization itself and its various interrelationships with other organizations in the society. In this we are faced with exactly the same problem as the adequacy of knowledge for high levels of centralization. We may not—indeed we do not—know enough of what we are about to have a completely explicit, empirical set of checks and balances for power and responsibility.

Insofar as balances of power and responsibility in terms of the government result from the nonempirical orientations of the members of the government, they depend on the socialization and self-will of those with strategic roles in the government. The implications of either dependency are relatively high levels of instability of the government involved. The problem of adequate socialization in this respect is a special form of the problem of socialization for an unknown future. In addition there is the problem of what happens if an individual achieves a strategic role in the government without adequate orientation to the usual nonempirical sources of balance. How, for example, could one devise a governmental organization such that only God-fearing men could rise to high position and such that, once there, they could only stay there if they continued to be God-fearing? Nonempirically oriented balances of power and responsibility in governmental organizations have classically been stable only in highly sedentary, relatively nonmodernized societies.

There have been many cases of governmental organizations with unbalanced structures of power and responsibility. Such governments have been unstable. On the modern scene, however, a new element injects. Increasingly the societies of late-comers to modernization are ones in which previously balanced structures of government become radically unbalanced as soon as new structures are introduced from relatively modernized social contexts—regardless of how they are introduced. In previous periods of history with relatively high degrees of isolation and self-sufficiency, these instabilities would either have resulted in elimination of the society or change to some more stable form. It is unlikely that such systems disappear altogether in the kind of world in which we live today. Given the high level of public opinion throughout the world against colonialism, it is also unlikely that these systems be absorbed overtly into other systems, as has been the case of various nations in Eastern Europe and elsewhere throughout history. In this day and time neither the overt absorption of such societies into others nor the elimination of their populations is likely to be permitted. In the modern world, populations may be permitted to die out in war, but never in peace.

Increasingly radical cases of governmental instability will be met by some sort of international cooperative stabilization of the system. The situation in the Congo today is an example of just this sort of phenomenon. Whether the structure of handling the next such situation will be similar to that employed in the Congo is a highly unsettled question. What is an increasingly settled question, however, is that the range of toleration by the representatives of the United Nations of unbalanced governmental systems in any particular nation has declined radically in recent years and will continue to decline. Furthermore, whereas at one time such questions, if intervention took place at all, were likely to be settled by the strongest of one's neighbors, increasingly such questions are likely to be settled by the representatives of some combination or set of nations whose members will act in concert. The drift in the world today is overwhelmingly in the direction of the development of some form of international government or governments. As the implications for a relatively modernized world of the instability of the government of any particular society for other societies and all their members become increasingly obvious and increasingly important, an imbalance in the government of any one society becomes an imbalance in the others. Under these conditions an international governments of stable dimensions will develop or else. . . .

In the balances of power and responsibility variations with regard to the level of specificity or the level of diffuseness have been mentioned above [pp. 304–307]. Today such variations have special implications for international capabilities. For example, given the governmental system of the Soviet Union the representatives of that state can alter the policies in terms of which they act with great rapidity by contrast with the degrees of flexibility open to the representatives of the United States government. On the other hand it is much more difficult for others to check the representatives of the Soviet Union, if the policies they select embark them upon a disaster course. By contrast with President Johnson, Comrades Brezhnev and Kosygin can move far and fast indeed. Short of a palace revolution which is likely to become a governmental revolution if not a general social revolution, who can stop them in terms of the Soviet Union? It has become quite clear in recent years that the governmental system of the Soviet Union has undergone important changes in this respect. Whatever the degrees of freedom presently open to Comrades Brezhnev and Kosygin by contrast with those open to President Johnson, the degrees of freedom open to them are fewer than those formerly open to Comrade Stalin or presently open to Comrade Mao Tse-Tung. In the Soviet Union with the increase of modernization, there has been an increase in specific rather than diffuse balances of power and responsibility. This has gone along with an increase in the emphasis on explicit empirical checks and balances there.

Diffuse balances of power and responsibility can become inexplicit and by lack of definition at least, perhaps, nonempirical. Here again the lack of perfect and adequate knowledge makes some inexplicitness, and some diffuseness, a necessity if the system is to operate at all, but increasingly this becomes an area of vagueness which must be eliminated if there is to be survival.

Finally, with regard to the implications of balances of power and responsibility for general governmental stability, it is necessary to return to some of the remarks made above about the use of mobs. The remarkable improvements in the technology of communications and the easy exportability of these techniques regardless of the levels of development of other aspects of modernization have made the rational use of mobs as an instrument of social change or the general exertion of social pressures more feasible than was ever the case before. The operation of individuals in terms of mobs always has implications of instability for the government in power. This is not to say that action carried out in terms of any mob will make any governmental organization unstable, but it is to say that action in terms of any mob contains some potentialities which point in this direction. It is never, therefore, rational for the members of a government in power who wish to preserve that government in power to use mobs. On the other hand, insofar as the instability of the government in power is desired, it is rational to attempt to use mobs. The less likely it is that those out of power, who wish power, are able to acquire power through legitimate channels in terms of their society, the more rational it is for them to attempt to use mobs in pursuit of power.

D. PROBLEM OF INSULATION OF THE GOVERNMENT FROM OTHER SPHERES OF ACTIVITY

For governments in general, as already indicated above, the major problem of insulation is always nepotism. How does one keep the level of objective performance sufficiently high in the face of the desire, whether legitimate or not, of members of the government to give preference to their relatives? Actually, of course, it is necessary to generalize the concept of nepotism to the implications of particularism in any form, but certainly the major form of particularism down through social history has been favoritism on the basis of kinship. Such preference has implications for the stability of governmental units insofar as it increases the levels of ineptness of the members of governments. There is no society for whose members in general kinship is unimportant, and there are a large number of societies whose members consider kinship to be more important than anything else outside the government, if not more important than the government itself. The problem is more likely to be solved if one approaches it from the point of view of how such influences can be minimized rather than from the point of view of how they can be eliminated. The probability of eliminating them is small, and any substantial diminution of them is out of the question save in terms of those societies whose members, ideally speaking, regard nepotism as a bad thing. Down through social history the most stable ways of handling these problems have been those which achieve the levels of ability and devotion to service necessary by judicious balances of particularism rather than by the attempt to eliminate them or to create a situation in which such pressures could be ignored.

The problem of particularism as epitomized by nepotism is well recognized and often commented upon in sophisticated forms. There is, however, another problem of insulation which is much more peculiar—one much less often commented on. This is the attempted separation of activities the implications of which foredoom them to high levels of mutual relevance. In terms of the ideal structures of societies this has been attempted again and again—usually with far-reaching implications for the stability of the governmental organizations of the societies concerned. The classic case of this is the attempt to separate certain predominantly economically oriented activities from predominantly politically oriented ones by making it illegitimate for the governing elite to dirty their hands in trade or for the specialist in exchange—the merchants—to become involved in government. This always results in graft and corruption. The ideal separation can never actually be achieved, much less maintained. The allocation of power and responsibility is always highly relevant to the allocation of goods and services and vice versa. In all societies of any considerable scale sufficient interdependency exists such that some specialization of roles emphasizing the exchange of goods and services is required. To attempt to separate the spheres of the merchants from the spheres of the governmental officials is to imply that the vulnerability to expropriation of the merchants is irrelevant to them and that the command over resources which the merchants can accumulate is irrelevant to governmental officials. Neither has ever been the case. The attempt to separate these spheres always builds elements of instability into the government concerned. Under these circumstances merchants can gain security from capricious allocations of power and responsibility via seduction of the members of the government. Once seduction is begun there is absolutely no reason to expect merchants to desist from their efforts when the minimum stable level of security has been achieved. After all, the very illegitimacy of their position with regard to the allocation of power and responsibility forces them to plan rationally insofar as their command over resources can be used to influence those with legitimate access to the allocation of power and responsibility.

On the obverse side, once governmental officials learn that power is a saleable commodity in some sense, if they are motivated to sell it at all, they are not likely to be motivated solely to sell it in limited and trivial quantities, however they reckon those quantities. Regardless of how or where initiated, transactions of this sort undermine the stability of the ideal structures of the governmental system. If it were easy to limit these transactions, the contacts so made might actually increase the stability of the governmental organizations specifically because those contacts provide the minimum necessary recognition of the relevance of the allocation of goods and services for the allocation of power and responsibility and vice versa. It is difficult to see how the motivation that gets individuals on both sides of these transactions involved in the first place can be stopped short at just those levels which might increase the prospects of stability of what would otherwise be an impractical set of distinctions. Either the specialized operations with regard to exchange must be a legitimate part of action in terms of the government, or if they are regarded as nongovernmental, those engaged in them must have some legitimate roles from the point of view of the members of the government and the members of the society in general, if governments are to be stable. The instability implicit in such impossible separations of relevant activities need not be dramatic and catastrophic in relatively nonmodernized contexts. They make themselves felt by long-run drains on the efficiency and objectivity of the operations carried out in terms of the governmental organizations. Such gradualism can not hold in relatively modernized contexts.

V
ASSOCIATED UNITS

A. ARMED FORCES

As associated units have been defined above [pp. 438–439] armed forces are not necessarily associated units.[17] Especially as rela-

[17] Unless otherwise noted I shall use the term *armed forces* to refer to the organizations involved rather than to the sets of personnel involved as members of the organizations concerned.

tively modernized nations emerge, armed forces are likely to be particular subsystems of the government. Nevertheless, there certainly have been many societies in which armed forces were present but not as a part(s) of the governmental organization. Whether armed forces are considered as associated units or as subsystems of the government, they are exceedingly likely to be present in all cases of societies or nations interesting to students of public affairs. I regard armed forces as so highly relevant to the matters discussed here that I have included a separate chapter on the armed forces [pp. 571–605], and I defer extended discussion of armed forces to it.

Armed forces have classically had dual functions, one of which is exceedingly likely to be overlooked in general discussions. The first is the classic and obvious one on which most comment is centered. This is the use of the members and materiel as an instrument of policy in relations between the members of one society and another or the relations between the members of one government and another. Whether such armed forces have been private nongovernmental armed forces or subsystems of the government, their relevance to governments is not obscure. The leaders of armed forces, whether public or private, generally have important relations with the members of the government. Nothing so drives home to a leader of the armed forces the potentialities of his position for strategic positions in his own government as the focus of attention placed on his position by involvement in a war. If these are popular armed forces and popular governments, a military man who seeks to seize a leadership role in the government is involved in a governmental revolution. If the government is characterized by little popular participation and little communication with the people, ambitious military leaders are likely to participate in what have here been called palace revolutions. They may, of course, participate in palace revolutions in cases of more popular governments, but such revolutions become governmental revolutions as well. I have nothing to add here, beyond emphasizing the fact that the concentration of power in the hands of military leadership in times of war makes some transfer of those powers to the sphere of domestic governments probable, even if initially those transfers are limited overwhelmingly to attempts to acquire the means necessary from the leader's point of view to prosecute the strictly military aspects of his operations efficiently.

Operations in terms of the armed forces have internal as well as external functions. We tend to ignore the internal functions because armed forces have figured relatively so little in the internal maintenance of order in our society [pp. 571–576]. Nevertheless for most societies of any considerable scale the armed forces have been the major organizations in terms of which force has been applied as a means for the maintenance of internal order. Members of armed forces, qua members, have also been used for the destruction or the alteration of the structures of internal order, but the important thing is that, ideally as well as actually, the men and materiel have been regarded as the last resort for the maintenance of governmental stability against programs and activities considered deviant by members of the government, if not by members of the society at large. The actual use of force is only the extreme form of the exercise of power is one direction, and the existence of no government and of no society can be understood in terms of applications of force alone, but the exercise of force is never irrelevent to the existence of governments, and armed forces are by definition never irrelevant to the exercise of force, real or potential.

If the armed forces constitute associated units rather than subsystems of the government, and if the members of a government seek the support of the leaders and/or members in general for the maintenance of internal order, they have in essence accomplished a palace revolution since the leader of such an armed force in actuality becomes a [or the] major power in that governmental organization whether he realizes it or not. Academic stereotypes about military intelligences to the contrary notwithstanding, military leaders have seldom been too obtuse to see the implications of such resorts. The situation is not completely different when the armed forces are subsystems of the government itself. Unless the leadership of the armed forces does constitute the major leadership of the government, the armed forces are likely to constitute a sufficiently discrete and easily definable subsystem of the government so that the members of the armed forces easily can and do think of their organization as an associated unit rather than a subsystem. If so, one implication of the use of the members of the armed forces for the maintenance of order is a palace revolution except insofar as the use of them for these purposes is required on a relatively small scale and in a relatively limited segment of the activities of the members of the society in general. The more general the disturbance members of the armed forces are called upon to quell, the greater is the likelihood that some of the leaders of the armed forces will become the leaders of the government if they are not already. The most relevant difference between armed forces as a subsystem of the government and associated armed forces is the fact that any occasion which causes the members of the government to rely upon the members of associated armed-force units alerts the military leaders to their opportunity to take power. As long as the armed forces are subsystems of the government, the dividing line between restricted opportunities and more general ones for the seizure of power is considerably less obvious.

Some of the special economic implications of armed-force systems are highly relevant for governments. Manpower is always a question of strategic significance for armed forces. To some extent the members of armed forces have to devote a considerable amount of their time, if they are to be effective, to special training in the bearing of arms, and those forms of special training cannot very well be combined simultaneously with other forms of productivity. In addition, the capital equipment necessary for the exercise of arms is never completely convertible to other purposes, is usually large in scale, and is expensive. In addition, in a number of social contexts, it is necessary to keep standing armed forces, if action in terms of them is to be effective. This necessity increases with the scale of the societies concerned, and it also increases radically with increases in the level of modernization attained. Finally, unlike other subsystems of the government, the members of the armed forces ordinarily spend only a small portion of their total time in being in either the external or internal functions toward which their activities are primarily oriented. Therefore, when armed forces exist, allocations of goods and services in terms of them constitute a considerable item in the general budget of the government; their members can only within limits accomplish the purposes for which they are primarily oriented in combinations with other purposes; and to the extent that such combinations are not possible, both the capital expended in terms of them and the maintenance of the services of all of the members of the armed forces are constantly consumed whether or not those services and the attendant capital are actively engaged in pursuit of the functions for which they are designed. There is no comparable cost of maintaining a constantly ready reserve, as it were, in any other area of governmental concerns in social history.

On the other hand—and not inconsistently with what has just been asserted—to some extent the forms of special training appropriate to armed-force personnel *can* be combined with other forms of productivity and to some extent the relevant capital equipment *is* convertible. Army engineers can build civilian as well as military bridges—indeed the same bridge may serve in both contexts—and army trucks can carry civilian loads while army bulldozers can clear land for farming as well as camping. The preoccupation of most statesmen and scholars with armed forces as an organizational instrumentality oriented to the exercise of force has obscured these possibilities. As will be discussed in Chapter 4 below, these possibilities may have little exploited implications for the development of late-comers to modernization. Although the problems involved are of a different kind and order, there may also be possibilities here relatively unexplored by the leaders of the governments of the most highly modernized societies.

B. PARTIES AND THE LIKE

Reference to political parties always raises the question of mass government—i.e., of mass participation in the government. Operation in terms of political parties is always such as to increase the *appearance at least* of predominantly universalistic selection. Political parties always become a sort of buffer between the general distribution of tastes in the population and the members of the government. Via activities in terms of party organizations the essence of the particularistic preferences associated with the individuals who belong to or act in terms of the party is distilled into some results which in a sense cancel out the detailed personal preferences of individuals into a more nearly universalistically defined general policy or selection of leadership. It is by no means true that political parties are organizations whose members function in such a way that the lowest common denominator of agreement always results, but to some extent a common denominator of agreement does result from the various individual preferences of the members who belong to such an organization. To the extent that this is the case, some indiosyncratic individual preferences are canceled out and the result is somewhat more nearly universalistically defined. This, of course, does not imply that the result is better or worse than would otherwise be the case. The increased emphasis on universalism may simply be that a candidate has been selected who offends the general public less than his competitors, but even this is to some extent an achieved rather than an ascribed characteristic. Wherever mass participation takes place, such a canceling out of particularistic elements is involved to some degree. The development of mass production, if it is viable, carries with it an inescapable channeling of tastes. The operation in terms of political parties is to the political aspects of behavior as large-scale mass-production firms and large-scale mass markets are to the economic aspects of behavior—with some important differences, of course.

From the point of view of this work the most important of these differences has to do with rationality. It has been argued above [pp. 263 and 329] that to some extent market structures mitigate the impact of lack of adequate knowledge in the allocation of goods and services via the decentralization and parcellation of decision making. Political parties have just the opposite effect. In a sense they always involve more people more of the time than would otherwise have been the case. Action in terms of political parties focusses their attention on influencing more large-scaled governmental systems than they would otherwise have taken an active interest in, etc. Such behavior often has common denominator effects, but insofar as political parties are not centralized, action in terms of them tends to maximize the influence of a number of sources of ignorance or special prejudice which might not otherwise have come into play. The extent to which a market mechanism is a suitable substitute for adequate knowledge is a function of the numbers of degrees of freedom in it, i.e., its lack of centralization. The lack of centralization of a political party has just the opposite implication unless the decentralization is such that activity in terms of the political party has little or no effect on action in terms of the government. Participation in political parties—however salutory in fostering democracy—has negative implications for any attempt to maximize rationality in this sphere whether in the service of bestial or blessed goals.

Political parties always pose a special problem for the members of government. While they are units of high relevance to the governmental organizations, they are always units outside governmental control structures. One may feel that this is contradicted by the so-called authoritarian cases, but actually their governments confirm this. In most of these governments it is the "political party" system so-called whose leaders in fact control the action in terms of the government rather than vice versa. Technically the Communist Party is outside the Soviet government in both China and Russia. Quite clearly in both these societies the party organization is the unit in terms of which the government is controlled rather than vice versa. Something of the same is true in the case of Nazi Germany, Fascist Italy, and Franco Spain. It is not true that either the members of the Democratic or the Republican Party, as a party, control the government, but it is true that the operations in terms of those parties are technically outside the government but highly relevant to operations in terms of it. In a two-party situation like that of the United States, the activities of the members of both parties are highly relevant to the leaders who are actually engaged in running the government. Often the problem for the government leaders of preventing deviant behavior on the part of the members of the party is a more serious one than the problem of coping with the opposition of the members of the party out of power. In United States society, at least, some of these problems are clearly visible in the fact that even the most responsible members of the two opposing parties feel obliged to forget partisan advantage primarily in matters conceived to be crucial for the future of the United States because of their international implications. There is a clear-cut realization on the part of the sophisticated members, and even the relatively unsophisticated ones, of both parties that their behavior is highly relevant to the stability of the government regardless of whether they are in or out of power. The responsible members of both parties are quite clearly convinced that there are many positions which they might take which would give them a partisan advantage only at the cost of a level and type of instability in the government which they are unwilling to countenance. In the case of modern authoritarian governments at least, this sort of thing is not a problem for the members of the government. If anything the roles are reversed. The government is something of a problem from the point of view of the members of the party. This may simply be another way of saying that in such societies the party organization is in effect the actual government whatever the ideal structures may be from other points of view.

In general the problem of the relation between governments and associated units is a special form of the problem of the relations between governmental organizations and other social systems in the society. To some extent the other social systems lie outside the government, but the action carried out in terms of them is relevant to the action carried out in terms of the government and vice versa. In the case of political parties and similarly associated units, the difference lies in the fact that both ideally and actually what goes on in terms of these units is highly relevant to what goes on in terms of the government. Despite that relevance, to some extent a separation is maintained as between the members of such organizations. Activities in terms of ordinary social systems in a society may or may not be highly relevant to what goes on in terms of the governmental organization, and to that extent the existence of some separation as between governmental jurisdiction and the jurisdiction in terms of those other units may not pose critical problems of coordination and control. The close implications for one another of activities in terms of the associated units and the governmental units themselves are far more likely to constitute critical problems. To some extent these problems diminish with the general increase of modernization. They diminish, however, not because of the decrease in the relevance of what takes place in terms of associated units for operations in terms of the government. They diminish rather by contrast, since what takes place in terms of all units of any considerable scale in relatively modernized societies, whether they are considered associated units or not, comes to have increasingly critical implications for operations in terms of the governmental organization and vice versa. As the degrees of centralization and interdependence increase, clear-cut distinctions between associated, as opposed to nonassociated, units and governments tend to disappear.

PREDOMINANTLY ECONOMICALLY

ORIENTED ORGANIZATIONS

I

DEFINITIONS

A. GENERAL

Any organization whose members view action in terms of it as ideally and/or actually predominantly preoccupied with the allocation of goods and services is for the present purposes defined as a predominantly economically oriented organization. An organization that is not predominantly economically oriented ideally and/or actually may be considered one, and one that is, may not. Such errors may be made by members and/or nonmembers of the organization. It is possible to differentiate degrees of orientation to the economic aspects of the behavior conducted in terms of the organization. One can speak of one organization as more predominantly economically oriented than another, although both of them may be specialized along these lines. One can also speak of an organization being predominantly economically oriented when considered in isolation but not so when considered in other contexts. For example, although a government is a predominantly politically oriented organization, there are many subsystems of governments that are correctly described as predominantly economically oriented organizations, e.g., factories that are specifically government factories in the sense both of ownership of associated means and of a membership who are government personnel. The implications of the predominant orientation to the allocation of goods and services of the members of these governmental subsystems may be quite different from the case of what we ordinarily consider a business firm or a nongovernmental predominantly economically oriented organization. Some of these differences will inhere in the relation of this sort of unit to the more general organization of which it is a subsystem. Correspondingly in a predominantly economically oriented organization such as a business firm, there may be a subsystem overwhelmingly oriented to the political aspects either of that organization itself or of the society in terms of which that organization operates. Organizationally speaking, for example, the board of directors of a large-scale corporation is the predominantly politically oriented subsystem par excellence of that organization, but it is a different subsystem from the one which involves as members the President of the United States and his Cabinet.

B. SPECIAL INSTANCES

In discussing the economic aspects of action generally, and predominantly economically oriented organizations in particular, I shall distinguish three special types of organizations: *production units, exchange units,* and *consumption units.* One may refer to organizations as *production units, exchange units,* or *consumption units* simply as a way of indicating that for the moment interest is in the production, exchange, or consumption that takes place in terms of these units. In any organization, however, elements of all three inhere, however irrelevant they may be from many points of view. Without being either clumsy or misleading, it is useful to be able to say that the family unit is ordinarily the major production unit in relatively nonmodernized societies. All such a statement means is that the family units in such a society are the organizations in terms of which the greater part of what is considered production by an observer and/or by the members of that society is carried out. It does not imply that the family is predominantly economically oriented, that the family is predominantly oriented to production, that the family is not also a unit in terms of which exchange and consumption takes place, or anything else. These distinctions, used in conjunction with the others defined, make possible several distinctions. *Specialized* and *nonspecialized* production, exchange, and consumption units can be distinguished. *Specialized production units* would be predominantly production-oriented predominantly economically oriented units, and nonspecialized production units would be ones considered in their aspects of production despite the fact that the organizations were either nonspecialized or specialized with regard to aspects other than economic ones. It may be fruitful to distinguish societies on the basis of whether or not important elements of production are carried out in terms of predominantly economically oriented organizations or not.[1]

On this score remarks made above (p. 248) about the special asymmetry of production and consumption as a specialized focus of orientation of social systems must be kept in mind. Despite the

[1] Since the concepts of production, exchange, and consumption used here are subcategories of the concept of economic allocation in general, by definition a predominantly production-oriented organization is a predominantly economically oriented organization.

fact that from an observer's point of view what is production in one sense is simultaneously consumption in another—and in this connection exchange can be thought of as a special form of production—there are no organizations which are specialized as being both predominantly economically oriented and predominantly consumption oriented, although there are quite important cases of organizations that are both predominantly economically oriented and predominantly production oriented. Whatever individual motives may be, in the structuring of social systems, consumption as a focus never clearly predominates over other orientations for the membership. Thus all predominantly economically oriented organizations are either predominantly production oriented in general or predominantly exchange oriented in particular.

When I speak of production units I mean organizations considered from the point of view of the goods and/or services which can be regarded as an output of the activities of the members of the organization acting in terms of the organization. In this sense *all* organizations are to some extent production units. The ones of most obvious importance to us are those whose members, and/or the other members in the society ordinarily *think of* as having an output as a function of the activities of the members. Of hardly less importance from my point of view, however, are those units whose implications for production [or exchange] are likely to be overlooked specifically because their members, and/or the members of other units with whom the former interact, and/or scientific observers tend *not to think of* the units as concerned with or involving production of goods and/or services. Ordinarily, for example, friendship units are not thought of in these terms. Family units usually are in part, though their members, and often observers, are never fully aware of all of the production aspects of activities carried out in terms of them. Although friendship units are not ordinarily considered production units [though they may be from the point of view of an observer] and family units frequently are, these family units are certainly no more predominantly economically oriented organizations than the friendships are.

Another qualification is important here. I have already pointed out above [pp. 210–211 and 231–232] that from a strict scientific observer's pont of view there is no distinction between production and consumption on the basis of the intrinsic nature of the activities involved. Nevertheless, it makes a difference, even in analyzing societies characterized by relatively little or no specialization of organizations or activities in terms of economic aspects, that certain activities are regarded as significant intrinsically for production rather than consumption and vice versa.

With regard to production units in the sense used here, one may further distinguish with regard to whether or not the production referred to is reckoned primarily in terms of goods or services. This is a generally useful distinction, but it has come to have a special utility in describing the economic aspects of highly modernized societies. As modernization increases, an increasing portion of those whose occupational roles are carried out in terms of specialized production units consists of those engaged in outputs of services rather than goods.

In the vast majority of societies the production units have been nonspecialized as social systems even if the goods and services concerned have been highly specialized. The organization in terms of which most individuals have carried out most of such action has been some sort of family unit until relatively modernized societies developed. Even in the context of relatively modernized societies some production, especially of the service sort, continues to be carried out in family terms, although in most discussion of economic allocation these forms of production are at one and the same time ignored and too important to be ignored. The present chapter, however, is concerned with production, exchange, and consumption as carried out in terms of predominantly economically oriented organizations. While these specialized organizations have existed as subsystems of other societies than relatively modernized ones, they are carried to great lengths in relatively modernized societies. Even in such societies characterized by complete government ownership of all of the means of production, factories and similar specialized organizations exist as predominantly economically oriented subsystems of the government. In societies in which structures of private ownership exist, again there is a very wide variety of factories, business firms, research laboratories, etc., which may be spoken of as production units in this specialized sense.[2]

___

[2] Whether a research laboratory qualifies as a production unit in the specialized sense of a predominantly economically oriented organization depends very much upon the context in which one finds it. The research laboratory of a major business firm qualifies as a specialized production unit in this sense as does almost any research laboratory whose corporate title includes the word consultant. On the other hand, an identical research laboratory which is a subcategory of say Princeton University would not be considered a specialized production unit in this sense specifically because, although it too is concerned with the production of ideas and the like, research takes place in terms of it as a subsystem of Princeton University which is a predominantly educationally oriented organization rather than a predominantly economically oriented organization. When universities are

With all the qualifications which have already been suggested about the term production unit in mind, the term *exchange unit* requires some special discussion. Actually an exchange unit, as the term is used here, is a special form of a production unit in terms of which the productive aspects of behavior are concerned with a particular kind of service, namely the allocation of goods and services as such. Action in terms of exchange units, from this point of view, is concentrated on distribution. The example par excellence of exchange units in this sense are merchant's organizations, brokers, department stores, etc. Although exchange units are closely related to the facilities for communication in any social context, they are not coterminous with those facilities. For example the railroad corporations or the American Telephone and Telegraph Company from this point of view fall primarily into the category of production units rather than exchange units. In the context of most societies both the producers and consumers of given goods or services tend to think of them in terms of some of their intrinisc qualities. The service of allocation, apart from the physical transport of goods and services or messages about them, although as observable in theory as any other empirical quality of the goods or services, is a great deal more ephemeral from the point of view of most members of most societies. For this reason, at least, specialists in exchange in this sense are more often than not regarded with suspicion.

I shall speak of *consumption units* in two senses. The first is simply the obverse of the term *production unit*. Any unit in terms of which any goods or services are dissipated or converted into

---

referred to as PhD. factories, the implication is explicitly derogatory, because it carries the implication that the preoccupation is with output rather than with knowledge and education as such. With the development of the modern university in the setting of relatively modernized societies, the great emphasis on the importance of research as well as teaching has carried with it a whole special set of problems for the members of the universities as well as for other members of the societies for which universities are important. There is the persistent questions of "What are the criteria which indicate that creative research is takng place?" and "If creative research is to be a measure of achievement and if a scholar's rewards in terms of the university are to be based on such achievement, how is creative research to be measured?" In hunting for standards, ease of measurement is always one of the most appealing aids to seduction. In the context of societies whose members place so much emphasis on objective measurement, it is not a matter of chance that the quantitative measures of a scholar's bibliography come to occupy such a role in his qualifications for rewards. The surprising thing is that such criteria do not play an even more important role. Nevertheless, it is still quite clear that the assertion that the estimate of true academic worth is primarily a function of precise quantitative measures of output is enough to put virtually any academic on the defensive immediately.

another form is, from the point of view of those considering those goods or services, a consumption unit. In this sense the members of the General Motors Corporation are consuming steel plates, department stores are great consumption units from the point of view of toy manufacturers, etc. This second sense of the term *consumption unit* is the ordinary layman's sense of the term. From the point of view of the layman there is a tendency to think of the unit as a consumption unit when from his point of view the process stops there, i.e., the distinct roles of the goods or services end. The layman's foremost conception of a consumption unit has always been the family—if he thinks in such terms at all. He may be well aware that consumption in his sense does take place in other organizational settings, but the vast majority of those are either regarded as contexts which are relatively specialized and rare and not for members of the general public or as contexts with overtones of dissoluteness and immorality.

As indicated above [pp. 247–248] there is an actual asymmetry about structures of production and consumption. In no society are there any predominantly consumption-oriented units ideally speaking. No hedonism has gone so far. Actually speaking, there may have been individual organizations of this sort, but even these are almost certainly rare. Such an organization would be considered deviant, and such a deviance, rare. It could only be manned by virtuosi of puristic sensualism and even the devout observances of some of the Existentialists have not yet produced a set of heroes to man such a unit.

Since there seem to be no predominantly economically oriented organizations which are viewed by their members or the other members of the society as primarily consumption units, consumption units as such will not be discussed in this chapter in any detail. As the terms production and consumption have been defined here, they have nothing whatsoever to do with any estimates of merit or demerit of the activities involved. There are plenty of specialized production units, especially in relatively modernized societies, whose members aim specifically at the production of goods and/or services for what the layman considers to be consumption in the most hedonistic sense. All sorts of specialized entertainment-producing facilities fall into this category, e.g., night clubs, bars, etc. Nevertheless, from the point of view of the individuals who manage and work in such organizations or who own them, their preoccupation is with an output of goods and/or services. They are concerned with increasing or maintaining their share of the market, etc. Their clients or customers are the consumers. They do not think of themselves as consumers in this context. A private club owned and operated by its members for their own recreation—operated in the sense that the members literally performed all the tasks necessary for operation in terms of the club—might approach a predominantly consumption-oriented organization. It would not be such a structure, however, because such a club would be primarily oriented to recreation rather than to consumption as such, Even an organization pre-dominantly oriented to the sort of thing that Veblen referred to as conspicuous consumption would hardly qualify for this special category, since as Veblen himself realized conspicuous consump-tion is likely to be an aspect of individual behavior or behavior in terms of organizations rather than the sole or major focus of any organization as such. Furthermore, from Veblen's pont of view, conspicuous consumption placed the accent on what is here con-sidered expression rather than on consumption as such. For there to be a predominantly consumption-oriented organization, there would have to be an organization for whose members consump-tion was conceived somehow as approaching an end in itself. Most consumption, like most production, is certainly regarded as a means rather than as an end in itself by most of the members of most societies.

What is interesting about this is the fact that, however much the distinction between production and consumption as viewed by scientists may be a question of the point of view from which one looks at the process, from the point of view of the vast majority of members of all societies, the distinction is, in some sense asymmetrical. It has certainly been possible for many members of relatively modernized societies as well as of some relatively nonmodernized ones to think of themselves as over-whelmingly oriented not merely to economic aspects of behavior but to those considered as production in particular. In the case of relatively modernized societies this is true for the vast majority of the members of the society for a portion of their lives which they consider to be one of the most important portions of their lives. It is characteristically that portion of their lives on which, insofar as action takes place according to the ideal patterns of the society, most of their livelihood, well-being, and general standing in the community depends. Ideally speaking, in relatively modernized societies an individual's performance in terms of his occupational role is one of the most important criteria for his standing in the community. Those occupational roles are considered as produc-tive roles whether they exist in predominantly economically oriented organizations or differently oriented ones. Thus the ordi-nary individual often considers himself to be predominantly oriented to production, and he is so considered by other members of the society as well. He never considers himself in comparable degree consumption oriented.[3] In the context of most societies it would take a most sophisticated sybaritic actor to admit to such an orientation without feeling self-conscious about it. Somehow, with or without an ascetic or spiritual ethic, production has always been considered more respectable as a focus of attention or even as an end in itself than consumption. There are all sorts of religious overtones involved; the widespread ethical belief that it is "better to give than to receive" must somehow be related.

One of the developments in connection with the leisure revolution already discussed above may be a change with regard to the attitudes of individuals toward what they consider as production and consumption. Insofar as the leisure revolution succeeds, a major measure of achievement will become the support of a properly luxurious way of life via the efforts of the husband or father or other individual concerned in an increasingly restricted time period of productive effort. Even in the present beginnings of the leisure revolution, the phenomenon of moonlighting is interesting from this point of view. A *moonlighter* is one who in the time left over after his regular thirty or thirty-five hour week takes a second job. At an earlier period of United States history such application on his part would have been considered the minimum level of asceticism associated with the person of good character. Today we are ambivalent about moonlighters. We do

[3] I would not want this discussion biassed by unconscious neglect of various implications of sex role differentiation or absolute-age role differentiation. As the argument is phrased, it rivets attention on adult males. The argument is not negated by taking into consideration adult females who are regarded as wives and/or mothers rather than as holders of occupational roles in the more specialized sense, or retired old folks or youngsters or infants considered as not yet properly fitted to undertake occupational roles. All are expected to lead productive lives in some sense. Derogation of various sorts is implied if one seriously refers to them as preoccupied almost exclusively with consumption. Even for the members of highly modernized societies who are overwhelmingly likely to think of the family as a consumption unit when considering it from the economic point of view, the idea that it be so oriented in general would connote all sorts of sordid qualities such as greed, selfishness, self-indulgence, improvidence, sloth, etc. The individual who is happy with his work is usually admired right up to the point of fanaticism. He who overworks may be regarded as lacking in a sense of humor, proper perspective—even as mad —but he who overconsumes is described by far more derogatory terms; greedy is one of the milder of these terms. Contemplation of this asymmetry leads me to speculate that there is a fundamental uniformity about human nature that guarantees a universal appeal to such mottoes as "Don't knock, boost" and "Accentuate the positive; eliminate the negative." There may be both a fundamental human bias toward optimism and some valid precipitate of insight in what Veblen called the instinct of workmanship.

not know quite whether to applaud them for their energy, re-sourcefulness, etc., or to consider them as pushing, overly ambi-tious, or even greedy. One result of the leisure revolution may very well be a situation in which for the first time in world history distinctions, between production and consumption, if made, are either truly symmetrical or the emphasis on consumption in fact becomes both ideally and actually more highly rated as a sign of cultivation and achievement than the time spent in productive effort. If so, this will be one of the most extreme general social revolutions in history. Approximations to this have hitherto been confined almost entirely to the orgiastic recreations of a restricted elite set. The leisure revolution will not be characterized by this re-stricted sort of behavior. It will probably be characterized by a gen-eral line of emphasis on familistic recreation for most of the mem-bers of the general society with the exception of the elite as far as leadership and income is concerned. It is more likely to be homey than frenetic. It is more likely to be a mass phenomenon than an elite one, since under the new regime to follow the leisure revolu-tion the elite will be much too busy to be homey or orgiastic.

The fact that no social organization is generally regarded as predominantly consumption oriented is important in understand-ing the relevance of economic aspects for other social aspects. Here again so-called differences between materialistically ori-ented and spiritually oriented peoples are quite misleading. For the most materialistic of peoples the allocation of goods and services is generally regarded as instrumental for other purposes rather than as an end in itself. It is no less instrumental for the spiritually oriented. Indeed, most of the so-called distinctions between these two are difficult to draw. The use of a person's income to obtain a good education for his children is somehow regarded as less materialistic than the use of his income for the purchase of an automobile. The two uses are certainly different, but a good education, as that is generally appreciated today, is every bit as materialistic as a new automobile. The problem is becoming more confused because increasingly, in some social contexts at least, a new automobile is coming to be considered a part of the "good education package." The facts that there is in general no society in terms of which the actual consumption of goods and services is regarded as an end in itself and that there are no specialized consumption units imply that the consumption aspects of goods and services both ideally and actually are highly relevant in all known societies to a wide variety of other functions apart from economic allocation as such. It also implies that they are so regarded by the members of any society. It may not occur to the members of any given society to take the position of an observer and comment on this sort of thing of his own free will, but if asked about it, he will have views about it.

This is a [the?] key to what Marx saw. In some respects the allocation of goods and services is always relevant to any other aspects of action considered by the members of a society. It by no means follows that the economic aspect constitutes the only relevant one or even that the economic aspect constitutes one of the most important ones in all situations, but it is true that goods and services always appear in any action as an ineradicable element of means for other ends. From the point of view of the members of a society, consumption in the economic sense consists explicitly of the utilization of goods and services considered as such for conversion into other action or other goods which are not necessarily regarded primarily or even importantly as goods and services subject to similar allocation. In some of the contexts of all societies the conversion is considered by the actors involved as an explicit further step in the allocation of goods and services and to that extent as predominantly economically oriented, but even for the most highly modernized of societies this is never the case in all contexts. When it is the case for the relatively modernized societies, it is a case of consumption in terms of an organization whose members regard their operations as primarily production oriented.

In all human action in which other orientations take precedence or in which the set of orientations is so mixed that an observer could only with great difficulty tell that one aspect as opposed to another took precedence, the relevance of the economic aspects tends to be ignored. Insofar as the allocation of goods and services as such becomes explicitly important in the predominantly politically oriented sphere, for example, the intrusion of those concerns tends to be resented and contemned. The same is true in the predominantly educationally oriented ranges of activity. One of the standard relevant clichés of discussions by university presidents of the difficulties of their position is that they must spend so much time as fund raisers. No university president, however lofty his ideals, can ignore his budget without dooming his ideals. It need not follow, however, that the budget of a great university determines her ideal structures or the ideals of her president. The Catholic Church which is certainly a predominantly religiously oriented organization has recently been rated highly for her managerial structures, and the handling of problems of the allocation of goods and services by her leaders was deemed especially noteworthy. Only a foolish cynic would essay to describe the Catholic Church on the basis of her structures of economic allocation alone, but only the most naïve true believer could take the position that these structures have nothing whatsoever to do with the case either. Much of the relevance of economic allocation for other aspects of action appears at precisely the point that goods or services are no longer regarded by the individuals concerned as subjects of economic allocation as such. No observer can afford to ignore this or be gulled by the fact that the peoples he studies may be unaware of it.

I I
GENERAL REMARKS

A. THE SPECIAL NATURE OF PREDOMINANTLY ECONOMICALLY ORIENTED ORGANIZATIONS IN RELATIVELY NONMODERNIZED SOCIETIES

By contrast with what the members of relatively modernized societies have come to take for granted, predominantly economically oriented organizations are not to be taken for granted in relatively nonmodernized contexts. In the first place, they are by no means general in all such societies, and they are certainly rare in the so-called primitive societies. In terms of these societies and of many other relatively nonmodernized ones, virtually all of the economic aspects of behavior are likely to be handled as functions of another kind of organization altogether—usually a kinship organization. In other words, from the point of view of members of such societies, virtually all allocations of goods and services are likely to involve transfers as among kin or two or more sets of kin on a basis considered primarily relevant to the fact that they represent different sets of kin. The actual allocation of goods and services involved may, from the point of view of the members of the society, be so incidental to the interrelationships among kin as not to be regarded as separable from those kinships as such. What an economist might regard as the foreign trade of the members of a given tribe might be considered by them an exchange of gifts incidental to visiting.

Although there have been many societies without any clearly specialized predominantly economically oriented units, some such specialization is characteristic of all societies of any considerable scale, whether they be relatively modernized or not. In relatively nonmodernized societies, such specialized organizations may be limited to merchant firms, and even given societies of considerable scale, predominantly economically oriented organizations need not be highly developed. Finally, even if these organizations are rather highly developed in a given relatively nonmodernized society, the overwhelming majority of what the members consider to be the productive activities does not take place in terms of those specialized organizations nor in terms of governmental organizations. In such social contexts the development of predominantly economically oriented organizations is likely to be carried furthest in terms of what have here been described as exchange units. In such contexts the overwhelming majority of individuals considered by other members of the society to be engaged in productive efforts are engaged in productive efforts in terms of the so-called primary industries, especially agriculture. Those activities are overwhelmingly likely to be conducted in terms of family organizations rather than a functionally specialized organization of any sort.

In this connection the levels of decentralization and self-sufficiency of subsystems are highly relevant to the general discussion. The degree of specialization achieved in the relatively nonmodernized society is in part a function of the degree of decentralization and self-sufficiency of the other subsystems in the society. The more highly decentralized and self-sufficient the other subsystems are, the less important such specialized units will be in the society. Here also lies the key to the fact that the developments of specialized organizations in relatively nonmodernized societies are so overwhelmingly likely to be, initially at least, exchange units in the sense of the term here. It is interesting to note that even occupations which appear to be intrinsically made for specialization if only because the people who labor in these terms cannot eat the fruits of their labor—occupations such as mining—are not ordinarily conducted on a relatively specialized basis in the absence of a fairly highly developed specialized set of exchange units. Prior to the development of those systems mining is likely to be carried out on a family unit basis. Mining operations which require mass-coordinated labor on a nonkinship basis does not develop in the absence of some specialized service of supply.

Prior to the development of relatively modernized societies, however, there have been some social organizations, which certainly appear to have been characterized by high levels of specialization of exchange units. These have, however been unusual in social history. The Venetian City-states and the cities of the Hanseatic League are some of the best examples of such large-scale social organizations. Whether one is well advised to consider these as distinct societies or as special subsystems closely integrated with other societies is a matter for technical experts. They certainly were highly developed organizations; they were important in social history; their members were to an extraordinary degree accustomed to operating in terms of predominantly economically oriented units, and they operated as if their organizations had considerable autonomy. So did the members of other societies. Like merchant firms within a given society, these merchant societies were important in early decreases of international self-sufficiency and early increases in international centralization.

B. UBIQUITOUS NATURE IN RELATIVELY MODERNIZED SOCIETIES

Whatever the frequency of predominantly economically oriented organizations in relatively nonmodernized societies, they are ubiquitous in all relatively modernized societies. As far as their presence or absence is concerned, the usual distinctions between socialist and capitalistic societies, between authoritarian and democratic societies, between welfare states and individualistic states, among monarchies, republics, dictatorships, etc., all such distinctions are quite beside the point. It makes quite a lot of difference from various points of view whether or not a given predominantly economically oriented organization is explicitly a subsystem of a government, a subsystem of some other predominantly economically oriented organization, or a separate organization existing as one of many subsystems of the society. Such differences as these may be the main difference as between socialist societies and capitalistic societies. Nevertheless, however important these variations from other points of view, they do not affect the fact that increasingly such units will be present as the level of modernization increases, nor does it affect the validity of the proposition that any factors which impede the development of such specialized economically oriented organizations will interfere with the development of modernization in general and the maintenance of general social stability. In no relatively modernized social context is there any substantial movement in the direction of increasing the allocation of goods and services in terms of relatively nonspecialized organizations such as the family organization.

The real problems in analyzing relatively modernized societies are those of the interdependencies of such economically specialized organizations and other organizations. The most general and critical of these is the problem of interdependency of such organizations and governments in general—regardless of differences between capitalist and socialist systems.

The problem of all such subordinations is to prevent preoccupation with the political implications of the operation in terms of such organizations from producing irrational or other nonrational results as far as the implications of economic allocation are concerned for the maintenance of stability in relatively modernized societies. Although the state of development of the field of economics is not all it will be, there are nevertheless some generalizations about such economic allocation which will hold true for any possible society. Thus there are some principles which, even if their implications are not followed or even realized by the leaders concerned, will still enable us to predict quite explicit results.

For example, unless one is able to change the social structure in general and the resource picture in particular of the world as it exists today, major preoccupation with steel production in the state of Israel is not economically feasible under any form of government or organization. This is not to say that it isn't conceivable for a government to exist despite the fact that its members decide to devote considerable effort and resources to building up a steel industry. If they do, however, certain implications for the allocation of goods and services in general in terms of the state of Israel as well as certain other features of that society can be clearly predicted. In the field of economic welfare, given quite general criteria of value such as an increasing standard of living, the provisions of sufficient protections via modern arms and the like of one nation from potential attack by others, etc., there are again rational as opposed to irrational policies which are not simply dependent variables of the state of the society in general or of the government in particular, though the former, has of course more implications than the latter. As the level of specialization increases and correspondingly as the level of self-sufficiency declines and that of interdependency rises, the degrees of freedom in organization of the allocation of goods and services on a relatively nonspecialized or on a specialized basis predominantly oriented to some other aspect of social action than the economic one declines increasingly, if the society is to be stable. Increasingly, somewhere along the line of organizational differentiation, there must be organizations whose members are predominantly preoccupied with what they regard as the most rational solution to the problems of economic allocation given some objectives, however set for them, in terms of which this performance in terms of the organization to which they belong will be judged by themselves and others—if the process of modernization is to continue. For those who have occupational roles in such an organization it comes to matter increasingly little whether that organization is a subsystem of a government, of another predominantly economically oriented organization, of a church, of a predominantly recreationally oriented organization, or of a predominantly educationally oriented organization. From this point of view one of the main distinctions which remains meaningful between a capitalistic and a socialistic society is that a term such as businesslike will be used as praise for the proper running of such an organization as a subsystem of any other specialized organization in the former case, whereas a different term is more likely to be used in the latter. In both cases, however, the terms will have the same meaning, i.e., that there has been a maximization of rationality with regard to the allocation of goods and services in terms of criteria set for the members of the unit concerned by others.

There is another respect in which the ordinary descriptive clichés increasingly lose their ability to inform as the level of modernization characteristic of the societies concerned increases. That socialistic governments cannot exist without subsystems which are predominantly oriented to economic considerations should go without saying. Again and again the importance of this is witnessed by the problems created in terms of a socialistic society when the manager of a given plant owned by the government reports that his quotas have been fulfilled, although they have not. It makes little difference whether his erroneous report is a function of political zeal or fear. From certain points of view the effect is exactly the same as that of pieing the books of a business firm to show profits when none exist.

Some role of politically oriented considerations in connection with the operations in terms of business firms in a capitalistic society is also unquestioned. The leaders of privately owned broadcasting companies, for example, are much concerned with the presentation of various political candidates at election time. It is true that explicit laws have been passed which to some extent regulate such matters, but even apart from those laws, the members of those broadcasting firms in their capacities as representatives of those firms would be involved in the presentation of a considerable amount of coverage of political events. By no means all of this could be justified on the basis of presentation of the news or of competing with other broadcasting forms plus the laws which require, for example, equal time. Within certain limits at least, the following questions may well be raised: "Is this in fact a private ownership system?" When are enough departures from *laissez-faire* involved so that in effect it is a socialistic rather than a capitalistic system? Correspondingly, insofar as the representatives of the government of a socialistic society alter their policies on the basis of what is economically feasible in terms of a particular subsystem of the government, has that system to that extent become a capitalistic system, or a business-dominated system?

The separation of ownership and control has been carried so far in all of the relatively modernized capitalistic contexts that the directors of business firms are as much a managerial or administrative elite as their counterparts in socialistic contexts. Increasingly in terms of all systems, whether they be subsystems of socialistic or capitalistic societies, strategic decisions in what Veblen referred to as the "closely concatenated processes" are made by sets of administrative elite. The greatest distinction which remains to these sets is that between those who are not owners as a matter of principle as distinguished from those who, though in principle they could be owners, are not in fact owners in any substantial degree.

With increases in the level of modernization there will always be an increase in organizations which can be spoken of as predominantly economically oriented both from the point of view of the members of the organizations themselves and from the point of view of the other members in the society as a whole. In addition, the integration of activities in terms of those organizations with activities in terms of other organizations in the society becomes an increasingly critical problem because of the implications of operations in terms of these organizations for operations in terms of other organizations and vice versa. As the levels of modernization increase, those problems become increasingly similar regardless of the form of government or ideology in terms of which they are carried out. Increasingly the problems have to do with the minimum levels of coordination and control required if modernization is to continue. At any given point in time, differences in the ideal structures of government may indicate whether change is likely to be in the direction of greater subordination of the activities to supervision by members of governmental organizations or in the direction of greater degrees of freedom of action in terms of the predominantly economically oriented organization. In the long run, however, the level of centralization will increase, and that increasingly in terms of governmental centralization. Under these circumstances the temptation for bureaucratization beyond the level necessary for a given stage of development [i.e., premature bureaucratization] for the members of societies who are late-comers to the process of modernization is, as a practical matter, likely to be irresistable even were this not the case for other reasons.

The presence of predominantly economically oriented organizations in relatively modernized societies is not likely to be altered by whether or not private owners or managers emphasize particularism or universalism. That is to say, the presence of such organization will not be altered by whether or not an attempt is made to have all such organizations owned on a family basis as opposed to having general distribution of stock ownership such that anyone is a potential holder of equity in a given firm. It is exceedingly unlikely that with increases in modernization any structure of highly particularistic ownership or management can be long maintained. Insofar as such ownership and management are incompatible with the development of predominantly economically oriented organizations, it is the maintenance of the former rather than the growth of the latter that will be stymied. Furthermore, the trend will be as indicated even if the society concerned is not one in terms of which increases in the level of modernization are attained smoothly and efficiently. Late-comers to the process of modernization are likely to attempt combinations of predominantly particularistic ownership and management of new specialized predominantly economically oriented organizations. This was clearly tried in the early attempts to modernize China. Despite all the nepotism involved, and despite the fact that the early attempts at modernization were spectacularly unsuccessful, there was still a steady trend in the direction of the development of predominantly economically oriented organizations. When combinations are attempted, they either break the family or the firm. If the firm is broken, however, it is not likely to go out of existence completely. After some reorganization via the bankruptcy courts or otherwise, it is likely to continue as some sort of predominantly economically oriented organization. For example, either the members of a given family learn how to conduct a shipping industry on an increasingly predominantly universalistic basis, breaking the emphasis on nepotism, or the organization changes hands. The shipping industry, however, is not permitted to go out of existence. The importance of organizations predominantly oriented to shipping in this sense, whether controlled abroad or by the members of the society concerned, increases regardless.

The history of the modernization of Japan furnishes a large number of examples of highly particularistic beginnings of this sort which were conducted with efficiency. Japan is a case par excellence where things were done on a family basis but where the family and the firms were not broken. Rather the family became a peculiar particularistic unit whose members operated in connection with a highly specialized set of predominantly economically oriented organizations characterized increasingly by predominantly universalistic criteria. The Japanese techniques for attaining predominantly universalistic results within a highly particularistic framework were ancient. The most prominent among these was the practice mentioned above as civil service by adoption. Even in Japan, however, the close connection between family organizations and these specialized organizations became more and more attenuated. Today in Japan the family names remain and family influence is perceptible, but discussion of modern Japanese society in terms of the old family-oriented *zaibatsu* [financial cliques] is primarily understandable as a peculiarity of Japanese social scientists and intellectuals with a traditional fondness for familiar ideological implications rather than as an objective scientific analysis. It is of more interest as *Wissensoziologie* than as a description of the general state of Japanese social structure. Not only are the Mitsui no longer what they once were, but the family names of those important in directing either established business firms or new ones of importance are no longer as highly predictable as they were.

These highly specialized predominantly economically oriented units are always foci of instrumental attitudes. Activity in terms of these organizations is relevant to all other activities of all of the members of the society. As these organizations develop, increasingly those goods and services which are means for the vast majority of the ends pursued by members of the society are produced by action in terms of these organizations. Take for example the services of communication. It really does not make any difference in modern United States society whether one is interested in philanthropy, religion, education, business, or helling about with the girls. Whatever his interests, one must use a communications system. The American Telephone and Telegraph Company is important to the wicked and the saintly alike. The allocation of goods and services is generally relevant in any social context, but when the allocation of goods and services becomes the focus of highly specialized organizations to the extent that holds in the case of relatively modernized societies, it is easy to see why notions of economic determinism are so exceedingly general.[4]

---

[4] Devotion to the principles of economic determinism and profound faith in them has nothing whatsoever to do with the distinction between the political right and the political left. Many of the most conservative

When the allocation of goods and services is ordinarily pursued in an organizational context in which the allocation of goods and services as such receives no greater emphasis or perhaps not as great an emphasis as other aspects of behavior, the picture is quite different. It is not that people who operate in such contexts are unaware of material factors. Here again the distinction between spiritually oriented and materialistically oriented people is nonsense pure and simple. Social scientists, especially anthropologists, have pointed out for years that even the members of societies characterized by myriad magical practices do not confuse what they regard as improperly performed magic with poor workmanship. Loss of a canoe in a sudden storm may be attributed to improperly performed magic, but difficulties attributable to badly cut paddles of improper materials are not attributed to improperly performed magic but rather to poor workmanship. Malinowski was famous for his insistance on this.

The failure to think in terms of economic determinism comes out quite clearly in the thinking with regard to activities in the family context even in the most highly modernized societies. It never occurs to the ordinary member of United States society, for example, or most social scientists, for that matter, to describe family structure primarily as a dependent variable of the allocations of goods and services which take place in terms of the family. The tendency is rather to consider it primarily as a focus of consumption and rarely of production. Ideally speaking, the directors of a major corporation in the United States are supposed to be preoccupied with making profits. Actually this is likely to be a radical oversimplification of what they are in fact preoccupied with. Those in charge of a steel factory in a socialistic society, ideally speaking, are generally considered to be preoccupied with the maximization of production and efficiency, etc. Again, ac-

---

members of modern United States society are every bit as much economic determinists as the Socialists and Communists whom they decry as accepting the works of Karl Marx as gospel. The argument between such conservatives and those whom they consider to be at the opposite pole is over an entirely different question. They agree on economic determinism. Disagreement between these two is on the basis of whether or not economic determinism works out for the best under *laissez-faire* conditions or under conditions of state control. This argument, of course, violates the central implication which would be obvious to any puristic true believer in economic determinism, namely that if economic determinism really works there could be no such thing as "monkeying with the process" or "accelerating the inevitable tendencies of history." In this sense none of the actionist believers in economic determinism have ever been rigorous and careful logicians. Their faith has been more notable than their reasoning, or perhaps they have been followers of the dictum that "reason and faith cannot contradict one another, but if they do, faith takes precedence."

tually this is undoubtedly a vast oversimplification. Many who accept this sort of oversimplification readily, balk at a description of the family as consisting of individuals primarily preoccupied with the efficiency with which the toilet training of the young is carried out. After all, toilet training of the young is a service, and properly turned out young are in one sense at least goods, just as much as the treatment of steel is a service and properly turned out steel is goods.

When activities having to do with the allocation of goods and services are characteristically conducted in terms of nonspecialized organizations such as the family, the instrumental role of goods and services and hence the instrumental leverage furnished by production of them is not so obvious. Once any considerable proportion of what may be considered the production of a given society is carried out in terms of organizations overwhelmingly specialized in orientation to that production, the significance of that production is hard to overlook. It is also tempting in recognizing that significance, to go to the other extreme of implying that virtually nothing else is relevant.

In this respect Karl Marx represents one of the great intellectual divides in history. Quite apart from whether or not his ideas were original, he proclaimed the relevance of economic variables in a form so striking that he stood the general prior tendency to overlook the actual significance of these considerations on its head. Given our development of predominantly economically oriented organizations, the enormous attention paid to their economic aspects has become its own worst enemy. The economic aspects of such organizations are so much a matter of preoccupation that we are likely to analyze them badly specifically because we pay so little attention to any other aspects of these organizations or the general settings in which their members perform other roles and pursue other interests.

Predominantly economically oriented organizations are always limited ones from several different points of view. The most obvious limitation of such organizations is the preoccupation of their members and of the nonmembers who nevertheless think in terms of them for various reasons with the economic aspects of the organization. While this limitation is, of course, true by definition, the existence of such units is not a matter of definition. It is interesting that units of this sort should have developed at all, and it is revolutionary that they should have developed on the widespread basis we take for granted.

Less obvious is limitation of these organizations. As indicated earlier, these organizations in general are never considered predominantly consumption-oriented by their own members or by others in the society. They are always considered as production units. Implicitly rather than explicitly most laymen and social scientists regard production as action oriented to some future state of affairs which its results in some way enhance or make possible. Consumption on the other hand is generally perceived as a process which stops where it takes place. It is easy to perceive in this another and somewhat more subtle source of the tendency to accept economic determinism, particularly when the arguments about economic determinism proceed in terms of the role of production in the process. Production is generally perceived as leading to other things; consumption is not. Though, of course, that is precisely what all consumption does too.

The other important limitation as far as these organizations are concerned is the fact that in terms of no society—no matter how highly modernized—is *all* production carried out in terms of such organizations. Some forms of production critically important for understanding social phenomena are *never* carried out in terms of such organizations. This brings up once again the role of family organizations in general social structure. Even in the most highly modernized of societies family units remain those in terms of which the initial socialization of children takes place as well as a considerable proportion of the preparation of food, of cleaning, etc. The family, however, is only the most obvious and perhaps the most likely to be ignored of these noneconomically specialized organizations in terms of which activities important from the point of view of production are in fact conducted. There are many other nonspecialized organizations which are important in this sense and many specialized organizations which, though specialized, are not predominantly economically oriented. For example, a considerable proportion of all education in highly modernized contexts is produced in terms of predominantly educationally oriented organizations.[5]

[5] In recent years in the United States realization of this has taken a clear-cut form. Those in control of many business firms have become increasingly aware of the contribution made by universities both private and public to business firms via the provision of trained individuals whose education was not conducted at the expense of the corporation in terms of which some of the fruits of that education are consumed. Even less obvious services are performed by the schools and universities from the point of view of the members of the corporation. For example, anyone who reaches the graduating level of one of the Ivy League universities has gone through a selection process which at the university level alone represents a screening of thousands of candidates. The results of this selection are more or less automatically made available to potential employers of the students. For the members of a private corporation to conduct such a set of screening activities entirely at their own expense would require budgets well into

The allocation of power and responsibility is itself, of course, a service from many points of view, and the most general organization in terms of which such services are produced in any society of any considerable scale is the government. Unlike the family illustration, production of this sort in terms of other organizations which, however specialized they may be, are not predominantly economically oriented is recognized in various ways of computing national income. Regardless of the orientation of the organization concerned, wages, salaries, etc., paid to the members of such organizations do figure in national income accounting and the like, and to that extent at least, the productive implications of actions in terms of these organizations are not overlooked. Despite this element of recognition of the economic aspects of such organizations, insofar as one consciously or unconsciously thinks in terms of economic determinism, the fact that these organizations are not predominantly economically oriented deflects attention from them in general explanations of the problems and possibilities of a given society.

I I I

PREDOMINANTLY PRODUCTION-ORIENTED ORGANIZATIONS

A. INTRODUCTION

I have used the word predominantly to emphasize that more is involved than an organization which can be considered as a production unit, and that alone. When such units exist in relatively nonmodernized societies, they are usually predominantly particularistic, and kinship is ordinarily the basis of the particularism involved. In the history of such organizations usually the various activities considered as production develop well submerged within the general family context, and the family basis of recruitment and organization may never become secondary to or highly separated from other aspects of the organization even though by contrast with other family-based organizations in the society the level of specialized economic orientation of the mem-

---

hundreds of thousands of dollars per year. With the growing realization of the quite practical contribution of the universities to the corporation in this sense and the realization of the increasing difficulty of financing universities out of private contributions, the popularity of the corporation grant to the general funds of the universities in increasing. The mainstay of private universities may still be contributions from individuals, but contributions of this sort from corporations as well as government funds are sure to play an increasing role in the future budgets of such organizations.

bers of these organizations may have increased radically. The units in terms of which craftsmen pursue their jobs, systems of domestic industry, merchant firms, etc., are examples of this sort. Even when these organizations attain high levels of orientation to economic aspects by contrast with the others in the society concerned, they are not likely to lose their predominantly particularistic basis in general nor their nepotistic character in particular as long as the society continues to be a relatively nonmodernized one.

There is one general type of exception to this in such societies. There are organizations, formed usually for extremely limited purposes, which may well have been considered predominantly production oriented without any confusion with other orientations to family interests or the like. One of the best examples of this are *corvées*. These are after all organizations. From the point of view of all concerned with them they are predominantly concerned with production. If they are continued for very long periods of time without radical changes of personnel, they change into slave organizations or something else quite different from *corvées*. These organizations are not generally stable in this form, and their stable utilization depends at least in part on the fact that as far as any given set of personnel is concerned they are mobilized and then dispersed after relatively short periods of employment for quite limited purposes.

In relatively modernized societies these predominantly production-oriented organizations are extremely common, varied, and numerous. The overwhelming majority of them are never organized on either the predominantly particularistic basis or for the limited time period characteristic of such organizations in relatively nonmodernized societies.

B. PRIVATE OWNERSHIP VERSUS GOVERNMENT OWNERSHIP

In the long run in any relatively modernized society differences between private ownership and government ownership are highly restricted, since the problems of coordination and control increase regardless of the form of ownership. Most of the societies with structures of private ownership and relatively high levels of modernization have probably already proceeded further into this long run than most of their members realize. The situation in the United States, for example, has long been puzzling. One finds quite conservative businessmen, who are ideologically devoted to having the government get out of business and leave prices alone, advocating the regulation of the price of natural gas at the wells, if those same businessmen are private public-utilities executives. Impeccably conservative salesmen for ordinary insurance companies frequently point out to potential customers that, although the purchase of insurance from a mutual company will provide their insurance more cheaply, because of the policy of selected risks associated with some of those companies, "if all good risks turn their business over to mutual insurance companies the 'general insurance function' could not be performed." Under these circumstances it becomes increasingly difficult to distinguish with any rigor between a private capitalistic point of view and a socialist one.[6]

There can be no denying, however, that in the short run and from many other points of view, the differences between private ownership and governmental ownership may be of great importance. Given the types and levels of capital formation necessary for late-comers to modernization, the attempt to handle matters on the basis of private ownership may create difficulties of coordination and control and make certain lines of development impossible. There are projects, absolutely necessary from the point of view of modernization, which either require amounts of capital which cannot be gotten together on a private basis or for which the kind of remuneration necessary given private ownership cannot be efficiently assessed. Both problems are likely to be involved in the development of a modern set of educational means for late-comers. Literacy must become universal as quickly as possible, schools must be developed to cover the entire population at the elementary level, and schools covering an increasing proportion of the population at the secondary and college levels must also be created. Even if the sums involved were not beyond the means of private coalitions, the assessment of tolls via tuitions or the like would defeat some of the main purposes of the development in the first place. Initially it would confine literacy to those best able to pay, whereas the important point is to make literacy as universal as possible as quickly as possible. At the more advanced levels it would again result in highly particularistic standards of recruitment for a period during which the broadest development of talent wherever it could be found is of the essence. Finally, even in the most highly modernized and wealthiest of societies [i.e., wealthy in the sense that they are the societies whose members

---

[6] This problem is generally quite well recognized though not usually discussed in such pedantic terms. See a cartoon in the May 5, 1962, issue of the *New Yorker* by cartoonist J. Mirachi, in which an elderly and apparently irate citizen sitting in his club says to a fellow member, "It just makes my blood boil to hear some wild-eyed radical like Goldwater referred to as a *conservative*."

have the highest per capita incomes] education, with rare exceptions, is notoriously more expensive than any set of tuition fees has ever been able to cover. In certain forms of education strategic for these purposes the gap is especially great. Even in the wealthiest of highly modernized societies basic tuition rates are generally below $2,000 per year, but the most conservative estimate of the cost of educating a medical student start at something like $10,000 per year. Given the end sought in terms of many societies, therefore, there are some things which simply cannot be done via predominantly economically oriented organizations whose associated assets are privately owned.

The distinction between private and governmental ownership is of considerable importance from another point of view. Again in the case of late-comers for whom problems of development are crucial, but to a lesser extent in more highly modernized contexts as well, private ownership permits of certain degrees of flexibility which are more difficult to attain in terms of governmental ownership. If the policies embarked upon in terms of a given organization turn out to be unwise, it may be far easier to wash out mistakes if the mistakes are widely distributed on the basis of private ownership than if the mistakes have been made by members of the government. Given private ownership, mistaken policies may force the owners out of the market, or those with whom they interact, such as their bankers, suppliers, labor unions, etc., may coax them into changing their policies. Mistakes of government leaders, however, are certainly not automatically wiped out by operation of the market, and there is a sense in which it may be more difficult to get them to admit a mistake than to get an individual businessman to do so. The implications of the mistake in the case of the government leader call into question the organization as a whole, and that organization is always considerably broader in scale and implications in the society than is any individual privately owned firm. Thus, if one likes, the pride of individuals in a governmental context may make it considerably more difficult to cut one's losses than in the case of smaller scale private businessmen.

There is still another sense, almost a bizarre one, in which these ownership differences are important. When regulation is decided upon, for whatever reason, it may be considerably easier for the members of a given government to regulate the members of private organizations, e.g., a given business firm or set of business firms, than to regulate activities of other members of their own government. First, in regulating the members of an organization radically separated from one's own, problems are likely to seem much simpler. One is not nearly so harassed by detailed knowledge of all possible complications within the organization to be regulated. Second, one is not nearly so likely to have personal relations with the members of the firm so regulated, especially if the criteria for probity in governmental officials have been carefully adhered to. Third, in regulating the behavior of members of a private business firm, even if that behavior is a function of operation of the members of those firms in terms of regulations previously advocated by the members of the government themselves, one is not so directly involved in calling his own governmental organization into question by the very advocacy and need for regulation implied in the activity.

Despite these differences as modernization increases, differences as between private and governmental ownership are not nearly so significant as is the extent to which these organizations become increasingly specialized out of the general social context. No amount of governmental control alters this tendency save at the price of lowered efficiency of operation and consequent problems for the stability of the governments of such relatively modernized societies.

C. COMBINATION OF FACTORS:
INTERNAL AND EXTERNAL

Organizations of any sort are systems of action, but if action is to take place in terms of those systems many different factors are involved. Most obviously, of course, the individuals who are considered to be members of the organization concerned constitute one set of these factors. There are also the various material resources with which these members operate in terms of the patterns of the organization concerned, and there are the very plans of operation which are a part of the organization as such. Insofar as various combinations of these factors involve the members of the organization with one another, the combination of factors will be considered *internal* to the organization. Insofar as the various combinations of factors involve members of two or more different organizations, on whatever level of generalization the problem is considered, and consequently involve to some extent other factors than the membership of two or more organizations, the combinations of factors will be considered *external* to the organization.[7] Internal combinations of factors are characteristic of every organization. Some external combinations are involved in operations in terms of any organization that is not

[7] These being the current adaptations of the general terms, *internal* and *external,* to this context [see above, pp. 294 and 419].

completely self-sufficient.[8] To the degree that a given organization approaches self-sufficiency, however, the extent of external combinations is minimized. In this sense the external combination of factors is considerably more relevant and strategic for predominantly economically oriented organizations than they would be for organizations which, though important in the allocation of goods and services, were not predominantly oriented toward this aspect of behavior and which were relatively highly self-sufficient. It is important, however, that we be careful about judgments of importance of this sort. In the case of highly self-sufficient units characterized by diffuse orientations, the very restriction of external combinations of factors may make those external combinations which do exist both more obvious and more strategic from the point of view of the members of the organization than would otherwise be the case. The rare appearance of a government tax collector may be one of the most important events in the lives of the members of an isolated traditional Chinese family. Members of any modern factory or business firm take an indefinite number of external contacts for granted. Nevertheless, as interdependency among organizations increases, including some clear-cut dependencies, the general implications for social stability of the smooth operation of external relations of the members of any one of the units for all or many of the other units in the society increase enormously. This carries with it radically increased problems of planning, coordination, and controls—usually under government auspices, but by no means confined to them.

These problems of planning, coordination, and control are ticklish. If the members of the government are not supposed to control, coordinate, and plan all allocation of goods and services in detail, a considerable amount of coordination, control, and planning actually occurs either on a governmental or some other basis regardless of what the ideal structures may be. In various ways, sometimes by direct agreement, sometimes by informal general understandings, and sometimes by the general dissemination of influence from what Veblen would have called key firms or industries, the level of centralization actually attained with regard to the operation of predominantly economically oriented organizations is a great deal higher than is implied in the ideal structures of law and government.

There are, in addition, other factors involved. The general lay-

[8] The possibility is neglected here since only a stable society existing in complete isolation from the members of all other societies would be a completely self-sufficient social organization.

out of the means of communications, the state of technology of those means, and many other factors of this sort carry with them far-reaching implications for levels of centralization of which many are unaware. For example, whether we like it or not, the combination of preferences for suburban living and private ownership of automobiles, the mass distribution of a sufficiently high standard of living so that the vast majority of all family groups can afford at least one automobile, and perhaps one or two additional factors imply supermarkets, as opposed to relatively small-scale corner grocery stores and the like, regardless of whether the form of society is a socialistic or a capitalistic one. Large-scale supermarkets are themselves, of course, instances of far higher levels of centralization than are corner grocery stores. Nor does the increase of centralization described by them stop there. For supermarkets to exist, there must be relatively high levels of centralizations of various sources of supply, transportation, etc.

The structures of centralization which lie outside the governmental sphere may be quite as strategic for the operation of the members of the society as those which are considered legitimately a part of the jurisdiction of governmental officials. From a general theoretical point of view it is amusingly paradoxical that, only if complete centralization were, ideally speaking, within the jurisdiction of members of the government, regardless of whether achieved or not, would it be conceivable that all other organizations be completely decentralized and independent relative to one another. This is never the case, however, and in general the higher the level of centralization required for operation in terms of the society in one area of its structures, the higher is likely to be the requirement for centralization in other supposedly distinct areas. The ideal professed by members of United States society, for example, is that all justifiable centralization be vested in the representatives of the government, and that all organization other than the government approximate as closely as possible in their lack of centralization, the situation of pure and perfect competition. This has, of course, never been the case. It is the objective of the antitrust laws in the United States to keep the departures from this ideal within certain bounds. It is hard to say what the situation might have been in the absence of these laws, but even in the presence of them, the actual departures from a state of pure and perfect competition have certainly been noteworthy. Ethical disputes abound in this area, but regardless of whether a utopian picture would be approached if from the beginning the natural forces of the market had never been interferred with,[9] there is absolutely no question as to what would happen if the degrees of centralization which exist outside the governmental spheres could be magically banished overnight in favor of a state of pure and perfect competition. The result would be chaos or as a minimum, radical change in social organizations as we know them. Unless some of those elements of centralization were restored via action in terms of the government or by a return to the previous status quo in terms of other organizations, there would almost certainly be a radical lowering of the standard of living and a raucous hue and cry over the radical increase in what would be certainly regarded as inconveniences.

One of the most obvious problems of internal combinations of factors has to do with the interrelations among the members of a given organization. Simply because they are so well accepted, I suspect that terms such as *labor, management, staff,* etc., probably beg some of the questions involved in these interrelationships as well as helping to elucidate others. Certainly if such distinctions imply that the major problems of internal combinations as far as personnel are concerned consist of the problems of relations among sets such as the set of laborers, the set of managers, the set of staff men, etc., the problems have been seriously oversimplified. Relations within each set and as between members of these different sets without reference to these set differences are also problems of internal combinations of factors in these organizational contexts. These internal combinations must be so arranged as to be consistent with certain levels of efficiency of operation relevant to the preservation of the organization and at the same time clearly differentiable from the relations that all of the individuals concerned have in organizational contexts other than the one under scrutiny.

However much, ideally speaking, the members of the organization may be predominantly economically oriented as far as their action in terms of the given organization is concerned, their actual behavior is never so purely specialized. Many problems arise from the tendency to take for granted that the ideal structures approximate the actual ones more closely than is in fact the case. This matter was brought dramatically to light by the famous studies of the Fatigue Laboratory of the Harvard University Business School some decades ago. Their findings and those which they stimulated have never been refuted, and they have never

---

[9] Terms like natural when applied in the area of human conduct are confusing. What is, after all, natural behavior by men as opposed to artificial behavior by men, since the conception of man-made is obviously involved in some sense in both these cases?

been fully explored either. As any plant manager knows, the combination of factors which can be referred to as human relations cannot be set and then ignored. They require unremitting attention. They present problems of special complexity, since in the nature of the case they pose problems on quite low levels of generalization [i.e., relatively non-abstract]. On those levels social science has not yet come up with theories which enable predictions so precise and so tenable that unpredicted idiosyncratic factors highly relevant to general operations do not arise or arise only rarely.

For operations in terms of organizations of this sort to continue, capital, as the economists use that term,[10] has to be accumulated. Quite apart from its source, the capital once accumulated has to be combined with the existing capital resources of the organization. This problem is further complicated by the fact that by no means all of the capital accumulated comes from sources external to the organization itself. In the United States recently we have seen a dramatic exchange among members of the government and members of steel-making firms in which the question of how much capital was to be accumulated by virtue of internal reallocation in terms of those firms as opposed to combinations external to the firms themselves. Capital accumulations are generally reflected in budgets and the like in monetary terms. This may give the impression that additions to capital may simply be dropped in among other units of capital, but this is never actually the case. Problems of capital combination would not be small if no more than the question of floor space for machines were involved, but the problem is never as simple as that. We are often told from childhood on that various uses of material cost or mean money. It is no less true that monies mean other things as well. In monetary terms an increase in capital accumulations may amount to twenty-five per cent of previous capital. Its meaning, however, will be quite different if it represents expansion of previous plant, equipment, and activities or the establishment of radically different ones.

This brings up a somewhat more general problem of combinations, what might be described as the engineering problem. Whatever the objectives or goals toward which the members of a given organization are supposed to work, insofar as those goals can be defined in terms of outputs of goods or services, there is the

10 It would not do to complicate this discussion with an attempt to clarify the concept of *capital*. I have tried that without effect elsewhere. See "Some Social Obstacles to 'Capital Formation' in 'Underdeveloped Areas,'" *Capital Formation and Economic Growth*, National Bureau of Economic Research (ed. by M. Abramovitz), Princeton, 1955, pp. 443–450.

problem of the most efficient possible combination of material, tools, power, and the efforts of human beings. This is an *engineering problem,* but it is not a problem simply of mechanical engineering. It is a problem of *human engineering* as well. Again, whether one likes to think of human beings as being handled in these terms or not, these are contexts, par excellence, in which human beings *have to be* manipulated, in which their behavior *has to be* carefully coordinated and carefully planned. Whatever the state of freedoms in other respects, operations in terms of units of this sort require far closer supervision and detailing of individual participation than any slavery-based systems the world has ever seen.

Somewhat distinct from the engineering problem as such, but closely related to it, is the general problem of management. This problem differs from the engineering problem by virtue of the fact that, either implicitly or explicitly, the managers set the goals and hence the problems which have to be worked out in engineering terms. In terms of some units, of course, the so-called managers are simply foci of communication who decide nothing but rather communicate decisions of somewhat more remote managers. Somewhere along the line, however, such decisions have to be made, and from the point of view of the members these decisions are never purely engineering decisions. To some extent, ideally speaking, those with the roles of managers must pay more attention to problems of political allocation than other members of the organization do. This is true both ideally and actually. When materiel, power, human efforts, and engineering plans exist, there still exists the general problem of administration which in terms of any given organization is the most general problem of combinations of factors internal to the organization itself.

All the problems mentioned above have comparable ones when the combinations of factors involving external relations of members of the organization are considered. From the point of view of labor, the problem here is not simply a question of how one combines the efforts of two or more individuals. There is the problem of where one gets these efforts in the first place. This poses the delicate question of how one gets individuals out of other contexts and into the context of the organization concerned. Corollary to this, of course, is the question of how the members leave this organizational context and return to others. In these organizational contexts this is generally done via predominantly universalistic and predominantly functionally specific occupational roles, that is by carefully delimited jobs open to anyone on the basis of achievement. Remuneration for effort is in terms of recognition and wages or salaries or other forms of income, and increasingly the amount of income from such sources becomes the most important form of general recognition. The source of labor in this sense may be other predominantly economically oriented organizations. Many modern labor unions are organizations of this sort, though in some societies and in many social contexts there is a difficult question of whether or not labor unions are predominantly politically as distinguished from predominantly economically oriented organizations. In the United States they have classically been considered predominantly economically oriented whereas in many European countries and in countries like Japan the emphasis seems, if anything, to be on the political aspects. Insofar as organizations such as labor unions become important, whether their members intend to do so or not, the organizations become predominantly politically oriented unless some of their members receive explicitly some legal standing as representatives of the general membership in bargaining for jobs and the like. Otherwise, by virtue of falling in an undefined if not explicitly illegal area, action in terms of such organizations actually becomes primarily relevant to changes in the general allocation of power and responsibility even though the aims of the general membership may be primarily an alteration in the allocation of goods and services. This was one of the critical problems during the struggle for unionization in the United States earlier in this century. The labor unions at that time had nothing which approached the legal position which their members and representatives enjoy today, so that virtually everything that the representatives and members of unions did in terms of their organizations was cast into a mold of illegality by contrast with the action of businessmen representing their firms.[11]

Apart from the recruitment of labor and other services via union organizations, in general the sources of labor are the memberships of relatively nonspecialized organizations. The usual

[11] The situation is, of course, quite different today. The distinction between business firms and unions has been blurred. It is not only that today in effect a position very close to a property right in jobs has been realized so that unions are in effect well recognized as having vested interests in certain types of positions in certain types of factories and business firms generally. It is also a fact that, in a world which union leaders never made, in which they pursued one set of ends, they ended up in a different position than they imagined. In the attempt to finance retirement plans, health plans, and the like, in the attempt to invest union funds wisely, the union leaders got into business as it were, even into business in the industry in which their members are employed. The stereotypes of villains and heroes in the *soi-disant* struggle as between capital and labor, generally make the banker the symbol par excellence of the foe of the humble working man, but union funds are now increasingly involved in banking.

sources are, of course, family memberships. For the average individual the family is the organizational context from which he goes out to participate in specialized organizations whatever the form of specialization those organizations take. Even if human services are recruited in terms of unions, they come to the union context from the family context. In societies whose members emphasize specialized organizations of this sort, ideally speaking, participation in predominantly economically oriented organizations is clearly separated from family considerations. Actually speaking, as pointed out in other connections above, this is in fact never the case. What goes on "on the job" in terms of these specialized organizations is highly relevant to family life and vice versa despite the ideals of clear-cut separation of the two spheres. Other problems of combination of human beings external to the organization are primarily a function of the problems of the sources of capital, the sources of materiel, the disposal of products, and the general problem of management of the foreign relations of the organization concerned.

The distinction between capitalistic and socialistic societies probably has its maximum implications when the question of sources of capital external to the organizations concerned is raised. In the case of socialistic societies, presumably these sources are always capital handled in terms of other subsystems of the government. For capitalistic societies they may be capital handled in terms of governmental organizations or other nongovernmental organizations or individuals. Increasingly the former comes to be a matter of great importance in all sorts of connections. In the development of new industries, for example, especially in areas highly tinged with the national interest such as the development of atomic energy, whether for military or domestic purposes, the development of rocketry, etc., a considerable portion of the capital is supplied from resources controlled in terms of the government. Nongovernmental capital is supplied by private investment, presumably. Regardless of whether or not the societies concerned are capitalistic or socialistic a substantial part of the capital relevant for organizations specialized on other than predominantly economically oriented grounds is supplied from resources controlled in terms of the government. This is ordinarily the case, for example, for predominantly educationally oriented organizations. Whatever the nature of the societies concerned in other respects, sources of capital external to the organization are exceedingly likely to involve the members of the organization concerned with the members of other organizations known as *banks*. The place of banks in socialistic societies may be quite different from the place of banks in capitalistic societies, but there are both attitudes and modes of operations characteristic of the members of banks in whatever kind of society one finds them.

Coordination of the sources of materiel external to the organization concerned constitute what might be called the major consumption aspect, apart from the consumption of human effort, of the organizations concerned. Again, whatever the form of the society in general, to the extent that specialized production-oriented units tend to appear in relatively modernized societies, the types of units interrelated via the combination of factors for these purposes are other predominantly economically oriented organizations, regardless of whether they happen to be subsystems of the government or to exist as relatively independent organizations. The important thing is that these organizations are to a high degree interdependent with others rather than highly self-sufficient. Relatively little of the materiel consumed in the process of production carried out in terms of these organizations is supplied by operations in terms of these organizations themselves. There are some notable cases of vertical integration of such organizations, but this process has never been carried to lengths such that action in terms of these organizations supplies virtually all of the materiel utilized. Correspondingly, the members almost never dispose of any considerable portion of their product internally among themselves. The general methods of disposal is via *sales*, again regardless of whether or not the society concerned is capitalistic or socialistic. The element of cost accounting as a method of keeping track of the flow of goods and services almost always involves some structure of disposal via some market mechanism. There is no denying, however, that, given socialistic governments, the amount of direct allocation is likely to be higher. In any type of society in which predominantly production-oriented organizations appear, however, the important thing is that the disposal of products generally involves relations with members of other organizations. This again is in sharp contrast with highly self-sufficient units such as family organizations in many societies.

Finally, there is the general problem of management considered from the point of view of the combination of factors external to these organizations. Increasingly these organizations can be thought of in terms of their domestic affairs as distinguished from their foreign affairs. In the sphere of their foreign affairs, the problem of the general interdependency with other organizations is posed in its most dramatic form. As the level of modernization increases, it becomes increasingly clear to the managers that, no matter what their capabilities in ruthlessness, the organizations in terms of which they act cannot survive if the attempt is made to "go it alone" without reference to the implications of their behavior for the members of other organizations with whom they must interact. In this sphere of management as well as in the sphere of management internal to the organization, regardless of the predominant orientation of the members of the organization in general, increasing preoccupation with the general allocation of power and responsibility is inescapable. Thus, a peculiar sort of multifunctional orientation reappears in relatively modernized social contexts. The more highly modernized the society in general, the larger the scale of the predominantly economically oriented organizations must be. The larger the scale of such organizations, the more alert must the managers be to problems having to do with the general allocation of power and responsibility, if the organizations they represent are to survive. Correspondingly for the members of the government, the more highly modernized the society, the larger the scale of the government must be. The larger the scale of the government, the more alert must the leaders of that government be to the problems of allocation of goods and services if that government is to survive. In general, as the level of modernization increases, whether ideally or actually, the tendency is always for predominantly economically oriented organizations to appear as or be or become subsystems of the governments of the societies in terms of which the members of these organizations operate.

I V
PREDOMINANTLY EXCHANGE-ORIENTED ORGANIZATIONS

A. MARKETS

Whenever there is any sort of specialization with regard to the production of goods and services on an organizational basis—regardless of whether the organizations concerned are predominantly economically oriented or not—there must be markets unless the allocation of everything is planned in detail in advance or completely determined by tradition. Even if the organizations in terms of which production is carried out are not predominantly economically oriented, if there is any form of product or service specialization, there must be some specific structures of exchange. Rarely if ever is the organization whose members specialize in this fashion an organization whose members also consume all of what they have so produced. There are certainly societies in terms of which exchange among members of different organizations is overwhelmingly determined on the basis of tradition, but so far the members of no planned society have carried their planning to the extent of completely eliminating markets.

Although it may not be advanced necessarily as an explanation of the above, as in all cases of planning, the problem of adequate knowledge places an upper limit on the amount of planning possible for any given state of knowledge short of omniscience. It is not true that people cannot plan beyond this point, but they cannot plan with any reasonable expectation of stability or orderly progress, or whatever it is they seek to achieve. When some production units are specialized in the sense of being predominantly economically oriented organizations, then the only alternatives are markets or total planning. Relatively modest development of predominantly economically oriented organizations carries the complexity of interrelationships beyond what is practical on a purely traditional basis. Furthermore, the level of specialization achieved increases the probability of rational calculation on the part of the members of the organization concerned to such a point that the easy maintenance of any predominantly traditional structure would be threatened by the ease with which some of the influential might expect manipulations in violation of those traditions to bring windfall gains.

The degrees and kinds of freedom available are the essence of the market situation. If everything is completely controlled, then by definition there is no market, but rather a structure of direct allocation. There are two alternatives: (1) Either some level of discretion in some respects is permitted to the individuals who participate in the market as representatives of either their own interests or that of the organizations to which they belong, or (2) one eliminates the market altogether and simply tells all such individuals what to send, where, and when. The existence of some degree of freedom in the market situation is highly relevant from the political point of view in any society in which markets exist. There are several reasons for this. In the most general sense, there is always the enormous relevance of the allocation of goods and services for the allocation of power and responsibility.

In the most extreme and direct form, there may be an overt attempt to purchase political influence. One of the most important reasons for insisting that the terms, *economic* and *political* refer to *aspects* of behavior rather than to *things* lies in the fact that, when action is looked at from certain points of view, the exercise of political influence is itself a service. Whenever the exercise of influence is not completely planned and/or completely determined by tradition, [and if planned or determined by tradition whenever the plans are not completely realized or the traditions not completely realized . . .], it is always to some extent negotiable in terms of the allocation of goods and services. The overt decision to use allocations of goods and services to purchase political influence which would otherwise be differently allocated is only the most extreme form in which market decisions can be highly relevant to the political aspects of society. Given the general relevance of goods and services as *the* major form of means, whatever the various ends of members of the society, decisions to utilize them or exchange them in some radically different way or even mildly different way may have far-reaching implications for the allocation of power and responsibility. This possibility inheres in social life even if there is no direct attempt or even intention to make exchange-oriented operations a means for new allocations of power and responsibility. For example, regardless of whether the phenomena involved are rational or not, if leading business figures in the United States business community feel threatened by the Chief Executive of the United States, this can quite conceivably lower what Veblen referred to as "putative profits" or what Keynes called the "schedule of marginal efficiency of capital" to such an extent that business activity is reduced with many consequences for unemployment, increases in capital formation, the level of national income, and other changes which cannot take a downward trend in the United States today without implications for the allocation of power and responsibility.

The implications of degrees of freedom in any market situation may be more subtle than the fairly obvious example just given. Differential decisions having to do with exchange may work through a variety of organizations with quite differing orientations and consequent effects both with regard to the allocation of goods and services, the allocation of power and responsibility, and other allocations as well.[12] A degree of freedom in the market is to some extent a degree of freedom in the political aspects of social behavior whether people like to admit it or not. From this

[12] A decision by university administrators and alumni to improve the standing of an economics department by increasing the funds available for faculty and graduate students may not only have that effect, thereby proving that, while money is not everything in education, it is not negligible either—but may subsequently influence political policy through the effects of educating economists who become government employees, etc. Allocations of goods and services sometimes take curious turns when academics are involved, since our ethics are such that we constitute an unusual sort of economic good—you can buy us, but you cannot sell us.

point of view those in charge of highly authoritarian societies whether of a socialistic kind or not are well advised, ideally speaking at least, to play down any elements of freedom in a market sense even though some are in fact permitted to exist. The leaders of capitalistic societies tend to be proud of their markets; those of socialistic societies tend to be ashamed of them, and those of authoritarian societies tend to be afraid of them. For the leaders of any highly authoritarian or planned society a situation in which no markets exist ideally, but actually markets are permitted to exist, is the most rational solution to a problem having essentially to do with the lack of adequate knowledge for the level of planning desired. Leaders of such societies can push planning as far as they know how and leave other allocations of goods and services to a market mechanism in which the degrees of freedom, however much tolerated at a given point in time, have no standing at law. Such degrees of freedom are subject to immediate abrogation as soon as the leaders have available, or think they have available, sufficient knowledge to handle the matter otherwise or as soon as they deem the situation so created to have become one likely to give them trouble on other scores.

Finally, the degrees of freedom implicit in any market situation, whether ideal or actual, always carry with them some potentiality for instability. Degrees of freedom in the market imply some combination of emphases on tolerance and rationality. Under these circumstances there is always the possibility that one or more individuals will attempt to utilize the tolerance so available to manipulate the general structure so as to bring about a general change in the system. Even if this is not attempted self-consciously, other members of the society may feel that it is being attempted. If it is attempted and the area of tolerance is not closed down, there is always the possibility of the alteration of the system by virtue of success in these attempts, if that success is possible. On the other hand if the other members of the society act in such a way as to eliminate the area of tolerance, whether the threat they deem to be present is real or fancied, the system has been altered at least to the extent that other features of the society are dependent upon those degrees of freedom in the market.

Markets do not necessarily exist because there are structures of freedom in a society, but unless there are *some* such structures, ideally and/or actually, markets cannot exist. The existence of structures of freedom in a society brings up again the importance of adequate knowledge. A basic problem implicit in societies whose members emphasize rational knowledge is that they may not have enough of it for their purposes. A problem of societies whose members emphasize freedom lies in the fact that from the point of view of both observers and members themselves they may have too much of it. Individuals who will do the right thing given freedom cannot be left free to do it unless individuals who will not necessarily do the right thing are also free to misbehave. Those who believe in freedom generally believe in their ability to prevent, curb, or correct the behavior of those who misuse their freedom, but it is the essence of the maintenance of freedom that the members of such societies must wait for overt acts. One of the general tragedies associated with the high evaluation of freedom is that there are always some misbehaviors which can neither be deterred nor corrected after they have taken place.

B. MONETARY ORGANIZATIONS [13]

The definition of money as a generalized medium of exchange has already been discussed above [pp. 257–262]. In the course of that discussion some attention was given to the variations possible in the degree of generalization of media of exchange. Whenever the specialization of the allocation of goods and services is carried to great lengths, even if this is done in terms of organizations which are not predominantly economically oriented, the need for some generalized medium [media] of exchange increases. The same is true with regard to increases in the scale of such specialized organizations, and it is even more necessary with the development of predominantly economically oriented organizations. Under such circumstances predominantly traditionally determined exchanges do not suffice, and direct allocation becomes increasingly difficult, if only because of the problems of adequate knowledge. Even given structures of direct allocation, however, if any sort of accounting procedures are to be followed, some types of monetary units have to be devised. The more clear-cut and highly generalized the monetary units become, the greater is the likelihood of rational calculation in the exchange of goods and services. Even if the monetary units are multiple, complicated, and relatively less generalized, the existence of such units increases the probability of rational calculation with regard to exchange possibilities on the part of some members of the society. If the monetary media are sufficiently complicated and diverse, only a small number of individuals are capable of manip-

---

[13] To avoid confusion between monetary units in the sense of denominations of media of exchange, organizations predominantly specialized with regard to money will be referred to as monetary organizations [or systems] but never as monetary units.

ulating them with any considerable amount of rationality, and this means of course, that a *monetary elite* will exist. Even if the units are comparatively simple, if the level of generalization is high, and the general level of specialization in economic terms is high, special sets of experts in monetary maniuplations will develop, and one form of organizational specialization is along monetary lines. The most obvious organizations of this sort in relatively modernized societies are *banks*, but banks are by no means confined to relatively modernized societies. All sorts of restricted versions of such organizations in the form of money lenders, exchange specialists of all sorts, etc., exist as members of any society in terms of which money has come into general use. Monetary organizations of this sort represent perhaps the most extreme possibility as far as preoccupation with exchange is concerned. Were a perfectly generalized medium of exchange possible, specialists in operations in terms of that money would be, as it were, pure specialists in exchange. Such a monetary unit would be devoid of all content save the exchange possibilities inherent in its application. Many of the remarks that will be made below about merchants in general tending to marginal positions, ideally speaking, despite wide variations in other respects, apply in quite an extreme form to monetary specialists. Ideally these specialists are frequently marginal members of the societies to which they belong, but actually they are almost inevitably persons of importance and power. All of the relevance of the degrees of freedom implicit in a market for allocations of power and responsibility and other aspects of social phenomena apply in a puristic sense to command over considerable amounts of the money or monies of any particular society. For any manipulations which ideally speaking are frowned upon, negotiations in monetary terms combine the possibilities of greater flexibility and maximum secrecy better than does specialization in any single commodity in the social context concerned. In all relatively modernized societies some of these specialized monetary organizations must develop if only because of their utility for keeping track of allocation and because of their utility in communicating allocations of money from one point to another. The increasing interdependency of all relatively modernized societies in international terms increases the strategic relevance of such monetary organizations enormously. All societies in the modern world must sooner or later have available to their members either the services of their own national bank, that of some other society, or some private bank whose members can function as though they were the national banking facilities of the society concerned.

The general literature on monetary organizations is much too technical and highly developed to be gone into here. For present purposes suffice it to say that the more highly modernized a society becomes, the more strategic are clear-cut monetary structures and highly generalized monetary units. The more generalized the monetary unit, the more strategic becomes the role of those individuals or those organizations specialized with regard to the exchange and manipulation of monetary units as such. There is, in theory, an upper limit on the level of generalization which any medium of exchange can attain [see pp. 259–262], but in all known cases of relatively modernized societies the achieved level of generalization increases. In addition, any restrictions on the level of generalization of the medium of exchange in a given society, like restrictions on the degrees of freedom in markets, increases the importance of general planning with the consequent problem of the adequacy of knowledge available to those in control of the government. The simpler and more generalized the medium of exchange, the greater is the probability that more individuals will spend more time in attempting rational calculations about the allocation of goods and services. From many points of view complications of the monetary unit may serve important functions for the leaders of the government, but they complicate it at their peril. A major element in that peril is the availability of adequate knowledge. In this sense a highly simplified, highly generalized money minimizes the need for special intelligence on the part of governmental leaders. In relatively modernized societies in the absence of the knowledge necessary for complete planning, highly generalized media of exchange may be one of the major forms of decentralization of decision open to members of the government long after older and more common forms of decentralization on a predominantly geographical basis have become impractical.

C. MERCHANT ORGANIZATIONS

I define *merchants* as specialists in exchange. Exchange in this sense is a special form of production, but it is a form of production focused entirely on the service of distribution. Merchants in the sense of the term used here are different from what are generally referred to as businessmen, although to some extent our present conception of businessmen developed out of merchant origins, and certainly many of the individuals who are considered businessmen are merchants in the sense intended here. Those with major roles in predominantly economically oriented organizations other than those of merchant types are always, of course, to some extent, concerned with questions of exchange. There is always the problem of the acquisition of the goods and services which are the means for the members of the organization as such, and insofar as the organization is production oriented there is always the question of the disposal of the products, whether they be goods or services, created by the operations in terms of the organization.

There are various degrees of exchange orientation. The individual who deals in anything is the epitome of the merchant role as that is conceived here. The leaders of a modern steel firm in the United States are much concerned with their sales department, but they regard themselves primarily as steel makers rather than as specialists in the exchange of steel for money or other goods and/or services. The distinction between merchants and those who regard themselves as specialists in production, for example, is somewhat less important for an understanding of the phenomena of relatively modernized societies, if only because the level of specialization with regard to predominantly economically oriented organizations is carried to such great lengths that specialization of this further sort is taken for granted on all sides. The special role of the merchants appears most clearly in relatively nonmodernized societies. In those societies their organizations are frequently the most striking cases of predominantly economically oriented organizations. In such settings the merchant is to a peculiar degree a person detached from the significance of given goods or services to either their producers or consumers. The goods as such are not intrinsically meaningful to the merchant, his primary concern is with their turn-over—their exchange. Merchants are often specialists in a single commodity, not because of its significance to them as something they have produced or as something they must consume in the context of a nonspecialized organization, but rather because exchange of a relatively restricted number of commodities may maximize the possibility of rational manipulation and hence profit from such exchanges.

Most of the goods and services produced in terms of relatively nonmodernized societies have an intrinsic significance to the individuals who produce them. The favorite example of this in social history is the importance to the craftsman of the product he makes. The pride of the craftsman in good workmanship has been so appealing that even Veblen was unable to avoid sentimentality about it. One story—almost undoubtedly apocryphal—always told as an actual experience of the teller or a friend of his, is the story of the member of a relatively modernized society who sees a craftsman of a relatively nonmodernized society making a chair [or the like]. He asks the price, and then orders a dozen just like it. The modern is surprised to find that the price of a dozen chairs is not less than twelve times the price of a single chair but considerably more. On commenting on this fact he is told by the simple but devoted craftsman that the price is higher for twelve identical chairs because it is boring to make twelve just alike. This tale is told to illustrate the fact that the craftsman is in general concerned with a complete product, whereas the modern workman frequently never sees more than a portion of whatever he works upon, has lost all sense of identification with the final product, etc. The merchant by definition does not have this sort of identification with the products he buys and sells. Correspondingly, the intrinsic significance of the goods or services from the point of view of those who consume them is not a matter of preoccupation as far as he is concerned. He is concerned with selling it, not with using it.[14]

When production is ordinarily carried out in terms of organizations that are not predominantly economically oriented, there is a special intangibility about the exchange service. Not only do the goods and services in which he deals lack the significance for him that they have for those who either produce or consume them, but to some extent his profit from the transaction lies in giving as little as he possibly can to the one and getting as much as he possibly can from the other. Thus, if there is any dissatisfaction at all, he is likely to be the focus of that dissatisfaction. To the consumer, the goods or services appear no different physically from what they did when they left the hands of their producer, and the producer sees no difference in them either. It is not a

---

[14] The absolute extreme of merchant attitude in this respect is the attitude of the probably apocryphal representative of a major soap firm who required a writer for television to cut from his script a scene in which the distracted heroine puts her soapy hands in her mouth and spits out the soap making a face as she does so. The script writer inquired as to why this was objectionable, and said to the representative of the firm, "After all, you don't want them to eat soap." The representative of the firm replied, "Don't discourage them." There is also more than a little of this implication in Fitzgerald's translation which states, "I wonder often what the Vintners buy, One-half so precious as the stuff they sell."

On the other hand, there are certainly those who combine what is here taken as the heart of the merchant orientation with other concerns. Connoisseurship is prominent among these. The art dealer who sincerely loves and appreciates painting and sculpture is a familiar figure. To the extent that he becomes preoccupied with the intrinsic qualities of the objects in whose exchange he specializes, he is likely to become a less skillful merchant, however much he may increase in people's regard in other respects. If a vintner changed his way to the poet's preference, he would certainly cease to be a vintner.

matter of chance that with relatively rare exceptions merchants have appeared, ideally speaking, at least, as marginal men, if not actual outcasts, in the context of most of the societies in world history.

The fact that individuals who specialize in exchange have often actually achieved both powerful and prestigious positions, despite ideal structures to the contrary, has simply made matters more complicated. To the general membership of the society, the fact that these individuals, who are ideally marginal, have prospered is an added indication that something is wrong and devious about their behavior. However naïve and sentimental it may appear, it is a uniform human expectation, ideally speaking, that the good prosper and the evil be found out and punished. The fact that this is frequently not the fate of those who are ideally regarded to be evil serves to magnify the extent of their evil in the eyes of such idealists.

United States society is one in terms of which in general the businessman is a person of high prestige, and this applies even to those who would be classified specifically as merchants in this sense. Remnants of this attitude toward merchants, however, are not difficult to discern. There are at least two contexts in which the interests of the merchant are not supposed to transcend the intrinsic significance of the goods or services in which he deals. One example of this sort is the case of the shopkeeper or businessman whose goods are religious objects. These may be statues of holy figures, various ritual objects, etc. No such shopkeeper or individual could stay in business and follow ordinary advertising practices quite acceptable where other goods are concerned. Such a merchant may reduce the price on some of his articles in order to clear his inventory, but to advertise such sales in the ordinary fashion would almost certainly indict him for having a sacrilegious attitude.[15]

Another example about which members of United States society are still quite sensitive has to do with landlords dealing in private housing. It may be that "a house is not a home," but it is true that, ideally speaking, to raise the price of a house or to threaten to dispossess the inhabitants of a house is often taken as threatening a home. Landlords are, after all, housing merchants. One of the services in which they specialize, i.e., making housing available for homes, even in terms of a highly specialized society like our own is so intimately tied up with conceptions of family

[15] Imagine signs reading, "Spring Clearance Sale, Torah Scrolls 50 per cent Off" or "Statues of the Holy Mother at Less Than Cost—While They Last."

life and its importance that, long after the public became apathetic about price controls in general, it was still comparatively easy to maintain controls over rent. It was felt that the state of the market would give housing merchants a special ability to ignore an interest in proper family life in favor of the pursuit of profits. For the members of most of the relatively nonmodernized societies virtually all goods and services with which merchants deal fall into the category which we still perceive in the case of ritual objects and housing. Specialists in exchange under these circumstances easily and frequently become targets of aggression regardless of whether the accusations against them are tenable.

Ideally speaking the position of the merchant is often a lowly one, but there has never been a society characterized by highly developed merchant pursuits in terms of which the merchants did not actually achieve considerable wealth and power and at least the high prestige ordinarily associated with these two. They might be regarded as *nouveau riche* or as undeservedly rich, but they were regarded as rich, and there has never been a society in terms of which being rich failed to carry with it some prestige. Here again examples of people who actually achieve considerable power and prestige as well as wealth though ideally speaking they are regarded as deserving of only lowly position should not be hard for members of a society like ours to understand. After all, the gangsters and corrupt political bosses of American history are figures of exactly this sort.

Whenever merchants have constituted a marginal or outcast set of individuals they have been associated with graft and corruption. In a sense for them to be marginal or outcast implies that they lack legitimate status as far as the government is concerned in the roles and activities in terms of which they operate. But the allocations of goods and services at which they are so expert are highly relevant to operations in terms of the government and vice versa. If they are to exist, they must seek some insulation against capricious exercises of power and responsibility as far as they are concerned by the legitimate prestigious members of the government. The generalized purchasing power at their disposal plus the important functions of exchange, at which they are expert, are in turn highly relevant to the members of the government. Insofar as there can be no ideal or legitimate combination of these interests, there will be actual illegitimate ones. Under these circumstances merchants will, as it were, always buy into government, and government officials will always coerce or threaten their way into merchant pursuits.

The uniformity with which the merchants are a marginal set of individuals, ideally speaking, and with which they become in their relations with members of the government a focus of graft and corruption is relevant to the problems of modernization for the members of relatively nonmodernized societies. Specialized expertise in exchange of goods and services is an absolute requisite for the process, regardless of whether it is to take place on the basis of private business or governmentally owned and directed enterprises. From this point of view differences as to the manner in which these experts fit into the preexisting social structure may be of the greatest importance. The convertibility of experts of this sort to modernized roles may actually be a function of the extent to which they were previously unable to hope for elevation to nonmerchant roles. However relevant social mobility may be to modernization, if the level of modernization is to be increased and sustained, a lack of social mobility from merchant to nonmerchant roles in terms of the basis from which change takes place may actually facilitate the convertibility of experts in the specialized handling of goods and services to modern purposes. Merchants who can make nothing but merchant pursuits pay off in terms of actual power and prestige are far more likely to convert readily to the roles required in relatively modernized societies than are merchants who can use merchant practices to get out of ideally marginal merchant roles altogether. In relatively nonmodernized societies the position of merchants has probably been more often of the latter kind than of the former. To the extent that this is true, the members of such a society have to develop their new experts in exchange from different sources.

D. VARIOUS FORMS OF EXCHANGE

1. INTRODUCTION

The exchange of goods and services has already been treated above in general, but there are two forms of exchange with sufficiently special and unusual characteristics to justify separate mention here. The first of these, of course, is the exchange of people and the second is the exchange of ownership and control separated in a sense from the goods and services over which the ownership and control are exercised.

2. EXCHANGES OF PEOPLE

There is a long literature concerned with the exchange of people. The members of many societies have shown ingenuity in these respects. All sorts of structures have existed varying from slavery and serfdom, through what we consider today to be a modern labor market and allocation of individuals in various occupational roles. One can discern a range of differentiation of structures with regard to the exchange of people. The range stretches all the way from what might be regarded as structures of the exchange of total individuals as such [i.e., a pure slavery structure] to structures of the exchange of highly specific services over a limited range of time of particular individuals or sets of individuals [i.e., a modern labor market or exchange of occupational roles]. The more the organizations involved are ones in terms of which individuals are exchanged as total individuals, the less predominantly economically oriented such organizations are likely to be, if they are in the long run stable. Over short-run periods in the presence of large numbers of, say, captives, it might be possible for those in control of a set of slaves to utilize them without regard to replacement cost or any other aspect of human interaction save those necessary to get a certain expenditure of energy. Even in this extreme case, however, because of the possibility of interaction between the guards and the slaves, any organization whose members utilize slaves is likely to be more general in its orientations than a highly specialized predominantly economically oriented organization. In general, organizations characterized by slavery, serfdom, etc., have been characteristic of sedentary, relatively nonspecialized forms of production. This has certainly been the case when these arrangements have been highly stable. In all relatively modernized social contexts, exchanges of people take place largely at the other end of the scale. The general increase of specialization and interdependency forces an approach to total planning as a feature of any organization whose members tend to deal with other members as total individuals.

Even comparatively small departures from the pure labor-market end of the scale are likely to involve radical complications. For example, no one in his right mind would describe a modern university as an organization characterized by slavery or serfdom as far as the members of its faculty are concerned. Ideally speaking, the member of the faculty secures his position on a predominantly universalistic basis. His relations as a member of his university organization are, ideally speaking, predominantly functionally specific and limited to his professional occupational role. In many instances, however, as a fringe benefit, if for no other reason, the administrative officials of the university organization are involved in the provision of housing facilities for the members of the faculty. Any departure from a straight salary arrangement with members of the faculty to a salary arrangement which includes housing or some elements of housing as a fringe benefit is a radical departure in the direction of involving the general membership of the university with the whole man. Most particularly, if he is married, the faculty member's wife becomes involved in a direct sense in which, at least ideally, she was not supposed to be involved prior to the prominence of housing in the salary package. The Dean of the Faculty of such a university may with perfect propriety refuse to have any discussion whatsoever with the faculty member's wife about the salary arrangement or promotion of the faculty member, but it becomes almost impossible for him to avoid any discussion of matters of housing with faculty wives with whom in the legal sense the university has no contractual arrangements of any sort. The compartmentalization of exchanges of individuals or rather of their services increases radically with modernization regardless of whether that modernization takes place under ideologies of private ownership or state ownership. If the ideology is one of private ownership, the compartmentalization may increase in terms of governmental, business, family, and other nongovernmental organizations. In a society whose members are dominated by an ideology of complete state ownership and control, the compartmentalization will also increase, although in this case, ideally speaking at least, the differentiation will be largely in terms of family organizations on the one hand and various different divisions or subsystems of the government on the other. Under conditions of increasing modernization, however, the members of no one subsystem of the government will ordinarily deal with the whole man in the sense that members of slavery and serfdom organizations have to in a relatively nonmodernized situation.

In terms of relatively modernized societies the most radical departure from the ordinary "labor-market-highly-differentiated-occupational-role" end of the scale is the case of organizations such as military organizations. Characteristically, even these organizations do not approach slavery or serfdom. Almost all such organizations are characterized by memberships consisting solely [or almost solely] of adults. Ordinarily recruitment is not by virtue of the reproduction of members of the organizations themselves, nor in many cases do the individuals concerned continue to be members of the organization after retirement, though this may be the case in predominantly ascetically oriented organizations.

Regardless of which end of the scale or what place along the scale a given society falls, the exchange of people always involves one problem which is not involved in the exchange of other goods. Exchanges of people, however restricted those exchanges may be in time or in the services concerned, always involve a special potential problem of deviance. The problem is different in kind from the problem of variations in quality, weight, etc., of other goods which are exchanged. Deviance in the services of people may be a function of the fact that reaction to the settings in which the services are ordinarily performed is not what those wishing to utilize the services have predicted. Any exchange of people always involves, a political aspect, the allocation of power and responsibility among the people involved. Allocations of goods other than people always involve political aspects among the individuals involved in making the exchange, but they do not necessarily involve political aspects of the relationship between the goods exchanged and the individuals involved in making the exchange.

3. EXCHANGES OF OWNERSHIP AND CONTROL

Ownership and control, we know now, are easily separated from the goods and services to which they pertain. Ordinarily ownership and control are not only closely coordinated with one another but are on the whole relatively little separated from consideration of the goods and services over which ownership and control are said to exist. On the other hand some recognition of the possibilities of separation have an ancient lineage. Titles to property in the form of land constituted frequent separations of this sort. From ancient times, the possibility of absentee ownership of land has been clearly recognized. Nevertheless, the radical separation of ownership and control from the things to which they refer via stocks, bonds, titles of various sorts, etc., were rarely highly developed until the development of relatively modernized societies. In such contexts on the other hand, a considerable portion of the most strategic decisions with regard to exchange are made by individuals in terms of ownership and control without ever seeing or handling the things over which ownership and control are exchanged.

In the context of a society whose members preserve structures of private ownership as ideal structures as well as structures of governmental control, the possibilities of exchange of ownership and/or control radically separated from the objects concerned carries with it enormous flexibility. Feats of capital formation, which might not otherwise be possible, are possible. A radical diversification of interests on the part of many individuals is possible. Above all, such exchanges permit individuals with high liquidity preferences in the economist's sense to invest rather than hoard. Development of these phenomena to a high degree depends on all sorts of attitudes toward property. Above all, if these attitudes are to exist, the attitude toward the government must be such that members of the government in their roles as members of the government must at one and the same time: (1) not interfere capriciously, especially via expropriations, with exchanges of ownership and control as such, and (2) stand ready to prevent others from conducting such exchanges in terms of applications of force and fraud. Unless one could count members perfectly socialized with regard to the sacredness of private property, there could be no high flexibility in exchanges of ownership and control without a highly developed governmental organization. At the same time, the more highly specialized and interdependent the society in general becomes with the development of modernization and the greater the desire to maintain exchanges of ownership and control under conditions of private ownership, the greater becomes the importance of governmental officials in both respects mentioned here. As the government becomes more important, the range of variation in fact left unfettered for the exercise of private ownership is reduced. The range of private discretion in ownership in the context of relatively modernized societies can only remain steady if the society stabilizes at a given level of development. If that is the case, however, the society will not be able to be stable in the long run for other reasons. Therefore: once modernization has begun to increase and relatively modernized characteristics have been acquired, the range of private discretion in ownership declines no matter what the ideals of the members of the society.

To the extent that societies are characterized by government ownership, all exchanges of ownership and control consist of struggles for power among the members of various governmental organizations. From this point of view under relatively modernized conditions societies whose members stress governmental ownership have more in common with feudal societies than do relatively modernized societies whose members stress private ownership. Feudal societies after all are societies in terms of which the allocation of ownership and control over goods and services is closely correlated, ideally speaking, with allocations of power and responsibility in terms of a specific hierarchy of loyalties. In societies in terms of which all property is owned by the government, presumably the question of ownership ceases to be relevant, and the question is, of course, correlated with the position of the individuals concerned in the governmental hierarchy just as in the case of feudalism. There are, of course, substantial differences between such modern governmental systems and feudal ones. Presumably the relatively modernized ones will not contain structures which determine succession to position by inheritance through kinship, but the parallel between the two types of societies in the close coordination between the allocations of power and responsibility on the one hand and allocations of goods and services in the other is inescapable.

In societies in terms of which there is relatively little development of exchange of ownership and control as such, the initial development of such exchange is likely to appear to the membership at large as some special form of chicanery. In particular the possibilities of separation of control from ownership are likely to be exceedingly difficult for the average member of the society to understand or appreciate. The possibilities of separation of ownership and control pose such a problem only in terms of those societies in which private ownership is an ideal structure. After all, in the context of societies whose members consider the government to own everything, there is no such thing as separating ownership from control. There is only the possibility of shifts of control from members of one subsystem of the government to another. In the context of relatively modernized societies of the capitalistic sort, however, the separation of ownership and control poses special problems. One of the main methods of enforcing responsibility on those who control property in their exercise of control over their property is the possibility and/or probability that, if they misuse their powers, they will or can be made to suffer in terms of the amount of property left to them. Once the separation between ownership and control has reached considerable lengths, this is no longer a practical possibility. Recognition of this implication of modern development made a volume entitled *The Modern Corporation and Private Property* by A. Berle and G. Means one of the classic texts in modern intellectual history. It should be reexamined now for its more general social implications as well as its special economic ones.

Increasingly in all relatively modernized social contexts, if private ownership is stressed at all, the separation between ownership and control via exchanges of stock titles and the like proceeds further and further as modernization continues. Today with regard to the large-scale organizations of such societies at least, owners do not ordinarily control, and controllers do not ordinarily own any substantial portion of the assets associated with the organizations involved. The separation of ownership and control which attends so inevitably upon these modern developments leads to a heavy stress on the role of members of the government acting in terms of the governmental organization as the major method of balancing the power which such control denotes with the responsibility which was once deemed to be implicit in the fact that ownership was closely coordinated with such control.

The increasing separation of ownership and control has to some extent been accompanied by developments hailed especially among those interested in the business schools of the United States. I refer here, of course, to the growing professionalization of the business role. Increasingly under the existing circumstances, more and more people feel that the continuation of private direction of predominantly economically oriented organizations requires a different view of the role of the businessman—a view more akin to that which ideally characterizes the doctor-patient relationship, the lawyer-client relationship, the architect-client relationship, etc. In the publications of businessmen as well as others an increasing emphasis on public responsibility as well as on responsibility to owners and other members of the firm is discussed by those leaders who in fact control and direct activities in terms of these organizations. In the long run the balance of power and responsibility which once inhered in the vested interest of controllers in the assets of their firms may reenter via the conception of a professional ethic in the sphere of private business. There already exists a model of such roles carefully separated from governmental control but differentiated from ordinary business ethics. I refer, of course, to the role of trustees for assets. It is significant that a trustee in this sense is specifically held to be responsible for the interest of those who on the basis of their own abilities are not considered capable of protecting their own interests in highly individualistic relationships with regard to the control of the assets which they own. Whether pleasant to contemplate or not, as relatively modernized societies become increasingly interdependent, the general membership of the society comes increasingly to feel that each and every one of them has a stake in decisions carried out in terms of private organizations which may have far-reaching effects on general welfare. Even the most cynical critic of private enterprise can hardly deny that a radical shift in point of view has taken place among the leaders of private predominantly economically oriented organizations. Only the most radical conservatives seek or contemplate a return to the relatively unfettered freedoms of people in comparable positions in the early part of the twentieth or the latter part of the nineteenth century. In the general sets of professional-client structures there exist relatively clear-cut models of methods of conducting relationships about which people are much concerned and in terms of which they are vulnerable to experts without having the balances of power and responsibility based primarily on the ownership of assets. As private ownership of assets of predominantly economically oriented organizations is increasingly diffused throughout the general population and increasingly separated from control, a similar relationship involving great concern, high vulnerability, and a responsible attitude by controlling experts will either be approximated, or those economic aspects will be brought under still more rapidly accelerated direct administration by members of the government. This will hold for all societies which are increasingly modernized and yet still characterized by private ownership and control of goods and services on a large scale.

V

GENERAL PROBLEMS FOR THE MEMBERS OF SOCIETIES WITH PREDOMINANTLY ECONOMICALLY ORIENTED ORGANIZATIONS

A. STRATEGIC PROBLEMS OF COORDINATION AND CONTROL

Although predominantly economically oriented units may be so institutionalized that actions in terms of them are carefully separated from actions in terms of other types of organizations in the society and from actions in terms of other organizations of their own type, behavior in terms of those organizations in a direct sense affects the behavior of members of the organizations from which it is carefully separated. Regardless of how behavior in terms of such organizations is interrelated with behavior in terms of other organizations—whether they exist as private organizations or as subsystems of government—there is always the question of how the members of such organizations draw on outputs produced in terms of other organizations from which they are separated. Problems of coordination and control of this sort never involve interrelationships solely among members of organizations of the same type actually speaking, though this may be the case ideally speaking. For those members of the organization who spend a considerable part of their time working in terms of the organization concerned, there is always some actual interrelationship between their roles in the organization itself and their roles in their own family units. To the extent that the set of members of the families of the individuals who work in such a fashion derive a considerable portion of what is viewed as family income as some sort of return for such services, the importance of such interrelationships *actually* is increased. I have emphasized the word *actually* in this connection because the relationship is the more significant because *ideally* speaking these spheres are kept separate from one another.

Since the members always consider these organizations to be primarily concerned with production rather than consumption, the problem of disposal of output is as much a problem of coordination and control for the members as the problem of input. The operations in terms of such organizations can be brought to a stop as clearly by interference with the disposal of goods and services as by interference with the sources of supply. Members of predominantly economically oriented organizations can neither consume what they produce nor support life on what they produce alone without interrelationships via market mechanisms or some structures of direct allocation. In all cases of modernization of relative late-comers to the process, the problems of initiating new and more efficient forms of production are comparatively simple by contrast with the problem of coordinating and controlling the interrelationships in terms of organizations of this sort once a considerable number of such new operations are under way. In highly sedentary social contexts characterized by relatively low levels of specialization and high levels of self-sufficiency of the units in terms of which production is carried out, problems of coordination and control are never as important as the problems of maintaining the requisites for a given relatively stable level of operation. As modernization increases, the problem of traffic control, as it were, always increases in importance relative to what are ordinarily considered problems of output. Increases in output simply set the stage for increased problems of traffic in this sense. All problems of coordination of this sort raise again the problem of adequate knowledge for coordination. In the absence of careful records and accounting procedures, it is impossible to have adequate knowledge for such coordination and control. Given the problem of accounting alone, regardless of differences of opinion about private versus government ownership, any relatively modernized system will be characterized by highly generalized monetary units and likely by some market(s) as well. Given governmental ownership, for example, competition for survival by the members of various subsystems primarily concerned with the production of goods and services may come increasingly to resemble the rivalry and competition as between members of different large-scale private predominantly economically oriented organizations or members of given subsystems of a single such private organization. I have no intention whatsoever to deny that differences between private and governmental ownership are significant from many points of view—but, increasingly as levels of modernization increase, the common features of predominantly economically oriented organizations, regardless of these other differences also increase.[16] The accent here falls heavily on this increase and the consequent similarities primarily because so many for so many important policy reasons are concerned with the differences that the common features are the more likely to be ignored.

B. PROBLEM OF CAPITAL FORMATION

For reasons to be discussed in Part IV, Chapter 1 below, I hold that relatively modernized societies cannot continue stable without a positive rate of capital formation. They cannot be stable in the face of stagnation or the regression of the national income in general, and they also cannot remain stable unless there is an increase in the portion of the national income that is distributed to the members of the general population in particular. To the extent that a considerable amount of that national income is a function of the operation of members of the society in terms of predominantly economically oriented organizations the individuals responsible for the conduct of those organizations are constantly faced with the problem of capital formation. Capital formation, from this point of view, is to general economic development what coordination and control are to political development. Regardless of the form of society being discussed, if new capital is not formed either stagnation or regression of the national income must follow. Once these organizations exist, the problem of capital formation is no longer one simply of the prosperity or lack of prosperity of individual specialized organizations of this sort. It is a problem of the stability of the societies of which they are subsystems. Whatever the varieties of capital formation have been in social history, the avenues in general have been two. The first of these was the investment at private discretion of assets previously accumulated, presumably in the interest of receiving an income in the form of interest or profits from such investments. The other major avenue of capital formation has been via what is generally referred to as forced saving. It is generally conceived to occur via the operations carried out in terms of governmental organizations, although one might raise the question as to whether or not there have not existed in some societies nongovernmental organizations

[16] Indeed, this holds true of all large-scale organizations under such conditions—regardless of specialized orientations.

of sufficient scale and influence as to effect, via operations in terms of their structures, something closely analogous to forced saving on the part of both members of the organizations themselves and other members of the society.

There are a wide variety of questions raised by the problem of capital formation on a private basis by contrast with capital formation on the basis of forced saving, but if capital formation does not take place on the one basis, it will have to take place on the other basis if the society is to be stable. In a sense the question of the marshaling of capital formation as far as this work is concerned may be broken down into the problem of capital formation in terms of three types of societies: (1) relatively nonmodernized societies in a stable state, (2) relatively nonmodernized societies in the process of increasing modernization, and (3) relatively modernized societies.

The problem of capital formation is minimized for the members of those societies which are relatively nonmodernized and are in a stable state. The level of capital formation need not exceed the level necessary to maintain the national income at roughly the level presently obtaining. The per capita national income need not rise at all, and the absolute national income need rise only sufficiently to take care of increases in the general population. The latter are likely to be relatively slow and relatively modest. The methods of capital formation characteristic of such societies are heavily traditionalized, imbedded in the structures of organizations which are not specialized with regard to economic orientation, and subject to interference primarily via behavior which is generally considered socially deviant. Such deviant behavior is likely to take the form of theft, graft and corruption, etc. Relatively well institutionalized structures of handling such deviants generally exist, at least ideally if not actually, and if the actual structures do not coincide rather well with the ideal ones in this respect, such societies cannot be stable. The most important thing about such societies as far as capital formation is concerned is that stability of the societies does not hang on the use of capital to secure constantly increasing rates of material productivity. Indeed, when such societies begin to modernize, one of the most unsettling influences is the fact that radically increased rates of material productivity are introduced into structures of production previously not characterized by such tendencies.

The problem of capital formation in terms of relatively nonmodernized societies in the process of increasing modernization is, of course, a critical problem. The level of capital formation necessary for the process radically exceeds the level previously necessary for the maintenance of stability. Indeed, it must be at such a level that, despite radical new departures in the type of capital utilized, the general organization of production, etc., the old levels of national income are at least maintained while increases and changes in a variety of new directions are also put into effect. Given the radically bimodal distribution of income characteristic of such societies—that is to say, a distribution of income such that the vast majority of the members of the society are living close to the margin of subsistence while a relatively small number have quite large incomes—it is unlikely that the necessary capital can be formed overwhelmingly on a private basis. On a private basis it is practically impossible to increase the saving of the individuals living close to the margin of subsistence, and given the nature of the high income receivers of such societies, it is unlikely that a sufficient portion of their income can be directed into new types of capital formation via private means.

Even were there no problems of personal motivation as far as those individuals were concerned, there would still exist in such social settings problems of the scale on which capital formation must be carried out and the fact that some of the uses to which capital formation must be put are not the sort that can be handled on a scale sufficient for modernization with any sort of private returns likely to motivate private capital formation on any save an eleemosynary basis. There has never been a society in terms of which one could count on sufficient capital formation on such a basis for the general operations of the members of the society. Unless the members of some outside society, on an eleemosynary or other basis, are prepared to make available the necessary capital formation, a considerable part of the capital formation necessary in terms of a society whose members are seeking to become relatively modernized must be carried out on the basis of forced saving, regardless of whether the members of that society attempt such a transition on the basis of complete government ownership or whether they attempt some combination of governmental and private ownership in terms of predominantly economically oriented organizations.[17]

In relatively modernized social contexts the problem of capital formation is likely to take place increasingly via forced saving or some general scheme of private motivation operated primarily via

[17] One of the reasons for this is that in terms of relatively nonmodernized societies most eleemosynary activities are carried out on highly particularistic grounds—most frequently on nepotistic grounds—rather than in terms of sufficiently large-scale organizations to be effective for purposes of such transitions. W. E. Moore suggests that large-scale predominantly religiously oriented organizations might constitute an exception to this.

action in terms of the governmental organization. At this point some definition of the concept of *forced saving* is necessary. Saving is defined as *forced saving* if income in which an individual has an equity is income which he cannot at his own discretion divert to purposes which he regards as consumption. In this respect, although we think of the United States as being a society in terms of which private capital formation is carried to its greatest lengths, forced saving takes place on a large scale in terms of private organizations of varied sorts as well as in terms of the government and is related to the separation of ownership and control. Retained earnings of corporations, funds poured into retirement schemes of various sorts, whenever discretion about participation in them is denied the individual by the leaders of his government, his university, his union, or some other organization to which he belongs, are all examples of forced saving in this sense. Forced saving is the method of marshaling funds for capital formation perhaps to the extent of eighty to eighty-five per cent of all funds so marshaled. Presumably in societies in terms of which predominantly economically oriented organizations are expected to be governmentally owned, the level of forced saving amounts to an even larger percentage of the total savings. In any case the increased centralization of saving via increases in forced saving—both public [i.e., governmentally forced] and private—is one critical form of increased centralization in relatively modernized contexts. That carried out on a private basis probably constitutes one of the most critical forms of centralization outside a governmental context.

Insofar as the level of saving is left entirely up to the individual owner's initiative, the problem of motivation of such saving is not necessarily altered with the actual level of vulnerability of the society concerned to the lack of saving. With increased levels of modernization, the more the decision to save is left to individual initiative the greater the risks of general social instability, if the individual's decisions about savings do not coincide neatly with the requirements for the development of the systems involved. It does not follow that, as the complexity and the delicacy of adjustment increases, some group of individuals on as rational a basis as possible will make the decision that the continuation of such initiative is far too risky. Many of the increases of forced saving undoubtedly have and will continue to come about as by-products of quite other interests. Retention of corporate earnings as a means of financing expansion constitutes a private increase in forced saving most directly and self-consciously oriented to programs of capital formation. Nevertheless, preference for this means of capital formation may be more easily explicable in terms of its convenience and degrees of freedom for the leaders of such enterprises than in terms of some rational preoccupation with forced savings as a preferable means of general capital formation.

Increases of forced saving via compulsory contributions to privately and governmentally controlled welfare programs of all sorts, including prominently, of course, social security, were almost certainly undertaken primarily with a view to the development of those programs for their own sakes rather than as a particular means of implementing some specific scheme of capital formation apart from those welfare objectives. Nevertheless, as degrees of modernization increase, whatever a preferred ideology may dictate to the members of a given society by way of leaving initiative for saving as completely as possible in private hands, if that initiative does not make possible levels of capital formation consistent with the minimal requirements for development consistent with general social stability, the level of forced saving will increase. It may increase following a general situation of social instability such that the previous ideology about private initiative is eradicated quite self-consciously, and it may result from less self-conscious and explicit programs, but come about it will. No level of capital formation is sufficient in and of itself to guarantee the social stability of any relatively modernized society. The implications of insufficient capital formation are, however, sufficiently stark that, if it cannot be approached on a relatively decentralized basis, the attempt will be made to approach that level on the basis of some form of increasingly centralized organization, whether or not that effort is successful.

C. PROBLEM OF INCOME DISTRIBUTION

With the possible exception of relatively small-scale societies geographically so situated that the general resources constituting the main factors in the income of the members of the society concerned approach the character of free goods, the distribution of income will be bimodal as described above [pp. 265–279].[18] I

---

[18] In the strict economic sense of the concept of *free goods* the material elements of a standard of living are never in fact free goods in any social context. If, however, diets are sufficiently simple, housing requirements sufficiently elementary, the elements of clothing abundantly at hand, and the labor for conversion of these materials for such uses not regarded as exceptionally irksome, some approach to the conception of free goods may be approximated. In all such cases there is still probably a bimodal distribution of income, but the few members of the society who are at the wealthy end of the distribution may not be much more wealthy than those at the poorer end, and those at the poorer end may well not be living at all close to what they themselves would regard as the bare margin of subsistence.

have asserted that a strategic portion of the capital formation making it possible to maintain even that general level of income for the vast majority of the members of the society is a function of the uneven distribution of income among its members. What is important here is the proposition that for relatively modernized societies, which are always characterized by a proliferation of predominantly economically oriented organizations, the trend must always be toward a unimodal distribution of income.

For reasons which will be further elaborated in Part IV, Chapter 2 below, it is exceedingly unlikely that the stability of relatively modernized societies can be maintained unless there is a constantly increasing standard of living for the members of the population as a whole. The levels of specialization and interdependency of the types of units of production which develop under these circumstances is incompatible with the lack of mass markets. The increase in heavy consumers goods such as relatively elaborate housing, domestic machines of all sorts, automobiles, etc., will constitute an important portion of the production in such societies. Such goods cannot be developed on a relatively modernized basis for a restricted elite unless their use becomes general. In all historical cases the curve of income distribution characteristic of such societies has changed from a bimodal one to an increasingly unimodal curve, with increasingly few people at the bare margin of subsistence and relatively few people with much higher incomes than those average in the population at large. The trend in this direction has, if anything, been more extreme in the societies less characterized by governments dominated by socialist ideology in explicit contradiction to the predictions of Marxist beliefs. This has nothing whatsoever to do with the altruism or love of humanity of those who believe in structures of private ownership by contrast with those who believe in structures of government ownership. It has rather to do with the possibilities of development in terms of societies with governments which have been characterized by different levels of centralization and modernization. The societies with the highest levels of governmental centralization today are in general those whose members were relative late-comers to the process of modernization and therefore were ones relative to which the level of governmental centralization necessary to achieve a given level of modernization was probably considerably higher than for those societies in terms of which relatively modernized characteristics were achieved more or less indigenously over a much longer period of time. This state of affairs is characteristically associated with high levels of forced saving, great concentration on the development of heavy industries, and much less attention on the development of predominantly economically oriented organizations specializing in the production of consumers goods in the usual sense. Even in those social contexts, however, insofar as any considerable level of modernization has been achieved, the average per capita income actually distributed has increased, and the tendency has been away from the extremes of bimodal distribution characteristic of relatively nonmodernized societies of considerable scale.

The methods in terms of which these shifts are carried out vary enormously, but regardless of ideology, there are certain constant features. Both the increase in per capita income and the increasingly unimodal distribution of that income are accompanied by an increased distribution of that income in the form of monetary units and an increased reckoning of it in monetary terms. The income is increasingly distributed as a payment for services carried out in terms of predominantly economically oriented organizations. It is spent in terms of quite different organizations. So far the history of relatively modernized societies, no society of any considerable scale has been characterized by high levels of modernization *and* distribution of income via direct allocations of goods and services. Many different degrees and kinds of direct allocation characterize different historical instances of such societies, but as the level of modernization increases, beyond the achievement of the lower levels of relatively modernized classification, the distribution of income, via monetary units, as increasingly generalized purchasing power increases rather than decreases. Control of uses of such income tends to be by centralized decision as to what goods and services will be made available in terms of markets rather than by direct allocation as such.

Once relatively unimodal curves of income distribution have been achieved and the production of goods and services has become interdependent with such distributions of income, without the development of social chaos, there can be no turning back to bimodal distributions of incomes such as were characteristic of relatively nonmodernized societies. This again has nothing whatsoever to do with private versus public ownership or the altruism or selfishness of owners or governmental officials. Once operations have been largely geared to the mass-purchasing of both general and heavy consumers goods rather than to highly self-sufficient family units, any sharp return to radically bimodal distributions of income could be achieved only by massive negations of capital formation. This could take place by the sort of mass destruction of capital goods and installations which would presumably be attendant upon a war fought with modern weapons, but it is exceedingly unlikely that the members of any known society would tolerate social decisions which negated capital formation by wiping out the demand and markets for the kind of goods and services to whose production the capital formed could be adapted. Once relatively modernized societies have been achieved, any schemes of exploitation which would imply a return to historical bimodal distributions of income would wipe out the basis of power of those who sought to bring the situation about as surely as it would wipe out the basis for existing structures of living on the part of those who were presumably to be used in this fashion. Once predominantly economically oriented units exist on any considerable scale, their existence can be continued only if in the long run the general standards of living in the population continually increase and become increasingly uniform. There is, however, no reason to believe that any limiting state of absolutely equal income distribution is possible.[19]

D. PROBLEM OF COORDINATION WITH GOVERNMENT

As predominantly economically oriented organizations proliferate, the problems of coordination of activities carried out in terms of them and those carried out in terms of governmental organizations become increasingly important. The importance of such coordination is frequently discussed in terms of the problems of graft and corruption, but as levels of modernization increase in relatively modernized societies, the role of graft and corruption becomes much less important than the general problem of coordination and control. If assets associated with predominantly economically oriented organizations are privately owned, the possibilities of graft and corruption are, of course, considerable. Use by those in control of such organizations of the goods and services at their disposal to affect action in terms of the government is always a possibility. Even if these organizations are subsystems of the government, manipulation by their directors of the goods and services at their disposal to affect action in terms of other subsystems of the government is always a possibility.

The very extent to which efforts in the direction of graft and corruption are likely to be narrowly, personally, and rationally

[19] The minimal correlation between gradations in income and other symbols of prestige, achievement, etc., already mentioned above [see pp. 156, 257–262, 277, and 403, etc.] clearly implies that inequalities in income distribution cannot be eliminated unless most [or logically, *all*] other invidious distinctions are also eliminated—if the society is to be stable.

conceived, in a sense minimizes the problem posed. Graft and corruption of this sort is not conducted unconsciously. In all societies the individuals directly involved are exceedingly likely to know what they are doing. The very rationality of these efforts increases the probability that such efforts can be coped with by attempts at rational countermeasures.[20] Furthermore, those involved in graft and corruption generally seek personal benefits, and if those benefits are being sought with a view to their relevance to economic allocation, that is to say, if an individual seeks to buy government favor for improvement of his economic position, however large the sums may be from the individual's point of view, they are likely to be relatively small in terms of the total national income or as an element in the governmental budget. The cases of graft and corruption of this sort which turn up in the United States today, for example, are in part remarkable as a demonstration of how cheaply some people can be bought and sold. The most spectacular cases which we can uncover are trifles by comparison with what could be achieved in this country fifty or seventy-five years ago by comparable levels of effort devoted to graft and corruption. Furthermore, none of the scandals of this sort uncovered have come even close to implying a financial panic, a major give-away of natural resources, or anything of comparable implication for the society at large.

On the other hand, the problem of lack of adequate knowledge to achieve the kind of coordination and control necessary if the general processes of production and distribution are to continue smoothly and at an ever increasing rate constitute an ever increasing problem. As the interstitial adjustments become finer and finer, as the levels of productivity achieved grow higher and higher, as the number of individuals involved become greater and greater, as the expectations of standards of living constantly rise, the implications of any mistake, regardless of how honest or well intended it may be and regardless of whether or not it is that of the director of a private corporation or of a wholly owned government subsystem, increase by leaps and bounds. The probability of any government in the world surviving such mistakes committed either by its own members or those of private organizations in the society is more a measure of the relative lack of modernization in that society than of the level of authoritarianism achieved by the members of the government. Under such circumstances the con-

[20] In general one should always pray that one's enemies or opponents be wicked. The wicked tend toward explicitly rational action. Hence the possibility of dealing with them by outthinking them is increased. [See p. 490.]

tinuation of private versus public discretion in predominantly economically oriented organizations is more a function of the lack of spectacular errors than of any ideological preference on the part of the members of the society in general for private enterprise as opposed to public ownership. Whatever that ideological preference may be, if the mistakes are sufficiently spectacular to threaten a rising national income there will be social change. The ideological preference for private enterprise may be wiped out, and/or there may be general social instability with a variety of possible consequences. In no case, however, will continuation of increases in modernization in that society be consistent with the previous degrees of freedom accorded privately controlled predominantly economically oriented organizations.

E. DEVELOPMENTAL TENDENCIES

Certain developmental tendencies characterize all predominantly economically oriented organizations in all societies characterized by the large-scale development of such organizations, regardless of whether these have developed as subsystems of a government or on a private basis ideally, at least, separated from the government. First, all such organizations tend either to increase in scale or to be wiped out. Whether one reckons scale in terms of the numbers of members involved, the amounts of capital involved, the amounts and variations of output, etc., such organizations cannot survive in a society in which organizations like themselves are increasingly frequent unless they grow. In the long run such organizations cannot survive either decreases in scale or stagnation. In the face of either they tend to become subsystems of other organizations or to go out of existence as organizations altogether.

Second, there is always an increasing emphasis on rationality in the relationships that comprise the organizational structures as such and in the relationship among the members of such organizations in their roles as members of the organization with the members of other organizations. Coincidences between predominantly traditional orientations and rational behavior cannot be counted upon to guarantee sufficient levels of rationality in terms of these organizations as it can in terms of the organizations in many relatively nonmodernized contexts. Balances of particularism as a means of arriving at predominantly universalistic solutions become increasingly impossible in terms of such organizations, despite the fact that particularistic elements are, of course, never even approximately eliminated from such settings.

Third, there is always an increasing emphasis on functional

specificity in these contexts. The extent of obligations among the members of such organizations may continuously proliferate, but ideally speaking at least, they never become increasingly functionally diffuse. The obligations, for example, to employees may come to cover health insurance, general welfare of various sorts, and increasingly detailed retirement plans, but it is always the essence of such increases that they are increasingly detailed. The number and scope of these obligations may increase radically but the emphasis on explicit definition and explicit delimitation never decreases in the long run. A considerable amount of friction of individuals in their relations with others involved in such organizations and a considerable amount of the complaints about operations in terms of such organization is a function of the fact that the responsibility of these organizations for general welfare and retirement is continuously deemed to increase by their members. Ideally speaking, especially from the point of view of those with administrative responsibility, those obligations however far-reaching are explicit, limited, and detailed. From the point of view of the individual whose welfare is concerned, however, the problems of his welfare can never be so precisely detailed and delimited. This constitutes an important element in the constantly reiterated complaint that such relationships involve the individual in endless amounts of red tape and that the provisions for his welfare never precisely fit the needs of his case. Such complaints will never decrease in the context of any increasingly modernized society, because welfare programs of this sort from the point of view of the maintenance of the organization must always be increasingly functionally specific whereas from the point of view of the individual, if they do not deal with the whole man and hence to some degree become functionally diffuse, they give rise to dissatisfaction expressed in such terms.

Fourth, relationships in terms of these organizations also become increasingly avoidant, ideally speaking. In this respect a curious sort of balance is restored by the discrepancy between ideal and actual structures. The general increases in scale already mentioned above probably imply increasing degrees of emphasis on rationality, universalism, and functional specificity. With regard to avoidance, however, there is probably a working level which once achieved is compatible with more or less indefinite further increases in emphases on rationality, universalism and functional specificity. On the other hand, in the presence of high emphases on avoidance in terms of relationships which nevertheless must be frequent and efficient, some departures on relatively isolated bases in the direction of intimacy are likely to be necessary, not only for the maintenance of morale, but also because relatively few individuals are capable of virtuosic avoidance.

At the same time, actual departures in the direction of predominantly particularistic relationships which involve increases in nonrational behavior, emphasis on particularism, functional diffuseness, and intimacy are characteristic of all such organizations. Such departures are most likely to exist without far-reaching implications for instability if they involve individuals in constant interaction and of very nearly identical rank in terms of the organization, or if they involve individuals constantly interacting with one another and of radically different ranks in terms of the organization. After the discussions above in Part II, Chapter 2, it should go without saying that no development of these organizations ever completely eliminates emphases on tradition, particularism, functional diffuseness, or in some cases intimacy.

Fifth, in the development of such organizations the tendency is always toward increasing emphasis on responsibility rather than individualism, regardless of whether private or governmental ownership is involved. This holds true regardless of how individualistic the emphasis may have been in the early history of the development of privately owned organizations of this sort. The greatest problem connected with increases in emphasis on responsibility is to maintain such increases without getting involved in predominantly particularistic and functionally diffuse relationships. The form par excellence of danger in this respect is an increase in paternalism. Relatively modernized societies have differed enormously in their compatibility with different levels of paternalism within such specialized organizations. The level of paternalism maintained in organizational contexts of this sort in Japan, by contrast with the levels maintained in the United States is one of the best examples of the possibility and extent of such variations. Nevertheless, with the continued development of modernization in Japan the level of paternalism characteristic of such organizations is declining. Increasingly the emphasis on responsibility takes the form of participation in welfare programs which are increasingly regulated and supervised in terms of other specialized organizations, usually ones in which governmental supervision, if not direct control, is increasingly evident.

Finally [sixth], these organizations become increasingly hierarchical in their organization. This is probably a function of increasing problems of coordination and control and the increasing significance of failures in terms of these organizations. The membership of different societies have differed radically in their degree of emphasis on egalitarian treatment. This is often taken to imply that nonhierarchical organizations or relationships are preferred to hierarchical ones. This is never the case in so simple a form. The vast majority of all organizations have been hierarchically organized. In a society like the United States, for example, friendship relations constitute one of the very few types of relationships not hierarchically organized ideally speaking, and even those relationships, as all men know, are actually frequently hierarchical. Family relationships are to some extent hierarchical and are a great deal more hierarchical in some societies than in others. School relationships are to some extent hierarchical, ideally as well as actually; relationships among governmental members are hierarchical, ideally as well as actually. There is virtually no organization of any major importance in any society which is not, ideally speaking, hierarchical in critical respects. The level of hierarchical emphasis carried out in actuality is even higher. Egalitarian emphases, where they exist, are overwhelmingly concerned with the equal availability on predominantly universalistic grounds of access to and/or protection of certain rights. The meaning of egalitarianism has never implied general participation in nonhierarchical organizations for the members of a society during any considerable portion of their lives. This has never been the case in terms of even the least modernized of societies. In the most highly modernized contexts the number of hierarchically ordered organizations in terms of which the average individual operates and the clarity of the hierarchical structures themselves constantly increase with the scale of the organization and the levels of modernization characteristic of the society as such.

The levels of coordination and control, seen as internal to the operation of such organizations, as well as the levels of coordination and control viewed from the point of view of the interrelations of operations in terms of these organizations with operations carried out in terms of other organizations constantly increase. Such increases are often perceived as increases in regimentation and displeasing to those not well-socialized to such developments. On the other hand, the number of individual members of any relatively modernized society not well-socialized to such developments is constantly decreasing. As these organizations develop, the large-scale allocation of power and responsibility internal to them with regard to the functionally specific areas covered by the relationships common to them increasingly take on the nature of the hierarchical relationships ordinarily associated with armed-force organizations. Indeed, if general developments in international affairs are such that war on the whole becomes unlikely and the memberships of armed forces as they are known today are to any considerable extent disbanded, large-scale organizations of a predominantly economically oriented character are likely to take on even further stiffening of their hierarchical nature by virtue of the fact that to some extent operation in terms of these organizations will acquire some elements of the emergency life or death character previously associated with membership in the armed forces. This is particularly likely to be so with elements of risk associated with radical new departures in technology.

III · CHAPTER · 4

ARMED FORCE ORGANIZATIONS

I
INTRODUCTION

A. GENERAL STATE OF THE SUBJECT

Curiously enough in academic discussions armed force organizations constitute one of the most generally ignored and overlooked areas of great importance despite the role of armed force organizations in budgets, despite the frequent figuring of members of such organizations as central figures in revolutionary situations, despite the decisive role played by operations in terms of such organizations during periods of war, etc. The vast majority of the work on armed force systems has been carried out by historians or persons interested in armed force systems per se [e.g., military experts] rather than by general social scientists. In recent years an increasing number of social scientists, especially in the fields of sociology and political science, have concerned themselves with armed force systems as such or with restricted interrelations between armed force organizations and other specific matters.[1] The fact remains that general social treatment of societies or nations in which the armed force organizations are obviously of considerable relevance are on the whole strikingly sparing in their mention of those organizations. For example, four major recent works on the Soviet Union specifically,[2] all of them general treatments, totaling 2,123 pages, contained references to armed force organizations on only 101 pages, of which one refers to the

---

[1] See for example, Morris Janowitz, *The Professional Soldier,* The Free Press, 1960, Glencoe, Illinois; Samuel P. Huntington, *The Soldier and the State,* Harvard University Press, Cambridge, Mass., 1957; John W. Masland and Laurence I. Radway, *Soldiers and Scholars, Military Education and National Policy,* Princeton University Press, Princeton, N.J., 1957; and John J. Johnson (ed.), *The Role of the Military in Underdeveloped Areas,* Princeton University Press, Princeton, N.J., 1962.

Professor Eli Chinoy does refer to the significance of armed forces in his elementary text [*Society, An Introduction to Sociology;* Random House, N.Y., 1961, pp. 263–265] and gives students initial bibliographical aid on this point.

[2] There is in addition a general work on Russia in transition—C. E. Black (ed.), *The Transformation of Russian Society,* Harvard University Press, Cambridge, 1960, 695 pp. This contains an essay [R. L. Garthoff, *The Military as a Social Force,* pp. 323–338] on the armed forces plus mentions reflected in the index on 12 other pages.

United States Air Force, if chapter headings and indices are to be relied upon. A major treatment of United States society of 575 pages contains no mention of armed force organizations important enough to be reflected either in chapter headings or the index. Another volume on United States society, consisting of 1,036 pages has mentions of the subject on 19 pages as indicated by subheadings and the index. A work on China of 611 pages contains references to armed force organizations on only 36 pages. Three volumes treating of Egypt and/or other countries in the Middle East of 941 pages contained references to armed force organizations in only one volume, and those references occur on no more than 37 pages. One volume on Brazil of 346 pages and a general treatise on the economy of Latin America of 434 pages indicate such interest on only one page with a reference there to "militarism." [3]

[3] The works referred to and the attention given to these matters are the following:

1. Inkeles, A., and Bauer, R.: *The Soviet Citizen*, Harvard University Press, Cambridge, Mass., 1959. This volume contains 533 pages. Interest in the Soviet armed force organization is indicated in no chapter headings. In the index there are references to armed forces on 6 pages. One of these is a reference to the United States Air Force.

2. Bauer, R., Inkeles, A., and Kluckhohn, C.: *How the Soviet System Works*, Vintage Books, New York, 1960 (reprinted by arrangement with Harvard University Press). This volume contains 312 pages, it has no chapter indicating any interest in any armed force system, and it has references reflected in the index on 11 pages.

3. Inkeles, A., and Geiger, K.: *Soviet Society: A Book of Readings*, Houghton Mifflin Company, Boston, Mass., 1961. This volume contains 703 pages. It has one 7½ page section in one chapter devoted to this subject plus mention on 12 additional pages including 3 which refer to World War II, as indicated by the index.

4. Fainsod, M.: *How Russia is Ruled*, Harvard University Press, Cambridge, Mass., 1953. This volume contains 575 pages including one chapter of 28 pages entitled "The Party and Armed Forces," and mentions reflected in the index on 36 other pages. The reference here to armed force organizations is considerably more serious and more important than all of the references in the other three volumes combined.

5. Williams, R.: *American Society, A Sociological Interpretation*, Alfred A. Knopf Inc., New York, 1960 (second edition). This work contains 575 pages and no indication whatsoever of any mention of United States armed force organizations in either index or chapter headings. In the index there are references to military powers of the federal government on 3 pages, to military society [caste structure of] on 3 pages, to the Salvation Army on 1 page, and to veterans' organizations on 2 pages.

6. Lerner, M.: *America as a Civilization*, Simon and Schuster, New York, 1957. This volume contains 1,036 pages. One section of Chapter XII, "America as a World Power," has a subheading "Landscape with Soldiers" of 9 pages. Under the headings, War, Military, and Army in the Index there are references to 11 other pages. There are no references there to Navy, Marines, or Air Force.

7. Berger, M.: *The Arab World Today*, Doubleday & Co. Inc., New York, 1962. This work contains 480 pages. It has one chapter of 28 pages entitled

As far as the works of American scholars are concerned, there are in the main two bases for this neglect. The first has to do with a peculiarity of United States society. As will be indicated below, armed force organizations have two major foci of significance in any society. One is the role of such organizations as far as external use, either for defense or aggression, is concerned. The

---

"The Military Regime." Armed force systems are mentioned on 9 other pages as indicated by the index.

8. Berger, M.: *Bureaucracy and Society in Modern Egypt, A Study of the Higher Civil Service*, Princeton University Press, Princeton, N.J., 1957. This work contains 271 pages and no mention whatsoever of armed force organizations as indicated by the chapter headings or indices. This is, of course, a volume on the higher civil service in Egypt, but given the general role of members of the armed forces in that country, a lack of reference to the armed forces even in such a volume indicates a certain level of restraint. Professor Berger has published an essay, *Military Elite and Social Change: Egypt Since Napoleon*, Research Monograph #6, Center for International Studies, Princeton University, 1960.

9. Harbison, F., and Ibrahim, I. A.: *Human Resources for Egyptian Enterprise*, McGraw-Hill Book Company, Inc., New York, 1958. This volume contains 230 pages with no reference to armed force organizations in either chapter headings or the indices.

10. Hu, C-t, et al.: *China: Its People, Its Society, Its Culture*, H.R.A.F. Press, New Haven, Conn., 1960. This volume contains 611 pages. According to its indices there are 36 pages on which there appear mentions of armed force organizations.

11. Schurz, W. L: *Brazil, the Infinite Country*, E. P. Dutton & Co., Inc., New York, 1961. This volume contains 346 pages. According to its index there is a reference to militarism on page 320.

12. Gordon, W. L.: *The Economy of Latin America*, Columbia University Press, New York, N.Y., 1950. This volume contains 434 pages. Neither chapter headings nor indices indicate any relevance of any armed force organizations to the economic aspects of any Latin American society.

These examples of the point do not constitute anything like a systematic survey. For purposes of this illustration I simply pulled off some of the more obvious volumes on my own shelves and added one or two others snatched from the shelves of colleagues. On the basis of this explicitly non-random sample, I would not hesitate to give good odds that a volume with a title such as *Dutch Society* would be unlikely to contain any treatment of the Dutch armed force system on any comparable level of generalization with other equally or perhaps less relevant features of the society. In general one could give considerable odds and still feel safe about almost any society that he might care to name save German society, Japanese society, the society dominated by Genghis Khan, and that of Napoleonic France.

Nothing could be more superficial than my examples or my use in them of measures such as chapter headings, numbers of pages cited in indices, etc., but even so superficial a case is damning in one major respect. If it reflects little attention to these matters by the scholars concerned, is that little attention the result of their having self-consciously considered the question of whether armed force organizations were no more relevant than indicated by their references to the matters they sought to treat? If so, we have an arguable question of judgment. But was the scarcity of attention a function of the fact that, for whatever reasons, the question of the relevance of the phenomena simply never got raised?

other is the use of such forces for the internal maintenance of order. As far as external use is concerned, until participation in World War II, members of United States society relied overwhelmingly on armed forces which could be called into being after an emergency became clear. The extent of armed force organization maintained during periods of peace was a relatively minor consideration as far as the general membership of the society was concerned. For a whole series of reasons too complicated to go into here, armed force organizations were not in general viewed as having any particular role in the internal maintenance of order. Even following World War II, there was a genuine sense in which it was much easier for Americans to envisage the sending of troops to Korea than to Little Rock. In general, Americans tended to denigrate armed force organizations save those which were considered as essentially citizens' armies in times of emergencies. Regularly and continuously maintained armed force organizations were on the whole suspect. In time of peace we Americans generally tended to regard armed force careers as undertaken only if one were unable to do any better.

To this general American tendency to look down on or ignore armed force organizations as a serious focus of consideration one must add the far more general parochialism of academics with regard to members of the armed forces. There are few subjects about which academics have more stereotypical views than about armed forces in general and the individuals who seek professional careers in terms of them in particular. We generally look down on professional military personnel; we regard them as unintelligent, humorless, authoritarian, and above all antiintellectual. Our average view of what armed force organizations or professional military personnel are like has little to do with the state of the facts. Actually, there are some amusing departures from the stereotype. A reasonable case may be made out for the fact that, particularly with the developments of modernization, the planners and members of armed force organizations are more likely to put stress on education and on various forms of intellectual training than are the members or planners of any other subsystems of their respective governments. After all, in times of peace, armed force organizations are explicitly organizations in terms of which training and planning take place. In any context in which the technologies on which some operations in terms of armed force organizations depend are constantly changing, sooner or later, the members of those organizations must increase their interest in new education at least with regard to the new technological frontiers. In the United States case at least, members of the armed force organizations have given more thought to continuous reeducation of the members of their organizations than have the members of any other subsystem of the government. In the public affairs field generally, Americans as a whole and American social scientists in particular have tended overwhelmingly to think of armed force organizations as at best a necessary evil rather than as organizations to be brought into creative attempts to analyze social phenomena in general. Unless specific crises and specific problems involving armed force organizations in the most obvious and direct sense have appeared, it has simply not occurred to most of us that they were likely to have any relevance.[4]

B. SPECIFIC INTERESTS HERE

I make no attempt whatsoever to treat armed force organizations at any length in the context of problems of war, since in that context they have received their most thorough and detailed treatment by military experts, historians, etc. The concern here is rather with possible relevances of armed force organizations in societies generally and in the process of development along increasingly modernized lines—especially the development of latecomers to the process of modernization. The potentialities of such organizations as foci of radicalism and of controlled development have seldom been explored.[5] With a degree of unanimity that is fascinating, both the professional military members of most societies as well as the civilians have viewed the armed force organizations as primarily of relevance in situations in which applications of force are of the essence. No doubt, both the military professionals and the civilian experts are quite correct that this will continue to be the major focus of interest as far as armed force organizations are concerned, but it may at least be interesting to raise questions.

I I
GENERAL SETTING OF ARMED FORCE ORGANIZATIONS

A. ARMED FORCE ORGANIZATIONS AS
OBJECTS OF EXPLICIT SOCIAL ENGINEERING

Armed force organizations, whenever found, appear almost inevitably as explicitly planned and carefully differentiated from other

[4] There are, of course, some exceptions. See, for example, *The Role of the Military in Underdeveloped Countries* (ed. John J. Johnson), Princeton University Press, Princeton, N.J., 1962, published after this chapter was written.

[5] Again, as an exception see *Ibid.*, footnote 4.

organizations. It is not true that organizations are generally explicit examples of social engineering. It is exceedingly doubtful, for example, whether an organization such as the family is generally an example of social engineering.[6] Whatever the case of organizations in general, armed force organizations are usually the result of explicit planning. Armed force organizations may vary enormously with regard to the range of actions appropriately carried out in terms of them, but they are not generally formed on the spur of the moment, and they are usually quite explicitly organized with a view to efficient functioning of their members in pursuit of relatively well understood ends. There are several reasons for this. In the first place, to a high degree armed force organizations are viewed as means by most of the members of the society most of the time. The means may be offensive or defensive or have to do with the general maintenance of internal order, but the organizations are instrumentally viewed. In the second place, these organizations are always specialized on the basis of sex and age, and therefore they are not organizations in terms of which every individual in the society can more or less casually grow up as a member. They are definitely organizations into which individuals are inducted for fairly explicit purposes. It is perfectly true that there are plenty of examples in social history of armed force organizations which are in a sense only called into being when needed, but in such cases what constitute needs in this sense are generally planned for and quite explicit. This sort of thing was quite prevalent as a characteristic of feudal societies. There might be no activity in terms of the armed force organizations at a given point in time, but when a given lord called into being the armed force organizations that he had the right to invoke, there were tables of organization in the form of the obligations owed him by his vassals. For example, each owed him a given amount of time or a given number of knights, horses, grooms, and so forth. Throughout the history of mankind few things have been as explicitly structured as religious ritual, magical practices, and armed force organizations.

[6] I feel quite sure, in fact, that family organizations in general were not examples of social engineering although certainly there are many cases in which specific structures of family organizations have been explicitly modified by social engineering. For example, in the period of Ch'in Shih-huang-ti in Chinese history explicit rules calling for the equal inheritance among all sons were set up in order to combat the continuous maintenance of large accumulations of land and the like. This one bit of explicit social engineering in family terms was quite enough to spell an end to feudalism in Chinese history. This particular bit of social engineering had quite far-reaching implications for Chinese society in general and Chinese family structures in particular.

B. TWO GENERAL FOCI

Operations in terms of armed force organizations are usually conceived to be oriented toward external *and* internal uses. It is the external applications of the efforts of the members of the armed force organization that tend to come immediately to mind when Americans consider these problems. We think of the members of the armed forces as being bent on aggressive exploits or defensive ones. Rightly or wrongly we have convinced ourselves that only defensive applications of armed forces externally are justifiable. As everyone knows, this attitude on the part of Americans in general constitutes one of the major realities as well as one of the major question marks of present-day international affairs. On the one hand there are those individuals who are thoroughly convinced that Americans are so bound by this point of view that, no matter how certain the knowledge may be that members of another society contemplate an attack, we cannot strike first, no matter how defensively such an initial strike might be conceived. There are also those who maintain that one of the real question marks in international stability is whether or not those in position to give orders to the members of our armed force organizations are in fact still bound by such thinking.

From this point of view both the society of Great Britain and that of the United States have been quite unusual. Neither society has been characterized for well over 150 years by any large-scale uses of armed forces for the internal maintenance of order. The closest approach to this on a large scale was our so-called *Civil War*, but at least from the point of view of the participants on both sides that has come somehow to be considered as involving external uses of armed forces and not as a use of the armed forces for the maintenance of order, regardless of what the views of an objective observer might be. The views of such an observer have not in any case shaped the attitude of Americans toward the legitimate applications of armed forces. For the members of the societies of both the United States and Great Britain it is in a quite genuine sense easier to contemplate the use of the members of armed force organizations abroad than at home.

For the members of most societies, however, the relevance of armed force organizations for internal uses is as much a matter of concern as their relevance for uses abroad. Generally the armed force organizations are clearly recognized as the main organizations in terms of which force is used for the maintenance of internal stability. One might maintain that even Americans and the English recognize this readily, if one discounts what some might almost consider a verbal distinction between internal as opposed to external armed force organizations, the external ones being generally recognized as armed forces in the ordinary sense, the internal ones being recognized as a police force. Even for us, operation in terms of various police organizations is certainly taken for granted as the means par excellence for curbing certain types of deviant behavior. The actual differentiation in organizational terms between *internal* and *external* armed forces is by no means rare, but it is probably unusual for the distinction to be carried to such lengths that the general members of the society regard it as especially shocking and unusual for the armed forces generally associated with external application to be called out in support of what is generally regarded as a problem of internal stability. Perhaps the members of highly stable societies generally regard members of the armed force organizations as having little to do internally. This would be a thoroughly expectable corollary of the fact that whenever actual force is exercised as a day-to-day way of securing conformity, the general internal stability of the society concerned is highly problematical.

The distinction between external and internal uses of members of armed force organizations is further important because in the present world situation no society of any considerable scale is going to be characterized by an absence of armed force organizations—regardless of the form of government or leadership or ideology expressed by the general membership. It is almost certainly true that in the present world situation fewer and fewer armed force organizations are of great significance for what might be called aggressive foreign uses. This may be obscured by all sorts of minor-scale applications of armed forces aggressively by the members of societies of some scale, or in some cases by members of societies of considerable scale. Without passing judgment on who is [or was] the aggressor, there are involvements of this sort between the Chinese and the Indians, the Israelis and the members of the surrounding Arab countries, and so forth. It is a fundamental thesis of this work, however, that the major problems of international relations may be divided into two general categories: first, those which are a function of the problems of modernization of relatively nonmodernized societies, and second, those which are a problem of the maintenance of the stability of the most highly modernized of societies.

The relatively small-scale uses of armed forces externally in the present state of technology are primarily possible because of potential instability between two or more of the camps capable of calling the most highly developed technologies of modern war into use against one another. I prefer to oversimplify this situation by discussing it in terms of the United States and The Union of Soviet Socialist Republics. Suppose that by some magic there were to be an agreement today between the members of those two societies that settled all existing differences between them, and suppose that one of the results of that agreement was not simply the settlement implied, but a state of mutual trust as between the strategic representatives of the respective governments of the order that exists, let us say, between the representatives of the government of Great Britain and that of the United States. In view of such a settlement, if the major parties to that settlement then felt that small-scale aggressions around the rest of the world served no purpose, would it really be difficult to put an end to such endeavors by international cooperation? I would not for a moment underestimate the seriousness of aggressive uses of armed forces scattered about the world today, but I would maintain that the major significance of those applications of force lies in the fact that they play around the potential instability as between camps consisting of the most highly modernized of societies. Phrases such as invincible Israeli or Arab nationalism are the emptiest substitutes for thinking in the international sphere I know. Even the current Chinese potential is primarily a function of this other major instability. I do not believe in miracles whether performed by people of whose conduct I approve or disapprove, and no information which has come out of mainland China has indicated that aggressive uses of modern Chinese armies would be excessively difficult to curb were it not for the potentiality that the attempt to curb them would touch off the far more awesome involvement of members of the United States and The Union of Soviet Socialist Republics in a third and perhaps final world war.

There is another reason why the external application of armed forces may be on the decline. The recognition of national interest as a major form of ideology justifying great extremes of conduct on the part of the members of the nations concerned is on the decline save within strict limits. Those limits now have primarily to do with the focus on national concern of the members of underdeveloped societies as a lever for the achievement of recognition of the right of their members to development and rapid modernization. Apart from this, national interest as such has ceased to be a major form of ideology. In Europe only one major statesman speaks of the glory of his nation as a major focus of policy, and his words sound impossibly old-fashioned in the world today. Other statesmen may think so, occasionally the recent leader of the Soviet Union, for example, used to state that something was necessary for the dignity of his country, but in general the really terrifying probability of international war is not viewed in simple national terms any more. Today, nationalism must be carefully separated from chauvinism. It may be that the underlying instability between the United States and The Union of Soviet Socialist Republics is simply old-fashioned nationalism, but it is significant at least that the members of both societies will find it necessary to clothe their causes in generalizations which presumably have to do with the good of all regardless of what society or nation they belong to. The members of the different nations may continue to think in terms of manifest destiny, but when they do, it is the destiny of man in general rather than the men of particular nations they have in mind—at least most feel they must put it that way.

Even if the significance of action in terms of armed force organizations for external aggression is becoming increasingly restricted and increasingly a function of one major instability in current international arrangements, armed force organizations are not likely to disappear as social phenomena, even if that general instability is settled to everyone's satisfaction. For a long time after an increasing number of individual members of an increasing number of societies have come to realize that they will not be permitted to utilize members of their armed force organizations for external aggression, the significance of such organizations as a potential means of defense against the aggression of others is not likely to be abandoned. It is unlikely, for example, that representatives of the United States and the Soviet Union be able to settle their differences within the near future, but it is even less likely that a state of firm mutual trust would come into being immediately, even following such an agreement. Even the known capacity of Americans for optimism beyond the call of duty is not likely to be that great. Armed force organizations are likely to be maintained for defensive purposes even if they become largely ceremonial organizations as far as any genuine immediate availability of their members for effective defense is concerned.

Much more important than the maintenance of armed forces for defensive foreign purposes is likely to be the continued maintenance of such organizations because of their internal significance for the general maintenance of order. People may cease to regard such organizations as armed force organizations in the ordinary sense, but if one is to judge from the state of the world today, even that seems unlikely. Reliance on members of the armed forces either by themselves or by others as the source of stability of government is quite widespread throughout societies enormously varied in other respects. The maintenance of armed force organizations for these purposes requires some of the same equipment necessary for such organizations conceived primarily in terms of operations abroad or in defense against members of other armed force organizations from abroad. The maintenance of such organizations in societies is not and never has been solely explicable in terms of international involvements. In societies of any considerable scale the maintenance of armed force organizations is always intimately involved with the question of general stability—especially in its political aspects.

In the early stages of the development of relatively modernized societies in the form of nations which prior to that time were to a high degree self-sufficient, one of the early effects was to make possible a sharper public differentiation of internal and external affairs at exactly the same point in history at which the developments were making the maintenance of the distinction meaningless. Today, when increasingly there are no domestic affairs of any importance without international implications and vice versa, the symbol of the last resort in international affairs—the employment of members of armed force organizations—may in the future become increasingly significant in the maintenance of the kind of internal solutions to problems of stability that keep the domestic situation of one nation from involving the intervention of members of another as an act of solution.

C. ISOLATION OF ARMED FORCE PERSONNEL

One of the most fascinating aspects of armed force organizations is the literal degree of isolation of members of these organizations from members of other organizations in the society. When operations takes place in terms of armed force organizations, to some extent their members are always isolated as clearly as possible from nonmembers. The significance of the uniform in this connection cannot be questioned.[7] The isolation takes other forms as

[7] There is not space here to go into any extended analysis of the significance of the uniform in armed force systems, but it is a subject virtually untouched by modern social analysis. In all sorts of ways the uniform is used to epitomize distinctions in office ["Salute the uniform not the man!"]. Appearance in or out of uniform in critical situations is prima-facie evidence of the most serious differences in intent [A soldier captured in enemy territory in uniform is supposed to receive honorable treatment of a given sort; a soldier of an enemy force captured out of uniform is likely to be shot as a spy]. The uniform in armed force systems is a specific instance of a very general social phenomenon of great significance but

well. To some extent members of the armed force organizations live in isolation from nonmembers, especially when what they are doing is conceived to be important in terms of the objectives of the leaders and planners of the organization and especially when they are involved in training.

Armed force organizations may be modernized well in advance of the extent of modernization elsewhere in the social contexts in which they are found. As that modernization proceeds, the importance of isolation for training and maintenance increases.[8] The isolation of armed force personnel means, among other things, that the interrelationships of armed force personnel and other members of the society are periodic and delimited. They are subject to enormous variation in these respects. For quite considerable lengths of time under crisis circumstances or even under training circumstances, members of armed force organizations may be kept in nearly complete isolation from other members of the society. Most of the other organizations in societies with comparable isolation of their members are generally characterized as ascetic organizations and usually as some form of predominantly religiously oriented organization.

The isolation of members of the armed forces is also in terms of the age classification of the members. Even when the members of the armed force organization are determined primarily by birth or class or the like, they generally belong to the armed force organization only for a limited age period. That period is usually all or a portion of their adulthood. This means, of course, that one of the problems universally associated with membership in armed force organizations is the problem of getting members from a general social context and of returning them to a general social context, if they survive to the age of retirement. Within the period of their membership in the armed force organization there may be other periodic returns to a general social context, but in

---

little appreciated in public affairs. This is the general phenomenon of making social distinctions literally and easily visible. Dress may not make the man, but it is almost inevitably an enormously helpful item in classifying him.

[8] For modern armed force purposes, the old United States conception of minutemen will not work, and other forms of emergency levies won't work either. Even members of United States society have learned that there must either be a peacetime armed force organization of more than token quality and scope or none at all. Until the beginning of World War II our attitude was generally that in time of peace the more complete the disbandment of members of armed force organizations the better. Something of this attitude was still perceptible in the rapid demobilization of the United States armed forces following the apparent settlement of world problems by the surrenders of Germany and Japan. The views of the place of armed force organizations in American life have changed radically since that time.

all such cases it is important that the rules governing the transition from one context to another be clear-cut and that the solidarity of the member of the armed force organization with other members of that organization take precedence over his other solidarities in the general social context.

Critical for an understanding of the fit of armed force organizations into general social structure is the fact that their members are frequently isolated for important periods of their time even when other members of the society except for religious ascetics and imprisoned criminals are never so isolated. Moreover membership in armed force organizations is not ordinarily confused with either religious asceticism or imprisonment except facetiously. Most armed force organizations are notoriously secular. The levels of regimentation in isolation of members of armed force organizations may approach or even surpass those characteristic of a prison, but regardless of personal attitudes toward armed force organizations, they are certainly radically different in kind from systems of imprisonment as such.

D. ECONOMIC ASPECTS

Almost inevitably armed force organizations are relatively lacking in self-sufficiency. This is true even of those armed force organizations whose members live off the land. The land referred to is usually inhabited by someone else, and a major strategy of modern warfare in some areas of the world is to remove the population ordinarily present in areas in which members of enemy armed force organizations live off the land. The interrelationships of members of armed force organizations with members of other organizations in the society or in other societies is therefore a matter of the greatest strategic significance from the point of view of operations in terms of those systems. Along with isolation and other special characteristics, logistics is a universal military problem.

The logistical problems of large-scale armed force organizations always constitute critical elements of economic allocation in terms of the societies in which they are found. Generally speaking, as far as members of the armed force organizations are concerned, the availability of the goods and services necessary for their efficient operation is someone else's responsibility. Their responsibility is to make use of these goods and services in particular ways. These two responsibilities do not coincide unless the leaders of the armed force organizations are also the leaders of the government of the society. This means that certain problems of economic allocation which are strategic from the point of view of other members of the society are not necessarily matters of concern from the point of view of members of the armed force organizations.

This difference of point of view may give rise to many problems. Members of armed force organizations are supposed to be rational in their uses of goods and services, but the criteria for rationality need not coincide with those which are generally accepted in other spheres of the society. For example, to use the simplest sort of misunderstanding, ordinarily a public official of the United States government who purchases shoes from one firm at a price double that at which they are offered by members of another firm is not only behaving irrationally from the economic point of view, but the irrationality is so extreme that one would ordinarily suspect that an explanation of it lies in graft and corruption rather than in stupidity. On the other hand, an individual member of an armed force organization responsible for supplies may be quite rationally more preoccupied with the dispersion of his sources of supply in a pattern invulnerable to foreign attack, despite radical differences in the cost curves of different supplying firms, than in buying at the lowest possible price. Particularly in the context of relatively modernized societies with their very high levels of interdependency, the different criteria of rationality with regard to the allocation of goods and services of members of the armed force organizations and of others concerned with the allocation of goods and services in terms of the society may become increasingly relevant to an understanding of such very diverse questions as capital formation in general, income levels, etc. These questions are ordinarily not considered to be a major sphere of concern of members of the armed force organizations at all. This in turn poses delicate problems with regard to training members for high office in such organizations. Whether one should attempt to train armed force leaders to be sophisticated economists is by no means a simple question. Its answer is in no sense directly given by the inescapably important involvement of members of armed force organizations in the allocation of goods and services of the society in general.

E. POLITICAL ASPECTS

Armed force organizations are always predominantly politically oriented organizations, whether regarded from the point of view of internal or external applications of force.[9] Armed force organi-

[9] The political aspect of social phenomena has been defined as having to do with the allocation of power and responsibility, and applications of

zations, as such, are usually regarded as instrumental by the members of the society. Although this matter has been relatively little discussed, the development of specialized armed force organizations is certainly one of the earliest examples in social history of an organization specialized along one aspect of social phenomena. Much more importantly, armed force organizations constitute one of the earliest developments and one of the most general developments of organizations in terms of which a considerable part of the action is expected to be overwhelmingly rational in its orientation. Armed force organizations vary widely in the degree of emphasis by members on traditional ways. One of the academic stereotypes of the nature of armed force officials is that they are overwhelmingly conditioned to thinking in nothing but traditional terms. Many instances of technological conservatism and of conservatism, not only in general strategy but also in what might almost be termed the philosophy of strategy as exemplified in such phrases as the "Maginot Line attitude," give some basis for this,[10] but the general inferences drawn from such data constitute a vast and misleading oversimplification.

The technology associated with applications of force and questions of tactics and strategy are always matters about which quite

---

force have been specifically delineated as an extreme in one direction of these allocations. Armed force organizations are always oriented toward applications of force.

[10] The actual role of conservatism and tradition in general in armed force organizations has not, as far as I know, ever been given a general examination by a modern social scientist. Again I would observe that until quite recently only historians and military experts as such have paid a great deal of attention to armed force organizations. Much of the literature has been highly polemic in its orientation. Not only are modern studies by social scientists just beginning and general studies of the relevance of armed force organizations for other social phenomena still virtually nonexistent, but fascinating clichés are accepted almost universally without critical examination. I am not qualified to pass on whether or not the technology available early in World War II was sufficient to crack the Maginot Line, as that line was presumably planned and heralded as invulnerable to the technology of its day. As far as I can make out, however, the line itself was never completed in the form called for by the presumed claims of invulnerability. Its failure in the defense of France was not the result of the kind of frontal assault through or over the line which would have been necessary had the line been completed as conceived. Rather, German military personnel went through areas not covered by the line, "turned it" as it were. If this is the case, the extent to which the experience of early World War II technology forever discredited the Maginot Line psychology is by no means a simple matter to determine. What is more important, the facile acceptance of this as a cliché may actually beg the question of what was wrong with the planning involved. It is one of the grim ironies of history that by the end of that war technological improvements had made the issue, as generally argued, quaint.

important elements of rational emphasis accrue. There are in the experiences associated with armed force organizations many of the elements that we associate so importantly with the development of science, although most academics prefer to think that the scientist and the army man are, intellectually at least, polar types of animals. Nevertheless, associated with the application of technology and the use of force generally in the terms of armed force organizations is consideration of the data, concern with generalizations, comparative analysis, etc. One would expect the emphasis on rationality to be marked under such circumstances. The objectives of leaders and planners of armed force organizations are in general relatively easy to specify, highly material, and in major respects easy to verify. They may be as easily defined as the death or capture of particular sets of individuals, control over the inhabitants of a given area, defeat of enemy army personnel, etc. Military history is full of bonehead plays, but the demonstration of the superiority of the long bow over mounted knights, for example, is the kind of demonstration that is decisive, clear-cut, and readily understood by the most conservative of witnesses. Furthermore, the fate in social history of those who cling to less than rational emphases is also clear-cut. Many have gone into battles determined that they would either kill like gentlemen or not at all, but the vulnerability of these to enemies more preoccupied with killing and less with aesthetics and ethics has been demonstrated again and again. Whatever the moral implications of such demonstrations may be, the implications of them for an emphasis on rationality or its approximation in the conduct of members of armed force organizations while seeking their major objectives have not generally been lost in history or seen in social science.

Interestingly enough, despite the tremendous emphasis throughout history on armed force organizations as the last resort of government leaders and the like, in the general structures of governments armed force organizations are rarely more than instruments in readiness for emergencies. Rarely do they become the direct focus of government. It has become popular for some to prattle about the power elite and the role of leaders in armed force organizations in that. In various highly authoritarian societies such as that of Germany under the Nazis, Russia under its present rulers, and the like, the armed force organizations have certainly been important centers of attention. Nevertheless, in none of these cases have the armed force organizations as such constituted the major focus of governmental leadership. In most societies armed force organizations have been instruments of governance rather than the government. Most of the cases in which the armed force organizations have been the general focus of the government have been relatively short-lived. Some cases have been spectacular. The leaders of the military organization took over control of the Japanese government in the late 1930's. In the period of Tokugawa Japan [1603–1868] that society had a government whose leaders explicitly consisted only of militarists, but actually this constituted one of the major jests of history, since they were militarists [bushi, samurai] who were explicitly forbidden to engage in military endeavors in general and who in fact constituted the civil bureaucrats of their various feudal leaders. In general the men and materiel associated in terms of armed force organizations have considerable value in taking over the control of the government of a society and in making the arrangements for another type of government and/or another set of leaders of the government. Professional soldiers and their subordinates have not been conspicuously successful in social history in long-run governmental administration conducted primarily in terms of armed force organizations.

This is exactly what one would expect if one considers the general emphasis characteristic of such organizations on rationality in the exercise of force. It is the essence of understanding the general political structure of a society as a whole that the allocation of power and responsibility cannot consist overwhelmingly of applications of force and threats of force. Applications of force and high levels of coercion constitute extremes in one direction. Preoccupation about the rational application of such extremes tends to preclude consideration of other measures. In the context of all viable armed force systems there is an emphasis on *command* which is never easily identifiable with an emphasis on *governing* in general.

The frequent emergence of armed force organizations and their leaders in central governmental positions in those societies whose members are late-comers to modernization is not a contradiction to the above. It is rather a function of the fact that, because of the general interest in armed force organizations and the importance of their being modern, the armed force organizations of such societies are likely to be foci of modernization and ladders of social mobility for talent, even if other organizations in the society are not.[11]

---

[11] This matter is pursued in Section IV of this chapter.

I I I
ARMED FORCE ORGANIZATIONS AS SUCH

A. THE HIERARCHICAL NATURE OF ARMED FORCE ORGANIZATIONS

There is a sense in which armed force organizations constitute perhaps the purest case of predominantly politically oriented organizations. Applications of the extreme form of power always constitute the main focus of action in terms of armed force organizations, ideally speaking at least. If these organizations are effective as a set of structures in terms of which individuals pursue such ends, the structures of the organization must stress allocations of power from the top down and allocations of responsibility from the bottom up. It is of the essence of armed force organizations that they are strictly speaking hierarchical in the purest sense of the word. It has already been pointed out that, regardless of ideologies about egalitarianism, most organizations are in fact hierarchical. The hierarchical nature of other organizations may or may not be stressed, may be carried much further actually than ideally, may not be fully appreciated by the individuals involved, etc. Most of the hierarchical characteristics of armed force systems are explicit, ideally speaking, and they tend actually to be clear-cut too. There are some departures from this emphasis on hierarchy. Leaders of some special units, for example, make much of the fact that relatively little attention is paid to rank among their members, but on the whole it is considered a mark of derogation of any armed force organization to imply that the chain of command is unclear. Emphasis on hierarchy is frequently associated with emphasis on tradition, authoritarianism, etc. These are frequently characteristic of armed force organizations too. Nevertheless, it is of the essence of understanding the importance of hierarchical structures in armed force organizations to realize that, given the goals of members and nonmembers alike, a concern for rationality would require an emphasis on hierarchical organization, even in the absence of other justifications of "rank" by the members of armed force organizations.

B. RATIONALITY

The emphasis on rationality may be especially high relative to that characteristic of the rest of the society. To some extent there is always an explicit emphasis on rationality in the action carried out in terms of armed force organization, no matter how traditionally oriented general relationships may be in general in a society. At least one reason for the emphasis on rationality is that the members of such organizations are always concerned with instrumental uses of weapons and physical skills in forms easily understood rationally. Efficiency in applications of force via tools [i.e., in this case, weapons] is most immediately and easily recognizable.

This heavy emphasis on rationality carries with it an actual emphasis of predominantly universalistic criteria, despite the fact that, ideally speaking, armed force recruitment may be overwhelmingly particularistic. For example, only individuals of a given class by birth are eligible to be military personnel in some cases. Nevertheless, once the organizations are formed, some relatively clear-cut delineations among the members on the basis of their actual or alleged military achievements are inevitably made. Probably no armed force organization has ever existed without being featured by contests of skill, tournaments, etc., among its members. Rank in terms of authority is often not clearly dependent upon rank in terms of these skills, but they are never irrelevant to one another either. The emphasis on predominantly universalistic criteria, however, may be largely a function of the actual structures rather than of the ideal structures in many cases.

C. BUREAUCRATIC ASPECTS

Armed force organizations, regardless of the general social setting, are likely to be pronouncedly bureaucratic in character. Even when they are not highly bureaucratic, the emphasis on bureaucratic qualities of the armed force organizations is likely to be much greater than elsewhere in societies not characterized by the general development of bureaucratic organizations. Whenever the development of bureaucratic organizations is general, such armed force organizations as exist are highly bureaucratic. These organizations to some extent are always characterized by specialization of functions, by great emphasis on office and on the hierarchy of authority and responsibility, by being regarded as highly instrumental, etc.

The bureaucratic character of armed force organizations is especially important in considering the problems of modernization of relatively nonmodernized societies. One of the inevitable changes in any society with an increase in the emphasis on modernization is an increased proliferation of bureaucratic organizations. In some relatively nonmodernized societies the armed force organization may be the major precedent for a bureaucratic or semibureaucratic experience.

D. THE PROBLEM OF CONTROL OF ARMED FORCE PERSONNEL

The problem of control of the general membership of armed force organizations is usually minimal as such problems go in societies. This is a function of the fact that the general socialization of members of societies is such that membership in an armed force organization is always viewed as something of a thing apart and in some sense in the service of the general membership rather than as an end in itself even in the most militaristically oriented of societies. Despite the fact that new members of armed force organizations receive additional socialization in terms of the organization itself, since they do not ordinarily join prior to an advanced level of maturity, their general socialization is highly relevant. Without general habituation of the members to hierarchial structures of authority and responsibility, it is difficult to see how discipline after joining could account completely for the relatively minimal problem of control of the general membership. Even in the United States, for example—and the general members of United States society have on the whole been about as actively anti-military-organizations as the members of any society in world history— [12] there has been little problem of control of the general membership of armed force organizations. Despite all the griping characteristic of American soldiers, we have lost more members of our armed force organizations by psychological discharges than by mutiny.

The vast majority of problems of control over members of armed force organizations are problems of palace revolutions rather than of mass mutiny. Mass mutinies are exceedingly infrequent. The famous Russian Prince Potemkin incident may have been such a case, but they have rarely occurred save under conditions of general social breakdown proceeding far beyond the armed force organizations themselves. Indeed, one may general-

[12] The general antimilitary-organization sentiments of United States citizens should not be confused with corresponding sentiments against violence in general. The social history of the United States has shown no recalcitrance to violence, but the emphasis has been on individualistic applications of violence rather than carefully regimented ones. Even mob violence places only short-run emphasis on organization. Within the context of large-scale armed force organizations, Americans are likely to single out as heroes ones who can be understood as individualistic virtuosi of violence such as the famous Sgt. York rather than geniuses of military organization. The latter, with rare exceptions, do not achieve great popular appeal in the United States.

ize as follows: The problem of control of the general membership of an armed force organization never reaches considerable proportions save under conditions of extremely general breakdown of the society of which the armed force organization is a subsystem.

The seizure of general control by one quite restricted set of the members of an armed force organization—almost inevitably its leaders of the moment—is a much more general problem in social history. The problem of military-led palace revolutions as a problem of control of armed force personnel is likely to be a problem when there is general social breakdown. It is also a problem under relatively stable conditions if recruitment or general operation in terms of armed force organizations has somehow managed to concentrate opportunistic personalities. Because of the extreme efficiency of applications of force for limited purposes, illegitimate acquisition of control of the armed force organizations always constitutes a considerable seizure of power in and of itself, but it always also constitutes a potential avenue to power in terms of the general society. After all, if a given individual seizes control of the armed force organization in an illegitimate fashion, it is necessary for him to alter some of the general structures of government even if he is merely to maintain the position he has illegitimately seized within the military organization. Thus palace revolutions within military organizations are quite likely to turn into palace revolutions for the society as a whole or in some cases into governmental revolutions as well. In extreme cases they may even turn into general social revolutions.

Far more serious as problems of general control are those of combating states of apathy or the general maintenance of morale. Military specialists for centuries have been well aware of the fact that no equipment and no numbers give the members of any armed force organization superiority over others if they lack the will to fight. It is the fate of the wisdom of the ages to turn into the clichés of the present, if that wisdom is not continually supplemented. One of the great hopes of the development of science was that these developments presaged continuous additions to the wisdom of the ages. In the military field at least the social sciences have not borne out this promise. The major problems of control in the context of armed force organizations are closely related to problems of social control in terms of the society as a whole. Mass apathy of armed force personnel, like mass mutinies, accompanies general social disorganization associated with the society in which these armed forces occur. Given general social disorganization leaders of large-scale organizations of armed forces cannot overcome problems among their own members, unless the level of isolation of their members from the general membership of the society can be radically increased and rigidly maintained. And even this is not likely to be successful. Indeed, one of the most important forms of dependence or interdependence of armed force organizations and the rest of the society is their extreme dependence on the general social organization for certain basic levels of morale in terms of which members of their own organization can operate.[13]

Insofar as problems of control of members of armed force organizations are not the result of general failures in socialization of the members of these organizations but are rather of the type of restricted mutinous outbreaks, the deviant behavior is extremely vulnerable to the use of secret police techniques. Such activities are likely to contain a high element of rational calculation, and that implies that they are to a high degree subject to rational prediction and rational offset. If secret police are necessary for the control of such phenomena, however, the set of secret police themselves become a major focus of the possibility of palace revolutions within the armed force organizations. Consequently they hold forth also the possibility of palace revolutions in the general government of which the armed force organizations are parts, and depending on the implications of that sort of palace revolution, their revolutionary implications may spread to the governmental level or even the general social level.

Consideration of the general problem of control of members of armed force organizations calls attention once again to an extremely general observation about subsystems of societies. Various organizations within a given society may become highly specialized and highly differentiated from one another. If an organization is of any considerable scale, however, and/or of any considerable stability, the variations possible in the social structures which characterize the organization are a function of the general social system in which they exist as subsystems. The general social structures constitute, as it were, the most crucial element in the general setting of any particular organization. There may seem to be a contradiction in the fact that armed force

---

[13] It is highly improbable that problems of the sort encountered in the behavior of Americans after capture in the Korean War can be offset by operation in terms of the armed force systems alone. The actual extent to which members of armed force organization can increase or lower their level of morale without reference to other social contexts, however, is nowhere thoroughly studied by modern scientific techniques as far as I know.

organizations are overwhelmingly oriented to applications of force and the general membership of the societies in which they are found may be much less specifically concerned with such applications. Nevertheless, armed force organizations are as much a mirror of general social structures as any other subsystem in a given society. Our armed force organizations are no less characteristic of our society than are our universities, our churches, our legislative bodies, our courts, or our families. The detailed organizational components of these systems constitute an important component in what one might consider their optical properties if the mirror metaphor is pursued, but the range of optical properties is never infinite and the properties reflected are never solely functions of the mirrors themselves. For those students of public affairs who feel that it is important that armed force organizations be kept under strict control and guidance, the importance of nonarmed force responsibility for the behavior of the members of armed force organizations cannot be ignored.

The utilization of the members of armed forces in the maintenance of general social internal control raises another problem. The more action in terms of armed force organizations is relied upon for general social control, the greater is the likelihood that the leaders of the armed forces will take over the leadership of the government as a whole. It is quite possible for leaders of the armed forces to take over direction of the general government under other circumstances. The history of Japan in the period of the 1930's is clear enough evidence of the possibility. Nevertheless, insofar as the armed force organization becomes the major organizational bulwark of general social control—not as a last resort but as a daily instrument—the general government is likely to become a subsystem of the armed force organization rather than the reverse. There are fairly obvious reasons for this. The day-to-day invocation of an organization overwhelmingly oriented to applications of force for the maintenance of general order is not likely to be the case unless there is a fairly general situation of social disintegration. The purely sadistic application of force generally cannot be long maintained in terms of any society. Under circumstances of such general and continuous application, it is impossible to maintain balances of power and responsibility, if the leaders of the armed force organization do not take over the general policy decisions. There is nothing inevitable about the balance of power and responsibility, but if it is not maintained, there will be widespread social change, usually of a revolutionary sort. If it is under the circumstances just mentioned, it can be maintained only if the members of the armed force organizations take a larger role in the domination of the general governmental system.

E. ISOLATION OF ARMED FORCE PERSONNEL

In the discussion of the general setting of armed force organizations I pointed out that some isolation of armed force personnel is ubiquitous but not ordinarily associated with either asceticism or imprisonment. The generally accepted kind and level of isolation of armed force personnel is extraordinary and it becomes the more extraordinary the more modernized the society.[14] There are many reasons for the relative isolation of armed force personnel. There is the obvious factor involved in the importance of twenty-four hour readiness, and vital to this is the availability of the members without need to separate them out of other sets of individuals. To some extent these ideas tend to fade into the background if the general situation is not regarded as one of emergency. Even if there is no felt emergency, however, another factor is generally in operation which carries with it the implication of relative isolation. This is the inordinate emphasis on training. The skills emphasized in the context of armed force organizations are generally speaking of a high order, and they degenerate rapidly if not constantly exercised. Not the least of these skills is the skill of coordination of large numbers of individuals under critical conditions. If action in terms of armed force organizations is to be effective, it is necessary not only to isolate new members of the organization from the general civilian populace in order to teach them new skills and to integrate them with the going members of the organization, but to some extent it is also necessary to keep them relatively isolated during their membership in order to keep their skills at the readiness level.

The implications of this isolation are quite far-reaching. Not the least of these implications is the inevitability of cliques based largely on armed force membership as such. If general civilian attitudes isolate the members of the armed force units still further, the relevance of cliques as a special form of particularism in armed force organizations is heightened.[15]

---

[14] In relatively modernized contexts, armed force personnel may in fact be less isolated and are certainly less isolable than in relatively nonmodernized contexts, but interdependency in general is so high in the former that any isolation becomes more extreme in its implications—whether for good or for evil.

[15] Prior to the beginning of World War II the situation of the armed force organizations of the United States illustrated this. Not only were there the ordinary cliques associated with relatively isolated membership units of any sort, but in addition the general civilian attitude can hardly be

Given the general isolation of armed force personnel and given the special emphasis on this isolation until basic training, at least, can be imposed upon the new members, the general social origin of the personnel has a special relevance for their behavior while members. After all, their origins constitute the source of the nonarmed-force opinions of the members of the armed force organizations. These opinions are of great importance when members of the armed force organizations operate in contexts other than those strictly military ones. Within the context of each of the societies in world history the social origins of the personnel concerned is likely to be relatively uniform. For some societies this uniformity results from the fact that only those with a given class standing could become members of the armed forces, as it were. For other societies, insofar as membership in the armed forces is generally open to members of the society, the vast majority of the members of a given society are likely to be individuals of a single class, and hence if the armed force organizations are large scale, most recruitment is likely to come from people of more or less common origins. This is especially true, of course, of relatively nonmodernized societies. In such societies armed force organizations are frequently elite organizations whose members are likely to come from representatives of a single elite class. If they are not elite organizations and recruitment is open class, the

---

described as responsible. Civilians felt that armed forces should and could be called into being on a moment's notice and that professional military careers were hardly calculated to appeal to anyone of ability or sensitive tastes. Regular officers were looked down upon with the exception of rare personalities who had somehow come to prominence in time of crisis and held over some residue of reputation as the heroes of past wars. The attitude toward enlisted personnel who constituted the largest portion of the membership was even more extreme.

Under these circumstances it was a minor miracle of American life that a sufficient skeletal organization of the armed forces in time of peace could be maintained to serve as a basis of rapid build-up in times of external emergency for essentially new armed force systems. The fact that there should be West Point and Annapolis cliques, that Army brats tended to marry other Army brats, etc., is by no means difficult to understand. The remarkable thing is that these tendencies did not go much further. With the end of World War II and the continuing crisis in world affairs following that period, the situation changed somewhat. Nevertheless, one of the strongest testimonies of the relevance of the general social setting for the character of the members of the armed force organizations is the fact that —despite the isolation inherent in armed force organizations as such, and the increased isolation by the general lack of public regard for armed force personnel in any time save times of crisis—the professional members of the armed force organizations did not come to consider themselves a breed apart and opposed to the general membership of United States society. It is difficult to understand why they did not do so, and their previous socialization is probably the only clue we have to such understanding.

vast majority of individuals concerned are likely to come from agrarian social backgrounds.

The armed force organizations of relatively modernized societies and the new ones of societies whose members are late-comers are overwhelmingly likely to be based on some structure of "universal conscription." For the late-comers this means that the membership is overwhelmingly likely to consist of individuals with peasant backgrounds, while members of the officers corps may be of middle-class background. Even this is on the whole unlikely since it is difficult to recruit a large-scale officers corps from persons of middle-class background because of the extreme bimodal character of the social structures of those societies prior to the beginnings of modernization. In an increasing number of cases, whatever the origins of the officer group may be at the outset, in the long run the officers corps is likely to consist increasingly of persons originally brought into the organization by general conscription and elevated to the officers corps on the basis of predominantly universalistic criteria. Thus, increasingly in these social contexts both officers and enlisted personnel are likely to have quite common views of what the general social structure and social problems of their societies are. During the years of their most intensive training in terms of the new organization, they are likely to be, relatively speaking, out of contact with the general social settings to which they were previously accustomed. Therefore if they get into discussions of general social problems outside strictly military ones, they are likely to have a uniform point of view that, though it may not in fact be a function of the military discipline or of any explicit indoctrination to which they have been subjected, is likely to be so uniform as to be mistaken for a function of regimented experiences in terms of armed force organizations.

Finally, this isolation keeps the members of armed force organizations separated from the general population of the society while the views, discipline, and knowledge of the members change, if and as they do. This is important both for them and for the general membership of the society from which they come. Since the members of armed forces are always to some extent kept in isolation, it is possible to minimize or control the feedback of the introduction of the relatively modernized structures in terms of which they act to the general population at large. In the context of both modernized and relatively nonmodernized societies in process of modernization there is no question but that the new training will be on as highly modernized a basis as possible. I have tried to point out again and again that there are always reasons why elements of modernization are never completely inexplicable to members of even the most nonmodernized societies. In this chapter I have already tried to indicate that, regardless of how traditional the orientations of the members of a given society may be, the emphasis on rationality by members of armed force organizations is likely to be carried to great lengths—that efficiency in weaponry, for example, is not difficult for people to understand even though they may not even have conceived of a given technology of weaponry before. In decisions on the type of training and the type of technology to be put at the disposal of members of the armed force organizations in such societies there will be few arguments about the degrees of modernization—as high a degree as possible will be aimed for. What is unusual in this situation is the extent to which the spread or impact of structures of modernization beyond the focus of immediate introductions can be restricted and controlled if the situation is clearly understood. The implications of this factor for armed force organizations in societies which are being modernized is sufficiently great to justify the devotion of the remainder of this chapter to this question.

I V
ARMED FORCE ORGANIZATIONS IN SOCIETIES UNDERGOING MODERNIZATION

A. THE UNIVERSAL PRESENCE OF ARMED FORCE ORGANIZATIONS IN SUCH SOCIETIES

I asserted at the start of this chapter that the analysis of the armed force organizations has been systematically affected by the American attitude that armed force organizations are necessary only in times of external crisis in particular, and the almost universal academic biases with regard to armed force organizations and their members in general. In the following discussion I do not wish to get involved in questions of whether militarism is good, bad or indifferent, but I do wish to point to some aspects of the special relationships between armed force organizations and societies in the transition to relatively modernized states.

Armed force organizations will be universally present in societies undergoing modernization regardless of whether or not their leaders and members take into consideration the radically diminished degrees of freedom open to them today for the employment of armed force organizations as instruments in external relations. They will in some form or other be universally present if only because of the importance of such organizations as instruments of internal control during a period of social change in which problems of internal control are likely to be maximized, regardless of how quiescent or turbulent the traditional basis from which change takes place may have been. It is extremely unlikely that armed force organizations be maintained only for this purpose. The external role of armed force organizations is likely to be a matter of prominent consideration, even if the leaders and members of these societies only contemplate defensive applications externally.[16]

B. MAXIMAL MODERNIZATION

No one, contemplating an armed force organization, wishes less than the most modern weapons. It is sometimes possible, though difficult, to convince the late-comers that the efficiency of modernization may actually be radically increased if initially they do not seek the most modern form of machines because of their comparative advantages for purposes of international trade in other combinations of resources. It is not possible, nor is it generally attempted, to convince them that less than the most modern weapons will serve them best in the planning of the development of their new and modern armed force organizations. When I hear those who deal with problems of modernization in relatively non-modernized societies complain about the difficulty of getting certain ideas across with regard to modern technology, I wonder why we have not capitalized on the much greater ease of getting across these ideas in the military sphere. Because of the ease of under-

[16] Quite apart from the specific features of United States society, it may be argued generally that the relevance of armed force organizations as an instrument of external relations is more clearly appreciated than the relevance of armed force organizations as means of internal control. There are one or two cases of societies in the world which give the appearance of the *reductio and absurdum* of the maintenance of armed force organizations for purposes of either internal or external control. The press of the world takes periodic pleasure in pointing to small countries whose annual military budgets consists of only a few pennies. Nevertheless, these are clearly not societies of any scale in the sense discussed here. They are actually quite clearly subsystems of some of the larger-scale societies whose associated territories are adjacent to theirs. As soon as observations depart from this set of extremely small nations and contemplate other quite small but not nearly *so* small nations, one contemplates a set of nations whose members guard their independence jealously. I doubt that the members of such societies as Denmark, Switzerland, etc., seriously believe that they could use their armed force organizations as protection against their larger neighbors, but the maintenance of armed force organizations oriented to such defensive operations does symbolize, at least, the determination of the members of those societies not to be easily engulfed. This symbolism increases the likelihood that their large neighbors agree in time of crisis on their neutrality or their protection.

standing of certain of the aspects of modernization insofar as it has to do with military transport and weaponry and because of the generally great emphasis on rationality in this sphere regardless of what the previous society has been like, the emphasis on modernization in general with regard to armed force organizations is an emphasis on modernization which generates little resistance. When one speaks of modernizing a government or a city, or in some cases even of agricultural production, there are always fundamentalist objections. There are even fundamentalist objections when one speaks of this with regard to the armed forces, but these objections are relatively rarely persistent or difficult to cope with.[17]

With weaponry as with anything else, modernization cannot be imported piece-meal at the whim of the modernizers. The easy recognition of the importance of modernization in weaponry and logistics in general means, however, that there will in general be an emphasis on the maximum amount of modernization as fast as possible in the development of the new armed force. In this respect the emphasis on modernization may be even greater in the case of some of the late-comers to modernization than in some of the more highly modernized societies. In the former, vested interest in the older technologies are so hopelessly out of date as not to pose a serious barrier to modernization. In the latter the gap between a somewhat older technology and more modern ones is sometimes not sufficiently obvious to make vested interest in older ways appear patently ridiculous.

C. UNIVERSAL CONSCRIPTION STRUCTURES

The new basis of recruitment for the armed forces of all societies undergoing modernization will probably be universal conscription. The recruitment procedures may be characterized by graft and corruption, though if universal conscription is attempted this is less likely. Acceptance of personnel will, ideally

---

[17] One of the few instances of violence in the course of the modernization of Japan was occasioned by just such a fundamentalist reaction to proposals to modernize the armed forces. One of the major older feudal leaders, Saigo, Lord of Satsuma revolted because he felt specifically that the new general conscript soldiers could not protect the integrity of Japanese society from threatening powers elsewhere in the world. When he finally received a convincing demonstration that ordinary peasant soldiers equipped with the modern rifles of that day could mow down fierce samurai warriors with their terrible long swords, he obligingly committed suicide to indicate his realization of error. His fearless peerless demonstration of good intentions was immediately recognized, and his reputation is forever enshrined as the Robert E. Lee of Japanese history. Military experts of relatively nonmodernized societies are not usually that difficult to convince.

speaking, be based on the predominantly universalistic criteria of physical fitness and mental ability. The general population from which conscripts will be drawn will be too poverty stricken to accumulate any considerable amount of economic resources to be used for graft and corruption. Furthermore, the increased survival of children accompanying new medical technology will remove some of the earlier resistance to conscription of any sort.[18]

Given the relevance of rationality about physical fitness and mental ability in the context of armed force organizations, it is not difficult to achieve relatively high levels of predominantly universalistic criteria based overwhelmingly on physical fitness and mental ability. Thus the armed force organizations are likely to have as their new membership not only a cross section of the general population, but also a cross section of the best talent available from such sources. It is part of the easy rationality of military matters in general that neither the sick nor the stupid make the best recruits. In the context of relatively modernized armed force organizations the emphasis on health is certainly not diminished, and the emphasis on mental ability is if anything increased radically. In addition, the easily comprehended relevance of these factors is as much as anything else likely to dictate a structure of universal conscription rather than some more particularistically based form of recruitment. The relevance of predominantly universalistic criteria for armed force organizations is no more difficult to understand than is the relevance of rational modes of thought.

D. HIGH SOCIAL MOBILITY

Armed force organizations in societies undergoing modernization will become major ladders—perhaps *the* major ladder—of social mobility. To the extent that these organizations are large in scale they cannot be confined to membership related via kinship to the elite of a relatively nonmodernized society. This is not a question of whether or not the elite care to maintain such a monopoly. There are simply not enough of them to man the armed force organizations let alone their other preferences. If physical fitness and mental ability are emphasized as a basis for original accept-

---

[18] As more sons and daughters survive, the relevance of any one of them to any one family organization either for his labor or for purposes of family continuity diminishes. Indeed, the structure of universal conscription may partially solve an otherwise embarrassing problem, the survival of children who were always wanted before the increased probability of survival.

ance, they will be emphasized as a basis for promotion in terms of the organization so formed.

Prior to increased modernization, any position of importance in the armed force organization of a relatively nonmodernized society is probably an elite position. Frequently the vast majority of the members of a society are considered too lowly to even aspire to such positions. If they are able to join the armed force organizations at all, ordinarily they join only in positions of extreme subordination, and mental ability or physical fitness do not necessarily promise advancement.[19] Thus in many contexts entrance into the armed forces alone is taken to be social mobility. In the effort to maximize modernization of armed force organizations, predominantly universalistic criteria for admission will be maintained for advancement.[20] If mobility is not on predominantly universalistic grounds, the price paid in terms of efficient, loyal, and dependable armed force personnel will be heavy.

If the armed force organization is important to the general government for maintaining internal order or for other reasons, high mobility in terms of the armed force organization means high mobility in strategic areas of control as far as the general society is concerned. The case of the modern Japanese Army may be the most extreme case. Nevertheless, in modern history the number of individuals who have come into positions of important leadership in their various societies via roles in the relatively modernized armed force organizations which their countrymen have attempted to set up—never mind what they had in mind in so doing—is far too great to be ignored. If promotion is predominantly universalistic and recruitment is on the basis of universal conscription, the large-scale armed force organizations are more likely than any other single avenue to be ones in terms of which, both absolutely and relatively, the possibility of general social mobility from the most humble levels to the pinnacles of prestige and power is offered and realized.[21]

---

[19] Caution is warranted here. Zeal for the point of the relevance of armed force organizations for social mobility during the process of modernization should not obscure the point that throughout history generally these organizations have been ladders of mobility. Individual cases, e.g., Napoleon, have been spectacular.

[20] This was notably the case in the history of the Japanese Army. Despite the closed class, feudal background of that society, at a time when it was difficult for a member of the United States Army to rise from enlisted status to officer status, the structures of the Japanese Army were far more highly universalistic.

[21] I would be willing to give considerable odds that some day we shall have at hand data indicating that the extent of social mobility on predominantly universalistic grounds in the armed force organizations of

E. ARMED FORCE ORGANIZATIONS
AS FOCI OF RADICALISM

If the use of the term *radical* is not restricted to the clichés of the political right and left, armed force organizations in societies undergoing modernization are likely to be foci of radicalism. The form such radicalism takes is more likely to be explicable in terms of the social backgrounds of the personnel of the armed forces than in terms of the general structures of the armed force organizations. The case of Japan is, again, an excellent illustration. Prior to the development of World War II the major focus of radicalism in Japanese society had nothing to do with communism or socialism in the ordinary sense. The major focus of radicalism in that society was national loyalty—patriotism. The most significantly radical personnel were to be found as members of the armed force organizations, and the leadership resided primarily in young officer cliques. These young officers were precisely examples of high social mobility in terms of the armed force organizations. Almost to a man they came from peasant backgrounds. Insofar as they were dissatisfied with Japanese society as they viewed it aside from their military environment, they were likely to think in terms of the problems which they considered typical of the agrarian peasant environment. Distribution of the fruits of modernization to the peasants may or may not have lagged, rate-wise, behind that to other members of the society, but those individuals constituted the vast bulk of the membership of the society, and such increased benefits as they received were not so dramatic as those in many more restricted urban environments.

The young officers behaved radically as far as the stability of the existing social structure was concerned. To describe them as

modern Japan was far greater than the social mobility on such grounds within Japanese universities. If one compares the various cliques characteristic of Japanese society prior to World War II, i.e., the financial clique [zaibatsu], the military clique [gumbatsu] and the university or scholarly clique [gakubatsu], there is little doubt that predominantly universalistic criteria—that rational objective recognition of achievement —were much more characteristic of the military cliques than of the other two, academic biases to the contrary notwithstanding. Something of the same may also be true of United States society. Because of the general attitude of civilians toward armed force organizations, such organizations in the United States are not ordinarily thought of as a major ladder of social mobility despite the number of individuals who have risen to the Presidency of the United States in part through their careers as important leaders of armed force organizations. Nevertheless, it would be interesting to compare social mobility in terms of armed force organizations and other general types in the society.

of rightist opinion is to misunderstand their position thoroughly, for it implies that in general they were conservative and supporters of the business and financial leadership of their society. Verbally, the subjects of their bitterest denunciations and, concretely, the targets of their bullets and the objects of their most spectacular exercises of sword-play were expressly members of the zaibatsu [i.e., financiers and businessmen], whom they regarded as betraying the true interests of the Japanese nation, and other military leaders whom they regarded as cravenly subservient to the zaibatsu. Their ideology was certainly not Marxist, but they did see the whole nation as betrayed and injured by the comparative disadvantage of the main body of Japanese—the peasants—relative to the always suspect city folk.

The important thing about the Japanese case is not whether these particular oversimplifications hold true, but rather that as an organization the Japanese Army constituted one of the major foci of radicalism within the society, and in this case at least it constituted *the* focus of radicalism which at the end of the 1930's saw its leadership control Japanese society as a whole. In other societies undergoing modernization, if universal conscription on a predominantly universalistic basis takes place, if promotion of those conscripted continues to be on a predominantly universalistic basis, and if modernization of the armed force organization is maximized, this picture of an armed force organization as a major focus of radicalism will be repeated in every case.

F. ARMED FORCE ORGANIZATIONS AS A SPECIAL FOCUS OF MODERNIZATION

Preoccupation with armed force organizations as instruments of offense or defense relative to the members of other societies has diverted attention from armed force organizations as the most efficient type of organization for combining maximum rates of modernization with maximum levels of stability and control. The new technology will be taught to the members of the new armed force organizations, and leaders will try to maximize modernization. Furthermore, military technology is not radically different from the technology that is in general characteristic of modernization. Specifically, one may teach the new army recruits, for example, to drive and handle military trucks, but when they have learned their lessons, they have learned to handle trucks in particular, and beyond that they have learned a considerable amount about modern machinery in general. Indeed if anything, the teaching of technology for military purposes puts greater emphasis on learning it well than does the teaching of technology within a more peaceful context. Within the military context one not only has to learn how to run a truck but also what to do with it in case of a breakdown under critical or near critical circumstances. In ordinary civilian contexts the leeway for less thorough training is much greater even [or, perhaps, especially] in the context of relatively modernized societies.

Not only will modernization in general be taught, however narrow the preoccupation may be with military technology as such, but the teaching will also be done outside of the general social context. Here the isolation of the members of the armed force organizations is of the greatest significance. This isolation not only minimizes the impedance of the effect of modernization on the men directly submitted to it. It also minimizes the feedback to the general social context. Both are of the utmost importance in modernization problems. The former is important because modernization outside such a restricted context may very well raise all sorts of considerations of fundamentalist reactions. Do the people concerned wish to see the new ways imported in this fashion? All manner of soul searching may ensue. Such soul searching is never in the last analysis able to stop the impact of modernization, but it can certainly impede the efficiency with which it is introduced. The isolation and extreme emphasis on authoritarianism characteristic of an armed force organization, the general lack of problems of controlling the individuals who are members of such an organization, and the like—all unite to minimize these problems.

The minimization of the problem of feed-back to the general membership of the society as a whole is perhaps even more important. No matter how isolated the members of the armed force organization may be kept, the spread of the impact of modernization beyond the membership of the armed force organization itself can never be eliminated. Nevertheless, feed-back to the general membership can be considerably restricted, especially if one deals with the members of armed force organizations explicitly with this in mind. The emphasis on modernization in terms of armed force organizations makes it possible to maximize the impact of modernization for the member of an organization in terms of which control over individual behavior is both maximal and simple. The general spread of such structures among the general members of the society, before controls for modern purposes are available and before some of the elements of modernization are better understood than formerly, can be impeded even though it cannot be eliminated. Thus the armed force environment makes possible the maximization of the impact of modernization while minimizing the uncontrolled spread of modernization with the consequent production of problems and crises presently difficult if not impossible to foresee.

In the course of these developments—regardless of whether they are carefully planned—the general membership of the armed force organizations always become a pool of skilled labor in the general modernized sense and not merely with regard to military tools. The officers or leaders of the armed forces always become a civil service of sorts, a set of skilled bureaucratic administrators, whether they like to think of themselves as such or not. Modern military leaders are primarily administrators rather than fighters.[22]

The focus on armed force organizations as things apart from general civilian concerns—as a necessary evil at best—has obscured attention to what may be the most efficient vehicle for the maximization of modernization with a minimization of the uncontrolled spread of side effects. In the past students of public affairs and men of public responsibility have thought in terms of armed force organizations as vehicles of offense and defense or organizations for the maintenance of internal order or some combination of the two. Their impact on the general process of modernization is generally taken to be peripheral at best. This may turn out to be one of the great mistakes of the twentieth century—one of the neglected opportunities of history.

[22] Some of these leaders maintain a sense of bravado by carrying pearl-handled side arms and the like, but it is quite clear that these are symbols of roles which the general can no longer play, rather than essential equipment for roles that he actually plays. At all levels of modern military organization the premodern emphasis on individualism in battle which has always been so strong a focus of the romantic appeal of combat is preserved primarily in the naming of vehicles rather than in individual exploits. Contrary to clichés about regimentation, loss of personality, etc., prior to modernization few spheres featured such emphases on individualism as the military, but with occasional exceptions modern warfare is as much a matter of mass production as is modern factory work or modern large-scale farming.

OTHER ORGANIZATIONAL CONTEXTS:

CHURCHES, SCHOOLS, PREDOMINANTLY

RECREATIONALLY

ORIENTED ORGANIZATIONS, ETC.

I

INTRODUCTION: SPECIALIZATION
OF ORGANIZATIONS

The specialized orientation of organizations to a single aspect of social structure, e.g., the economic, political religious, educational, or recreational, has been stressed above. In the contexts of relatively nonmodernized societies, organizations predominantly oriented to economic and political aspects are more likely to occupy obviously central positions in the general social structure than are organizations specialized along the lines discussed in this chapter. Nevertheless, some specialized organizations along these lines are characteristic of virtually all societies of any considerable scale. Such organizations are more often than not strategic in the general social structure. Those of us reared in the context of relatively modernized societies tend to take it for granted that organizations in terms of which these aspects of behavior are at all emphasized will in fact be specialized just as are those in terms of which the allocation of goods and services and the allocation of power and responsibility are emphasized. When the term *religion,* for example, is mentioned we think of *churches;* when the term *education* is mentioned we think of *schools.* Even in the context of our highly modernized society, by no means all the religious aspects of action are conducted in terms of churches, nor is all of education carried out in terms of schools. Nevertheless, the idea of there being religions not characterized by churches such as the religion having to do with household and field gods in China or of there being education not having to do with schools as is the case of the vast majority of all education carried out in the context of all relatively nonmodernized societies—such an idea considered explicitly is foreign and strange to us. In this, however, it is our structures that are exotic and strange.

I I
RELIGION AND CHURCHES

A. DEFINITIONS

I would define *religious action* as action directly oriented to ultimate ends. Such a definition would include the devotional behavior ordinarily associated with the concept of religion, whether such devotions be directly oriented to the reverence of a deity as such, toward attainment of a heaven of some sort, toward the maintenance of general ethical standards regarded as good in and of themselves, etc. I would define a *church* as any predominantly religiously oriented organization. Given these definitions the positive or benign connotation which the term religion frequently has for the layman need not inhere in the concept as defined here. By this definition Communism and Nazism must both be considered religions for the party faithful, and in some interesting and important senses the party organizations associated with both of those religions must be considered churches. It is also important to note that much activity ordinarily associated with the concept of religion from the point of view of the layman is not included in this definition. The invocation of the aid of a deity for the restoration or maintenance of health, for example, is from the point of view taken here *magical* rather than religious behavior. The distinction involved may do great violence to the point of view of the average devout layman, but the implications for behavior of the distinctions made here are important though different. What is here defined as religious action is action that from the point of view of the actor involves the use of nonempirical means for the attainment of *nonempirical* ends. Their action itself is quite empirical. There is nothing mystical about saying that some people believe that a certain type of behavior is pleasing in the sight of the deity in whom they believe and conducive to their participation in life eternal after death. Whether such a deity exists or whether in fact their behavior is conductive to such participation, no scientist can say, but a scientist may say, and must say if he is to understand human behavior, that such beliefs on the part of the actor are certainly predictive of some differences in the behavior of those actors and even that different sorts of such beliefs have radically different implications for the behavior of actors. Thus it makes quite observable differences whether an actor has such orientations or not, what they are like, etc. What has here been referred to as *magic* on the other hand involves the use of nonempirical means such as the invocation of deities and the like for *empirical* ends. Here a scientist again cannot tell whether the *means are in fact effective,* but he can tell whether or not the given end is in fact achieved. Furthermore, as in the case of religious action above, the belief that empirical ends can be attained by nonempirical means can be shown to characterize some actors and not others in some circumstances and not in others. It can also be shown that whether the actors concerned have such beliefs or not is highly predictive of differences in their behavior.[1]

B. CHURCHES AS A SPECIAL FEATURE OF A SOCIETY

It is a truism of the approach taken here, that although there may be religions without churches, there are no churches without religions. As a minimum the presence of an organization which can be termed a church always raises the question of specialist roles for individual actors, even for such egalitarian sects from the religious point of view as the Baptists.[2] Wherever there are churches, of course, there must be religious specialists. To some extent there may be specialization of roles on a religious basis connected with religions which are not characterized by churches. For example, the family head is the family priest of ancestor worship, as it were, for the traditional Chinese family, but the family head is not a predominantly religiously oriented figure as such. His role as chief of the ancestor cult of the family is only one of his special roles as family head.

---

[1] If the specific use of terms here causes offense to anyone because of his sincere beliefs and unavoidable connotations of the two terms *religion* and *magic* used here, he should feel free to substitute any other symbols he might wish for the concepts as defined. I have used these terms to avoid being unduly obscure, but any letters from any alphabet or any characters from any language could stand for these definitions equally well as far as the treatment here is concerned.

[2] From the point of view of social structure a study of the Baptist sect and its various modes of organization is enlightening. Ideally speaking, from the point of view of Baptist theology, religion is a completely individual matter incompatible with any shred of authority from the religious point of view or in religious terms of one individual relative to another. This makes any sort of church organization an extremely ticklish question among Baptists. The erection of organizations which in a sense organize individual churches is an even more ticklish question. An excellent volume on this subject by Paul M. Harrison: *Authority in Power in the Free Church Tradition,* Princeton University Press, Princeton, N.J., 1960, treats this whole question in fascinating detail. The problems of organization given such specially anarchic views require new conceptions in the field of bureaucracy including additions to Weber's conceptions of authority in terms of bureaucratic organizations.

At least some of the roles distinguished as elements of a church organization are likely to be close approximations to full-time roles as far as the people occupying them are concerned. Indeed, one of the standard aspects of church organizations is that a considerable number of the members of the administrative staff of the organization, as well as specialized nonadministrative personnel, are expected to be so preoccupied with the religious aspects of action as to withdraw more or less completely from involvement in roles falling outside the church context. Some cases of religious asceticism are indictive of enormous human ingenuity.

Specialization of roles in terms of a predominantly religiously oriented organization implies problems of interdependency of churches with other organizations. Such interdependencies may be viewed in terms of competition, for example. A church is, by definition, never an organization whose membership is primarily concerned with either economic or political aspects of behavior, but these aspects are never irrelevant to the church as an organization any more than they are irrelevant to any other organizational context. The development of a church on any given scale will have effects on the general structures of allocation of goods and services in the society as a whole. Those effects may be strategic ones. For example, at certain periods of European history a considerable amount of capital formation consisted of erection of various buildings for church purposes. There are periods in Chinese history of which it is alleged, at least, that the appeal of life in the context of the Buddhist monasteries was so great as to create not only labor shortages, but more importantly for the Chinese, a shortage of individuals crucial for the continuation of various families.

The problems of interdependency of churches with other organizations in the society mean, of course, that religions characterized by churches are always specially differentiated from religions not characterized by churches. For example, some students of traditional Chinese society would hold ancestor worship to be the most fundamental form of worship generally practiced by the members of that society. Ancestor worship as a religion is not primarily a church affair, although there certainly do exist individual instances of temples or churches which might be considered predominantly ancestor-worship-oriented organizations. Relative to ancestor worship in general, however, any churches associated with it were of relatively little consequence. The major organizational focus of ancestor worship in that society was the family organization, and the typical Chinese family unit certainly did not constitute a church. On the other hand the relation of family members with members of Buddhist churches, and in some cases members of Taoist temples and the like as such did constitute problems of special interrelationships. This was particularly true since, in some types of families characteristic of that society, the feminine members of the family were more likely to be devout Buddhists than the males in general or the family head in particular.

There is neither time nor space here to discuss the variety of problems connected with the interdependencies of churches and other organizations in a society. It must suffice for the present to point out that these in fact always constitute problems. Furthermore, churches cannot ordinarily be organized on a family basis. Like armed forces, the leaders of churches must count on obtaining some of their most crucial members as exports from other organizational contexts in the society—most notably from the family. When churches exist, the interdependencies between churches and the government may or may not be a problem, but the interdependencies between the church and families in the society concerned is always a question about which there must be special institutional structures, if there is to be social stability. In the remaining discussion of churches other aspects of this general problem of interdependency will be brought up. It is, properly speaking, a subject for treatment in general terms by social scientists who are experts in the field of religion with a broad comparative background in religious history. Despite the importance of religion in human history generally and the considerable preoccupation of many social scientists with the subject there exists no highly generalized treatment of this sort in anything approaching modern scientific terms.[3]

C. EXCLUSIVIST VERSUS NONEXCLUSIVIST CHURCHES

An *exclusivist religion* may be defined as one such that a person recognized as a true-believer in that religion, ideally and self-consciously speaking, may believe in one and only one religion at any given point in time. People in what is generally referred to as the Western World, are accustomed to thinking of religion in

[3] Most of the work in the field has never exceeded that of Max Weber in the generality of its focus. Weber, however, was not primarily interested in religion in general but rather in the light he could throw on a specific problem of development by reference to religious aspects of behavior. For some it seems to imply the fault of *lèse majesté* to try more general approaches than Weber's. Future intellectual historians may find it odd that in a period of new and proliferating forms of religion so little attempt to analyze the associated phenomena has been made by us.

exclusivist terms. One of our most fundamental ethnocentrisms is thinking all religions to be exclusivist ones. We feel that one may be either a Catholic or a Jew or a Mohammedan, but not two or more of them at one time. Even the differences within the Christian religion are exclusivist distinctions in this sense. One may not be both a Baptist and a Methodist at the same time. Professed belief in two or more such religions at a given point of time is prima-facie evidence of religious insincerity. There are, however, nonexclusivist religions known to world history. Buddhism, Taoism, Ancestor Worship, and the religion of household and field gods in China are all examples of such religions. The list may be made extremely long. Shintoism in Japan is also a nonexclusivist religion, and there are many religions which are nonexclusivist despite the fact that in the social context in which they exist no other religions have been invented or imported.

Apart from explicitly nonexclusivist religions, many quite sincere and devout believers in exclusivist religions, without realizing it have other religious beliefs outside the strict theology of the religions to which they think of themselves as belonging. Nevertheless, as long as they are unaware of these as different religions, however different such participation may be from the point of view of a scientific observer, it does not constitute a problem of conscience from the point of view of the true-believer. There is one extremely general case of such unconscious dual devotion in the history of European and American societies during the last century or two. This is the extreme form of patriotism or nationalism which does not ordinarily occupy a place in the theology of exclusivist religions as such. For an enormous number of true-believers in various exclusivist religions the existence of their nations is also an ultimate end as far as they are concerned. Insofar as there are religious aspects of this orientation, it is not generally viewed as violating the exclusivist religious orientation specifically by virtue of the fact that an emphasis on loyalty or patriotism as such is not regarded as a religious preoccupation. Nevertheless, there are questions in which the ethical implications of the theology of a given religion do seem to pose clear-cut conflicts of implication with the dictates of national interests. So far these unconscious conflicts have not in general posed serious problems of social stability.

The distinction between exclusivist and nonexclusivist religions is relevant to the general question of social change. In this connection, of course, the problem is posed by the point of view of the true-believers in exclusivist religions rather than by the true-believers in nonexclusivist religions. From the point of view of the latter the development of some new religion, whether introduced by contact with outsiders or indigenously developed, is not a matter requiring immediate readjustment. On the other hand, the presence of other religions, from the point of view of the true-believer in an exclusivist religion, is generally a focus of friction. However little interest the true-believers in an exclusivist religion may have in proselytizing, close contact between true-believers in an exclusivist religion and true-believers in any other recognized religion, whether exclusivist or nonexclusivist, poses the possibility of contamination. Exclusivist religions are not inevitably proselytizing religions, but proselytism is one of the most general forms of protection against contamination by belief in another religion. It is difficult for true-believers in exclusivist religions not to regard any other recognized forms of religion as competing religions.

Religions generally may or may not be characterized by churches. Certainly nonexclusivist religions sometimes have associated churches, and sometimes they do not. Exclusivist religions probably always involve churches. They need not involve and many do not involve predominantly religiously oriented organizations such that all of the true-believers in the religion are conceived to belong to a single church or its explicit subsystems, though this is sometimes the case. So great is the emphasis placed by true-believers in exclusivist religions on adherence as opposed to nonadherence that it is quite difficult to contemplate the stable existence of such a religion without some form of organization in terms of which members may be distinguished from nonmembers with clarity and ease. If churches are present in a given social context, and if the churches are based on exclusivist religion, there exists not only the problem of interdependency with other organizations characteristic of any specialized organization of any sort. There is also, explicitly, the problem of the kinds of interrelationships probable or possible among the members of these churches and other churches, if any others exist within the society. As a minimum the possibility of conflicts among true-believers in two or more exclusivist religions or between those in exclusivist and those in nonexclusivist religions inhere in such situations. It is essential to bear in mind that all of these true-believers are oriented to ends which they take to be good in and of themselves and not open to question. Parties to such conflicts almost inevitably take their own motives for the purest and those of their opponents as threatening all that is sacrosanct. Self-questioning always skirts close to the question of heresy. From the point of view of the true-believer holy wars, crusades, holy inquisitions, and saintly massacres are the most self-justified forms of violence. It is not a matter of chance that such conflicts have been bloody, bitter, and baneful even as wars, tortures, and massacres go, nor that these side phenomena of exclusivist religions fail to vary as one might expect with the tone of the associated theologies. True-believers in humility and the Golden Rule are as prone to massacres of innocents as are those worshiping violence and might, rough-hewn racial qualities, or sadistic deities. There are remarkable aspects of religion which do not inhere in religious doctrine as such.

D. THIS-WORLDLY VERSUS OTHER-WORLDLY RELIGIONS AND CHURCHES

The distinction between *this-worldly* and *other-worldly* religions is familiar to all students of Weber. Weber used this distinction to point the difference between religions whose true-believers paid as little attention as was compatible with the ethics associated with the religion to the things of this world as they found them and rather focused their aspirations and hopes on life after death or life in some form of existence other than the ordinary empirical state of affairs as perceived by the average individual. The this-worldly religions, however much emphasis their true-believers might place on life after death and conceptions of other worlds, are characterized by theologies such that the attention of the faithful is firmly fixed on dealing with the problems and affairs of the world in which they find themselves in the ordinary empirical sense. Weber, of course, was preoccupied with the different implications of ascetic behavior in terms of either other-worldly or this-worldly religions. From his point of view the implications of true-belief in the Protestant Ethic were what he considered to be this-worldly ascetic behavior. Such behavior was one of the major factors in the development of what he considered to be modern capitalistic, industrial society.

Whether one agrees or disagrees with Weber, for the particular case he had in mind, his distinction is a useful one. It makes a difference in understanding social behavior whether or not the theology of a given religion is other-worldly in this sense or this-worldly. Other-worldly orientations, when carried to a high pitch, are best suited, as far as social stability is concerned, to highly sedentary situations in which the individual has few prospects for mobility, either social or physical, little or no control over problems of health, and little probability of change in his general social situation save for the different roles which he will ordinarily assume during his life cycle. In this connection it is quite important not to confuse the other-worldly orientation of the religion with a complete lack of interest in the material world or complete lack of concern with problems of rationality. Indeed, one may say that the level of *asceticism* in terms of other-worldly religions is likely to be measured by the lack of concern with matters having to do with the material world and a lack of concern with rationality. The general adherents of an other-worldly religion are not likely to be characterized by any considerable development of asceticism. Their other-worldly belief is itself their asceticism. High levels of other-worldly asceticism require virtuosi just as do high levels of accomplishment in other respects. It is, however, legitimate to infer that even for the average believer the emphasis implicit in other-worldly theologies is on adjustment rather than reform, on passive reaction rather than on active desire to change the environment as one finds it. Apart from its virtuosi, however, the leaders of such churches by no means encourage a complete lack of concern for the affairs of this world or for rationality on the part of the general membership of their churches.

This-worldly religions on the other hand are not generally characterized by ascetic religious virtuosi or ascetic religious specialists. Insofar as asceticism is associated with this-worldly religions, the individuals concerned are likely to be ascetic generalists. Ideally speaking, religion is not a thing apart from anything done in terms of a this-worldly ascetic-generalist approach to life. The this-worldly emphasis of these religions makes for an activist preoccupation with social reforms. Religion, by definition, is preoccupied with the ideal state of affairs from the point of view of the actors who believe in it, and as has already been mentioned above, in no general social context do the ideal and actual states of affairs coincide. To the extent that one believes in a religion which dictates the working out of religious ideals in the world in which he lives, he is constantly challenged to bring the ideal and actual states of affairs into closer correspondence, presumably by alteration of the actual state of affairs in the direction of the ideals concerned. Furthermore, only an emphasis on this worldly asceticism makes it possible for asceticism to become vulgar.

If there is anything in this contrast at all, it would argue that other-worldly religions are incompatible with any considerable level of modernization. With increasing levels of modernization, the problems of coordination and control constantly increase as indicated. Problems of active participation are of the essence of many matters for the members of relatively modernized societies. Above all, however, for the first time in world history, social change as such becomes a major general ideal, perhaps even an end in itself; failure to be preoccupied with such change and its furtherance becomes a special form of sin—a special source of guilt and embarrassment.

E. SUPERNATURAL VERSUS SECULAR RELIGIONS

Religions vary as to whether or not their associated theologies involve deities and other nonempirical forces of various sorts or refer more or less directly to general value orientations with quite empirical referents. The former I would refer to as *supernatural* religions, the latter I would refer to as *secular* religions. It is essential for the analyst to realize that without exception the supernatural religions in this sense contain, as an important component of their theologies, references to value orientations quite as empirical in their referents as those associated with secular religions. The main difference between the types of religion has to do with whether or not forces conceived to operate in terms other than the activities of human beings and to some extent beyond the control of human beings are also conceived to intervene and control the affairs of men in the world. Most of the religions which we ordinarily consider to be religions in the layman's sense are supernatural religions. Christianity, Judaism, Buddhism, Ancestor Worship—all of these are supernatural religions. Ethical Culture, Humanism, Nazism, Communism, and frequently Nationalism in general are secular religions in this sense. The same terms which have here been used as examples of secular religions contain important supernatural elements in some of their associated theological formulations. To this extent they are not purely secular religions but rather constitute mixed forms with important supernatural elements. For example, the mystic invocation of racism as a supernatural force in the case of Nazism, and some of the references to the process of history and the dialectic in connection with Communism constitute supernatural elements associated with those faiths.

Secular religions tend to be ambivalent in a sense that is not characteristic of supernatural religions. All supernatural religions legitimize some core of secular ethics in terms of the will, desires, etc., of the deities involved. There need not, therefore, be any further strain toward secularism as far as supernatural religions are concerned. On the other hand, there is a considerable tendency for supernatural elements to creep into the theology associated with secular religions. For reasons that I do not pretend to understand, few individuals believe in rigorous theologies stated solely in terms of certain ethical ideals regarded as good in and of themselves.[4] Only virtuosi are capable of maintaining such a puristic orientation without succumbing to the temptation to explain on some higher plane the tenability of the ethical ideas which they regard as good in and of themselves.

Despite this ambivalence the difference between the two types is important. In the history of the world as far as conscious orientations of believers have been concerned, supernatural religions have been far more important than secular ones. Secular religions have on the whole been believed in by individuals who regarded this set of beliefs as something quite different from their supernatural beliefs. They tend to identify only their supernatural religions with religion in the sense discussed here. Secular religions tend to be directly oriented to faith in standards of conduct about which to some extent rationality and critical appraisal must be emphasized as the levels of modernization increase. Insofar as secular religions do not acquire important supernatural elements, they tend to leave all but highly individualistic believers bereft of answers to some of the classic problems for which most individuals have found answers in terms of supernatural religious beliefs. These are answers to the problems of evil in the world, of uncertainty, and of adjustment to the death of important individuals. Supernatural religious beliefs sometimes constitute obstacles [in the form of traditional modes of thought highly legitimized] to the kind of constant departures in empirical practices that must be characteristic of highly modernized societies. On the other hand, no large-scale stable society has been characterized solely by an overwhelmingly secular religion. One thing is absolutely clear, and that is that the secular components of supernatural religions must be heavily emphasized if the religion is to be highly compatible with high levels of modernization. Insofar as religious asceticism is emphasized by the general membership of the relatively highly modernized societies, the only form that that asceticism takes is this-worldly asceticism in terms of which, of course, the secular emphasis is of a high order.

F. CHURCHES AND GOVERNMENT

Religion in the most general sense is never separated from government. Religion as a general statement of basic value orienta-

---

[4] The statement here refers to the point of view of the believer. Whether or not others like or dislike the ethics involved, the true-believer may regard them as good in and of themselves. The conception that "might is right" which was such a fundamental element in the Nazi theology has limited appeal for some of us, but it has certainly served as an ideal for many.

tion is closely associated with the questions of authenticity and legitimacy of governments as of other forms of social organizations. This is true regardless of whether or not the church as an organization is separated from the government. The government of the United States is about as secular a government as has been attained in social history, but it is viewed by its members and the members of the society in which it is found as a government under God and a government of individuals who trust in God. In Imperial China the whole doctrine of sovereignty had to do with the Will of Heaven. According to this doctrine the government was a legitimate government as long as the ideal structures of the society were being approximated. Deviation from those structures was in and of itself indication that the leaders of the government lacked the Will of Heaven, and therefore the government was not the legitimate government. The Emperor participated in various ceremonies invoking the Will of Heaven, but in most respects the government of Imperial China was about as thoroughly a secular government as has been seen in world history. Supernatural religions may not have much greater connection with the government than a relevance as a sort of ideological source of authenticity, but in modern times at least the relation between secular religions and governmental organizations always goes much further than this. One might almost say that some subsystem or associated organization of the government tends to become the church as it were of the major secular religions of modern times. This was true of Nazism considered as a religion; it has been true of Communism in those countries in which Communism is the major religion.[5] It has also been true of Nationalism in those societies in which that set of beliefs constitute a major secular religion.

Although religion is never completely separated from government, churches may be. Actually the churches of a given society are never as separate from the government as they may be ideally speaking. The United States represents an extreme form of the ideal separation of Church and State. The situation in Great Britain represents a somewhat intermediate form. The state of affairs in medieval Europe, modern Spain, modern Italy, represent general cases in which the Church and State are not separated, ideally speaking. In those areas of the world in which Mohammedanism is the major form of religion, the members of only one major nation, Turkey, have succeeded in carrying out

[5] One might well consider the question of churches as governments versus governments as churches and even vary a famous question to ask, "How many churches does the Secretary of the Communist Party have?"

the separation of Church and State to any considerable length. In recent years there have been signs of reversal of that state of affairs in Turkey. When Church and State, ideally speaking, are not separated, the religion involved is likely to be an exclusivist one. If it is in fact exclusivist, influence in governmental terms is aligned in a specific position with regard to religious questions. Differences of opinion with regard to economic and political aspects as well as other aspects of social behavior tend under these circumstances to be translated directly into matters of religious concern.

A number of the religions of world history are international religions in that their adherents are by no means confined to the citizens of a single nation. Not all religions which are international in this sense are characterized by international churches, but international churches pose special problems of relationships between the members of the churches and those of the government. Many of the possibilities of overlapping and nonoverlapping memberships are obvious enough. It is, perhaps, a sign of the extreme recognition of and sensitivity to secular elements characteristic of the adherents of even the most highly supernatural of modern religions that international churches, insofar as they exist, no longer pose the kind of challenge to sovereignty which was once considered characteristic of them. The adherents of almost any recognized religion are placed on the defensive in the modern world if they can be accused of subordinating the interests of the nations of which they are citizens to the interests of the churches to which they belong. In modern times some of the secular religions have come closest to avoiding this conflict, but despite an important international element in its theology, whatever the actual practices of its religious leaders, even Communism as a secular religion has seen a deemphasis of its international theme in favor of national interest and a justification of its emphasis on international control in terms of national and domestic interests.

G. CHURCHES AND ECONOMIC ASPECTS

Although a church is a predominantly religiously oriented organization by definition in this treatment, it always has important economic aspects, as does any other organization. A church may become an organization characterized by substantial accumulations of goods and services. In medieval Europe the Catholic Church represented perhaps the largest single concentration of goods and services associated with any organization in the world at that time—certainly in the European world. Even today, from the economic point of view, the Catholic Church is a major organization in terms of the command of its leaders over goods and services. In a somewhat more restricted sense the Mormon Church also represents a major concentration of goods and services.

The economic aspects of a church are likely to raise specific problems of the mutual implications of churches and the governments concerned. Churches are likely to be tax exempt, and sometimes this applies to sources of income wholly owned in terms of a church organization. At many periods in history this constituted a major basis for large-scale accumulations as far as a given church was concerned and an increasing problem with regard to the financing of operations in terms of the government. More than once, for example, it has been possible for a man to contribute his land to his church thereby gaining tax exemption from his government while he continued to operate the properties as a tenant or on some other basis. Not only has the financial basis of the government been to some extent undercut thereby, but a new major relation of allegiance has also been established. Frequently this led to churches becoming in some special sense governmental subsystems or even governments themselves.

Quite apart from a tax problem, if the church is an organization of considerable scale in terms of the allocation of goods and services, although it is not predominantly oriented to such allocations, operations in terms of that church have all of the implications of large-scale operations having to do with the allocation of goods and services in general. Regardless of religious preoccupations, one factor which cannot be ignored is the obvious relevance of the allocation of goods and services for allocations of power and responsibility. Insofar as the representatives of churches occupy strategic positions in the allocation of goods and services, the relevance of the action of their representatives, and hence of these organizations themselves to allocations of power and responsibility can no more be ignored than can the relevance of the action of merchants as discussed above. So far as I know, there have been no major modern attempts to use church organizations as vehicles of economic development especially within societies whose members have been late-comers to modernization. The roles played by church representatives as such in these respects have so far been confined largely to matters of education and health plus, of course, the interest of the members of the churches concerned in the religious loyalties of the members of these societies.

One can hardly touch on the economic aspects of the church

without bringing to mind immediately the implications of action in terms of churches for capital formation. The things which are built in the name of churches are of importance for reasons other than their religious significance. Again from the economic point of view, apart from the question of tax exemption, the position of the churches with regard to capital formation is more a function of the size of operations in the name of the churches than of the fact that these organizations are not predominantly economically oriented. In the modern world except for the capital formation involved in the creation of facilities for direct use by members of the churches themselves, capital formation based on church sources is overwhelmingly likely to be handled not by members of the churches themselves in terms of the church organizations but rather in terms of specialized predominantly economically oriented organizations through which administrators of the churches handle church investments, etc. Under modern conditions, if separate organizations of this sort are not utilized, the members of the church concerned must develop church subsystems that are predominantly economically oriented.

At various times in church history organizations of strategic importance in the general allocation of goods and services have been directed as subsystems of churches and not as predominantly economically oriented organizations. In the world in which we live today, with the increasing likelihood that organizations of great relevance to the allocation of goods and services will be specialized on the basis of economic orientation, it is unlikely that churches will continue to maintain the position they have had in these respects in the past. It is much more unlikely that this sort of activity in terms of churches be increased in the future. Even when church and state are not actually separated as in the case of some of the modern secular religions, organizations in terms of which major capital formation is likely to be carried out are much more likely to be subsystems of the government as such than of the church [or party] as such.

From the economic point of view one of the most important aspects of church organization has been the part played by the members of such organizations in what in modern terms might be considered the *relief* structures characteristic of the societies concerned. From the beginning of time men have been faced by various conditions of distress of which the victims, no matter how exemplary their behavior prior to their plight, have been unable to shift for themselves and improve their lot. Such conditions sometimes attend natural disasters such as floods, famines, etc. There are the technological disasters of explosions. There are the disasters associated with that special form of social interaction, war. Finally above all, there are those disasters that are endemic in social life—the sick, the helpless aged and the helpless young, etc., who for some reason or other lack the expected care they need. For all of these activities the members of church organizations, especially the full-time members have been an important source of labor and of funds. In most societies the primary organizational focus of *relief activities* has probably been the family organization. If it has not been the family organization, it has probably been some other kinship organization, and when that has failed, the slack, if taken up, was probably taken up by members of some form of government or of churches, where these exist.

In relatively modernized social contexts these problems of relief are increasingly likely to fall outside the family and kinship context because of changes in family and kinship structures in general, but also because the scale of these problems is out of all proportion to the previous experience of them along certain lines. To some extent the enormous productivity of increasingly modernized methods of producing goods and services can cope with the sheer material deficiencies of natural disasters with an ease not possible in periods of more primitive technology. There have, after all, been famines simply because it was impossible to move sufficient food from a neighboring area with sufficient rapidity to save those in distress. This is no longer the case. At the same time, the operation of medical technology alone has increased out of all proportion to previous history the problem of the helpless aged members of a society at exactly that period of social development in which family organizations both ideally and actually are quite unlikely to be the organizations in terms of which these problems are successfully taken care of. In the relatively modernized societies there may well be no organization of sufficient scope to handle these problems efficiently apart from the context of government. Private insurance schemes will be so tinged with the public interest that the members of no society will tolerate such schemes without structures of close regulation by officials of the government. To the degree that that regulation is close enough and participation in such schemes is sufficiently general many of the distinctions between private and public methods of handling these problems will disappear.

In many societies churches will continue to occupy an important position in these fields. First, operations in terms of churches will remain more distinct from operations in governmental terms than operations in terms of other private or parti-private organizations. This will be the case because the sacred aspect of church organizations will be considered a more reliable guarantee of responsible behavior on the part of church members in these areas than the self-interest of the leaders of a private predominantly economically oriented organization. There is, however, another reason why churches will continue to be important in relief activities which in and of themselves will become increasingly important. Both ideally and actually, church representatives are almost inevitably committed to such activities, but they are also generally committed to come to such activities with certain attitudes which, though they are a focus of much sentimentality and the basis of much cynicism, are nevertheless particularly important for relief activities. Prominent among these is a heavy emphasis on tender loving care. Representatives of churches, insofar as they are committed to such activities, are not simply committed to them as problems that must be handled efficiently if there is to be social stability. In general neither church representatives nor other members of the society regard one of the most important religious aspects of the commitment to these problems as properly served unless the religious behave in these spheres with tender loving care for those they serve. From this point of view the churches, unlike the government, may replace one of the most important elements characteristic of societies in terms of which these activities are ordinarily carried out on a family or kinship basis—the emotional environment in which the labor and funds available are utilized for relief purposes. Care for the feelings of the recipients as individuals is more likely to be a feature of church care rather than of government care in these spheres. Despite wide variations in theologies church care almost always features self-abnegation by the caretaker. Despite wide variations in political ideologies, government care almost never does.[6]

Quite apart from the relief activities and capital formation carried out in terms of churches, their memberships may be enormous concentrations of manpower. I would separate out of this enormous concentration of manpower those sets which, though frequently organized in terms of the subsystems of churches, might alternatively have been organized in terms of other systems in the society. For example, the individuals who

[6] There are many different aspects of such situations about which individuals feel strongly. From certain points of view individuals prefer to be treated with tender loving care and self-abnegation by the caretakers. From others such attitudes are regarded as placing the recipient in undignified roles etc. In general few qualities make men more uneasy than humility. Psycho-sociologesically, men are ambivalent about this quality.

work church lands frequently consist of peasants or serfs not radically different from other peasants or serfs acting in terms of nonchurch organizations. These individuals may well be [and usually are] church members in the sense of being true-believers in the religion associated with the church, but they are certainly not ordinarily church members in a sense of being full-time specialists in ecclesiastical activities as such.

If one turns attention to full-time ecclesiastical personnel as such, the amount of manpower involved still reaches considerable proportions. As mentioned, there have been periods in Chinese history in which the expansion of Buddhist monasteries allegedly threatened something of a labor shortage. Much of this ecclesiastical manpower has been concentrated on the administration of church organizations, on the relief activities associated with the churches, on the educational aspects of activities associated with the churches, etc. This pool of manpower is an important element in the national income even for some of the most highly modernized societies. By modern methods of computing the national income this pool of manpower is probably largely ignored. This may not make much difference since the proportion of such manpower to the total labor force is generally small and more importantly since the associated uses of materiel, power, and services would be measured via national income accounting. In many of the relatively nonmodernized social contexts neither of these propositions necessarily holds true. To fail to consider such sources of manpower in national income accounting is probably always a mistake from the point of view of students of public affairs.

Finally, with the possible exception of extremely unusual societies of quite small scale such as that of Iceland, the literacy rates associated with relatively nonmodernized societies are low. Given low literacy, ecclesiastical personnel will almost certainly have a far higher level of literacy than is characteristic of the general population. Often the level of literacy of the ecclesiastical personnel is higher than the general level of literacy of the members of the government. Whatever the general level of literacy, the literate have many advantages by contrast with the illiterate. When literacy is highly restricted, full-time church personnel are exceedingly strategic personnel for this if for no other reason. From the point of view of the allocation of goods and services, one of the most important services over which church personnel are likely to have a considerable command are those in which literacy is strategic. This specialized advantage of the labor force of the church diminishes radically as the general level of literacy rises in the context of relatively modernized societies. For those societies universal literacy is a requisite. Shortly after such changes have gotten underway, the distinction between literate and nonliterate members of the society loses a considerable amount of its previous significance.[7] This is one of the more important changes associated with such transitions.

I I I
SCHOOLS

A. DEFINITION

Schools have already been defined above [pp. 342–344] as predominantly educationally oriented organizations. Structures of education exist in all societies, but schools do not necessarily exist as subsystems in all societies. When they do exist in relatively nonmodernized societies, they may be comparatively pauce and involve only a small minority of the population. It is one of the peculiar characteristics of relatively modernized societies that in them schools fall into the category of basic organizations as well as into the category of intermediate organizations. The average member of a relatively modernized society always participates in one or more schools at some time during his life cycle. In addition, there exists a large number of special schools in terms of which only relatively specialized members of the society are educated. As in the cases of churches, governments, predominantly economically oriented organizations, etc., the fact that schools are defined as predominantly educationally oriented organizations in no way implies that economic allocations, political allocations, solidarity, and other aspects of action are irrelevant to schools. This is no more the case of schools than of churches. Here again the ideal-actual distinction is useful. It is possible for organizations to exist which, ideally speaking, are schools but which actually are organizations of quite another sort. Conversely it is conceivable that there be organizations which actually are schools although, ideally speaking, they are taken to be something quite different. In the general discussion of schools the ideal-actual distinction will not be raised unless these variations are specifically relevant. Generally when I refer to an organiza-

[7] In other senses the distinction increases in importance. Apart from preliterate children, the illiterate members of a relatively modernized society are radically disadvantaged. This, incidentally, is a sort of socially inherent inequality that no egalitarian good intentions can fully correct once it exists—for whatever reasons.

tion as a school, I take it for granted, if only as a hypothesis, that, from the point of view of its own membership as well as that of the society at large, it is both ideally and actually a predominantly educationally oriented organization.

B. THE NATURE AND FREQUENCY OF SCHOOLS IN SOCIAL HISTORY

I have just pointed out that, although *education* is always present if a society exists, *schooling* is not necessarily always present. On the other hand, in societies of the scale of interest here, there is no society in which schools are totally lacking. Usually in relatively nonmodernized societies the development of schools is restricted. The extent may be reckoned many different ways. The most striking restriction is that only a small proportion of the general population is in fact educated in terms of schools given such societies. The distinction between relatively modernized and relatively nonmodernized societies with regard to schools is not so significant in most other lines of variation [e.g., the subjects taken up, the specialization of schools, the source of their support, their governance, etc.] as it is with regard to the one chosen here.

One of the elements in the restricted extent of schooling in terms of the ordinary relatively nonmodernized society has to do with its cost. The distribution of income is pronouncedly bimodal with the vast majority of the population living at the bare margin of subsistence. The vast majority of those with small incomes are engaged in agrarian pursuits or some other form of food and raw material production. In addition to the ordinary cost of schooling associated with the phenomenon in relatively modernized societies, that is to say in addition to the actual cost of tuition, materials, etc., there are two other types of cost usually of considerable importance for the members of these societies. The first of these is the cost of labor of the person who receives the schooling and hence must forego active participation in the economic aspects of the family organization. Ordinarily this is not an inconsiderable item, especially since the years of his schooling are likely to coincide with the years in which his labor contribution might really begin to amount to something in terms of the general income of the family members. The structure of death rates characteristic of the membership of such societies is generally such that there is not ordinarily a labor surplus at points of time that are considered critical [e.g., planting and harvest times] from the point of view of the members of the organization [i.e., usually family units] in terms of which most laboring takes place, despite the fact that there may be many slack times of the year.

As important as the cost of foregone labor is the potential cost involved if the individual receives education in the form of schooling but is then a failure in his attempt to utilize it in the kind of elite roles generally open to those who have received such an education. His success or failure in these attempts is not likely to be known in time for him to recover the kind of day-to-day habituation to a rather hard way of life which he will have lost by virtue of his involvement in schooling. Furthermore, even if he is a failure in the more optimistic sense of the elite who have received schooling, he may not be able to return to the roles he might have been expected to fulfill had such education never been attempted. Not only will he be unacclimated, but having attempted such specialized education at all he will in a sense be too prestigious for the ordinary roles of a totally unschooled adult. His family members or those of some other organization may be faced with the problem of supporting him in some way through-out the remainder of his life as something of a loss. Thus when education via schools is open to persons of low degree in terms of a given society, high motivation to seek such advantages for one's children may be offset by these elements of cost.

Universal schooling or well-nigh universal schooling is rare in history, despite the fact that members of relatively modernized societies take it for granted. Furthermore, the development of universal schooling within a society is never simply a matter of having available from whatever source the means of meeting the costs of schools, the costs of released labor for the young to attend schools, and the costs of handling the failures. The problem is always considerably more complicated than that. To develop universal schooling without a planned utilization of the educated products carries with it a special additional set of problems in the form of the wide creation of individuals who from their point of view bear certain of the symbols of elite position without well-defined positions in terms of which to put their new talents to work. Closely associated with this is the fact that in a social context in which schooling has been restricted indeed and highly symbolic of elite status, the initial reaction to universal schooling may be that it confers elite status on all those who receive it. In those social contexts in which universal schooling has come to be taken for granted in its elementary forms at least, it confers no elite status. It is simply a requisite for nondegraded status. In transitional situations, unless careful thought is given to the matter, the situation may result in one of all Chiefs and no Indians—a specially created set of cadets.

C. TYPICAL DIFFERENTIATIONS

There is neither time nor space to treat of the types of differentiation important from many points of view as far as schools are concerned. Four bases of differentiation are of some importance here. First, all schools are graded in some fashion, and the grading characteristic of school systems in the ordinary sense, i.e., in organizations which consist of sets of schools, is always carried a great deal further. As a minimum this grading must be differentiated on some basis of elementary, middle, and higher education. Elementary education must focus on what may be considered to be the various forms of simplest literacy. These are, everywhere, literacy in the literal sense, arithmetical literacy, and cultural literacy in the simplest sense. Also characteristic of elementary schools is early if not initial experience of treatment on a radically more predominantly universalistic basis than has been characteristic of the previous treatment of the individual in his family context. Initial introduction of a general school system or set of schools ordinarily involves at the elementary level a substantial number of individuals who have already reached the stages of adult development, but in the long run and in most settled situations, elementary schooling is primarily a matter involving teachers and quite young children.[8] Middle schooling ordinarily develops the basis for considerably more differentiated skills than does the elementary schooling. In addition, differentiated skills beyond the level of the simplest literacies are commonly also developed in terms of the middle schools. The higher schools are those in terms of which the differentiation of schooling is carried to its greatest and most highly refined lengths. In addition to other functions the higher schools are also the schools' schools. Both elementary and middle schools are organizations not only overwhelmingly oriented to education, but to the teaching aspects of education as such. In any viable school system characterized by higher schools, those higher schools must in addition to the preoccupation of some of their members with teaching also be importantly oriented to the preservation of learning and the acquisition of new knowledge. The special position of the higher schools in a school system or set of schools poses special problems for those societies whose members are relative late-comers to highly and generally devel-

[8] And, of course, the parents or guardians of the children in special forms of symbiosis.

oped sets of schools. In the initial stages of such development elementary and middle schools may be of far greater importance than higher schools, but the prestige of participation, both as a student and as a professional member of the staff, in terms of higher schools is so much greater than participation in the other two that the problem of adequate attention to the elementary and middle schools is something of a special problem. Never underestimate the power of academic snobbery—whatever its basis!

Second, is the distinction between what might be called *vocational* schools as distinguished from *intellectual* schools. In this sense the teaching associated with vocational schools emphasizes the detailed learning and skills necessary for specific occupational roles. These roles are skilled occupational roles, and there is pressure from the members of some of the most highly developed of the vocational schools to consider them as *professional* or *semiprofessional* schools. The intellectual schools are not so specifically oriented, and their leaders claim at least to be concerned more with the basis for the preservation of learning and the acquisition of new learning. The distinction between vocational as opposed to intellectual schools tends to appear full blown in the middle schools. Whatever the ideal distinction may be, the actual distinction is frequently one of degree and difficult to draw. In the context of any relatively modernized society the need exists for both types, but in the early period of transition from relatively nonmodernized status, vocational schools are probably a great deal more important actually for purposes of smooth transition.

Third, various detailed differences may be noted among schools. There are, for example, secular as distinguished from religious schools. There are medical as distinguished from law schools and so forth. One of the most important of these distinctions is that between higher schools of the *professional* type and higher schools of a *general intellectual* type. Professional schools in the sense intended here may be differentiated from vocational schools in that ordinarily speaking participation in professional education in relatively modernized societies presupposes participation to some extent in higher education in predominantly intellectual schools as distinguished from vocational schools. The professional schools, however, have in common with the vocational schools an enormous emphasis on the detailed mastery of carefully specified skills, whereas the professional staff of the higher general intellectual schools are more oriented to the maintenance of knowledge and the acquisition of new knowledge, ideally, that is.

Fourth, one may distinguish among *private* and *public* schools and schools which are mixed in these respects. The distinction here is usually based on the source of funds required for the operation in terms of the school and the governance of the schools. If the source of income is, ideally speaking, primarily from private contributions and the tuition of the students, and if the direction of the school is ideally independent of the government of the society concerned, we tend to think of them as private schools. The reverse in both cases tends to mark the schools as *public* schools.[9] As in the case of churches, the problem of tax exemption alone introduces an element of public nature into the most private of schools in most societies. In relatively modernized societies a strict line between public and private schools is increasingly difficult to draw.

It is quite clear that in sketching the typical differentiations of schools, I have in mind the schools characteristic of relatively modernized societies. This is partly because the development of schools in relatively nonmodernized societies is so much more restricted. What appears on the surface to be a curious contradiction accompanies this. In terms of relatively modernized societies the development of schools, as of so many other organizations, is characterized by a level of specialization out of all context with developments in terms of any relatively nonmodernized societies. Nevertheless, apart from the differentiation implicit in this high level of specialization of schools, variation in the organization and orientation of schools themselves may well be greater if read across the pages of the social history of relatively nonmodernized societies than if read in terms of relatively modernized societies alone. The extent in relatively modernized social contexts to which schools, as other specialized organizations, are crucially interdependent with other aspects of social life cuts down the level of idiosyncratic features tolerable in the more strategic school organizations.

D. THE STRATEGIC NATURE OF LEARNING

There is no doubt a target for irony in the shrill insistence of academics on the importance of learning, but it is nevertheless a tenable position from the point of view of social structure, regard-

[9] For the English reader some different set of terms should be selected. Any symbols will do.

less of the source. The strategic nature of learning is always high in the case of any large-scale society. The problem of records alone and the importance of literacy in the efficient maintenance of records is enough to explain this.[10] In the context of relatively modernized societies, of course, the problem is always considerably greater than the mere keeping of records.

Even in the context of relatively nonmodernized societies of considerable scale there are some activities that must be carried out on a centralized basis, and those require planning as well as execution. In the context of relatively modernized societies the number of such activities is multiplied beyond relatively nonmodernized imagination. The enormous development of specialization requires an enormous variation in the details of learning. The problems of interdependency and adjustment also require an enormous uniformity in certain learning. In relatively modernized social contexts both basic and intermediate cognition as distinguished above [p. 217] are enormously proliferated. Furthermore, although the variations in learning are carried far, there must be an enormous uniformity with regard to the details of the learning in terms of the variation. For example, what lawyers learn is sharply differentiated from what medical doctors learn save possibly for the courses in medical jurisprudence, but within strict limits what lawyers learn must be highly uniform from one law school context to another, and the same is true for what doctors learn from one medical school context to another.

I cannot think of any actual case of a relatively nonmodernized society of any considerable scale totally lacking in schools, but it is not impossible, at least, to imagine that in some relatively nonmodernized societies of considerable scale all of the learning conducted in terms of schools *could be* conducted on the basis of some relatively nonspecialized organizations or on the basis of some specialized ones not necessarily predominantly educationally oriented. In relatively modernized social contexts the amount, the importance of uniformity, and the extent of the

---

[10] One of the greatest vulnerabilities to analysis of Mr. Orwell's vision of life in 1984 lies in his telling gibe at certain aspects of highly authoritarian societies by the device he referred to as the "memory hole." These were holes into which any inconvenient record was dropped and immediately destroyed. Without losing the point about the willingness of certain types of political leaders to alter history whenever they feel it convenient, it is important to realize that the method suggested is not feasible. Even the most authoritarian of leaders cannot control a society of any considerable scale on the basis of capriciously kept records. As the ironists of bureaucracy are fond of pointing out, it is perfectly all right to destroy old records to make space provided one first makes a copy of the records to be destroyed.

variations in learning remove forever the possibility of learning entirely confined to relatively nonspecialized units or to specialized ones not predominantly educationally oriented. These requisites also remove another possibility which in fact was generally realized in the context of most relatively nonmodernized societies—the possibility that virtually all of the education for the vast majority of the members of the society will be carried out in terms of relatively nonspecialized organizations. No society ever has been—or will be—such that no education is conveyed in terms of family structures. It is certainly possible to maintain, however, that in all relatively modernized societies an ever-increasing amount of both basic and intermediate learning will be conducted in terms of schools rather than in terms of nonspecialized organizations or organizations specialized on bases other than educational ones.

E. SCHOOLS AND OTHER ORGANIZATIONS

An increase in the development of schools always weakens the control exerted in terms of family units. Specifically education outside the family context removes some of the reinforcement of the precedence of some of the family members over others. The ordinary member of a society, in the absence of specialized schooling, receives his education from older members of his own family. This is an additional respect in which quite unconsciously, perhaps, he is dependent upon them and takes them for granted as people who know more than he, etc. Furthermore, if they do not perform their teaching roles properly, he may have no alternative method of repairing these deficiencies. As soon as the individual begins to receive a portion of his education from individuals who are members of other organizations outside the family context, this reinforcement of family orientation is removed. Furthermore, those teachers, especially in transitional cases may violate his ordinary expectations of relative age and the like in teaching figures. To the extent that general control structures in the society are a function of the stability of family controls, the introduction of schools in a society tends to undermine the general structures of control quite apart from the substantive content of new ideas presented, the ideology of the specialized teachers, etc.

Schools are a focus of interactions considered significant by the members of the schools whether those be students, faculty members or any other members. Whenever schools are highly developed, they are important foci of cliques. Perhaps one of the purest examples of this is the famous *gakubatsu* or academic cliques of

Japan. In various fields of endeavor different universities are the foci of cliques, but overwhelmingly more important than any of the others in the society as a whole is Tokyo University. Operation in terms of cliques based on common participation in education in terms of Tokyo University is especially significant in the manning of the various offices of the government. The importance of cliques based on Harvard University in the United States today is not solely a matter of jest either. Participation in schooling, especially in terms of relatively modernized societies, provides the means for an increasing emphasis on predominantly universalistic standards of selection, but it also carries with it new bases for predominantly particularistic selection. General realization of this in the English language is clearly implied in such phrases as "the old school tie." The development of cliques as an inevitable by-product of teaching, learning, and researching in terms of schools is closely related to the fact that action in terms of schools always provides new bases for peer group solidarities and similarities. This is not necessarily confined to individual schools. It may very well be, at least in part, a function of certain common aspects of the learning experience. In recent years some social scientists have maintained that in the United States at least, regardless of differences in colleges and universities, and regardless of how long an individual has gone to a college or university, there are more tastes and other characteristics in common on the average between any two or more individuals who have had any college experience whatsoever than between any two individuals one of whom has had some college experience and the other not. If this is so, it is a quite extraordinary generalization and quite incompatible with the conventional snobbism about the different qualities of different schools and the differences different schools make for those who attend them.

In addition to becoming a general focus for solidarity on the part of the people who have belonged to them, schools have frequently been the basis of a very particular sort of solidarity—a solidarity which finds its special expression in predominantly politically oriented activities. How far this extends back in social history I do not know. It has certainly been marked from the time of the social revolution of political liberalism at the end of the eighteenth century on. It has grown in intensity since that time, and appears in some of its strongest manifestations in the student bodies of schools of higher education in those societies whose members are relative late-comers to modernization. This would argue that the predominantly politically oriented activities specifically associated with students are closely related to the general process of modernization. There is every reason to suspect that this would be the case, since the universities are bound to become special foci of the new forms of learning and the like. In general the politically active students, regardless of their specific ideology, have regarded themselves as radicals rather than as conservatives. Here again the tie-up with modernization in general is an important factor, since the processes of modernization in general are, according to the position taken here, inevitably radical with regard to the social systems which preexist those changes.

The question of the higher schools as a special focus of predominantly politically oriented activity on the part of the student body is considerably more complicated than this, however. With two particular exceptions the student bodies of institutes of higher education even in quite highly modernized societies are on the whole quite active in the political arena. Those two exceptions are the United States and Great Britain. Furthermore, the faculty members of these universities and colleges might in a sense be regarded as even more in the forefront of radical views than their students are, since many of the former are working at the frontiers of the new learning whereas the students receive their initial indoctrination in terms of much better established and hence to some extent less radical information. Nevertheless, despite the fact that the faculty members are also quite active in some of these movements, they seem on the whole to take considerably less initiative and are of considerably more mixed minds about general participation in such activities than are the students under their guidance.

Whatever the answer to such questions may be, there is absolutely no question but that schools in general and the various forms of higher schools such as universities, colleges, etc., in particular are going to occupy an increasingly important position in all the societies in the world. One of the marks par excellence of the modernization that is increasing throughout the world is that universal education always accompanies it—or rather is part of it. For the members of the most highly developed of those societies a college education comes to be taken for granted as a general right rather than a wish of those capable of sustaining such education. Furthermore, what constitutes that capability is increasingly liberally interpreted. In the earlier stages, elementary education for the simplest forms of literacy is first considered to be a right and a necessity, then secondary education is so considered, and so forth. This happens in a social setting which many feel is increasingly fragmented. This increasing fragmentation is widely regarded as creating special problems of adjustment for the individual. Under the circumstances any influence so general as that of schools as a basis for clique structures, for peer group solidarity, and as a focus of politically oriented activity, is a matter of the greatest immediate concern to anyone interested in public affairs.

IV
PREDOMINANTLY RECREATIONALLY ORIENTED ORGANIZATIONS

A. DEFINITION

Recreation has been defined above [p. 361] as that aspect of behavior which has to do with relaxation and relief from the usual duties and concerns of daily life. In that chapter there was a fairly extended discussion of recreational aspects considered as an aspect of activities in general and of recreational aspects as constituting a basis for the development of specialized organizations and activities. The preoccupation in this portion of the work has to do only with those social settings in which recreation does become a basis for such specialized organizations.

B. THE FREQUENCY OF PREDOMINANTLY RECREATIONALLY ORIENTED ORGANIZATIONS

In relatively nonmodernized societies such organizations are rare in two senses. First, they are rare in the usual sense that such societies contain few specialized subsystems in general. Second, they are rare in that there is a general lack of distinction of recreation from other aspects of action both with regard to activities and in terms of organizations themselves. Here it is necessary to draw a distinction which might be easily overlooked. Specialized organizations such as theaters, opera troops, circuses, and the like are not predominantly recreationally oriented organizations from the point of view of their performing members, though they certainly are predominantly oriented toward the provision of a specialized service which will be consumed in a predominantly recreational context by their audiences. If one wishes to think of the audience of a given theatrical performance as belonging in some sense to the same organization to which the performers belong then one has in such organizations a special distinction among the members. They fall into at least two clear-cut classes; those for whom participation is predominantly recreational and those for whom participation is predominantly production or otherwise oriented.

Those organizations with important recreational aspects such as orientation to performance before an audience and the like involve a set of professional members who are predominantly oriented to production rather than recreation, but there are organizations which are in fact predominantly recreationally oriented, which do emerge on a specialized basis. Amateur sports teams, various picnic clubs, hobby organizations, private chamber music ensembles, and thousands of other types of organizations come readily to mind in this connection. In relatively nonmodernized societies such organizations are most likely to involve a small minority of the members of the society. At adult and even childhood levels the mass of members of the society are likely to be too preoccupied with activities of which recreation is only one aspect—if that—to have time for participation in such specialized systems. Insofar as such specialized systems involve the general members of the society, they are likely to be organizations of short duration, e.g., drinking parties, feasts, etc. In relatively nonmodernized settings more enduring organizations along these lines are likely to involve an elite membership.

In relatively modernized settings, on the other hand there is a radical proliferation of such organizations. This proliferation is partly a function of the general increase in specialization characteristic of relatively modernized societies and partly a function of the increased availability of time regarded as leisure time for individuals of all ages in such social contexts.

C. VICARIOUS AND PARTICIPANT FORMS OF RECREATION

The distinction here is between forms in which the recreational aspects inhere in essentially audience-type activities as opposed to the detailed activities being regarded as predominantly recreational. The most direct relationship of this distinction to the discussion immediately above is that those organizations which can be spoken of as predominantly recreationally oriented for the membership as a whole are on the whole organizations centered around participant forms of recreation as opposed to vicarious forms of recreation. The organizational settings for vicarious recreation always involve a distinction between those members overwhelmingly engaged in recreation from their point of view and those members for whom the production of recreation for others is a specialized form of occupation.

Obviously the distinction between vicarious and participant forms of recreation does not emerge as a matter of general relevance save in those social contexts in which recreation takes on highly specialized aspects. This is not generally true until one encounters relatively modernized society. Nevertheless, some form of predominantly recreationally oriented behavior emerges in all societies, and certainly some predominantly recreationally oriented organizations emerge in all societies of any considerable scale. Even in societies of quite small scale some predominantly recreationally oriented organizations primarily based on participant recreation are to be found. Such organizations may be of considerable importance in understanding the general social structure. Usually they are rather short lived as specific organizations. Various feasts, orgies, dances, etc., fall into this category, though similar organizations may also be accompaniments of predominantly religiously oriented activities, predominantly politically oriented activities, etc. In small-scale relatively nonmodernized societies developments of specialized organizations oriented to the production of vicarious recreation for an audience is usually limited, if present. They are, however, never absent from societies of any considerable scale. In such cases what may appear from the point of view of relatively modernized observers especially as activities in terms of organizations overwhelmingly significant from the recreational point of view may in fact have a significance for understanding the society concerned which goes far beyond the relevance of recreation as a form of release and adjustment. These matters have been so little studied on a comparative basis by those interested in modern analysis rather than descriptive or anecdotal accounts that general hypotheses—even free-wheeling ones—are scarce. Nevertheless, one striking case of this sort associated with traditional Chinese society will serve to illustrate such possibilities.

Prior to the present period, there has probably never been a society whose members placed a higher emphasis on literacy than did the traditional Chinese for at least two and possibly three thousand years.[11] Despite this great emphasis on literacy only a minority of the membership of Chinese society was literate. That minority was probably as high if not higher than the corresponding portion of any other relatively nonmodernized society, with the possible exception noted in the footnote above. Nevertheless, whether one sets that minority at 20 per cent of the total population or 30 per cent or 10 per cent—a minority it was. One would expect that minority to be relatively well informed about Chinese history and the great works of Chinese civilization in

[11] The society of Iceland may be an exception to this statement [see above, p. 87]. It is true that Icelandic society is a small-scale society indeed by contrast with the types of society generally under discussion here, but any relatively nonmodernized society characterized by well-nigh universal literacy would constitute such a special exception to general social history as to be well worth exploration in depth from this point of view alone.

general, but judging from the history of other relatively nonmodernized societies one would not expect a high level of diffusion of that knowledge to the general nonliterate members of the society. Nevertheless, to a perfectly extraordinary degree the nonliterate members of the society were informed about Chinese history and the Chinese classics.

In the recreational sphere the place of the wandering and local story tellers is an important one in China. So is the position of traveling opera troupes and the like. Most of the stories told and most of the operas performed are based on the major events and themes of Chinese history as the Chinese saw them. Even the various popular Chinese novels were to a high degree diffused among the illiterate members of the society by such means. The monolithic sense of cultural unity attributed to Chinese is certainly importantly related to these elements. The implications of rates of illiteracy for elements of social structure vary markedly with the presence or absence of such recreational forms as these. In Chinese society this was vicarious recreation dependent on more or less professional personnel. In a society characterized by highly self-sufficient family units and village organizations, the common and detailed awareness of history, so inculcated, was as vital an element in the interdependency of the society as a whole as the set of roads, canals, and irrigation devices which are so justly famous. Such recreational specialization as exists in relatively nonmodernized societies may constitute some of the most important general structures of communication of the society.

D. RECREATION AND MODERNIZATION

Whatever the situation may have been before, with the development of specialized occupational roles, especially those organized in terms of predominantly economically oriented organizations whose members consider them to be predominantly concerned with production—with that sort of development—recreation always emerges as a focus of specialization too. The increase of specialized forms of recreation is as much a mark of relatively modernized societies as is the increase in specialization of other sorts. This specialization takes two forms. First, there is a radical increase in organizations which, either from the point of view of the membership in general or at least the audience-type members, are regarded as predominantly recreationally oriented. Second, and perhaps more important, is the specialized differentiation of recreational aspects from other aspects of behavior. In relatively modernized social contexts this latter development is carried to such greater lengths that terms such as *work* and *rec-*

reation are automatically assumed to refer to radically differentiated things. To say of a member of a relatively modernized society that his work is his recreation is to differentiate him from the ordinary members of his society. It carries with it overtones of special asceticism, of an especially narrow outlook on life in general. Or, if it is said with a positive overtone, the observation implies that he is in an especially and unusually fortunate position.

With this increase of specialized differentiation between work and recreation, there is also in some sense a growing distinction between what are regarded as recreational contexts and other social contexts as well as that of work. Thus ordinary interaction in the family context is not generally considered as recreational any more than activity carried out in such contexts is considered as productive from the economic point of view. From the point of view of the family members, for example, family recreation is both specialized and differentiated from ordinary family behavior. This lends increasingly to recreationally oriented activities an aspect of escapist orientation in the technical sense used here. Recreation increasingly is viewed by those who participate in it as somehow taking one out of all other social contexts as much as possible. There is an interesting contrast between recreation so considered and what is ordinarily considered as other-worldly asceticism. In the latter, the emphasis is on getting the actor as far from the material world as possible, completely released from the "wheel of life" as one formulation puts it. The emphasis on predominantly recreationally oriented activities characteristic of the members of relatively modernized societies is not in this sense oriented to getting clean out of this world. The forms of recreation which are preferred usually place a high emphasis on material factors including an especially high emphasis on specialized equipment the contemplation and preparation of which becomes almost a specialized form of recreation in and of itself. It does, however, place an increasing emphasis on getting away from every other aspect of the material world ordinarily associated with the individual's behavior. The emphasis is increasingly placed on going somewhere different and doing something different. At one and the same time, this tends to develop specialized devotees of particular recreational forms such as fishermen, skiers, sailing enthusiasts, ocean travelers, etc. In the ordinary case this means that the recreational form is likely to shift radically and quickly. In these contexts both specialization and faddism in the recreational sphere become quite marked.

With the marked increases in productivity and the increasingly high unimodal distribution of income characteristic of relatively modernized societies whatever their forms of government, there is always an increase in what comes to be regarded as leisure time, that is to say, time away from work. This means, of course, time away from participation in what is increasingly a specialized occupational role. As indicated above, not all time spent away from work is regarded as leisure time. Indeed, in relatively highly modernized social contexts, only time spent in what are specifically regarded as recreational activities is considered to be leisure time properly spent. Nevertheless, the radical increase in released time from activities directly oriented to the maintenance of sufficient income to support life itself and the accustomed standard of living certainly does increase the time available for recreational development. In the most highly modernized contexts the leisure revolution referred to above [pp. 77–78, 487, 510–511] is a salient feature. Two spheres of preoccupation tend to develop. One is the occupational role sphere, identified with work. The other is the nonoccupational sphere, and an important part of that is identified with ordinary family life. Increasingly ordinary family life in relatively modernized contexts is disassociated from recreation, but with the advent of the leisure revolution in the most highly modernized social contexts, the time available for this recreation is increasingly likely to be spent in a family context. Family life itself under these circumstances, tends to become increasingly differentiated on the basis of what might be regarded as family work as distinguished from family recreation. Under these circumstances some of the forms of behavior ordinarily associated with family productivity come to be considered as recreational rather than as parts of ordinary family life. Gardening, do-it-yourself household repairs, hobbies of all sorts, and the like fall into these categories. In these contexts, there is every appearance of an increasing emphasis on family life but it is a special form of emphasis. Prior to the development of relatively modernized societies the distinction between one's occupational involvements and the other forms of behavior was not ordinarily considered to be a difference between working and really living. Increasingly that is the case for the members of relatively modernized societies. In the most highly modernized of the relatively modernized societies a corresponding distinction within the context of family life is also developing. The rearing of children, the care of the house, cooking, participation in meals, under ordinary circumstances increasingly come to be considered a thing apart from real family living which is increasingly identified with what the individual regards as recreational activi-

ties carried out on a family basis. This development in specialized recreational emphasis may be something new under the sun
in family life.

Closely connected with this implication of the leisure revolution in general is another development. United States society is
perhaps the most extreme case. As already indicated above [pp.
77–78] the vast majority of Americans take the forty-hour
week for granted. The movement in favor of a thirty-five-hour
week is well advanced. For Americans as for others the seven day
week contains one hundred sixty-eight hours. If one deducts forty
hours for work, fifty-six hours for sleep, and twenty-one hours for
meals, one is still left with fifty-one hours which constitute more
time for recreation than for work. Some of the time allocated to
sleeping and eating in this example is, of course, time for ordinary family life. Some of the remaining fifty-one hours for those
involved in occupational roles would also have to be allocated to
these purposes. Nevertheless, a moments' contemplation of these
figures indicate once again that the major problem of keeping
individuals well adjusted insofar as it is a function of the time at
their disposal is for the members of United States society increasingly a problem of individuals who if not at play are certainly not
at work. For this point of view what individuals tend to regard as
the recreational sphere may increasingly become a focus of the
problems of integration second only to those of the initial socialization of children.

E. RECREATIONAL ASPECTS AND VARIOUS ORGANIZATIONAL CONTEXTS

Recreational aspects of behavior or behavior regarded as predominantly recreational by the individuals concerned are always
to some extent carried out within a family context. This is likely
to be true of the vast majority of recreational aspects in relatively
nonmodernized societies, and no matter how highly specialized
relatively modernized societies become, separation between recreational aspects or activities considered as predominantly recreational and family contexts is never complete. In the discussion of the family above in Part III, Chapter 1, the strategic role
of the family in many contexts was emphasized. This context is
no exception. Initial socialization with regard to recreation characteristically for all societies takes place in family terms.

With increases in modernization, the combination of recreational and economic orientations as self-conscious matters diminish. Occupational roles become increasingly a source of prestige
rather than of relaxation. If anything, the higher the prestige the

lower the possibilities of relaxation as such. From the point of view of the strict Protestant Ethic according to Max Weber, the posession of fortune was at best a stewardship not to be enjoyed as such by its owner or accumulator. The same has come to be true in relatively modernized societies with regard to positions of high prestige and responsibility. A famous member of the Medici family is reputed to have said on becoming Pope, "God has given us the Papacy, let us enjoy it." It is doubtful that any major public figure could survive the expression of this sort of attitude toward important office today. Positions of high public prestige carry with them the sort of responsibility once involved in the possession of great wealth. One of the many reasons why the Presidency of the United States, at least in the United States, is referred to as the "most onerous job in the world" is specifically the fact that no incumbent of the office can "get away from it even for a minute." Recreation for individuals in such important positions is as much a question of strategic planning and complicated logistics as other large-scale operations.

With increases of modernization the combination of recreational aspects and political orientation in the long run diminishes. As pointed out in another connection [pp. 372–374], politics was a major form of recreation in United States society in the nineteenth century. If anything today the picture is reversed. In terms of relatively nonmodernized societies in general predominantly politically oriented activities are much more closely identified with recreation, and the identification has held true of activities up to and including war. In terms of relatively modernized societies, however, the allocation of power and responsibility is carried out increasingly in specialized contexts and increasingly is neither a laughing nor a relaxing matter.

Activities considered predominantly religious are also increasingly separated from recreational connotations in terms of relatively modernized societies. In this respect there has been something of a switch like that from politics as recreation to recreation as politics. There was a period of time in modern United States history, for example, when special recreationally oriented occasions were closely associated with predominantly religiously oriented organizations. The church picnic, for example, was a common occasion. Today there is an appearance of a return to such combinations, but the combination has a different emphasis. Whereas previously predominantly religiously oriented behavior had associated with it many strikingly recreational occasions, today the preoccupation with specialized predominantly recreational behavior is made a basis for attracting and holding members of a congregation to occasions of worship. The community house is often every bit as important as the church or synagogue to which it is attached. Sometimes it is built first.

As recreational aspects of behavior are increasingly specialized outside the context of other organizations, recreation becomes an increasingly serious business.[12] To this extent criteria for achievement in recreation become an increasing focus of attention. As this development continues, it becomes increasingly important for the forms of recreation for the individual to change, if the element of relaxation is to persist—if specialized recreationally oriented behavior is not to turn into some other form of specially oriented behavior. This is a major source of the faddism associated with recreation in highly modernized contexts.

F. THE RELEVANCE OF THE RECREATIONAL ASPECTS OF BEHAVIOR TO THE PROBLEM OF INTEGRATION IN GENERAL

To the extent that recreational aspects of behavior are differentiated from others, the activities regarded as recreational become increasingly relevant as far as the reduction of tensions is concerned. One of the major problems with regard to recreation is to keep the element of relaxation sufficiently high with loose enough organization so that the organizational aspects as such do not become a source of serious preoccupation. In relatively modernized social contexts, where such specialization is increasingly emphasized, the vicarious forms of recreation may be more significant in the long run than participant ones. One of the major characteristics of vicarious recreation is that, from the point of view of the individual, the organization in terms of which he participates is an exceedingly fleeting one—one in which he need not get highly involved.[13] On the other hand participant

---

[12] The grim seriousness of both adults and children about such presumably predominantly recreationally oriented activities as little-league baseball and football has already become a focus of alarm in some circles. College football at most colleges in the United States has long been a matter of high seriousness. One of the fascinations of family touch football as practiced in some circles lies in the fact that for all of the devotion to it, the casualness of dress, the informality about size and type of personnel of the teams, etc., still mark it as predominantly participant recreation.

[13] In relatively modernized contexts one has to be cautious even on this score. The epitome of vicarious recreation from certain points of view lies in behavior as an athletic fan, as a Yankee or Dodger fan, for example. The average fan of this sort goes to an occasional game and enjoys himself. The rabid fan is quite another matter. Sooner or later he feels it necessary to attend every possible game; he becomes recognized as a virtuoso of villification of his team's opponents, umpires, etc.; or he may come to be a participant in an amateur band or some other activity of

recreation probably has considerably more relevance as reinforcing other structures of social organization in the society. The optimum balance between recreation as a form of integration via its escapist aspects as distinguished from recreation as a form of integration by virtue of its direct reinforcement of the values of everyday life is a difficult question at the present stage of development of social science. The solution to this problem will vary with the kind of society and the position of recreational structures within the general social structure. In general as modernization progresses, the relevance of recreation to integration via its escapist aspects probably increases steadily.

As work is increasingly confined to highly specialized social settings, the individuals thought of as having leisure time become increasingly those who have specialized occupational roles. When one speaks of the increased leisure time in the United States, for example, one has in mind the shortened work week within the specialized occupational role context. The productive aspects of the efforts of others, for example in the family setting, have probably increased in efficiency also by virtue of the use of various mechanical aids, but productivity in other spheres is not a major focus for the definition of increased leisure. It is also characteristic of these societies that the family units, ideally speaking, are small ones generally involving as members father, mother and nonadult children. Unlike the economic aspects of other family units in relatively nonmodernized societies the major source of income for family members under these circumstances becomes overwhelmingly the income earned in a specialized occupational role by the father or husband. In the life of the father or the husband, under ordinary circumstances, the two organizational contexts of greatest significance from his point of view are the one in terms of which he pursues his specialized occupational role and the family context. From this point of view a felt increase in leisure time defined primarily as far as the individual is concerned by shorter hours in his specialized occupational role means increased time within the family context. Regardless of what has actually happened to the work load within the family context, the increased release time for

---

equally devoted fans. Whatever the case may be, what was at one time vicarious recreation for him and others becomes participant recreation for him. It involves the maintenance of standards, questions of reputation, etc. Such participation takes on more and more of the overtones of a typical occupational role. Above all, a sense of responsibility comes to be associated with such participation and from that point on the distinction between relaxation and work is difficult to maintain.

family interaction by the father and husband is regarded as an increase in leisure time generally and hence increased opportunity for activities viewed as importantly if not predominantly recreational. Insofar as this is true the family organization seems destined for a return as a focus of recreationally viewed activities. This may become a major specialized orientation within the family context as indicated above. To some extent this may off-set the tendency for the development of predominantly recreationally oriented organizations which to some extent have gone along with the increase in specialization of organizations in general in such societies. In recent developments in the United States, where these trends have perhaps been pushed to their furthest developments, the popular literature in magazines, newspapers, and other forms of mass communication have laid enormous stress on the word *togetherness* in discussions of ideal family life. Togetherness has in its turn had two major subemphases: the togetherness of the family members in religiously oriented activities and the togetherness of the family members in recreationally oriented activities. As indicated above, the development of the family as the special context for increased recreationally oriented activities promises to bring with it a new form of specialization within the context of family structure: an increasingly sharp division between the serious business of family life and the recreationally oriented activities carried out on an overwhelmingly family-oriented basis. This development may constitute a brake on tendencies which have generally been taken to connote family disintegration in relatively nonmodernized societies as they become relatively modernized and in relatively modernized societies as they become still more highly modernized. Initally in the development of increased modernization all relatively nonmodernized societies will be characterized by a radical alteration and restriction of the extent to which general behavior is overwhelmingly family or kinship oriented. As degrees of modernization are approached which are compatible with unimodal distributions of high levels of income with a considerably shortened highly specialized work week, the time spent by the average individual in a family context, albeit in relatively specialized recreationally oriented activities, will increase. The family and kinship orientation of the average individual will thereby be increased.[14]

[14] So far none of the large-scale attempts at radical restriction of family influence, such as the commune plan in Communist China, have been either stable or in general successful. Far from the tendency toward restriction of behavior in terms of family orientations continuing, there will be an enlargement of family-oriented behavior characterized by heavy emphasis on the recreational aspects of family life as indicated above. This is likely to take place within a special context of new departures in family

V
MISCELLANEOUS ORGANIZATIONS

A. INTRODUCTION

In the discussions above I have concentrated on the most strategic organizations, if not for all societies, at least for all societies of any considerable scale. Except for the discussion of kinship organizations in general and the family organization in particular, all of the discussion has focused on organizations specialized with regard to one aspect of behavior such as the economic, political, recreational, etc. These specialized organizations are those overwhelmingly likely to be strategic for students of public and international affairs. Attention has been focused on only one nonspecialized type of organization—the family—because a reasonable case can be made to the effect that it is overwhelmingly more important in understanding social organizations of

structures of other sorts. Given the medical technology characteristic of relatively modernized societies, the limitation of actual size of family membership primarily via high death rates over which the individual has little or no control is out of the question. From time to time these technological changes may be partially off-set by the phenomena of large-scale wars, but such events are not likely to have exactly the same implications for the discrepancy between ideal and actual family structures characteristic of quite primitive, inexplicit medical technology.

Under relatively modernized conditions the ideal family as well as the actual one will become increasingly the multilineal conjugal unit whose members will consist of father, mother, and nonadult children, or of husband and wife before children are born and after the children become adults. A radically new element may well be injected into this picture, however, by a fluctuating set of ideal family structures within this broad outline. In the past, for any given ideal family type, the number of children desired has tended to be either indefinitely large or in the cases of some relatively modernized societies, two children, preferably one of each sex. Under the new conditions of high modernization with the great emphasis on the family organization as a focus of recreationally oriented behavior there may well be a predictable fluctuation of ideal family size without departure from the ideal structure of multilineal conjugal family units as such. If this develops, it will take the form of the individuals of one generation, probably those reared in a family context of one or two children at most, desiring families of procreation involving three to five children. The children reared with several siblings may well return in their own ambitions to a preference for a family of procreation involving only two to three children. If such a tendency should develop, it would constitute something new under the sun in the general field of kinship phenomena. It would have nothing to do in the direct sense with the economics of family organization save for the fact that in the absence of a society in terms of which the average standard of living was an extremely high one with an extremely even distribution, the ideal number of children for any given generation would to a greater extent be a function of the potential role of children as contributors to family income. It would be directly related to the experiences of the children reared in one of these family contexts as opposed to the other and the impression made upon them by the recreational aspects of several as opposed to few siblings.

any sort in any sort of society than any other type of organization. The implications of action in terms of families are far-reaching for both specialized and nonspecialized organizations ideally and/or actually. Nevertheless, this treatment has ignored an enormously varied set of organizations which are not specialized with regard to any single aspect of behavior, however specialized they may be in other respects. These organizations are probably the more important the less highly modernized a given society is, but they are certainly not without significance in understanding even the most highly modernized of societies.

B. VARIED BASES FOR MISCELLANEOUS ORGANIZATIONS

We do not as yet have any typology of such organizations which is useful in the comparative analysis of any societies or even of any societies of considerable scale. Most of the taxonomies of organizations which we have are limited to quite restricted types of organizations in quite specific types of societies. Some of the most important of the organizations ignored here are those whose membership is based on age, friendship, neighborhood, and appendency to other organizations [e.g., The Parent Teachers Association which may be regarded as an appendent organization to schools]. These organizations are only examples of miscellaneous organizations although they have been selected as four types of special significance throughout history. Friendship and neighborhood organizations, for example, are undoubtedly universal in social history and of enormous and varying significance in understanding the general implications of social structure in both relatively modernized and relatively nonmodernized societies.

In a general sense a simple basis for distinction among these organizations is that between predominantly functionally specific organizations and predominantly particularistic ones. The former would cover a whole range of relatively specialized organizations such as those devoted to saving our forests etc. The latter would contain those organizations not only recruited on a highly particularistic basis, but also oriented to the bases of that recruitment. Age and neighborhood organizations would be examples of this sort, friendship organizations would generally fall into this category, and in a more detailed sense organizations such as Daughters of The American Revolution would be included. Predominantly functionally specific organizations are specialized in a different sense from the organizations discussed above as predominantly economically, politically, religiously, or otherwise oriented. The organizations under consideration here are not so much oriented as far as their members are concerned to an aspect of behavior as to a specific well-defined goal. These limited functional organizations are much more highly developed in relatively modernized social contexts than in relatively nonmodernized ones.[15]

The overwhelmingly particularistically based organization, however, are of enormous significance in all societies. For example, in most of the societies in which the interest is greatest here a great deal of what would have to be taken up from the point of view of societies in general under the heading of neighborhood organizations can be subsumed under the discussion of governmental type organizations. In societies of considerable scale whether relatively nonmodernized or not some governmental subsystems on a local or neighborhood basis are universal. Nevertheless, in both relatively nonmodernized and relatively modernized societies these predominantly particularistically oriented organizations will be of considerable significance for operation in terms of those organizations characterized by structures of highly specialized orientation to aspects of behavior. Thus, no matter what the governmental organization on a local basis may be, there will, ideally and/or actually, always be some local or neighborhood organization(s) of great significance for the actions carried out in terms of the governmental units, whether this is generally recognized or not.

C. THE SIGNIFICANCE OF MISCELLANEOUS ORGANIZATIONS

The significance of miscellaneous organizations in general social structure varies with whether or not societies are relatively modernized. In societies of any considerable scale the organizations of greatest and most obvious significance are always kinship [espe-

---

[15] The specialized organizations discussed in Chapter 2, Section V of this Part are usually predominantly functionally specific in the relationships of their various members qua members, but the criteria for membership is not orientation to nearly so specific and identical a goal. Any modern bureaucratic organization, ideally speaking at least, is characterized by subsets of relationships that are overwhelmingly functionally specific but what the leaders and others regard as the goals of the organization may be very broad and the individual members may be recruited on bases quite other than orientation to those goals which they are expected to seek once they have joined. The goal of a modern government is quite broadly defined by contrast with a "Save Our Forests Club" though it is predominately functionally specific in many respects. Furthermore, members join or are selected for membership in the government because they seek power, wealth, are drafted, have degrees in economics, etc. Ideally speaking at least, members join the "Save Our Forests Club" because they wish to save their forests. Other actual reasons are denigrated as meretricious.

cially family] organizations and specialized organizations of the type previously discussed in some detail. Miscellaneous organizations of the type discussed here are of considerable significance in understanding the integrative aspects of any society. In relatively nonmodernized societies, however, a considerable part of the interdependency of the general social structure at both local and broader levels inheres in organizations of this sort—especially those of a highly particularistic nature. Because of the ubiquity, frequency, and relevance of family orientations in such societies, these organizations form a set of organizations in terms of which members of different family organizations are interrelated with one another. Some such structures of interrelationships are probably essential if large-scale organizations of a specialized sort such as governments are to be viable in societies in which kinship orientations constitute the most numerous ones of the average individual even if, ideally speaking, they are not absolutely overriding ones from his point of view. Indeed, quite apart from the preceding problem, such miscellaneous organizations are probably essential in providing comparatively universalistic actual balances of predominantly particularistic factors.

In relatively modernized social contexts on the other hand the development of high emphases on predominantly universalistic criteria in general and on interdependency reduce the relevance of such organizations as intermediate forms of organization for more highly specialized organizations and ones of larger scale. Under these circumstances, however, the miscellaneous organizations have a different significance. The predominantly functionally specific organizations have a fairly obvious instrumental relevance to the accomplishment of the goals which define them as well as contributing to the general aspects of integration in the society by constituting a focus for like-minded individuals with so restricted a concern that all their other differences may be held to be irrelevant. Thus, social cohesion in general is increased by virtue of separating out of the extremely divided interests of many individuals various bases on which narrow but quite effective agreement is both possible and satisfying.

The predominantly particularistic organizations are primarily significant in relatively modernized social settings for the release action in terms of them affords the individual from the generally high emphasis in such social contexts on predominantly universalistic criteria. In the context of these organizations, no matter how humble an individual may be, it matters who he is. The basis for determining who he is is the more personal and detailed the more highly particularistic the orientation of the organization. In this sense, in relatively modernized societies, these predominantly particularistically based organizations are likely to be much oriented to recreational aspects of the behavior of their members. Even though they may not begin as predominantly recreationally oriented organizations, in relatively modernized social contexts they frequently turn into such specialized organizations.

Insofar as these organizations are in fact primarily significant in societies because of their integrative implications, the frequency of such organizations is relevant as indicating a setting in which charismatic leaders are likely to develop. Especially in relatively modernized societies, if the frequency of such organizations increases radically, that increase connotes a search for identity and meaning. Identity and meaning are exactly one of the major contributions of charismatic leaders to their followers. There is exactly the same sort of significance in the proliferation of such organizations in societies undergoing modernization from a relatively nonmodernized past.

There are many problems of the interdependencies of organizations of these sorts with the sorts of organizations discussed in greater detail above. Even in relatively nonmodernized societies in which organizations of this sort are intermediate organizations between family or kinship organizations on the one hand and more specialized organizations of the sort previously discussed on the other, the direct problems of interdependency tend to be minor save possibly in the case of the interdependency as between neighborhood organizations and governments. In both relatively modernized and relatively nonmodernized societies these organizations tend to stay separated from the other organizations discussed above. If this is not the case, organizations of this sort are converted into organizations of the type previously discussed or become subsystems of them. These miscellaneous organizations are just as much an essential of general social structure as organizations of the types discussed above. If the integrative aspect of these organizations is of the importance alleged in either relatively modernized or relatively nonmodernized societies, it would be difficult to understand how societies could remain stable in the absence of such organizations. In that sense they are just as much requisites of societies as any other form of organization. On the other hand, almost any radical change in either the kinship organization or any of the highly specialized organizations such as governments, churches, schools, etc., is likely to mark a social revolution on practically any level of generalization in which a student of public affairs would be greatly interested.

This is considerably less likely to be so of these organizations if only because of their more restricted scale and a greater likelihood of their being local in nature. These are organizations, par excellence, in terms of which interstitial adjustments take place. As such they are essential and highly relevant to operations in terms of other organizations, but no single interstitial adjustment as such is likely to be crucial for the entire social structure.

PART · IV

THE COMMON ELEMENTS,
VARIATIONS, AND PROBLEM FOCI

COMMON ELEMENTS AND MAIN LINES

OF VARIATION IN SOCIETIES

I

INTRODUCTION

Parts II and III are concerned with the categories of analysis which I hold to be the most basic and general ones for students of public and international affairs. In the discussion and elaboration of these matters I have emphasized the elements common to all societies and some of the major lines of variations of particular significance in understanding problems in this field. The next chapter treats the major problem foci in international affairs seen from the point of view of general social structure. Here, in summary form, I reiterate the respects in which all societies are everywhere alike and many of the major respects in which societies everywhere differ in their implications for behavior in terms of them. At the outset of this work I asserted that the two views—(1) that human beings and societies were everywhere the same and (2) that human beings and societies were everywhere different—are neither of them true as posed, nor do the two statements taken together constitute a paradox. It is trivially easy to demonstrate. Individual instances of societies like any other units are always the same when considered on the most general or abstract level. If they were not, we would have no basis for calling them all instances of the set of societies. The differences among societies become increasingly apparent and are increasingly great as more detailed description of them is sought. It is possible to go beyond the trivial level, however, and specify in greater detail some of the elements common to all societies and some of the main lines of variations among them. It is also possible to state in general form the main relationships between these common elements and main lines of variation. It is even possible to go into some detail with regard to less abstract statements of that interrelationship. The most general position here from this point of view holds that the main lines of variation among societies are in fact variations in the details of the common elements which characterize all societies. The variations among societies are never independent of the elements that characterize all societies.

The remainder of this chapter is divided in two parts. The first is concerned with the common elements characteristic of all societies. It is subdivided into the common aspects, the common units, the common aspects of any relationship, and the common problems faced by the members of any society. The second part is divided into a discussion of the range and nature of substantive variation, and the range and variation of the aspects of societies.

I I
THE COMMON ELEMENTS OF ALL SOCIETIES

A. THE COMMON ASPECTS OF ALL SOCIETIES

The common aspects of all societies have been treated in some detail above with some admixture of remarks about the ranges of variations among societies. The members of all societies have in common some concentration of attention on five aspects of behavior: role differentiation, solidarity, economic allocation, political allocation, and integration and expression [including such categories as socialization, religion, education, and recreation]. The members of a given society do not ordinarily think in terms neatly differentiated along these lines, but these aspects of their behavior are always highly structured. There is room in terms of any society for many idiosyncracies, but general behavior from these points of view is never random or chaotic if the society is at all stable.

1. ROLE DIFFERENTIATION

The structures of role differentiation furnish the most general lead to the aspects common to all societies. As a minimum in terms of all societies roles are differentiated on the basis of age, generation, sex, economic allocation, political allocation, and cognition.

a. AGE Not only are the roles of the members of societies always differentiated on the basis of age, but they are always differentiated on the basis of what has here been called absolute age as distinguished from relative age. In some fashion as a minimum the age categories of infancy, childhood, adulthood, and old age are distinguished and become an important focus for roles considered from many different points of view. The number of absolute age distinctions characteristic of any society is proliferated into at least five to seven categories, but whatever the details of those categories they always cut across and exhaust the four presented here. Thus, even if the exact categories characteristic of a particular society, are unknown, questions asked in terms of these four will elicit the different categories ideally and/ or actually distinguished by the members of the society as well as the most strategic roles and many of the less strategic ones associated with them. As a minimum the absolute age distinctions are always made within a family context in terms of every known society, but they are also frequently a major focus of organization in terms of other organizations. Roles distinguished on the basis of infancy and even those on the basis of childhood can be confined to the family context, but in every known society there are interrelationships that as a minimum involve members of two or more families and usually members of other families and other types of organizations. Some of these interrelationships must be focused on adulthood. Because of this focus on adulthood or the various subcategories into which it may be divided, in the more general nonfamily context there must also be some distinctions oriented to old age. The distinction of old age outside the family context as a minimum has to do with the ending of eligibility for holding adult roles in these contexts. The increasing imminence of death in general and the problems attendant on senility in particular make it essential that some attention be given to this sort of distinction if a society is to be stable.

In addition to the absolute age distinctions discernable in every family organization in every known society and carried over to some extent to organizational contexts other than the family, there are usually absolute age distinctions based on length of membership in a given organization. This is familiar in the form of retirement structures which are frequently reckoned on the basis of a given amount of time spent as a member of a given organization or is correlated with one of the age distinctions already mentioned. These distinctions often take the form of designation of those who have held a given office for a given number of years as having appropriate to their positions roles specifically differentiated on this basis [e.g., membership in the "twenty-five years of service club"].

Absolute age distinctions facilitate clear-cut classifications of sets of individuals. In addition the roles of members of all societies are also differentiated on the basis of their relative ages, that is to say, on the amount of elapsed time that one individual as opposed to another is considered to have spent in a given context. The most general form of such distinctions is elapsed time from birth, however birth is reckoned. Unlike the absolute age distinctions mentioned above, distinction on the basis of relative age is capable of indefinitely fine gradations in terms of any society. Absolute age distinctions on the other hand are always made in terms of a definite and relatively limited number of categories, whether that number be five or fifty. Not only are some of the roles always differentiated on the basis of relative age, but again as a minimum, some of those differentiations always take place within a kinship context in general and a family context in particular. In the kinship context relative age is always to some extent reckoned from the actual or presumed date of birth. In addition to relative age reckoned on the basis of elapsed time from birth and considered in a family context, relative age is always the basis for some differentiation of roles in some other organizational contexts. The members of nonfamily organizations always reckon relative age role differentiations on the basis of elapsed time as a member of the organization concerned or elapsed time as the holder of a particular role within the organization. Perhaps the most familiar form of this in our own society is the reckoning of seniority among the members of a particular organization. In relatively modernized contexts relative age is not so obvious a focus of role differentiation as it is in relatively nonmodernized ones, but no reasonably well-informed layman is unaware of the importance of seniority in such varied contexts as government, labor unions, business firms, universities, etc., let alone the family.

Differentiation of roles on the basis of relative age always have implications for the allocation of power and responsibility. All societies, and to some extent most if not all of the subsystems of a society are characterized by some differentiation of political roles on the basis of relative age, ideally and/or actually. Any subsystems of which this is not the case must either be small in scale or relatively casual and fleeting in importance. After all, knowledge about a given organization and operation in terms of it is always to some degree a function of the acquaintance that goes with membership. Imagine, for example, what it would mean to try to start even a local telephone company office with personnel all of whom began on exactly the same day. In some contexts relative age is assumed without ground to correlate highly with increased knowledge, skill, etc. In our revolt against such forms of particularism, we sometimes approach the opposite extreme of implication that relative age distinctions have nothing to do with predominantly universalistic criteria. That is not the case. It is quite obvious that there must also be some differentiation of the allocation of power and responsibility on the basis of absolute age distinctions; after all, infants cannot exercise power nor can they be held effectively responsible. Given the emphasis placed on predominantly universalistic criteria by the members of relatively modernized societies, however, the importance of relative age distinctions in the allocation of power and responsibility is not nearly so obvious.

b. GENERATION Within the kinship context in general and the family context in particular some roles are always differentiated on the basis of generation. As the term generation is defined here, role differentiation on the basis of generation is never identical with role differentiation on the basis of absolute age distinctions. Unlike such differentiation, role differentiation on the basis of generation is always confined to the kinship and family context, and only extends beyond that context when the area of extension is on an actual or simulated kinship or family basis. Frequently differentiations on the basis of generation and absolute age overlap, but from the point of view of the individuals concerned they are never taken as identical. Within the kinship and family contexts, people of the same absolute age classification but different generational categories always have some different roles. Furthermore, individuals of the same generational category but different absolute age classifications also always have some differentiated roles. These distinctions are characteristic as both ideal and actual structures of every known society although the members of the most highly modernized societies generally pay less attention to them than do the members of relatively nonmodernized societies. Not only is the generational basis of role differentiation not extended beyond the kinship and family context, but unlike the age distinctions referred to above there is no close analogy to this distinction outside those contexts save in the case of kinship simulation.[1] Role differentiation on the basis of generation is a matter of great importance from a wide variety of points of view in general social analysis. From the point of view of the student of public affairs in particular, however, it is generally relevant because the individual member of any society initially learns to behave in terms of distinctions between authority and responsi-

---

[1] As indicated above [see p. 99] there are social contexts in which generational and other kinship distinctions are widely simulated in a favorable spirit outside the kinship sphere. This always indicates an exceedingly heavy emphasis on kinship as the [or a] major form of proper and respectable identification. The absolute and relative age distinctions characteristic of nonkinship contexts are not necessarily simulations of those appropriate in the kinship sphere. For example, the term *freshman* is now widely exported from the educational sphere. If one goes into sufficient descriptive detail, there must be some absolute and relative age distinctions peculiar to each organization. This does not hold of generational distinctions.

bility in the context of generational distinctions. No matter how predominantly universalistic may be the bases for roles of authority and responsibility in other contexts such as government, predominantly economically oriented organizations, etc., the individual always learns to react to such distinctions initially in a family context in which generational distinctions, ideally or actually, realistically or simulatively, are of the essence of the learning involved. In this sense the emphasis placed by modern psychiatrists and psychoanalysts on the relation between authority in general and father figures [or mother figures] may be quite tenable despite the fact that many of the contexts in which authority is exercised have nothing else to do with the kinship or family context.

c. SEX In family and other social contexts some roles are always differentiated on the basis of sex. As a minimum sex roles are differentiated on the usual dual basis, though social history is not without examples of more Byzantine distinctions on the basis of sex. Not only are roles always differentiated on this basis to some extent, but ideally speaking at least, there are always some roles which are exclusively male as distinguished from female roles and vice versa. Given the long revolt against the more simple forms of biological determinism, no social scientist today can state unequivocally to what extent the differentiation of roles on the basis of sex has a clear-cut purely biological basis. Whatever such a basis may be, the actual and ideal differentiations of roles on the basis of sex always go well beyond any such purely biological basis. The fact that some sex roles are exclusively identified with individuals of one sex, quite apart from any purely biological basis of the distinction concerned, is quite enough to account for the fact that even in those roles in which individuals of either sex may participate, distinctions on the basis of sex continue to have social effects. In our own society, for example, females as well as males may become university professors and medical doctors. There is also no question that actually, even if not ideally, the role of a female doctor or professor is different from that of a male doctor or professor. Not only are roles differentiated on the basis of sex, but from the point of view of the members of every known society to some extent personality differences are also conceived to cut along these lines, even though the personality traits considered muliebrous by the members of one society may be considered virile by the members of another.

Finally, the differentiation of these roles begins for the average member of any society in a family context, as might be expected. Contrary to any materials which may be given in any literature on the equal treatment of infants of different sexes, this differentiation of roles always begins with some of the earliest perceptions by the infant of differentiations in his [or her] treatment by others. There is no society for whose members in general role differentiation on the basis of sex has not been almost certainly firmly fixed by the time the child is two years of age reckoned from his [or her] biological birth. This is not to argue that the attitudes of an individual in these respects cannot be radically altered subsequent to this time, but merely that some attitudes on this score are set by this stage in the life cycle. Anent every society the inculcation of role differentiation on the basis of sex is always an actual barrier, even if not an ideal one, to puristically universalistic treatment of individuals. Sex role differentiations always make a difference, and some of the differences are bound to be nongermane for some purposes of selection.

d. OTHER COMMON BASES [ECONOMIC ALLOCATION, PO-LITICAL ALLOCATION, COGNITION, AND THE NONHUMAN ENVIRONMENT] Beyond the categories of role differentiation on the basis of age, generation, and sex, role differentiation on the basis of economic allocation, political allocation, cognition and the nonhuman environment is characteristic of all societies as has been brought out in Part II, Chapter 2. Beyond a brief reiteration of what has been said there it is only necessary to add one special item. Role differentiation on these bases is frequently primarily determined on the basis of role differentiation of the three general types mentioned above. The reverse is not necessarily true. Indeed, it is seldom true. Thus, who does what and when with regard to the allocation of goods and services is frequently primarily determined by criteria of age, generation, or sex. The same is true of political allocation, cognition, and role differentiation on the basis of a nonhuman environment. On the other hand, although age role differentiation may have to do with different roles in economic or political allocation, etc., indeed they commonly do, one is not ordinarily classified in a given age category in a given relative age position, in a given generational position, or in a given sex position, primarily on the basis of economic allocation, political allocation, cognition or the nonhuman environment.

There are a few exceptions to this. The most universal of these exceptions has to do with the relation between role differentiation on the basis of political allocation and role differentiation on the basis of absolute age. In some cases, ideally if not actually, a given individual is classified by other members of his society as an adult upon being classified as having certain roles of authority, regardless of whether or not he would ordinarily be classified as an adult at that stage of his life cycle. In this sense role differentiation on the basis of age, generation, and sex may be considered to underlie the role differentiations of all societies on all other bases.[2] Although one wishes to avoid naive forms of biological determinism, it is hard not to contemplate some form of explanation with strong biological overtones for this state of affairs.[3] Although with the exception noted, differentiations on the basis of age, generation, and sex are not ordinarily determined by other forms of role differentiation, there is no question but that other forms of role differentiation are so identified with various combinations of role differentiation on the basis of age, generation, and sex that departures from the ordinary ideal structures in these respects will alter the overtones appropriate to roles differentiated on the basis of age, generation, and sex. For example, in the context of a society in terms of which women do not ordinarily hold roles of command in armed force organizations, a woman who actually commands an army unit will not be classified as a male, but she is overwhelmingly likely to be considered as having acquired certain virile attributes specifically regarded as incompatible or contradictory to her roles as a woman. The same sorts of observations may be made with regard to differentiations on the basis of age and generation. In any situation of general social change, the increase in what previously would have been considered contradictory combinations of this sort radically heightens the sources of stress and strain which may at one and the same time further undermine the old order and impede the stable

[2] Since basic role differentiation on the bases of age, generation, and sex always takes place in a family context for the average individual, the view taken here of the strategic position of the family in general social structure is reinforced.

[3] Insofar as this line of hypotheses is tenable, it has interesting implications for the vulgar or more simplistic forms of economic determinism at least. It argues that age, generational and sex distinctions always influence action to some extent, that economic roles, political roles, etc., are frequently a function of age, sex and generational roles, but that an individual's age, generation, and sex roles are rarely a function of those former role differentiations. This would imply that to some extent at least economic allocation may be a dependent variable of sex role differentiation whereas an individual's sex roles are rarely, if ever, a dependent variable of his [or her] economic roles. Q.E.D. there are some instances at least in which economic factors are not the sole causal factors—are even dependent variables.

attainment of a new order. This is, of course, especially likely to be true of transitions toward radically greater modernization.

Within the category of role differentiation on the basis of economic allocation the most general distinction useful for analysis in all societies is that between consumption roles and production roles, granted the sense in which one of these is the obverse of the other as previously discussed [pp. 210–211, 231–232]. Some role differentiation on the basis of economic allocation is always present in the context of family organization, and in all societies there is always some differentiation of roles on this basis outside a family context. For the vast majority of the members of a relatively nonmodernized society, however, role differentiation on the basis of economic allocation outside a family context may be highly restricted. Such nonfamily roles in such societies usually mark a highly specialized category of members in the society. Frequently it is the mark of an elite category.

In the sphere of role differentiation on the basis of political allocation the most important distinction has to do with the roles of authority as distinguished from roles of responsibility. Exactly the same sort of additional remarks made about role differentiations on the basis of economic allocation and the family context may be made. Here, however, some additional remarks can be made. Some of the role differentiation on the basis of political allocation outside the family context is always the mark of elite members of the society, if only because of the implication of such roles for governmental leadership. This holds true both ideally *and* actually in all known societies. There is a further addition with regard to role differentiation on the basis of political allocation. These roles are always hierarchical rather than egalitarian. No society consists of members all or most of whom have mutually reciprocal roles of authority and responsibility. Moreover, hierarchical distinction in terms of authority and responsibility is always considered from the point of view of the members of the society to constitute an invidious distinction. In this respect if no other, some elements of stratification inhere in every known society.

Finally, with regard to role differentiation on the basis of political allocation, it is important for students of public affairs to realize that such roles exist in all organizations, not just in governments and organizations associated with governments. In relatively modernized social contexts we are so accustomed to speaking of both the economic and political aspects of behavior as specialized realms that we tend to loose sight of both the importance and the legitimacy of politically differentiated roles in nonpolitically specialized organizations. They always do exist, however, and the members of societies not used to our highly specialized way of looking at things often find us difficult to understand for this reason—and we them. Furthermore, even in the context of our own highly specialized society the relative insensitivity to these matters displayed by general laymen and academics by contrast with the sophistication in these respects of professional politicians with a great deal of practical experience leads to a considerable amount of misunderstanding and even disillusionment with things as they exist in terms of our own society.

All societies exhibit a differentiation of roles on the basis of knowledge at least to the extent that there is a distinction between basic and intermediate knowledge. There is a special relationship between those who are in possession of the basic knowledge of the society, and those who incorporate the intermediate or more specialized knowledge characteristic of the members of the society. As a minimum the basic knowledge must contain sufficient relevance for the intermediate knowledge so that the more restricted personnel who command the latter may communicate with some of the former sooner or later—if the society is to be stable or if the intermediate knowledge is to be maintained. Again, those of us who live in highly modernized contexts are so accustomed to an unbelievably proliferated range of specialized knowledge taught, preserved, and increased in highly specialized predominantly educationally oriented organizational contexts that we tend to ignore the enormous substratum of basic knowledge that is more or less taken for granted.

The degree of specialization and proliferation of intermediate knowledge may vary enormously from one society to another, but if a method of measurement could be found, the ratio of intermediate to basic knowledge for the members of any given society probably approaches a constant. What is most striking to the observer of a highly modernized society by contrast with an observer of a relatively nonmodernized society is the enormous proliferation of highly specialized learning. At least as noticeable, however, is the fact that the basic learning taken for granted by the average member of the society, if he is to operate normally in that environment, is a breadth of general learning quite out of all context with that taken for granted for the average member of the average, or even of *any*, relatively nonmodernized society. The members of traditional Chinese society probably carried the development of the private scholar to its highest point in social history, but even there the urge to publish was marked, and the importance of a basis for communication between the have's and the have-not's of specialized knowledge was clear-cut.[4]

There is another special feature about role differentiation on the basis of knowledge characteristic of any society about which the members of relatively highly modernized societies are likely to have an especially biased set of views. Regardless of what one's views on epistemology or ontology may be, from the point of view of members of a society, knowledge or cognition is never confined to what we consider rationally defensible knowledge, i.e., scientifically tenable knowledge, or its opposite, i.e., errors scientifically demonstrable. Because of the tremendous developments in the scientific field, never has scientific and its closely associated technological knowledge seemed so clear-cut to so large a section of the planet's population as is the case today. Nevertheless, the general membership of even the most highly modernized of societies does not consider that sort of knowledge to be the only sort of knowledge at either the basic or the intermediate level. What might be termed *arational* knowledge [as quite distinct from *irrational* knowledge] is important for understanding the ideas, the attitudes, and the action of the membership of all societies including the most highly modernized ones. The fact that knowledge about ethics, religion, artistic productions of all sorts, and the like may well not appear in rational form never means that such knowledge is of negligible importance. Even though the knowledge involved appears to be arational or even irrational from the point of view of a given student of a given situation, it does not follow that the situation can easily be altered by presenting alternative knowledge in a rational form.

Role differentiation on the basis of knowledge has one special aspect in all societies because of the importance of the distinction between basic and intermediate knowledge. From one point of view roles are not generally differentiated on the basis of basic knowledge, since it is assumed that this is the case of knowledge that every individual in the society will acquire at some stage of

[4] As indicated in the discussion of recreation in the preceding chapter, the average Chinese, even though illiterate, was to an unusual extent informed about the history and the classics held to be of such importance in his society by those in possession of more specialized knowledge including literacy. Typically, I have probably pushed too far in maintaining that there must exist some sort of constant relationship between the intermediate and the basic knowledge characteristic of any society. Certainly it would not be nearly so rash to maintain that the expansion and specialization of intermediate knowledge cannot vary independently of the basic knowledge characteristic of the members of a society, that the elaboration and increase of the former tend always to vary directly with elaboration and increase of the latter.

his life cycle. Nevertheless, there are important distinctions on this basis. The major role differentiation with regard to this kind of knowledge is that between the *have's* and the *have-not's*. There are those who do not have this knowledge because they are unable to acquire it or utilize it. This defect may be the result of a social situation considered pathological by the members of the society, that is a given set of individuals may simply be deprived of legitimate opportunity for acquiring such knowledge [i.e., the *socially pathological have-not's*], or it may be the result of biologically pathological conditions which restrict the individual's ability to learn [i.e., the *biologically pathological have-not's*]. Neither category can ever amount to a substantial proportion of the society if that society is to be stable. The members of a society who are have-not's in these senses always require special treatment and handling even if they are ruthlessly disposed of.

Apart from this special consideration, there is always a set of *normal have-not's*. These are the individuals who have not yet reached the stage in the life cycle at which they are expected to acquire the given portion of the basic knowledge about which they are classified as have-not's. The most obvious case of this sort are the newborn members of all societies. At birth they are always normal have-not's in this respect. The role of *normal cognitive have-not's* is closely correlated in all societies with role differentiations on the basis of absolute age. Indeed, some age distinctions of this sort may be based on whether a particular kind of knowledge has been acquired or not. Apart from the *pathological cognitive have-not's*, have-not's with regard to basic cognition are primarily differentiated on the basis of the timing and rate at which they acquire this knowledge.

Role differentiation on the basis of intermediate knowledge in all societies is quite different. Questions of timing and rate are certainly involved, and conditions considered pathological are also involved. Apart from these differentiations, however, the essence of intermediate cognitive role differentiation has to do with substantive distinctions about the knowledge at the disposal of the individuals concerned. The state of typologies of knowledge for analyzing problems of this sort leaves much to be desired.

Basic knowledge is a *sine qua non* for general communication in terms of a given society. In drawing a distinction between relatively modernized and relatively nonmodernized societies on the basis of uses of inanimate sources of energy and of tools, I have accented the hypothesis that since some evidences of both of these measures are associated with any society—that some more developed applications of them are to some extent understandable across even the greatest gaps in such developments as between the members of one society and another. In addition the common elements in role differentiation on the basis of age, generation, sex, economic allocation, and political allocation as well as cognition give some common bases of communication with regard to social structures as between any members of any two societies regardless of how different these may be in other respects. One must add to this an additional element of general communication on the basis of cognition. Different types of arational knowledge may be more or less completely opaque to individuals of radically different social backgrounds, but there are no differences in social background so radical that some rational knowledge is not a part of the basic knowledge of the members of the societies concerned. Apart from biologically pathological cases of cognitive have-not's, there are no individuals in any society completely incapable or completely without experience of applications of rational knowledge. Furthermore, the breadth and depth of rational knowledge as a part of the basic knowledge characteristic of every society is never narrowly confined to a single item or element of behavior. Across any and all differences of social custom and languages the common elements of rational emphasis of the basic knowledge associated with all societies and the acquisition of this knowledge as an important element in the ordinary roles of every individual make communication possible across any known social gulfs. Once that communication is begun it can always be expanded.[5]

In all societies to some extent role differentiation is based on variations in the nonhuman environment. Some of these variations are so exceedingly general that here again we have one of the basic elements in the possibility of communication among people of radically different social experiences. Variations in night and day, seasonal variations, topographical variations and the like are all examples of factors in the nonhuman environment on the basis of which roles are differentiated. Even if the members of a society are all located in a physical environment such that seasonal variations are minimal, all of the nonhuman environmental factors are never constant. The extent of role differentiation on the basis of these factors varies enormously, of course, but there is always some. Developments in technology may make it possible in relatively highly modernized social con-

[5] This sort of hypothesis has long been both implicit and explicit in the writing of science fiction. Now it is a matter of quite serious study by natural scientists who have become preoccupied with establishing communications with other sentient beings from other worlds. Some common core of rational knowledge is assumed by these scientists—across space.

texts to set aside role differentiations that were previously taken for granted.[6] Some may change radically or be eliminated altogether, but no technological developments known or envisaged hold any promise whatsoever for eliminating all such role differentiations. Indeed, as indicated above [see p. 219] some of these new departures make for new role differentiations oriented to such factors.

2. SOLIDARITY

It is possible to go far beyond the statement that in all societies structures of solidarity exist both ideally and actually. There is some exploration of these matters in Part II, Chapter 4. One of the most general observations about solidarity is that the strengths of solidarities do not necessarily vary directly with the intensities of the solidarities concerned. Furthermore, in all societies, actually if not ideally [but probably to some extent in both respects], the strengths and intensities of some solidarities have an inverse relationship to one another rather than a direct reinforcement of one another. To put this matter simply, in the histories of all societies there are always some people with whom an individual sticks despite the fact that he doesn't feel strongly about them in a positive sense or despite the fact that he feels very strongly about them in a negative sense, even to the extent of strong dislike, fear, etc. Many have held that the emotional attitudes of participants in particular relationships must be positive and strong if those solidarities are important for the maintenance of a given system and if the system is to be maintained. What is equally true, if not equally important in some statistical sense, is that the strength of some solidarities is enormously important regardless of what the emotional attitudes of the participants in the solidarity may be.[7] It is so obvious and so striking that this cannot be true of all solidarities in any society that the qualification emphasized here may be overlooked or underemphasized.

Some common foci of solidarities are characteristic of all societies. The most obvious one of these is kinship, and the minimal organizational focus of kinship solidarities for every known society is some sort of family. For all societies of any relevance here, some form of government is also a focus of solidarities. Even in

[6] Professional baseball playing, well within the memory of man, was exclusively a daytime role, for example.

[7] In the context of societies whose members pride themselves on their general democratic procedures, members of the armed forces who are made uneasy by the fact that the precedence of rank is not necessarily highly correlated with ability are told that they must learn to salute the uniform and not the man.

societies characterized by specialized predominantly economically oriented organizations, these are not necessarily a focus of solidarity for more than a small proportion of the general membership of the society. The same may be said of predominantly religiously oriented organizations, predominantly educationally oriented organizations, etc. In understanding any society, family organization as a focus for solidarity is of special importance because in all societies the family context is the first context in which behavior in terms of structures of solidarity are learned. In some contexts governmental structures of solidarity may be learned at an early age as well, but this is certainly not true of any and all societies—whereas it is of the family.

One of the major reasons for treating role differentiation as the first of the common aspects is that it affords a set of concepts in terms of which all of the other aspects common to all societies can to some degree be treated. This is particularly obvious in the case of the structures of solidarity. In all societies a minimal set of solidarities may be derived in terms of minimal combinations of role differentiations necessary if any society is to persist.[8] There must as a minimum be solidarities between adults and infants, between adults and children, between adults and the aged, that there must be some solidarities among family members of the same generation and family members of different generations, some on the basis of sex role differentiation, and so forth. As a minimum if the society is to survive those solidarities must be such as to support a viable form of family organization and some minimal organized types of relationships among the members of two or more families.

3. ECONOMIC ALLOCATION

In all societies there are discoverable structures of allocation of goods and services. Contrary to the usual presuppositions of the members of highly modernized societies, these structures are not necessarily specialized out of the general social structure and confined to predominantly economically oriented organizations. Such specialization need not exist in all cases though some does exist in all societies of any considerable scale. In all societies

---

[8] Once again it is important to emphasize the fact that the survival of no given society is guaranteed in advance, as far as we know. The statement that something is necessary for a given society if it is to persist does not even imply that if that particular condition is present the society will necessarily continue. It only implies that if that condition is absent or is going out of existence, the society cannot continue to survive or will shortly be going out of existence. Particularly when questions of modernization are relevant, the societies concerned can be unstable.

there are some organizations of strategic significance in the allocation of goods and services which are not specialized on an
economic basis, and the examples par excellence of this are
families and governments. Not only are there always some cases
not specialized on an economic basis, but there are always some
cases not specialized relative to any particular aspect of social
behavior, that is to say there are always some units such as family
units which are not predominantly oriented to any single aspect
of behavior. Finally, there are always some organizations that are
strategic for understanding the allocation of goods and services
characteristic of a given society and that are not specialized with
regard to economic orientation though specialized with regard to
some other aspect of behavior. The minimal example of this is, of
course, the government, but other examples such as churches,
schools, etc., frequent social history.

Without getting involved in economic determinism, regardless
of the language used, and despite the lack of economic specialization in some cases, there is always some self-conscious awareness
on the part of the members of the society of some problems of
economic allocation. Moreover, they are always aware of some of
the general relevance of allocations of goods and services for
other aspects of behavior. The general membership of a society is
never indifferent to the allocation of goods and services. Finally,
the general membership of every known society share some
conception (s) of social improvement, and one criterion of social
improvement is always some sort of increase in the allocation of
goods and services. Increased wealth has never been identified
solely as an evil or a matter of indifference by the general membership of any society.

Regardless of differences in language the general membership
of all societies distinguish between the production of goods and
services and the consumption of goods and services. If and insofar as predominantly economically oriented organizations exist,
they are always regarded as foci of production. Consumption is
always considered an aspect of behavior in terms of a relatively
unspecialized or multipurpose organization or of an organization
specialized on the basis of an aspect of behavior other than a
strictly economic one.

Some action in terms of the structures of economic allocation
is always actually rational in all societies. Ideally speaking, that
action may also be predominantly traditional, if the traditions
happen to coincide with what is rational under the circumstances. To the extent that the rational and the traditional structures coincide there need not be any self-conscious recognition by

the members of the society of an emphasis on rational behavior. They behave rationally with regard to economic allocation because the traditional structures do in fact coincide with rational ones. Nevertheless, there is always some self-conscious recognition of rational behavior in this sphere by the general membership of any society, and hence probably there is always some action which both ideally and actually is rational in this sphere. The likelihood of the sphere of economic allocation as a special focus for rationality is based on the extremely instrumental attitude general among members of all societies toward some allocations of goods and services and on the clear-cut empirical nature of some at least of the processes involved in handling goods and services. It is doubtful whether any such strong statements about the inevitability of both ideal and actual structures of rationality can be made about either the structures of role differentiations or solidarity except insofar as they focus on economic and political allocation as will be indicated below. Given the general importance of any emphasis on rationality as a basis for communication across radically different social lines, the high probability of some rational behavior with regard to economic allocation [9] is of great importance not only because of the intrinsic importance of problems of economic allocation themselves, but also as the basis for establishing clearly defined and mutually intelligible bases of communication as between individuals of radically different social backgrounds.

For the average individual the family organization is the main focus of what he regards as consumption although there may be important additional organizational foci of consumption as far as he is concerned. The family is also actually always an important focus of what may be regarded as production, but the average individual does not necessarily regard it as such. Failure to regard the family as a focus of production for the average member of a society is overwhelmingly a development characteristic of the members of relatively modernized societies. It exists in relatively nonmodernized social contexts, but there it is ordinarily confined

[9] It is not really reckless to push this matter further. Not only must there be *some* rational behavior in the allocation of goods and services; there must be a quite considerable absolute amount and a quite considerable proportion of all such behavior—even if much of it is actually rational only because the rational and traditional ways happen to coincide. Even when the two coincide, the individuals concerned may appreciate what they are doing quite rationally. There can, of course, be no gainsaying the considerable force of traditional preferences, but some of what is taken to be purely traditional behavior without self-conscious rationality may be more a function of a difficult language barrier than of accurate observation of a lack of rational understanding.

to relatively restricted types of individuals—usually an elite group. Finally, for all societies the family is the organization in terms of which most initial and basic learning about allocations of goods and services take place.

4. POLITICAL ALLOCATION

At least in all societies of any considerable scale, there always exists at least one organization predominantly oriented to the allocation of power and responsibility. Such organizations always constitute a special focus of the allocation of power and responsibility as far as the members of the society as a whole are concerned, even though the government may not in fact be an organization in terms of which a monopoly of the use of force is concentrated. There can be nongovernmental organizations in the society which are stronger. Never completely apart from, but always in addition to, these specialized predominantly politically oriented organizations, there exist in every society well-defined structures of the allocation of power and responsibility characteristic of every other organization both ideally and actually. All organizations also always have some structures of allocation of power and responsibility that are not well defined ideally and/or actually. There are always some relationships whose members have mutually equal powers and responsibility, but egalitarian relationships never constitute more than a special and restricted set of the total relationships in the society. Regardless of different emphases on authoritarianism as opposed to democracy, regardless of mottoes such as liberty, equality, and fraternity, the vast majority of all relationships are hierarchical as far as the allocation of power and responsibility are concerned. Regardless of Utopian or other ideal structures, no large-scale organization in any society has ever actually been organized on an egalitarian basis or even on a close approach to such a basis. The larger the scale of any given organization, the smaller is the likelihood of egalitarian structures of organization. Relatively restricted friendship-type relations constitute the major models for egalitarian allocations of power and responsibility. However important these organizations may be to their members, and hence to the societies which they characterize, they are always restricted in extent, in scale, and in their proportion to other types of relationships. Furthermore, the members of egalitarian relationships always participate in hierarchical relationships with others. Some of the latter always take precedence over the nonhierarchical relationships. Some of the demands placed on the individual in terms of some of his hierarchically defined relationships always take critical precedence over his obligations in terms of egalitarian friendships. *Egalitarian friendship is never a general organizing principle in any society.*

It has become commonplace to think of political allocation in general and governments in particular in terms of specialized foci such as the executive, the legislative, and the judicial functions. These are certainly distinguished on a specialized organizational basis by the members of many societies. Nevertheless, often such specialization does not occur at all or is not highly developed. Anent such societies the only distinctions possible on this basis are those made by an observer as an aid to analysis rather than those made by the members as a template for action. If that is the case, however important analysis in those terms may be, the form taken by the analysis will not ordinarily be a form in terms of which a member of that society does or can understand either his own behavior or the behavior of his fellow members from the political point of view. Furthermore, even when such specialized organizations exist, there are always other important allocations of power and responsibility in the organizational contexts in which distinctions of this sort are not drawn. Thus, although these distinctions are strongly drawn in the context of the government of the United States both ideally and actually, we do not ordinarily distinguish predominantly executively, legislatively, and judicially oriented subsystems of the family. They are also frequently not drawn in the context of organizations such as business firms, schools, churches, etc.

The position of the family is again strategic. Initial learning and some of the most important basic learning of structures of political allocation takes place in a family context in all known societies for nearly all individuals. The political aspects of behavior so learned may be offset and even reversed, but all other behavior from this point of view represents some alteration or incorporation of these early experiences. Within the family context political allocation is always differentiated on the basis of age, generation, and sex. The experiences of the individual on the basis of age and sex role differentiation with regard to political allocation is always generalized beyond the family context as well. Authority generally varies directly with both absolute and relative age distinctions.[10] Within the family context exactly the

[10] This requires some qualification to take care of problems of senility and death of the aged, if the society is stable. Usually this is handled via retirement structures or structures whereby the aged have ideal though not actual power. After all, tales of true gerontocracies not withstanding, it is possible to give the aged both ideal and actual power, but it is not possible

same thing is true with regard to generational differences, precedence going to individuals of the older generation. This generational distinction is not, of course, directly transferred outside a kinship context, but outside of the kinship context it does tend to reinforce the precedence of authority on the basis of absolute age distinctions. For example, ordinarily the distinction between adults and children is reinforced by the distinction within a given family between individuals of older and younger generations.[11]

There is another universal distinction in social history, regardless of how predominantly universalistic the ethical views of the members of any society about sex differences may be. The members of every known society have preferred to grant precedence with regard to the allocation of power within the family context on the basis of sex, and that allocation has always favored some individuals of the male sex over females. This has also always been generalized to some contexts outside the family sphere.[12] Societies are always male dominated ideally and actually. The actual extent of male domination may be less than the ideal extent, of course, but the reverse is more likely to be the case, since the males are more likely to favor male domination and to some extent so are the females. All extant descriptions of Amazonian and matriarchal societies require qualification.

As in the case of economic allocation, regardless of the degree of specialization of organizations from the political point of view within a given society, there always exists members who from their own points of view self-consciously aim at rationality with regard to the allocation of power and responsibility. Here again, regardless of the importance of tradition or other nonrational concerns, there always exists some action that is both ideally and

---

to balance those with actual responsibility. From this point of view the real problem is senility rather than death. The aged cannot be held effectively responsible after death, but they cannot continue to wield power in a capricious fashion either. The senile person cannot be held effectively responsible, but he can continue to exercise power in ways that can be quite upsetting. No true gerontocracy could be stable since a balance of power and responsibility could not be maintained reliably over any extended period. All apparent gerontocracies are characterized by special retirement structures and/or structures in terms of which ideal and actual powers and responsibilities are carefully separated, with the ideal ones devolving on the aged and the actual ones on younger adjutants of some sort.

[11] It is possible, of course, for individuals of an older generation to be younger in absolute age terms than individuals of a younger generation, but ordinarily these two reinforce rather than contradict one another.

[12] I do not intend this mode of statement to imply that male precedence in this sense can have no other origin than experience in the family context, though as a minimum it always does have that basis.

actually rational with regard to the allocation of power and re-sponsibility. Thus regardless of the strength of tradition for the members of a given society, some communication about political allocation in purely rational terms is always possible. It may, of course, be difficult for individuals from radically different social backgrounds in radically different societies to locate the minimal basis on which such communication is possible.

5. INTEGRATION AND EXPRESSION

There are always well understood structures of integration and expression in any society. From the point of view of the members of the society, these are differentiated in terms of education, religion, recreation, etc. In all societies once again the family is the focus of the initial learning and of some of the most impor-tant action in terms of these aspects of behavior. However much the family may be a special focus of these aspects of behavior, it is never the sole context of importance in these respects. Every individual in every society must be socialized so that he can interrelate with individuals who are not members of his family and express himself in such contexts without causing undue friction. In the context of some societies, the opportunities for such associations may be highly restricted by contrast with oth-ers, but some are always present and crucial if the society is to be stable.

B. COMMON ORGANIZATIONS

1. FAMILY

It will come as no surprise if I suggest the family as the surest and most fundamental of the organizations common to all societies. The family is always a major focus of social structure in general and most of its special aspects in particular, and for most of the members of most of the societies the family has been *the* major focus of social behavior. It is not necessary to reiterate certain universally strategic characteristics of the family already empha-sized in this chapter, though those generalizations are relevant here. In all societies the family is a type of organization in terms of which the average individual has roles at every stage in his life cycle, and the family is the only type of organization of which this generalization holds true for all societies. In addition, the roles the individual has in the family context are always relevant ideally and/or actually for his roles in all other organizations distinguished by the members of his society. In the context of most societies his roles in the family have been relevant to his roles in other organizations ideally speaking as well as actually speaking. Even given those societies in terms of which family considerations are not supposed to intrude on an individual's behavior outside the family context, however, it is well known that they do in fact influence the individual to some extent, whether he wishes that to be the case or not.

Sometimes generalizations about the family which will be relevant in all societies seem hopelessly blocked by the enormous variations in the ideal structures of family structure at least. This enormous variation need not be so great a cause for concern as it has generally been. Regardless of variations in ideal structures, in terms of all matters having to do with behavior in a family context that are affected by the numbers of individuals involved, the age distribution, the sex distribution, the generational distribution, the number of siblings and the number of spouses involved, etc., the actual structures throughout history have been far more similar than has generally been suspected. The vast majority of all actual families in social history have probably consisted for most of the time of father, mother, and nonadult children with the average number of the latter living at any point in time being two or slightly more. The sex distribution of those children has been such that roughly 50 per cent of the families involve one boy and one girl, roughly 25 per cent two boys, and roughly 25 per cent two girls. Insofar as the ideal structures have differed from these, the discrepancy between ideal and actual structures can be looked to to explain certain sources of stress and strain in the family context, but they must also be looked to to explain certain possibilities of integration and adjustment within the family context. The enormous developments in the field of anthropology in the last few decades have lent great emphasis to the richness of variety of ideal family structures around the world. Nevertheless, the core of uniformity with regard to family structures emphasized here implies, just as does the common existence of tools which are to some extent rationally understood, a focus of behavior about which communication can be established among individuals from the most diverse backgrounds. Thus, for example, although it may not be true that the members of all societies maintain that "a boy's best friend is his mother," it is true that in all known societies the concept of mother is always meaningful to the boys and that it has some common core of meaning.

To the extent that the hypotheses presented here about the family are correct, analysis of family organizations is not only the most general lead-in that one can establish to the analysis of any society, but it is also a lead-in in terms of which individuals of any two different societies have one of the highest probability of communication in mutually understandable terms.

2. GOVERNMENT

Governments are mentioned here and before because the argument for the universality of governments as well as their level of development is on a much sounder basis than any corresponding argument for predominantly economically oriented organizations. Governments, if not characteristic of all societies, are certainly characteristic of all societies of any considerable scale. In addition, governmental organizations are never confined in their membership solely to restricted elite individuals or restricted outcast individuals. Only two items about governments need be reiterated here. First, governments always involve a combination of centralization and decentralization. Closely related to this is the fact that, appearances to the contrary notwithstanding, all governments of any considerable stability in relatively non-modernized societies have been characterized by critical elements of decentralization. Never until relatively high levels of modernization have been reached, has overwhelming centralization been a characteristic that *could be* combined with stability. Second, there are always associated with governmental organizations problems of predominantly particularistic selection regardless of whether, ideally speaking, governmental organizations are predominantly universalistic or predominantly particularistic. There are two problems about particularistic criteria as far as governmental organizations are concerned. First, insofar as the governmental organizations are, ideally speaking, predominantly universalistic, departures in the direction of particularism always undercut these ideal structures. However, even if the governmental organizations are, ideally speaking, predominantly particularistic, there always intrude on operations in governmental terms some predominantly particularistic factors other than those that, ideally speaking, are supposed to intrude. The key to some problems of governmental reorganization is not necessarily conversion of government officials to predominantly universalistic standards but rather the insistence that they hold to the predominantly particularistic standards which they profess.

Finally, in trying to understand the level of centralization which can be attained and maintained in terms of a given society, the level of knowledge at the disposal of the leaders of the government is as important as the amount and type of force at the disposal of the leaders. High levels of centralization can sometimes be maintained with relatively low levels of exercise of force, but they can never be maintained with relatively low levels of exercise of intelligence. Knowledge is not necessarily power, but there is no power without it.

3. PREDOMINANTLY ECONOMICALLY ORIENTED ORGANIZATIONS

One of the most important distinctions between predominantly economically oriented organizations in societies in general and either governments or families lies in the fact that these predominantly economically oriented organizations, if present, may be regarded, ideally speaking, as illegitimate organizations, whereas neither families nor governments are ever so regarded, even though some members of a given society may oppose the government or oppose given family structures. Whether considered legitimate or illegitimate, whenever predominantly economically oriented organizations do exist, they are important in understanding the behavior of the members of the society. If they are considered, ideally speaking, to be illegitimate, there will always be relationships between their members and the members of legitimate organizations which will also be considered illegitimate. Under these circumstances predominantly economically oriented organizations will always be a major focus for graft and corruption. Whatever other organizations have members who are involved in such graft and corruption, the members of the government will always be involved. It may also be added, parenthetically, that such organizations never exist unless there is also a government in the society, regardless of whether or not there is in fact a government in every society.

4. OTHER ORGANIZATIONS

In all societies, in addition to the first two or three of the organizations mentioned here, there are always some others that are organized on a predominantly particularistic basis. Usually some will be organized on the basis of family particularism, but there are other particularistic bases such as neighborhood and the like which are also likely to be important. Some of these organizations may be organized on a predominantly universalistic basis. Outside of relatively modernized societies these are relatively rare by contrast with those organized on a predominantly particularistic basis. Although there are always some organizations other than the first three types, it is quite important to realize that they are by no means necessarily the same organizations from one society to another. Some of the types of organizations most frequent are those one would expect from the various discussions above. In societies of any considerable scale armed force organizations, schools, churches, etc., are exceedingly likely to be present. Whenever organizations of this sort exist, the other three types of organizations previously mentioned above will always be present too. Furthermore, there will always exist problems of interrelationships of the members of these organizations and the members of the other three types of organizations. Relations with members of the government and members of specific family organizations will no doubt be the most important of these relationships for societies as a whole, but relations with the members of specialized predominantly economically oriented organizations can never be ignored. Rarely, if ever, are organizations of this sort characterized by the level of economic self-sufficiency that would be necessary to make them to a high degree independent of the action of members of predominantly economically oriented organizations.

C. COMMON RELATIONSHIP ASPECTS

1. THE UNDERLYING SET OF RELATIONSHIP ASPECTS

In all societies there is always an observable cluster of relationships that are predominantly traditional, predominantly particularistic, and predominantly functionally diffuse. Not only are these ideally of this form [hereinafter referred to as Y_1, Y_2, and Y_3 type relationships],[13] but they are actually of this form as well. The actuality may not coincide exactly with the ideal structures from other points of view—indeed it never does—but whatever the discrepancies may be, they do not affect the argument at this level. Sometimes relationships of the Y_1, Y_2, and Y_3 types are considered the only legitimate ones by the members of a given society. That is to say: in some social contexts even though predominantly rational, universalistic, functionally specific, and avoidant relationships [hereinafter referred to as X_1, X_2, X_3, and X_4 type relationships] are sometimes actually found, they may not in fact exist, ideally speaking, in that context. In the context of any society, whenever relationships of the X_1, X_2, X_3, and X_4 type are found ideally and/or actually, there are always underlying relationships of the type Y_1, Y_2, and Y_3 [The relationships emphasizing these Y categories may or may not also be Y_4 or X_4 types]. In other words, ideally speaking, there may be no emphasis on any of the X-type relationships save for X_6 [hierarchical] relationships, but whenever those emphases do exist ideally and/or actually, they exist only for individuals who have already learned to interact

[13] See above, p. 153 for identification of the symbols X_1 . . . X_6 and Y_1 . . . Y_6.

over a wide range of behavior in terms of relationships of the Y_1, Y_2, and Y_3 types. This is true for the members of all societies regardless of whether they are highly modernized or not.

There is nothing mysterious about this. As a minimum, kinship and family organizations always take the form of emphasizing the Y_1, Y_2, and Y_3 type relationships mentioned here. The members of any society receive some if not the vast majority of their most intense and formative experiences within just such kinship and family settings. In the context of any society action in terms of the X_1, X_2, X_3, and X_4 aspects, whenever it exists, is always something learned after the individual has learned to act in terms of relationships emphasizing the Y_1, Y_2, and Y_3 aspects mentioned above. In all known societies relationships emphasizing these characteristics constitute the initial major focus of socialization. Transition, if one will, of the infant from a biological entity to a social being is always in terms of relationships emphasizing Y_1, Y_2, and Y_3 aspects. Since the family context is so important in these respects one may add another Y-type category to this list, i.e., Y_5. Initial experience in the family context is always predominantly responsible as far as the goal orientation aspects are concerned. Therefore, as far as the family elements of this argument are concerned, these relationships are always characterized by Y_5 aspect. As far as the infants in society are concerned, many of their initial formative relationships are also predominantly intimate as far as affective aspects are concerned. In this respect Y_4 aspects are stressed as a minimum in terms of the relationship between mother and infant. Predominantly avoidant or X_4 aspects may be emphasized in terms of other relationships, but we have increasing evidence in the findings of modern psychology to the effect that mature and stable adults cannot develop if infants are not the objects of a great deal of intimate affective display from some source, usually their mothers as a minimum. In addition, there is no convincing material available on any society to indicate that infants are treated in a totally avoidant or predominantly avoidant structure by every member of the society.

The predominantly hierarchical aspect, X_6, must be added to this underlying set of relationship aspects. The vast majority of all relationships characteristic of any society are of the hierarchical sort save for casual and fleeting relationships on the one hand and limited relationships in terms of organizations of small and restricted scale on the other. Predominantly egalitarian or nonhierarchical relationships, Y_6 relationships, always develop within some larger more pervasive context of relationships characterized by hierarchical aspects. Initial socialization both within and without the family context is always in terms of predominantly hierarchical relationships, both ideally and actually [though the ideal and actual aspects of these relationships may diverge in other respects]. Family relationships as a set are always predominantly hierarchical.

2. COMMON SPECIALIZED SETS OF RELATIONSHIP ASPECTS

In addition to the underlying types of relationships stressed above, there are always some specialized sets of relationships in all known societies. For example, there is always some set of relationship aspects to cover the possibility of contacts with strangers. This is certainly the case for any society of considerable scale or of any society whose members are in reasonably close contact with the members of other societies. It is almost certainly true at least by default even of societies whose members ordinarily know each other by sight, since they would treat any stranger differently from those with whom they have relatively well-understood and well-institutionalized relationships. Contact with strangers may take the form of relationships characterized by predominantly traditional, particularistic, functionally diffuse, either avoidant or intimate, either individualistic or responsible, and either hierarchical or nonhierarchical aspects. If Y_1, Y_2, and Y_3 aspects are emphasized, X_4 aspects and X_6 aspects are exceedingly likely to be emphasized as opposed to Y_4 and Y_6 ones. In other cases it is possible that the members of a society may govern these contacts by emphasizing predominantly rational, universalistic, functionally specific, avoidant, individualistic or responsible, and hierarchical or nonhierarchical aspects. If X_1, X_2, X_3, and X_4 characteristics are emphasized it is difficult to generalize about the goal orientation or stratification aspects. I would guess that they would be predominantly X_5 and X_6 ones rather than Y_5 and Y_6 ones. When it is considered proper to be predominantly rational, universalistic, and functionally specific in the treatment of strangers, an individual is also likely to be able to act without very much regard for the interests of those strangers and in as hierarchical a fashion as he can get by with. Relationships of this sort are far more likely to be characterized by exceedingly ruthless forms of rationality than by any considerable amount of responsibility.

The problem of relationships with strangers is a well-nigh universal problem, although it is carried to vastly greater lengths in the context of relatively modernized societies. After all, in the context of relatively modernized societies, it is absolutely certain that the average individual will, during the course of every day of his life, have some contacts with a large number of individuals whom he may not have any recollection of even having seen before. Furthermore, it is also certain that a large number of those will be most fleeting *and* casual. In relatively nonmodernized contexts the probability of contact with strangers for the average individual is relatively small even though he may always be aware of it.

Quite apart from the problem of the possible contact with strangers, there is always the possibility that every society include some relationships characterized by emphases on rationality, universalism, functional specificity, and avoidance. These may be actual structures even if they are not ideal structures. When such structures do not exist, ideally speaking, they are always to some extent approximated by the balancing of aspects already referred to above [e.g., pp. 448, 458, and 462–465]—by the juxtaposition of Y-type emphases, one may get the equivalent of X-type relationships. One of the most prominent examples of this is the balancing of various family interests against one another or by the balancing of neighborhood as against family interests. For example, for village governmental systems the villagers, ideally speaking, frequently emphasize Y_1, Y_2, Y_3, X_4, Y_5, and probably X_6 aspects. The Y_2 aspects, i.e., the particularistic bases of selection that are crucial here are frequently primarily kinship criteria. If, however, in the membership of the village council many different families are represented, the balance of interests of the representatives of different families may result in a person being selected for a given task primarily because he is in fact the person best fitted to serve the whole set of interests represented most equitably. This is a case of a balance of family particularisms leading to a selection that actually has highly universalistic emphases. Sometimes in these situations actions in terms of a village governmental organization which, though predominantly particularistic in the emphases of the members, may nevertheless curb the activities of the members of a particular family bringing about a more nearly universalistic solution to a given problem than might have otherwise been the case. Observers of societies of a highly modernized sort in terms of which emphases on X_1, X_2, X_3, and X_4 aspects over a broad variety of behavior are taken for granted, on seeing comparable results within the social context of relatively nonmodernized societies may well feel that those results have in fact been obtained because the point of view of the members of those societies is the same as the point of view to which they are accustomed. This is not the case. Under these circumstances a break-down in the stability of the various predominantly particularistically recruited organizations, the balancing of interests of whose members has resulted in such actual emphases on X aspects, may radically increase the role of predominantly particularistic factors as well as other Y emphases—to the great surprise of the observer. The observer under these circumstances sees relatively high emphasis in effect, at least, on what he regards as predominantly universalistic criteria. He sees in terms of the organizations which various individuals represent heavy emphasis on particularistic factors, and assumes frequently that if those organizations become more universalistic, the general emphasis on universalistic criteria will be that much further increased. Such changes, however, inevitably break down the organizations whose members participate in such balances, and the result is overwhelmingly likely to be a far more highly particularistic selection primarily based on that organization or set of organizations whose members remain strongest in the face of such changes.

Another one of these balancing possibilities is the type of civil service by adoption alleged of Tokugawa Japan. This kind of balance is a far more rationally oriented one than the type discussed above. It is highly vulnerable to the instability of the predominantly particularistically oriented relationships in terms of which balance has been achieved. Thus by cutting down the role of inheritance of office in individual families under such circumstances, one may actually increase the role of favoritism in selection rather than decrease it.

Such balances constitute one of the reasons why the process of modernization is so highly disruptive of relatively nonmodernized societies. Part of that process is always increased emphasis by ideal on X_1, X_2, X_3, and X_4 aspects of relationships as a combination. Sometimes it is the first time such emphases have been introduced by ideal at all even though actual results of that sort may have been achieved. Inevitably it is an increased emphasis *and* an emphasis on these aspects in areas where they have not been emphasized before. This frequently increases the amount of graft, corruption, favoritism, etc., specifically because such introduction may break down the old balances before new safeguards have been created. Rational social engineering does not necessarily call for moving as directly as possible toward a given change in social structure.

With regard to both the fundamental set of relationship aspects emphasizing Y_1, Y_2, Y_3, X_4 [or Y_4], Y_5, and X_6 aspects as well as with regard to specialized sets emphasizing some of the X aspects mentioned above, the actual experience, as well as the ideal structures, always give some fundamental bases for communication as between the members of any two societies. Regardless of differences on other scores, the overwhelming familiarity to all people of the fundamental sets of relationship aspects is quite enough to account for the probability of some communication. The X_1, X_2, and X_3 type emphases may be a far less reliable basis for mutual understanding, but in this respect understanding can at least in theory always be established by referring to these aspects as emphases moving in the opposite direction from the Y-type aspects within these first three categories. For this reason it is worth the redundancy to repeat a warning. The emphasis on X_1, X_2, and X_3 aspects has been carried to such dramatic lengths over such a broad range of relationships in relatively modernized social contexts that social scientists as well as others, whether they use this or related jargon or not, give the impression that these societies by contrast with relatively nonmodernized ones are wholly or almost wholly defined by X_1, X_2, X_3, and X_4 type relationships. This is never and can never be the case. A remarkable characteristic of relatively modernized societies is not that their members have eliminated relationships characterized by heavy emphases on Y_1, Y_2, and Y_3 aspects but rather the high degree to which they have combined the maintenance of these in some contexts with high emphases, both ideally and actually, on X_1, X_2, X_3, and X_4 aspects in other contexts. To treat these categories as though they were binary and as though, for a society or anything else, these constitute an either-or set of distinctions is to miss the heart of the problem. From the point of view of social science and of general theoretical implications one of the fascinating things about such societies is that such a combination ever developed at all. Really tight rigorous theories explaining how or why such a combination developed would constitute a major break-through.[14]

For policy questions what is a great deal more interesting is whether or not the combination of radically increased emphases on these X_1, X_2, X_3, and X_4 aspects within a continuing context of high emphases on Y_1, Y_2, and Y_3 aspects in the context in which the earliest and certainly a considerable part of the most fundamental socialization of the average individual takes place can be maintained with stability. We know from the long history of

[14] It is not difficult to give *reasoned accounts* for these purposes, but no elegantly [in a mathematical sense] formulated theory on this score is yet available.

many societies that quite high levels of stability can characterize societies in terms of which the emphases are overwhelmingly on Y_1, Y_2, and Y_3 aspects, with the emphasis on X_1, X_2, X_3, and X_4 aspects existing ideally and/or actually only in quite restricted spheres. So far no societies characterized by the kind of overwhelming emphasis in highly specialized areas such as predominantly economically oriented organizations, governmental organizations, churches, schools, etc., on the X_1, X_2, X_3, and X_4 type aspects has ever existed stably for much more than fifty years.[15]

D. COMMON PROBLEMS

It is possible to treat the common problems associated with all societies at considerable length even in the present state of development of social science. For present purposes, given what has been said earlier in this work, I should like to touch only four such common problems: (1) socialization, (2) economic allocation, (3) political stability, and (4) discrepancy between ideal and actual structures. These four problems constitute a focus of general theoretical significance and of general implications for policy questions.

1. PROBLEM OF SOCIALIZATION

There is a reference in the social sciences to infants as constituting a periodic barbarian invasion of any society.[16] That metaphor states unforgettably the minimal problem of socialization associated with any society. Unless one wishes to fall back on so far unverified assumptions of infants born with innate substantive ideas, racial memories, and the like, it is necessary to assume that the mind of an infant at birth is a *tabula rasa* as far as the substantive ideas current among the members of his society are concerned. Not only will an infant abandoned at birth die, but there is every reason to believe that if it were possible to keep a human infant alive without the intervention of any other human being whom that infant could perceive, the resultant organism would in no way, save the physiological, resemble what we ordinarily equate with the more mature individual. The problem of socialization exists in the context of all societies as far as infants are concerned, and a considerable part of the socialization char-

[15] After all, very high emphases of the sort we are speaking about here for the population at large do not greatly antedate the year 1910 for any known society.

[16] I once located the source of this metaphor; I have since lost it. *Mea culpa.*

acteristic of all known societies is carried out within a family context. This is all obvious enough, but what is not equally obvious is that in some respects socialization continues throughout the life cycle of the individual. The most important part of the socialization of an individual may be that which takes place in his earliest most formative years, but the member of any society probably learns some new social structures as life continues, and for the members of some societies the rate of socialization even at quite advanced ages is considerable.

The problem of socialization is least obtrusive, of course, in highly sedentary societies characterized by restricted social mobility, existing within a highly constant physical environment. The structures of socialization of such societies may be so constant from one point in time to another as to be taken entirely for granted and to be as far as the average individual is concerned, the focus of no highly specialized organizations whatsoever. As pointed out above in other connections [pp. 79, 433, 478, and 491], the opposite extreme as far as societies are concerned is the problem of socialization in relatively modernized social contexts in which increasingly the members of the society are faced with the problem of socialization of individuals for an unknown future. Although I assert with fervor that this is new under the sun, it is nothing but a new special form of the extremely general problem of how social structures are inculcated on individuals not previously acquainted with them. The most general problem of socialization is, of course, to get this inculcation carried out for everyone not pathologically incapable of achieving it.

In addition to this general problem of socialization there are characteristic of every society special problems of socialization. The most general of these special problems of socialization is the way in which specialized structures are inculcated on a selected set of individuals. Some individual members of all societies have to be specially prepared for intermediate roles as opposed to basic roles in the society. The problem here ranges all the way from specialized forms of knowledge through specialized attitudes of a wide variety. The fact that there are associated with every known society specialized problems of socialization carries with it as a corollary another special problem of socialization. To the extent that there is specialized socialization in the context of a given society, some individuals are bound to suffer special frustrations by virtue of the fact that they will be trained for roles which they will in fact not be able to occupy. This set of special problems with regard to socialization is a function of the fact that for some specialized roles there must be "substitutes-in-being" in case of emergency.[17] Thus, in all societies, the existence of specialized role differentiation is likely to have as an accompaniment sources of stress and strain since many members cannot in fact hold the roles for which they have been socialized. Given societies characterized by many alternative avenues of occupation and achievements, this problem may be diminished, but it cannot be eliminated. Regardless of whether the specialized roles in a society are allocated largely on the basis of predominantly universalistic or predominantly particularistic criteria, some of the people prepared to assume some of them are bound to have their feelings hurt. The higher the level of prestige of the roles in question the greater is likely to be the sense of frustration and hence the greater the potential focus of discontent.

Finally, there is another problem closely associated with the general problem of socialization. It is a problem for the members of any and all societies, but the less sedentary, the more complicated, and the more highly modernized the society, the greater this problem is. This again is the problem of adequate knowledge. Never do the members of a society know all that they would in fact need to know to socialize new members of the society as they develop perfectly. For the members of highly sedentary societies these problems may be minimal, especially if the societies are relatively small in scale. The larger the scale of the society, other things being equal, the greater the problem, and the more highly modernized the society, regardless of what other things are equal, the greater will the problem be. The pressure for practical accomplishment within the sphere of the social sciences must build up year by year in the relatively modernized societies. This factor alone would account for such a build up, let alone others.

2. PROBLEM OF ECONOMIC ALLOCATION

The problems of economic allocation associated with any society may for present purposes be discussed under two headings: (a) the problem of capital formation and (b) the problem of distribution. There must be sufficient capital formation for the general functioning of the members of the society if any society is to remain stable. For some societies of small scale and primitive stages of technology, the amount of capital formation involved may be slight. It is never negligible, however. The members of every society regard some material items as of considerable productive significance, as ones on which considerable time and

---

[17] One of the best examples of this sort of problem is the problem of cadets already discussed above [see pp. 202, 400–403, 416, and 459–460].

effort must be lavished. In addition to the capital formation necessary if general functioning is maintained, there must also be some capital formation if the growth and development characteristic of some societies are to take place. It is difficult to envisage a society so precisely sedentary and stable that neither degeneration [that is in the sense of change into a subsystem of another society or in the sense of the organization ceasing to exist] nor growth or development of any sort is taking place. It is characteristic of all societies that some technological equipment is associated with the members of the society as well as there being capital formation in the form of the preparation of new land or the redevelopment of old land. If the society is not in one way or another in the process of going out of existence as a separate society, its rate of capital formation must be in excess of that necessary for general functioning, unless an exquisitely and precisely sedentary society is possible. There can be no simpler tautology than this.

This extremely general problem of capital formation has one clear-cut implication for students of public affairs. The forms of capital formation characteristic of the vast majority of relatively nonmodernized societies may not be ones readily understood by the members of highly modernized societies. Manipulations of the distribution of income and the like with one set of implications for the members of one kind of society may have a different set of implications for observers who are members of another. Unless policy planning in this realm is careful and sophisticated, one may disrupt the minimal level of capital formation necessary for general functioning without repairing or improving the situation for increased and different forms of development. As indicated above [pp. 269–273, 558–559, 561–563] this is one of the problems involved in radical redistributions of income in the context of societies characterized by strongly bimodal distributions of income. Under those circumstances until radical new structures of economic allocation have taken firm roots in one form or another, bimodal distribution will in fact remain, and if they do not, there will be radical interference with the process of effective capital formation.[18]

[18] This is in no sense a statement to be taken as an injunction against any change in structures of income distribution which may, for a variety of reasons, be considered grossly inequitable. It does indicate quite specifically that, regardless of questions of equity, bimodal distributions of income, especially in social contexts in which the vast majority of the people exist close to the margin of subsistence, are closely and directly related to problems of capital formation—whatever other problems they may be closely related to. To tamper with them without having this consideration

The problem of distribution of goods and services is often considered quite apart from or in addition to the problem of capital formation. The problems are, of course, never so neatly separable since one of the most critical questions about income distribution is the implications of a particular set of structures of distribution of goods and services for capital formation and vice versa. Nevertheless, the problems associated with the distribution of goods and services constitute an importantly different way of looking at the general problems associated with economic allocation in general. The distribution of goods and services must be sufficient for a balancing of the activities carried out in terms of the society. No society has any completely self-sufficient subsystem save for extremely isolated self-limiting cases.[19] One of the major forms of interdependency of these subsystems is in terms of different structures of distributions of goods and services among their members. This is by no means the only form of interdependency, and in many cases it is by no means the most important form, but it is always *a* form of interdependency.

In all societies some of these structures of distribution are asymmetrical. One important example of such asymmetry has been discussed above (pp. 278–279). This is the asymmetrical distribution of goods and services between towns and cities on the one hand and villages or other predominantly agrarian settings on the other. As far as the flow of goods and services is concerned, characteristically to a high degree the members of all of the relatively nonmodernized societies have viewed this as a one-way flow. Not only have these individuals seen goods and services flow out of the agrarian setting in the form of rent, taxes, interest, and the like, but they have seen considerably less in absolute amounts come to them from the towns and cities. Above all, however, what has come to them from the city and town environments has at most contributed to the maintenance of a given level of productivity. Relatively infrequently—and if present at all, on a discontinuous basis—have the goods and services received from the town and city folk raised local productivity progressively. This latter kind of distributive relationship is characteristic only of relatively modernized societies.

As indicated above, some asymmetrical structures of distribu-

---

specifically in mind in all probability will not merely fail to eliminate the bimodal distribution of income. It may actually prevent even the previous level of productivity which from the point of view of desired policies posed so many problems in the first place.

[19] The problems of intermarriage alone will force some departures from self-sufficiency or the membership of the isolated system will die off.

tion are always characteristic of every society. Furthermore, to some extent, the members of every society not only accept asymmetrical distributions of goods and services as nothing unusual, but also consider many asymmetrical distributions to be right and proper both ideally and actually speaking. For example, the distributions of goods and services between husband and wife and parents and children are always asymmetrical in some important respects. Nevertheless, for any given society, from the point of view of the members, the tolerable range of asymmetry in the distribution of goods and services is never indefinite. There are always some increases and changes in such asymmetry that the members of the society will not tolerate. Even if the tolerance of the members knew no bounds, if they never revolted, and if they never showed dissatisfaction, there are always some increases and changes in the forms of asymmetry of distribution of goods and services such that the social systems in terms of which the individuals operate could not continue to exist. Sometimes the attitudes of rulers have been pushed quite far in these respects. Certain Tokugawa leaders [Iyeyasu] in Japan were famous for the view that there should be left to the peasants only enough goods and services so that they could neither live nor die. Such a precise balance is difficult to maintain regardless of whether one thinks of it as good, bad, or indifferent. The major problem of the maintenance of order during the Tokugawa period was above all else a function of pushing this sort of asymmetry too far. For the leaders of that society one of the major problems of social control was the problem of peasant revolts which almost inevitably focused around pushing just this sort of asymmetrical distribution one step further in the direction of a one-way flow from the farmers to the urban centers.

Another problem of distribution of goods and services in any society is the problem of distribution in such a form that special surpluses for large-scale but episodic emergencies are maintained. If this is not done it is quite conceivable that emergencies may wipe out the membership of such societies or important segments of it at least. These emergencies are subject to wide variation. Some of the more obvious sources of emergencies of this sort have to do with floods, crop failures, and the classic instances of pestilence, famine, and the like. These are emergency problems in the sense that, as far as the general population is concerned, they are on the whole unpredicted in detail and probably to a high degree unpredictable in precise detail. From the point of view of the members of the societies concerned these are often capricious events. As such, it is difficult to plan distribution so as to allow for these situations. Most societies of any considerable scale have in their catalogue of social heroes some individual who whether by dream [like Joseph] or other form of foresight made allowances for just such emergencies.

Until relatively high levels of modernization were reached, large-scale but episodic emergencies have usually been only partially offset by the general distribution of goods and services. Frequently such emergencies are in fact characterized by some portion of the general population being wiped out. Depending upon the extent and kind of such elimination, a similar society may continue to exist, the society may go out of existence or the society may continue to exist though radically changed. Structures of distribution in terms of which the members can, or attempt to, deal with emergencies of this sort will ordinarily have radically different implications for the members of different societies under all sorts of circumstances in times of both peace and war.

Quite apart from large-scale but episodic emergencies, the distribution of goods and services characteristic of any society, if that society is to be stable, must be sufficient to take care of what might be called the endemic relief problems characteristic of every society. These are the problems that have to do with the care of the incapacitated aged, the sick, and the care of infants and children who are not so much incapacitated as not yet capacitated. These are the highly predictable relief problems as opposed to the large-scale but episodic emergencies. For the vast majority of all societies the organization par excellence in terms of which these problems are handled is the family organization. Even for the most highly modernized societies this continues to be the case for the handling of the incapacitated sick apart from the aged and the handling of the not yet capacitated infants and children.

One of the special developments characteristic of relatively modernized societies is that increasingly in terms of all of them the problem of handling the incapacitated aged is a problem of handling them on a nonkinship basis. The fact that these relief problems are endemic is, of course, another respect in which the distribution of goods and services must be asymmetrical if the society is to survive. It is conceivable that the aged and some of the sick, and no doubt some of the infants and children for that matter, can simply be permitted to die and the society can continue to be viable, but regardless of how ruthless one may become with the aged, one cannot be correspondingly ruthless with the general run of the sick and all of the infants and children. For the vast majority of societies, next to the family, some local form of organization is usually the major focus of relief of this sort. These problems are frequently not viewed as problems of relief by the members of the society concerned. It is usually taken for granted that these activities will be carried out in a family context. To that extent, however desirable it may be under certain circumstances to alter the form of family organizations, it is rarely possible to do so without creating immediately an increased relief problem where a special relief problem was not distinguished out of the ordinary social context before.

Finally, for present purposes, in some minimal sense the distribution of goods and services must be such as to maintain the motivation of individuals for active participation in social life. Here again, I would emphasize the fact that motivation is rarely, if ever, solely explicible in terms of the distribution of goods and services, but it is equally tenable to maintain that rarely, if ever, is the distribution of goods and services completely irrelevant to motivation. As emphasized above [e.g., pp. 68, 91, 125–126, 511, and 521] the distinction between societies or individuals as spiritually as opposed to materially oriented is always a spurious distinction if one means by that that material factors are completely irrelevant to the spiritually oriented. Material factors can never be completely irrelevant in any maintainable situation of action. No society can survive in the face of complete apathy on the part of its members or in the face of an active withdrawal from the material factors of life. To this may be added another generalization: in the context of any society, if the relevance, ideally and/or actually, of the distribution of goods and services to motivation is ignored or radically altered, intentionally or unintentionally, one result for a relatively extended period of time will be an increase in the relevance of the distribution of goods and services for motivation to a wide variety of forms of social participation.

3. PROBLEM OF POLITICAL STABILITY

As pointed out above in Part II, Chapter 6, the allocation of power and responsibility is a strategic point of view from which to tackle general problems of stability in social systems. The basis for maintaining this in so general a form is the hypothesis that systems in terms of which power is not balanced by responsibility and vice versa [either internally to the system or by virtue of the interrelationship among the members of that system and those of some other system] are inherently instable. This hypothesis does not maintain that *only* the allocation of power and responsibility is relevant to problems of instability and stability. There are, in fact and in theory, other sources of instability of social systems than imbalances of this sort. Moreover, it does not imply that, if power and responsibility are balanced, the systems concerned will be stable. It merely states that if they are not, the system will be instable as a result of either capricious exercises of power or ineffectual assessments of responsibility.

The most general problem as far as political stability is concerned in any society is the problem of how and to what degree such balances of power and responsibility are in fact maintained—or what takes place if they are not maintained. There is absolutely no reason to believe that there are any foreordained qualities of social systems which guarantee that such balances will be achieved or maintained. One of the most fundamental objections to the practice of *defining* social systems as equilibrium systems or homeostatic systems lies precisely in the fact such a definition implies that the systems concerned *must* be stable and thereby rules out consideration of the possibility of radical imbalances in the allocation of power and responsibility. "Men have died from time to time, and worms have eaten them . . ." and no less surely have social systems changed radically or even ceased to exist altogether—because of such imbalances of power and responsibility as well as for other reasons. Nevertheless, insofar as social systems are stable over any extended period of time they are not in fact characterized by considerable imbalances of this sort and certainly not by imbalances of this sort on the level of generality on which the system is being studied.

One of the most remarkable aspects of this problem lies in the fact that although societies vary radically in the extent to which explicit planning has been devoted to such balances by the members of the society or their forebears, for no society have we any evidence that either the ideal or the actual structures, and certainly not the combination of the two, have in fact been completely thought out and rationally planned. The system of checks and balances so carefully developed by the Founding Fathers of modern United States society—Founding Fathers who founded a society they hardly envisaged at all—certainly was explicitly worked out with great sophistication. Nevertheless, in founding that system of checks and balances, they focused their attention overwhelmingly on the governmental organization rather than on the society as a whole. Even with regard to the government, actually [if not both ideally *and* actually], there are many aspects of the balances of power and responsibility which were not explicitly delineated. There have, however, been few attempts to push politically oriented social engineering further than was attempted in this instance. There are other outstanding examples in social history of social engineering. The focus of such attention on governmental organizations by the members of such societies as Tokugawa Japan, modern Turkey, the Soviet Union, early modern Japan, etc., all furnish examples of fairly explicit attempts along these lines. Everyone of these examples, however, shares with that of the United States the feature that, however remarkably explicit the leaders were, they never came close to an explicitly planned, let alone executed, set of structures for the balance of power and responsibility throughout the society.

This state of affairs is to be expected; it is revealing; and in addition most of us would probably consider the state of affairs on the whole fortunate. It is to be expected because in fact there has never existed a set of social studies or social sciences so highly developed as to make available the necessary knowledge for such explicit and detailed planning with regard to this aspect of behavior. It is revealing because one of the implications of this state of affairs is a built-in social dynamic—that is to say, a built-in tendency toward social change. There is nothing mystical whatsoever about balances of power and responsibility, however difficult they may be to understand thoroughly, given the present state of our knowledge. Unless one invokes some assumption of a nonempirical sort such as the beneficence of a "Guiding Hand," in the absence of quite careful planning and execution in broad areas of this sort, on a probability basis alone, one would expect some of the balances of power and responsibility which were especially strategic for the societies concerned to get out of kilter and result in instabilities. Some of these instabilities would lead to relatively minor social changes, and some of them presumably to major alterations. Certainly there is a great deal of evidence in social history subject to this interpretation. Although the interpretation leaves much to be desired as far as detailed relevance and rigor are concerned, there is at least nothing nonempirical or romantically vague about it. Again this line of argument does not hold that *all social change* can be interpreted as a function of imbalances of power and responsibility. It does say that, lacking perfect planning and execution with regard to such matters, in the long run there will be social change as a result of such imbalances, if there is not social change attributed to other states of the system. Since I hold it unlikely that we ever achieve perfect knowledge let alone execution in this field or any other, this is tantamount to saying that any social system will change for this reason if not for others. If this position is not trivially false, it has another implication for uses of equilibria hypotheses and assumptions with regard to social systems. This implication may be stated bluntly as follows: Unless equilibrium [or homeostatic] conditions are attributed to social systems by definition, the general problems of maintaining balances of power and responsibility place limits on the range within which any social system *can be* an equilibrium system or a homeostatic system.[20]

[20] It is quite important that the position taken here *not* be construed as maintaining that it is irrelevant to use the concept of equilibrium, or even perhaps that of homeostasis with regard to social systems. In general I would avoid the latter specifically because it perpetuates the habit of conceiving of social systems as close analogies to organisms and hence preserves in full flower the pathetic fallacy of referring to social systems as though they had an organic life of their own. This commission of the pathetic fallacy is not merely displeasing from the point of the aesthetics of scientific theory. As maintained above [p. 4], it always involves some begging of some important questions of social analysis. There certainly are social systems such that the behavior of members in terms of them within limits tends to reinforce and maintain the structures of behavior in terms of which their action takes place. One of the most important distinctions, both from the point of view of the pure scientist in the social field *and* from the point of view of the student of public affairs, is the distinction between social systems which, on the level that they are being studied, are not characterized by equilibrium tendencies as opposed to those which within some limits are. To define all social systems as equilibria systems is to rule out this important distinction unless one ignores the definition or subsequently, implicitly or explicitly, defines the term equilibrium to mean what is frequently understood by this term in scientific discourse and its residual category as well. If one defines social systems as equilibria systems, or assert of social systems that they are always characterized by equilibria states and then defines equilibrium as consisting of stable, partial, and unstable equilibria, one is left in one of the following two positions. (1) Some range of the phenomena covered by the terms partial equilibria and unstable equilibria is equivalent to disequilibria in which case the definition or assertion about equilibria means nothing since the term has now been defined as itself and its opposite [or residual category]. With regard to any defined empirical quality, one may always make the assertion that any system either has it or doesn't have it, assuming, of course, that having *part of it* is not having *it*. There are, after all, some legitimate uses of the law of the excluded middle. Even in the world of the fanciful, all snarks are either boojums or nonboojums [Russell's problem of the "set of all μ-sets" is not germane to this question]. To proceed so is to reduce the assertion or definition about equilibria conditions to a meaningless state. (2) On the other hand, if one uses the term unstable equilibrium, not as a residual category of stable equilibrium, but in the precise sense of an equilibrium state quite easily disturbed, and one which if disturbed by relatively slight displacement is likely to depart further and further from the original state [e.g., a cone balanced on its vertex (or Columbus's egg) is a usual example of unstable equilibrium in this sense], then the implication is quite extreme in another direction. Any social system characterized by unstable equilibria properties in this sense, if displaced, ceases to be a social system or even social until some future equilibrium is established. Since the next more general frame of reference after the social is usually the biological, and after that the

Apart from the general problem of the balance of power and responsibility which is both endemic and to some extent always unplanned in every society, there is always the problem of control of deviant behavior. In the context of every society some deviant behavior will arise if only because of the ignorance of some of the people some of the time.[21] As members of relatively modernized societies, because of the enormous development of specialization of government, we tend to think of control of deviance as overwhelmingly centered in the activities of members of the government. Although the position of members of our governmental organizations in handling cases of deviance is highly developed, in relatively modernized societies the role played by members of the governmental organizations in this respect is never all of the story. Indeed it never encompasses all of the strategic controls over deviance in the society. For example, family organizations are always significant in the control of deviance, but they are never simply subsystems of the government.

I have asserted above that deviant behavior would exist if only as a result of ignorance. Whatever the many other reasons de-

---

physical, such social theorists are either in the position of saying nothing comprehensible or of asserting, by implication if not intention, that many instances of what others consider social change are for them purely biological or physical changes.

These are at any rate the implications if all social systems are defined as equilibria systems. If the equilibrium aspect of all social systems is asserted as a theorem or hypothesis about those systems otherwise defined, then precise use of the concept of unstable equilibrium will almost certainly refute the theorem as posed. If there is any displacement from any unstable equilibrium, the system concerned is in disequilibrium, temporarily at least. Unless the thinker concerned is prepared to assert that social unstable equilibria constitute an unusual set of unstable equilibria, namely those unstable equilibria which in fact *never* are displaced, it is untenable to assert that all social systems are characterized by equilibria conditions.

Finally, there is a trivial way in which scholars who take these positions can defend them. If one makes the time interval small enough, with regard to anything of interest—or certainly with regard to the vast majority of things—one can arrive at a time span such that nothing can be said to have changed save the age of the thing contemplated. In this sense not only all social systems but all empirical entities of any sort can be called equilibrium systems. Usually neither social scientists nor students of public affairs are interested in such restricted time spans. In some of the social sciences such as economics the concept of equilibrium is generally used with a high level of precision and sophistication. In many of the other social sciences the concept of equilibrium is both too important to be used carelessly, and too carelessly used to be important.

[21] There are, of course, in any social context many sources of deviance other than ignorance. For example, no society is characterized solely by members who are so well socialized that they would never, apart from failures of knowledge, deviate from any of the ideal structures characteristic of the society and not all the ideal structures are mutually consistent.

viant behavior has, does, and will exist in every social context, past, present, and future, if one source establishes its inevitability, for present purposes the development of others would be beating a dead horse. The two most general statements about deviant behavior are: (1) that it has, does, and will exist in the context of every known society, and (2) that some of the deviant behavior which has, does, and will exist will make the stable existence of a social system impossible if it is not curbed.[22] Some of the members of every society are always motivated to try to ensure the continued stability of the system concerned. The fact that they are so motivated certainly does not mean that they will be successful, but it does mean that some of them will at least try. Finally, in the last analysis the use of force is the extreme in one direction of the means which can be used to control deviant behavior. In the context of every known society, whether effectively or ineffectively, to some extent force has, is, and will be used for such purposes. Thus in terms of applications of force alone, the structures of allocation of power and responsibility are always to some degree involved in the attempt to control deviant behavior. Less extreme exercises of power and responsibility are also always so involved.

The instrumental aspects of allocations of power and responsibility, especially in attempts to control deviance, whether these involve clear-cut applications of force or less extreme exercises of power, are always to some extent so clearly instrumental from the point of view of the members of a society that the probability is extremely high that there will be quite important elements of rationality in the allocations of power and responsibility which are oriented to the control of deviant behavior. This is one of those realms of behavior in which traditional methods of procedure may coincide with rational ones. It is also one in which some rational procedures are an explicit ideal and one in which, if the rational structures no longer coincide with traditional ones, the traditional ones will have to change if the society is to be stable. Not only are the members of all societies faced with problems of control of deviant behavior, but some of that control is always rationally thought out, if it is effective.

There is an additional line of hypotheses about the role of rationality in this realm of behavior. Perhaps the most effective control of deviance in any social context is that which prevents its

---

[22] This is not to imply that it is good to be stable, nor to deny the less general hypothesis that some forms of deviance and/or conflict contribute to some stable states.

occurrence altogether. There are always important elements of rationality in socialization, but particularly in highly sedentary societies, these structures may be overwhelmingly traditional. Apart from the underlying structures of control of deviance by prevention of its occurrence—structures which are characteristic of any society —there is always some control of deviance after overt acts have taken place. It is in the realm of control of deviance after overt acts of a deviant sort have taken place that some rational applications of power and responsibility are inevitably characteristic of any society which is maintained. What the future may bring in social development in this field is hard to predict, but for the present and the past as well as for the realistically predictable future, there has never been, is not, and is not likely to be a society in terms of which rationally developed means of ensuring conformity are as highly developed as rational means for handling deviance once it occurs. In some social contexts, of course, neither has been developed to any remarkable extent, but societies in terms of which control over overt deviance is not rationally developed to *any* considerable degree are likely to be highly unstable societies. The members of relatively modernized societies will also have to place increasing emphasis on rational socialization if their societies are to be stable.

Given a society characterized by political instability there are two extreme possibilities. The first possibility is that the society will cease to exist either because the members of the society are wiped out or because they are somehow taken over or incorporated into subsystems of some one or other existing societies. The other possibility is the possibility of social change such that the society continues to exist but in changed form. Here again there are two extreme possibilities, the first of which is on the whole quite unusual in social history. The first possibility is that via what has been described above as either palace revolutions or governmental revolutions, the previous governmental leadership is swept out of power, but the basic social structure of the society as a whole is renovated and reactivated. Some of the more extreme forms of deviance are eliminated; some of the discrepancies between ideal and actual structures are reduced. The most extreme example of this in social history is traditional Chinese society. For over two thousand years internal revolts against ruling dynasties and external conquests resulted essentially in the elimination of some of the more extreme forms of graft and corruption, a reallocation of land ownership and consequently of rents, a refurbishment of the ideals of objectivity and probity characteristic of the bureaucratic organization, etc., but an extraordinary number of the main social structures were constant.

The other possibility is more usual. It is that of general social revolution. Governmental instability as distinguished from simple leadership changes, usually leads to important alterations in the general social structure. Palace revolutions and even governmental revolutions, as those have been defined above [pp. 480–481], may take place without effective renovation and without general social revolution, but in the long run if these continue to crop up, there will be social changes of the type which constitute a general social revolution. Such revolutions are by no means inevitably accompanied by violent outbreaks, but those that are primarily a function of governmental instability are extremely likely to be featured by violence and some chaos—to be what the connotations of the term *revolution* call for.

Not only does the problem of political stability hinge on problems of balance of power and responsibility. The problems of political stability always involve problems of balancing solidarities.[23] For a society to be stable, the balancing of solidarities for the average individual most of the time must be a relatively simple matter. One of the special problems associated with relatively modernized societies is that this balancing probably reaches a complexity never before realized in social history. Traditional Chinese society was classically elegant in the simplicity of its ideal pattern of balancing solidarities. The individual, ideally speaking, was expected to be loyal first, last, and always to the interests of his family, i.e., to the perpetuation of the unit and the improvement of the lot of its members. The allocation of solidarities within the family sphere need not detain us here. The role par excellence of the Emperor as a symbol of government was to ensure the existence of a general social situation such that the average individual by putting his devotion to family interests and his solidarity with other family members first could not possibly behave in a way which would endanger either the government or the society as a whole. The doctrine of Chinese sovereignty, the famous Will of Heaven concept, rested on just this. The Emperor had the Will of Heaven just as long as this situation was maintained. Any indication that it was not—any indication that a person who, though properly filial, could behave in a fashion damaging to the prospects of the continued existence of the government or the society was prima-facie evidence that

[23] These problems may also be considered as problems of balancing loyalties in the layman's sense of the term.

the Emperor no longer had the Will of Heaven and consequently that he was not the legitimate Emperor.

In Tokugawa Japan as well as in modern Japan, there was a great deal of talk about the difficulty of balancing loyalties. This was, however, primarily a focus for romanticism. For the average Japanese the ideal hierarchy of solidarities was clear-cut. For the vast majority of the population the initial and overriding solidarity was with their immediate overlord who was the *daimyo* or head of a fief; the *shogun* was the focus of solidarity for the daimyo and various other top feudal lords; and presumably the Emperor was the focus of solidarity for the shogun and the Emperor's court nobles. After this hierarchy of solidarities an individual's loyalty was due his family members as a group. Other solidarities took a back seat to these two types. The vast majority of individuals, that is to say the peasants, ideally speaking were not supposed ever to be put in a position where even the possibility of a conflict between their solidarity with their overlord and their solidarities with other members of their families could arise. In the Tokugawa period the great novels and dramas which focused around the themes of conflicting loyalties rested largely on the lives of the *samurai* class and on the lives of merchants and other urban folk who in a certain sense committed the sin of *lèse majesté* by implying that they could legitimately have problems of conflicting solidarities which were to be taken seriously. During that period of history the actual disturbances of balances of solidarities were so restricted, the emphasis on proper fulfillment of one's obligations so high, and the literature and the arts of the period so preoccupied with conflicts of this sort, that it is hard not to come away with the feeling that the literature and the arts represent a special form of fantasy life and wish-fulfillment in this regard. The average individual had so few opportunities to demonstrate his virtuosity in loyalty in real life that identification with literary figures who lived out protean struggles in these arenas came as a sort of blessed relief.

In the context of relatively modernized societies—especially insofar as the societies concerned are characterized by relatively nonauthoritarian ideal structures—the possibility of conflicting loyalties is carried to its highest pitch in social history, and partly by default. That is to say, some of the possibilities of conflict lurk in the fact that memberships in different organizations, ideally speaking, are regarded as such separate matters for the individual as to have no relation one to the other. However much a virtuoso of compartmentalization modern man may be, he is still an individual. Solidarities with members of two or more organizations always contain the possibility of conflicting loyalties regardless of whether they are ideally irrelevant to one another. As long as an individual's solidarity with some member of some central organization does not take a clear and overriding precedence over any and all of the others, these conflicts by default inhere. This is one of the aspects of the attitude generally described as nationalism which is so characteristic of the members of all of the relatively modernized societies. In such social contexts, considerations of chauvinism to one side, to a surprising degree national loyalty, at least ideally speaking, takes precedence over all other loyalties distinguished by the members of the society. This simplifies the problem of balancing loyalties even for the members of relatively modernized societies. Despite all of the possibilities of simplification of balances of solidarities, other things being equal, the greater the number of differentiated organizations to which an individual belongs, the greater is the problem of balancing solidarities from his point of view and from that of other members of the society, actually if not ideally.

4. PROBLEM OF THE DISCREPANCY BETWEEN IDEAL AND ACTUAL STRUCTURES

As indicated above [pp. 26–30], there is no society whose members do not distinguish between ideal and actual structures, i.e., between how they feel individuals should behave and how individuals actually behave. Furthermore, no society is characterized by ideal and actual structures that coincide in all cases. No society could exist if there were *no* discernible approximation of actual structures to ideal structures, but no society and no subsystem of a society exists or ever has existed in which the coincidence is exact. The discrepancies between ideal and actual structures always constitute a major focus of stress and strain for the members of any society. That is to say, to some extent the members of every society are aware of these discrepancies, and to some extent they are upset by them. Insofar as stress and strain are accountable in terms of these discrepancies, they always constitute one of the first studies if one is interested in predictions of social change and/or in what will result from such changes. Direct inference from these discrepancies to problems of social change is by no means simple. The sorts of disturbances caused by such discrepancies may appear to have their effects in areas quite different from the focus of disturbance itself. For example, there are a variety of different views about individual psychology compatible with the expectation that upsets traceable to a given area of social interaction result in changes of behavior in areas of social action which may be at a considerable remove from the genesis of the disturbance itself. In various connections above, examples have been given of changes thought to be entirely external to the one sphere with far-reaching implications for that sphere [e.g., see p. 395 for relevance of changes of family structures to general structures of government].

The problem of these discrepancies is further complicated by the fact that some of the possibilities of integration and adjustment in terms of any society depend on the fact that the ideal and actual structures do not in fact coincide. Since some of the ideal structures are mutually incompatible, approximations to ideal structures which do exist are at least in part a function of the fact that the approximation of actual structures to other ideal structures is not great. For example, as indicated [p. 27], if the average Chinese had been able to have the number of children he wished, the structure of equal inheritance among sons could not have been maintained to the degree it was in fact maintained. In this case one of the major structural obstacles to feudalism in the classical sense would have been abolished had the actual family size in fact approximated the ideal family size.

The problem of these discrepancies is further complicated by the role of rationality in social behavior. While the members of a given society are always to some extent aware of such discrepancies, they are never completely aware of the extent of them. Furthermore, the fact that they are not completely aware of the discrepancies does not mean that these discrepancies do not have implications both for stress and strain and for the possibilities of integration. Neither the implications of the discrepancies between ideal and actual structures nor the set of discrepancies themselves are ever a simple function of rationality in the sense that these discrepancies and their implications can be explained by the hypocrisy of individuals who profess one set of ideal structures but do not in fact believe in them. The problem of discrepancies is never primarily a function of the fact that ideal ideal structures do not coincide with actual ideal structures.

One of the nasty problems facing both social scientists and people primarily concerned with policy questions is the undoubted fact that some, if not all, members in any society are capable of hypocrisy. Therefore, some discrepancies do result from hypocrisy. Nevertheless, the general membership of a society is never so rational or so self-conscious about the ideal structures which they hold that they are capable of being hypocritical about every instance in which their ideal structures do not coincide with their actual structures. Virtuosity in hypocrisy is probably as rare as other forms of virtuosity. There is, therefore, always a problem of separating out the problems which involve hypocrisy from those which do not. This problem is to some extent simplified by the fact that the major endemic problems of these discrepancies can never be accounted for solely in terms of hypocrisy. For purposes of both social analysis and policy decisions, cynics to the contrary notwithstanding, one is more likely to be correct if one assumes that these discrepancies are not the result of hypocrisy than if he assumes the reverse. Such an assumption need not become dangerous unless one is inalert to the possibility of hypocrisy.

There are in the main two reasons why the approximation of actual to ideal structures can never be complete. The first of these is the problem of adequate knowledge. Knowledge of the individual members of a society is never sufficient for them to be completely aware of all of the possibilities of ideal and actual structures. Therefore, they are never able by purely rational means to eliminate the possibility of discrepancies which arise simply from lack of knowledge. One of the inevitable results of lack of knowledge in this sphere is the fact that some of the ideal structures are always inconsistent with one another.

There is another reason why this coincidence cannot exist. If the ideal and actual structures did coincide, the resultant social system, regardless of whether characterized by the kind and levels of interdependency characteristic of relatively modernized as opposed to relatively nonmodernized societies, would be such that the resultant set of social structures would be unbelievably brittle. Any change in the setting of such a social system with any implication for any other structures would have to result in immediate and far-reaching changes in the whole set of ideal and actual structures if they were to continue in coincidence with one another. Almost any conceivable adjustment in any structure would require an extremely general social revolution.

The critical problem with regard to these discrepancies is never the problem of trying to eliminate them altogether. From the point of view of policy formulation the critical problem is always the problem of eliminating those discrepancies which interfere with the aims of policy without that elimination having unintended and/or unrecognized effects which interfere with the ends of policy immediately aimed at or with other equally or perhaps more relevant aims of policy. It is especially important to avoid preoccupation with the elimination of such discrepancies. The best policy solution in a given case may be the substitution of a different set of discrepancies for those currently in existence.

Finally, on a much more specific level, detailed awareness of the discrepancies between ideal and actual structures plus knowledge about those which can be manipulated easily as opposed to those which cannot lie at the heart of much of what is meant by sound political judgment, a sense of political reality, etc. The essence of the conception of compromise in the realm of public affairs, as elsewhere, is a solution to a given problem in terms of a new set of discrepancies between ideal and actual structures.

I I I
MAIN LINES OF VARIATIONS AMONG SOCIETIES
A. SUBSTANTIVE VARIATIONS
1. INTRODUCTION

The range of substantive variation of social structures is too great to be discussed in any detail here. As yet no highly developed taxonomy of demonstrated scientific utility has been generally accepted. The distinction between the structures of relatively modernized and relatively nonmodernized societies is at most a beginning of such a taxonomy. Here I shall only discuss these variations in broad terms, drawing together the material previously presented.

In this discussion certain relations between the elements common to any society and the main lines of variation must be kept clear. First, the common elements always underlie the variations. This is the sense in which men are everywhere the same, and societies everywhere like men. Every variation as between one society and another is either a variation in the special form taken by one of the common elements already discussed above or a special form of some less general element. If the latter, the common elements will still be requisites for its existence. The particular treatment of an infant by a mother or the particular institutionalization of leadership in a governmental organization may constitute a special variation unique to a given society of the common elements already stressed above. On the other hand the variation may in a given society represent a social structure that is not classifiable under the heading of role differentiation, solidarity, economic allocation, political allocation, or integration and expression. I find it difficult to give examples of this last category because, in devising the scheme of analysis used here, had I been able to think of so general an exception, I would have revised the scheme of analysis itself. Nevertheless, it would be radically misleading to imply that this scheme of analysis rigorously rules out the possibility of such an additional form of variation in any particular society.[24]

Although the common elements of societies always underlie the variations among societies, the common elements never exhaust the elements in any particular society.[25] That is to say, there is no society in which the elements consist solely of those elements which that society has in common with all other societies. This is not true of any society [societies] unless one is considering societies solely on the level of the common elements of all societies, and this sense of common elements exhausting the elements of the societies concerned is simply a case of sterile tautology. The fact that the common elements never exhaust the elements in any society on the level of generalization of interest for specific analyses constitutes the sense in which societies, like men, are everywhere different from one another. In some comparative analyses the variations appear on more general levels of interest than on others, but there are no comparative analyses in which elements of variation fail to appear on any and all possible levels.

For purposes of policy decisions it is quite important to know in what respect policy questions focus on the common elements which underlie variations in any societies and in what respect they focus on the variations themselves. There is a sense in which, unless policy makers are able to come up with some alternative to a society as a form of social organization, the common elements which are essential for all societies if they are to be stable set an unbreachable set of limits on the possibilities of effective policy formation. For example, given the present state of our knowledge in the fields of biology, psychology, and various of the social sciences, it is not far-fetched to hold that it is not possible to have a society in which there is no family organization. Furthermore, there is some question as to whether or not conceivable improvements in that knowledge would make such a variation possible.[26]

It was possible on these grounds alone to conclude that a policy

[24] The scheme in its present stage of development is as a minimum theoretically deficient to the extent that, although I cannot think of exceptions on this level, I cannot present a general principle other than a tautological one to rule out such a possibility.

[25] Even if the types of variation which I find it so difficult to envisage do exist, they exist in addition to and at lower levels of generalization than those presented as the common elements of any society. Hence the common elements can still be said in principle to underlie the variations.

[26] Even the most cavalier theoreticians pause before generalizing about presently inconceivable alterations in our knowledge.

program such as that originally announced in Communist China about the communes would be a failure if actually introduced as called for in the prospectus. Although one cannot rule out the possibility of a policy doomed to failure being instituted, in many such cases in general and in this one in particular, it may be [and was] quite reasonable to predict that the policy as called for could not or would not in fact be fully introduced. On the other hand, alterations in the variations do not place this sort of limit on policy decisions. Many of them are quite compatible with the continued existence of some sort of society. The crucial question with regard to policies calling for alterations in the variations among societies is the ordinary policy question rather than the *catastrophic policy* question, that is to say it is a question of whether or not the results of such alteration will in fact be what the policy makers predict and seek, without raising the question of the viability of any society.

In Part I, Chapter 2 above I have discussed certain distinctions among relatively nonmodernized societies which on the whole I have held to obscure rather than advance the problem of substantive variation among such societies. That contention bears iteration here with regard to these classifications of the main variations in societies in general. For example, within the range of variation of relatively nonmodernized societies, the distinction between Chinese and Japanese social structures is considerably greater and more general than the distinction between Chinese *and* Japanese social structures on the one hand and those of certain relatively nonmodernized European societies on the other hand. If one wishes to be more cautious, one might state that if the difference is not greater it would at least be difficult to demonstrate that it is not as great. The same sort of objection may be raised about classificatory terms such as European society unless that term is actually used to mean those societies whose associated territories exist on that particular continent. In discussions of this sort the term is rarely used with so precise a geographical referent, and endless clever and erudite academic exercises have turned on such questions as whether or not the society of Great Britain or the society of Russia, particularly the latter, is in fact a European society. The really important thing about designations of this sort is that they were not devised without motive, however inutile they may be as a basis for a scientific taxonomy. These designations recommended themselves because there was at least an element in each distinction which in some manner, however inexact, conveyed to those who took it up a sense of distinction of which they felt in need. The great problem of such distinctions, of course, is that they not only get passed on from teacher to student, but they get passed on quite readily to the general public and to practitioners in the field of public affairs. At this stage it is the very inexplicitness of such terms which in part recommends them. Finally, a sort of intellectual closure is reached in which a considerable number of people assume that these terms must have had some precise and useful meaning or they would not be in such general use. At that point the terms are not only firmly set; they have also become a means for begging the question, quite unintentionally of course, rather than of bringing students progressively closer to grasp with distinctions difficult to phrase. One of the most dramatic examples of clichés of this sort turning into a major point of view and attitude relevant to public affairs is embodied in the use of the phrase *the mysterious orient* to cover Chinese society. The traditional Chinese placed perhaps as little emphasis on the mysterious as any people in history. Furthermore, because of the careful creation, maintenance, collection, and constant interpretation of records and broad historical treatises, Chinese society, is perhaps the least mysterious society of any considerable scale prior to the middle of the nineteenth century.

Classifications such as primitive, nonprimitive societies, literate, nonliterate societies are important in general social analysis if carefully and rigorously used. As far as general usage is concerned such classifications are almost never accompanied by rigor and care. For most of the purposes here distinctions of this sort are of relatively little use since most societies of great concern from this point of view are neither primitive in the most careful sense of that term nor nonliterate. For all the importance of these distinctions carefully used, relatively nonmodernized literate societies and nonprimitive societies have more in common with their opposites in these taxonomies than they have with any relatively modernized literate or nonprimitive societies.

There is another set of social taxonomies which are misleading, or relatively useless in their represent form for an entirely different reason. These are the cases which suffer from the fallacy of misplaced dichotomies. There are classifications such as the gemeinschaft–gesellschaft, mechanical–organic, folk-urban societies, etc. These classifications are improper dichotomies in the sense that although the societies at one pole of the distinction may be said in some cases to lack elements at the other pole of the distinction, the reverse has never been the case. Thus, although improbable, there might conceivably be gemeinschaft, mechanical, folk societies totally lacking in gesellschaft, organic, urban characteristics. *But,* there never have been, and never will be, any societies of the gesellschaft, organic, urban types totally lacking in gemeinschaft, mechanical, folk characteristics.[27]

These dichotomies almost always contain a useful element, however. One end of the dichotomy is almost always overwhelmingly concerned with some sort of set of what has here been called common elements in any society. Those common elements are usually considered in a form readily recognizable as characteristic of many relatively nonmodernized societies, especially primitive ones. The other category in the dichotomy, however, as ordinarily used, tends to imply that these elements are totally lacking in other types of societies, and usually relatively modernized societies are being referred to by the other category in the dichotomy. This can, of course never be the case. The societies classified under the heading of the other category pose some of their most interesting and peculiar problems both for social analysts and for students of public affairs specifically by virtue of the fact that despite these elements which they have in common with all other societies, they are also characterized by such peculiar and special variations in other respects. It would, for example, perhaps make matters much simpler if one could say of gesellschaft [roughly, relatively modernized] societies that strong fam-

[27] One of the major claims of Emile Durkheim to fame as a sociologist lies in the fact that of the many creators of such misplaced dichotomies, he is the only social analyst to have seen through his creation, abandon it for improved formulations, and continue work utilizing the important element of insight in his earlier set of concepts without continuing to bollix the analysis by further use of the thoroughly confusing and fallacious implications of his original formulation. In a famous early volume entitled *The Division of Labor* (translated from the French by George Simpson, The Free Press, Glencoe, Ill., 1947) he distinguished between mechanical and organic societies, and went on to a discussion of the modern contract as typical of the organic societies. Part way through that discussion he realized, and pointed out, that contracts could not be generally used were it not for what he called the "noncontractual elements in contracts," i.e., general standards of honesty such that contracts would ordinarily be fulfilled without the requirement of court enforcement, etc. These noncontractual elements were exactly the sort of elements which he had previously held to characterize mechanical rather than organic societies. Once having seen the relevance of the one type to the other, he never again fell into this particular simple form of the fallacy of misplaced dichotomies. In this respect Durkheim demonstrated his superiority as a theorist to other thinkers who misplaced this dichotomy. He did not beg questions with it or make *ad hoc* qualifications. He saw through it, salvaged what was fruitful, and went on. It is one of the ironies of intellectual history that this dichotomy is still taught as one of Durkheim's contributions. His contribution as one may judge from reading Parsons [Talcott Parsons, *The Structure of Social Action*, McGraw-Hill Book Company, Inc., New York, N.Y., 1935, pp. 308–323] lay not in devising the dichotomy, which had several more or less independent discoverers, but in seeing through it.

ily feelings were relatively irrelevant to their members whereas such feelings were the essence of the attitudes of members of gemeinschaft societies. If this were the case, it would be very easy indeed to understand how, *ideally speaking,* you might expect so many areas of social activity to be ideally [or actually] uninfluenced by family matters in relatively modernized contexts. It would, however, make a mystery [the "mysterious West"?] of the fact that family feelings have so much *actual* influence. Actually the interesting thing about relatively modernized societies in this respect is that, in the face of important family concerns, their members are able to maintain such separations even on the ideal level. The fact that such separations are carried as far as they are on the actual level is even more surprising under the circumstances. To use a dichotomy that, even by implication, detracts attention from this is to use a dichotomy that diverts attention from critical interrelationships and gives to many problems an air of original caprice and malice.

There are various and numerous taxonomies which focus on a single aspect of societies. The distinction between capitalist and socialist societies focuses on questions of the form of ownership of property; that between democratic and authoritarian societies focuses on certain elements of the allocation of power; that between Christian and non-Christian societies focuses on religious distinctions; etc. Most of these dichotomies have been devised on an *ad hoc* basis for quite limited purposes of analysis whether those who have devised these classifications have realized it or not. Whatever the intentions of the authors may have been, these dichotomies have not been chosen with a view to their general relevance to social structure except insofar as those who devise and use them have tended to think monistically. All such dichotomies focus attention on a single variable. To the extent that a single variable is relevant to general social structure, these dichotomies are also relevant. As generally treated, however, these classifications lend themselves to monistic treatments which inevitably turn out to be either true but meaningless or meaningful but false. They are true but meaningless if one takes the basic element on which the classification is devised and by definition, in effect, makes it *the* relevant variable in any and all cases. If, for example, *the* religious variable is defined as the only one that can cause change, then it is perfectly true but perfectly meaningless that religious differences are the only ones important in explaining variations. If on the other hand one defines the single variable in any other way, some difficult person will always turn up with an exception to the generalization that "only religious differences explain variations," and therefore show the statement, though quite meaningful, to be untenable.

Dichotomies of this sort when used for quite limited purposes, however, are frequently the source of important advances in social understanding. The scholarship and analysis based on the distinction between societies characterized by common-law structures versus Roman-law structures are of a very high order and important from many points of view. The same may be said about numerous studies in terms of the three dichotomies mentioned above, but when these dichotomies are used as though they were derived on general bases rather than on a limited *ad hoc* basis they tend overwhelmingly to fall into the type of difficulty alleged.

2. VARIATIONS IN MODERNIZATION

Although it is a taxonomy only just begun, I find the gross distinction between relatively modernized and relatively nonmodernized societies the most general and useful taxonomy. It is a polar taxonomy permitting of indefinite distinctions of degree as between theoretical extremes, it is possible to speak specifically of the variations in structures among the types of societies which in general cluster at one end of the scale by contrast with those which cluster at the other—and it is possible to treat differences and similarities within and between those clusters in terms of several relevant variables as well as a set of constants characteristic of all societies. The possibility of continuous variation between the polar extremes—the fact that it is not a binary distinction as emphasized by the use of the term *relatively* prior to the terms *modernized* or *nonmodernized*—emphasizes at one and the same time the possibility of variations and the inevitability of common elements. Throughout this treatment I have tried to emphasize again and again these common elements as well as the variations. With a view to more detailed relevance I have constantly reiterated that were it not for the common elements which extend across these categories, however great their variations, it would be impossible to understand how individuals from backgrounds in these different types of societies could possibly communicate with one another—especially given difficult language barriers as such.

Before treating the major lines of variations in terms of the aspects of societies classified in terms of this distinction, I would pull together the discussion of this classification with the following hypotheses:

(1) Whatever the variations among them, any two relatively

nonmodernized societies have more in common with one another on more general levels of social structure than any one of them has in common with any relatively modernized society even though that society may have developed out of one of the relatively nonmodernized societies under consideration.

(2) Corollary to the previous hypothesis (1) is the proposition that any two or more relatively modernized societies, regardless of variations among them have more in common with one another at more general structural levels than any one of them has in common with any relatively nonmodernized society even though it may have developed out of the relatively nonmodernized society concerned.

(3) As the level of modernization increases, the level of structural uniformity among relatively modernized societies continually increases regardless of how diverse the original basis from which change took place in these societies may have been. In other words, the more modernized relatively modernized societies become, the more they resemble one another.[28]

(4) It is not possible to maintain an hypothesis similar to (3)

[28] This does not imply that they are all becoming more like any particular relatively modernized society at any given point in time. In general U.S. society is the most highly modernized society extant. I assume that it will continue to be more highly modernized than the others and to modernize more rapidly most of the time, though this is not germane to the present discussion. The point intended is illustrated in the graph on the following page. Great Britain, Japan, Russia and the United States are chosen solely for illustrative purposes. Early in the process Great Britain was undoubtedly ahead of United States society in these respects. American society started out well behind that of Great Britain and passed her somewhere in the late nineteenth or early twentieth century. Both Russia and Japan were late-comers with steep upward curves. I assume all converge asymptotically toward some impossibly high level of modernization [at point M on the curve]. As they do—even though American society may be well in the lead in the process—I do not consider the others as becoming more like American society in any sense save that all are becoming more modernized. Thus the difference between American society and that of Great Britain in 1920 [represented by A'B' on the graph] is not as great as the difference between American society of 1920 and 1950 [represented by C'A'' on the graph] or between 1950 and 1980 [represented by D'C'' on the graph]. All of the relatively modernized societies become increasingly similar to one another as the process continues and increasingly different from their own pasts. As this convergence increases, the requisites for the various stages of modernization rather than the historical bases from which these changes started in say the nineteenth century become increasingly relevant in the analysis of all of them. The differences which remain at any stage, however, remain explicable largely in terms of the differing implications for modernization of the historical bases from which those changes took place.

It is quite conceivable that these curves cross and recross one another. Although the curves are drawn as smooth continuous curves, they need not be, etc. A three dimensional curve would be more informative.

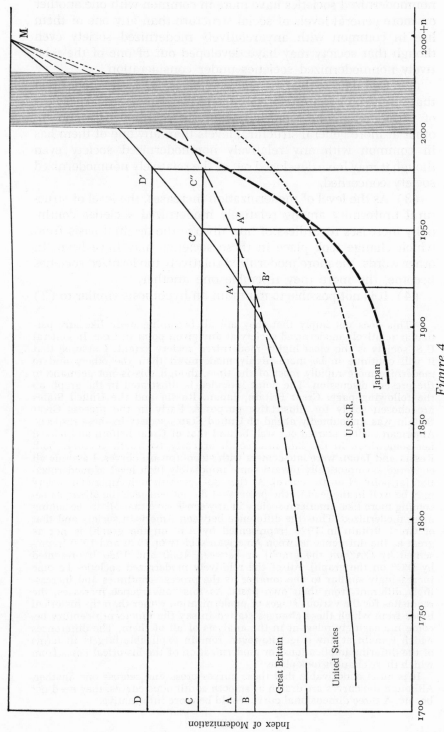

Figure 4

about relatively nonmodernized societies. Within the range of nonmodernization known to us there is relatively little basis for believing that the range of variation tends to diminish unless one invokes special additional factors such as extremely limited geographical environments, etc.

(5) Not only do relatively modernized societies tend to become more similar to one another as modernization progresses, but endemic in relatively modernized societies, if they are at all stable, is a constant increase in the level of modernization.

(6) In principle there are various upper limits on the extent to which modernization can increase,[29] but so far no case has reached such limits.

(7) Although it is not possible to maintain that there is a general tendency toward greater uniformity in structure among different cases of relatively nonmodernized societies, it is possible to maintain that the structural variations among such societies are on the whole confined to certain types of variations. For example, there is some variation among relatively nonmodernized societies with regard to how much their members emphasize predominantly universalistic criteria either ideally or actually, but they never emphasize them highly by contrast with such emphases by the members of relatively modernized societies. The most important variation among relatively nonmodernized societies in this respect is not so much variation in the ratio of emphasis of their members on predominantly universalistic as opposed to predominantly particularistic criteria but rather upon the substantive nature of the particularistic criteria themselves.

Although I hold this classification to be more relevant to more general structural distinctions than any other, it has not been developed beyond the level of the major distinction itself. Subcategories have hardly been developed at all. Insofar as predominantly modernized societies tend to become increasingly similar, this lack may not be a matter of great concern to the policy maker as far as they are concerned. Even here, however, it would be enormously useful for further development of analysis to have a highly developed taxonomy on the basis of different stages or levels of modernization, etc. No tendency toward general uniformity apart from the most general classification as relatively nonmodernized societies characterizes all such societies and thereby mitigates the shortcomings of lack of further develop-

[29] For example, the requisite level of centralization can conceivably exceed the possibility of adequate knowledge to plan effectively and/or the rate of change might exceed the capacity of men to adjust to change.

ment of the taxonomy from any point of view. Insofar as the distinction has been developed, the discussion above has gone into some detail with regard to the implications of both the common and the variable elements characteristic of societies. The summary reiteration of the variations touched upon is carried out below.

B. VARIATIONS IN THE ASPECTS OF SOCIETIES

1. VARIATIONS IN THE POSITION OF ORGANIZATIONS AS SUBSYSTEMS OF THE SOCIETY

One of the major lines of variations among societies has to do with the manner in which the importance of given organizations is stressed by the members of the society. As a minimum variation along these lines takes the form of differences in the persons by whom the importance is stressed and differences in the purposes or respects for which the importance of the organization is stressed. Something of the range of variation in these respects may be illustrated by reference to families as organizations.

As far as family organizations are concerned we know perfectly well that they are always considered to be crucially important organizations by the vast majority of the membership of any given society. Nevertheless, there remains an enormous variation with regard to the questions "By whom is the family stressed and for what purposes." In the context of relatively nonmodernized societies, for example, as far as the vast majority of the population is concerned, for both adults and children alike the family is likely to be the major unit in terms of which most of their behavior is reckoned. In the context of relatively modernized societies this is much more likely to be true of very young children than of adults. Insofar as it is true of adults, it is true in a different sense than it is true of children. For example, among adults sex role differentiation is more important in this connection than among children. The family in these contexts is much more of a focus of behavior for adult females than for adult males. At an early age it becomes less true of children in the context of relatively modernized societies than in the context of relatively nonmodernized societies.

To use another example, governmental organizations in some societies are organizations such that the average member of the society minimizes as much as possible, or has minimized for him, his direct contact with members of the government, whereas in other societies scholars stress the fact that mass participation in action in terms of governmental organization and well-nigh universal interaction among the members of the society and the members of the government is essential to stability.

At least two types of organizations are always stressed by the members of any society. These are family organizations and governmental organizations. Several others are also characteristic of any society of any considerable scale. The family is always stressed as important by virtually everyone, and we know some of the respects in which this emphasis is important. Even in a comparison of family and governmental organizations, however, clear-cut variations in emphasis can be shown. The members of relatively modernized societies emphasize types of organizations which may not even be present in relatively nonmodernized societies. Finally, there is considerable variation among relatively nonmodernized societies in that the members of some emphasize types of organizations which are not stressed by the members of others at all.

In addition to the question of which organizations are stressed, there is the closely related question of how much given organizations are stressed. Again the questions may be raised by whom and for what purposes. Finally, there is the question of how given organizations are stressed relative to one another. Both within the context of a given society and in the contrast between two or more societies again the questions of by whom and for what arise. It is easy to illustrate both points from the cases of China and Japan. In the context of traditional Chinese society the family was stressed more than the government for the vast majority of individuals in the society both ideally and actually. In the context of Tokugawa Japan the government, at least ideally speaking, was stressed more than the family. In this sense at least it is possible to maintain that the position in the general social structure of the family in China received greater stress than the position of the family in Tokugawa Japan. In all statements of this sort, however, one must be prepared to stipulate with some precision exactly what is meant by more important or by more stress. If this is not done, such discussions are more likely to beg than answer questions.

Finally, cutting across all questions of differing emphases on organizations by the members of societies, it is essential to keep in mind the distinction between ideal and actual structures. One of the most important types of variations among societies with structures which seem to be quite similar on initial inspection has to do with variations in the approximation of the actual to the ideal structures.

2. VARIATIONS IN THE SPECIALIZATION OF ORGANIZATIONS

Organizations vary greatly in the manner in which from the point of view of their members, from the point of view of others in the society, and/or from the point of view of an observer, they are specialized with regard to the various aspects of behavior discussed above in Part II. First, organizations vary with regard to how much emphasis is placed on specialization in terms of them. If they are predominantly economically oriented organizations, how highly specialized are they with regard to the economic preoccupation? Who among the members of the society emphasizes this specialization? In the context of societies many of whose members interact little if at all in terms of specialized organizations, it is difficult for *those* members to understand or appreciate the fact that there are organizations so specialized. Initial reaction of people not accustomed to the structures of such specialized organizations may be to regard action in terms of them as laid open to individualism by default—to be cut loose from all ordinary restraints by virtue of this peculiar emphasis on specialization not generally understood by them.

The other major variation in this regard has to do with what is specialized and again by whom, etc. The range of specialized organizations characteristic of relatively nonmodernized societies tends to be quite restricted, and the proportion of the members of the society who actually become members of such organizations is also on the whole quite restricted. In relatively modernized societies on the other hand relatively few organizations remain nonspecialized, ideally speaking. Apart from organizations like the family, other organizations tend overwhelmingly to become specialized as they develop.

Consideration of the question of specialization in terms of ideal and actual structures is relevant here in the general sense that it is always relevant. It is, however, especially relevant as a focus of stress and strain. With new developments in such specialization one of the major bones of contention is likely to be among those members of the society who feel that, ideally speaking, a given organization should not be specialized in this sense by contrast with those who feel that it should. In the social change characteristic of modernization some of the greatest foci of nostalgia for the good old days are organizations such as the family which were once able to symbolize all things to all people.

3. VARIATIONS IN EXPLICITNESS

Societies vary enormously with regard to how explicitly the social structures are known and understood by the members of the society. In this connection all sorts of distinctions are relevant. The emphasis on law as contrasted with an emphasis on tradition, an emphasis on status as distinguished from one on contract, an emphasis on functionally specific as opposed to functionally diffuse relationships as those terms have been used in this work—all of these have importantly to do with variations in the explicitness of social structures.

There is, of course, some explicitness throughout the social structures of any society. Marked efforts to make as many things explicit as possible are characteristic of the members of some societies as can be judged from the emphasis on checks and balances in terms of the governmental organization of the United States. On the other hand there are also certainly societies whose members do not emphasize explicitness but rather the qualities of judgment inculcated by a proper acquaintance with the classics. There are also an indefinite number of possibilities of combining the two.[30]

Some inexplicitness about social structures is characteristic of all societies, and in some cases the degree of inexplicitness is carried quite far. Nevertheless, it is doubtful that inexplicitness is ever erected into a general principle either in the ordinary ideal sense or in the utopian sense to the extent that the principle of explicitness sometimes is. The emphasis on inexplicitness in general is more often a matter of default than of self-conscious ideal. It requires highly developed intellectual sophistication to place self-conscious emphasis on inexplicitness as a preferred state with regard to social structures.

Variations in the approximation of actual to ideal structures are highly relevant to variations with regard to explicitness in

[30] A case of what begins as an emphasis on explicitness and turns into a case of judgment based on the classics is the story of a famous but highly individualistic self-constituted judge in the early history of West Texas. The Judge was learned in the law in terms of only one volume in that field, *The Law of Negotiable Instruments*. The Judge claimed that the law was a remarkable thing, that no case arose which could not be settled in terms of a precedent to be found in *The Law of Negotiable Instruments*. On one occasion the Judge was faced by a difficult paternity suit in which the plaintiff freely admitted that the defendant had probably begun his relations with her after the child in question had been conceived. The Judge, after careful search of *The Law of Negotiable Instruments* found in favor of the plaintiff by holding that the case was clearly provided for in the ruling to the effect that, as he interpreted it, "If you can't find the maker of a note the last endorsee has got to pay."

societies. After all, one of the more poignant forms of inexplicitness by default is that inexplicitness which arises when an individual is willing to be explicit, wants to be explicit, is wanting in
explicitness, and is unaware of his inexplicitness.

4. VARIATIONS IN KNOWLEDGE

Variations in cognitive aspects among societies are closely related
to the variations in explicitness about social structures discussed
immediately above. Explicitness about social structures is, after
all, one major form of knowledge characteristic of any society. In
the context of all societies, quite apart from the general question
of explicitness, there is some emphasis on both basic and intermediate knowledge. The arguments underlying the general
relevance of the common elements of knowledge in all societies
have been discussed above. The distinction between basic and
intermediate knowledge applies to all societies, but what constitutes basic knowledge and what constitutes intermediate knowledge varies enormously. It has been suggested above [p. 662] that
the ratio between basic and intermediate knowledge probably
approaches a constant. It would be more temperate to say that as
a minimum they vary directly with one another. It is certainly
correct to say that there are major differences among societies
with regard to the content, the degree of differentiation, etc.,
in both the categories of basic and intermediate knowledge.

It is popular today among the most sophisticative social thinkers in relatively modernized social contexts to point the finger of
scorn, don the look of alarm, and cry havoc at the state of mass
learning and mass culture, but the fact of the matter is that even
taking into consideration relatively rare cases such as the average
Chinese peasant's unusual knowledge of Chinese history and the
classics, the breadth and variety of basic knowledge among the
members of any of the relatively modernized societies is out of all
context with the breadth and variety of basic knowledge in any of
the relatively nonmodernized societies. Exactly the same sort of
observation may be made about the breadth and variety of the
various forms of intermediate knowledge. The level of specialization of knowledge associated with the so-called natural sciences
alone probably equals, if it does not far surpass any comparable
refinement or specialization in learning previously whether one
contemplates the scholastic philosophers and theologists of the
Middle Ages, the field of Talmudic scholarship, the resources of
Chinese historiography, the field of alchemy, or whatever. Modern physicists for example, in different fields of specialization no

longer really expect to be able to communicate in great detail with one another, let alone with nonphysicists.

Here again in the face of enormous variations we are bereft of fruitful taxonomies for treatment of the wealth of material we know to exist. No attempt is made here to alter this general state of affairs. It is important for students of public affairs and educated laymen as well as scholars everywhere, however, to realize that we are already in general enormously sensitive to a far greater variation in knowledge than we have any well-worked-out set of concepts to handle. This whole field of study has progressed little beyond concepts such as wealth, depth, richness, varied, refined, sophisticated, etc. The categories I intend to use here are a selection from this set of clichés of three distinctions of some relevance to students of public affairs. All of these distinctions have to do with types of cognitive emphases. The first is the distinction between rational and arational emphases, the second is between scientific, technological and common-sensical emphases, and the third is the distinction between long-run cumulative attitudes toward knowledge and *ad hoc* or stagnant ones. Obviously all three distinctions are closely related.

The rational-arational distinction has been used above. Rational knowledge is knowledge which at least in theory could be analyzed scientifically. At any given state of development one could observe about a given bit of allegedly rational knowledge: (1) that it was in fact rational [i.e., that it contained no logical fallacies and its allegations of fact, if any, were correct], (2) that it was irrational [i.e., it contained a logical error and/or an error in allegation of fact], or (3) that at the present stage of our knowledge of logic and of fact, although there was no reason to believe that one could not in principle find out whether it was logically consistent or not or whether the facts were tenable or not, for the present one lacked the necessary logical techniques or data gathering techniques to make a definitive decision. It is important to realize that whenever rational knowledge is heavily emphasized, there are bound to be a large number of cases of irrational or erroneous knowledge around. Indeed, it is the very emphasis on rational knowledge that radically increases the ability to detect actual instances of irrationality.

Arational knowledge, on the other hand, has to do with that knowledge which is not in principle testable in one or both of the two senses referred to above. Regardless of what others may think about such knowledge, the people who believe in it may not believe the test of logical consistency or of empirical verifiability to be relevant to what they are thinking about. As already indicated above, there is no society whose members are completely lacking in use of and appreciation of either rational or arational knowledge. Wherever one runs into terms such as *fate* one is likely to be dealing with arational knowledge. It is not, in principle, possible to prove or disprove scientifically the existence of God.[31]

Although societies are identical in that the members of all societies place some emphasis on both rational and arational knowledge, they vary radically in the types of each and in the relation of each to the other. Sometimes the emphasis is overwhelmingly on arational knowledge with rational knowledge in a subsidiary position insofar as it is consciously recognized. Members of other societies appear to have held that "faith and reason cannot contradict, but that if they do faith takes precedence." In other social contexts the emphasis is so overwhelmingly on rationality that many become self-conscious and embarrassed if it becomes clear in certain contexts that they are relying heavily on arational knowledge. This last state of affairs is typical, increasingly, of members of relatively modernized societies. Regardless of the nature of the enormously varied cognitive structures in societies, there is one generalization of great relevance for those concerned with public affairs. If one wishes to change the point of view of others in a realm of action in which the emphasis is on rational cognition, the problem is different in kind than if the emphasis is on arational cognition. In the former case efforts involving logic, demonstration, etc., methods to which the policy

---

[31] There is absolutely no point whatsoever for present purposes in getting involved in the epistemological question of whether or not questions which cannot be handled in terms of rational knowledge are meaningless questions. Whatever the definitive answer in philosophical terms may be to such questions there is absolutely no question that, from the point of view of some members of all known societies, indeed the vast majority of all known members of all known societies, questions of this sort have been considered germane and in some respects have been considered radically different from what have been here called rational ones. Malinowski was fond of pointing out that no people confuse bad magic with bad workmanship, that no people, for example, were so dominated by arational beliefs that they felt that magical rites would make corn grow if seeds were not planted or weeding neglected. For present purposes, whether or not arational knowledge *is* meaningless is quite beside the point. The vast majority of members of all known societies feel that some elements of arational knowledge quite relevant to their behavior in terms of social structures are meaningful. Without becoming involved in any ontology whatsoever, it is possible here to quote W. I. Thomas' remark that, "If men define situations as real, they are real in their consequences." Thomas, W. I. and D. S.: *The Child in America*, Alfred A. Knopf, Inc., New York, 1932, p. 572.

maker is accustomed, are highly relevant and often effective. In the latter case, before such arguments can take effect, there is a problem of conversion, of redefinition of the situation from the point of view of the persons to be convinced. They must either be converted to an emphasis on rationality as opposed to arationality in this connection, or they must be made to believe that what they previously regarded as a proper subject for the realm receiving arational emphasis really did not belong in that category at all, or they must be converted to a new form of arationality, if the effort to convince is to be effective.

The distinction between scientific, technological knowledge as opposed to common-sensical knowledge is closely related to the previous distinction in that it is largely concerned with special ways of looking at the rational sphere. This is not to say that the ordinary common-sensical point of view contains no elements of arational knowledge, but this point of view tends to be held in that area of knowledge most closely associated with the realistic connection between empirical means and empirical ends. People assert that the world is flat because that's the way it looks to almost everybody. Common-sensical knowledge is frequently rational within limited spheres of application. It tends to be made up of views specifically adjusted to a specific state of affairs. Scientific, technological knowledge on the other hand is characterized by the tendency, self-consciously, of the people who practice it to eliminate irrational and arational elements as far as possible, to eliminate them as systematically as possible and to arrive at particular solutions at least in part by deduction from and further elaboration of more general explicit principles. Common-sensical knowledge is usually the form of rational knowledge that happens to coincide with the traditional way of doing things. The history of science and technology is not without its important elements of traditionalization, but they are always getting overturned by new practitioners with new ideas. The justification of common-sensical knowledge is frequently that "we have always known this" or "this is the way our people have always done this." The justification of scientific, technological knowledge usually takes the form of someone asserting, "I can 'prove.'. . ."

The pair of terms just discussed above, when elaborated, develops into the distinction between a long-run cumulative attitude toward knowledge as distinguished from an *ad hoc* or relatively stagnant one. It is the essence of modern science that the central concern of the elite practitioners is with a body of extremely general theory. It is also an essential of the scientific attitude that one expects the body of general theory to develop and change.[32]

Another important feature of the history of science has been the fact that one of the major effects of the emphasis on a system of general theory has been to make the collection of knowledge cumulative in its effect in these fields. The rate of development of the natural sciences, for example, has in the last few decades outstripped their rate of development in all previous times. As these developments continue, the mutual relevance of exceedingly diverse bits of knowledge become increasingly important. For the vast majority of the members of the vast majority of societies in world history, the emphasis on long-run cumulative additions to rational knowledge has on the whole been absent. Today in relatively modernized contexts whole segments of university personnel are preoccupied with just such development; special laboratories and other organizations of all sorts abound. Most societies, however, have been as highly sedentary with regard to the state of the knowledge associated with them as with regard to other aspects. Even in the context of a society like Chinese society, whose members placed an enormous emphasis on knowledge in general, with certain notable exceptions the general attitude of the members toward knowledge was both *ad hoc* and stagnant. In certain fields of which the most notable is perhaps the field of historiography, the attitude of the scholars was a long-run and a cumulative one.[33] In other fields, however, the Chinese scholars were typical of scholars in relatively non-

[32] One of the wry ironies of modern propaganda lies in the simultaneous insistence from certain quarters that the works of Marx represent *the* development of scientific method par excellence in the social field and at the same time that these works have never been shown to be importantly in error since handed down. This is tantamount to taking pride in a science in which nothing of great theoretical importance has been discovered in over 100 years. The additional assertion that these works can never be shown to be false would take them clean out of the scientific realm altogether since one of the rules of the game of science is that scientific propositions are always, at least in theory, conceivably falsifiable. Though less dramatic than faith in a nonfalsifiable scientific theory, pride in a stagnant one is inconsistent enough.

[33] The enormous development of historiography by the traditional Chinese scholars constitutes a genuine puzzler for those scholars who maintain that the Chinese, for one reason or another, were simply incapable of doing scientific work. The field of historiography in general and the closely related questions of the authenticity of texts and the like were developed to a high point while Western scholars "were still hanging by their tails from the trees," as it were in these respects. Nothing about either the Chinese mind or Chinese society kept the Chinese scholar from being highly scientific in a quite modern sense about matters of considerable interest to him.

modernized societies. By fits and starts all sorts of brilliant discoveries were made so that scholars today can find all sorts of intriguing anticipations of quite modern scientific discoveries in fairly ancient works. Nevertheless, these isolated discoveries frequently appear as a pastime by private scholars. They were frequently not pursued systematically by the discoverer himself or even communicated generally to his colleagues.

When the members of a society accent a long-run cumulative attitude toward knowledge, there is always a heavy emphasis on communication of findings in general. For the most modernized of these societies that communication generally takes the form of publication in particular. This is no place to argue the virtues and shortcomings of publication as a cornerstone or as a fetish of the modern academic disciplines, but only to assert the enormous relevance of such an attitude for the cumulative aspects of modern knowledge. For the first time in world history the greatest threat to cumulative development in scientific fields is not the lack of communication but its plethora. Scholars are not only concerned because of their inability to read the journals of people in slightly different fields. They are growing increasingly alarmed at their inability to keep up with the flood of material directly oriented to the field in which they consider themselves expert. Periodic reviews of the state of discipline have become a fixed and important part of intellectual work. With each passing year in these more developed scientific disciplines this work becomes increasingly difficult for the individual scholar to carry out. It is quite predictable that one of the new forms of specialization in academia is going to be the individual who is especially good at writing general reviews of the state of his discipline. Such individuals need not be the most creative scholars themselves, but they are certain to be thought of affectionately by other scholars whose creativity may be flyingly buttressed by their efforts.

The distinctions with regard to the discrepancy between ideal and actual structures apply to variations in knowledge no less than to any other variations characteristic of societies. There is one special aspect of this discrepancy in connection with variations in knowledge, however. As the emphasis on rationality increases, in the areas of action in which it increases the discrepancy between ideal and actual structures consistent with stability is considerably less than in areas of activities with heavy emphasis on arationality, areas characterized by *ad hoc* stagnant knowledge on a common-sensical basis, etc. The greater the emphasis on rationality, the greater is the clarity of what constitutes ignorance and error. The more individuals accent rationality in

their ideal structures, the more clearly does irrationality constitute one of the discrepancies between ideal and actual structures.
Finally, the greater the emphasis on rationality, the greater is the
denigration of irrationality. To the extent that reason becomes
the hero, ignorance and error become villains. This constitutes
one of the sources of dynamism in the development of modern
science. When science is emphasized, the casting out of ignorance and error assumes some of the aspects of the struggle with
sin, but in this field any successful struggle with sin not only
removes an obstacle to virtue, it adds a specific increment to
virtue. In this specific sense there is no such thing as destructive
criticism from the point of view of a scientist. To learn that
something previously held tenable is untenable is to know more
than one knew before. The scientist holds that the disproof of any
proposition not previously known to be trivially false is highly
constructive.

5. VARIATIONS IN AFFECTIVE DISPLAY

Variations in affective display from one social setting to another are enormous. Here too, we have neither highly developed
taxonomies of great scientific fruitfulness nor generalizations
which have proved to be powerful tools of analysis across the
lines of social differences, despite marked advances in knowledge
of the emotions along certain lines. Variations in affective display
are especially noteworthy for students of public affairs. They are
usually literally highly modernized Westerners who find both
extremes of restraint and license in affective display quite discon-
certing. In considering the behavior of Japanese, for example,
persons from the United States are generally astonished by what
they consider to be the impassive aspect of Japanese affective
display in some contexts and its extreme lack of discipline in
others. Theoretically and practically one of the interesting things
about variations in affective display is that the distinction between relatively modernized and relatively nonmodernized societies is not as indicative in this sphere of concern as it seems to be
in most others—with one exception. Avoidance rather than intimacy of affective aspects, and hence to some degree restraint
with regard to affective display, tends to be emphasized in the
context of all organizations in terms of which heavy emphasis is
placed on rationality, universalistic criteria, and functional
specificity. This need not be the case of behavior in terms of other
organizations, however. Outside this sphere of behavior in terms
of relatively specialized organizations, variations in affective display are probably as great among different instances of relatively

modernized societies as among different instances of relatively nonmodernized societies or as between instances of relatively modernized and relatively nonmodernized societies. For quite general theoretical reasons it is unlikely that the trend toward similarity of relatively modernized societies can be as strong as has been asserted here without that trend also engulfing variations in affective display. Nevertheless, it certainly has not done so as yet, and few items are so frequently cited in attempts to distinguish national character among relatively nonmodernized societies and/or relatively modernized societies as terms descriptive of affective displays—terms such as volatile, excitable, phlegmatic, dour, calm, imperturbable, mercurial, genial, etc.

As far as variations in affective display are concerned the discrepancy between ideal and actual structures has a systematic bias. Discrepancies of this sort generally take the form of greater intimacy or greater lack of restraint where the ideal structures call for greater avoidance or restraint. Emphases on avoidance and restraint in affective display are frequent in social history, but virtuosity in attaining ideals of avoidance would seem to require greater talent than approaches to ideal structures which emphasize intimacy and lack of restraint. When the ideal structures emphasize intimacy and lack of restraint, insofar as the ideal and actual structures do not coincide, the discrepancy is more likely to be that the actual structure of intimacy and lack of restraint are different ones than the ideal structures call for rather than that more restraint and more avoidance is present than is called for. Actual affective displays in terms of the traditional Chinese family organization are generally characterized by higher levels of intimacy than the ideal structures call for. In the context of highly modernized, highly specialized organizations whose members emphasize avoidance, again, the departures from the ideal structures generally take the form of much greater intimacy than the ideal structures would lead one to expect.[34]

Some of the structures characteristic of every society always stress intimacy in affective displays, especially structures of the relations between some adults and infants and small children. Some relationships characteristic of every society are also predominantly avoidant, but there is every reason to believe that these are learned later in the life cycle of the average individual

[34] The development of the concept of the particularistic nexus which constituted such an important part of the studies carried out in association with the Fatigue Laboratory of The Harvard University Business School some decades ago gave evidence of this. See, for example, the studies of Roethlisberger and Dickson: *Management and the Worker,* Harvard University Press, Cambridge, Mass., 1939.

and that these are more difficult to maintain than the display of more intimate and less restrained affects. Whenever high levels of restraint and avoidance are stressed ideally, there is some area of activity in which the members of such relationships find relief in more intimate, less restrained displays, e.g., office parties.

6. VARIATIONS IN THE INTERDEPENDENCE OF ORGANIZATIONS

While there is no society in which interdependence among the organizations is totally lacking [that is to say, there is no society made up entirely of self-sufficient subsystems], a high level of self-sufficiency attained in terms of a large number of the organizations is characteristic of many societies. When this occurs, the units of highest self-sufficiency are usually family or village units in a relatively nonmodernized agrarian society. The level of interdependency always increases with increases in modernization, and even in relatively nonmodernized societies the level of interdependency is higher in town and urban environments than in the agrarian setting.

The two main lines of variations in interdependency have to do with the degree and kind of interdependence. It is possible to discuss these types of variations in scientifically fruitful ways even though these discussions would be immensely furthered by better ideas for measurement and better taxonomies. There is always much more actual than ideal interdependence. This is true of both relatively nonmodernized and relatively modernized societies. The ideals of self-sufficiency characteristic of relatively nonmodernized societies are never equalled by the actual levels of self-sufficiency attained. Ideally speaking, the traditional Chinese family unit in the countryside involved members who would have liked to see the family unit as completely self-sufficient as was compatible with the marriage system based on family exogamy.

Members of relatively modernized societies have a more curious ambivalence about interdependence. Both ideally and actually the level of interdependence that one would expect is high. The very level of specialization attained, however, has led to an expectation that the specialized organizations be much more completely separated from other organizations than is in fact possible. The very specialization of these organizations means that their members in their activities in terms of the organization will be interdependent with the members of many other organizations. The ideal, however, that these organizations be completely separate and distinct from others, for example, from family organizations, implies a self-sufficiency which, of course, can never actually be attained. The implications of what happens to an individual in his family setting for his behavior in terms of a government job, a university position, or a role in a business firm—and vice versa—are actually far greater than the ideal structures would lead one to expect. One of the most unusual aspects of relatively modernized societies is the extent of ideal separation actually achieved among many specialized organizations, but quite apart from the types of interdependence which are expected by the members under these circumstances, there are additional inescapable elements of interdependence which violate the ideal structures.

7. VARIATIONS IN GENERAL DEFINITIONS OF THE SITUATION [WELTANSCHAUUNG]

Some of the typical general definitions of the situation have already been mentioned in one or another connection above. Societies vary widely in the emphasis placed by their members on other-worldly versus this-worldly orientations, on ascetic versus nonascetic orientations, on determined [fatalistic] versus voluntaristic orientations, and on hostile versus benign orientations. There are, no doubt, many other distinctions which might be suggested.

The other-worldly versus this-worldly orientations are frequently discussed as the distinction between spiritual and materialistic orientations. I have placed great emphasis on the fact that there are no societies whose members are not oriented to material or this-worldly factors at all. Insofar as the members of a given society are oriented to other-worldly concerns, they are so oriented within a specific set of orientations to this-worldly matters. If a society is to continue to exist, some minimal orientation to the matters of this world is absolutely essential for the general membership. At the same time within a context of material orientations of this sort the members of societies vary enormously in the emphasis placed on other-worldly orientations. There are not only important variations among societies, but within any given society there are important variations among the members.

The ascetic versus nonascetic orientations are closely related to the ones just discussed above, but there is an additional element in this distinction. Ascetic performances are never indulged in by more than a small minority of the population. The ascetic way of life requires virtuosity just as much as piano playing does. Societies, however, vary widely from one another as to the emphasis placed by their members on the desirability of ascetic virtuosity.

The type of asceticism emphasized also varies widely. Hindu society, for example, was one whose members placed a very much higher emphasis on religious asceticism than is generally placed by the members of any of the relatively modernized societies. Insofar as asceticism is emphasized by the members of any relatively modernized society it is likely to be what Max Weber referred to as this-worldly asceticism, that is to say, they are likely to accent ascetic mastery over material events in a nonsensuous fashion. No relatively modernized society is distinguished by a membership placing heavy emphasis on other-worldly asceticism.

Determinism, insofar as it is accented by the members of a society, tends to take one of two forms. Either there is an accent on the physical determination of events or on the determination of events by the role of ideas in the lives of individuals. Idealistic determinism has always been much more popular on the part of philosophers of history than on the part of the members of the general population. Insofar as the general population is fatalistically oriented, even though fatalism is expressed as a function of the Will of the Gods, from the point of view of the members of such societies the Will of the Gods is usually worked out in a quite material fashion via the operation by people in terms of their social structures and via forces of the physical environment such as floods, storms, etc.

Closely related to this sort of determinism is a closed-class structure as opposed to one in terms of which ideally and actually there is some emphasis on social mobility among different class positions. In those societies whose members emphasize a voluntaristic as opposed to a fatalistic point of view there are always important elements of social mobility ideally as well as actually. Relatively nonmodernized societies vary widely with regard to the accent by members on determinism versus voluntarism, although throughout social history they have placed greater emphasis on determinism than on voluntarism. The members of all relatively modernized societies place a considerable emphasis on voluntarism even though the society may be highly authoritarian. The individual member of a society whose members emphasize voluntaristic definitions of the situation may feel hemmed in and trapped by factors over which he has no control, but characteristically individual members of such societies are highly frustrated by this state of affairs. Individuals in predominantly deterministically oriented societies may feel themselves to be the helpless pawns of fate, but that state of affairs is taken for granted. The person who knowingly resists fate is a fool rather than a heroic or tragic figure, though the person who unknowingly resists fate may be both heroic and tragic.

The distinction between hostile and benign definitions of the situation takes various forms. One of the most obvious forms in which this appears has to do with the type of proposition which is frequently central to the set of theological ideas characteristic of a society. In this form the extremes are the concepts of "men born good" as distinguished from "men born evil." This distinction has a great deal to do with the way in which the members of a given society conceive of social controls. Insofar as this definition of the situation is conceived to determine action, positions taken in terms of it are closely related to the fatalistic point of view. In general, societies characterized by the point of view that men are in a sense the masters of their fate are likely to have a benign definition of the situation. The members generally feel that, if man can command his own fate, he can command it for his good.

Such a definition of the situation is obviously closely related to the problem of evil, and there are no people of any society who have been totally uninterested in such problems. From one point of view members of all societies, regardless of the variations in this respect, come to some specific combination of the two definitions. If they regard their setting as essentially hostile, there is always to some extent the possibility that the combination of ideal and actual structures will result in more benign results. It is difficult to see how if the members of the society regard the environment as essentially hostile and feel that there is no possibility of offsetting it, they can avoid apathetic reactions. Societies vary enormously with regard to how much apathy on the part of the members can be tolerated if the society is to survive. In theory at least, however, there are always limits to tolerable apathy. Insofar as the members of a society regard the definition of the situation as benign, to some extent discrepancies between the ideal and actual structures are always looked to for an explanation of why evil can result despite such a benign environment. Despite the fact that these combinations frequently approach one another, the difference in point of view still remains of great significance in understanding action and hence in the formulation of any policies oriented to the alteration of the structures of action. In the one case orientation is to self-conscious behavior on the part of men to offset the disabilities into which all mankind is born. In the other case actors are more or less drawn to the point of view that the presence of evil is the result of a plot on the part of some more or less unaccountably wicked individuals to subvert the benign environment. The logical consistency of neither of these points of view is in question here. From a strict logical point of view there are, of course, questionable elements in both. Whatever their logical inconsistencies, each has implications for understanding the action of the individuals who believe in it.

There is a further implication of this distinction. Insofar as either position is held in an extreme form, and insofar as apathetic adjustments to the situation are avoided, both tend to predispose the members of the societies concerned to rational or pseudo-rational views of social problems. If the definition of the situation is regarded as hostile and apathy is avoided, some important set of the members of the society concerned are likely to devote their time and attention to explicit attempts to figure ways around the implications of hostile environment. To the extent that the definition of the situation is regarded as benign, explicit attention on the part of some set of the members of the society is overwhelmingly likely to be devoted to more or less rational consideration of how the individuals whose behavior contradicts the benign implications of the environment can be offset.

In the distinction between hostile and benign definitions of the situation the implications for the distinction between relatively modernized and relatively nonmodernized societies are not conclusive. I have no theoretical basis, not even a plausible one, for maintaining that the members of relatively nonmodernized societies are more likely to be characterized by one of these definitions of the situation, whereas the members of relatively modernized societies are likely to be characterized by the other. I do not even have a basis for maintaining that relatively nonmodernized societies may be characterized by either extreme, whereas relatively modernized societies can only be characterized by one extreme or the other. I suspect that relatively modernized societies are more likely to be characterized by a benign definition of the situation, simply because a belief in the possibility of ascetic mastery over the situation for the benefit of the members of the society is so characteristic of the members of relatively modernized societies. Other than a personally fatuous optimism, however, I see no sound reason to believe that this point of view is not as readily combinable with a Weltanschauung which holds man's general setting to be hostile—unless, of course, one follows the implications alleged above [see pp. 504–513] of the asymmetry about production and consumption.

All of these variations in the definition of the situation contain the possibility of considerable subvariations, but none of these definitions of the situation can be pushed to the extremes of the distinctions mentioned here, if the society is to survive. Men cannot live by faith alone any more than they can live by bread alone—at least they never have. This rules out the extreme of either the other-worldly or the this-worldly point of view. The extremes of the ascetic versus the nonascetic and the deterministic versus the voluntaristic points of view imply levels of virtuosity, a devil-may-care attitude, a complete sense of apathy, a complete lack of realism, or some combination of the four—none of which are compatible with the maintenance of any society. The fact that hostile definitions are always combined with some fudging in the direction of benign definitions of the situation has just been delineated. The inevitability of combinations of these points of view, however, does not alter the tenability of the proposition that variations in emphases on these extremes may be of the essence of understanding problems as viewed either from the point of view of the members of a given society or from the point of view of outsiders who would in some way alter the state of affairs characteristic of the members of a given society. It would hardly be necessary to emphasize the importance of these combinations were it not for an extremely general tendency to the fallacy of misplaced dichotomy in this connection. There are few radically false clichés about human points of view more generally believed in than the one which holds the members of some societies to be spiritually or other-worldly oriented as opposed to members of others who are materialistically or this-worldly oriented. Were either of these extremes possible for the members of a society as a whole, without any middle ground of combination, the contemplation of many social problems with a view to their solution would be a waste of time.

8. VARIATIONS IN THE EMPHASIS ON PARTICULARISM

Societies vary enormously in *how much* emphasis their members place on particularistic criteria of selection as well as the ranges of social relationships on which these emphases are placed. The discrepancy between ideal and actual structures certainly guarantees that there will be some actual emphasis on relatively universalistic criteria, but it is at least in theory possible that there be societies whose members, ideally speaking, place no emphasis whatsoever on universalism. In the context of such societies some predominantly universalistic results can be obtained by balances of various particularistic emphases and by violations of the ideal structures. There is no reason to believe, however, that the ideal structures themselves must contain specific universalistic elements. Such societies could not, of course, be relatively modernized societies, and the difficulty of maintenance of such purity of particularistic orientations would almost certainly increase with increases in scale reckoned either in terms of number of members involved or the size of the area inhabited by the members of the societies concerned. To the extent that the emphasis on particularism is high, as it is exceedingly likely to be in the context of all relatively nonmodernized societies, any shift in the direction of more nearly universalistic criteria is certain to undermine important elements in the general structures of control.

9. VARIATIONS IN ATTITUDES TOWARD ECONOMIC ASPECTS OF SOCIAL ACTION

This category is introduced here on a more or less *ad hoc* basis. It is really a subcategory of the discussion of variations with regard to specialization of organizations. Unlike discussions of variations in political aspects, religious aspects, etc., this category has to some extent been less fully explored in the social sciences if only because of the power of the development of the field of economics, emphasizing one general type of attitude toward economic aspects. This situation is being rapidly altered by the preoccupation of many economists with the problems of underdeveloped areas, but it still merits special mention here.

First, societies vary enormously with regard to the extent to which the economic aspects of action are specialized respectably. There is probably no society of any considerable scale without some specialized predominantly economically oriented organizations, but it is certainly not essential that the members in general of relatively nonmodernized societies, even though they be of considerable scale, regard such specialized organizations as respectable. It is quite conceivable that, from the point of view of the overwhelming proportion of the membership, if not all of it, the allocation of goods and services be regarded, ideally speaking, as only one of many concerns of the members of relatively nonspecialized organizations.

Closely related to this observation is the question of the extent to which economic preoccupations as such are regarded as respectable. Quite apart from the question of whether or not the allocation of goods and services *is* carried out in terms of specialized organizations, there is the question of whether or not individuals may be considered to be respectably preoccupied with the allocation of goods and services to the exclusion of or to the substantial subordination of other considerations. For example, even if merchants operate in terms of relatively nonspecialized organizations, their preoccupation with exchange as such may be regarded as disreputable by the general membership of the society and perhaps even by themselves. This point is somewhat more ticklish than the previous one because it is also true that there can be no society whose members in general are either totally unconcerned with the allocation of goods and services or relegate their concerns for the allocation of goods and services to an insignificant position in their general set of concerns. Nevertheless, it is possible for there to be societies in terms of which, ideally speaking, neither organizations nor individuals are regarded as overwhelmingly specialized with regard to the economic aspects of behavior.

Finally, societies vary enormously with regard to the extent to which specialized economic aspects of behavior are separated, ideally speaking, from what the members of the society regard as the legitimate sphere of action of members of a government and other organizations. When such specialization exists despite the fact that it is a violation of the ideal structures, it exists outside the legitimate order as far as the members of other organizations are concerned. United States society is an extreme in the opposite direction. We not only consider such specializations highly legitimate, but their legitimacy specifically vis-à-vis the government and other organizations is well buttressed by ideal structures. Many societies in social history, however, have tended toward the opposite extreme in these respects.

Feudal societies generally and the societies of traditional China and Tokugawa Japan are fairly obvious examples of this sort, but there are also some examples, at least ideally speaking, among relatively modernized societies. Those societies whose members consider their societies to be Communist or Socialist societies to some extent approach this category. It is not true in the relatively modernized cases of these societies that economic specialization is illegitimate ideally speaking, but it is true that any economic specialization that is not a subsystem of the government as such tends to be regarded as illegitimate, or at least a violation of the ideal structures.[35] So far in social history all known cases of such

[35] In this respect the similarity with traditional China is most striking. Many predominantly economically oriented subsystems of the Imperial government were recognized. The production of salt under the direction of the scholar-officials was a different kettle of fish from the production of salt or other commodities privately directed. A bureaucratic executive who sought to maximize productivity in the former was likely to be considered a meritorious servant of the state; a merchant executive who sought to maximize productivity in the latter was likely to be considered a meretricious servant of his own [or his family members'] best interests.

societies have been characterized by some elements of this sort which were not directly subsystems of the government. To this extent, for these societies, as for all other societies in social history, in which such elements exist and for whose members such elements are regarded as illegitimate in a narrow legal sense or as violations of the ideal structures in a more general sense, the implication is inevitably a set of relationships characterized by graft and corruption.

I V

SUMMARY

The emphasis throughout the treatment here is on the consideration of variations in societies as an overlay of the common elements which characterize all societies. An understanding of the common elements is essential to understanding social structures and the possibilities and probabilities of their change, even when the overlays of variations result in diametrically opposite behaviors. Consideration of the variations alone may easily lead the student of public affairs to overlook vital elements of the problem. Quite recently in social history, for example, the leaders of one society—a major one as far as current world problems are concerned—apparently convinced themselves that, because of the ostensible irrelevance of elements of family organization for social life as they saw it and desired it in other respects, they could dispense with family organizations altogether. They announced that they were doing so and some of their less cautious statements implied that indeed they had already done so. A considerable segment of observers throughout the world took these statements at face value or at least assumed that the Chinese Communist leaders were well along the road to achieving what they claimed. Those leaders themselves have since withdrawn to other doctrinal positions.

Preoccupation with the overlying variations in general predisposes the student of public affairs to overlook the common elements requisite for all stable societies, that is to say the elements which are as essential as the foundation for one set of variations as for their opposites, near opposites, or apparent opposites. It also predisposes the student of public affairs to overlook the implications of the variations in one area of social behavior for another.

Preoccupation of the student of public affairs with variations rather than the common elements is, however, thoroughly understandable. Students of public affairs in general and policymakers in particular must be so preoccupied. It is the variations that the former seeks to understand, and the latter must use his understanding as a basis for coping with the variations directly or indirectly. Nevertheless, failure to consider such variations in the context of the commonalities which underly them constitutes the major reason why the professional social analyst as well as the amateurs have rarely, if ever, given policy-makers more than an *ad hoc* basis for policy work in general and policy work in the sphere of international affairs in particular.

THE PROBLEM FOCI OF

INTERNATIONAL AFFAIRS:

MODERNIZATION AND STABILITY

I

INTRODUCTION

The choice of problem foci is always a special one—combining creativity and pretentiousness. There are, after all, always an infinite number of problems to choose among in the field of international affairs as in any other. I have chosen the two problems I see as the most general problems of international affairs in our time. All problems of international affairs in our time are special cases of one or the other of these two problems or—more likely given the state of interdependence of the world in which we live—some combination of both. The problem foci are those of the modernization of the relatively nonmodernized societies and of the maintenance of stability within [and consequently among] the relatively modernized societies. If all of our problems in international affairs can be shown to be special cases of one or some combination of the two of these problems, these are *the* problem foci of our times.

These problems can be stated simply. Modernization is the problem par excellence for the vast majority of the world's peoples whether they are aware of it or not. Apart from the possibility of life on this planet being wiped out or catastrophically reduced [which is a conceivable function of the second of these two problems or of the combination of both of them], the members of relatively nonmodernized societies are not faced with a choice of whether to modernize or not. They will modernize to some extent, whether they like it or not, unless they die out or in rare cases of small-scale societies dwell in regions with no contacts save the most sporadic ones with the members of other societies. Whether and to what degree they modernize successfully from their point of view or that of anyone else is quite a different question. The *whither* of their modernization is in doubt by contrast with the question of *whether*. The question of whither is also one about which many will not care to be optimistic. From the point of view of the members of relatively nonmodernized societies as well as from the point of view of members of the modernized societies, the degree, kind, and rate of success with modernization are the essence of policy questions. Leaders who feel either that total resistance is possible or that only superficial elements of change are involved will fail foolishly.

The problem of stability is not a problem from the point of view of the members of relatively nonmodernized societies in one sense. The process of modernization into which all of them have entered or are entering is a general social revolution in as far-reaching a sense as is possible without destruction of their societies altogether. Stability in the sense of the avoidance of general social revolution is out of the question for these people. Whether there will be stability in the sense of an orderly nonviolent revolution is another, different, less general question. The possibility certainly exists, though the probability is not one about which I would care to be optimistic. Social stability is the essence of problems from the point of view of the members of the relatively modernized and highly modernized societies, whether they realize it or not. There are no ideals or goals of the members of relatively modernized societies for which stability is irrelevant, and instability is implicit in many of their goals. The problems of modernization of the relatively nonmodernized societies—quite apart from any ideals they may have—pose a problem for the members of highly modernized societies because of the implications of the process for the stability of their own societies. Correspondingly the stability of the relatively modernized societies is a problem for the members of relatively nonmodernized societies. The stability of relatively or highly modernized societies is *the* problem for everyone in a quite genuine sense—one quite conceivable result of internal instability in any one of two and possibly in any one of several of these societies could result in holocaust. Apart from predictions of the end of the world by supernatural direction, never before in history has mankind accepted and made a cliché of so realistic a possibility of world-wide holocaust.

There is a great deal of talk about central problems in international affairs which makes no sense at all considered apart from potential instability as between some combination of the relatively modernized societies which might result in a war utilizing the weapons presently at hand only for the members of such societies. Much of this talk, especially as it reaches the layman, is not only foolish but also states the problem in such a way that solutions, if possible, are almost certainly obscured and ignored. Phrases such as irresistible Arab Nationalism and unconquerable Zionist Spirit, issues at stake among Pakistan and India and China, between Pakistan and Afghanistan, in Southeast Asia and elsewhere are problems today primarily by virtue of the possibility that decisive action in any of these areas could touch off or could be touched off by instabilities which could lead to a war among the members of two or more of the highly modernized societies.

At the risk of some oversimplification, I would exemplify the possibilities of that instability by the potentiality of conflict as between the representatives of a government of the Soviet Union and those of a government of the United States. All of the problems of international affairs mentioned immediately above, and the problems in the Middle East, the Far East, and Southeast Asia are problems of high seriousness. Nevertheless, let me conjure up a dream world of wishful thinking [as above on pp. 578–579]. Suppose there were a fairy godmother of the world, and suppose she waved her wand. Suppose that once she had waved her wand a sleep descended on the peoples of the world and when they awoke they were refreshed and different in several and various respects: First, neither the members nor the leaders of either United States society or Russian society hated, feared, or distrusted one another as individuals or as representatives of different societies. Let us suppose that instead these peoples liked, respected, and trusted one another and now felt secure and self-confident in helping one another. Furthermore, let us suppose one other feat, perhaps even more difficult, even for a fairy godmother. Let us suppose that there was nothing going on in terms of either social system which would recreate the previous set of attitudes between the sets of members of these two societies. How difficult would it be under these circumstances to conceive of enforceable settlements in terms of some world organization like the United Nations of the outstanding problems of international affairs? How much less perplexing would these policy problems be if one could feel that they lacked one dimension, namely the possibility of touching off a major world war in which the members of United States society would be the leaders of one side and those of the Soviet Union of the other?

Whether the members of so miraculously united a camp of the highly modernized of societies would use the powers at their disposal wisely or humanely in international affairs would remain as perplexing as ever, but given the means at their disposal, it can hardly be doubted that the members of these societies would have at their disposal the power to handle many of the outstanding international problems with dispatch. They might not be able to avoid the first outbreak of violence in the Middle East, for example, but they ought to be able to make a second radically unlikely. To curb what many regard as the menace of the Chinese Communists to the members of neighboring societies would not be difficult given the overwhelmingly probable actual state of development of that society were it not for the possibilities of involving the participants of such corrective action in a world war of combatants with nuclear weapons at their disposal.

Even without a fairy godmother, if anyone knew with certainty under exactly what circumstances either the representatives of the United States or of the Soviet Union would go to war with one another, the problem of international relations would be immensely simplified. Never have the crucial problems of all international relations headed up so clearly in the hands of the members of two major governments. All previous incidents in history seem to have been clearly divided into two categories by virtue of the fact that major segments of the world population either were not involved or at least at the outset of difficulties were not nearly so neatly bifurcated. The extent to which the general problems of international affairs were importantly a function of the potential instability of the members of two societies or nations would have seemed, ere now, to be a typical oversimplification of a complex situation by a naïve social scientist; it may still be.

These two major problems—modernization for the relatively nonmodernized societies and stability for the relatively modernized ones [1]—have been misunderstood for very general reasons in both cases. Apart from the general lack of development of the social sciences and the failure to consider variations in the context of common elements, which impede knowledge of both problems, the greatest source of difficulty in understanding the problem of modernization lies in confusions of the type mentioned in the footnote on p. 106 above. I should now like to consider them in more detail.

Any student of modernization must realize that the requisites for maintaining relatively high levels of modernization are not necessarily the same as the prerequisites for achieving it. One cannot discover the techniques best adapted to increasing the rate of efficiency [however efficiency may be judged] of modernization simply by looking at the structures of a relatively modernized

---

[1] Even those who disagree with the overriding importance which I give to these two problems, would hardly care to consider them unimportant.

society and attempting to put those directly into effect in the relatively nonmodernized context. It is obvious in the analysis of this or any sort of problem in social change that if one narrows the time span sufficiently and is interested in sufficiently descriptive detail, the possibility of discrepancies between the requisites and the prerequisites of a given state of affairs diminish toward the vanishing point. It is also important to realize that some of the requisites for maintaining relatively high levels of modernization probably are prerequisites in a given case for achieving it. There is relatively little danger of ignoring requisites and prerequisites which are identical. The major source of difficulty lies in the tendency to overlook the fact that the requisites and prerequisites may be different in a given case. From the point of view of the members of both relatively nonmodernized and relatively modernized societies, prerequisites for achieving modernization which are not requisites of high levels of modernization may often appear to be a senseless detour. In a climate of opinion highly charged with emotion, no matter how rational such detours may seem to be on other grounds, they are exceedingly likely to get bogged down in recriminations having to do with the attempt of one set of individuals from one social context attempting to exploit those from another, with attempts to reinstate imperialism or colonialism, etc. The problem of the divergence between requisites and prerequisites in a given case is quite difficult enough as a purely intellectual problem. Even when considerable certainty can be achieved on this score, it does not follow at all that those findings, however tenable, can be translated into workable policy directives with any ease—if at all. Furthermore, even if they can be translated into workable policies, they will often not be palatable policies from many points of view.

Second, the prerequisites for achieving a relatively modernized state in one case are not necessarily the same as the prerequisites for achieving such a state in another case. There are two important distinctions within this generalization. The first is that the prerequisites for late-comers to relatively modernized status are not necessarily the same as the prerequisites were for those societies whose members carried out these transitions more or less indigenously over a relatively long period of time. As will be indicated below in the general discussion of modernization, the members of those societies who may be described as late-comers to the process have certain obvious advantages in the form of developed knowledge about the process, etc. They also, however, inevitably encounter certain special problems. Thus, it is always naïve to assume, in contemplating the problems of modernization in terms of a given relatively nonmodernized society today that one can simply translate, as it were, from the experiences recorded in the social history of the United States, France, or Great Britain to viable policy in the case under consideration.

The second special form of the problem of the discrepancy in prerequisites from one instance to another is that the prerequisites for achieving relatively high levels of modernization for one late-comer are not necessarily the same as the prerequisites for another late-comer. What worked in Japan will not necessarily work in Turkey. Since the structures which tend to be introduced from outside in the case of the late-comers are quite uniform in very general respects [e.g., increasing emphasis on universalistic criteria, specialization, interdependence, etc.], the most important source of enlightenment as to the difference in prerequisites from one case to another is to be found in a thorough understanding of the historical basis from which change takes place in the various instances. Most of the available analyses of attempted transitions to relatively modernized social systems have focused attention overwhelmingly on the early stages of the process and later ones. Relatively scant attention has been paid to the last stable or relatively stable formulation of the structures before the process of change in direction of a relatively modernized state began—unless that formulation immediately preceded. In the early stages of the process, there is usually enormous confusion about these old structures. The vulnerability of the previously prevailing structures to the new forces and the rapidity with which they get wiped out have tended to obscure the vital roles that a thorough knowledge and analysis of those structures have in understanding the process of transition in any given individual case or in understanding different results in different cases.

Closely related to the hypothesis that the requisites for maintaining relatively modernized societies are not necessarily the same as the prerequisites for achieving them and that prerequisites for achieving such levels of modernization in one case are not necessarily the same as in the other case is another much more specific generalization. The presence of a type of social structure which is precisely analogous to a social structure which is a requisite of a relatively modernized society does not mean that the late-comers concerned are thereby advantaged for achievement of a relatively modernized society. For example, high levels of social mobility and therefore of open-class structures are requisites of any relatively highly modernized society. Nevertheless, a society characterized by closed-class structures may be a much better basis for rapid transition than a society in terms of which in fact there is a great deal more social mobility both ideally and actually. The presence of social mobility in one case may be in detail a close analogy to the social mobility necessary for relatively modernized societies, but the position that those structures have in the relatively nonmodernized social setting may be such that action in terms of them obstructs a rapid transition.[2]

The major special obstacle to an understanding of the problems of stability in relatively highly modernized contexts is of quite another sort. It too may be subdivided into two parts. In the first place it is by no means clear that any example of such a society can be stable in the sense that one speaks of stability in societies in general. After all, no cases of this sort of society are of any considerable age. To some extent the age which can be attributed to a society of this sort is a function of how far along the scale implied in the definition of modernization used here one wishes to place the beginning of any relatively modernized society. If one does not wish to consider a relatively modernized society very highly modernized until the advent of mass production and mass communication, no such society has a record of stability of as much as fifty years. In the most empirical sense, therefore, we do not know whether any case of very high levels of modernization is in fact stable.

The second problem obscuring an understanding of this point has to do with the characteristics of social change—even of general social revolution—within relatively modernized societies in general and highly modernized societies in particular. Frequently, [e.g., pp. 126, 380, 461, 475–488, etc.], I have emphasized factors extremely likely to result in social change in any society. I have also pointed out the extreme rarity of any relatively nonmodernized society with the kind of record of general social stability which characterized traditional Chinese society [pp. 696–697]. Nevertheless, it is quite possible that relatively nonmodernized societies have extensive periods of stability. In terms of certain types of social change that is out of the question for

---

[2] See my article entitled "Contrasting Factors of the Modernization of China and Japan," *Economic Development and Cultural Change,* vol. 2, no. 3, Oct., 1953, pp. 161–197. In the light of research undertaken since that article was written I would alter many of the statements it contains. Nevertheless, the main outlines of the argument about the differential advantage in the process of modernization which fell to the Japanese at least in part because of the fact that ideally as well as actually speaking Tokugawa Japan was characterized by closed-class structures while traditional China was both ideally and to a considerable extent actually characterized by open-class structures seem to me still to hold. In any case, the argument can be taken as an illustration of the point attempted here.

relatively modernized societies. I have pointed out and repeat that the problem of socialization of individuals for an unknown future is a special and peculiar problem in social history. There has even been speculation [e.g., pp. 79–82] as to whether or not there is some limit on the ability of members of societies to tolerate rapid and far-reaching changes in general social structure of the sort characteristic of relatively modernized societies whose members take it increasingly for granted that there will be roughly the equivalent of a general social revolution every twenty or thirty years.

Apart from the fact that some society is being maintained, on what level of generality can we speak of any society being stable with such an endemic set of changes? Traditional Chinese society is fascinating because, for reasons that are by no means clearly understood, for a period of roughly two thousand years there was the periodic expectation, roughly every two hundred some odd years, of a dynastic change in terms of which a systematic renovation of the traditional social structure would be realized. In the case of relatively modernized societies we may be faced with a type of society whose structures in some general sense remain highly stable despite a systematically built-in general social revolution with a periodicity of three decades or less. This would be a fascinating sort of moving social equilibrium. On the other hand, operations in terms of these societies and in terms of the interrelationships among the members of two or more of them may simply not yet have reached the literal explosion toward which they are tending. There are certainly limits, as mentioned, on the extent to which this process can be pushed. I do not know exactly or even approximately what they are. Insofar as I speculate about them I do not have any idea as to whether the process, if it continues, at present is likely to stabilize at or near those limits.

Lastly, if the process is not likely to stabilize at those points as it goes today, I do not have any ideas based on any highly generalized knowledge as to what changes in present procedures we might attempt in order that the tendency would be toward some stabilization.

I I
THE PROBLEM OF MODERNIZATION

A. MODERNIZATION AS A UNIVERSAL SOCIAL SOLVENT

1. THE UNIVERSALITY OF THE SOLVENT

The process of modernization as it is conceived here is something new under the sun. Although elements of modernization have accumulated throughout social history, and sometimes in the course of social history have been destroyed, the general process of modernization conceived of as a transition from relatively nonmodernized to relatively modernized societies is new and peculiar in the most precise sense of that much abused word. Considerable effort has been taken in this work to point out the elements of continuity—and consequently the possibilities of communication—between various elements in relatively nonmodernized and relatively modernized societies. Nevertheless, the type of society which the vast majority of us take for granted as normal, ordinary, and more or less readily understandable to anyone from anywhere is actually the most exotic type in the most general respects. Travelers from these social contexts leave the strangest social environment in history to find recreation in observing customs strange to them. Any society would be unique if one could consider it in completely descriptive detail, but relatively modernized societies, and especially the most highly modernized cases, constitute unique types when considered on quite general levels. Throughout this work no point has been raised without considering its relevance in terms of possible variations to the distinction between this type of society and all others. At present rather than relist these elements I prefer to dwell on one of the unique characteristics of this set of structures which is the central core of the problem of modernization as recognized and/or unrecognized by the individuals who are affected by this problem. This is the characteristic of the structures of modernization as a sort of universal social solvent.

Social history has seen many spectacular conquests. Those best known to the members of the most highly modernized societies tend to be those general conquests which have issued from the West or threatened the West. Alexander the Great in the diffusion of Hellenic structures, Ghenghis Khan and the spread of destruction,[3] Napoleon and the spread of French conceptions of law—all of these are sometimes referred to as "world conquerors," and there are others. No single figure among them conquered the known and inhabited world of his day—not even the world known to him. Alexander the Great was certainly one of the most dramatic of these individuals. He went so far as to control most of the area within his original ken and to extend it so that the social structures characteristic of his society lastingly affected the costumes of Indian statuary and bas relief and from that influence

---

[3] It is not a matter of chance that Ghenghis Khan is far better known as a non-Western example of this sort of thing to the members of Western societies than any other figure of social history and that he is always associated with the idea of destruction.

eventually affected some important Chinese sculpture as well. He had, however, no direct contacts with Chinese society which was certainly a large-scale society and from almost any point of view a highly developed society, perhaps even as highly developed as his own.[4]

Not only did none of these conquerors extend their influence to the then known world [i.e., known to them, let alone the world of civilizations such as those in Central and South America which were presumably isolated from them], but also the export of structures from the societies of which these conquerors were members never constituted anything like a general social solvent of the structures of the societies among whose members they were introduced. Probably the closest analogy to the impact of the structures of relatively modernized societies on those of the relatively nonmodernized is the impact which the structures characteristic of traditional Chinese society sometimes had on individuals and even whole peoples from radically different social backgrounds. One of the clichés of social history is to speak of the Chinese as absorbing all others.[5] Despite direct contact, however, and even direct control at some periods, the structures of traditional Chinese society were not a general solvent as far as the structures of Korean society were concerned. Even more dramatically they were not a solvent as far as the structures of Japanese society were concerned, despite the fact that at one period of Japanese history there was a deliberate attempt on the part of the rulers of that society to make it over in the Chinese image as completely as possible.

The structures of the relatively modernized and of the highly modernized societies are quite another matter. In every single

[4] The term *highly developed* when used in this context tends overwhelmingly to refer to either ethical or aesthetic standards. Whether traditional Chinese society or the society of the Chou Dynasty represented as high a peak of civilization as that of classical Greece is not primarily a question for social scientists until and unless the preferences of the parties to the arguments with regard to standards of judgment have been made explicit.

[5] There is no intention in this to denigrate the unusual structures of the members of traditional Chinese society. The social structures of the Chinese certainly did have this sort of solvent effect on some with whom they came in contact. There is very good reason to believe that a considerable number of the members of a Jewish society [sometimes considered unassimilable] disappeared, not as a result of compulsion, but without a trace save for the preservation of a few Torah scrolls which of course the Chinese preserved because written materials in general were to be treated with the greatest reverence. The fate of some of the Mongols when they decided to rule the Chinese, of various non-Chinese people from the North before them, and of the Manchus even before they decided to rule the Chinese is well known.

instance in which there has been contact between the members of relatively modernized and relatively nonmodernized societies, apart from a brief meeting and the extermination of the representatives of one society or the other, a single general type of social change has ensued. Whatever the basis from which change took place has been, the structures of the relatively nonmodernized society have begun to change and that change has always been in the direction of the structures of the relatively modernized society. Furthermore, the contacts of members of these different types of societies have now reached such a state of development that there is not a single example of any relatively nonmodernized society of any considerable scale whose members have not experienced some such contacts and whose social structures have not begun to dissolve and change. There is absolutely no reason to believe that prior to the development of relatively modernized societies in the West that contact with the structures of the relatively nonmodernized societies of the West had any such effect whatsoever on people in all other types of social settings. To this extent it is not *any* Western influence; it is specifically only a modern Western influence—and not just any modern Western influence [e.g., not that of modern Portugal] but only the influence of modern Westerners who are relatively modernized. This set of structures constitutes a universal social solvent in the sense that whenever there are contacts among the members of this sort of society and those of other sorts of societies, the structures characteristic of those other societies dissolve and change and always in a given direction. It is possible to state why, as a minimum, this always occurs. It is also possible to state in some general respects, despite variations in the historical backgrounds from which changes take place, how this always occurs.

2. THE SOURCE OF APPEAL

The nature of modernization as a process has been obscured by the fact that the structures of the relatively modernized societies have frequently been introduced to the members of relatively nonmodernized societies by what the vast majority of the people in the world today would agree to call the excesses of imperialism. Indeed, until recent decades hardly any of the contacts between the members of the relatively modernized and the relatively nonmodernized societies took any other form. It is understandable, therefore, that it is exceedingly difficult to get discussions of the phenomena apart from resentment about, guilt feelings about, or defensive attempts to reinterpret the myriad situations associated with the term *imperialism* throughout the world. I neither desire nor intend to apologize for, defend, or deny the excesses so generally associated with imperialistic endeavors. I do, however, assert flatly that: (1) except in the sense that what is past and done is past and done, this need not have been the case, (2) the invasion of the structures of relatively nonmodernized societies by the structures of the relatively modernized societies via contact between the members of those societies would have taken place with or without the excesses of imperialism, (3) the structures of the relatively modernized societies would still have constituted the sort of general social solvent they constituted whether introduced by forcible or peaceful means, and (4) regrettably, an enormous amount of human dissatisfaction, unrest, and misery would have accompanied those invasions had they occurred under the most benign, well-intentioned of auspices.

As the structures of modernization were developed further and further in terms of those few societies such as Great Britain, the United States, France, etc., whose members developed them indigenously and gradually, quite apart from previous habits of exploration, increased contacts among the members of relatively nonmodernized and relatively modernized societies were inevitable. Nothing could have been more unlikely than the possibility that the members of the relatively modernized societies with their increased facilities for communication, with their increased interest in sources of raw material, in markets, and the like would have been uninterested in the kind of exploration that would bring them into contact with the members of the relatively nonmodernized societies. Thus for a whole series of reasons, far too obvious to go into here, the members of the relatively modernized societies were overwhelmingly likely to be so motivated as to bring them into contact with the members of less modernized societies. This is in fact what happened in terms of what we today call imperialism. It is perhaps conceivable that those contacts could have been made with a more altruistic interest in the future of the members of the relatively nonmodernized societies. The important thing for present purposes is that the contact was inevitable, not that it was done wickedly. Whatever one's judgment of how it was done, even if one takes into consideration only the point of view of the members of the relatively modernized societies, it was bound to be done.

The members of the relatively nonmodernized societies might never have initiated increased communications. Even after contacts were established, the members of the relatively modernized societies might, as was frequently the case, have no greater interest in introducing their new structures to the members of the relatively nonmodernized societies than necessary for their own narrow self-interests. Regardless of their motivations, however, the contacts alone would have made known to some of the members of relatively nonmodernized societies structures previously unknown to them. Once those structures were known, regardless of whether the members of the relatively modernized societies consciously attempted to export them, some would have been imported by the members of the relatively nonmodernized societies. This turns the discussion to the other side of the relationship.

I have already pointed out above that the supposed distinction of peoples into those who are purely materialistically as opposed to those who are purely spiritually interested is utter nonsense. All people throughout the history of the world have had some material interests. No peoples have ever failed to distinguish between material and spiritual matters. No members of any society taken as a whole have ever been completely indifferent to material matters. Quite beyond the fact that human beings are capable of feeling pain and reacting to it, of experiencing hunger and reacting to that, etc., one may push the matter further. Not only are people never indifferent to material matters, not only do they distinguish between material and spiritual matters, but the general membership of any society, indeed probably every conscious member of any society, to some extent distinguishes between being relatively better off and relatively worse off materially. Finally, the vast majority of the members of all known societies, and perhaps everyone capable of conscious thought, have *to some extent* always preferred to be better off materially than worse off. There is absolutely no denying the fact that the members both of a given society and of different societies vary widely as to how much they prefer to be better off rather than worse off materially, as to what methods they are willing or anxious to take in pursuit of such preferences, of the extent to which they regard it as within their powers to improve the situation materially [i.e., their horizons of material improvement], etc. Nevertheless, the vast majority of them always have some interest in material improvement, and some of them will always seek to implement that interest if the opportunity seems to be afforded.

The members of relatively modernized societies acting in terms of their peculiar and specialized structures achieve a higher level of material productivity over a broader range of allocation of goods and services than has ever been characteristic of the members of any previous type of society. By contrast with all previous methods the methods characteristic of these societies may be described as inordinately productive. Thus, quite apart from the nefariousness or the altruism of the members of the relatively modernized societies—quite apart from their chauvinism, their national pride, their interest in the welfare of others, their missionary zeal, or their desire to live the lives of other people for them—once the contacts are made and the structures of the relatively modernized societies and the results of behavior in terms of them are put on display, as it were, some of the members of any and all of the relatively nonmodernized societies are always motivated to try to import some of the products and some of the structures of use or production of those goods and services—never mind what the level of sanctimony may be. At this point, however convenient and simple it is to think in terms of economic aspects or purely material factors, the other aspects of the process in fact relevant all along are inescapable. It has proved impossible in every case simply to borrow new techniques of inordinate productivity without importing at the same time structures having to do with other aspects of social organizations—structures which once introduced have in every known case been implicated in the general disintegration of the *status quo ante*.

Once modernization has been developed to the level characteristic of relatively modernized societies, those structures will be disseminated. The people who have become accustomed to acting in terms of them will be motivated to disseminate them whether from good or bad motives. The members of societies in terms of which these structures have not yet developed will be motivated to accept some of these structures or some of their results once they are aware of them—whether wisely or unwisely. There always appears to be something in such transfers for somebody, and frequently there appears to be something in it for everybody. Once the process has begun, previous conceptions of sovereignty, independence, maintenance of tradition, and the like are doomed. It is by no means certain that the fruits of the importation looked for by those importing these structures voluntarily will be forthcoming, but social change will be forthcoming, and increasing interdependence, including in the initial stages more noticeable elements of dependence than otherwise, will ensue for the members of the relatively nonmodernized societies.

Moreover no matter how well intentioned all of the parties to the transition may be, during the transition some individuals will always be hurt, and from the point of view of many individuals things will have gotten worse rather than better. The past history of these events ensures that feelings on all sides will be exacerbated by sensitivities about real or fancied imperialistic behaviors, however much such attitudes may be beside the point. Short of a war coming close to destruction of life on this planet, statesmen, patriots, and scholars have all failed completely to come up with any suggested methods which threaten to halt this process and restore the meaning which concepts such as sovereignty and independence had two centuries ago.

3. THE NATURE OF THE SOLVENT

The structures of modernization are always subversive of the status quo of relatively nonmodernized societies for several reasons. First, as indicated above, if there is contact between the members of a relatively nonmodernized society and the members of a relatively modernized one, or if the structures of a relatively modernized society are communicated to the members of a relatively nonmodernized society in any other way, some of them always will invade. Second, the structures of modernization are such that they can never simply be imported piecemeal. That is to say, the members of relatively nonmodernized societies—even assuming they are not subjected to any coercion by others—can never simply take over what they want or what fits in well with the rest of their social structures and leave the rest. This is the fatally romantic element best propounded by F. S. C. Northrop. He holds that a good and proper state of mankind inheres in a combination of what he seems to regard as a sort of combination of the best of the East and of the West. For Professor Northrop the West in this sense refers to the societies with the structures of modernization developed to quite high points and the East refers to relatively nonmodernized societies. What Professor Northrop regards as the best of the East and the West includes some of the more radically incompatible elements as far as any conceivable amalgam is concerned. With or without an achievement of what he considers to be the best of the West there is not a single case of the members of a relatively nonmodernized society in contact with the structures of a relatively modernized society, in which disintegration of the structures regarded as the best of the East has not begun even though attainment of the best of the West may not seem at all close at hand.

Third, what may be referred to as the historical or *status quo ante* structures never coincide exactly with the relatively modernized structures. Even in cases in which in many details the traditional structures are identical with those of the relatively modernized society, there are other elements which differ radically. Above all, the fit of those historical structures into the general social structure is always different from the fit of their corresponding structures in the relatively modernized society. Thus in the process, even when similarities seem greatest, disintegration of the historical structures will take place. Details similar to the old ones are likely to be reintroduced in a different form.

Fourth, with rare exceptions, the major sources of control over the members of the relatively nonmodernized societies are exceedingly likely to be eroded. This erosion alone can make contacts with the structures of the relatively modernized societies highly subversive of the *status quo ante*—even in the absence of any notable attainment of modernization. These contacts are capable of disintegrating the old without substantial achievements of the new and without the possibility of the reestablishment of the old.

Some of the basic sources of the erosion of the structures of the relatively nonmodernized societies as a result of these contacts have been discussed above in Part 1, Chapters 1 and 2 in general, and points relevant in greater detail have characterized the remainder of the treatment throughout this work. Before drawing some of the more prominent of these together in summary fashion here, I would like to discuss quite briefly some of the special advantages and disadvantages of late-comers to the process. Most of the statements here hold true for the general problem of modernization, in terms of any society, but the most pressing problems of modernization as far as public affairs are concerned have to do with either the achievement of structures of modernization by late-comers or the maintenance of modernization in stable form by the members of societies regardless of whether they have achieved that state indigenously or as late-comers. There are, of course, important variations in both the advantages and the disadvantages to the members of those societies who can be described as late-comers to the process of modernization by contrast with the members of those societies who can be spoken of as having achieved modernization more or less indigenously over a long period of time.[6]

[6] The following six pages are a nearly verbatim adoption of material which I presented in a paper entitled "Some Structural Problems of Modernization and 'High Modernization': China and Japan," *Economic and Social Problems of the Far East* Edited by E. F. Szczepanik, Hong Kong University Press, Hong Kong, 1961, pp. 445–458. This volume constitutes publication of the proceedings of a symposium of the Golden

The principal advantage of late-comers lies primarily in the fact that the process of modernization is no longer the sort of terra incognita it was for the indigenous developers. The late-comers are faced by different problems—many of them vastly different—but they have some conception of the elements involved in the transition by virtue of their inescapable observations of the discrepancy between the state of their own societies and the state of the societies which are regarded as relatively modernized. In the second place, there exists inescapably for the late-comers the possibility of borrowing at least the initial expertise in planning, capital accumulation, new materials and machines, general skills, and associated structures of organization.

Closely connected with this is a third advantage—that of being able to skip some of the early stages associated with the process of modernization as developed indigenously and gradually. The late-comers are in a position to take over the latest inventions. This advantage frequently—but by no means inevitably, especially in the early stages of modernization—is the equivalent of a major amount of capital formation by the avoidance of major initial elements of obsolescence. No less important, however, is the advantage of being able to take over the latest inventions of social structures even when the inventiveness involved is incompletely appreciated by either the borrowers or the developers. For example, the members of no relatively nonmodernized society need be in the dark about the need for a general set of schools and almost certainly a set of public ones at that.

A fourth advantage of late-comers also involves knowledge of where the process may lead. The members of a relatively non-modernized society who are most interested in bringing about such changes may at least attempt to win support, bolster morale, etc., by offering known prospects of the fruits of the changes they foster. They may not in fact know what they are doing, but if they are able to think they do and convince other members of the society, substantial advantages in terms of possibilities of coordination and control inhere.

As a fifth advantage not only are the late-comers in a position to borrow elements already developed elsewhere, but, of course, the members of the relatively modernized societies are in a position to lend or give assistance, if so inclined. This is, of course, a banal deduction from the fact that one can distinguish late-

Jubilee Congress of the University of Hong Kong, Sept. 11–16, 1961. Use of these remarks is possible via the courtesy of the Hong Kong University Press.

comers in the first place. What is not banal, however, is that to some extent some of the members of some of the relatively modernized societies are always motivated either to lend or to give assistance to the late-comers. Sometimes this motivation does not take a form calculated to appeal to the late-comers, but whether one likes the form it takes or not, it does constitute an advantage from the point of view of getting on with the process.

The disadvantages for late-comers are also marked. First, there are problems of scale. There are many developments such as facilities for education, means of communication, etc., which must be carried out on a fairly large scale if there is to be any prospect of a smooth transition to a relatively modernized state. Furthermore, these elements will have to be attempted on a relatively large scale even if the transition is not going to be smooth and easy. Gradual development of these elements after the fashion of the indigenous developers is not open to the late-comer. Various problems—not the least of which are usually called political problems—will militate against overwhelming reliance on the members of other societies to train experts who require high levels of education in their occupational roles. The development of educational facilities necessary for the production of such experts is out of the question except through a generally developed set of schools at the primary and secondary levels. Those primary and secondary schools are in turn necessary for the vast proportion of the membership of the relatively nonmodernized societies if the specialized or nonspecialized roles they will have to fulfill in the future are to be provided for. All problems of transition not only require experts; they also require generally high levels of literacy among the general members of the society. When these structures developed more or less indigenously over a more or less extended period of time, the general level of education could be raised gradually concentrating a bit at a time on the sets of experts necessary. This is out of the question for the late-comers. Excepting an unusual case like Icelandic society, the members of the relatively nonmodernized societies will be characterized by high rates of illiteracy which have to be overcome fast.

The scale of operations alone poses obvious problems of capital formation and also of coordination and control in general. In addition, many of the factors posed by the problems of scale are the sort which preclude operating on a nonpublic basis partly for reasons other than that of scale. Means of communication might conceivably be set up on a private toll basis, but it is exceedingly difficult to devise a set of schools of the right sort for which the operating costs are borne by either the recipients of the education or by the major utilizers of its products. The magnitude of these requirements inevitably carries with it the necessity of public management. Even if this could be avoided in the most direct manner, there would remain the general problems of coordination and control, and some public organization must take care of these and other derivative problems.

The second special problem for late-comers is that of the interdependence of the various levels and sectors of the society in which change will inevitably take place in the course of the process. Despite the advantages of having before them examples of the achievements of members of relatively modernized societies, the members of no modernizing society have had a clear-cut picture of all that was involved for them in the process. One might expect that they would profit from what is known on this score, but the state of the social sciences is such that relatively little has been learned, and even that has not always been communicated. Quite apart from the factors involved in this minor cognitive tragedy, a more subtle problem arises. The members of a relatively nonmodernized society see before them many and various results of the process in which they are, or are about to become, involved. These appeal to them in varying degrees, and almost inevitably the popular leaders, the influential persons, or the society's members in general are obsessed with the belief that they can take what they please and leave the rest. The result is likely to be an interplay among old and new factors of a particularly explosive character. Although it is advantageous to know something of the results of modernization, and although that is an advantage which late-comers may have whereas indigenous developers did not, the late-comers have a special disadvantage in that they, much more than the indigenous developers, are likely to think that they know where they are going. The very discrepancy between their planning and their results constitutes a special disruption for them.

Many of these interdependences are well known. The switch to different emphases in relationship aspects, the disintegration of the historical family structures, the development of predominantly educationally oriented organizations and bureaucratic forms of organization in general, etc., are all examples familiar to anyone who reads the growing literature of this field. Among these interdependences two are especially important from the present point of view. The first is the fact of general interdependence itself. Again it is essential to emphasize the fact that the myth of easy independent selectivity from among the social structures of highly modernized societies must be recognized for what it is and has always been—a hybrid of wishful thinking and sentimental piety. It is essential that thinking not be confined to concepts such as capitalism, communism, or socialism. These terms refer to quite important differences among some of the structures of relatively modernized societies [as well as those of some relatively nonmodernized ones]. It is also true that all of those societies in terms of which modernization was carried out more or less indigenously were of the capitalist type. In the present stage of these developments, however, it is relatively easy to see that these distinctions and the clichés formed in terms of them [regardless of our preferences for one type rather than another] do not point to the strategic factors in the structures of the highly modernized or to the prerequisites for modernization in the relatively nonmodernized societies. The relevance of diminished levels of self-sufficiency of organizations in general, the growth of highly specialized orientations of specific organizations in particular, the proliferation of specialization of occupational roles, the development of professional roles, and the like carry us much further into the basic questions of social structure than do questions of private versus public ownership. Indeed, in the case of very high modernization, distinctions between such categories become increasingly hard to apply.[7] Whether modernization is attempted on a socialist or on a capitalist basis, all of these factors and many others combine.

The second is a problem of special interdependence for late-comers—the interdependence between the various structures involved in the process on one hand and the general structures of control on the other. With rare exceptions such as that of Japan, the structures of control characteristic of the relatively nonmodernized societies are among the most vulnerable to modernization. They become vulnerable at just the point at which close coordination and control is essential if the process is to be smooth, efficient, and rapid. Without going into detail, the methods of control are usually highly dependent on family loyalty which in turn is highly vulnerable to modernization in general.

---

[7] For example, the leaders of many labor unions in the United States, which is generally regarded by its members as well as by the members of other societies as highly capitalistic, have far greater power to disrupt communications than have the leaders of a giant corporation such as The American Telephone and Telegraph Company. Despite what may be considered to be domination of the government by businessmen, representatives of labor seem on occasions to exercise a power and independence of both business organizations and the government unequaled in terms of any non-capitalistic society.

Most late-comers are in fact going to be faced by a period of decay, violence, etc., during which the main prevailing structures of coordination and control are destroyed without the development of new stable forms of organization.

Finally, there is a third special disadvantage for late-comers. This is the special frustration in store for late-comers in the certainty of the long continued existence of gaps between what the members of highly modernized societies have achieved and what the late-comers attain to the extent that they are successful. Even when this gap is being closed in relative terms, in absolute terms the gap may both grow and seem to grow rather than lessen with the passage of time. Running so hard without even catching up is especially relevant to questions of morale. The problems of running at all are often exceedingly severe.

With so much by way of the discussion of the advantages and disadvantages of late-comers, some of the basic sources of erosion of the structures of relatively nonmodernized societies during the process of modernization become especially relevant. First, there is always the radical increase in the amount and level of specialization of organizations. In many relatively nonmodernized societies few such organizations exist prior to the change in the direction of relatively modernized societies. Those which do exist are often not specialized to any great extent. For an increase in such organizations and an increase in the level of specialization of other organizations previously in existence, there must be a radical increase in compartmentalized thinking on the part of the members of the society. Not only must they learn to think in this fashion about the new organizations. They must simultaneously learn to think differently about the existing organizations in terms of which they operate. The fact that the average individual now acts in terms of a larger number of organizations than he did before, for example, alters his general view of his family organization. The mere fact that he is aware of more alternative organizations to his own family makes a difference.

There is another universal difference attendant on increases in specialization. Prior to the development of relatively modernized societies, although there were some specialized organizations in any society of any considerable scale, the vast majority of the members of those societies may have had few or no contacts with members of those specialized organizations. With increases of modernization, increasingly the average individual comes into contact with the members, not of one, but of many such organizations. Although prior to the transition some members of the society operated with the knowledge of both specialized and relatively nonspecialized organizations, now virtually everyone must act with an awareness of this distinction. This awareness alone raises possibilities of alternatives to thinking solely in terms of a relatively nonspecialized organization or a set of such organizations, even though the alternatives so conceived may in fact not be viable or practical ones. The general contact of the average member of such societies with specialized organizations does not eliminate relatively nonspecialized organizations, nor does it necessarily make the position of such organizations in the general social structure less strategic—especially in the case of the family. It is, however, certain to make the vast majority of individuals *feel* that this is the case. Therefore, the position of the relatively nonspecialized organizations in the general social structure is radically changed. For example, the extent to which the members of such a society continue to be predominantly family oriented always declines despite the fact that the new structures incorporated into family organizations may be just as strategic for the changed society as the previous structures were for the particular case of the relatively nonmodernized society in question.

Only analytically speaking is the problem of interdependence separable from the problem of specialization as such. As the level of specialization increases, the interdependence of the subsystems and hence in that sense the interdependence of the system as a whole increases. To put the matter another way, the level of self-sufficiency of the various organizations is lowered. It becomes increasingly difficult to conceive of the operation of the members of any organization if they are cut off from contact with the members of other organizations. Any increase in the interdependence of organizations increases the relevance of actions in terms of one such organization for the state of the members of other organizations. Many of the characteristics of relatively nonmodernized societies are closely tied to relatively high levels of self-sufficiency of family units, villages, etc. There is a special feature of interdependence in the form characteristic of a relatively modernized society. As the level of interdependence increases, problems of maintenance in a given organization become quite as relevant and as strategic for the society as a whole as the problems of initial planning. In relatively nonmodernized social contexts, for example, it takes a certain amount of planning to create a new village, to start a new family, etc. If well thought out in the first place or established according to well-accepted traditional structures, maintenance may be much less explicitly devised. As organizations become more highly interdependent the day-to-day maintenance of the interstitial adjustments among the members of these organizations become as much a matter for constant attention as the establishment of the organizations themselves. Thus it is, relatively speaking, easy to plan a given new factory or even a set of factories for the members of a relatively nonmodernized society. It is even not too difficult to start operations in terms of these organizations. It is much more difficult to keep them operating and to keep levels of coordination of increasingly interdependent organizations constantly rising.

The increase in interdependence usually undermines motivation to self-reliance within the context of the previously existing structures. For those unfamiliar with highly interdependent organizations increases in interdependence are likely to appear as increasingly capricious situations over which the individual has no control and in which he has no hope. As the level of interdependence characteristic of the society as a whole increases, members who are not yet used to the new find themselves increasingly incapable of coping with implications of these interdependences for organizations with which they once felt themselves thoroughly familiar.

With the increase in specialization and interdependence, there is always a change in the emphases on relationship aspects. There is always an increase in the emphasis on rationality, universalism, functional specificity, and avoidance beyond the previously existing level.[8] These changes need not be complete alterations of the *status quo ante* to be important. As indicated above, the new emphases never completely replace emphases on predominantly traditional, particularistic, functionally diffuse, and intimate relationships. One of the most puzzling forms of erosion of the *status quo ante* lies in the fact that the new emphases may destroy some of the balances maintained in terms of balances of the old without members of the society having become accustomed to operation even in limited spheres in terms of the new. As already discussed above [e.g., pp. 680–681], the emphasis on predominantly universalistic criteria, for example, may undermine selection on the bases of particularistic criteria which were so balanced as to in fact result in predominantly universalistic results. This undermining may take place without operation in terms of predominantly universalistic criteria being self-

---

[8] There might be societies characterized by so high and general an emphasis on avoidance that that emphasis would need no increase, but even so, the much greater density of interrelationships per person per day would radically increase the density of avoidant relationships even if this were only the avoidance characteristic of the casual contact.

consciously understood. The net result may actually be considerable increases in capricious and/or ultimately particularistic criteria.

There is a further special problem about emphases on predominantly rational, universalistic, functionally specific, and avoidant
relationships. Many of the leaders of the transition and many of
the students of these matters, both in relatively nonmodernized
and relatively modernized social contexts, will conceive of these
emphases as all or none matters and implicitly or explicitly seek a
total transition for the members of the society from one type of
emphasis to the other. This cannot be achieved either ideally or
actually; it is not characteristic either ideally or actually of the
most highly modernized of societies. The untenability of such
views is nevertheless never proof against attempts to act in terms
of them. Such thinking may contribute to the erosion of the
previously existing structures without a notable contribution to
the attainment of modernization in general.

There is no single type of organization in terms of which the
subversive effects of the introduction of the structures of relatively modernized society emerges more clearly than the family.
For the vast majority of members of all of the relatively nonmodernized societies, few if any other organizations compete with the
family as a focus of orientation. If there is a competitor in this
sense, it is likely to be a governmental organization. Even if
family considerations do not take precedence over orientations to
another organization, the possibility of conflict in which the other
organization will take precedence is rare for the average individual. Thus the increase in alternative organizational foci of attention constitutes in and of itself a radical change in family structure. This is perhaps the most general and the most inescapable
alteration.

Many others have been mentioned in this work. For example,
with the introduction of structures of modernization, the role of
members of the family in education, especially for adult roles, of
younger family members is curtailed. The family structures
of control over individuals are modified. The increased possibility
of alternative employment on relatively nonnepotistic grounds
increases the degrees of freedom of disgruntled individuals who
belong to a given family. The comparative stability and importance of the family organization prior to the beginning of change
is likely to accentuate any departure from the previous state of
affairs.

The most telling of the implications of change in family structure for the problems of modernization lies in the implication of

these changes for general problems of social control. Even if family solidarities are not the strongest solidarities, ideally speaking, for the average member of any society of any considerable scale, they are certainly second only to the solidarities that he has or may have with some members of some governmental system or subsystem. Governmental controls may be, therefore, to a considerable extent independent of family controls, but almost literally nothing else is. Even governmental controls are unlikely to be independent of structures of family control. The vast majority of governmental organizations in relatively nonmodernized societies are ones whose members exert control over members of the society largely via some references to kinship organizations in general and family organizations in particular. During a transition in which problems of coordination and control are of strategic importance, changes in family structures generally undercut the probabilities and possibilities of controls over individuals. Family change during transition is accompanied by a radical increase in the amount of individualism by default.

In general considerations of the problems of modernization, the interference with efficiency which is so obviously inseparable from so many nepotistic practices has on the whole obscured the relevance of family structures for the general structures of social control. The leaders and planners of modernization must and will seek to reduce the incidence of nepotistic practices, but when and if they reduce nepotistic practices, they also wipe out important controls over deviance among strategic individuals.[9]

With the development of modernization there must also be changes in the literacy characteristic of the members of the society and in closely associated matters. Literacy must become universal, a component of basic knowledge, if the society is to become a relatively modernized one. In general the members of the society must also learn to think in terms of a critical rational approach as far as broad areas of their actions are concerned. In addition, literacy sufficient for highly developed intermediate forms of knowledge must also be present. This means, of course, that the general basic knowledge of the members of the society must be radically explanded. Finally, some of the members of the society at least must be highly developed in their ability to think critically. The relevance of general literacy and the critical ap-

[9] They are extremely likely to do so without any awareness of any connection between the two. In this arena of public affairs we frequently hear that "things just seem to come apart at the seams." This bewilderment is primarily a function of the fact that so little is known about where the "seams" are and what they are like.

proach for the processes of modernization need not be elaborated here. What is important as far as the process of erosion is concerned lies in two directions. First, there is the departure from previously existing structures by virtue of the generally increased level of literacy and the general increase in disseminated emphasis on the critical approach. Second, there are many problems inherent in the fact that no one has ever devised a neat and easy way to keep applications of either literacy or the critical approach carefully confined to those areas in which they are essential if modernization is to take place at all. The increase in literacy opens up new avenues for the centralized control of propaganda, but it also opens up new avenues for individuals to get hold of materials which other members in their society would inevitably prefer to keep from them. One of the great vulnerabilities of authoritarian systems lies in these aspects of literacy and the critical approach. Thought control in one form or another is always a major preoccupation of the leaders of authoritarian organizations. Problems of thought control may be no less a concern for the members and the leaders of nonauthoritarian organizations. The exercise of critical faculties in a situation of general literacy and intellectual freedom is not necessarily either responsible or rational.[10] For the members of relatively or highly modern-

[10] The intellectual ferment in Japan in 1960–61 is an exceedingly interesting one from this point of view. Some of the most articulate Japanese intellectuals of the day were conspicuously silent in the 1940's as far as expression of criticism of what was then an explicitly militaristic authoritarian regime, whose leaders were characterized by no discernible scruples about free expression. Had they not been unobtrusive at that time, they would probably not be with us today. In the face of a governmental organization in 1960–61 whose members, whatever their faults might have been on other scores, certainly did not abridge freedom of expression in any highly authoritarian fashion, the criticisms of the intellectuals were vociferous and frenetic. A considerable amount of the criticism and even the allegations of fact under these circumstances is more readily explicable in terms of the determination on the part of these thinkers never to be caught being uncritical as they or their elders had been in another period of history. Neither careful logical nor empirical analysis of the content of the criticisms tendered makes these acts of criticism seem so rational as does the assumption of the desire of the critics to avoid being found uncritical.

From the point of view of the maintenance of high rates of economic development, of rapid rates of generally peaceable social change, and of virtually unrestricted areas of freedom of expression, such criticisms may constitute a capricious element. One of the great differences between a relatively authoritarian government and one whose members interfere little if at all with freedom of expression lies precisely in the fact that in the face of capricious criticism of this sort the members of the latter cannot cope with the situation directly without to some extent becoming the former. The uncritical exercise of the critical faculties poses a special problem for leaders who value freedom of expression.

ized societies as well as for the members of societies in the process of becoming relatively modernized, emphasis on literacy and a critical approach constitutes at one and the same time a requisite and a problem. It is an emphasis which the members of such societies cannot live without, but under certain dispensations it can be exceedingly difficult for them to live with too.

In the course of modernization the members of all known societies today experience radical changes in their demographic situation. For the members of relatively nonmodernized societies the problems posed here are popularly referred to in terms of the concept of the population explosion. The members of these societies have generally had exceedingly high birth rates. The increase of their numbers has been held in check by factors which resulted in exceedingly high death rates. Especially infant mortality and many of the endemic diseases which sap resistance to other ailments are exceedingly vulnerable to relatively inexpensive forms of modern medical technology. Characteristically in the process of transition of the late-comers, the decline in the death rate is dramatically faster than any decline in the birth rate. Prior to the beginning of the process, the birth rate or at least the rates of conception have been close to the biological maximum for mature female members of these societies. Sooner or later, as the process of modernization increases, factors affecting the birth rates come into play. So efficient has modern medical technology become, however, that the lag in decline in birth rates behind death rates is dramatic.

Many of the ideal structures of family life have in fact been preserved because some of the actual structures varied considerably from the ideal ones. In Chinese society, for example, the emphasis on equal inheritance among all sons could be preserved at least in part because relatively seldom did enough sons survive to make operation in terms of these structures impossible. The advent of modern medical technology alters these situations radically. Enormous pressures are exerted on the ideal structures specifically because, for the first time in the general history of the society, the actual structures, in terms of the availability of the individuals called for, approximate the ideal structures. This sort of problem of population explosion for the maintenance of the general social structure is at least as far-reaching in its implication for social change as the problem of increased mouths to feed.

Authors of popular articles are fond of illustrating the problems involved in the population explosion by some projection pointing out that, at present rates of increase, by the year 2650, approximately, the population increase will have gone to such lengths that new individuals will have to stand on the heads of their forebears, and within sixty some odd years of that date this will hold true even if they can stand on water.[11] So dramatic has this example been with its focus of attention on problems of space with the closely allied questions of food supply, etc., that little attention has been given to equally relevant questions. Long before such densities of population are approached, we shall be faced with much more detailed consideration of the problems of the minimal implications for viable social structures of such numerous members of the social systems of this earth. Apart from discussion of small groups such as dyads, triads, etc., for which the number of individuals constitute a part of the problem by definition, the implications of the numbers of members involved in a social system for the substantive aspects of the social structure has been little if at all explored. There clearly are such implications long before physical saturations in spatial densities are approached. The population explosions characteristic of the members of the relatively nonmodernized societies in the transition toward relative modernization are the most dramatic examples of this problem, but some of the population increases characteristic of the members of some of the relatively modernized societies also raise questions of this sort.[12]

There is another implication of the demographic changes in the process of modernization which contributes to the erosion of the previously existing social structures. This one is also closely connected with family structures. With the improvements of modern medical technology far more individuals survive to be-

[11] Ansley J. Coale, adapting an image first presented by P. C. Putnam [see: Putnam, P. C., *The Future of Land Based on Nuclear Fuels*, Oak Ridge, 1955, p. 18] has observed: "In about 6500 years, if current growth continues, the descendents of the present world population would form a solid sphere of live bodies expanding with a radial velocity that, neglecting relativity, would equal the velocity of light" [see: Coale, A. J., "Increases in Expectation of Life and Population Growth," *International Population Conference*, Vienna, 1959, pp. 36–41, esp. p. 36]. C. F. Westoff informs me that calculations based on a more recently available figure on the annual rate of increase [i.e., 2 per cent instead of 1.7 per cent] would lower that figure to roughly 5400 years. A. J. Coale has pointed out that all such illustrations are special cases of Malthus' insight of some one hundred fifty years ago, regardless of whether the illustration is in terms of space, weight of bodies, etc. Long before any of these dates could be reached, life would of necessity become "crowded, poor, nasty, brutish, and short."

[12] For example, what are the implications of the demographic structures characteristic now of United States society for United States family structures, megalopolitan developments, transportation structures, etc. These matters certainly do not vary at random relative to one another.

come aged. In the past in an overwhelming majority of relatively nonmodernized social contexts the aged, when they existed, have been taken care of in terms of family structures. Part of the possibility of such care lay in the fact that only relatively rarely did the aged members of the ordinary family long survive, if indeed they reached the stage of being aged at all. At the same time that ideal family units are frequently characterized by a decreasing size of membership and individuals of the younger generation are detaching their families of procreation from those of their parents, an increasing number of parents survive to the point of helplessness. In the context of all such societies there develops quickly the problem of public care for the aged. These problems have implications not only from the economic point of view. They have implications from the point of view of respect for the aged, and hence for what were at one time considered structures of authority in those societies, family solidarity, etc.

Finally, one of the special factors in rapid erosion of the status quo is the radical increase in the generalization of the medium of exchange. Among the members of relatively nonmodernized societies the extent of the use of money may have been quite limited. Some form or forms of money are certainly present in all societies of any considerable scale, whether relatively modernized or not. Among the members of the relatively nonmodernized societies, however, the use of money never approaches the generality, either in terms of the number of goods or services which can be exchanged in monetary terms or in terms of the number of the members of the society who are involved in such exchanges, which is taken for granted by the members of a relatively modernized society. As modernization proceeds, more members use money for more things all the time.

The increase in specialization and interdependence possible under these circumstances is obvious enough. Somewhat less obvious are two other implications of the increased use of money by the general membership of the society. First, the increased use of money always increases the comparability of diverse goods and services as far as the membership of a society is concerned. No matter how diverse two items may be in other respects, if one is priced at $5,000 and the other at $10,000 the latter is in some sense—if only the monetary sense—twice the former. In this sense an increase in the use of money broadens men and quickens their imagination—even if we call the latter greed. Not only is the comparability of goods and services which at one time might not have been considered comparable at all increased, but also the tendency to compare quite diverse elements in monetary terms is radically increased. I have already [pp. 66–71] stressed the fact that it is not surprising how much the members of the relatively modernized societies judge diverse items in monetary terms as it is surprising that they do not do so to an even greater extent [see also pp. 257–262]. To the extent that this criterion for evaluation increases among the members of relatively nonmodernized societies, important alterations in the criteria of judgment take place.

Inseparable from the increased sense of comparability and the alteration in standards of judgment which accompany increasingly general uses of increasingly general forms of money is an increase not only in specialized orientation to economic allocation but also an increase in the conscious awareness of uses of economic allocation as means to diverse ends. This is the second aspect of importance here. Among members of most of the relatively nonmodernized societies an enormous amount of the allocation of goods and services takes place on a relatively nonspecialized basis and is considered by them to be incidental to quite other matters. With increases in the generalization of the medium of exchange and increased uses of money, there is an increased awareness of the efficiency of money as a generalized means. Without going to the naïve extreme of assuming that it is possible to have a society in terms of which anything can be bought and sold, it is nevertheless quite tenable to take the position that an increase in the number of things which the average member of the society regards as *capable* of being bought and sold has radical implications for a wide variety of social situations. For example, ends which at one time could only be achieved by a marshalling of the efforts of family members, fellow villagers, or the like may now be achieved by hard labor. With an increase in the range of applications of money for different purposes, individuals who at one time were reluctant to sell land to strangers within the village setting may have their reluctance offset by the increased possibilities of what they can do with the funds so obtained. If the monetary units available to the members of the society are relatively difficult to counterfeit and stable in value, some of the reluctance previously felt to deal with strangers lest one be cheated may be overcome.

I stress the importance of the increased use of money as a source of the erosion of the status quo of the relatively nonmodernized societies for two reasons. First, for the reasons already given above, I think it is of especial importance. Second, I think its importance is likely to be overlooked by students of public affairs, whether they are members of relatively modernized or relatively nonmodernized societies. Students of public affairs who are members of relatively modernized societies overlook the importance of increased uses of money for general changes in the social structure for two reasons. First, they take the highly generalized use of highly generalized media of exchange so much for granted that its peculiarity as a highly developed phenomenon in social history tends to be ignored. Second, the use of monetary criteria as a basis for evaluation has come so much under moral fire as an example of crass materialism that there is a tendency to regard phenomena relative to which uses of money have broad implications as somehow crassly materialistic and shameful for that reason. At one and the same time the members of relatively modernized societies tend to overlook the extent to which money is important as a social device and to be ashamed of it.

Students of public affairs who are members of relatively nonmodernized societies, unless they have become sophisticated via education in the context of relatively modernized societies, tend to overlook the importance of money as a social device for two reasons also. On the one hand, they tend to overlook the implications of its generalized use because such uses of money are so unfamiliar to them. On the other hand, if they do not overlook them, they are also exceedingly likely to regard attaching major significance to the introduction of monetary structures as somehow crassly materialistic and shameful. If the students of public affairs of the relatively nonmodernized societies have received their education in relatively modernized social contexts, they are likely to overlook the importance of these implications for the same reasons characteristic of those who are members of relatively modernized societies. If one wishes to understand modernization—regardless of why one may wish to understand it—the implications for social change of increased uses of money must not be overlooked for any reasons. It is easy to combat overlooking these matters either because of excessive familiarity or lack of familiarity with them. That is a simple cognitive problem. The other problem is not so easy to combat. Whether or not the relevance of increases in uses of money for other aspects of social life is shameful or crassly materialistic, unless its relevance can be refuted, students of these problems must learn to discuss it frankly without getting involved in casting ideological aspersions on one another.[13]

[13] Social scientists in general might be well advised to reconsider the implications of uses of money and increases in generalization and general use of media of exchange for other aspects of social life. On the whole, money tends to be regarded as something which narrows your develop-

B. STRATEGIC PROBLEMS OF TRANSITION.

The *three most strategic problems of transition* are those of *control, capital formation,* and *elements of ambivalence* created by the process of modernization itself.

1. CONTROL

Enough has been said above to make clear the importance of control and coordination of the efforts of the members of a society if transition to a relatively modernized state is to be smooth and efficient. At just the point in time at which such control, and coordination are most vital, the general structures of control and the ones in terms of the government in particular, are usually radically undercut by the social changes taking place—even if

---

ment. Thinking in monetary terms is not only regarded as crass but as limiting our perspective and our cultivation of the finer things of life. By contrast with social scientists and philosophers some of our more pragmatic and humorous wealthy have pointed out that while it may be perfectly true that "money cannot buy happiness, it nevertheless makes unhappiness a great deal easier to bear." Without getting involved in this sort of discussion the relevance of money and the use of money for the finer things of life might well be reconsidered.

The relevance in one sense is quite obvious. The higher the standard of living, the greater is the possibility of utilizing leisure as well as converting other goods and services to whatever may be defined as the finer things of life. While it may remain true that one cannot buy culture in one sense, it is certainly not true that one cannot buy culture in any sense at all. However narrowing and demeaning it may be if an individual concerned himself only with the accumulation of money, the transition from thinking overwhelmingly in nonmonetary terms to thinking of an increasing range of phenomena as calculable in monetary terms and subject to manipulation in terms of exchange may be an exceedingly broadening transition from all sorts of points of view. Realization, for example, that education is available at a price may make some aware of the possibility of achieving an education, whereas before they considered that completely out of the question. The best things in life are frequently not nearly so free as some would have us believe. Nevertheless, the fact that such things can be acquired makes a great deal of difference for the general orientation of most members of the population toward such things. To be freely available on an exchange basis, even given the difficulty of acquiring the means of exchange, may be to have a far higher level of accessability than might otherwise be considered possible. Increase in the general use of a more generalized medium of exchange may radically increase that *horizon of the possible* [see p. 126] which is essential to ambitious striving. The view that money is the root of all evil is an ethical monism and no less a form of naïve economic determinism in the ethical field than the explanation of all social phenomena in terms of their economic aspects in social science. Quite apart from the evaluation of its products, neither money nor its use produces or is responsible for *all* of anything. Nevertheless—and neither paradoxically nor quixotically —the explanatory relevance of money and its use has been far underestimated in the social science literature of every field save economics.

the structures institutionalized among the members of the society are highly authoritarian ones. During the transition and what is to follow, the governmental organization and increases in centralized control are probably more important than ever before in the history of the society concerned. The transition, the greater centralization and greater emphasis on government, as well as the greater interdependence of the various organizations in a society with the governmental organization constitute radical changes which are not easy to make. If the governmental structures of these societies are not considerably more authoritarian than those of us who prefer relatively nonauthoritative structures wish to contemplate, it will be impossible for the members of the government to get done the job which has to be done if the transition is to be at all smooth.

The problems of scale for late-comers already discussed above virtually ensure that the members of no subsystem of the society other than the government will be capable of exerting the coordination and control necessary for these purposes. The minimal emancipation of the members of such a society from previous forms of control necessary if they are to participate in new roles, become members of new organizations, and literally move about at a rate not previously contemplated also makes it possible for them to behave in ways not conducive to such developments. Furthermore, the members of these societies are not realistically faced with the alternative of not getting involved in the process of modernization at all. If lack of control, whether authoritarian or not, interferes with the smoothness of such transition, the alternative is not to go back to the *status quo ante* but rather to exist in a kind of social limbo in which the advantages sought in terms of modernization are not available and a return to the previous forms of integration is not possible. Those societies whose members are ineffective in their attempts to modernize are certainly "more to be pitied than scorned." Nor can one argue that even if either relatively nonauthoritarian or authoritarian governments could be effective as a set of structures in terms of which governmental leaders can carry out modernization, a return or the creation of a less authoritarian form of government in the social limbo which results is possible. It is almost certainly not possible. Throughout history the kind of unrest and dissatisfaction characteristic of this state of affairs has more often resulted in the acceptance of highly authoritarian forms of governance than otherwise.

So far one of the few sets of late-comers who have been successful with modernization, and the only ones radically out of contact with the members of those societies in terms of which modernization developed more or less indigenously while those developments took place, have been the Japanese. To a remarkable degree the structures of control in Tokugawa Japanese society were convertible to modernized forms with little loss of effectiveness. There is, however, every reason to believe that the case of Japan is rare—not likely to be copied or repeated.

In the case of Japan, as of other cases, the fact that the form of the government was authoritarian at the outset of the process is certainly not enough in and of itself to explain this result. Social history furnishes many cases of highly authoritarian governments which unlike that of the Japanese were undercut just when it was most important in the process that control be maintained. In the process of transition it is critically important that the structures of control be overwhelmingly on a governmental basis and be highly effective whether authoritarian or not. It is also unlikely that control on a governmental basis will be highly effective whether authoritarian or not when the transition begins. One of the implications of the period of social limbo which so often attends ineffective efforts in terms of governmental control may be to prepare the way for the acceptance of viable elements of control in terms of a government—usually on a fairly authoritarian or highly authoritarian basis—whether one likes to think so or not.

2. CAPITAL FORMATION

Among the strategic problems of transition the problem of capital formation is to the economic aspects of modernization as the problem of control is to political aspects. In any process of development two forms of capital formation are always involved. First, sufficient capital must be formed to take care of deterioration and obsolescence. Second, additional capital must be formed as a basis for further increases in productivity. The members of any society are faced by the first problem. The members of any society in terms of which the level of income or the level of productivity of the members is increasing are faced by problems of the second sort as well. The members of societies in transition toward modernization are faced by quite special problems of the second sort. For them not only must there be additional capital formation, it must also be *new* capital formation in the sense that the actual devices and materials involved are likely to constitute radical departures from previous ones. From the point of view of latecomers the old forms of capital will no longer do. Among the members of relatively modernized societies, even if levels of productivity are rising, the types of capital formed—with occasional discontinuities of invention—are to a high degree familiar. During the course of transitions to relatively modernized societies, this is no longer the case.

In this connection there is a special contrast between the late-comers and the indigenous gradual modernizers. In the latter case the members of the society concerned were able to convert quite directly the materials and the skills of one stage of their development to those of the next. There were thousands of steps of this sort in the process—all of them quite gradual by contrast with the vast majority of those facing the members of any relatively nonmodernized societies. The first steam engines could be constructed and were constructed out of the metals available and by the blacksmiths available. This kind of direct conversion of the materials and skills at hand is often out of the question in many cases for late-comers. It is not possible to construct a modern milling machine out of the materials and skills available among the members of relatively nonmodernized societies. Not only are many of the new kinds of capital which are to be formed not ones which can be formed out of existing materials at hand, but also some of the new forms are absolutely necessary if the developments are to take place at all.[14]

Since the old forms of materials and skills are not directly convertible into the new ones necessary, the late-comers in one form or another become further involved with the members of other societies. Ordinarily this takes the form of involvement in international trade. Either the late-comers change some of their forms of production so that export of goods and services in which they have a comparative advantage can be used in exchange for imports of the goods and services which are necessary, or they must seek these imports via borrowing or via gifts. In the long

[14] There is an important qualification necessary here. One of the more naïve mistakes of those in charge of these processes is to insist on using the very latest ideas, the most modern tools, etc., in the development of relatively nonmodernized societies. Frequently it is necessary to do this, but it is not always necessary. For the members of some of these societies at least during a considerable portion of the process they will have a considerable comparative advantage in international trade via combinations of machines and workers which are not so labor saving as those characteristic of some of the most highly modernized societies. Thus it is a mistake to assume that it is absolutely necessary in every case to jump as far as possible from the kind of capital at the furthest remove from the most modern forms. Nevertheless, in every case there will be gaps between the materials and skills available among the members of a relatively non-modernized society and the materials and skills necessary if the process is to go ahead. There will be some gaps which these members cannot bridge on a self-sufficient basis.

run, if the development is to be stable, some of the first of these possibilities must take place. This means, of course, that late-comers are not only involved in the reorientations occasioned by the introduction of new forms of capital, but there must be important alterations in the orientation of production in terms of the older and more familiar forms as well. Thus *three things* are involved. First, there is need for additional capital and probably on a scale beyond that previously conceived. That is to say, the rate of formation of additional capital, if the transition is to be successful, is probably considerably in excess of the rate of additional capital formation previously taken for granted by the members of the society. Furthermore, additions to capital formation, once this process has begun, cannot be viewed as constituting some absolute goal. Once the process is started, if the society is to be stable, there must be a continuing rate of additions to capital formation. Under the conditions of relatively modernized societies one cannot simply increase productivity by the creation of an irrigation works and let the level of productivity so achieved rest for decades or even centuries.

Second, entirely new forms of capital must be created and the members of the society concerned must learn to operate in terms of those new forms.

Third—and this is more often overlooked than the first two—because of the lack of direct convertibility from the old forms of materials and skills to the new necessary forms, the orientation of production in terms of the old forms must be altered. Sometimes this involves the use of old methods to create new products; sometimes it merely involves a greater preoccupation with export than before. It almost inevitably involves consideration of the older forms of productivity in terms of much more highly specialized predominantly economically oriented organizations than before. All three of these requirements are implications in the general social context of the problems of capital formation implicit in any transition from a relatively nonmodernized society to a relatively modernized one.

These requirements of capital formation raise the complicated question of private versus public effort. It is obviously closely tied to questions of centralized control of the members of these societies and hence to the problem of the kind of government in terms of which the members can operate effectively during the process. There are also the obvious preoccupations of individuals with a differing ideology about how much of such effort should be in private as opposed to public terms. Quite apart from these ideological preferences certain general considerations can be laid down. First, some of the problems of scale almost certainly rule out sole reliance on private effort. Whole communications networks for the territory occupied by the members of the society, whole sets of schools to create a situation of general literacy, etc., are not only necessary, but if the transition is to be accomplished with expedition, these must be achieved quite rapidly. Among the members of most of these societies, despite radically bimodal distributions of income with outstanding examples of exceedingly wealthy individuals, there do not in general exist individuals or sets of cooperating individuals sufficiently wealthy to handle these projects alone. The financial capacity of these individuals is a question apart from whether or not the general membership of the society or the leaders of the governmental organizations wish, or should wish, to leave matters of such general significance in private hands. Whether justified or not, in the current world situation it is exceedingly unlikely that the public in any of these areas will be willing to leave such important matters so closely and privately held.

Second, quite apart from the problem of scale there is another problem which almost certainly would dictate handling a considerable portion of these matters on a public rather than a private basis, unless the private basis is a strictly charitable one. Some of the requirements of capital formation of larger scale such as the creation of schools for the entire membership of the society, constitutes enterprises which it would be exceedingly difficult to make pay on a private basis. The vast majority of the individuals who must be educated lack the means to pay for their education, even should they wish to. The leaders of organizations or others utilizing the educated products produced in terms of these schools do not know in any precise sense how to reckon the value added by the education received, etc. Handled on a private basis it is difficult to see how many of these enterprises could be made to pay for themselves, unless this were done via grants of funds collected as taxes or in some other form in terms of a governmental organization. One of the virtues of handling some of these matters on a private basis might be the possibility of washing out, via bankruptcy, failures in such efforts by private individuals, but many of these organizations are not ones which the members of the society can permit to be wiped out even though they are not doing as well as might be expected. Nor is it likely to be economically feasible to duplicate facilities sufficiently to create a competitive situation in these areas of activity.

Third, the problems of international trade raised for the members of these societies probably require some considerable level of public participation at least in the form of regulation. I have tried to point out above that the members of these societies are faced not only with the problem of entirely new forms of economic allocation. They are also faced with radical reorientations of many of the existing forms if they are to take the fullest possible advantage of their comparative advantages in international trade to facilitate the capital formation necessary for these developments.[15]

Fourth, there is the question of errors. Here there is a great deal to be said for the handling of matters on a private rather than a public basis. A public basis as that term is ordinarily understood means a governmental basis. If a competitive basis can be created, it is much easier to wash out individual cases of error on the part of private individuals than to get members of the government to desist from practices which prove to be in error. To some extent the private individuals will be washed out by their competitors. This will not be true of the persons responsible in terms of the government. On the other hand, as the need for coordination rises, and given the immediate requirement for high levels of

---

[15] In this connection there exists a special problem. This may be described as commercialization versus industrialization. Given the extreme bimodal distribution of income characteristic of most of these societies, there is a profitable market for what might be considered luxury goods from abroad. These constitute imports which are at one and the same time expensive and of little significance in raising general levels of productivity. In the field of automobiles, for example, the importation of large and luxurious private passenger vehicles is not only desired by many of the personally wealthy, but the possibility of converting such vehicles to uses alternative to luxurious private transportation are exceedingly restricted. Second, these are usually societies in terms of which the role of specialists in exchange, that is to say of merchants, are, ideally speaking, marginal roles at best. The specialists in exchange are generally subject to exploitation and expropriation by the members of the government. Under these circumstances, since it is easier to conceal inventory than plant plus inventory, these specialists are highly motivated toward deals in terms of inventories with considerable possibilities for concealment, rapid turnover, and high margins of profit. The importation of luxury items for quick exchange rather than investment in plants for indigenous production is quite appealing under these circumstances. The importation of expensive items generally irrelevant to increases in productivity among the members of such societies can consume considerable amounts of foreign exchange without substantially furthering the formation of new capital or the acquisition of new capital necessary during the process of modernization. Especially to the extent that specialists in the exchange have lacked prestige in the relatively nonmodernized societies prior to this time, to the extent that the government has been characterized by the commission of graft and corruption by its members, to the extent that there has been a bimodal distribution of income, etc., income from international trade is exceedingly likely to be dissipated unless members of the government step in and handle these matters on a public basis.

planning, the toleration of error on a private basis feasible under other circumstances is not likely to be feasible under these. The reversibility of error and the stimulation of initiative are perhaps two of the most solid bases for high levels of private participation in these matters. In the context of the other requirements, however, and in the general context of requirement of control in terms of an increasingly centralized governmental organization, it is unlikely that any set of late-comers will ever again be able to attain the level of private participation in an efficient process of this sort which was characteristic of the modernization of Japan. Even that case, of course, was characterized by high levels of public participation and a peculiar and close coordination of public and private efforts.

3. AMBIVALENCE TOWARD MODERNIZATION

I have stressed the fact that as far as modernization is concerned there is always something in it for some of the members of any relatively nonmodernized society. It is also true that there are always some members of the society who are against it. There is more to the matter than that, however. Some of the people who start out in favor of the process inevitably end up as its bitterest opponents, and some of the people who may not have thought much about it one way or the other come to be opponents. The very feelings stirred up and given mass expression during the process are in some respects inimical to the process. Nationalism in its extremistic form is a prominent example. The positive implications of a nationalistic spirit for transition have been commented on at length by both laymen and scholars in profusion. The extent to which preoccupations of this sort can impede the process has not been explored in anything like so much detail. The extent to which the implications of nationalistic fervor are dysfunctional for the process of modernization is probably inseparable from the extent to which this type of fervor is eufunctional for the process. The time wasted by individuals in attempts to be specifically different from others and preserve their separate identity may be the price paid for the morale necessary to get certain things done which have to be done if the process is to continue.

The enthusiasm for things modern may also carry with it its own excesses. In the discussion of capital formation above, I have indicated that it is not always the most modern technique that is best adapted to a given set of problems of transition. Nevertheless, if the necessary admiration for things modern is to be approximated, especially given nationalistic pride, almost any suggestion that something less than the most modern be utilized in a given situation is likely to be viewed with suspicion as an attempt to keep the people concerned backward. The emphasis on education and social mobility may have as an important side effect new forms of snobbism which to some extent interfere with further development. All of the fervors attendant to the process probably have some dysfunctional implications for the process.

There is yet another kind of ambivalence—radically different from these just mentioned but characteristic without exception of all of those who have made progress along these lines. In the process of modernization, however great improvement may be from certain points of view, some individuals always get hurt or think of themselves as having been hurt. In addition others are frustrated not so much by direct deprivation as by the fact that, no matter how great progress may be, it does not live up to the expectations of those who contemplated it nor does it reach the goals sought as fast as was hoped for. In all cases sooner or later these two types of diappointment result in fundamentalistic reactions.[16] I would define a fundamentalistic reaction as one in which the actors concerned regard the solution to present problems as they conceive them to lie in a return to the good old days from which they feel departure never should have been made. With or without understanding the process, these members feel that all would have been better off had it never begun—that salvation lies in a return to tried and true ways. A long history furnishes a thousand levers with which to prize a nation about. The longer the historical background of a given set of individuals, the greater the variation in bases for fundamentalistic reactions. Members of United States society rarely go back more than a hundred years in their view of what constitutes the good old days. For the members of a society with as long a history as French society, for example, fundamentalistic reactions may focus on periods as remote as the Carolingian in the case of virtuosi of fundamentalism.

Some of the more extreme forms of ambivalence about modernization call for a total abandonment of participation in the

[16] My use of the concept of fundamentalistic reaction, though no doubt modified, stems unquestionably from two sources. One is the use of the concept by Talcott Parsons more than two decades ago. See: T. Parsons, "Some Sociological Aspects of the Fascist Movements," *Social Forces*, vol. 21, no. 2, Nov., 1942, pp. 138–147, reprinted in T. Parsons', *Essays in Sociological Theory*, revised edition, 1954, The Free Press, Glencoe, Ill., pp. 137 ff. The other is the work of Veblen. The idea involved with or without the term is a recurrent theme in his work, *Imperial Germany*, *Absentee Ownership*, *The Theory of Business Enterprise*, etc.

process. This extreme form has never characterized anything like the majority of the membership of any of the societies whose members have begun along this road. There is, however, a mixed form of this ambivalence which is highly characteristic of many of the members of such societies. This is the kind of ambivalence characteristic of individuals who, as far as modernization is concerned, wants its *results* but not *it*. By no means all of the members of a given society ambivalent in this respect have in mind the same *results* or the same *it*, but this kind of ambivalence constitutes a major problem of morale, especially during transition. In many instances this ambivalence results in major problems of control.

There is a special form of ambivalence in the process of modernization which is especially characteristic of late-comers in the situation of international affairs today. This is an ambivalence which results in considerable part from the very feelings stirred up and given mass expression in the course of modernization, but it is an ambivalence by virtue of the fact that it involves a specific kind of ignorance of what the situation is. I refer in this connection to something already discussed above in other connections [e.g., pp. 284–286]. This is the definition of the situation as seen by many of the members of the new underdeveloped nations. Many of these individuals are preoccupied with conceptions of independence, national sovereignty, and freedom which for all of their overtones are frequently meaningless in the context of international affairs today. The concepts of independence, freedom, and sovereignty which made a certain amount of sense in the eighteenth and early nineteenth centuries, when to a high degree the members of what we consider nations today approached self-sufficiency make little sense in that form in the context of daily increases in interdependence among the peoples of the world. It is no longer possible for the representatives of any nation to "go where they want to go, do what they want to do, I don't care" as a popular song once had it. The problem facing the representatives of all nations is how to create the kind of structures of interdependence in terms of which the interest of the members of the societies relatively smaller in scale are not subject to capricious sacrifice at the whim of the members of the societies of much larger scale. The conception that all men are equal before the law is a specialized and restricted form of equality. It by no means implies equality across the board in social life. Whether such conceptions can be applied to nations or their representatives or whether entirely new ways of looking at these problems have to be devised is by no means certain. What is absolutely certain, however, is the fact that individuals with points of view, which find expression because the process of modernization has begun to move forward throughout the world, cannot effectively insist that the situation for them must be what it approximated for some others before modernization had developed far any- where. The development of modernization cannot make possible the achievement of a type of social situation which the devel- opment of modernization destroyed and revealed as destroyed insofar as it had previously been approximated.

C. SOURCES OF PESSIMISM

The problems of modernization are not ones about which we have cause for optimism. Unless one wishes to consider the members of nations such as Sweden, Denmark, and Holland as consisting of late-comers in this sense, none of the late-comers have so far been peaceful, prosperous, and stable. Few of the true late- comers have so far shown any considerable success with this transition. Of those societies whose members really were out of contact with the process of modernization as it developed more or less indigenously among the members of societies like that of the United States, Great Britain, France, etc., only the Japanese has been markedly successful in the transition. The way in which this was done by the Japanese was closely related to their involvement in World War II. Whatever the implications of that involvement, one may add further of the Japanese that after that war they went on to achieve much higher levels of modernization at a greater rate than they had ever done before. The Russians had far more continuous contact with those societies in terms of which these structures developed more or less indigenously, but despite the fact and despite unequal developments of modernization along certain restricted lines as an overall matter, present-day Russian society is not as highly modernized as present-day Japanese so- ciety. Certainly it has not gone so far if the development of mass markets for heavy consumers goods is an improtant part of the process. Outside of these two examples and a few European cases or cases strictly derivative from the European cases, it is difficult to find other examples of dramatic progress in these respects. At the same time there are no cases in which the members of the societies concerned have shown no successes whatsoever. As a minimum the old structures begin to disintegrate and change. In all of these societies parts of the previously existing structures have eroded with little or no chance of recovery. The extent of this erosion is not necessarily directly related to the extent of success with modernization in a positive sense. From the point of view of the members of the relatively nonmodernized societies, this process may be a true Pandora's Box. Quite apart from the question of whether the states of affairs achieved by the members of the most highly modernized societies are worth seeking in the first place, there is the question of whether or not most of the people involved as late-comers do not come to regard themselves as importantly worse off than before. The dilemma of the members of the relatively nonmodernized societies lies in the fact that they cannot leave the process alone, and yet they cannot carry it out anywhere nearly so effectively as they would like. With regard to that dilemma, the dilemma of the members of the relatively modernized countries is very similar. They, in their turn, are unable to leave the members of the relatively nonmodernized societies alone and yet the very contacts they make, which carry with them inevitably the beginnings of modernization among the members of those societies, are not necessarily ones which they can see through to the finish. They too "can't do it and can't leave it alone." At least so far neither the members of relatively modernized or relatively nonmodernized societies have devised plans which ensure that they can do with efficiency and dispatch what they cannot refrain from starting.

I I I
THE PROBLEM OF STABILITY

A. AS A PROBLEM FOR MODERNIZING SOCIETIES

There is an important sense in which one of the characteristics of relatively modernized societies is that their members too must continue the process of modernization, but for present purposes I refer to the relatively nonmodernized societies in transition to relatively modernized ones as modernizing societies. For the members of these societies the problem of stability focuses on whether or not they are going to achieve relatively high levels of modernization and on the question of how difficult it is going to be for them to do so. From one point of view stability is not possible at all for them. Achievement of considerably advanced levels of modernization itself constitutes as radical a social revolution as is possible in human affairs. Stability as far as individuals in this situation are concerned consists primarily in the avoidance of bloodshed and the achievement of an efficient general social revolution. Furthermore, for the time being at least, whether their societies are stable or not is primarily *their* problem from one quite cold-blooded point of view. Instabilities in terms of one of these societies are not likely in and of themselves to create a situation of general world instability. The members of other societies can play on such a situation, but the instabilities leading to this state of affairs cannot be created internally via the instabilities characteristic of any one of the relatively nonmodernized societies. Were it not for sources of instability elsewhere, in this cold-blooded sense, their instabilities could be left to their members. After all, from this cold-blooded point of view, they are bound to be undergoing social revolutions in any case, and we have little reason to expect that, even with the best of intentions from all of us, their transitions will be easy or pleasant.

If one takes a less cold-blooded point of view the major problem of stability for the members of these societies is the problem of modernization for late-comers as stated above.

B. AS A PROBLEM FOR RELATIVELY MODERNIZED SOCIETIES

From one point of view a major form of instability is built into operations in terms of relatively modernized or highly modernized societies. It is not possible to consider the general question of stability in these societies apart from the question of these built-in tendencies toward continuous social revolution. Even if it is possible to consider changes of such magnitude as a characteristic of the societies concerned, there remains a question as to whether the prognosis for stability in other more general respects is bright. From many points of view the accomplishments within the grasp of members of societies such as these seem to offer bright prospects for the solution of the classic material problems, which have beset mankind or which men have considered to beset them. Nevertheless, despite unparalleled control over technical means for material ends, I see no clear scientifically reasoned basis for an optimistic prognosis as far as the general stability of societies of this sort is concerned. Such highly complicated, highly interdependent systems of action are well beyond our present capacities for explicit planning on a rational basis. The levels of complexity and interdependence of these systems increase daily, unaccompanied by any direct variation in the amount of knowledge at our disposal about such systems. Increasingly the members of such societies participate with one another in terms of systems of action of unbelievable complexity, operations in terms of which, insofar as they are directed at all explicitly, are directed largely on an *ad hoc* basis by members who often do not know what they are doing that is relevant and often cannot communicate their knowledge when they believe it to exist.

There is an enormous amount of concern in public discussions of morality with gaps between the development of our scientific technological knowledge and our knowledge of ethical and moral concerns—especially with regard to the proper criteria for judgment. In this great concern over this gap a gap in our scientific knowledge has been overlooked. The gap between our scientific knowledge in fields associated with the so-called natural sciences and our knowledge associated with the so-called social sciences is every bit as great as the gap between our scientific knowledge on the one hand and our ethical knowledge on the other. The field of economics is incomparably the most highly and rigorously developed theoretically of the various social science fields. Furthermore, on the side of applied economics the aggregate of highly intelligent talent specifically devoting their efforts to conscious rational prediction and planning of action with regard to the allocation of goods and services is almost certainly greater than characterizes aggregates of talent orienting efforts to the rational appreciation of all other aspects of social behavior put together.

In the context of both predominantly socialistic and predominantly capitalistic societies, however, the individuals who comprise such aggregates of talent, by their own standards, fall far short of the mark they have set themselves. Phenomena having to do with the stock market in the United States, with agrarian problems in the United States and the Soviet Union, with all sorts of problems of international trade, and the like furnish ample evidence. The inadequacy of the knowledge at our disposal for application in the natural science field falls short of our desires there as well. I do not know how one could measure with precision the differences between this gap and the one I assert to exist relative to the social sciences. Nevertheless, it would probably not be difficult to get general agreement that we are worse off in the latter respect than in the former.

Whatever the criteria for errors may be, the implications of errors in judgment in the context of the relatively modernized societies increase each day. So does the actual level of centralization whether one likes to admit it or not. Progress in the last few decades in the development of the social sciences has certainly not been negligible, but the gap between that progress and our needs for increased knowledge grows rather than diminishes. As members of these societies, we may discover a new problem of evil in the world. We may not prove to be bright enough to be able to live in terms of what we and our forebears have created.

There are many possibilities for disruption of such systems. In the past disruptions in the allocation of goods and services epitomized in the context of predominantly capitalistic societies by what are generally referred to as depressions have been one of the most spectacular types of disruption. There are experts who feel that the knowledge at our disposal is sufficient to cope with these situations today, but there are also experts who disagree. One of the most difficult sources of disagreement among the experts in regard to such phenomena is whether the criteria for rational action have changed or whether the type of action which poses a problem of this sort is correctly described as nonrational.[17]

The disruption of economic allocation is not a new problem for anyone, but for the members of relatively modernized societies there are others in the face of which men seem to feel more uneasy. *Juvenile delinquency* as that term is generally used today shows every sign of being a special characteristic of every relatively modernized and every modernizing society in the world. In different social contexts the juvenile delinquents bear different names, but they seem to share certain characteristics. They do not seem so much to care to overthrow existing structures, which in general they do not challenge, as they seem to wish to develop structures of their own. They do not seem to develop these structures so much as a challenge to the structures of other members of their society as because they are apathetic or unconvinced about the generally accepted structures. Their behavior is frequently revolutionary, but by default rather than by ideal. Despite considerable differences among such societies as the United States, England, France, the Soviet Union, Japan, etc., they exist and puzzle the general membership of the society. Attempts to account for their special form of deviance on the bases of such social characteristics as class background, income, religion, etc., do not seem to be effective. These individuals share one characteristic—they are young. They also share another. Insofar as they move toward middle age without becoming identified as criminals in other respects, they give up their special form of deviance and become more or less like others who share their social characteristics in all other respects save a lack of previous participation in the activities of juvenile delinquency.

This problem, whatever else its basis, is closely related to the general problem discussed above of socialization for an unknown

[17] Among some of the best economic adepts in the world of 1962 the movement of stock prices downward was neither generally explained nor was it generally predicted. The puzzlement that those movements have caused has raised further questions as to whether the previous upward movement was well understood or posed as few problems as seemed to be implicit in the relative lack of concern during the rise.

future. It is not at all difficult for young people to realize that the adults who direct the young see the problems of the young as they conceived of their own some two to three decades before and that they are therefore out of touch with the current situation. There must be some special lack of communication in the fact that what is relevant for one of these sets of individuals is not necessarily relevant for the other. The young are acutely aware of the irrelevance, whereas their elders probably aren't. The elders are probably as much disturbed by the reaction of the youths who do not see the relevance of the direction they receive in many cases as by anything else the youths do. The youths are no doubt in turn disturbed by the irrelevance of that direction as they see it, for at some stage prior in their development, if they developed at all, they must have gotten in the habit of expecting relevance from their elders. Whatever other factors operate in the context of juvenile delinquency, the cognitive problem also operates. Either the whine or defiant shout of "how was I to know?" is probably as characteristic of these youths as any other statement expressing their problem. Furthermore, under these circumstances the youths who come to be identified as juvenile delinquents or their equivalent probably constitute only the extreme cases of malintegration and strain among the young members of such societies.

There is another kind of problem characteristic of these societies. We speak glibly of those societies in terms of which we regard the rights of men as having been trampled upon. We speak of the lives of men as counting for nothing under the circumstances. We point to the masses of nameless slaves, serfs, peasants, etc. In doing so our preoccupation with certain concepts of freedom and independence, certain criteria for the proper recognition of the dignity of man, etc., becloud our judgment. However misused men may have been under these circumstances by other criteria, they were almost inevitably identified as individuals. The lack of surname, for example, meant that individuals were identified on the basis of personal or family characteristics or village characteristics or the like. Within the interrelationships in terms of which the average individual moved there was only one "Fat Charles," one "Lame Tinker," one "Big Red," etc. Within the context of the most complete bondage, individuals were on the whole predominantly particularistically identified and considered, however demeaning the consideration, as whole men.

In the context of relatively modernized societies this particular form of individual identification becomes rarer and rarer. Increasingly the individual is identified in predominantly universalistic terms over a broad range of his activities. In his occupational sphere he is identified as an able surgeon, or a fast typist, or a slow office boy. Most of the individuals who identify him in that context have no contact with him whatsoever in many of his other contexts. Even in those strongholds of his identification on a predominantly particularistic basis, those areas in which he is judged as a whole individual, of which the family context is overwhelmingly the most important—even there most of the members of his family will have little or no knowledge of him as an individual in the context of his occupational role which is so important a factor as far as the social position of the family members are concerned, the income which they utilize, etc.

There are important differentials on the basis of sex in this respect in these societies. The fact that women are less identified with occupational roles outside the family context means that their identification as whole individuals is carried much further both within and without the family context than is that of the husband and father. But for all the sex differential, over a broad sphere of his behavior the average individual becomes from his point of view a depersonalized cog, but there is in a sense a depersonalization of the individual even within his most highly personalized context. The average family member knows little save in a highly derivative fashion, the bias of which is immediately obvious to the subject, of the life of the family member outside the family context—especially not of his life in terms of those nonfamily roles which are most significant to him. To the extent that action in terms of those roles takes the individual outside the family context, that individual in turn also understands less well the identification of the other individuals who operate more fully in terms of the family context. In the context of relatively modernized societies the most extreme form of this depersonalization is characteristic of the father and husband, but in qualified respects it pertains to all of them. As the children get involved in schools, they are treated in an increasingly objective fashion—they become cogs—they increasingly have lives apart from that of their parents and from one another. As the wives shop in supermarkets rather than neighborhood stores, as they spend more and more time separated from all save the youngest members of the family, they too lead lives important elements of which are simply out of contact with the other members of the family.

The members of all of these societies place an increasing emphasis on the objectivity of criteria in terms of which the individual judges and is judged, in terms of which he behaves and others behave toward him. Prior to the development of such societies such levels of depersonalized behavior and treatment were rarely achieved. We have no reason to believe that men adjust easily to such depersonalization or compartmentalization of their lives or whatever you may wish to call it. No matter what the ideal structures are with regard to universalistic criteria in the most highly specialized predominantly universalistic spheres of behavior, particularistic nexus [i.e., cliques] always arise. It is quite obvious to all that action in terms of these cliques interferes with the ideal structures of operation of well-worked-out tables of organization, but there is also good reason to believe that if they were unable to develop, it might be even more difficult to operate in terms of those ideal tables of organization. It is clear that one cannot operate in terms of relatively modernized societies without radical increases in depersonalized treatment, but there is also a question as to whether in the long run men can adjust stably to such treatment. We do not know whether increasing estimates of the level of mental illness in relatively modernized social contexts is the result of better diagnoses, different definitions of mental illness, or increased levels of pathology. If it represents a general and genuine increase in the incidence of such illness, however, that difference is certainly related to these phenomena, and that state of affairs poses the question of how far these trends can continue as well as whether present levels of them can be maintained. The question of how far and how long these trends can continue is especially grim since there is no indication in any of the relatively modernized societies that the accent on such depersonalized predominantly universalistic treatment is either leveling off or decreasing in some of the most important areas of activity as far as the average individual is concerned.

Oddly enough, closely related to the question of depersonalization is the general question of individualism. Individualism in the sense of identification of the total individual declines continuously with the development of the structures of relatively modernized societies. Individualism in the sense that the actor is the major focus of decisions rather than his family organization or the like probably continually increases even in highly regimented relatively modernized societies. As indicated above [pp. 227–230], individualism may be considered as ideal and/or actual individualism, and one special form of actual individualism highly relevant to social stability is individualism by default. In relatively modernized societies the extreme specialization of roles and the interdependence of roles requires an increasing emphasis on individualism in the actual sense and probably in the ideal sense as well. Furthermore, the probability of individualism by default is radically increased under such circumstances. The flexibility of manoeuver required for the specific individual is hard to achieve in the absence of individualism, but the presence of individualism or an emphasis upon it increases the problem of the individual making the correct decision. Individualism in this sense may undercut the stability of solidarities necessary if the society is to survive. Individualism in this sense is not necessarily synonymous with an emphasis on freedom and independence as it is in terms of some of its connotations for many if not most laymen. Whether it has or has not these connotations, the question remains as to whether societies of this sort can be stable with or without such emphases on individualism.

Not only is the emphasis on social change unremitting in relatively modernized contexts: the emphases on constantly increasing technological changes in general and of increasingly even distribution of increasing income among the members in particular are unremitting. One of the major problems for stability characteristic of the relatively modernized societies lies in the fact that the members of such societies cannot live with stagnation or depression in the economic aspects of their lives. This is not merely one aspect of the general importance of change characteristic of these societies. One of the strongest integrations of the types of stresses and strains discussed immediately above lies in the possibility of preoccupation of the members of such societies with continuously increasing material acquisitions. In this sense the members of these societies probably are more materialistically oriented than are the members of many other types of societies though of course this does not mean that they are solely oriented to such considerations. To some extent individuals can have their preoccupation with other problems alleviated by increased acquisitions of goods and services in general and of new and different goods and services in particular. The appeal of both sorts follows from two exceedingly general aspects of the behavior of human beings wherever they are found. One is the irreducible interest always found in material goods and services and in being relatively better off in terms of them. The other is the fascination with novelty. The extent to which the novel is likely to be regarded with fear and suspicion varies widely from the members of one society to the members of another, but there has never been a society whose members were indifferent to novelty or found it totally lacking in a favorable fascination for them.

For the members of all of the relatively modernized societies there is an enormous preoccupation with material well-being, and this does not seem to be a function of such classic distinctions as capitalism and socialism. Arguments as to the type of system whose members can maximize material well-being need not detain us here. The members of all these systems who favor their respective systems give as one of the most important elements in justification of their preference the contribution which they see their type of organization making to an increase in material welfare.

Not only do the members of these societies find some integration in continuously increasing standards of living composed of continuously novel elements. They also find integration in the appearance if not the actual achievement of social mobility. One of the most important forms of the appearance of social mobility has to do with one type of allocation of goods and services very characteristic of these societies. I have in mind here Professor Lloyd A. Fallers' brilliantly and suggestively phrased analysis of the *trickle effect*.[18]

The trickle effect refers to the following phenomena. In the context of relatively modernized societies new goods and services are frequently first produced at relatively high prices and in relatively small quantities. When these new goods and services become available, they tend to be identified with the elite members of the society. One of the reasons for this is that during their early appearance they tend to be relatively more expensive since many of the economies of mass production which will characterize them if they are popular are not possible when they are originally introduced. Therefore, during their early appearances they tend to be available to the members of the society with the larger incomes at their disposal. As I have indicated above, regardless of the ideology characteristic of the society concerned, there is for all societies, and especially relatively modernized ones, a correlation between income [or favored position with regard to scarce goods and services] and general social prestige. Insofar as demand operating either through state decision or free private purchases results in increased production at lower cost, these goods and services become available to members of society who are lower down in the income scale and hence to a considerable extent likely to be lower down in the prestige scale as well.

As these goods and services which have acquired a high prestige by virtue of their identification with the members of the

[18] See L. A. Fallers, "A Note on the Trickle Effect," *Public Opinion Quarterly*, vol. 18, no. 3, Fall, 1954, pp. 314–321. I have never ceased to be amazed at the fact that after this publication by Professor Fallers so little use has been made of the implications of the "trickle effect" for the maintenance of stability in relatively modernized societies.

society who are considered to constitute an elite, the acquisition of such goods and services by persons lower down in the scale of social prestige conveys an impression of upward social mobility much as one has the illusion that he is moving when the train next to the stationary one in which he is sitting in the station begins to move. The illusion of movement is in the opposite direction of the movement of the train which is actually moving, and so in this case, if the goods continue to trickle down in the scale of social prestige as it were, those who acquire them have something of the feeling of upward mobility and with it, of course, a feeling of achievement which in the context of these societies is expected to be the major basis for upward social mobility. It is of the essence of this process, if it is to operate in this fashion, that the flow of these goods and services be continuous and varied and that they continuously trickle down through the social hierarchy.

Closely connected with this whole phenomenon is the importance of the increasingly unimodal distribution of income characteristic of such societies. This has already been discussed above [pp. 265–279]. It is difficult to conceive of increasingly broad mass markets of the type which make possible the economies of mass production in societies with radically bimodal distributions of income or other radically discontinuous forms of the distribution of income. If the trickle effect is to operate, a unimodal distribution of income, preferably one increasing rapidly and becoming more unimodal is preferable, but there is an important limit to such an evolution. If income distribution were so unimodal as to be absolutely equal among all the members of such a society, the trickle effect could not operate at all, but then neither could the society be stable unless many of the arguments above about the importance of hierarchical arrangements, the relevance of income distribution as a reflection of social evaluation, etc., are untenable.

The trickle effect has been noteworthy in terms of United States society, for example, in all sorts of goods and services. It has operated with regard first to automobiles in general and now it is operating with regard to second automobiles and sports cars. It was characteristic of all sorts of household appliances from washing machines to television sets [and now to color television sets]. It has operated in connection with air travel domestically, travel abroad, higher education, etc. There are many examples of it characteristic of Japanese society today, and it is characteristic, though at a much less frenetic pace, of the Soviet Union.

If the operation of the trickle effect is as important as I judge it to be for stability in terms of these societies, it is one of the most important elements in understanding the problems of stability in terms of relatively modernized societies posed by any stagnation or lowering of income levels. The trickle effect ties in the integrative possibilities of increasing income and its use to acquire increasing material goods and services and increasingly novel ones with the important structures of motivation of individuals to strive for achievement. This structured striving for achievement is also of the essence of these societies. The constant striving for achievement is at one and the same time essential, if these societies are to be stable systems of action and a constant source of frustration to the members of the society, as is symbolized by the fine line dividing the properly ambitious from the overly ambitious, by the fine line dividing the driving personality from the driven personality, the dynamic from the obsessed, etc. Actually, in terms of all such societies, there is much more social mobility than is characteristic of relatively nonmodernized societies, but the systematic and ever increasing, and ever increasingly rapid, operation of the trickle effect makes possible all of the integrative effects characteristic of upward social mobility with relatively few of the drawbacks characteristic of other realizations of social mobility. Above all it permits the illusion of social mobility, if one wishes to consider it such, to exceed far the level of actual mobility as measured by other criteria, though from the point of view of the members concerned this illusion of social mobility may be quite as real as any other measure of social mobility might be. This is important because, however great the absolute amount of social mobility as measured by other criteria, regardless of political ideologies, it is never as great as the members of relatively modernized societies wish it to be or feel that it should be. In the absence of the trickle effect, desire would outrun performance by an even larger margin.

The trickle effect is one other factor relevant to the problem posed by stagnation or decrease in the standard of living. To the extent that the trickle effect operates, not only does stagnation and the decrease in distributed income have far-reaching effects, but also, if the rate of increase slows down appreciably over long periods of time, the implications for stability must be negative. Rates of the trickle effect like rates of material acquisition in general come quickly to be taken for granted. The integrative implications of the trickle effect vary directly with the rate of the effect. Thus, if the rate has been going up, a slackening of the rate may result in as genuine a feeling of deprivation as absolute stagnation or decrease. In this respect too the phenomenon is a relative one.

Only in times of great crises from their point of view have the members of relatively modernized societies adjusted stably to decreases or stagnation of levels of income. Under any save extreme conditions, it is much more difficult to cut back the achieved standards of living among the members of relatively modernized societies than among the members of relatively non-modernized ones. One of the great differences confronting the leaders of the Soviet Union and the leaders of United States society as far as capital formation by one avenue or another of forced saving is concerned lies in the fact that the standard of living and the rate of the trickle effect to which the members of the one society are in general accustomed is far in excess of that to which the members of the other are used. Whatever the difference in the degrees of freedom characteristic of these two societies, in these respects the degrees of freedom characteristic of both of them are declining all the time. Short of the special morale possibilities of involvement in open war, neither the leadership of the governments nor, possibly, the general structures of the societies themselves, could survive substantial stagnation or cut-back or even declines in rates of increase in either case. Furthermore, talk about ideological differences to the contrary notwithstanding, if and when the level of distribution characteristic of the Soviet Union reaches those characteristic of the United States, as the leaders of the Soviet Union claim it shortly will, differences in authoritarianism and centralization as between the forms of the government of the two societies will make little or no difference in the degrees of freedom in these respects from that point on. The leaders of the Soviet Union, no matter what force is at their disposal, will have lost one of their major comparative advantages in freedom of manoeuver—the range within which forced savings can be increased at the expense of what are regarded as the consumption aspects of economic allocation.

In the long run the leisure revolution will characterize all of the relatively modernized societies. We have seen so little of it so far that prediction of some of its implications for stability is even more problematical than other statements which have been made here. One of the special problems for stability implicit in the leisure revolution is the peculiar problem posed by the fact of the peculiar altruistic character of the leadership of this revolution mentioned above [pp. 77–78]. To what extent can an increasingly professionalized leadership be motivated to provide the leadership necessary for the increase of desired material advantages which they, by contrast at least, cannot share? Are such individuals likely to become so preoccupied with other considerations such as power as to become subversive of the very organizations they lead? Furthermore, with regard to the membership of these societies in general, how does one keep them out of deviant activities which threaten the stability of the society when an increasing portion of their lives is ostensibly not taken up with the serious side of life but rather with its lighter side? In virtually all societies the problem has generally been the other way around.

My usage of the term *leisure* is out of phase with that of a recent writer [19] who defines the term according to his own preferences as to what people might do with free time at their disposal, maintains that leisure has not increased, and points more in pity than in scorn to the seriousness, doggedness, and workman-like way at which members of United States society appear to be driven to recreation. If the free time available to the members of a society becomes an increasing proportion of the time available to them and is occupied in ways which do not directly reinforce the structures increasingly crucial in the diminished remainder of their time, will the result have greater or lesser implications for the continued existence or development of the society than if those members spend their time in the sort of contemplation of literature, the arts, the pleasures of the mind in general, and the contemplation of nature which takes them clean out of themselves? The plasticity of human beings is enormous, but it is by no means certain that men adjust well to the state of affairs characteristic of relatively modernized societies.

This brings up once again the problem of change in general. Quite apart from the problems of socialization for an unknown future, from the problems of economic stagnation, and the problems of adjustment to increasing leisure there is the problem of adjustment to change in general. A point has already been reached in terms of the most highly modernized of these societies, at which it is possible to speak of something close to a general social revolution taking place at least once every three decades. The hypothesis that the periodicity of these revolutions is growing shorter rather than longer is reasonable. Although one may conceive of the form of a given relatively modernized society being revolutionized periodically without the society ceasing to be a relatively modernized society and without ceasing to be a society

[19] See Sebastian de Grazia, *Of Time Work and Leisure,* Twentieth Century Fund, New York, 1962.

altogether, by definition societies have no existence whatsoever apart from the operations of members in terms of the structures of action which comprise these societies. Is there a rate of social change so rapid and so general as to be inconsistent with stable adult behavior? There is some rate of change endemic in relatively modernized societies and requisite for them. Can that rate be so slowed or handled as to approach no more than asymptotically some absolute limit consistent with the existence of a society? There is surely some lower limit to the rate of change compatible with a relatively modernized society. Is there not just as surely some upper limit on the rate of change—some rate to which members cannot adjust stably? As these societies become increasingly specialized and interdependent, one of the special problems placing a limit on such rates of change is not simply that to which the human individual can adjust, there enters once again the problem of adequate knowledge. Is there, or can there be, the knowledge necessary for the conscious level of planning which must characterize operations in terms of such societies with unlimited rates of change? If these amounts of knowledge about social phenomena cannot be available to the leaders of these societies and to the membership in general, there can be no possibility of stability in the face of indefinitely increasing rates of change—quite apart from other elements of plasticity.

Finally, there is another consideration relevant to the problem of stability of the relatively modernized societies. Whatever the sources of instability may be—whether the initiation of instability is a function of the interaction of the members of the society with one another or of the interactions of the members of one society with those of another or from some combination of the two—those instabilities once begun spread easily and rapidly throughout these highly interdependent systems. Increasingly along with the increase of the anonymity of the individual, of his depersonalization, etc., there is a general increase in the actual comradeship of the common fate which faces all of the members of such societies. As these societies become increasingly more and more highly modernized, increasingly what affects one member of one of these societies affects all of the others. Given the increasing interdependence characteristic of all of the societies and all of their subsystems and hence of all their members, the effects of the instabilities characteristic of one or more of the relatively modernized societies spreads inevitably to the individuals of the world in general. The more highly modernized the society concerned, the more involved in the process of modernization, the greater is the implication of instability emanating from any social context for its members. The most backward and least advantaged in these respects are the societies whose members are most nearly invulnerable to the spread of such instabilities. Increasingly, however, elements of invulnerability diminish with the remarkable assault being made at an ever increasing rate on the sorts of backwardness which makes such invulnerability possible. Vulnerability inheres increasingly in any contact the members of such societies have with those of relatively modernized societies. Any such contacts increase interdependence. This brings us directly to the implications of the problems of instability of the relatively modernized societies for the problems of the world today.

C. AS A PROBLEM FOR THE PEOPLE OF THE PLANET

The prospects for stability of a relatively nonmodernized society undergoing the transition to modernization are not good; the transition itself is a major form of instability. More pessimistically, the instability which is certain to characterize these societies is certain to characterize them regardless of whether or not the transition to modernization desired by so many of their members and so many others is achieved as they wish it or not. The problems of modernization always involve the members of the relatively nonmodernized societies with those of the relatively highly modernized societies, not only because of the borrowing relationship, but also because of the general increase in interdependence characteristic of increases in the levels of modernization, which are in turn increasingly characteristic of social systems generally. The problem of stability of the relatively nonmodernized societies would be in at least one hardhearted sense primarily a problem for their members as far as general world stability is concerned, were it not for the prospects of those instabilities exacerbating or being exacerbated by the instabilities characteristic of relatively modernized societies. Such restriction of significance—even from a hardhearted point of view is not conceivable with regard to the implications of the instabilities characteristic of the relatively modernized societies. If those instabilities exist, they will spread with massive effects for all other individuals on the planet given the levels of interdependence already characteristic of the members of the different societies of the world. Although instabilities characteristic of a particular relatively nonmodernized society in the process of modernization would surely spread to some extent, given increased degrees of interdependence, in many, many cases assured stability among the members of the relatively modernized societies could damp down those effects. While the increasing interdependence of the relatively nonmodernized societies has revolutionary implications for their members, many individual cases are not significant for the members of relatively modernized societies apart from the kind of instabilities which might find reflection in a major outbreak of hostilities between or among the members of relatively modernized societies.

To some extent—rationally, irrationally, or arationally—the members of highly modernized societies can use the state of their relationships with the members of other societies for internally instrumental reasons. The important thing for the moment is to keep in mind that this continues to be true despite high levels of modernization. Problems of stability in a sense internal, i.e., specific, to the members of a given society and the interest which they conceive to flow from those problems may be a major cause of relations with the members of other societies. Those relations may increase the export of instability not only via the existing network of interdependence but via direct acts regarded as threatening or dangerous by members of other societies. Members of one society are no doubt quick to exaggerate the extent to which the members of another behave in such a fashion, but the use of such techniques as international scapegoating for their domestic relevance by government leaders from Hitler to less extreme examples is surely beyond question.

The stability of foreign relations, whether deliberately interfered with for domestic reason or not, now constitute the primary question given the state of modern military technology. In general, those who have been kept informed about the developments of modern military technology do not require further demonstration of the catastrophic possibilities of application of these technological advances. There are, of course, important differences of interpretation. There are those who feel that any major war fought with modern weapons would wipe out all life on the planet today; there are those who think there there would be survivors but that the state of society as generally known today in terms of relatively modernized societies would be out of the question, perhaps for centuries. There are even experts who are more sanguine, but none of them predict casualties running to smaller figures than tens of millions with never mind what aftereffects genetically as well as socially.

At present the major possibility of warfare of this order lies in potential instabilities between the members of two of the more highly modernized societies at least in terms of the military technology at their disposal, that is to say the United States and her associates and allies versus the Soviet Union and her associates and allies. At present no easy basis for the restoration of stability in the form of some third force viewed as an overwhelming threat by the members of both camps is apparent. Apart from the literature of science fiction there is little prospect of a threat appearing which so frightens the members of these two camps as to make them see their current fears and distrusts of one another as of comparatively minor significance. With the best of intentions all around, an instability generated within the range of activities of the members of a single one of these societies can touch off planet-wide effects in such interdependent systems. For example, a major economic depression could certainly have such an effect, without the set of leaders of any given society in their right minds attempting to touch off such a chain deliberately. Without the best intentions, the possibility of the members of one camp becoming involved in hostilities with members of the other is even less out of the question.[20] In addition any instability specific to the members of one of these societies is almost certain to see radical rises in the anxieties, aggressions, etc., of its own members with a consequent increase in the possibility that they will see—never mind how irrationally—all of their problems as having been created for them by members of the opposing camp.[21]

Under these circumstances members of the public in general and the leaders specifically in the two most probable foci of radical instabilities of this sort operate in a continual lather of suspicion and distrust, which might have made itself into something approaching rationality—after the nature of other self-fulfilling prophecies—were it not for the irrationality in the cer-

[20] But perhaps not. There is a question of how rationality varies with good intentions and what constitutes rationality under these circumstances.

[21] The extent to which members of societies on both sides of this instability are prepared to invoke references to the others in an inflammatory context has not only reached the point of attribution of most major difficulties to the members of the society seen as threatening, it has permeated life in general in quite a surprising fashion. Some years ago a radio personality encouraged his listeners to increase their religious observances by holding, roughly, "This weekend go to the church or synagogue of your choice; make the Commies mad!" Representative L. Mendel Rivers, South Carolina Democrat, commenting on a recent decision of the Supreme Court ruling unconstitutional a prayer used in the New York public schools—a decision of which many were adversely critical—said, "I know of nothing in my lifetime that could give more aid and comfort to Moscow than this bold, malicious, atheistic, and sacrilegious twist of this unpredictable group of uncontrolled despots." [New York Times, p. 10e, July 1, 1962]. Hardly a day goes by during which one could not glean from any respectable newspaper of record many quotations indicative of such opinions of leaders of the opposing camps or members of the public generally.

tainty of high levels of mutual destruction should hostilities break out.

I speak of major instabilities among the members of any one of the relatively modernized societies largely in terms of those instabilities eventuating in hostilities among the members of several of those societies—in the current world situation between the members of the two major camps. I think the possibility of containment of such instabilities without hostilities is well nigh out of the question. First, scapegoating or its equivalent is far too frequent a concomitant of the kind of anxieties and aggressions which are likely to accompany such instabilities. Second, the effects of such a set of instabilities on the members of other societies by virtue of the interdependence of the systems involved may make some form of retaliation more or less inevitable. Third, the kind of opportunism which is often the essence of political leadership favors the attempt of some leaders of any one of these societies to court measures likely to result in hostilities in order to achieve or maintain power among the members of his own society. Finally, there is the problem raised by the lack of adequate knowledge generally. Especially in an environment of anxieties exacerbated by such instabilities, a chain of actions and reactions resulting in hostilities could result from a clear-cut mistake either literally by accidental discharge of a weapon or by the apprehension, perhaps quite erroneously, that members of the other society were about to attack.

The problems of modernization for the members of relatively nonmodernized societies are exceedingly serious ones about which we have little reason to be optimistic. We do not know nearly as much as we need to know to solve these problems to the satisfaction of anyone. We could be more careful, more systematic, and even more hardhearted were that necessary for rational behavior in planning modernization, were it not for the potentiality of hostilities among the members of relatively modernized societies. The problems of modernization are guaranteed to generate continuous dissatisfaction among the vast majority of the population of the world today. All sorts of leaders can fish in these troubled waters. It is already a well-recognized element of statecraft to play off the members of one camp of the relatively modernized societies against those of the other plus an enormous number of intermediate arrangements that can be made with the leaders of societies whose members regard themselves as more or less neutral in these matters. The fact that the problems occasioned by the problems of modernization within the context of any relatively nonmodernized society can result in the exacerbation of the potentiality of hostilities between the members of the major relatively modernized camps makes any problem of modernization, potentially, a major world problem. Solution of the problems of instability of the members of the relatively modernized societies will not solve other world problems automatically, but it will vastly increase the possibility of many other problems being solved or even being permitted to run on without catastrophic consequences for the population of the planet in general —however catastrophic they may be for the members of the society immediately concerned.

There is one other quite important possible implication of instabilities which can eventuate in hostilities among the members of relatively modernized societies. I have asserted that: (1) the processes of modernization constitute a sort of universal social solvent, (2) no social structures have yet proved an insuperable barrier to this process, (3) modernization breeds increased modernization in the context of any society it touches, whether relatively nonmodernized or relatively highly modernized, (4) there would seem to be signs of upper limits to which such a process could go, but (5) there are no signs of members of such societies not pushing heedlessly toward those limits. A major outbreak of hostilities utilizing current military technology could change that picture. Life could be a return to relatively nonmodernized social existence. There would be memory on the part of some individuals of the structures characteristic of relatively modernized societies, but the means to reachieve those structures might be out of the question for some centuries. Were this to be the case, one might expect the Chinese or what was left of them to revert to some of the structures characteristic of traditional China. Those would be well within the memory of survivors, they would be achievable on the basis of the means which would survive, and those methods of organization were the most stable for the longest period of time of any of the structures of any of the relatively nonmodernized societies of any considerable scale.

I

INTRODUCTION

This summary is a recapitulation of reiteration. This work has been an attempt to derive some implications for applied problems of a set of theories in an inchoate stage of development. The most general objective of all the material above has been to create in the student of public affairs a sensitivity to the implications of considering societies as wholes. Most social analysis is confined to restricted aspects or organizations characteristic of a single society. Most of the discussions of societies as wholes tend to be mystical, resting heavily on inadequately defined terms such as spirit, ethos, culture, ideology, etc. The approximation of rigor sought here is often unachieved, but lapses into animism and mystery are infrequent.

In order to create this sensitivity to the implications of considering societies as wholes I have taken up a set of topics, everyone of which has turned on all the others. The first was the distinction between relatively modernized and relatively nonmodernized societies. I present it as the most general distinction relevant to the analysis of societies considered as wholes. At the opposite pole, the aspects of any relationship were discussed as a means for the analysis of organizations, however complicated, when such organizations were encountered in forms not suggested to the observer by ones with which he was already familiar. There followed a lengthy treatment of societies viewed in terms of the aspects of societies and societies viewed in terms of the subsystems which enter their composition. In all of this treatment one distinction was kept in mind. What are the aspects or units which are characteristic of all societies, and what are the major lines of variation which overlie them? The treatment of the second in turn turned on the distinction between relatively modernized and relatively nonmodernized societies. A reiteration of the more striking common factors and the more striking lines of variation in summary form followed. Finally, in quite general form, two central foci of problems in public affairs—modernization and stability—were discussed in terms of all the groundwork laid before. I should like to close with some general observations and a final warning which I would not see lost in the length of what has gone before.

I I
SOME GENERAL OBSERVATIONS

A. THE IDEAL-ACTUAL DISTINCTION

The distinction between ideal and actual structures is the most general tool of analysis used throughout this work. There is hardly a page on which it does not appear in one form or another. It is not a new distinction. Laymen and social scientists alike have used it in some form or other well nigh universally—but it is more often used implicitly than explicitly. Many apparently paradoxical accounts of social phenomena lose the element of paradox if these distinctions are made explicit. Apart from the definition of the concepts themselves the main proposition in this tool of analysis are the following: (1) The members of all societies distinguish between ideal and actual structures. (2) The ideal and actual structures never coincide completely for any society or any subsystem of a society. (3) Some of the sources of stress and strain characteristic of the members of any society inhere in the fact that the ideal and actual structures do not coincide. This proposition has two subsidiary elements. (a) To some extent the members of any society are aware of the fact that not all ideal and actual structures coincide, and to some extent are upset by the lack of coincidence. (b) Even if the members are not aware of the lack of coincidence in a given respect they may nevertheless be upset by the implications of the discrepancy. (4) Some of the possibilities of integration in terms of any society inhere in the fact that the ideal and actual structures do not coincide perfectly. Again the members of the society may or may not be aware of the relevant discrepancies, but when the discrepancy is relevant for integration the members of the society are not likely to be aware of the discrepancy or at least are not likely to be aware of the relevance of the discrepancy for the possibilities of integration. (5) Discrepancies between the ideal and actual structures in general are never adequately explicable in terms of hypocrisy. Some discrepancies may be a function of hypocrisy; it is important to distinguish between those which are and those which are not; but the charge that the general discrepancy is a function largely of hypocrisy always involves a greater implicit allegation of rationality than can in fact be supported. (6) A part of the discrepancy is always explicable in terms of inadequate knowledge of the members of the society about the structures of their society and about the experiences which they are likely to have. It is questionable whether the members as a whole are capable of the amount of knowledge which would be necessary were such discrepancies to be eliminated completely. (7) Were there to be a society for whose members these discrepancies did not exist, that society would be impossibly brittle in the face of any changes in the setting of the society with any implication for the activities carried on in terms of the society.

The implications of any or all of these propositions may be raised relative to any of the structures in terms of which action takes place. The answers to such questions almost inevitably yield information relevant to the student of public affairs. Detailed precision with regard to the ideal structures, especially in cases of discrepancy, may be hard to acquire, but difficulties about measurement to the contrary notwithstanding, it is enlightening simply to raise questions by hypotheses in these terms.

B. SOCIAL CHANGE

The concept of social change always refers to changes in the system of action, that is to say, to changes in the structures in terms of which actions take place. No society is immune to social change. The greater the detail in terms of which one considers a given society, the greater is the amount of change taking place. Even if societies are considered on exceedingly general levels, however, change is always possible. The most extreme form of change is that in terms of which a given society becomes a subsystem of another society or ceases to exist altogether. Short of such extreme changes even at general levels of consideration all known societies have been characterized by social change.

Once the structures characteristic of relatively modernized societies have been developed in terms of one society and the members of relatively nonmodernized societies can come in contact or be brought in contact with those structures, all such societies are especially vulnerable to the structures characteristic of relatively modernized societies. As a class, relatively nonmodernized societies are not so vulnerable to any other type of social change.

Social changes characteristic of any society are more likely to be revolutionary changes than renovating changes. When social changes take place, on any given level of generalization, they are more likely to usher in a new set of structures than to restore a previously existing set of structures. Not all social changes have implication for more general levels of social consideration than the one on which the change is originally identified. The more highly modernized a society, however, the greater is the likelihood that such implications will exist for more general levels, if only because of the increased level of interdependence characteristic of increased levels of modernization.

By no means all changes which are revolutionary are carried out in terms of physical violence. Changes which are revolutionary in terms of any given level of consideration of any given society may be carried out relatively gradually and quite peacefully.

No social structures are inherently slow-changing as opposed to fast-changing. It is true that in social history some structured aspects of action as well as some of the organizations in terms of which action ordinarily takes place have on the whole tended to change more slowly than others, but it is fundamentally naïve to assume that either given aspects or given organizations can only change slowly. There are two situations in which any conceivable structure might be fast-changing. One is a situation in which for whatever reason there develops a charismatic leader. The other is a situation in which the reinforcement of previously existing social structures is destroyed. This latter is exceedingly likely, if not inevitably the case, when the structures of relatively modernized societies are introduced into the context of relatively non-modernized societies. To assume, for example, that family organizations in a given society will change only slowly because in social history family organizations have ordinarily changed slowly is to run a grave risk of misunderstanding the situation.

Few social changes of any considerable magnitude or generality occur without important implications for the allocation of power and responsibility in general and for the government of the society in particular. Social changes of any sort are exceedingly likely to erode the general structures of control in the society concerned, even though the area of behavior in terms of which the changes are first noticed or in terms of which they are induced do not seem in any obvious and direct sense to be closely related to the general structures of control.

One of the problems always connected with social change—quite apart from the substantive nature of the change itself—is the rate at which the change takes place. There are upper limits on the rate of social change to which human beings can adjust. Save for short-run periods in social history this has probably never been an endemic problem until the development of highly modernized societies. Nevertheless, apart from this extreme case, societies vary radically as to the rates of change to which their members can adjust readily. There is no reason to believe that the greater the rate of change to which people have previously been accustomed, the greater is the ease of adjustment to increased rates of change. The substantive nature of the changes may be more relevant than the previous rate of change to which the members of a given society were accustomed. In the case of the members of highly modernized societies, within certain limits, a decrease in the rate of change may be as difficult to adjust to as an increase would be for persons accustomed to a different situation.

Finally, actions in terms of all changing social systems—especially social systems undergoing revolutionary changes—stimulate and are somewhat vulnerable to fundamentalistic reactions. The more revolutionary a set of changes, the greater is the likelihood that some individuals, who for one reason or another are disgruntled in the face of the changes, will conceive some past state of affairs to be preferable to the current ones, and push for restoration of that state of affairs. Stress on the good old days is always to some extent subversive of the status quo. In general, until the development of relatively modernized societies, the term *old-fashioned* has never been a general term of derogation, but even some of the members of the most highly modernized of societies conceive of a return to the old-fashioned as a solution to current problems. The more highly modernized a given society, the more radical are the implications of fundamentalistic reactions. In this sense the development of high levels of modernization makes radicals of conservatives and vice versa.

C. THE STRATEGIC NATURE OF ECONOMIC AND POLITICAL ASPECTS

It is quite out of the question for any student of public affairs to overlook the relevance of economic and political aspects for the problems he seeks to solve. Frequently if not inevitably, especially in the social contexts of today, these aspects set the most obvious and best recognized limits for most of the pressing policy problems. To some extent this has to do with our comparatively greater sophistication about questions of economic and political science in general at the operating level. Our knowledge in these fields leaves much to be desired, but nevertheless, particularly with regard to the economic aspects, fairly considerable levels of scientific sophistication have been achieved. The political aspects at the operating level have been a focus for a considerable portion of the world's wisdom for more than two millennia. Without pressing the present limits of sophistication in economics as a science or the field of politics as wisdom one can be quite certain, for example, that the production of steel cannot be made self-supporting in the state of Israel, and one cannot operate efficiently in a large-scale program of modernization with an ineffective governmental organization. So obvious is the relevance of the allocation of goods and services and the allocation of power and responsibility for practically any problems, and so sensitive have we become to such considerations today that we run relatively little danger of completely overlooking the economic and political aspects of variables. These aspects are so strategic, and we think so easily in terms of them, that the real danger is of confusing the strategic nature of these aspects with a completely deterministic role for them. Our knowledge, both descriptive and theoretical of these fields is so much greater than our knowledge about other aspects in the social context that we are overwhelmingly likely to ignore the others or at best to consider them as perpetually relegated to the category of other things being equal. The latter practice poses a special danger all its own. With regard to these aspects as with others, it is frequently of the essence of scientific procedure, either by actual experimentation or by hypothetical reconstruction, to hold other things equal. The danger of this procedure lies not in its use but in forgetting that it is a specific procedure and in no way constitutes an acceptable alternative to examinations into the question of whether other things are in fact equal or not.

Two injunctions are certain. (1) No student of public affairs and no individual of responsibility in public affairs can afford to ignore economic variables, political variables, or a combination of the two. (2) The student of public affairs and the man of responsibility in public affairs can never afford to ignore variables other than the economic and political ones. To this second injunction two corollaries may be added. (a) When economic and political variables seem most adequate for the treatment of a given problem that is perhaps the best time to be most alert for the possible relevance of other variables. One of the greatest dilemmas of the policy maker after all is the fact that at one and the same time he must be self-confident and hence to some extent confident of his solutions to a given problem, but to the extent that he is confident in those solutions he is highly vulnerable to ignorance. (b) Whenever the analysis of a situation in terms of economic and political variables rests overwhelmingly on the assumption or actual appearance of rational behavior on the part of the persons concerned, and the persons concerned constitute a considerable number of individuals, the tenability of those assumptions about rationality or those observations of rational behavior should be reexamined. This is particularly important with regard to current phenomena, since never before has so much emphasis both ideally and actually been placed on rational behavior, and probably never before has so high an achieved level of rational behavior characterized so large a proportion of the activities of men.[1]

D. THE INERADICABLE ELEMENT
OF MATERIAL INTERESTS

Material interest is an ineradicable element of behavior. Individuals always orient their behavior to some elements or aspects of the empirical world which can be perceived by an observer. This ineradicable element of material interests is in no way inconsistent with enormous differences in degree and kind of preoccupation with material interests. It is in part the ineradicable element of material interest which makes the strategic nature of economic and political variables so obvious in all social situations. To some extent it is also this ineradicable element of material interest which makes the confusion of the strategic nature of these variables with determinism plausible. Two aspects of this ineradicable element of material interest are of special interest here: the vulnerability of nonmaterial interests to material interests and the vulnerability of material interests to nonmaterial interests.

Although members of one society as well as members of different societies can vary enormously in the degree to which they orient their behavior to nonmaterial concerns, those nonmaterial orientations are always vulnerable to some material interests. Even ascetic virtuosi are not completely indifferent to material factors, and the average member of a society has a much more limited tolerance of extremes of nonmaterial orientation. Sooner or later any program which pushes nonmaterial orientations to great lengths with a consequent denial of material interests will result in either apathetic or violent reaction on the part of the population at large. The motto often attributed to Tokugawa Iyeyasu, the founding father of that famous line of Shoguns, is a model of callous sophistication in these respects. As mentioned above, in response, presumably to a question of how much should be left to the peasants for their own support he is said to have replied that they should be left with an amount such that "they can neither live nor die." [2] History knows no more carefully calculated

---

[1] As a corollary to the second corollary: To the extent that a given situation regarded as evil is the result of action based on rational calculations, that situation is relatively easy to cope with. Irrational or arational behaviors are far more difficult to deal with.

[2] The feudal lords of this period did not always calculate this amount cleverly, as may be judged from the number of peasant revolts which characterized the last 100 years of the regime.

statement of the limits to which material denial can be pushed without fatal implications for operation in terms of the system concerned.

The vulnerability of the nonmaterial interests varies enormously from one society to another. These interests are never completely vulnerable, but they are certainly more vulnerable in terms of relatively modernized societies than in terms of relatively nonmodernized ones in general. In theory at least the vulnerability of nonmaterial interests may be as great in terms of a relatively nonmodernized society as in terms of a relatively modernized one, but the degree of invulnerability of nonmaterial interests cannot be as high in terms of a relatively modernized society as in terms of a relatively nonmodernized one. From this point of view the constant allegation that complete materialism is characteristic of the members of relatively modernized societies, though quite untenable, is quite understandable.

Because of the predominance of the structures characteristic of the process of modernization and of relatively modernized societies, few individuals run the danger of overlooking the vulnerability of nonmaterial interests to material ones whether voluntary or enforced. The danger is rather that this vulnerability will be overemphasized rather than overlooked. It is meet therefore, to point to two forms of vulnerability of the material interests to nonmaterial ones: The one form of vulnerability being a specific form of the other more general form. The most likely specific form of vulnerability of materialistic orientation to nonmaterialistic ones is what has been referred to above as a fundamentalistic reaction. This reaction is in and of itself never completely devoid of materialistic orientations. To some extent fundamentalists look to a previous time as a period during which they were better off [or people like them were better off] materially. Nevertheless, the fundamentalistic reaction is nonmaterial in the sense that the previous period looked to represents for the fundamentalist a state of affairs considered good in and of itself—an exemplification of a particular set of basic value orientations. For the fundamentalist it is the current indifference to these values which constitutes the core of evil as they see it. Exhortations to return to the good old days always involves the allegation that a return to the good old days constitutes a return to greater emphasis on spiritual values.

More generally speaking from the point of view of the individuals concerned, action always takes place in terms of standards of evaluation. Sooner or later, if pressed, the members of any society will justify some of those standards as good in and of themselves, that is to say, for nonmaterial reasons. However an observer may explain those standards, from the point of view of the individual they contain a nonmaterial element. The limits on the extent of material interests never consist solely of the nonmaterial element of evaluation inherent in basic value orientations. Some of the members [and it is overwhelmingly likely that they be the vast majority of the members] always orient to nonmaterial elements either in the form of literal concepts of supernatural deities and the like and/or in the form of glorification of various causes, movements, or concepts such as the nation, etc., as ends in themselves. These orientations are subject to change and vulnerable to elements of material interest, but such elements are quite vulnerable to them as well. Social history has not only furnished examples of individual ascetics who, in their virtuosity of nonmaterialistic orientations, have sat on pillars for years at a time and contemplated the nonmaterial verities as they saw them. Even among the members of quite highly modernized societies in time of war, for example, social history has also borne witness to the willingness of men in quite large masses to disregard material factors to the extent of being willing to court certain death for a glory considered good in and of itself.

The members of different societies react differently to such orientations, but none fail to appreciate them altogether. For example, during World War II Americans reacted differently to such sacrifices than did the Japanese. As long as Americans can pretend that there is any chance for survival in mass activities of this sort, or an individual independently chooses for patriotic reasons to commit suicide, as it were, for the glory of his cause, Americans understand and applaud such behavior as worthwhile salutary patriotism—good in and of itself despite the material sacrifice involved. After all, one of the favorite slogans of our society is: "My country may she always be right, but right or wrong, my country." [3] Despite approval of such sacrifices as these, Americans generally regarded the formation of an explicit suicide corps, the kamikaze pilots of World War II, and the constant fighting to the death of the last man once positions had become indefensible by the Japanese as examples of the bizarre extremities of Japanese character.

In this sense the quest for bread is always to some extent vulnerable to the quest for heaven and vice versa.

[3] The members of some societies do not invoke the introductory qualification.

E. THE STRATEGIC NATURE OF FAMILY
ORGANIZATIONS AND GOVERNMENTS

The two most strategic organizations for those concerned with public affairs are always the family organizations and the government characteristic of a given society. Acceptance of the relevance of the governmental organization will require little support, since ordinarily those concerned with public affairs must operate in terms of the governmental organizations of the societies concerned. Furthermore, the relevance of governmental organizations to the general problem of control tends to be taken for granted in the present-day world. It is so much taken for granted that many people define the government of a society as that organization in terms of which members exercise a monopoly of the legitimate use of force in the society [pp. 290–293]. If this definition is used, there are many societies of considerable scale which have not been characterized by governments, that is to say, there have been societies of considerable scale in terms of which the members of more than one general organization have legitimately exercised force in such a way that no clear-cut monopoly of the exercise of force can be said to have existed in terms of that society.

The relevance of the family organizations of any society may be considerably less acceptable at the conscious level, especially to those who have become accustomed to hearing relatively modernized societies described and decried as societies in terms of which family organizations have been reduced to more or less meaningless positions, in which their members are more or less impotent as long as they operate in terms of the family. I have mentioned these two types of organizations specifically because it is just as important to realize that all societies have such subsystems just as surely and just importantly as they are characterized by differentiable aspects such as the economic and the political. These two types of organizations are both characteristic of and strategic for the existence of any society of any considerable scale if not, indeed, for any society at all.

Governmental organizations have a special characteristic which recommends them for these purposes. The greater becomes the allocation of power and responsibility at the disposal of the members of any nongovernmental organization, the greater becomes one of two probabilities: (1) either there will be an increase in the importance of the governmental organization in the general society, or (2) the nongovernmental organization(s) whose members have become increasingly important in the allocation of power and responsibility will become a governmental organization(s). In addition to this there is no case of a society which has changed from a relatively nonmodernized state to a relatively modernized one in which the governmental organization has not radically increased in significance relative to other organizations characteristic of the society. Furthermore, except for possibilities referred to above [pp. 55–60, 100–107, 310–316, etc.] as premature centralization, the long-run tendency in every known relatively modernized society is for the centralization of the society in general to increase and for the importance of the government as the main focus of that increase in centralization to increase.[4] Thus, all concerned with problems of stability and/or of modernization in the world today will increasingly have to think and operate in terms of governmental organizations, insofar as the problems with which they concern themselves are deemed to be important by others or are in fact important from the point of view of an objective observer.

The deemphasis of the strategic nature of family organizations in every society is a function of the tendency to confuse an important change in the position of family organizations in general social structure characteristic of relatively modernized and modernizing societies with a general lack of significance of such organizations. Despite the fact that, ideally speaking, the proportion of the average individual's orientation in family terms diminishes in the context of every relatively modernized society and every modernizing society by contrast with any relatively nonmodernized society,[5] family organizations remain from many points of view the most important type of organization both ideally and actually for the vast majority of all individuals in the society. The family organization continues to be the organization in terms of which the average individual receives initial classification in social terms. Whatever emphasis is later placed on his achievements, his initial placement is in terms of his family membership. The individual, ideally speaking, receives the overwhelming proportion of his basic socialization including all sorts of learning of the initial sort in a family context. The family remains the one organization in which the average individual always has roles throughout his life cycle despite the fact that

[4] In this connection both the extreme left with its concept of the withering away of the state and the extreme right with its concept of a return to laissez-faire have been curiously and identically naïve.

[5] If the leisure revolution sees a return to increased activity in a family context, this trend to some extent may be reversed in relatively highly modernized societies, though it is not likely ever again to approximate the proportion characteristic of relatively nonmodernized societies.

virtually all of the members of relatively modernized societies have families of procreation which are separate and different from their families of orientation.[6] Finally, in the context of relatively modernized societies as of all other societies actually if not ideally speaking what happens to an individual in terms of his family roles is overwhelmingly likely to affect his behavior in terms of his other roles. Although there are differences characteristic of relatively modernized societies as opposed to relatively nonmodernized ones in the extent of actual influence as well as in the extent of ideal influence, the fact remains that, even when, ideally, the influence of family roles is not expected to carry over to behavior in terms of other roles, it actually does carry over often.

There is another aspect to relatively modernized societies which tends to be overlooked. Despite the number of social contexts in which, ideally speaking, family considerations are not expected to intrude, and despite the number of organizational orientations which in special circumstances take precedence over one's orientations to his family ideally speaking, the fact remains that both ideally and actually the average individual is expected to orient his behavior more to his family than to any other organization in terms of which he operates. In certain contexts solidarity in terms of other organizations take precedence over solidarity with family members, but these contexts are not expected to be the contexts in terms of which the individual ordinarily operates. Thus in time of war, family interest to the contrary notwithstanding he is expected to respond to a draft call, but this is specifically expected to be an emergency state of affairs or one of limited duration. It is not a matter of chance that one of the aspects of modern totalitarian societies which has appeared most shocking to individuals who dislike such social structures has

[6] This is not so great a change as it has sometimes been made to appear. In terms of all societies roughly 50 per cent of the population as a minimum changed families when they married. For example, ideally speaking, in traditional China all women left their father's family context and joined that of their husband's at marriage. Whenever stem families and the like existed considerably more than 50% of the population had families of procreation which were different from their families of orientation since individuals of one sex were selected to "marry out" of their families of procreation and individuals of the other sex save for one member of the family left their families of orientation and set up separate families of procreation as well. Finally, the proportion actually living in more discontinuous family units was even higher because even in the context of those societies in terms of which individuals of at least three generations were, ideally speaking, always involved in a single family organization, the death of grandparents before the birth of grandchildren frequently prevented this.

been the extent to which family members of all totalitarian societies, regardless of the type, have been motivated [or attempts have been made to motivate them] to place solidarity with others in terms of the government ahead of solidarity with other family members. The loyal totalitarian is expected to inform systematically on family members to members of the government in matters both serious and trivial.[7]

There are two other sources of special family importance for those concerned with public affairs. The family is always the context in terms of which the average individual in every known society learns to respond to structures of power and responsibility. In this sense the family organization is always strategic to the general structures of control in any society. In a considerable majority of the societies still in existence, however, that is to say, in the relatively nonmodernized societies, the family may still remain one of the most strategic organizations as far as the general structures of control are concerned in another sense. Control over the behavior of individuals generally in terms of the society may to a high degree remain a function of the extent to which the family head or the members of the family in general can control the actions of the individual family member.

The second consideration is somewhat less obvious but nevertheless inherent in the material stressed here. Action in terms of the elements common to all societies has been stressed as a matter of the first significance in understanding the possibility of communication among individuals of radically different social backgrounds in terms of a given society or more importantly in terms of two radically different societies. The fact that all people have some material interests, that the members of all societies are to some extent aware of what tools are, and of inanimate sources of power, that rationality is not unknown to the members of any society, etc.,—all of these elements are important if communications across such radical differences of backgrounds are to be established. These problems of communication exist in addition to language differences as such. In the modern world no person

---

[7] The extent to which societies can be stable under these conditions remains to be determined. It is undeniable that a considerable amount of such systematic informing has been motivated in terms of such societies. It has never yet been proved that the extent to which this has been motivated equals either the claims or the desires of the leaders of such societies. When and if it does, there will remain the question as to whether family organizations can be stable under these circumstances, and if they cannot, whether the societies concerned can be stable. While we have no dearth of new instances of such societies, the fact remains that several within the memory of man have already passed from the scene.

concerned with public affairs is immune to such problems of communication in a world in which no international questions lack domestic implications and no domestic questions lack international implications. The vast majority of the elements common to all societies which form a minimal base for such communication find at least a part of their exemplification in terms of every society in the family organizations characteristic of the members of that society. Though somewhat more likely to be ignored, the fact that the average public official in any society is overwhelmingly likely to have had experiences both as a son and as a father may be as significant for the ability of these individuals to communicate as the fact that they have shared the experience of roles of public responsibility.

I I I
FINAL WARNING

At its present stage of development what has been attempted here is presented primarily as a sensitizing tool. The theoretical propositions on which it rests are not nearly well enough worked out or logically interrelated to claim more. The greatest vulnerability of this work does not inhere in the fact that hypotheses about the facts, though carefully labeled as such, have been flatly asserted without any accompanying attempt at empirical demonstration. We are not close to having adequate empirical materials for the definitive verification of many if any of the hypotheses about the facts presented here. A broad set of hypotheses, however, carefully taken for what they are, may serve far more fruitfully as a sensitizing tool than any small selection of them presented in terms of carefully marshaled data. This is not to say that the whole effort would not be immensely improved by the careful marshaling of data. It would, of course, and a more positive role of all that has been attempted here must wait until basic research on the general structures of a broad sample of the major societies in the world is carried out in some such general terms as those suggested, rather than having the material from these societies presented in terms of detailed descriptions of more or less isolated aspects and organizations with the interconnections among them left largely on an *ad hoc* basis. At least the hypotheses about the facts presented here may serve as challenges to the data which may some day be collected. Although I have not knowingly presented any hypotheses about the facts which I suspect to be false, I have tried to present hypotheses such that either their confirmation or disproof would teach us a great deal more than we now know. If such basic research on societies in general can be done even in such elementary and partially developed terms for handling societies and the various subsystems characteristic of them as wholes, the implications for making isolated bits of knowledge cumulative in their impact will be enormous. If the past history of other sciences holds for ours, the possibility of direct application of such increased knowledge will be greatly increased—whether for good or evil.

age (*Continued*)
665, 654–57, 657, 672; aged (old age), 185–86, 197, 201, 385, 417, 654–55, 667, 671, 762; age variable, 393; armed forces and, 576, 582; distribution of, 674; generation and, 195, 654–57; 659–60; organizations based on, 646; political allocation and, 671; reinforcement of roles and, 195; relative age, 197, 201, 654–57, 665; sex and, 195, 659–60

aggression, 547, 573, 580, 792

agrarian [*see also* agriculture, farmers, peasants, rural], definition of, 234; elements, 234–38; enterprises, 391; problems (U.S. and U.S.S.R.), 778; production, 234–38; productivity, 252; products, 69, 234–38; pursuits and schooling, 625; society, 87–88, 245, 724

agriculture [*see also* agrarian], 9, 514

air force, 438, 572

alchemy, 716

alchohol(-ism), 365, 366

Algeria, 37

alliance, 308

allocation, chain of, 240; distributive sense of, 240–42; economic, *see* economic allocation; *see also* allocation of goods and services

allocation of goods and services [*see also* economic allocation], 21, 24, 41, 48, 69, 160, 168, 176, 179, 181, 194, 209, 212–13, 233, 241, 283–84, 290, 314, 334, 359, 361, 391, 414, 454–55, 494–95, 498, 500, 503, 507, 511–13, 515–17, 520–22, 528–29, 533–34, 537–41, 547, 553, 584, 606, 609, 619–20, 623, 659, 667–70, 730–31, 763, 779, 784, 800

allocation of loyalty, 282

allocation, political [*see also* political allocation, and power and responsibility], 21, 41, 105, 147, 176, 179, 182–83, 194, 206, 207, 209, 212–13, 241–42, 281–84, 290–91, 303, 313, 319, 325, 335, 360–61,

allocation (*Continued*)
414, 454–55, 494–95, 524, 537–41, 542, 551, 553, 569, 584, 587–88, 606, 619, 656–57, 669–72, 690–91, 695, 707, 798, 800, 805

allocation of property, 281–84

allocation, relevance of economic to political allocation [*see also* exchange units], 241–42

allocation services, 241–42

Almond, G. A., 316

altruism, 148, 562–63

amateur psychoanalysis, 386

amazonian societies, 672

ambitious, 765, 786

ambivalence toward modernization, 772–75

Americans, 26, 92, 152, 303, 389, 574, 575, 577, 580, 640

American scholars, 573

America, Central and South, 743

American life, 595

American scholar, 573–75

American society [*see also* U.S. society], 147, 303, 611

American soldiers, 370

American Telephone & Telegraph Co., 472, 507, 520, 753

analogy, 22, 175, 322

analysis, of action, 243; comparative, 5, 138, 152–53, 160, 357, 646; dynamic, 380; most casual, 305; most modern social science, 292; of order and change, 295; requisite, 223; scientific social, 177; of social structure, 147; of societies, 249; status, 380

analytic apparatus, 133

analytic structural requisites, 223

analytic structures, 20, 175

anarchy, 83, 467–68, 608

ancestor(s), spirits of, 301; worship, 216, 378, 608, 609, 611, 615

anger, 324, 371

Anglo-Iranian Oil Co., 328

animal husbandry, 236–38, 251

Annapolis, 595

anonymity, 324, 789

antagonism, 179

anthropology(-ists), 86, 140, 219, 260, 310–11, 357, 377, 404, 412, 521, 674

anthropomorphism, 4

anti-monopoly, 160, 168

anti-trust, 530

centralization(-ed) (*Continued*)
60, 100–07, 310–16, 805;
problems of and information
theory, 251
sedentary societies, 102; states,
292; system, 264
technology of communication
and, 102–03; tyranny and,
17
variations, 55–60
ceremonies, 262
certainty, 358–60
Ceylon, 15
challenge to traditionalism, 109
change, 31, 127, 166, 302, 347,
352, 380, 539, 540, 589, 690–
99, 788–89; as an approach,
175; balances of power and
responsibility and, 692; built-
in tendency toward, 692–93;
charisma and, 127; explicit
orientation to a rarity, 477,
614; fast vs. slow, 127; general importance of, 783–90;
governments and, 475–88; as
an ideal, 477, 614; level of
abstraction and, 479–80; limits, 81–82; orderly, 475, 487–
88; problem of, in general,
788–89; rapidity of, as a
problem, 789; rate of, 81–82,
789; revolutionary, 476, 479–
88, 797–99; role of, 81–82,
347; social [N.B. all change
referred to throughout is "social" unless otherwise noted];
and stability, 380; in taste,
69; technological, 783–88
characteristics, 38
charisma(-tic), definition of, 350–
51; fast change and, 127;
governments, 456–66, 476;
leader(-ship) 127, 301–02,
320, 350–53, 450–52, 460,
461, 476, 483, 485, 649, 798;
miscellaneous organizations
and, 649; organizations and,
456, 649; recruitment, 450
charity, 452
chauvinism, 116, 579–80, 699,
747
checks and balances, 303, 490–91,
691, 715
chief executive, 539
chiefs, 450, 627
childhood, 19, 197, 201, 385, 654–
55
children, 19, 74 ff., 667; bearing,

children (*Continued*)
39; buying, 259; care, 205;
rearing, 39
Ch'in Shih-huang-ti, 576
China [*see also* Chinese], 6, 12,
15, 19, 37, 45, 47, 73, 86–87,
94, 98, 100–01, 103, 106, 118
120, 122, 124, 146, 147, 150,
152, 162, 166, 169, 189, 195,
201, 216, 224, 225, 237, 245,
252, 278, 288, 302, 308, 311–
14, 318, 331, 332, 337, 348,
352, 354–55, 362, 379–82,
385, 389, 394, 395, 401, 405,
406, 427, 429, 434, 457, 458,
476, 488, 500, 519, 529, 572,
579, 606, 611, 636–37, 713,
731, 736, 70, 749, 794
as absorbing all others, 743;
and Alexander the Great,
743; armed forces and, 572
balancing of solidarities, 697–
98; Buddhist monasteries,
609, 623
cadets, 401; clans, 413; cognition and peasants, 716; centralization, 100, 313; civil
service, 106; Communist, 15,
37, 275, 462, 500, 644, 704,
732, 737; contrast with other
societies, 704
dynastic cycle, 741
export of kinship terms, 99,
657; extended form, 416
illegitimate combinations of
economic and political aspects, 731; Imperial, 71; incest, 421; and India, 578–79,
736
lines of descent, 407
mysterious, 705
open class, 740
position of organizations in,
713; private scholar, 663
renovating change, 19, 488,
696–97; reversion to traditional, 794
sedentary knowledge, 720; self-
sufficiency and external factors, 524; social engineering
and, 576; stability of, 696–
97, 740
will of Heaven, 476, 617, 697
Chinese, 91, 197, 207, 224, 225,
228, 237, 390, 578, 697, 700
ancestor worship, 609; Army,
579, 572
bureaucracy, 73, 101, 106, 117,

hierarchy(-ical) (*Continued*)
  archical aspect], 150, 162,
  568–69, 588
high modernization, 753
high priest, 216
high school, 627–28
highlighting, 423
highly general theory, 69
highly modernized nations, 9
highly developed, 743
Himes, J. R. 260
Hindu, 91, 190, 349, 726
historical data, 270
history, 3, 31, 50, 107, 120–21,
  123, 452, 460, 615, 773
Hitler, 308, 320, 351, 451–52, 791
hoarding, 551
hobbies, 639
Hoffer, E., 347
holistic, 4
Holland, 285, 573, 775
holocaust, 58, 735
holy inquisitions, 612–13
holy wars, 612
homeostasis, 123, 221–22, 691,
  693–94
homosexual, 98, 419
honesty, 148, 159, 706
Hong Kong, University of, 749
honke, 383
honor, 261, 300
honorific expression, 369
horizon, 126, 746, 765
horizontal proliferation, 428
hostility, 725, 727, 728
house, 546
household and field Gods, 606,
  611
Hu, C-T., 573
human, action, 217, 326, 512;
  activity, 239; behavior, 28,
  217, 303, 333, 607; beings,
  12, 276, 341, 535; conduct,
  531; creation, 84; dignity,
  31, 277; engineering, 533;
  heredity, 21, 234, 345; nature, 5, 394; organization,
  249; power, 36; relations,
  249, 532; societies, 84, 303;
  species, 139, 223
humanism, 346, 615
humor, 409
hunting, 236, 391
Huntington, S. P., 571
husband-wife, 62, 164, 165
hydraulic theory of emotion, 369
hypocrisy (def. of, 28), 346, 700–
  01, 796

hypothesis, vii, 7, 10, 26, 37, 58,
  69, 103, 136, 137, 138, 154,
  170, 230, 251, 277, 294, 309,
  357, 384, 625, 636, 660, 664,
  665, 674, 690, 709, 788, 797,
  808, 809; about the facts, 7,
  26, 37, 154, 270, 808; façade,
  429

Ibrahim, I. A., 573
Iceland, 87, 623, 636, 751
ideal [*see* actual], definition of,
  26, 37, 154, 270, 808; façade,
  and actual structures, 26–30;
  individualism, 228
idealistic determinism, 726
identification, 53–55, 98, 99, 110,
  192, 209, 261, 282, 285, 349,
  365, 545, 698
identity, 648–49
ideological, aspersion, 764; differences, 48, 53, 58, 69, 72, 82,
  83, 256, 264, 272, 274, 287,
  387, 435, 471–72, 503–18,
  525–28, 530, 535, 550, 556–
  57, 559, 561–66, 568, 578,
  588, 662, 633, 707, 753, 769,
  778–79, 784, 787; sentiments,
  72; wishful thinking, 83
ideology, 58, 60, 69, 72, 82, 83,
  280, 374, 471–72, 518, 550,
  561–63, 566, 578, 579, 588,
  603, 784, 795
Ieyasu [*see* Iyeyasu]
ignorance [*see also* adequate
  knowledge, inadequate knowl-
  edge], 359, 694, 800
illegitimate(-cy) [*see also* graft],
  41, 71, 402, 483, 494–95, 676
illiteracy, 43, 86–87, 636–37
imagination, 459, 630
impedance, 604
Imperial China [*see* China]
imperialism, 125, 285, 324, 738,
  744–45, 748
impersonal bases, 54
impersonality, 73
importance, 10–11, 75, 529
impracticality, 199
imprisonment, 583
improper allocation of goods and
  services, 41
inadequate knowledge [*see* also adequate knowledge], 493, 692
inanimate products, 233, 238
inanimate sources of power [*see
  also* modernization (def. of)]
  35–36, 63, 95

modernization (*Continued*)

family, 644; hostile-benign definition of situation and, 728

inanimate sources of power and, 35; indigenous, 16; in international affairs, 734–94 Japanese, 396

latecomers [*see also* latecomers], 738; level of, 49, 239, 260, 273, 275, 310, 319, 515, 517, 518, 536–37, 557, 560, 562–63, 569, 614, 616, 709, 711, 737, 739, 776, 790, 798

maximal, 598–99

national governments and, 469–71

pessimism about, 775–76; problem of, 5–6, 31–32, 125, 190, 232, 548, 578, 741–76; process of, 8, 16, 44, 127

relative, 31; requisites and prerequisites of, 106, 737–40; research, 637–40; role differentiation and, 199–200

special problems, 319; stability, 5, 31–32, 129, 734–94; structures of, 13, 97, 106, 125, 199, 200, 745, 748, 749, 757; tools and, 35

variations between centralization and modernization, 58–60, 708–12

Western influence and, 743–44; whither and whether of, 734–35

modernized, more or less, 11

Mohammedanism, 346, 347, 611, 617

momism, 409

monarchy, 453, 456, 515

monasteries, 350, 609, 623

monetary [*see also* media of exchange, money], basis, 259; criteria, 764; measurement, 261; organization, 541–43; specialists, 542; structure, 543, 764; unit, 67, 69, 70, 541–43, 556, 563

money [*see also* media of exchange], 66–68, 257–62, 455, 541, 556, 762, 763, 763–65; definition of, 66, 257; ashamed of, 763–64; accounting, 556; broadening, 126; criteria of judgment, 762–65; denigrated, 763; ed-

money (*Continued*)

ucation, 539; elite, 541; feudal societies, 67, 258; government and, 66, 70, 257–58, 455; Great Britain and, 67; happiness, 765; income distribution, 563; increased use of, 762–65; limitation on generalization of, 542; measure of merit, 277; perfectly generalized, 259, 542; root of all evil, 765; secrecy and flexibility, 542; simple and general money minimizes need for planning, 543; social prestige and, 67–68; symbol of success, 156; U.S. and, 67; why ignored, 763–65

Mongols, 88, 251, 743

monism(-istic), ethical, 765; determinism, 380; misplaced concreteness and, 707; monoply of, force, 292, 335, 436, 455

moonlighting, 510

Moore, O. K., 357

Moore, W. E., 274, 280, 559

moral, fire, 764; indignation, 156; standard, 225

morale, 364, 463, 568, 591–92, 754

morality, 114, 126, 778

morals of imperialism, 125

Mormon Church, 619

mortality and government derecruitment, 441

Mossadegh, 324, 328

"mother," 658, 674

motion pictures, 365–67

motivation(-al), 126, 147, 320–21, 344–57, 449, 559, 690, 786; definition of, 344; aspects, 147; capital formation and, 559; economic allocation and, 690; for stability, 695; sanctions, 353; strive for achievement, 786; structure, 363; voluntary basis of, 353

motives, good or bad, 747

multifunctional orientation, 537

multilineal conjugal family, 74–79, 120, 407, 645; descent, 407

multiple spousage, 428

Murdock, G. P., 428

music, 367

mutiny, 590–92

religion, 21, 39, 49–50, 94, 216,
345–46, 353, 389, 397, 451,
520, 576, 607–24, 641, 654,
663, 673, 707, 779; definition
of, 345; Catholic, 52, 115,
216, 345, 347, 451, 512–13,
611, 618–19; Christian, 611;
churches and, 607–24, 666;
communications, 520; ethical, 345–46; exclusivist, 346,
610 (def. of), 612; family as
a focus of, 397; governments
and, 616–19; international,
618–19; juvenile delin-
quency and, 779; knowledge
and, 663; nonexclusivist, 346
(def. of), 610, 612; organizational context, 607, 624;
organized, 345; particularism
and, 389–90; predominantly
religiously oriented organizations [see church]; recreation and, 641; religious ritual,
576; remarkable aspects
which do not inhere in doctrine as such, 612; secular,
615–16; supernatural, 345,
346, 347, 615–16; taxonomy,
707; this worldly—other-
worldly, 612–14

religious, action, 345, 607–08; af-
filiation, 389; behavior, 607;
belief, 345; discrimination,
143; element, 216; history,
610; ritual, 576; role differentiation, 216, 230; schools,
628; structure, 346–47; systems, 155

remuneration, 533
Renaissance society, 35
renovating change, 488
rents, 244, 696
representatives, 55, 59, 257, 297,
436, 455
Republican(s), 72, 500
requisites, 106
research laboratories, 72, 506
residence, 277, 411, 423
residual definition, 3
resources, 271, 276, 287
respect, 146, 200
responsibility, 74, 148, 167–68,
182, 199, 207, 211, 213, 235,
241, 251, 290–92, 320, 325,
449, 454, 553, 567–68, 583,
641, 643, 658, 661, 680, 690–
92, 694, 696; definition of,
211, 290; assessor of, 310;

responsibility (Continued)
balances of, 293, 310; common elements and, 669, 673;
increasing emphasis on, 568;
private enterprise and emphasis on, 167; public, 554;
recreation and, 643; role, 212;
technology of allocating, 304
responsible, predominantly, relationship [N.B. involved
whenever Y_5 is used in discussing relationships, pp.
133–74, 677–83], 147–49,
157, 160
restricted involvement, 95
restriction of function, 75
retirement, 441, 655, 671
revenue, 455
reversal of trend to increased
specialization, 94–95
revolts, 73
revolution, 19, 476, 477, 479–88;
definition of, 480; armed
force leaders and, 496–98,
590–93; by default, 779;
change, 476, 479–88, 797–99;
French, 485; general social,
77, 476–88, 492, 511, 591–93,
697, 740–41, 776–90; governmental, 476–88, 496–98, 591,
696; leisure, 77–78, 250, 487,
510–11, 639–40, 787; mass
production, 77, 486; palace,
476–88, 492, 496–98, 590–92,
697; "political," 77, 435; political liberalism, 486; War,
487
rich, 547
right(s), 144, 235, 280, 286, 486,
780; of businessmen, 41; extreme, 805; political, 520
rites de passage, 262
Rivers, L. M., 792
Roethlisberger, F. J., 170, 196,
364, 723
role, 44–46, 49, 54, 95, 97, 107,
111, 157, 160, 178, 188–200,
212–15, 294, 297, 299, 343,
391, 398, 434, 451, 501, 509,
516–17, 522, 555, 566, 574,
608–09, 631, 640–43, 656,
658, 660, 685, 695, 700, 753,
757; definition of, 44;
achieved, 190–92; adult, 51,
54, 398; ascribed, 190–92;
conflicts, 193–94; consumption, 660; coordination of,
44–46; differentiation [see

role (*Continued*)
 role differentiation]; employee, 189; family, 46, 188, 194–95, 806; female, 188; feudal elements, 107; friendship, 299; governmental, 214; kinship, 191; leadership, 212, 451; male, 188; military chain of command, 198–99; occupational, 46, 178, 189, 509, 516, 640, 643, 753; parents, 434; political, 215, 656; power, 212; production, 509, 660; rationality, 695, 700; reinforcement, 194–200, 215; responsibility, 212; scholarship, 190; separation, 44–46; sex, 658; specialist, 608; specialized occupational, 391; teaching, 631
role differentiation, 25, 149–50, 178–79, 185, 187–219, 223, 230, 249, 384–87, 410, 510, 654–69, 685, 702; definition of, 178; age, 200–04; basic, 187–88; cognition, 217–18; consumption, 209; economic, 209–10, 230, 658–60, 667–69; family as a focus of, 384–87, 654–66; foci of, 193–94; generation, 204, 657, 658; intermediate, 188–90, 387; nonhuman environment, 218–19, 230, 659–66; occupational, 208; political, 207–08, 211–16, 230; production, 209; relative age, 202; relatively modernized societies, 201–04; religion, 216, 217, 230; sex, 188, 206–10, 213, 387, 403, 410, 510, 658–59, 667; solidarity, 221–22, 230, 667; types, 200–19
Roman, Catholic Church [*see* Catholicism]; law, 53, 100, 708; roads, 103; society, 95, 115, 318, 464
Rome, 318, 464
romanticism, 698
ronin [*see also samurai*], 121
Roosevelt, F. D., 366, 480
Royal Family of Japan, 166
Rubaiyat, 545
rule, adjudication, 316; application, 316; making, 316
ruler, 96, 146, 322

Russia [*see also* Soviet Union, U.S.S.R.], 72, 351, 352, 430, 500, 586, 590, 704, 736, 775
Russians, 72, 775
ruthlessness, 537, 689

sabotage, 168
sacred figure, 146
sadistic despot, 322
St. Thomas Aquinas, 182, 521
saintly massacres, 613
sales, 536
samurai, 99, 117–18, 121, 225, 312, 410, 442, 587, 599, 698
sanction, 155, 181, 211, 290, 320, 353
saving, forced, 557–561 (def. of, 560), 787
scale, government and, 675; large, and egalitarianism, 670
Scandinavia, 37, 156
scapegoating, 791, 793
schedule of marginal efficiency, 539
Schneider, D. M., 379, 428
scholars [*see* academic(s)]
scholarship, role of, 190
scholastic, 716
school(s)(-ing), 20, 26, 39–40, 60, 72, 76, 125, 185, 342–43, 393, 606, 624–34, 649, 668, 671, 677, 751, 770; definition of, 342–44, 624; secular, 628; semi-professional, 628
Schurz, W. L., 573
science, 6, 7, 23, 90, 91, 140, 586, 665
scientific, analysis, 177, 316, 419; concepts, 152, 173, 280; ethic, 110; fallacy, 176; guesses, 83; knowledge, 155, 358, 778; method, 720; solution, 140; -technological, 719–20; thinking, 63
scientists, 32, 77, 586
sculpture, 367
seasons, 218–19
secondary schools, 39
secrecy, 542
secret police, 592
security markets, 69
sedentary, agrarian societies, 61; agriculture, 251, 254; nature, 95; precisely, 686; society, 87, 191, 459, 556, 684, 685, 696; structures, 236, 465